ETHICAL TRADITIONS

ETHICAL TRADITIONS

Paul A. Newberry
California State University, Bakersfield

Mayfield Publishing Company
Mountain View, California
London • Toronto

Library of Congress Cataloging-in-Publication Data
Newberry, Paul A.
    Ethical traditions / Paul A. Newberry.
       p. cm.
    Includes bibliographical references.
    ISBN 0-7674-0748-2
    1. Ethics.   I. Title.
BJ1012.N487 1999
170' .9—DC2l

Manufactured in the United States of America
10   9   8   7   6   5   4   3   2   1

Mayfield Publishing Company
1280 Villa Street
Mountain View, California 94041

Sponsoring editor, Kenneth King; production, Publication Services; manuscript editor, Dave Mason; design manager, Jean Mailander; text designer, Anne Flanagan; cover designer, Diana Coe; manufacturing manager, Randy Hurst. The text was set in 10/12 Sabon by Publication Services and printed on 50# Butte des Morts by The Banta Book Group.

99-31547
CIP

Preface

As a historical anthology of moral philosophy suitable for an introductory class in ethics, this book is designed to demonstrate that the tradition of philosophy is central to the enterprise, not an arcane interest of certain historically minded individuals. Philosophy, by its very nature, is a shared effort in which ideas are created, questioned, analyzed, and synthesized by an entire community over time. A common analogy is that philosophy is like a conversation that builds on the talk that has gone before.

This analogy suggests that progress will be lineal and teleological, and to some extent this is true. Yet in this anthology I want to stress a different aspect of the conversation analogy. When we think of a conversation as long-term or ongoing, a further essential point of correspondence becomes apparent: What may be said early on in the conversation reappears at a later time and in a different context, taking on a new perspective as a result of the intervening dialogue. It is this aspect of the Western tradition in philosophy that this historical anthology stresses. Ideas arise, provoke a response, and may disappear for a time, only to emerge later with a renewed interest conceived in a new context. For example, concerns about ethical relativism that were initially addressed by Plato figure prominently in current writing and thinking about ethics. However, today's philosophers do not merely rehash Plato's arguments. Instead, this ancient issue has developed a new urgency because of the rise of science and increased multicultural sensitivity.

Many of us who teach philosophy are concerned with showing our students that philosophy is, and should be, applicable to their lives. One of the areas of greatest applicability must certainly be ethics. This applicability is often seen in an ethics course's emphasis on controversial ethical issues such as abortion or euthanasia. Yet, as those of us who love philosophy already know, the applicability of philosophy is not limited to current hot topics. Plato, Kant, and Mill still speak forcefully to us, albeit in language that is often difficult to penetrate. This book is designed to serve those who wish to show their students that the effort to understand these apparently ancient writings will let these great thinkers speak to them directly. The primary purpose of this book is to show that writings throughout the history of the philosophical endeavor are serious efforts to make sense of the very real ethical concerns of real people, just like those of the students reading the text. Thus, to demonstrate that historical treatments of ethical issues can still resonate with meaning and vitality, I have chosen issues from historical readings that are of most interest to beginning students, rather than focusing on issues that currently fascinate philosophers.

The majority of the works in this text are core works in the history of Western moral philosophy. Representative works in ethics from the primary philosophers of the last 2500 years are included, and each work is edited as lightly as possible. Since space is a major factor in deciding which works to include, I have shortened readings when necessary while cutting as little as possible within any chosen selection. For example, I chose to begin Plato's *Euthyphro* some lines into the dialogue, but I have let the reading speak for itself once it begins. Each selection is of sufficient length that students may experience the true flavor of the original work and get a more accurate understanding of each writing's place in the philosophical conversation. The usual fare of mere snippets and sound bites favored by many other introductory texts has been studiously avoided.

Along with the major works in ethics recognized by virtually every philosopher, I have included some more recently rediscovered historical pieces from women authors. Merely because the historical selection process has resulted in a canon written exclusively by males, one should not think that women were not interested in philosophical issues throughout the history of Western philosophy. I do not wish to make a claim as to whether these works are better or worse than those works recognized as the canon. Rather, they are included to demonstrate that philosophy belonged (and continues to belong) to both men and women. This may help dispel the notion that our students inadvertently receive, that women took up an interest in philosophy only in the latter half of this century.

Besides the historical works, both canonical and noncanonical, the book includes works representative of current debates in normative ethics. My aim is to show a continuity of themes, problems, and rational attempts to discern answers that began with the ancient Greeks and continues to this day. Thus works chosen from the twentieth century (particularly the second half) represent the history of moral philosophy amid its current concerns. These particular selections may or may not be of lasting interest and value (only time will tell), but they illustrate accurately the state of the enduring ethics conversation in the last decades of the twentieth century.

A brief word should be said about what the book makes no attempt to cover. I have chosen to limit the scope of the book to the history of the Western tradition in philosophy. Certainly, moral philosophy exists outside of this tradition, but I have not included any representations outside the Western tradition for two primary reasons. First, the length of the text limits the number of selections that can be included, and, since the canonical works are extensive and I am mindful of the need to include some noncanonical works as well, I leave myself no room for work outside the historical tradition in the West. Second, although much work outside of this tradition is of interest to those in the Western tradition and of lasting value, it takes place largely outside the context of concerns (outside of the conversation, if you will) within which the readings composing the text arose. Thus it is my belief that selections from outside of the tradition could display little if any regard for their cultural and historical context, which is necessary for the work to be best understood and appreciated.

This book is designed for an introductory course in ethics, at either a two- or four-year college or university. The following principal features ensure that the book is suitable to this audience.

1. The book is arranged chronologically so that ideas and problems of ethics can be read, discussed, and understood within the historical context in which they were written. It can be very misleading for students, I believe, to encounter side-by-side works by philosophers separated by millennia in both years and culture, as if they were contemporaries.

2. Each selection is preceded by an introduction that situates the work in the proper historical context. Studying texts in historical context is the most powerful and effective way of entering the philosophical conversation. These introductions also identify and define issues that figure importantly in the work and provide links to related material.

3. The canonical works by the most prominent philosophers in ethics are included, all with as little editing as possible. This enables students to read and learn from the real masters of our discipline in their own words without having the works rearranged so that they appear differently than the authors intended.

4. Examples of historical works of noncanonical status are included so that students can see that women, throughout the history of philosophy, also engaged in the philosophical enterprise, even though they may have occupied a lesser status than their male contemporaries have both within the discipline and within society.

5. Questions suitable for journal, homework, or class discussion follow each selection. The purpose of the questions is twofold. First, they help direct students to the important sections and issues of the reading. Second, and most important, they help students develop the reading, thinking, and writing skills essential for understanding philosophy.

6. A separate teacher's guide is available with summaries of the readings, answers to the reading and discussion questions, and sample test questions. It may be obtained either by contacting your local Mayfield sales representative or by phoning Mayfield's customer service department.

Despite its chronological ordering, the material is adaptable for ethics courses that do not treat the subject historically. Following is a suggestion for reading order in a course that focuses on prominent ethical theories.

1. Utilitarianism: Hume, Mill, Moore, and Williams

2. Kantian deontology: Kant and Hill (perhaps Ross as an alternative)

3. Virtue ethics: Aristotle, Anscombe, and Wolf

4. Social contract theory: Hobbes and Rawls

5. Feminist theory: Wollstonecraft and Held

I would like to acknowledge people who helped make this book possible. Janice Daurio, of Moorpark College, and my colleague at California State University–Bakersfield, Jeffrey Paris, gave useful advice on the introductions. Lorna Clymer, also of California State University–Bakersfield, offered wise counsel and editing throughout the process. I thank the following people for their thoughtful review of the manuscript: John R. Danley, Southern Illinois University at Edwardsville; Richard Eggerman, Oklahoma State University; Joyce Henricks, Central Michigan University; Bruce Landesman, University of Utah; Walter H. O'Briant, formerly of the University of Georgia; Curtis H. Peters, Indiana University Southeast; Dr. Michael Pinner, East Tennessee State University; Hal Walberg, Mankato State University; and Edward Walter, University of Missouri at Kansas City. Of course, any remaining mistakes are mine alone. My thanks go to Ken King and the rest of the Mayfield staff, who gave me great advice and support from start to finish. Finally, and most important, thanks to my wife, Joanne (who read every word), and daughter, Madeline, for their unceasing support and love.

Contents

MEDIEVAL ETHICS

MODERN ETHICS

EARLY TWENTIETH-CENTURY ETHICS

CONTEMPORARY ETHICS

ETHICAL TRADITIONS

Introduction to Ethics

A ll of the writings in this text are on the subject of ethics, or moral philosophy. (I will use these terms interchangeably in this text.) They are arranged chrono-logically, beginning with the earliest known written examples of ethics in the Western tradition and extending through the last years of the twentieth century. Before you begin to read, it might be helpful to have some idea of what ethics is, what particular ethical problems you should expect to encounter in these pages, and some explanation of the reason for the historical nature of the text. Additionally, a few words about how to go about reading these often intimidating and perplexing works will make your excursion through this text more fruitful and effective.

Before I explain what ethics is, let me say something about what philosophy is. Philosophy is distinctive both for what it studies and for the way it studies it. What philosophy studies is nothing but the most fundamental and important concepts un-derlying all of human existence. What is reality? What is the nature of God? How did the universe come to exist? How should we live? What is knowledge? How is knowledge different from belief? These are just a few of the questions philosophers ask and attempt to answer. So we could say that philosophers study life, but they study it by examining ideas, concepts, and words. The way in which philosophy studies these fundamental ideas, concepts, and words is unique. Philosophers use reason and logic, particularly in the form of *arguments*. Philosophers don't run ex-periments or take surveys; instead they give arguments. And arguments are nothing but statements that attempt to prove a conclusion.

Philosophers now distinguish three main areas of study: metaphysics (the study of reality), epistemology (the study of knowledge), and axiology (the study of val-ues). Ethics, the topic of this text, is a field of philosophy in the area of axiology. This tells us, at least initially, that ethics concerns itself with values.

As anyone who has taken an introductory philosophy class can tell you, phi-losophers hardly ever agree about anything, and they certainly wouldn't agree about anything as important as the definition of a term such as *ethics*. You will find a slightly different, slightly nuanced meaning for *ethics* in just about any ethics text you pick up. The very broad meaning that I will assign it here does not say every-thing that could be said, but it does, I think, give a flavor of the enterprise that ex-plains both its scope and its importance. My definition harkens back to the man you will learn about in the first reading of this book, Socrates. Some two and one-half millennia ago, Socrates declared that ethics was the study of how we ought to live.

Ethics can be defined simply as that: the rational search for how we ought to live. But what appears to be such a simple question becomes much more complex the longer you think about it. As you proceed through this book, you should remind yourself of that definition, because the men and women whose words you will read say very important things about how you and I should direct our lives. You will not agree with all of them, of course. But among these words you will likely find some that will resonate to your core.

Now that we have at least some idea of what ethics is all about, we can pursue the second question. Why does this book contain historical works of moral philosophy, and why is it arranged chronologically? There are several reasons for choosing the material included here and for arranging it by date. The most important reason for the historical nature of the book concerns philosophy's unique relationship to its own past. Philosophy as a discipline relates to its past in a way that most other academic disciplines do not. Scientists, for example, seldom care about who had the wrong idea about the way the heart worked or the various reasons that the person came to that erroneous conclusion. For scientists the past is a museum where quaint notions can be displayed. But philosophers seldom reach a point where all past efforts to answer a question can be universally rejected as irremediably wrong and of little further interest to anyone. Progress, in any kind of overarching, for-all-time sense, is slow indeed in philosophy. So philosophers continually return to ideas from philosophy's past. Philosophy, as it is conceived of as a tradition in the culture of the Western world, is best thought of as a continual process. A useful metaphor for describing philosophy is a conversation. Just as you would miss something vital should you enter a conversation in process without any idea of where the conversation began, you would be missing something vital if you were to pick up a work on philosophy without some understanding of its place in the ongoing dialogue that is philosophy. Sure, you might find something important in it, but you would be missing something as well. To ensure that you have the opportunity to enter the conversation at its beginning, the works in this volume cover the entire span of the history of philosophy in the Western tradition. The text is arranged chronologically so that you can learn about moral philosophy in a way similar to the way the conversation unfolded.

Something else should be said about the nature of historical works. History is necessarily selective. The winners of the battle write the histories of that conflict. This means that one side's perspective is likely to be slighted or ignored altogether. History is dependent on what gets saved. If something is written down on a papyrus roll or printed in a book, its chances of being saved and later deemed important are much greater than if those ideas are merely told and retold to others.

Philosophy is not timeless, although its problems may be. Ideas are the products not only of the minds that produced them, but also of the time and culture in which they are formed. Some of the ways we think about things would still be completely comfortable for a Greek of the classical era, some 2500 years ago. Other ideas would be so foreign as to be incomprehensible.

This book attempts to show how one particular area of philosophical interest, the study of moral philosophy, has developed over time. This history will be, like any history, selective. What is available for us to read is that which has been written down, preserved, transcribed, and deemed important by other people over the course of two and one-half millennia. Some of the thinkers you will encounter here are familiar to most educated people and perhaps even to most people in our society. Many will recognize names such as Socrates, Plato, and Aristotle even if they don't know who these individuals were or what they did. St. Augustine and St. Thomas Aquinas are also names familiar to many, as are the names of Kant and John Stuart Mill. Yet even if the names of these figures are unknown, their ideas will be familiar because they form the stock of ideas that has created the world as we know it today. You will discover here the origins of the ideas that many take for granted today—that what is good is relative to a culture or an individual, that God determines right and wrong, that might doesn't make right, and that the right thing to do is to bring the most pleasure to the most people.

Along with these familiar people, some less familiar thinkers will be introduced in these writings. Many of them are well known to those trained in philosophy. You may not have heard of Epicurus or G. E. Moore, but most of those who have seriously studied philosophy have. However, some of the names will be unknown to almost everyone. These are people who engaged in the study of ideas, who did philosophy, but who were not selected by the historical process to be remembered through the ages. Their exclusion may have been due to a number of factors: They may not have written down anything, or very much of anything; what they wrote may have been destroyed by fires, floods, or wars; their thoughts may not have been original or inspiring to those who followed; or they may have been neglected because they weren't on the winning side. One group that was seldom, if ever, on the winning side in the history of philosophy is women. If one looks at a traditional list of famous ethical philosophers of the Western tradition, nary a woman's name will be found until late in the twentieth century. However, women as well as men engaged in the study of ethics. And some of that work by some of those women has come down to us. Not a great deal exists; but a few selections are included in this text to demonstrate that women did do work in moral philosophy that has survived the ages, and that work can still speak to us today. The fragments are small because women seldom published books prior to the last couple of centuries; more likely they corresponded with others more famous or wrote shorter works that have been preserved. But these selections are given here, first, as a reminder that women were thinkers and writers in all ages, and second, to make us wonder what the history of ethical philosophy would have looked like had women been encouraged to participate in this most wondrous of scholarly endeavors. Who knows what progress could have been made?

All of this discussion about history is important for our study of moral philosophy. You will see, if you study ethics historically, that problems of the ages are problems for the ages. Ideas that Plato grappled with are ideas that we grapple with today. The study of important ideas is not something that is understood and then moved beyond. Old ideas reappear, but in new contexts. With new understandings about one issue, an old issue takes on a different meaning or expression. What looks unimportant in one era becomes of central concern in a later one. By reading this book, you will encounter a process. This process expands and narrows, it looks one way and then another, it moves forward and back, it makes progress that soon begins to slide away. Most important, the study of ethics is a dynamic enterprise, one that can engage us all and in which there is room for all to engage.

Issues in Ethics

Before you begin reading the text and encountering moral ideas, a rough outline of some perennial issues and questions may help you understand the terrain. First, moral philosophers are often searching for a foundation for ethics. What that means can be shown by a simple example. To answer the question about how we should live, one might say that we should do whatever makes us happy. But philosophers are people who ask questions like children do—they always want you to tell them why. Why should we do what makes us happy? For many people the questioning ends here: "I don't know why—because I said so, that's why." But that is not much help for a philosopher. Maybe one could say that we should live like that because it is the right thing to do. Again comes the question: What makes that way of living right? This can go on and on, but the nature of this kind of questioning requires that moral philosophers search for a foundation. Moral philosophers, many of them at least, want to reach the point where the "why" questions end—"Here's why," they want to say. Unfortunately, someone always manages to keep asking why. Fortunately, the possibility of arriving at that foundation is intriguing enough for some people that they are willing to keep searching for answers.

In addition to the search for a foundation, but related to that issue, ethics is continually concerned with whether ethical truths or ethical values exist for everyone for all time, or whether values and truths are related to individual people or particular societies. This debate is about whether, to use more specific terms, ethics is objective (delivering timeless truths and values) or relative (delivering truths and values that are specific to individuals and cultures). This issue has been an integral part of the history of moral philosophy.

A third major issue for ethics involves the kinds of value judgments we make. We may say that an action is good or bad; we might say that doing this or that is right or wrong. People can be described as evil, courageous, good, or perhaps virtuous. What do we mean by these words? Because these kinds of words are so troublesome, which you will discover as you read, a great deal of attention is paid by moral philosophers to the meaning of ethical terms.

Other important issues for ethics will arise further on in the conversation. For example, you will encounter moral philosophers concerned with the relation of ethics to religion, the place of reason in ethics, human free will, and the source of moral motivation. The subject is broad, touching on a number of intriguing issues, and is of critical importance to anyone who wants to get the most out of his or her life. A world of ideas awaits you.

How to Read the Text

Reading philosophy in any form promises to be challenging. The search for truth about fundamental, important issues such as the ones studied by philosophers can be abstract, deep, and painstakingly detailed. Along with the everyday problems of reading philosophy, reading philosophical works from times long past poses additional problems. But I want to assure you that, first, reading these texts is not done with a magic "key" possessed by some and forbidden forever to others. Nothing could be further from the truth. Reading philosophy, ancient or modern, is just like reading any other text. One learns the skills gradually and, with practice, becomes more and more adept at applying those skills. If you follow the steps that I will describe shortly, you too can develop these skills, no matter how foreign the process seems to you initially. It isn't easy, but it can be done by anyone willing to work at it.

The second thing about which you may wish some reassurance is the value of learning to read these texts. It will be wonderful if you learn and remember some of the famous men and women who wrote philosophy, if you can relate names and movements with certain philosophical ideas, at least long enough to pass the tests and get good grades in your classes. Yet beyond this useful information, you can learn how to develop skills that will help you think deeply and critically about extremely important questions that arise from the study of moral philosophy. How you choose to live your life is of the utmost importance to you. Learning to think systematically and creatively about vital questions is a skill you can use for your entire life. These same reading and thinking skills will also transfer to every other text you pick up throughout your college career. Indeed, they will apply to whatever you read throughout your lifetime. Learning to read a philosophical work well will increase your ability to read well any other book in any other field.

How should you read these texts? I will list the steps you should follow:

1. Read the work in its entirety, trying to grasp the major issues and main themes. These readings are relatively short so that you can read them more than once. No one will get much out of philosophy by reading a selection once.

2. On the second time through, take note of the editor's comments that highlight important points in the text. These comments do not point out everything of importance; what they do is point out some places where you should take special care to read carefully.

3. By looking carefully at the areas to be given special attention, take care to note the kinds of ways philosophers indicate that they are doing something important. Attention to the way language is used to indicate important points will make your reading of the text much more productive and interesting. For example, authors often signal the main thesis, an overview of the chapter, an argument summary, and conclusions. Knowing and recognizing these kinds of signals will make it much easier for you to make your way through the readings with maximum understanding.

4. Take note of the kinds of questions that are asked about the text. You should learn to ask questions of the text as you read. What does the author mean here? How is this consistent with what was just said? Does this seem true to my experience? These kinds of questions help you read the text with a critical, engaged mind.

5. Have a good dictionary available whenever you read. Look up the meanings of words with which you are unfamiliar.

6. Philosophy, because it is so dense and demanding, should be read only for brief periods. Don't rely on marathon reading sessions. You must study what you read, not merely pass your eyes over it; therefore, several reading periods of a shorter length will be much more effective (and tolerable) than one longer period.

Socrates

Ancient Greece is the birthplace of Western civilization. Almost every important facet of Western culture can trace its roots to the society that occupied that dry, rocky land in the eastern Mediterranean. Painting, sculpture, literature, theater, science, and even the study of history flourished in the eastern Mediterranean some 2500 years ago. Philosophy, too, began here. Our civilization still resembles that of Greece in some important ways. Beginning with this section, we will read some of the most important works in moral philosophy created by the Greek mind. However, to better understand these works, we will first investigate some of the similarities and differences between the society of ancient Greece and our own. Such an investigation will be helpful for better understanding anything we read by the Greeks, whether it be drama or philosophy. Yet it is especially important for reading Greek moral philosophy because society produces the moral life in which people, including philosophers, are born and raised. A good way to begin is to look briefly at the political organization of Greek society and at Greek religion.

Although the ancient Greek people were religious and Greek democracy was the basis for our own democratic government, Greek religion and Greek society differed greatly from the religions and societies we know today. The Greek people lived in small city-states, each of which they called a *polis*. The *polis* consisted of a city fortified by walls, the surrounding farms and countryside, and numerous nearby small towns. Athens and Sparta are two well-known Greek city-states. The Greek people considered their foremost allegiance to be to their *polis,* but they all spoke a common language and recognized each other as Greeks, a people superior to all others, whom they called *barbarians.* Barbarians included those uncivilized peoples who surrounded them to the north and west, as well as the civilized Egyptians, Persians, and others whom they encountered along the eastern end of the Mediterranean Sea.

The political life within the *polis* was democratic, yet this democracy demanded a much greater involvement on the part of its citizens than does current Western democracy. However, not all inhabitants of a Greek city-state were citizens. In fact, true citizens were a distinct minority. The population consisted of slaves (usually foreigners captured in battle), immigrants who were free but who were not allowed to participate in political affairs, and native citizens. Only male citizens were allowed a say in the running of the city-state. Whereas we elect people into government offices to represent our interests, the Greek male citizens participated directly in the governing of their nation. Greek male citizens made up the governing bodies of the city-state; they considered service to the *polis* to be both a privilege and an obligation. This helps explain why the Greek philosophers were apt to blur the distinction between ethics and politics: political involvement was usually considered a necessary part of the good life. It also explains why it was often taken for granted that the highest virtue for a man was the ability to govern well.

To properly understand Greek philosophy, we must also know something about Greek religion. Greek religious belief postulated a whole other world filled with deities. The Olympian gods, headed by Zeus, are the most familiar to us. Being immortal and extraordinarily powerful, the gods were superior to humans. But they were quite humanlike as well, especially in their failings. They quarreled with each other, spitefully interfered with people who had offended them, lied, and could be petty and jealous. Some of these gods belonged to all Greeks, but others were more personal. Athena, for example, the goddess of Athens, was especially close to the people there.

Along with the Olympian pantheon, various shadowy deities and spirits also occupied a place in the religion of the common people. So, too, did the gods of what are called the "mystery religions," such as Dionysus, whom people worshiped in a more wild and frenzied way than they did the gods of the pantheon residing at Olympus. This wide variety of gods, many hardly recognizable to us as godlike at all, provided a background to the morality of the Greeks. Like many people today, most Greeks viewed their religion as the source of their moral code.

From this society emerged individuals who determined the course of Western civilization by changing the way people thought about the world and their place in it. The earliest philosophers may not have been the first people to ask fundamental questions about the nature of reality, the origins of the universe, and the basis of human knowledge. They were the first, however, to refuse to rely on answers given by historical legends, by priests, or by soothsayers. Instead, these people uniquely strove to find the truth about fundamental questions through the resources of their own minds. They employed *reason* to arrive at the truth. The first of the philosophers, Thales, lived around 600 B.C. He and his successors, such as Anaximander, Heraclitus, and Pythagoras (collectively called **pre-Socratics**), devoted their attention to answering the kinds of questions we tend now to classify as **cosmological** (how did the universe come into existence?), **ontological** (what does it mean for something to exist?), and **metaphysical** (what is the ultimate nature of reality?). Neither Thales nor his immediate predecessors appear to have been particularly interested in ethical issues. It took more than a century, until the fifth century B.C., for philosophers to seriously tackle the questions of ethics.

Philosophers eventually began to think seriously about ethics, in part because Greeks increasingly encountered non-Greek civilizations. The Greeks, whose colonies occupied most of the eastern Mediterranean and extended to parts of the Black Sea coast, were familiar with the ancient civilization of Egypt and felt the powerful reach of Persia. With this interaction with other societies came the growing awareness that these people had different customs, traditions, and values from those of the Greeks. What appeared right and proper in one society—burning one's dead relatives, for example—scandalized other people who believed it was proper to eat the bodies of their dead fathers. How could it be that values differed so widely among different societies? It began to appear that valuing one set of practices over another was merely a matter of tradition and nothing more. Values, it seemed, were relative to society. Moral philosophy began as this increased exposure to diverse cultural practices forced thoughtful Greeks to examine the source of their own values.

Another factor that helped bring about moral philosophy was the increased popularity of traveling teachers known as **Sophists**. The Sophists were experts in rhetoric, the art of persuasive argumentation, and made their living by teaching the young men who hungered for advancement in society. Sophists taught *success*. Those who were not born with money, power, and status knew that such things were attainable only with the right knowledge. Knowing the ways of the government and how to persuade people in the courts were essential tools for those who wished to prosper in Greek society. Because the Sophists accepted pay for their teaching and because they called into question the traditional values and societal roles—indeed, they taught their students how to manipulate these roles and values for their own advantage—they were often looked down upon by those who already occupied high positions. Nonetheless, the services of Sophists were sought after, and many became wealthy and powerful. At least partly because of the success of the Sophists, philosophers began to turn their attention to problems of ethics. When values are called into question, as Athenian ones were by Sophists and their students, the subject of ethics takes on increased importance.

So who was the first moral philosopher in the Greek world? The answer is not obvious. The Sophists—philosophers such as Protagoras, Gorgias, and Thrasymachus—studied morality. But it's hard to see their work as moral philosophy since, for the most part, they used their knowledge of ethics to lead their pupils into successful lives and careers by manipulating ethical arguments. Their interest lay not in the moral life, but in success. We could say that they studied ethics, but as a means to an end, not as an end in itself. Yet in a way, the Sophists brought about the conditions for the first moral philosopher. That title, most would say, belongs to an incomparable figure of Western civilization, the great Socrates.

We can find several reasons for placing Socrates at the top of the list for the title of first moral philosopher, but two main reasons stand out. The first is philosophical: he initiated a style of philosophical inquiry that was to have lasting and profound effect on the history of subsequent thinking. This method is sometimes called the Socratic dialectic, but it is usually known as the **Socratic method.** This method, which is exemplified in the dialogue *Euthyphro* in the next reading, forcefully examines important philosophical concepts by scrutinizing the meanings of words. For example, Socrates would respond to someone who claimed to know what courage was by asking him to provide a definition of the word. After Socrates' opponent set out a definition, Socrates would lead him to discover a contradiction or inconsistency in the definition. The person would attempt to improve the definition, only to have Socrates find an underlying flaw in it too. On and on this would go until the target of this inquiry, always someone who claimed to have knowledge, was forced to admit that he, in fact, did not really know the meaning of the word. Seldom, apparently, did the Socratic method establish a definition that was unassailable. But for Socrates, the first step to knowledge is the admission of ignorance. This the method usually exposed.

We may consider Socrates the first moral philosopher merely on the basis of the influence the Socratic method had on the subsequent history of philosophy. However, another reason for designating him first is perhaps even more powerful. For Socrates, moral philosophy was his life. The key to *the* good life—not *a* good life, one among many possibilities—lay in the proper knowledge of what was good. Socrates believed that people would do the right thing if they could. And the reason that they do bad, do harm, or do evil, is out of ignorance of what is good. Perhaps you can think of a time when you harmed a friend or relative and later looked back on your actions only to realize "Boy, was I stupid." This is the case, thought Socrates, with every bad act. This is the reason that Socrates made as his motto "The unexamined life is not worth living." Such a life will be one of ignorance, and therefore not a good life.

Many people use fancy words and have high ideals but fail to live according to them. Not Socrates—the philosophy of Socrates guided his life. This can most clearly be seen in his death at the hands of the Athenian government. Accused by envious leaders of corrupting the youth and not believing in the gods, Socrates was found guilty and sentenced to death by drinking hemlock. In the powerful dialogue written by Plato, the *Crito,* Socrates refuses to allow his friends to spirit him out of the jail and into exile. To thwart the law that he had lived his whole life by, just to gain a few years of breath, was to lose his integrity. He must live by the rules even when they were against him, so he would drink the hemlock. He did and became a model for all time by doing so.

One problem accompanies the choice of Socrates as the premier moral philosopher. Because he wrote nothing, we have no words of his own that we can be assured represent his ideas. Instead, we know the philosophy of Socrates mostly through dialogues written by his most famous student, Plato, in which a character named Socrates usually plays a significant role. But even scholars are unsure of where Socrates' ideas leave off and those of Plato begin. Is Plato representing the philosophy of Socrates, or is he merely using the character named Socrates as a mouthpiece for his own views? Most specialists agree that the earlier Platonic dialogues most likely represent Socratic philosophy, and that the middle and later dialogues represent developments made by Plato himself. We need not concern ourselves too much with this problem. The reading is meant to characterize an important facet of the Socratic character even if it fails to include his exact words.

Before we begin with the reading, a final word should be said about the influence of Socrates on subsequent moral philosophy. Socrates formed no school of his own, preferring to teach in the open marketplace to anyone who would listen. However, four schools were founded in ancient Greece by followers of Socrates. The **Megarian** school belonged to Euclides, Aristippus led the **Cyrenaics,** Antisthenes headed the **Cynics,** and Plato, his most brilliant student, founded the **Academy.** All claimed Socrates as their inspiration, although each emphasized a different aspect of the master's teaching. These schools and the philosophers associated with them exerted a tremendous impact on the more than two millennia of subsequent philosophy. Even in our own day the great civil rights leader Martin Luther King, Jr., invokes the memory of Socrates in his famous "Letter from Birmingham Jail" and reminds us that the life and death of Socrates give testimony to his deep moral convictions and his belief in the incorruptibility of philosophy.

Crito

In a selection from the *Crito,* a dialogue written by Socrates' student Plato, we get a close view of the moral character of Socrates. This dialogue also supplies rich moral philosophy, including the first written argument about an issue that has played an important role throughout the history of moral philosophy, even to this day. This is the question of our **debt to the society** in which we live.

From Plato, *Crito,* translated by Benjamin Jowett.

Every government seems to require a great deal from its citizens. We must obey its laws, pay its taxes, and fight (perhaps die) in its wars. But do we follow the laws and serve in the military only because we will be punished if we do not? Or do we instead have a duty to pay our fair share and fight when needed? If there is such a duty, what is it that obligates us to serve our country in these various ways? In the *Crito,* Plato discusses what we owe to the state. The dialogue takes place in the jail cell of Socrates, who has been condemned to death by an Athenian court. His followers think he has been accused and sentenced unjustly. And because the government has no real wish to execute this flamboyant figure, Socrates' friends believe that they can easily break him out of jail. The government, they believe, will look the other way if Socrates is spirited out of Athens to spend his remaining years in exile.

As the scene opens, Socrates is approached by Crito, his student and friend, who urges Socrates to accept his help and avoid this unfair death sentence. Plato, through the character of Socrates, introduces the idea of an implied contract between each citizen and the state. By living in the state and accepting its institutions, each citizen enters into a binding contract, or a promise, with the state. To act against the rule of law, then, is to break the contract. This idea figures prominently in the ethical work of Thomas Hobbes and in contractarian theories from the twentieth century. Also see the selection from John Rawls in this volume.   ✒

PERSONS OF THE DIALOGUE

SOCRATES   CRITO

SCENE:—THE PRISON OF SOCRATES

SOCRATES: Why have you come at this hour, Crito? it must be quite early?

CRITO: Yes, certainly.

SOC: What is the exact time?

CR: The dawn is breaking.

SOC: I wonder that the keeper of the prison would let you in.

CR: He knows me, because I often come, Socrates; moreover, I have done him a kindness.

SOC: And are you only just come?

CR: No, I came some time ago.

SOC: Then why did you sit and say nothing, instead of awakening me at once?

CR: Why, indeed, Socrates, I myself would rather not have all this sleeplessness and sorrow. But I have been wondering at your peaceful slumbers, and that was the reason why I did not awaken you, because I wanted you to be out of pain. I have always thought you happy in the calmness of your temperament;

but never did I see the like of the easy, cheerful way in which you bear this calamity.

soc: Why, Crito, when a man has reached my age he ought not to be repining at the prospect of death.

CR: And yet other old men find themselves in similar misfortunes, and age does not prevent them from repining.

soc: That may be. But you have not told me why you come at this early hour.

CR: I come to bring you a message which is sad and painful; not, as I believe, to yourself, but to all of us who are your friends, and saddest of all to me.

soc: What! I suppose that the ship has come from Delos, on the arrival of which I am to die?

CR: No, the ship has not actually arrived, but she will probably be here today, as persons who have come from Sunium tell me that they left her there; and therefore tomorrow, Socrates, will be the last day of your life.

soc: Very well, Crito; if such is the will of God, I am willing; but my belief is that there will be a delay of a day.

CR: Why do you say this?

soc: I will tell you. I am to die on the day after the arrival of the ship?

CR: Yes; that is what the authorities say.

soc: But I do not think that the ship will be here until tomorrow; this I gather from a vision which I had last night, or rather only just now, when you fortunately allowed me to sleep.

CR: And what was the nature of the vision?

soc: There came to me the likeness of a woman, fair and comely, clothed in white raiment, who called to me and said: O Socrates,

"The third day hence to Phthia shalt thou go."

CR: What a singular dream, Socrates!

soc: There can be no doubt about the meaning, Crito, I think.

CR: Yes; the meaning is only too clear. But, Oh! my beloved Socrates, let me entreat you once more to take my advice and escape. For if you die I shall not only lose a friend who can never be replaced, but there is another evil: people who do not know you and me will believe that I might have saved you if I had been willing to give money, but that I did not care. Now, can there be a worse disgrace than this—that I should be thought to value money more than the life of a friend? For the many will not be persuaded that I wanted you to escape, and that you refused.

soc: But why, my dear Crito, should we care about the opinion of the many? Good men, and they are the only persons who are worth considering, will think of these things truly as they happened.

CR: But do you see, Socrates, that the opinion of the many must be regarded, as is evident in your own case, because they can do the very greatest evil to any one who has lost their good opinion.

SOC: I only wish, Crito, that they could; for then they could also do the greatest good, and that would be well. But the truth is, that they can do neither good nor evil: they cannot make a man wise or make him foolish; and whatever they do is the result of chance.

CR: Well, I will not dispute about that; but please to tell me, Socrates, whether you are not acting out of regard to me and your other friends: are you not afraid that if you escape hence we may get into trouble with the informers for having stolen you away, and lose either the whole or a great part of our property; or that even a worse evil may happen to us? Now, if this is your fear, be at ease; for in order to save you, we ought surely to run this, or even a greater risk; be persuaded, then, and do as I say.

SOC: Yes, Crito, that is one fear which you mention, but by no means the only one.

CR: Fear not. There are persons who at no great cost are willing to save you and bring you out of prison; and as for the informers, you may observe that they are far from being exorbitant in their demands; a little money will satisfy them. My means, which, as I am sure, are ample, are at your service, and if you have a scruple about spending all mine, here are strangers who will give you the use of theirs; and one of them, Simmias the Theban, has brought a sum of money for this very purpose; and Cebes and many others are willing to spend their money too. I say therefore, do not on that account hesitate about making your escape, and do not say, as you did in the court, that you will have a difficulty in knowing what to do with yourself if you escape. For men will love you in other places to which you may go, and not in Athens only; there are friends of mine in Thessaly, if you like to go to them, who will value and protect you, and no Thessalian will give you any trouble. Nor can I think that you are justified, Socrates, in betraying your own life when you might be saved; this is playing into the hands of your enemies and destroyers; and moreover I should say that you were betraying your children; for you might bring them up and educate them; instead of which you go away and leave them, and they will have to take their chance; and if they do not meet with the usual fate of orphans, there will be small thanks to you. No man should bring children into the world who is unwilling to persevere to the end in their nurture and education. But you are choosing the easier part, as I think, not the better and manlier, which would rather have become one who professes virtue in all his actions, like yourself. And indeed, I am ashamed not only of you, but of us who are your friends, when I reflect that this entire business of yours will be attributed to our want of courage. The trial need never have come on, or might have been brought to another issue; and the end of all, which is the crowning absurdity, will seem to have been permitted by us, through cowardice and baseness, who might have saved you, as you might have saved yourself, if we had been good for anything (for there was no difficulty in escaping), and we did not see how disgraceful, Socrates, and also miserable all this will be to us as well as to you. Make your mind up then, or rather have your mind already made up, for the time of deliberation is over, and there is only one thing to be done, which must be done, if at all, this very night, and which any delay will render all but impossible; I beseech you therefore, Socrates, to be persuaded by me, and to do as I say.

---

1. Now that Crito has given his reasons for coming at this hour, Socrates questions the value of common opinion. Why be concerned with what people may say?

SOC: Dear Crito, your zeal is invaluable, if a right one; but if wrong, the greater the zeal the greater the evil; and therefore we ought to consider whether these things shall be done or not. For I am and always have been one of those natures who must be guided by reason, whatever the reason may be which upon reflection appears to me to be the best; and now that this fortune has come upon me, I cannot put away the reasons which I have before given: the principles which I have hitherto honored and revered I still honor, and unless we can find other and better principles on the instant, I am certain not to agree with you; no, not even if the power of the multitude could inflict many more imprisonments, confiscations, deaths, frightening us like children with hobgoblin terrors. But what will be the fairest way of considering the question? Shall I return to your old argument about the opinions of men? some of which are to be regarded, and others, as we were saying, are not to be regarded. Now were we right in maintaining this before I was condemned? And has the argument which was once good now proved to be talk for the sake of talking;—in fact an amusement only, and altogether vanity? That is what I want to consider with your help, Crito:—whether, under my present circumstances, the argument appears to be in any way different or not; and is to be allowed by me or disallowed. That argument, which, as I believe, is maintained by many who assume to be authorities, was to the effect, as I was saying, that the opinions of some men are to be regarded, and of other men not to be regarded. Now you, Crito, are a disinterested person who are not going to die tomorrow—at least, there is no human probability of this, and you are therefore not liable to be deceived by the circumstances in which you are placed. Tell me then, whether I am right in saying that some opinions, and the opinions of some men only, are to be valued, and other opinions, and the opinions of other men, are not to be valued. I ask you whether I was right in maintaining this?

CR: Certainly.

SOC: The good are to be regarded, and not the bad?

CR: Yes.

SOC: And the opinions of the wise are good, and the opinions of the unwise are evil?

CR: Certainly.

SOC: And what was said about another matter? Was the disciple in gymnastics supposed to attend to the praise and blame and opinion of every man, or of one man only—his physician or trainer, whoever that was?

CR: Of one man only.

SOC: And he ought to fear the censure and welcome the praise of that one only, and not of the many?

CR: That is clear.

SOC: And he ought to live and train, and eat and drink in the way which seems good to his single master who has understanding, rather than according to the opinions of all other men put together?

CR: True.

SOC: And if he disobeys and disregards the opinion and approval of the one, and regards the opinion of the many who have no understanding, will he not suffer evil?

CR: Certainly he will.

SOC: And what will the evil be, whither tending and what affecting, in the disobedient person?

CR: Clearly, affecting the body; that is what is destroyed by the evil.

SOC: Very good; and is not this true, Crito, of other things which we need not separately enumerate? In the matter of just and unjust, fair and foul, good and evil, which are the subjects of our present consultation, ought we to follow the opinion of the many and to fear them; or the opinion of the one man who has understanding, and whom we ought to fear and reverence more than all the rest of the world: and whom deserting we shall destroy and injure that principle in us which may be assumed to be improved by justice and deteriorated by injustice; —is there not such a principle?

CR: Certainly there is, Socrates.

SOC: Take a parallel instance: —if, acting under the advice of men who have no understanding, we destroy that which is improvable by health and deteriorated by disease—when that has been destroyed, I say, would life be worth having? And that is—the body?

CR: Yes.

SOC: Could we live, having an evil and corrupted body?

CR: Certainly not.

SOC: And will life be worth having, if that higher part of man be depraved, which is improved by justice and deteriorated by injustice? Do we suppose that principle, whatever it may be in man, which has to do with justice and injustice, to be inferior to the body?

CR: Certainly not.

SOC: More honored, then?

CR: Far more honored.

SOC: Then, my friend, we must not regard what the many say of us: but what he, the one man who has understanding of just and unjust, will say, and what the truth will say. And therefore you begin in error when you suggest that we should regard the opinion of the many about just and unjust, good and evil, honorable and dishonorable. —Well, some one will say, "but the many can kill us."

CR: Yes, Socrates; that will clearly be the answer.

SOC: That is true: but still I find with surprise that the old argument is, as I conceive, unshaken as ever. And I should like to know whether I may say the same of another position—that not life, but a good life, is to be chiefly valued?

CR: Yes, that also remains.

SOC: And a good life is equivalent to a just and honorable one—that holds also?

CR: Yes, that holds.

SOC: From these premises I proceed to argue the question whether I ought or ought not to try and escape without the consent of the Athenians: and if I am clearly right in escaping, then I will make the attempt; but if not, I will abstain. The other considerations which you mention, of money and loss of character and the duty of educating children, are, as I fear, only the doctrines of the multitude, who would be as ready to call people to life, if they were able, as they are to put them to death—and with as little reason. But now, since the argument has thus far prevailed, the only question which remains to be considered is, whether we shall do rightly either in escaping or in suffering others to aid in our escape and paying them in money and thanks, or whether we shall not do rightly; and if the latter, then death or any other calamity which may ensue on my remaining here must not be allowed to enter into the calculation.

CR: I think that you are right, Socrates; how then shall we proceed?

SOC: Let us consider the matter together, and do you either refute me if you can, and I will be convinced; or else cease, my dear friend, from repeating to me that I ought to escape against the wishes of the Athenians: for I am extremely desirous to be persuaded by you, but not against my own better judgment. And now please to consider my first position, and do your best to answer me.

CR: I will do my best.

———

2. Socrates begins to question whether he will be acting rightly or wrongly in following the advice of Crito. Notice that he has already argued that his life will be valuable only if he retains his honor. As he said, not life, but "a good life" is to be valued.

———

SOC: Are we to say that we are never intentionally to do wrong, or that in one way we ought and in another way we ought not to do wrong, or is doing wrong always evil and dishonorable, as I was just now saying, and as has been already acknowledged by us? Are all our former admissions which were made within a few days to be thrown away? And have we, at our age, been earnestly discoursing with one another all our life long only to discover that we are no better than children? Or are we to rest assured, in spite of the opinion of the many, and in spite of consequences whether better or worse, of the truth of what was then said, that injustice is always an evil and dishonor to him who acts unjustly? Shall we affirm that?

CR: Yes.

SOC: Then we must do no wrong?

CR: Certainly not.

SOC: Nor when injured injure in return, as the many imagine; for we must injure no one at all?

CR: Clearly not.

SOC: Again, Crito, may we do evil?

CR: Surely not, Socrates.

SOC: And what of doing evil in return for evil, which is the morality of the many—is that just or not?

CR: Not just.

SOC: For doing evil to another is the same as injuring him?

CR: Very true.

SOC: Then we ought not to retaliate or render evil for evil to any one, whatever evil we may have suffered from him. But I would have you consider, Crito, whether you really mean what you are saying. For this opinion has never been held, and never will be held, by any considerable number of persons; and those who are agreed and those who are not agreed upon this point have no common ground, and can only despise one another when they see how widely they differ. Tell me, then, whether you agree with and assent to my first principle, that neither injury nor retaliation nor warding off evil by evil is ever right. And shall that be the premise of our argument? Or do you decline and dissent from this? For this has been of old and is still my opinion; but, if you are of another opinion, let me hear what you have to say. If, however, you remain of the same mind as formerly, I will proceed to the next step.

CR: You may proceed, for I have not changed my mind.

SOC: Then I will proceed to the next step, which may be put in the form of a question:—Ought a man to do what he admits to be right, or ought he to betray the right?

CR: He ought to do what he thinks right.

SOC: But if this is true, what is the application? In leaving the prison against the will of the Athenians, do I wrong any? or rather do I not wrong those whom I ought least to wrong? Do I not desert the principles which were acknowledged by us to be just? What do you say?

CR: I cannot tell, Socrates; for I do not know.

---

3. Socrates personifies the laws and the government of Athens and imagines them questioning him about the justice of his escaping punishment. Why do they accuse him of attempting to overthrow the government and the laws?

SOC: Then consider the matter in this way:—Imagine that I am about to play truant (you may call the proceeding by any name which you like), and the laws and the government come and interrogate me: "Tell us, Socrates," they say; "what are you about? are you going by an act of yours to overturn us—the laws and the whole state, as far as in you lies? Do you imagine that a state can subsist and not be overthrown, in which the decisions of law have no power, but are set aside and overthrown by individuals?" What will be our answer, Crito, to these and the like words? Anyone, and especially a clever rhetorician, will have a good deal to urge about the evil of setting aside the law which requires a sentence to be carried out; and we might reply, "Yes; but the state has injured us and given an unjust sentence." Suppose I say that?

CR: Very good, Socrates.

SOC: "And was that our agreement with you?" the law would say; "or were you to abide by the sentence of the state?" And if I were to express astonishment at their saying this, the law would probably add: "Answer, Socrates, instead of opening your eyes: you are in the habit of asking and answering questions. Tell us what complaint you have to make against us which justifies you in attempting to destroy us and the state? In the first place did we not bring you into existence? Your father married your mother by our aid and begat you. Say whether you have any objection to urge against those of us who regulate marriage?" None, I should reply. "Or against those of us who regulate the systems of nurture and education of children in which you were trained? Were not the laws, who have the charge of this, right in commanding your father to train you in music and gymnastic?" Right, I should reply. "Well then, since you were brought into the world and nurtured and educated by us, can you deny in the first place that you are our child and slave, as your fathers were before you? And if this is true you are not on equal terms with us; nor can you think that you have a right to do to us what we are doing to you. Would you have any right to strike or revile or do any other evil to a father or to your master, if you had one, when you have been struck or reviled by him, or received some other evil at his hands? —you would not say this? And because we think right to destroy you, do you think that you have any right to destroy us in return, and your country as far as in you lies? And will you, O professor of true virtue, say that you are justified in this? Has a philosopher like you failed to discover that our country is more to be valued and higher and holier far than mother or father or any ancestor, and more to be regarded in the eyes of the gods and of men of understanding? also to be soothed, and gently and reverently entreated when angry, even more than a father, and if not persuaded, obeyed? And when we are punished by her, whether with imprisonment or stripes, the punishment is to be endured in silence; and if she lead us to wounds or death in battle, thither we follow as is right; neither may any one yield or retreat or leave his rank, but whether in battle or in a court of law, or in any other place, he must do what his city and his country order him; or he must change their view of what is just: and if he may do no violence to his father or mother, much less may he do violence to his country." What answer shall we make to this, Crito? Do the laws speak truly, or do they not?

CR: I think that they do.

---

4. Socrates imagines the laws telling him of the implied contract he has agreed to by remaining in Athens. What do the laws answer to the person who denies having made any contract with the government?

SOC: Then the laws will say: "Consider, Socrates, if this is true, that in your present attempt you are going to do us wrong. For, after having brought you into the world, and nurtured and educated you, and given you and every other citizen a share in every good that we had to give, we further proclaim and give the right to every Athenian, that if he does not like us when he has come of age and has seen the ways of the city, and made our acquaintance, he may go where he pleases and take his goods with him; and none of us laws will forbid him or interfere with him. Any of you who does not like us and the city, and who wants to go to a colony or to any other city, may go where he likes, and take his goods with him. But he who has experience of the manner in which we order justice and administer the state, and still remains, has entered into an implied contract that he will do as we command him. And he who disobeys us is, as we maintain, thrice wrong; first, because in disobeying us he is disobeying his parents; secondly, because we are the authors of his education; thirdly, because he has made an agreement with us that he will duly obey our commands; and he neither obeys them nor convinces us that our commands are wrong; and we do not rudely impose them, but give them the alternative of obeying or convincing us; —that is what we offer, and he does neither. These are the sort of accusations to which, as we were saying, you, Socrates, will be exposed if you accomplish your intentions; you, above all other Athenians." Suppose I ask, why is this? they will justly retort upon me that I above all other men have acknowledged the agreement. "There is clear proof," they will say, "Socrates, that we and the city were not displeasing to you. Of all Athenians you have been the most constant resident in the city, which, as you never leave, you may be supposed to love. For you never went out of the city either to see the games, except once when you went to the Isthmus, or to any other place unless when you were on military service; nor did you travel as other men do. Nor had you any curiosity to know other states or their laws: your affections did not go beyond us and our state; we were your special favorites, and you acquiesced in our government of you; and this is the state in which you begat your children, which is a proof of your satisfaction. Moreover, you might, if you had liked, have fixed the penalty at banishment in the course of the trial—the state which refuses to let you go now would have let you go then. But you pretended that you preferred death to exile, and that you were not grieved at death. And now you have forgotten these fine sentiments, and pay no respect to us the laws, of whom you are the destroyer; and are doing what only a miserable slave would do, running away and turning your back upon the compacts and agreements which you made as a citizen. And first of all answer this very question: Are we right in saying that you agreed to be governed according to us in deed, and not in word only? Is that true or not?" How shall we answer that, Crito? Must we not agree?

CR: There is no help, Socrates.

SOC: Then will they not say: "You, Socrates, are breaking the covenants and agreements which you made with us at your leisure, not in any haste or under any compulsion or deception, but having had seventy years to think of them, during which time you were at liberty to leave the city, if we were not to your mind, or if our covenants appeared to you to be unfair. You had your choice, and might have gone either to Lacedaemon or Crete, which you often praise for their good government, or to some other Hellenic or foreign state. Whereas you, above all other Athenians, seemed to be so fond of the state, or, in other words, of us her laws (for who would like a state that has no laws), that you never stirred out of her; the halt, the blind, the maimed were not more stationary in her than you were. And now you run away and forsake your agreements. Not so, Socrates, if you will take our advice; do not make yourself ridiculous by escaping out of the city.

"For just consider, if you transgress and err in this sort of way, what good will you do either to yourself or to your friends? That your friends will be driven into exile and deprived of citizenship, or will lose their property, is tolerably certain; and you yourself, if you fly to one of the neighboring cities, as, for example, Thebes or Megara, both of which are well-governed cities, will come to them as an enemy, Socrates, and their government will be against you, and all patriotic citizens will cast an evil eye upon you as a subverter of the laws, and you will confirm in the minds of the judges the justice of their own condemnation of you. For he who is a corrupter of the laws is more than likely to be a corrupter of the young and foolish portion of mankind. Will you then flee from well-ordered cities and virtuous men? and is existence worth having on these terms? Or will you go to them without shame, and talk to them, Socrates? And what will you say to them? What you say here about virtue and justice and institutions and laws being the best things among men. Would that be decent of you? Surely not. But if you go away from well-governed states to Crito's friends in Thessaly, where there is a great disorder and license, they will be charmed to have the tale of your escape from prison, set off with ludicrous particulars of the manner in which you were wrapped in a goatskin or some other disguise, and metamorphosed as the fashion of runaways is—that is very likely; but will there be no one to remind you that in your old age you violated the most sacred laws from a miserable desire of a little more life. Perhaps not, if you keep them in a good temper; but if they are out of temper you will hear many degrading things; you will live, but how? —as the flatterer of all men, and the servant of all men; and doing what? —eating and drinking in Thessaly, having gone abroad in order that you may get a dinner. And where will be your fine sentiments about justice and virtue then? Say that you wish to live for the sake of your children, that you may bring them up and educate them—will you take them into Thessaly and deprive them of Athenian citizenship? Is that the benefit which you would confer upon them? Or are you under the impression that they will be better cared for and educated here if you are still alive, although absent from them; for that your friends will take care of them? Do you fancy that if you are an inhabitant of Thessaly they will take care of them, and if you are an inhabitant of the other world they will not take care of them? Nay; but if they who call themselves friends are truly friends, they surely will.

"Listen, then, Socrates, to us who have brought you up. Think not of life and children first, and of justice afterwards, but of justice first, that you may be justified before the princes of the world below. For neither will you nor any that belong to you be happier or holier or juster in this life, or happier in another, if you do as Crito bids. Now you depart in innocence, a sufferer and not a doer of evil; a victim, not of the laws, but of men. But if you go forth, returning evil for evil, and injury for injury, breaking the covenants and agreements which you have made with us, and wronging those whom you ought least to wrong, that is to say, yourself, your friends, your country, and us, we shall be angry with you while you live, and our brethren, the laws in the world below, will receive you as an enemy; for they will know that you have done your best to destroy us. Listen, then, to us and not to Crito."

This is the voice which I seem to hear murmuring in my ears, like the sound of the flute in the ears of the mystic; that voice, I say, is humming in my ears, and prevents me from hearing any other. And I know that anything more which you may say will be in vain. Yet speak, if you have anything to say.

CR: I have nothing to say, Socrates.

SOC: Then let me follow the intimations of the will of God.

READING QUESTIONS

1. Why has Crito come to Socrates' cell?
2. How did the state bring Socrates into existence?
3. What self-interested motives does Crito admit to?
4. What conclusion does Socrates draw from the fact that he never left Athens?
5. What is Socrates' point when he brings up the analogy of the gymnast?
6. At the end of the dialogue, Socrates gives a speech about what the laws would say to him if he should escape from jail. One thing that the laws say is "Think not of life and children first, and of justice afterwards, but of justice first. . . ." What *self-interested* reason do the laws present to convince Socrates?

Plato

Plato was born in Athens in 427 B.C. into a family of aristocrats and distinguished Athenian leaders. His family expected that he would adopt the political life, but due to his contempt for all sides engaged in an ongoing struggle for power, he turned his formidable talents to philosophy. He decided to train the next generation of rulers, not to be one. This training would be according to Socratic principles.

The student of Socrates and the teacher of Aristotle, Plato possessed an unsurpassed intellect that in large part determined the entire course of Western philosophy. A twentieth-century philosopher, Alfred North Whitehead, once remarked that the entire history of Western philosophy is but "a footnote to Plato." In other words, Plato laid out the central issues and problems in philosophy; subsequent philosophers have criticized and analyzed but not strayed far beyond his original ideas. Although this may be an exaggeration, in the field of ethics Plato certainly presented us with a very broad range of concerns that still elicit intense philosophical interest. No philosopher would claim that Plato solved all the problems of ethics, but few would deny the enormous debt that subsequent ethicists owe to him. Numerous fundamental ethical issues received their first significant philosophical treatment in his dialogues. Here we will focus on three of these issues that are still relevant to moral philosophy almost 2500 years later: the proper definition of moral terms, the divine command theory of ethics, and ethical relativism.

Plato did not publish a systematic theory of ethics in any of his dialogues. Yet he had a consistent view of the subject built upon what he learned from his teacher Socrates, and various ethical issues appear in his writings. The foundation of Plato's moral philosophy resides in his **metaphysics** (theory of reality) and **epistemology** (theory of knowledge)—in particular, his **Theory of Forms,** which is central to both. Because Socrates had been asking such questions as "What is courage?" and "What is justice?" it was relatively easy for Plato to assume that there must exist some real thing, distinct from mere examples of courage and justice, that one could ask such questions about. With his Theory of Forms, Plato postulated a world of Forms (or Ideas), known by the intellect, that were more real than the material things of the world that we perceive through our senses. The Idea of courage, for example, was the model for the instances of courage we observe in the world. When one attained knowledge of courage, one became courageous. Furthermore, if a person attained knowledge of Goodness, the highest of all Ideas, one would be virtuous in every aspect and be able to teach others how to reach the same goal.

With his Theory of Forms, then, Plato lends support to Socrates' claim that not only can virtue be known, but that people who know what is good will always do the right thing. For when people do wrong, they mistakenly think they are acting for their own benefit, when actually the act is self-defeating. Virtues such as courage, justice, and temperance are knowable by humans who are given the right kind of training by a teacher who has already attained the highest knowledge. The kind of training that makes such knowledge possible is philosophy.

Even though Platonic metaphysics is no longer a particularly credible theory in philosophical circles, its influence is still widely felt in many of our common notions such as the superiority of reason over sense experience and the immortality of an immaterial soul contained within a material body. Plato's tremendous influence on moral philosophy cannot be discounted. It was he who first framed many of the important issues in moral philosophy that still interest us today; the fact/value distinction, the objectivity or subjectivity of values, the attainment of moral knowledge, and understanding moral responsibility are just a few of the still vibrant issues that concerned Plato. Further, many consider Plato to be the founder of political philosophy and the *Republic* to be its founding document.

The influence of Plato extends beyond the fact that he introduced many perennial issues in moral philosophy. His philosophy directly and indirectly influenced important subsequent philosophers, many of whom are presented in this text. Directly he affected the many students of his own school, the **Academy**—in particular, his prize student, **Aristotle.** Later we will read some of the moral philosophy of Aristotle, whose ideas in ethics are currently experiencing renewed interest. In addition to Aristotle, Plato's ideas profoundly influenced a group of philosophers known as the **Stoics.** Ethical ideas of a famous Roman member of this school, **Epictetus,** are included in this text. Through the **Neoplatonists** (Roman-era followers of a philosopher named Plotinus, who revived Plato's ideas), Platonic philosophy inspired **St. Augustine** and thereby played a significant role in the intellectual history of Christianity. The influence of Plato is also seen in more modern philosophy—for example, in the ethics of the group of British moralists of the seventeenth century known as the **Cambridge Platonists** and the nineteenth-century intuitionist **G. E. Moore.** Representative works by St. Augustine and Moore are also included in this volume.

In the following two readings, we again encounter the difficulty of separating the ideas of Plato from those of Socrates. We will be reading from two dialogues by Plato in which the character Socrates has the leading role. In these two dialogues, Plato anticipated several issues of lasting importance to philosophy. The first is exemplified by the Socratic Method; what we may call a search for **the proper definitions of moral terms** takes place in the first selection, from the *Euthyphro.* Also in this dialogue, the character of Socrates sheds light on the relationship of ethics to religion. Those philosophers who argue that whatever is commanded by God is morally right advocate what is known as **the divine command theory of ethics.** This theory is investigated in the second selection from the dialogue. In the final reading, from his most famous work, the *Republic,* **ethical relativism** captures the spotlight.

Euthyphro

Why is it that people do bad things? For Plato, as for Socrates, the answer was relatively simple. People do the wrong thing because of ignorance of what is right. No one, not even a murderer or thief, does wrong knowingly. Thus, the first step for these moral philosophers was to show that

---

From Plato, *Euthyphro,* translated by Benjamin Jowett.

what people think they know about ethics is not correct. If it were, why would we have so much badness?

The method employed by Socrates and showcased in this Platonic dialogue is known as the Socratic dialectic, or **Socratic method.** This method is a search for truth by question and answer, but usually the kind of truth that Socrates was interested in was the definition of a concept. For example, knowledge of ethics would mean an understanding of all ethical concepts such as courage, justice, and the like. That is, people would know what trait each courageous act has and each cowardly act lacks. Philosophically, this is a search for universal definitions of moral concepts. The Socratic method begins with the questioning of an expert, someone who professes to know the meaning of courage, justice, or some other moral concept. Define the term, demands Socrates. The definition given is then subjected to scathing criticism, and the questioned person is urged to try again. More criticism follows until, ultimately, the expert is forced to acknowledge the inconsistency in his ideas and, thus, his ignorance.

In the *Euthyphro,* we see a fine example of the Socratic method. The dialogue begins with Socrates encountering Euthyphro on his way to the Athenian court to prosecute his own father for murdering a slave. The word under discussion is *piety.* As you read, notice how Euthyphro must keep offering new definitions of piety as he attempts to satisfy Socrates' objections.

SOC: I suppose that the man whom your father murdered was one of your relatives; if he had been a stranger you would never have thought of prosecuting him.

EUTH: I am amused, Socrates, at your making a distinction between one who is a relation and one who is not a relation; for surely the pollution is the same in either case, if you knowingly associate with the murderer when you ought to clear yourself by proceeding against him. The real question is whether the murdered man has been justly slain. If justly, then your duty is to let the matter alone; but if unjustly, then even if the murderer is under the same roof with you and eats at the same table, proceed against him. Now the man who is dead was a poor dependant of mine who worked for us as a field laborer at Naxos, and one day in a fit of drunken passion he got into a quarrel with one of our domestic servants and slew him. My father bound him hand and foot and threw him into a ditch, and then sent to Athens to ask of a diviner what he should do with him. Meantime he had no care or thought of him, being under the impression that he was a murderer; and that even if he did die there would be no great harm. And this was just what happened. For such was the effect of cold and hunger and chains upon him, that before the messenger returned from the diviner, he was dead. And my father and family are angry with me for taking the part of the murderer and prosecuting my father. They say that he did not kill him, and if he did, the dead man was but a murderer, and I ought not to take any notice, for that a son is impious who prosecutes a father. That shows, Socrates, how little they know of the opinions of the gods about piety and impiety.

SOC: Good heavens, Euthyphro! and have you such a precise knowledge of piety and impiety, and of divine things in general, that, supposing the circumstances to be as you state, you are not afraid that you too may be doing an impious thing in bringing an action against your father?

EUTH: The best of Euthyphro, and that which distinguishes him, Socrates, from other men, is his exact knowledge of all these matters. What should I be good for without that?

SOC: Rare friend! I think that I cannot do better than be your disciple, before the trial with Meletus comes on. Then I shall challenge him, and say that I have always had a great interest in religious questions, and now, as he charges me with rash imaginations and innovations in religion, I have become your disciple. Now you, Meletus, as I shall say to him, acknowledge Euthyphro to be a great theologian, and sound in his opinions; and if you think that of him you ought to think the same of me, and not have me into court; you should begin by indicting him who is my teacher, and who is the real corruptor, not of the young, but of the old; that is to say, of myself whom he instructs, and of his old father whom he admonishes and chastises. And if Meletus refuses to listen to me, but will go on, and will not shift the indictment from me to you, I cannot do better than say in the court that I challenged him in this way.

EUTH: Yes, Socrates; and if he attempts to indict me I am mistaken if I don't find a flaw in him; the court shall have a great deal more to say to him than to me.

SOC: I know that, dear friend; and that is the reason why I desire to be your disciple. For I observe that no one, not even Meletus, appears to notice you; but his sharp eyes have found me out at once, and he has indicted me for impiety. And therefore, I adjure you to tell me the nature of piety and impiety, which you said that you knew so well, and of murder, and the rest of them. What are they? Is not piety in every action always the same? and impiety, again, is not that always the opposite of piety, and also the same with itself, having, as impiety, one notion which includes whatever is impious?

EUTH: To be sure, Socrates.

1. Euthyphro makes his first attempt at defining piety.

SOC: And what is piety, and what is impiety?

EUTH: Piety is doing as I am doing; that is to say, prosecuting any one who is guilty of murder, sacrilege, or of any other similar crime—whether he be your father or mother, or some other person, that makes no difference—and not prosecuting them is impiety. And please to consider, Socrates, what a notable proof I will give you of the truth of what I am saying, which I have already given to others:—of the truth, I mean, of the principle that the impious, whoever he may be, ought not to go unpunished. For do not men regard Zeus as the best and most righteous of the gods?—and even they admit that he bound his father (Cronos) because he wickedly devoured his sons, and that he too had punished his own father (Uranus) for a similar reason, in a nameless manner. And yet when I proceed against my father, they are angry with me. This is their inconsistent way of talking when the gods are concerned, and when I am concerned.

SOC: May not this be the reason, Euthyphro, why I am charged with impiety— that I cannot away with these stories about the gods? and therefore I suppose that people think me wrong. But, as you who are well informed about them approve of them, I cannot do better than assent to your superior wisdom. For what else can I say, confessing as I do, that I know nothing of them. I wish you would tell me whether you really believe that they are true?

EUTH: Yes, Socrates; and things more wonderful still, of which the world is in ignorance.

SOC: And do you really believe that the gods fought with one another, and had dire quarrels, battles, and the like, as the poets say, and as you may see represented in the works of great artists? The temples are full of them; and notably the robe of Athene, which is carried up to the Acropolis at the great Panathenaea, is embroidered with them. Are all these tales of the gods true, Euthyphro?

EUTH: Yes, Socrates; and, as I was saying, I can tell you, if you would like to hear them, many other things about the gods which would quite amaze you.

SOC: I dare say; and you shall tell me them at some other time when I have leisure. But just at present I would rather hear from you a more precise answer, which you have not as yet given, my friend, to the question, What is "piety"? In reply, you only say that piety is, Doing as you do, charging your father with murder?

EUTH: And that is true, Socrates.

SOC: I dare say, Euthyphro, but there are many other pious acts.

EUTH: There are.

---

2. Here Socrates objects to the definition of piety given by Euthyphro. What does Socrates say is wrong with Euthyphro's definition? Here, also, Socrates tells what the proper definition of piety must do: It must explain the "general idea" of piety. What does he mean by that?

SOC: Remember that I did not ask you to give me two or three examples of piety, but to explain the general idea which makes all pious things to be pious. Do you not recollect that there was one idea which made the impious impious, and the pious pious?

EUTH: I remember.

SOC: Tell me what this is, and then I shall have a standard to which I may look, and by which I may measure the nature of actions, whether yours or any one's else, and say that this action is pious, and that impious?

EUTH: I will tell you, if you like.

SOC: I should very much like.

———

3. Euthyphro tries once again to define piety. This time the definition is of the type that Socrates is seeking, so he begins to closely examine it. Remember, if this is the correct definition, it will allow us to distinguish any pious act from an impious one. Does it do the job?

———

EUTH: Piety, then, is that which is dear to the gods, and impiety is that which is not dear to them.

SOC: Very good, Euthyphro; you have now given me just the sort of answer which I wanted. But whether it is true or not I cannot as yet tell, although I make no doubt that you will prove the truth of your words.

EUTH: Of course.

SOC: Come, then, and let us examine what we are saying. That thing or person which is dear to the gods is pious, and that thing or person which is hateful to the gods is impious. Was not that said?

EUTH: Yes, that was said.

SOC: And that seems to have been very well said too?

EUTH: Yes, Socrates, I think that; it was certainly said.

SOC: And further, Euthyphro, the gods were admitted to have enmities and hatreds and differences—that was also said?

EUTH: Yes, that was said.

SOC: And what sort of difference creates enmity and anger? Suppose for example that you and I, my good friend, differ about a number; do differences of this sort make us enemies and set us at variance with one another? Do we not go at once to calculation, and end them by a sum?

EUTH: True.

SOC: Or suppose that we differ about magnitudes, do we not quickly put an end to that difference by measuring?

EUTH: That is true.

SOC: And we end a controversy about heavy and light by resorting to a weighing-machine?

EUTH: To be sure.

SOC: But what differences are those which, because they cannot be thus decided, make us angry and set us at enmity with one another? I dare say the answer does not occur to you at the moment, and therefore I will suggest that this happens when the matters of difference are the just and unjust, good and evil, honorable and dishonorable. Are not these the points about which, when differing, and unable satisfactorily to decide our differences, we quarrel, when we do quarrel, as you and I and all men experience?

EUTH: Yes, Socrates, that is the nature of the differences about which we quarrel.

SOC: And the quarrels of the gods, noble Euthyphro, when they occur, are of a like nature?

EUTH: They are.

SOC: They have differences of opinion, as you say, about good and evil, just and unjust, honorable and dishonorable: there would have been no quarrels among them, if there had been no such differences—would there now?

EUTH: You are quite right.

SOC: Does not every man love that which he deems noble and just and good, and hate the opposite of them?

EUTH: Very true.

SOC: But then, as you say, people regard the same things, some as just and others as unjust; and they dispute about this, and there arise wars and fightings among them.

EUTH: Yes, that is true.

---

4. *Again, Socrates objects to Euthyphro's definition. Notice that this is an objection on different grounds from the first one.*

SOC: Then the same things, as appears, are hated by the gods and loved by the gods, and are both hateful and dear to them?

EUTH: True.

SOC: Then upon this view the same things, Euthyphro, will be pious and also impious?

EUTH: That, I suppose, is true.

SOC: Then, my friend, I remark with surprise that you have not answered what I asked. For I certainly did not ask what was that which is at once pious and impious: and that which is loved by the gods appears also to be hated by them. And therefore, Euthyphro, in thus chastising your father you may very likely be doing what is agreeable to Zeus but disagreeable to Cronos or Uranus, and what is acceptable to Hephaestus but unacceptable to Here, and there may be other gods who have similar differences of opinion.

EUTH: But I believe, Socrates, that all the gods would be agreed as to the propriety of punishing a murderer: there would be no difference of opinion about that.

SOC: Well, but speaking of men, Euthyphro, did you ever hear any one arguing that a murderer or any sort of evil-doer ought to be let off?

EUTH: I should rather say that they are always arguing this, especially in courts of law: they commit all sorts of crimes, and there is nothing that they will not do or say in order to escape punishment.

SOC: But do they admit their guilt, Euthyphro, and yet say that they ought not to be punished?

EUTH: No; they do not.

SOC: Then there are some things which they do not venture to say and do: for they do not venture to argue that the guilty are to be unpunished, but they deny their guilt, do they not?

EUTH: Yes.

SOC: Then they do not argue that the evil-doer should not be punished, but they argue about the fact of who the evil-doer is, and what he did and when?

EUTH: True.

SOC: And the gods are in the same case, if as you imply they quarrel about just and unjust, and some of them say that they wrong one another, and others of them deny this. For surely neither God nor man will ever venture to say that the doer of evil is not to be punished:—you don't mean to tell me that?

EUTH: That is true, Socrates, in the main.

————

5. Many people in our society, when asked where they learned right and wrong, will point to their religious upbringing. These are people who believe that a supreme being is the source of ethical values and the determiner of right and wrong. The right action to take is the one that follows God's wishes, rules, or plans. A wrong act, conversely, is one that goes against God. A philosophical theory that holds that the commands of God (or the gods) is the source of ethical values is called a divine command theory of ethics. *For such a theory, moral rules and moral values are considered to be immutable, absolute, and universal. That is, they are unchanging; they apply to all people, regardless of time and circumstance, and are not dependent on humankind.*

Next we will encounter a famous question asked by the character Socrates to undercut a divine command theory of ethics. The question poses a dilemma: neither possible answer appears acceptable to the divine command theorist. Socrates asks Euthyphro whether God loves a pious act because it is pious, or whether the act is pious because God loves it. Either way in which the divine command theorist answers the paradox shows the theory to be on a very shaky philosophical foundation.

————

SOC: But they join issue about particulars; and this applies not only to men but to the gods; if they dispute at all they dispute about some act which is called in question, and which some affirm to be just, others to be unjust. Is not that true?

EUTH: Quite true.

SOC: Well then, my dear friend Euthyphro, do tell me, for my better instruction and information, what proof have you that in the opinion of all the gods a servant who is guilty of murder, and is put in chains by the master of the dead man, and dies because he is put in chains before his corrector can learn from the interpreters what he ought to do with him, dies unjustly; and that on behalf of such a one a son ought to proceed against his father and accuse him of murder. How would you show that all the gods absolutely agree in approving of his act? Prove to me that, and I will applaud your wisdom as long as you live.

EUTH: That would not be an easy task, although I could make the matter very clear indeed to you.

SOC: I understand; you mean to say that I am not so quick of apprehension as the judges: for to them you will be sure to prove that the act is unjust, and hateful to the gods.

EUTH: Yes indeed, Socrates; at least if they will listen to me.

SOC: But they will be sure to listen if they find that you are a good speaker. There was a notion that came into my mind while you were speaking; I said to myself: "Well, and what if Euthyphro does prove to me that all the gods regarded the death of the serf as unjust, how do I know anything more of the nature of piety and impiety? for granting that this action may be hateful to the gods, still these distinctions have no bearing on the definition of piety and impiety, for that which is hateful to the gods has been shown to be also pleasing and dear to them." And therefore, Euthyphro, I don't ask you to prove this; I will suppose, if you like, that all the gods condemn and abominate such an action. But I will amend the definition so far as to say that what all the gods hate is impious, and what they love pious or holy; and what some of them love and others hate is both or neither. Shall this be our definition of piety and impiety?

EUTH: Why not, Socrates?

SOC: Why not! certainly, as far as I am concerned, Euthyphro. But whether this admission will greatly assist you in the task of instructing me as you promised, is a matter for you to consider.

------

6. Prompted by Socrates, Euthyphro announces another definition of piety. Socrates, of course, is going to examine this new definition.

EUTH: Yes, I should say that what all the gods love is pious and holy, and the opposite which they all hate, impious.

SOC: Ought we to inquire into the truth of this, Euthyphro, or simply to accept the mere statement on our own authority and that of others?

EUTH: We should inquire; and I believe that the statement will stand the test of inquiry.

SOC: That, my good friend, we shall know better in a little while. The point which I should first wish to understand is whether the pious or holy is beloved by the gods because it is holy, or holy because it is beloved of the gods.

EUTH: I don't understand your meaning, Socrates.

SOC: I will endeavor to explain: we speak of carrying and we speak of being carried, of leading and being led, seeing and being seen. And here is a difference, the nature of which you understand.

EUTH: I think that I understand.

SOC: And is not that which is beloved distinct from that which loves?

EUTH: Certainly.

SOC: Well; and now tell me, is that which is carried in this state of carrying because it is carried, or for some other reason?

EUTH: No; that is the reason.

SOC: And the same is true of that which is led and of that which is seen?

EUTH: True.

SOC: And a thing is not seen because it is visible, but conversely, visible because it is seen; nor is a thing in the state of being led because it is led, or in the state of being carried because it is carried, but the converse of this. And now I think, Euthyphro, that my meaning will be intelligible; and my meaning is, that any state of action or passion implies previous action or passion. It does not become because it is becoming, but it is becoming because it comes; neither does it suffer because it is in a state of suffering, but it is in a state of suffering because it suffers. Do you admit that?

EUTH: Yes.

SOC: Is not that which is loved in some state either of becoming or suffering?

EUTH: Yes.

SOC: And the same holds as in the previous instances; the state of being loved follows the act of being loved, and not the act the state.

EUTH: That is certain.

---

7. Socrates begins to undercut the new definition with a criticism of a divine command theory of ethics.

SOC: And what do you say of piety, Euthyphro: is not piety, according to your definition, loved by all the gods?

EUTH: Yes.

SOC: Because it is pious or holy, or for some other reason?

EUTH: No, that is the reason.

SOC: It is loved because it is holy, not holy because it is loved?

EUTH: Yes.

SOC: And that which is in a state to be loved of the gods, and is dear to them, is in a state to be loved of them because it is loved of them?

EUTH: Certainly.

SOC: Then that which is loved of God, Euthyphro, is not holy, nor is that which is holy loved of God, as you affirm; but they are two different things.

EUTH: How you mean, Socrates?

SOC: I mean to say that the holy has been acknowledged by us to be loved of God because it is holy, not to be holy because it is loved.

EUTH: Yes.

SOC: But that which is dear to the gods is dear to them because it is loved by them, not loved by them because it is dear to them.

EUTH: True.

SOC: But, friend Euthyphro, if that which is holy is the same as that which is dear to God, and that which is holy is loved as being holy, then that which is dear to God would have been loved as being dear to God; but if that which is dear to God is dear to him because loved by him, then that which is holy would have been holy because loved by him. But now you see that the reverse is the case, and that they are quite different from one another. For one is of a kind to be loved because it is loved, and the other is loved because it is of a kind to be loved. Thus you appear to me, Euthyphro, when I ask you what is the essence of holiness, to offer an attribute only, and not the essence—the attribute of being loved by all the gods. But you still refuse to explain to me the nature of piety. And therefore, if you please, I will ask you not to hide your treasure, but to tell me once more what piety or holiness really is, whether dear to the gods or not (for that is a matter about which we will not quarrel). And what is impiety?

EUTH: I really do not know, Socrates, how to say what I mean. For somehow or other our arguments, on whatever ground we rest them, seem to turn round and walk away.

SOC: Your words, Euthyphro, are like the handiwork of my ancestor Daedalus; and if I were the sayer or propounder of them, you might say that this comes of my being his relation; and that this is the reason why my arguments walk away and won't remain fixed where they are placed. But now, as the notions are your own, you must find some other gibe, for they certainly, as you yourself allow, show an inclination to be on the move.

EUTH: Nay, Socrates, I shall still say that you are the Daedalus who sets arguments in motion; not I, certainly, make them move or go round, for they would never have stirred, as far as I am concerned.

---

8. *Socrates will now begin to relate piety to justice.*

SOC: Then I must be a greater than Daedalus; for whereas he only made his own inventions to move, I move those of other people as well. And the beauty of it is, that I would rather not. For I would give the wisdom of Daedalus, and the wealth of Tantalus, to be able to detain them and keep them fixed. But enough of this. As I perceive that you are indolent, I will myself endeavor to show you how you might instruct me in the nature of piety; and I hope that you will not grudge your labor. Tell me, then,—Is not that which is pious necessarily just?

EUTH: Yes.

SOC: And is, then, all which is just pious? or, is that which is pious all just, but that which is just only in part and not all pious?

EUTH: I don't understand you, Socrates.

SOC: And yet I know that you are as much wiser than I am, as you are younger. But, as I was saying, revered friend, the abundance of your wisdom makes you indolent. Please to exert yourself, for there is no real difficulty in understanding me. What I mean I may explain by an illustration of what I do not mean. The poet (Stasinus) sings—

"Of Zeus, the author and creator of all these things, You will not tell: for where there is fear there is also reverence."

And I disagree with this poet. Shall I tell you in what I disagree?

EUTH: By all means.

soc: I should not say that where there is fear there is also reverence; for I am sure that many persons fear poverty and disease, and the like evils, but I do not perceive that they reverence the objects of their fear.

euth: Very true.

soc: But where reverence is, there is fear; for he who has a feeling of reverence and shame about the commission of any action, fears and is afraid of an ill reputation.

euth: No doubt.

soc: Then we are wrong in saying that where there is fear there is also reverence; and we should say, where there is reverence there is also fear. But there is not always reverence where there is fear; for fear is a more extended notion, and reverence is a part of fear, just as the odd is a part of number, and number is a more extended notion than the odd. I suppose that you follow me now?

euth: Quite well.

soc: That was the sort of question which I meant to raise when asking whether the just is the pious, or the pious the just; and whether there may not be justice where there is not always piety; for justice is the more extended notion of which piety is only a part. Do you agree in that?

euth: Yes; that, I think, is correct.

soc: Then, now, if piety is a part of justice, I suppose that we inquire what part? If you had pursued the injury in the previous cases; for instance, if you had asked me what is an even number, and what part of number the even is, I should have had no difficulty in replying, a number which represents a figure having two equal sides. Do you agree?

euth: Yes.

soc: In like manner, I want you to tell me what part of justice is piety or holiness; that I may be able to tell Meletus not to do me injustice, or indict me for impiety; as I am now adequately instructed by you in the nature of piety or holiness, and their opposites.

euth: Piety or holiness, Socrates, appears to me to be that part of justice which attends to the gods, as there is the other part of justice which attends to men.

_____

9. An extended analogy, using several examples, begins here.

_____

soc: That is good, Euthyphro; yet still there is a little point about which I should like to have further information, What is the meaning of "attention"? For attention can hardly be used in the same sense when applied to the gods as when applied to other things. For instance, horses are said to require attention, and not every person is able to attend to them, but only a person skilled in horsemanship. Is not that true?

euth: Quite true.

soc: I should suppose that the art of horsemanship is the art of attending to horses?

euth: Yes.

SOC: Nor is every one qualified to attend to dogs, but only the huntsman.

EUTH: True.

SOC: And I should also conceive that the art of the huntsman is the art of attending to dogs?

EUTH: Yes.

SOC: As the art of the oxherd is the art of attending to oxen?

EUTH: Very true.

SOC: And as holiness or piety is the art of attending to the gods?—that would be your meaning, Euthyphro?

EUTH: Yes.

SOC: And is not attention always designed for the good or benefit of that to which the attention is given? As in the case of horses, you may observe that when attended to by the horseman's art they are benefited and improved, are they not?

EUTH: True.

SOC: As the dogs are benefited by the huntsman's art, and the oxen by the art of the oxherd, and all other things are tended or attended for their good and not for their hurt?

EUTH: Certainly, not for their hurt.

SOC: But for their good?

EUTH: Of course.

SOC: And does piety or holiness, which has been defined as the art of attending to the gods, benefit or improve them? Would you say that when you do a holy act you make any of the gods better?

EUTH: No, no; that is certainly not my meaning.

SOC: Indeed, Euthyphro, I did not suppose that this was your meaning; far otherwise. And that was the reason why I asked you the nature of this attention, because I thought that this was not your meaning.

EUTH: You do me justice, Socrates; for that is not my meaning.

SOC: Good: but I must still ask what is this attention to the gods which is called piety?

EUTH: It is such, Socrates, as servants show to their masters.

SOC: I understand—a sort of ministration to the gods.

EUTH: Exactly.

SOC: Medicine is also a sort of ministration or service, tending to the attainment of some object—would you not say health?

EUTH: Yes.

SOC: Again, there is an art which ministers to the ship-builder with a view to the attainment of some result?

EUTH: Yes, Socrates, with a view to the building of a ship.

SOC: As there is an art which ministers to the house-builder with a view to the building of a house?

EUTH: Yes.

SOC: And now tell me, my good friend, about this art which ministers to the gods: what work does that help to accomplish? For you must surely know if, as you say, you are of all men living the one who is best instructed in religion.

EUTH: And that is true, Socrates.

SOC: Tell me then, oh tell me—what is that fair work which the gods do by the help of us as their ministers?

EUTH: Many and fair, Socrates, are the works which they do.

SOC: Why, my friend, and so are those of a general. But the chief of them is easily told. Would you not say that victory in war is the chief of them?

EUTH: Certainly.

SOC: Many and fair, too, are the works of the husbandman, if I am not mistaken; but his chief work is the production of food from the earth?

EUTH: Exactly.

SOC: And of the many and fair things which the gods do, which is the chief and principal one?

EUTH: I have told you already, Socrates, that to learn all these things accurately will be very tiresome. Let me simply say that piety is learning how to please the gods in word and deed, by prayers and sacrifices. That is piety, which is the salvation of families and states, just as the impious, which is unpleasing to the gods, is their ruin and destruction.

SOC: I think that you could have answered in much fewer words the chief question which I asked, Euthyphro, if you had chosen. But I see plainly that you are not disposed to instruct me: else why, when we had reached the point, did you turn aside? Had you only answered me I should have learned of you by this time the nature of piety. Now, as the asker of a question is necessarily dependent on the answerer, whither he leads I must follow; and can only ask again, what is the pious, and what is piety? Do you mean that they are a sort of science of praying and sacrificing?

EUTH: Yes, I do.

SOC: And sacrificing is giving to the gods, and prayer is asking of the gods?

EUTH: Yes, Socrates.

SOC: Upon this view, then, piety is a science of asking and giving?

EUTH: You understand me capitally, Socrates.

SOC: Yes, my friend; the reason is that I am a votary of your science, and give my mind to it, and therefore nothing which you say will be thrown away upon me. Please then to tell me, what is the nature of this service to the gods? Do you mean that we prefer requests and give gifts to them?

EUTH: Yes, I do.

SOC: Is not the right way of asking to ask of them what we want?

EUTH: Certainly.

soc: And the right way of giving is to give to them in return what they want of us. There would be no meaning in an art which gives to any one that which he does not want.

EUTH: Very true, Socrates.

soc: Then piety, Euthyphro, is an art which gods and men have of doing business with one another?

EUTH: That is an expression which you may use, if you like.

soc: But I have no particular liking for anything but the truth. I wish, however, that you would tell me what benefit accrues to the gods from our gifts. That they are the givers of every good to us is clear; but how we can give any good thing to them in return is far from being equally clear. If they give everything and we give nothing, that must be an affair of business in which we have very greatly the advantage of them.

EUTH: And do you imagine, Socrates, that any benefit accrues to the gods from what they receive of us?

soc: But if not, Euthyphro, what sort of gifts do we confer upon the gods?

EUTH: What should we confer upon them, but tributes of honor; and, as I was just now saying, what is pleasing to them?

soc: Piety, then, is pleasing to the gods, but not beneficial or dear to them?

EUTH: I should say that nothing could be dearer.

soc: Then once more the assertion is repeated that piety is dear to the gods?

EUTH: No doubt.

soc: And when you say this, can you wonder at your words not standing firm, but walking away? Will you accuse me of being the Daedalus who makes them walk away, not perceiving that there is another and far greater artist than Daedalus who makes them go round in a circle; and that is yourself: for the argument, as you will perceive, comes round to the same point. I think that you must remember our saying that the holy or pious was not the same as that which is loved of the gods. Do you remember that?

EUTH: I do.

soc: And do you not see that what is loved of the gods is holy, and that this is the same as what is dear to them?

EUTH: True.

soc: Then either we were wrong in that admission; or, if we were right then, we are wrong now.

EUTH: I suppose that is the case.

soc: Then we must begin again and ask, What is piety? That is an inquiry which I shall never be weary of pursuing as far as in me lies; and I entreat you not to scorn me, but to apply your mind to the utmost and tell me the truth. For, if any man knows, you are he; and therefore I shall detain you, like Proteus, until you tell. For if you had not certainly known the nature of piety and impiety, I am confident that you would never, on behalf of a serf, have charged your aged father with murder. You would not have run such a risk of doing wrong in the sight of the gods, and you would have had too much respect for the opinions of men. I am sure, therefore, that you know the nature of piety and impiety. Speak out then, my dear Euthyphro, and do not hide your knowledge.

EUTH: Another time, Socrates; for I am in a hurry, and must go now.

SOC: Alas! my companion, and will you leave me in despair? I was hoping that you would instruct me in the nature of piety and impiety, so that I might have cleared myself of Meletus and his indictment. Then I might have proved to him that I had been converted by Euthyphro, and had done with rash innovations and speculations, in which I had indulged through ignorance, and was about to lead a better life.

READING QUESTIONS

1. What does Euthyphro accuse his father of doing?
2. What does Socrates say is wrong with Euthyphro's first attempt to define "piety"?
3. What is Socrates' point when he charges that Euthyphro's chastising of his father may be agreeable to Zeus but disagreeable to Cronos?
4. State in your own words the paradox that Socrates draws for the divine command theorist.
5. What are the implications of each of the answers posed by the paradox?
6. What is the distinction Socrates is making between fear and reverence?

Republic

Have you ever noticed how many moral issues are highly controversial? Why is it that in a democratic country such as ours, where people can speak openly about issues such as abortion, capital punishment, and the rights of property owners over the environment, people on different sides of the issues think that their position is the only moral one? One possible reason is that people have different moral values and different standards, depending on where they were raised, what race or ethnic group they belong to, or their religion. You might be tempted to say that there is no one answer to any of these controversial moral issues: people have their own answers to each moral question, and that answer is right for them. This position, when taken up by philosophers, is known as **ethical relativism**. Values and standards are relative, either to individuals (each person has

From Plato, *Republic,* translated by Benjamin Jowett.

his or her own standards) or groups (religions, ethnic groups, socio-
economic groups, etc., have their own values or standards). No universal
moral values or standards exist by which we can judge one set of values
better or worse than another.

Opposed to this position is **ethical objectivism.** According to this
view, standards exist for all people regardless of their country of origin,
religious beliefs, or upbringing. Objectivists claim that relativists trivialize
ethics because relativism appears to render it impossible for anyone to
criticize the moral position of another. What is right is right for me, or my
group, and you cannot criticize.

Plato was an ethical objectivist who contested the increasingly popular ethical relativism associated with the teachings of the Sophists. In the
following selection, taken from Book I of Plato's famous work the
Republic, we are introduced to a character named Thrasymachus (a famous Sophist of the day), who argues for a version of "might makes
right." Socrates, as the voice of Plato, opposes that view.

The issue of ethical relativism has been a concern of moral philosophers throughout the history of philosophy. Thomas Hobbes was a
prominent philosopher who argued that values are relative, whereas
Immanuel Kant and John Stuart Mill are examples of ethical objectivists.
In the United States in the twentieth century, relativism is a view espoused
by many people, due in part to the enormous diversity in the belief systems of its citizenry.

Several times in the course of the discussion Thrasymachus had made an attempt to
get the argument into his own hands, and had been put down by the rest of the
company, who wanted to hear the end. But when Polemarchus and I had done
speaking and there was a pause, he could no longer hold his peace; and, gathering
himself up, he came at us like a wild beast, seeking to devour us. We were quite
panic-stricken at the sight of him.

He roared out to the whole company: What folly, Socrates, has taken possession of you all? And why, sillybillies, do you knock under to one another? I say that
if you want really to know what justice is, you should not only ask but answer, and
you should not seek honor to yourself from the refutation of an opponent, but have
your own answer; for there is many a one who can ask and cannot answer. And
now I will not have you say that justice is duty or advantage or profit or gain or
interest, for this sort of nonsense will not do for me; I must have clearness and accuracy.

I was panic-stricken at his words, and could not look at him without trembling.
Indeed I believe that if I had not fixed my eye upon him, I should have been struck
dumb: but when I saw his fury rising, I looked at him first, and was therefore able
to reply to him.

Thrasymachus, I said, with a quiver, don't be hard upon us. Polemarchus and I may have been guilty of a little mistake in the argument, but I can assure you that the error was not intentional. If we were seeking for a piece of gold, you would not imagine that we were "knocking under to one another," and so losing our chance of finding it. And why, when we are seeking for justice, a thing more precious than many pieces of gold, do you say that we are weakly yielding to one another and not doing our utmost to get at the truth? Nay, my good friend, we are most willing and anxious to do so, but the fact is that we cannot. And if so, you people who know all things should pity us and not be angry with us.

How characteristic of Socrates! he replied, with a bitter laugh;—that's your ironical style! Did I not foresee—have I not already told you, that whatever he was asked he would refuse to answer, and try irony or any other shuffle, in order that he might avoid answering?

You are a philosopher, Thrasymachus, I replied, and well know that if you ask a person what numbers make up twelve, taking care to prohibit him whom you ask from answering twice six, or three times four, or six times two, or four times three, "for this sort of nonsense will not do for me,"—then obviously, if that is your way of putting the question, no one can answer you. But suppose that he were to retort, "Thrasymachus, what do you mean? If one of these numbers which you interdict be the true answer to the question, am I falsely to say some other number which is not the right one?—is that your meaning?"—How would you answer him?

Just as if the two cases were at all alike! he said.

Why should they not be? I replied; and even if they are not, but only appear to be so to the person who is asked, ought he not to say what he thinks, whether you and I forbid him or not?

I presume then that you are going to make one of the interdicted answers?

I dare say that I may, notwithstanding the danger, if upon reflection I approve of any of them.

But what if I give you an answer about justice other and better, he said, than any of these? What do you deserve to have done to you?

Done to me!—as becomes the ignorant, I must learn from the wise—that is what I deserve to have done to me.

What, and no payment! a pleasant notion!

I will pay when I have the money, I replied.

But you have, Socrates, said Glaucon: and you, Thrasymachus, need be under no anxiety about money, for we will all make a contribution for Socrates.

Yes, he replied, and then Socrates will do as he always does—refuse to answer himself, but take and pull to pieces the answer of some one else.

Why, my good friend, I said, how can any one answer who knows and says that he knows, just nothing; and who, even if he has some faint notions of his own, is told by a man of authority not to utter them? The natural thing is, that the speaker should be some one like yourself who professes to know and can tell what he knows. Will you then kindly answer, for the edification of the company and of myself?

Glaucon and the rest of the company joined in my request, and Thrasymachus, as any one might see, was in reality eager to speak; for he thought that he had an excellent answer, and would distinguish himself. But at first he affected to insist on my answering; at length he consented to begin. Behold, he said, the wisdom of Socrates; he refuses to teach himself, and goes about learning of others, to whom he never even says Thank you.

That I learn of others, I replied, is quite true; but that I am ungrateful I wholly deny. Money I have none, and therefore I pay in praise, which is all I have; and how ready I am to praise any one who appears to me to speak well you will very soon find out when you answer; for I expect that you will answer well.

1. Thrasymachus gives his definition of "justice."

Listen, then, he said; I proclaim that justice is nothing else than the interest of the stronger. And now why do you not praise me? But of course you won't.

Let me first understand you, I replied. Justice, as you say, is the interest of the stronger. What, Thrasymachus, is the meaning of this? You cannot mean to say that because Polydamas, the pancratiast, is stronger than we are, and finds the eating of beef conducive to his bodily strength, that to eat beef is therefore equally for our good who are weaker than he is, and right and just for us?

That's abominable of you, Socrates; you take the words in the sense which is most damaging to the argument.

Not at all, my good sir, I said; I am trying to understand them; and I wish that you would be a little clearer.

Well, he said, have you never heard that forms of government differ; there are tyrannies, and there are democracies, and there are aristocracies?

Yes, I know.

And the government is the ruling power in each state?

Certainly.

And the different forms of government make laws democratical, aristocratical, tyrannical, with a view to their several interests; and these laws, which are made by them for their own interests, are the justice which they deliver to their subjects, and him who transgresses them they punish as a breaker of the law, and unjust. And that is what I mean when I say that in all states there is the same principle of justice, which is the interest of the government; and as the government must be supposed to have power, the only reasonable conclusion is, that everywhere there is one principle of justice, which is the interest of the stronger.

Now I understand you, I said; and whether you are right or not I will try to discover. But let me remark, that in defining justice you have yourself used the word "interest," which you forbade me to use. It is true, however, that in your definition the words "of the stronger" are added.

A small addition, you must allow, he said.

2. Socrates questions whether rulers always make laws in their own best interest.

Great or small, never mind about that: we must first inquire whether what you are saying is the truth. Now we are both agreed that justice is interest of some sort, but you go on to say "of the stronger"; about this addition I am not so sure, and must therefore consider further.

Proceed.

I will; and first tell me, Do you admit that it is just for subjects to obey their rulers?

I do.

But are the rulers of states absolutely infallible, or are they sometimes liable to err?

To be sure, he replied, they are liable to err.

Then in making their laws they may sometimes make them rightly, and sometimes not?

True.

When they make them rightly, they make them agreeably to their interest; when they are mistaken, contrary to their interest; you admit that?

Yes.

And the laws which they make must be obeyed by their subjects,—and that is what you call justice?

Doubtless.

Then justice, according to your argument, is not only obedience to the interest of the stronger but the reverse?

What is that you are saying? he asked.

I am only repeating what you are saying, I believe. But let us consider: Have we not admitted that the rulers may be mistaken about their own interest in what they command, and also that to obey them is justice? Has not that been admitted?

Yes.

Then you must also have acknowledged justice not to be for the interest of the stronger, when the rulers unintentionally command things to be done which are to their own injury. For if, as you say, justice is the obedience which the subject renders to their commands, in that case, O wisest of men, is there any escape from the conclusion that the weaker are commanded to do, not what is for the interest, but what is for the injury of the stronger?

Nothing can be clearer, Socrates, said Polemarchus.

Yes, said Cleitophon, interposing, if you are allowed to be his witness.

But there is no need of any witness, said Polemarchus, for Thrasymachus himself acknowledges that rulers may sometimes command what is not for their own interest, and that for subjects to obey them is justice.

Yes, Polemarchus,—Thrasymachus said that for subjects to do what was commanded by their rulers is just.

Yes, Cleitophon, but he also said that justice is the interest of the stronger, and, while admitting both these propositions, he further acknowledged that the stronger may command the weaker who are his subjects to do what is not for his own interest; whence follows that justice is the injury quite as much as the interest of the stronger.

But, said Cleitophon, he meant by the interest of the stronger what the stronger thought to be his interest,—this was what the weaker had to do; and this was affirmed by him to be justice.

Those were not his words, rejoined Polemarchus.

Never mind, I replied, if he now says that they are, let us accept his statement. Tell me, Thrasymachus, I said, did you mean by justice what the stronger thought to be his interest, whether really so or not?

Certainly not, he said. Do you suppose that I call him who is mistaken the stronger at the time when he is mistaken?

Yes, I said, my impression was that you did so, when you admitted that the ruler was not infallible but might be sometimes mistaken.

You argue like an informer, Socrates. Do you mean, for example, that he who is mistaken about the sick is a physician in that he is mistaken? or that he who errs in arithmetic or grammar is an arithmetician or grammarian at the time when he is making the mistake, in respect of the mistake? True, we say that the physician or arithmetician or grammarian has made a mistake, but this is only a way of speaking; for the fact is that neither the grammarian nor any other person of skill ever makes a mistake in so far as he is what his name implies; they none of them err unless their skill fails them, and then they cease to be skilled artists. No artist or sage or ruler errs at the time when he is what his name implies; though he is commonly said to err, and I adopted the common mode of speaking. But to be perfectly accurate, since you are such a lover of accuracy, we should say that the ruler, in so far as he is ruler, is unerring, and, being unerring, always commands that which is for his own interest; and the subject is required to execute his commands; and therefore, as I said at first and now repeat, justice is the interest of the stronger.

Indeed, Thrasymachus, and do I really appear to you to argue like an informer?

Certainly, he replied.

And do you suppose that I ask these questions with any design of injuring you in the argument?

Nay, he replied, "suppose" is not the word—I know it; but you will be found out, and by sheer force of argument you will never prevail.

I shall not make the attempt, my dear man; but to avoid any misunderstanding occurring between us in future, let me ask, in what sense do you speak of a ruler or stronger whose interest, as you were saying, he being the superior, it is just that the inferior should execute—is he a ruler in the popular or in the strict sense of the term?

In the strictest of all senses, he said. And now cheat and play the informer if you can; I ask no quarter at your hands. But you never will be able, never.

And do you imagine, I said, that I am such a madman as to try and cheat Thrasymachus? I might as well shave a lion.

Why, he said, you made the attempt a minute ago, and you failed.

---

3. Using a variety of examples, Socrates argues about the role of the ruler.
Whose interest should the ruler be mindful of, according to Socrates?

Enough, I said, of these civilities. It will be better that I should ask you a question: Is the physician, taken in that strict sense of which you are speaking, a healer of the sick or a maker of money? And remember that I am now speaking of the true physician.

A healer of the sick, he replied.

And the pilot—that is to say, the true pilot—is he a captain of sailors or a mere sailor?

A captain of sailors.

The circumstance that he sails in the ship is not to be taken into account; neither is he to be called a sailor; the name pilot by which he is distinguished has nothing to do with sailing, but is significant of his skill and of his authority over the sailors.

Very true, he said.

Now, I said, every art has an interest?

Certainly.

For which the art has to consider and provide?

Yes, that is the aim of art.

And the interest of any art is the perfection of it—this and nothing else?

What do you mean?

I mean what I may illustrate negatively by the example of the body. Suppose you were to ask me whether the body is self-sufficing or has wants, I should reply: Certainly the body has wants; for the body may be ill and require to be cured, and has therefore interests to which the art of medicine ministers; and this is the origin and intention of medicine, as you will acknowledge. Am I not right?

Quite right, he replied.

But is the art of medicine or any other art faulty or deficient in any quality in the same way that the eye may be deficient in sight or the ear fail of hearing, and therefore requires another art to provide for the interests of seeing and hearing—has art in itself, I say, any similar liability to fault or defect, and does every art require another supplementary art to provide for its interests, and that another and another without end? Or have the arts to look only after their own interests? Or have they no need either of themselves or of another?—having no faults or defects, they have no need to correct them, either by the exercise of their own art or of any other; they have only to consider the interest of their subject-matter. For every art remains pure and faultless while remaining true—that is to say, while perfect and unimpaired. Take the words in your precise sense, and tell me whether I am not right.

Yes, clearly.

Then medicine does not consider the interest of medicine, but the interest of the body?

True, he said.

Nor does the art of horsemanship consider the interests of the art of horsemanship, but the interests of the horse; neither do any other arts care for themselves, for they have no needs; they care only for that which is the subject of their art?

True, he said.

But surely, Thrasymachus, the arts are the superiors and rulers of their own subjects?

To this he assented with a good deal of reluctance.

Then, I said, no science or art considers or enjoins the interest of the stronger or superior, but only the interest of the subject and weaker?

He made an attempt to contest this proposition also, but finally acquiesced.

Then, I continued, no physician, in so far as he is a physician, considers his own good in what he prescribes, but the good of his patient; for the true physician is also a ruler having the human body as a subject, and is not a mere money-maker; that has been admitted?

Yes.

And the pilot likewise, in the strict sense of the term, is a ruler of sailors and not a mere sailor.

That has been admitted.

And such a pilot and ruler will provide and prescribe for the interest of the sailor who is under him, and not for his own or the ruler's interest?

He gave a reluctant "Yes."

Then, I said, Thrasymachus, there is no one in any rule who, in so far as he is a ruler, considers or enjoins what is for his own interest, but always what is for the interest of his subject or suitable to his art; to that he looks, and that alone he considers in everything which he says and does.

When we had got to this point in the argument, and every one saw that the definition of justice had been completely upset, Thrasymachus, instead of replying to me, said: Tell me, Socrates, have you got a nurse?

Why do you ask such a question, I said, when you ought rather to be answering?

Because she leaves you to snivel, and never wipes your nose: she has not even taught you to know the shepherd from the sheep.

What makes you say that? I replied.

---

4. Thrasymachus states his view of the relationship between the just and the unjust person.

Because you fancy that the shepherd or neatherd fattens or tends the sheep or oxen with a view to their own good and not to the good of himself or his master; and you further imagine that the rulers of states, if they are true rulers, never think of their subjects as sheep, and that they are not studying their own advantage day and night. Oh, no; and so entirely astray are you in your ideas about the just and unjust as not even to know that justice and the just are in reality another's good; that is to say, the interest of the ruler and stronger, and the loss of the subject and servant; and injustice the opposite; for the unjust is lord over the truly simple and just: he is the stronger, and his subjects do what is for his interest, and minister to his happiness, which is very far from being their own. Consider further, most foolish Socrates, that the just is always a loser in comparison with the unjust. First of all, in private contracts: wherever the unjust is the partner of the just you will find that, when the partnership is dissolved, the unjust man has always more and the just less. Secondly, in their dealings with the State: when there is an income-tax, the just man will pay more and the unjust less on the same amount of income; and when there is anything to be received the one gains nothing and the other much. Observe also what happens when they take an office; there is the just man neglecting his affairs and perhaps suffering other losses and getting nothing out of the public, because he is just; moreover he is hated by his friends and acquaintance for refusing to serve them in unlawful ways. But all this is reversed in the case of the unjust man. I am speaking, as before, of injustice on a large scale in which the advantage of the unjust is most apparent; and my meaning will be most clearly seen if we turn to that highest form of injustice in which the criminal is the happiest of men, and the sufferers or those who refuse to do injustice are the most miserable—that is to say tyranny, which by fraud and force takes away the property of others, not little by little but wholesale; comprehending in one, things sacred as well as profane, private and public; for which acts of wrong, if he were detected perpetrating any of them singly, he would be punished and incur great disgrace—they who do such wrong in particular cases are called robbers of temples, and man-stealers and burglars and swindlers and thieves. But when a man besides taking away the money of the citizens has made slaves of them, then, instead of these names of reproach, he is termed happy and blessed, not only by the citizens but by all who hear of his having achieved the consummation of injustice. For mankind censure injustice, fearing that they may be victims of it and not because they shrink from committing it. And thus, as I have shown, Socrates, injustice, when on a sufficient scale, has more strength and freedom and mastery than justice; and, as I said at first, justice is the interest of the stronger, whereas injustice is a man's own profit and interest.

Thrasymachus, when he had thus spoken, having, like a bath-man, deluged our ears with his words, had a mind to go away. But the company would not let him; they insisted that he should remain and defend his position; and I myself added my own humble request that he would not leave us. Thrasymachus, I said to him, excellent man, how suggestive are your remarks! And are you going to run away before you have fairly taught or learned whether they are true or not? Is the attempt to determine the way of man's life so small a matter in your eyes—to determine how life may be passed by each one of us to the greatest advantage?

And do I differ from you, he said, as to the importance of the inquiry?

You appear rather, I replied, to have no care or thought about us, Thrasymachus—whether we live better or worse from not knowing what you say you know, is to you a matter of indifference. Prithee, friend, do not keep your knowledge to yourself; we are a large party; and any benefit which you confer upon us will be amply rewarded. For my own part I openly declare that I am not convinced, and that I do not believe injustice to be more gainful than justice, even if uncontrolled and allowed to have free play. For, granting that there may be an unjust man who is able to commit injustice either by fraud or force, still this does not convince me of the superior advantage of injustice, and there may be others who are in the same predicament with myself. Perhaps we may be wrong; if so, you in your wisdom should convince us that we are mistaken in preferring justice to unjustice.

READING QUESTIONS

1. How does Thrasymachus initially define justice?
2. According to Thrasymachus, what do the laws of all three types of government have in common?
3. What is the point of Socrates' charge that rulers are not infallible?
4. What analogy is Socrates making when he questions whether we call a physician who makes an error a physician?
5. What analogy is Socrates making when he contends that the true physician considers the needs not of himself, but of the patient?

Aristotle

The third towering figure of early Greek philosophy is Aristotle, Plato's most brilliant student and the one he recognized as "the mind of the school." Aristotle was born in 384 B.C. in Macedonia, near the northern frontier of the Greek world. His father was the physician to the Macedonian king. At the age of seventeen, Aristotle moved south to Athens and joined Plato's Academy. There he remained as student and, then, teacher until the death of Plato, twenty years later.

When Plato died in 347 B.C., Aristotle left Athens. He spent his time in a variety of activities, including investigations in biology and zoology. He also took a position as tutor to the son of the new Macedonian king. For about a year, Aristotle taught the thirteen-year-old prince, who was later to become the most famous conqueror and ruler the ancient world had ever known: Alexander the Great. Apparently, they remained in contact after Alexander attained the throne. Legend has it that Alexander had specimens of exotic flora and fauna sent to Aristotle from his military expeditions to far-off lands. By the spring of 334 B.C., Aristotle had returned to Athens to found his own school, the **Lyceum.** Here he taught until the rising tide of anti-Macedonian sentiment among Athenians convinced him to flee. He died a year later in exile, in 322 B.C.

Aristotle most naturally was influenced by the powerful ideas of his teacher, Plato. Like his teacher, Aristotle had broad philosophical interests. Also like Plato, Aristotle's primary interests concerned the nature of external reality and the nature of the good life for humans. Aristotle was influenced by Plato's Theory of Forms (although his later philosophical works repudiated the Forms). In the main, however, the philosophy of Aristotle differed from that of Plato. For example, whereas Plato downplayed the reality of the material world in favor of an idealized immaterial realm to which he gave primary importance, Aristotle had the earthly interests of the true scientist. His attention was focused on the material world, and it is to that realm that he gave primary importance. Aristotle's interests included what we would now call scientific investigations, such as biology and zoology, but which in his time were all considered parts of the rational inquiry of philosophy. In fact, Aristotle's work in the natural sciences was so powerful that he remained the unquestioned authority in biology until the nineteenth century. If Plato was the speculative philosopher, Aristotle was the philosopher with his feet firmly planted on the ground.

In ethics, too, Aristotle's thought reflects the influence and interests of his illustrious teacher yet differs enough to deserve classification as a separate philosophy. Although Plato wrote and thought about numerous ethical issues (several of which we encountered in the preceding selections), his writings do not illustrate a systematic account of ethics. Aristotle, on the other hand, offers the first systematic account of ethics in the history of philosophy. Perhaps both their similarities and differences are illustrated in their thoughts on the meaning of the word *good*.

The meaning of ethical terms (such as *good*) constitute an enterprise we now call **metaethics.** That is, metaethics is an investigation into the concepts and methods of ethics rather than a study of how people ought to behave. Both Aristotle and Plato recognized the necessity of understanding what is meant by "the good." They arrived, however, at divergent conclusions. Plato argued that the word *good* represents a single concept, one in which all that is considered good "participates." The Idea of good is the model and inspiration for all the earthly instances of goodness. Aristotle begins the *Nicomachean Ethics,* his premier work in moral philosophy, with the search for the common features of everything good. But he concludes that the word contains not one sense, but many. Goodness is defined differently for each area in which the term applies. For example, if you declare that a particular hammer is a good hammer, you use a different sense of the word than when you declare a musician to be a good one. Good hammers are efficient pounders of nails whereas good musicians are adept at playing music. This distinction is important for Aristotle's ethics because if something is good only in relation to fulfilling its intended purpose, then good people must be good only in relation to fulfilling the intended purpose of people. His ethics, therefore, demands an understanding of the purpose (or ends) of human beings.

Like Plato, and unlike Socrates, Aristotle wrote down his philosophy for publication. Unfortunately, almost nothing remains of these works but short fragments. The dozen volumes that make up the English versions of the writings we now attribute to Aristotle were probably lecture notes, written down either by Aristotle or by students. This may account for the dryness and brevity of Aristotle's writings. Aristotle wrote on many subjects, and his titles include works on logic (the *Organon*) and natural science (the *Physics*), but his work in ethics is best represented in the *Nicomachean Ethics*. Excerpts from that work are reprinted here.

The writings of Aristotle have provided a springboard to philosophical discussion and contemplation even to this day. Aristotle's ethics has received a great deal of recent attention, in large part because his approach is seen as an alternative to the two dominant ethical theories in contemporary Western moral philosophy. **Utilitarianism** (associated with **Jeremy Bentham** and **John Stuart Mill**) and **Kant's duty ethics,** representations of which are included in subsequent readings, focus on the rightness or wrongness of particular actions. That is, they try to answer the ethical questions "How should I act in this situation?" and "What is the right thing for me to do?" Aristotle's ethics focuses instead on developing the proper character of a person. The attention of Aristotelian ethics is aimed less toward questions of how one should act or what one should do and more toward what kind of person we should strive to become. Aristotle's theory is called **virtue ethics** because it concerns itself with the attributes (or virtues) that a good person should have. When you read the following selections from Aristotle, notice how he concerns himself with issues of good character. Notice, too, how he investigates how one learns to be the best person he or she can be.

In addition to his refreshing influence on ethics in the last twenty or thirty years (a resurgence that began with an article by G. E. M. Anscombe, reprinted in this text), Aristotle's ethics directly affected other moral philosophers, most notably the **Stoics** and **St. Thomas Aquinas.** Quite important, by influencing St. Thomas, Aristotle had an effect on the entire subsequent history of Christianity.

Nicomachean Ethics

If someone were to ask you why you are reading this book, your answer would probably be something like "because it was assigned." If you were then pressed as to the reasons that you read what is assigned, you would probably reply that you read because you want a good grade. Why do you

want a good grade? Because, you would say, it will enable me to get my
bachelor's degree from this college or university. Why do you want to obtain a bachelor's degree? It will, you answer (probably irritated by now),
make it more likely that I'll get a decent, well-paying job. Why do you
want a good job? So I can buy a house, a decent car, and maybe raise a
family. Why do you wish these things? Ultimately, you say, so I'll be happy.

It is just such a train of means to ends that Aristotle argues lies behind all that humans do. In the end, we do what we do because we think
doing these things will make us happy. Not happy in the sense of joy-
ously, bouncily, laughingly pleased, but content, satisfied, or with a sense
of well-being. The Greek term to indicate this human flourishing, translated perhaps unfortunately as happiness, is **eudaimonia**. This, says
Aristotle, is what good means for human beings.   ✍

Book I

1. Every art and every inquiry, and similarly every action and pursuit, is thought to
aim at some good; and for this reason the good has rightly been declared to be that
at which all things aim. But a certain difference is found among ends; some are activities, others are products apart from the activities that produce them. Where there
are ends apart from the actions, it is the nature of the products to be better than the
activities. Now, as there are many actions, arts, and sciences, their ends also are
many; the end of the medical art is health, that of shipbuilding a vessel, that of strategy victory, that of economics wealth. But where such arts fall under a single capacity—as bridle-making and the other arts concerned with the equipment of horses
fall under the art of riding, and this and every military action under strategy, in the
same way other arts fall under yet others—in all of these the ends of the master arts
are to be preferred to all the subordinate ends; for it is for the sake of the former
that the latter are pursued. It makes no difference whether the activities themselves
are the ends of the actions, or something else apart from the activities, as in the case
of the sciences just mentioned.

---

1. After defining "the good," Aristotle tells us what constitutes the highest good.

---

2. If, then, there is some end of the things we do, which we desire for its own sake
(everything else being desired for the sake of this), and if we do not choose everything
for the sake of something else (for at that rate the process would go on to infinity, so
that our desire would be empty and vain), clearly this must be the good and the chief
good. Will not the knowledge of it, then, have a great influence on life? Shall we not,
like archers who have a mark to aim at, be more likely to hit upon what is right? If so,
we must try, in outline at least, to determine what it is, and of which of the sciences or

From *The Works of Aristotle,* translated by W. D. Ross, 1915. Reprinted by permission of Oxford
University Press.

capacities it is the object. It would seem to belong to the most authoritative art and that which is most truly the master art. And politics appears to be of this nature; for it is this that ordains which of the sciences should be studied in a state, and which each class of citizens should learn and up to what point they should learn them; and we see even the most highly esteemed of capacities to fall under this, e.g., strategy, economics, rhetoric; now, since politics uses the rest of the sciences, and since, again, it legislates as to what we are to do and what we are to abstain from, the end of this science must include those of the others, so that this end must be the good for man. For even if the end is the same for a single man and for a state, that of the state seems at all events something greater and more complete whether to attain or to preserve; though it is worth while to attain the end merely for one man, it is finer and more godlike to attain it for a nation or for city-states. These, then, are the ends at which our inquiry aims, since it is political science, in one sense of that term.

3. Our discussion will be adequate if it has as much clearness as the subject-matter admits of, for precision is not to be sought for alike in all discussions, any more than in all the products of the crafts. Now fine and just actions, which political science investigates, admit of much variety and fluctuation of opinion, so that they may be thought to exist only by convention, and not by nature. And goods also give rise to a similar fluctuation because they bring harm to many people; for before now men have been undone by reason of their wealth, and others by reason of their courage. We must be content, then, in speaking of such subjects and with such premises to indicate the truth roughly and in outline, and in speaking about things which are only for the most part true and with premises of the same kind to reach conclusions that are no better. In the same spirit, therefore, should each type of statement be *received;* for it is the mark of an educated man to look for precision in each class of things just so far as the nature of the subject admits; it is evidently equally foolish to accept probable reasoning from a mathematician and to demand from a rhetorician scientific proofs.

Now each man judges well the things he knows, and of these he is a good judge. And so the man who has been educated in a subject is a good judge of that subject, and the man who has received an all-round education is a good judge in general. Hence a young man is not a proper hearer of lectures on political science; for he is inexperienced in the actions that occur in life, but its discussions start from these and are about these; and, further, since he tends to follow his passions, his study will be vain and unprofitable, because the end aimed at is not knowledge but action. And it makes no difference whether he is young in years or youthful in character; the defect does not depend on time, but on his living, and pursuing each successive object, as passion directs. For to such persons, as to the incontinent, knowledge brings no profit; but to those who desire and act in accordance with a rational principle knowledge about such matters will be of great benefit.

These remarks about the student, the sort of treatment to be expected, and the purpose of the inquiry, may be taken as our preface.

4. Let us resume our inquiry and state, in view of the fact that all knowledge and every pursuit aims at some good, what it is that we say political science aims at and what is the highest of all goods achievable by action. Verbally there is very general agreement; for both the general run of men and people of superior refinement say that it is happiness, and identify living well and doing well with being happy; but with regard to what happiness is they differ, and the many do not give the same

account as the wise. For the former think it is some plain and obvious thing, like pleasure, wealth, or honor; they differ, however, from one another—and often even the same man identifies it with different things, with health when he is ill, with wealth when he is poor; but, conscious of their ignorance, they admire those who proclaim some great ideal that is above their comprehension. Now some thought that apart from these many goods there is another which is self-subsistent and causes the goodness of all these as well. To examine all the opinions that have been held were perhaps somewhat fruitless; enough to examine those that are most prevalent or that seem to be arguable.

Let us not fail to notice, however, that there is a difference between arguments from and those to the first principles. For Plato, too, was right in raising this question and asking, as he used to do, 'are we on the way from or to the first principles?' There is a difference, as there is in a race-course between the course from the judges to the turning-point and the way back. For, while we must begin with what is known, things are objects of knowledge in two senses—some to us, some without qualification. Presumably, then, *we* must begin with things known to *us*. Hence any one who is to listen intelligently to lectures about what is noble and just and, generally, about the subjects of political science must have been brought up in good habits. For the fact is the starting-point, and if this is sufficiently plain to him, he will not at the start need the reason as well; and the man who has been well brought up has or can easily get starting-points. And as for him who neither has nor can get them, let him hear the words of Hesiod:

> Far best is he who knows all things himself;
> Good, he that hearkens when men counsel right;
> But he who neither knows, nor lays to heart
> Another's wisdom, is a useless wight.

---

2. Aristotle discusses various views of the highest good. Can you identify the three types of lives he mentions?

---

5. Let us, however, resume our discussion from the point at which we digressed. To judge from the lives that men lead, most men, and men of the most vulgar type, seem (not without some ground) to identify the good, or happiness, with pleasure; which is the reason why they love the life of enjoyment. For there are, we may say, three prominent types of life—that just mentioned, the political, and thirdly the contemplative life. Now the mass of mankind are evidently quite slavish in their tastes, preferring a life suitable to beasts, but they get some ground for their view from the fact that many of those in high places share the tastes of Sardanapallus. A consideration of the prominent types of life shows that people of superior refinement and of active disposition identify happiness with honor; for this is, roughly speaking, the end of the political life. But it seems too superficial to be what we are looking for, since it is thought to depend on those who bestow honor rather than on him who receives it, but the good we divine to be something proper to a man and not easily taken from him. Further, men seem to pursue honor in order that they may be assured of their goodness; at least it is by men of practical wisdom that they seek to be honored, and among those who know them, and on the ground of their virtue; clearly, then, according to them, at any rate, virtue is better. And

perhaps one might even suppose this to be, rather than honor, the end of the political life. But even this appears somewhat incomplete; for possession of virtue seems actually compatible with being asleep, or with lifelong inactivity, and, further, with the greatest sufferings and misfortunes; but a man who was living so no one would call happy, unless he were maintaining a thesis at all costs. But enough of this; for the subject has been sufficiently treated even in the current discussions. Third comes the contemplative life, which we shall consider later.

The life of money-making is one undertaken under compulsion, and wealth is evidently not the good we are seeking; for it is merely useful and for the sake of something else. And so one might rather take the aforenamed objects to be ends; for they are loved for themselves. But it is evident that not even these are ends; yet many arguments have been thrown away in support of them. Let us leave this subject, then.

6. We had perhaps better consider the universal good and discuss thoroughly what is meant by it, although such an inquiry is made an uphill one by the fact that the Forms have been introduced by friends of our own. Yet it would perhaps be thought to be better, indeed to be our duty, for the sake of maintaining the truth even to destroy what touches us closely, especially as we are philosophers or lovers of wisdom; for, while both are dear, piety requires us to honor truth above our friends.

The men who introduced this doctrine did not posit Ideas of classes within which they recognized priority and posteriority (which is the reason why they did not maintain the existence of an Idea embracing all numbers); but the term 'good' is used both in the category of substance and in that of quality and in that of relation, and that which is *per se,* i.e., substance, is prior in nature to the relative (for the latter is like an offshoot and accident of being); so that there could not be a common Idea set over all these goods. Further, since 'good' has as many senses as 'being' (for it is predicated both in the category of substance, as of God and of reason, and in quality, i.e., of the virtues, and in quantity, i.e., of that which is moderate, and in relation, i.e., of the useful, and in time, i.e., of the right opportunity, and in place, i.e., of the right locality and the like), clearly it cannot be something universally present in all cases and single; for then it could not have been predicated in all the categories but in one only. Further, since of the things answering to one Idea there is one science, there would have been one science of all the goods; but as it is there are many sciences even of the things that fall under one category, e.g., of opportunity, for opportunity in war is studied by strategics and in disease by medicine, and the moderate in food is studied by medicine and in exercise by the science of gymnastics. And one might ask the question, what in the world they *mean* by 'a thing itself,' if (as is the case) in 'man himself' and in a particular man the account of man is one and the same. For in so far as they are man, they will in no respect differ; and if this is so, neither will 'good itself' and particular goods, in so far as they are good. But again it will not be good any the more for being eternal, since that which lasts long is no whiter than that which perishes in a day. The Pythagoreans seem to give a more plausible account of the good, when they place the one in the column of goods; and it is they that Speusippus seems to have followed.

But let us discuss these matters elsewhere; an objection to what we have said, however, may be discerned in the fact that the Platonists have not been speaking about *all* goods, and that the goods that are pursued and loved for themselves are called good by reference to a single Form, while those which tend to produce or to preserve these somehow or to prevent their contraries are called so by reference to these, and in a secondary sense. Clearly, then, goods must be spoken of in two ways, and some must be good in themselves, the others by reason of these. Let us separate, then, things good in themselves from things useful, and consider whether the former are called good by reference to a single Idea. What sort of goods would one call good in themselves? Is it those that are pursued even when isolated from others, such as intelligence, sight, and certain pleasures and honors? Certainly, if we pursue these also for the sake of something else, yet one would place them among things good in themselves. Or is nothing other than the Idea of good good in itself? In that case the Form will be empty. But if the things we have named are also things good in themselves, the account of the good will have to appear as something identical in them all, as that of whiteness is identical in snow and in white lead. But of honor, wisdom, and pleasure, just in respect of their goodness, the accounts are distinct and diverse. The good, therefore, is not some common element answering to one Idea.

But what then do we mean by the good? It is surely not like the things that only chance to have the same name. Are goods one, then, by being derived from one good or by all contributing to one good, or are they rather one by analogy? Certainly as sight is in the body, so is reason in the soul, and so on in other cases. But perhaps these subjects had better be dismissed for the present; for perfect precision about them would be more appropriate to another branch of philosophy. And similarly with regard to the Idea; even if there is some one good which is universally predicable of goods or is capable of separate and independent existence, clearly it could not be achieved or attained by man; but we are now seeking something attainable. Perhaps, however, some one might think it worthwhile to recognize this with a view to the goods that *are* attainable and achievable; for having this as a sort of pattern we shall know better the goods that are good for us, and if we know them shall attain them. This argument has some plausibility, but seems to clash with the procedure of the sciences; for all of these, though they aim at some good and seek to supply the deficiency of it, leave on one side the knowledge of *the* good. Yet that all the exponents of the arts should be ignorant of, and should not even seek, so great an aid is not probable. It is hard, too, to see how a weaver or a carpenter will be benefited in regard to his own craft by knowing this 'good itself,' or how the man who has viewed the Idea itself will be a better doctor or general thereby. For a doctor seems not even to study health in this way, but the health of man, or perhaps rather the health of a particular man; it is individuals that he is healing. But enough of these topics.

7. Let us again return to the good we are seeking, and ask what it can be. It seems different in different actions and arts; it is different in medicine, in strategy, and in the other arts likewise. What then is the good of each? Surely that for whose sake everything else is done. In medicine this is health, in strategy victory, in architecture a house, in any other sphere something else, and in every action and pursuit the end; for it is for the sake of this that all men do whatever else they do. Therefore, if there is an end for all that we do, this will be the good achievable by action, and if there are more than one, these will be the goods achievable by action.

So the argument has by a different course reached the same point; but we must try to state this even more clearly. Since there are evidently more than one end, and we choose some of these (e.g., wealth, flutes, and in general instruments) for the sake of something else, clearly not all ends are final ends; but the chief good is evidently something final. Therefore, if there is only one final end, this will be what we are seeking, and if there are more than one, the most final of these will be what we are seeking. Now we call that which is in itself worthy of pursuit more final than that which is worthy of pursuit for the sake of something else, and that which is never desirable for the sake of something else more final than the things that are desirable both in themselves and for the sake of that other thing, and therefore we call final without qualification that which is always desirable in itself and never for the sake of something else.

Now such a thing happiness, above all else, is held to be; for this we choose always for itself and never for the sake of something else, but honor, pleasure, reason, and every virtue we choose indeed for themselves (for if nothing resulted from them we should still choose each of them), but we choose them also for the sake of happiness, judging that by means of them we shall be happy. Happiness, on the other hand, no one chooses for the sake of these, nor, in general, for anything other than itself.

From the point of view of self-sufficiency the same result seems to follow; for the final good is thought to be self-sufficient. Now by self-sufficient we do not mean that which is sufficient for a man by himself, for one who lives a solitary life, but also for parents, children, wife, and in general for his friends and fellow citizens, since man is born for citizenship. But some limit must be set to this; for if we extend our requirement to ancestors and descendants and friends' friends we are in for an infinite series. Let us examine this question, however, on another occasion; the self-sufficient we now define as that which when isolated makes life desirable and lacking in nothing; and such we think happiness to be; and further we think it most desirable of all things, without being counted as one good thing among others—if it were so counted it would clearly be made more desirable by the addition of even the least of goods; for that which is added becomes an excess of goods, and of goods the greater is always more desirable. Happiness, then, is something final and self-sufficient, and is the end of action.

3. We must discover the proper function of a human being. In the paragraph, Aristotle gives his definition of human good.

Presumably, however, to say that happiness is the chief good seems a platitude, and a clearer account of what it is is still desired. This might perhaps be given, if we could first ascertain the function of man. For just as for a flute-player, a sculptor, or any artist, and, in general, for all things that have a function or activity, the good and the 'well' is thought to reside in the function, so would it seem to be for man, if he has a function. Have the carpenter, then, and the tanner certain functions or activities, and has man none? Is he born without a function? Or as eye, hand, foot, and in general each of the parts evidently has a function, may one lay it down that man similarly has a function apart from all these? What then can this be? Life seems to be common even to plants, but we are seeking what is peculiar to man. Let us exclude, therefore, the life of nutrition and growth. Next there would be a life of perception, but *it* also seems to be common even to the horse, the ox, and every animal. There remains, then, an active life of the element that has a rational principle; of this, one part has such a principle in the sense of being obedient to one, the other in the sense of possessing one and exercising thought. And as 'life of the rational element' also has two meanings, we must state that life in the sense of activity is what we mean; for this seems to be the more proper sense of the term. Now if the function of man is an activity of soul which follows or implies a rational principle, and if we say 'a so-and-so' and 'a good so-and-so' have a function which is the same in kind, e.g., a lyre-player and a good lyre-player, and so without qualification in all cases, eminence in respect of goodness being added to the name of the function (for the function of a lyre-player is to play the lyre, and that of a good lyre-player is to do so well): if this is the case, [and we state the function of man to be a certain kind of life, and this to be an activity or actions of the soul implying a rational principle, and the function of a good man to be the good and noble performance of these, and if any action is well performed when it is performed in accordance with the appropriate excellence: if this is the case,] human good turns out to be activity of soul in accordance with virtue, and if there are more than one virtue, in accordance with the best and most complete.

But we must add 'in a complete life.' For one swallow does not make a summer, nor does one day; and so too one day, or a short time, does not make a man blessed and happy.

Let this serve as an outline of the good; for we must presumably first sketch it roughly, and then later fill in the details. But it would seem that any one is capable of carrying on and articulating what has once been well outlined, and that time is a good discoverer or partner in such a work; to which facts the advances of the arts are due; for any one can add what is lacking. And we must also remember what has been said before, and not look for precision in all things alike, but in each class of things such precision as accords with the subject-matter, and so much as is appropriate to the inquiry. For a carpenter and a geometer investigate the right angle in different ways; the former does so in so far as the right angle is useful for his work, while the latter inquires what it is or what sort of thing it is; for he is a spectator of the truth. We must act in the same way, then, in all other matters as well, that our main task may not be subordinated to minor questions. Nor must we demand the cause in all matters alike; it is enough in some cases that the *fact* be well established, as in the case of the first principles; the fact is the primary thing or first principle. Now of first principles we see some by induction, some by perception, some by a certain habituation, and others too in other ways. But each set of principles we must try to investigate in the natural way, and we must take pains to state them definitely, since they have a great influence on what follows. For the beginning is thought to be more than half of the whole, and many of the questions we ask are cleared up by it.

8. We must consider it, however, in the light not only of our conclusion and our premises, but also of what is commonly said about it; for with a true view all the data harmonize, but with a false one the facts soon clash. Now goods have been divided into three classes, and some are described as external, others as relating to soul or to body; we call those that relate to soul most properly and truly goods, and psychical actions and activities we class as relating to soul. Therefore our account must be sound, at least according to this view, which is an old one and agreed on

by philosophers. It is correct also in that we identify the end with certain actions and activities; for thus it falls among goods of the soul and not among external goods. Another belief which harmonizes with our account is that the happy man lives well and does well; for we have practically defined happiness as a sort of good life and good action. The characteristics that are looked for in happiness seem also, all of them, to belong to what we have defined happiness as being. For some identify happiness with virtue, some with practical wisdom, others with a kind of philosophic wisdom, others with these, or one of these, accompanied by pleasure or not without pleasure; while others include also external prosperity. Now some of these views have been held by many men and men of old, others by a few eminent persons; and it is not probable that either of these should be entirely mistaken, but rather that they should be right in at least some one respect or even in most respects.

With those who identify happiness with virtue or some one virtue our account is in harmony; for to virtue belongs virtuous activity. But it makes, perhaps, no small difference whether we place the chief good in possession or in use, in state of mind or in activity. For the state of mind may exist without producing any good result, as in a man who is asleep or in some other way quite inactive, but the activity cannot; for one who has the activity will of necessity be acting, and acting well. And as in the Olympic Games it is not the most beautiful and the strongest that are crowned but those who compete (for it is some of these that are victorious), so those who act win, and rightly win, the noble and good things in life.

Their life is also in itself pleasant. For pleasure is a state of *soul,* and to each man that which he is said to be a lover of is pleasant; e.g., not only is a horse pleasant to the lover of horses, and a spectacle to the lover of sights, but also in the same way just acts are pleasant to the lover of justice and in general virtuous acts to the lover of virtue. Now for most men their pleasures are in conflict with one another because these are not by nature pleasant, but the lovers of what is noble find pleasant the things that are by nature pleasant; and virtuous actions are such, so that these are pleasant for such men as well as in their own nature. Their life, therefore, has no further need of pleasure as a sort of adventitious charm, but has its pleasure in itself. For, besides what we have said, the man who does not rejoice in noble actions is not even good; since no one would call a man just who did not enjoy acting justly, nor any man liberal who did not enjoy liberal actions; and similarly in all other cases. If this is so, virtuous actions must be in themselves pleasant. But they are also *good* and *noble,* and have each of these attributes in the highest degree, since the good man judges well about these attributes; his judgement is such as we have described. Happiness then is the best, noblest, and most pleasant thing in the world, and these attributes are not severed as in the inscription at Delos—

> Most noble is that which is justest, and best is health;
> But pleasantest is it to win what we love.

For all these properties belong to the best activities; and these, or one—the best—of these, we identify with happiness.

Yet evidently, as we said, it needs the external goods as well; for it is impossible, or not easy, to do noble acts without the proper equipment. In many actions we use friends and riches and political power as instruments; and there are some things the lack of which takes the luster from happiness, as good birth, goodly children, beauty; for the man who is very ugly in appearance or ill-born or solitary and child-less is not very likely to be happy, and perhaps a man would be still less likely if he had thoroughly bad children or friends or had lost good children or friends by death. As we said, then, happiness seems to need this sort of prosperity in addition; for which reason some identify happiness with good fortune, though others identify it with virtue.

4. How do we acquire happiness? Why aren't animals capable of being happy?

9. For this reason also the question is asked, whether happiness is to be ac-quired by learning or by habituation or some other sort of training, or comes in virtue of some divine providence or again by chance. Now if there is *any* gift of the gods to men, it is reasonable that happiness should be god-given, and most surely god-given of all human things inasmuch as it is the best. But this question would perhaps be more appropriate to another inquiry; happiness seems, however, even if it is not god-sent but comes as a result of virtue and some process of learning or training, to be among the most godlike things; for that which is the prize and end of virtue seems to be the best thing in the world, and something godlike and blessed.

It will also on this view be very generally shared; for all who are not maimed as regards their potentiality for virtue may win it by a certain kind of study and care. But if it is better to be happy thus than by chance, it is reasonable that the facts should be so, since everything that depends on the action of nature is by nature as good as it can be, and similarly everything that depends on art or any rational cause, and especially if it depends on the best of all causes. To entrust to chance what is greatest and most noble would be a very defective arrangement.

The answer to the question we are asking is plain also from the definition of happiness; for it has been said to be a virtuous activity of soul, of a certain kind. Of the remaining goods, some must necessarily pre-exist as conditions of happi-ness, and others are naturally cooperative and useful as instruments. And this will be found to agree with what we said at the outset; for we stated the end of politi-cal science to be the best end, and political science spends most of its pains on mak-ing the citizens to be of a certain character, viz. good and capable of noble acts.

It is natural, then, that we call neither ox nor horse nor any other of the ani-mals happy; for none of them is capable of sharing in such activity. For this reason also a boy is not happy; for he is not yet capable of such acts, owing to his age; and boys who are called happy are being congratulated by reason of the hopes we have for them. For there is required, as we said, not only complete virtue but also a com-plete life, since many changes occur in life, and all manner of chances, and the most prosperous may fall into great misfortunes in old age, as is told of Priam in the Trojan Cycle; and one who has experienced such chances and has ended wretchedly no one calls happy.

10. Must no one at all, then, be called happy while he lives; must we, as Solon says, see the end? Even if we are to lay down this doctrine, is it also the case that a man *is* happy when he is *dead?* Or is not this quite absurd, especially for us who say that happiness is an activity? But if we do not call the dead man happy, and if Solon does not mean this, but that one can then safely *call* a man blessed as being at last beyond evils and misfortunes, this also affords matter for discussion; for both evil

and good are thought to exist for a dead man, as much as for one who is alive but not aware of them; e.g., honors and dishonors and the good or bad fortunes of children and in general of descendants. And this also presents a problem; for though a man has lived happily up to old age and has had a death worthy of his life, many reverses may befall his descendants—some of them may be good and attain the life they deserve, while with others the opposite may be the case; and clearly too the degrees of relationship between them and their ancestors may vary indefinitely. It would be odd, then, if the dead man were to share in these changes and become at one time happy, at another wretched; while it would also be odd if the fortunes of the descendants did not for *some* time have *some* effect on the happiness of their ancestors.

But we must return to our first difficulty; for perhaps by a consideration of it our present problem might be solved. Now if we must see the end and only then call a man happy, not as being happy but as having been so before, surely this is a paradox, that when he is happy the attribute that belongs to him is not to be truly predicated of him because we do not wish to call living men happy, on account of the changes that may befall them, and because we have assumed happiness to be something permanent and by no means easily changed, while a single man may suffer many turns of fortune's wheel. For clearly if we were to keep pace with his fortunes, we should often call the same man happy and again wretched, making the happy man out to be a 'chameleon and insecurely based.' Or is this keeping pace with his fortunes quite wrong? Success or failure in life does not depend on these, but human life, as we said, needs these as mere additions, while virtuous activities or their opposites are what constitute happiness or the reverse.

The question we have now discussed confirms our definition. For no function of man has so much permanence as virtuous activities (these are thought to be more durable even than knowledge of the sciences), and of these themselves the most valuable are more durable because those who are happy spend their life most readily and most continuously in these; for this seems to be the reason why we do not forget them. The attribute in question, then, will belong to the happy man, and he will be happy throughout his life; for always, or by preference to everything else, he will be engaged in virtuous action and contemplation, and he will bear the chances of life most nobly and altogether decorously, if he is 'truly good' and 'foursquare beyond reproach.'

Now many events happen by chance, and events differing in importance; small pieces of good fortune or of its opposite clearly do not weigh down the scales of life one way or the other, but a multitude of great events if they turn out well will make life happier (for not only are they themselves such as to add beauty to life, but the way a man deals with them may be noble and good), while if they turn out ill they crush and maim happiness; for they both bring pain with them and hinder many activities. Yet even in these nobility shines through, when a man bears with resignation many great misfortunes, not through insensibility to pain but through nobility and greatness of soul.

If activities are, as we said, what gives life its character, no happy man can become miserable; for he will never do the acts that are hateful and mean. For the man who is truly good and wise, we think, bears all the chances of life becomingly and always makes the best of circumstances, as a good general makes the best military use of the army at his command and a good shoemaker makes the best shoes out of the hides that are given him; and so with all other craftsmen. And if this is the case, the happy man can never become miserable—though he will not reach *blessedness,* if he meet with fortunes like those of Priam.

Nor, again, is he many-colored and changeable; for neither will he be moved from his happy state easily or by any ordinary misadventures, but only by many great ones, nor, if he has had many great misadventures, will he recover his happiness in a short time, but if at all, only in a long and complete one in which he has attained many splendid successes.

Why then should we not say that he is happy who is active in accordance with complete virtue and is sufficiently equipped with external goods, not for some chance period but throughout a complete life? Or must we add 'and who is destined to live thus and die as befits his life'? Certainly the future is obscure to us, while happiness, we claim, is an end and something in every way final. If so, we shall call happy those among living men in whom these conditions are, and are to be, fulfilled—but happy *men.* So much for these questions.

READING QUESTIONS

1. What does Aristotle claim is that which we desire, not for the sake of something else, but for its own sake?
2. Why isn't an ox happy?
3. Why isn't a child said to be happy?
4. What is metaethics?
5. What reason does Aristotle give for saying that a happy person can never become miserable?

Book II of Nicomachean Ethics

Have you noticed that some people seem able to stand up courageously for their convictions whereas others timidly acquiesce in the face of opposition? While one person leads the crowd, others are content, it seems, to follow. Do you know a person who would steal anything that wasn't heavily guarded and another who could be relied on to return intact a wallet belonging to a stranger? What accounts for these kinds of differences in character? Perhaps we are born with certain character traits—some bad, some good. Or maybe they are somehow instilled in us as we grow. In Book II of the *Nicomachean Ethics,* Aristotle argues that character traits, virtues and vices, are learned. And, of course, if

From *The Works of Aristotle,* translated by W. D. Ross, 1915. Reprinted by permission of Oxford University Press.

virtues and vices are learned, that implies that they can be taught. Could we use Aristotle's insights to teach young children to grow up to be better people?   ✍

Book II

1. Virtue, then, being of two kinds, intellectual and moral, intellectual virtue in the main owes both its birth and its growth to teaching (for which reason it requires experience and time), while moral virtue comes about as a result of habit, whence also its name (ἠθική) is one that is formed by a slight variation from the word ἔθος (habit). From this it is also plain that none of the moral virtues arises in us by nature; for nothing that exists by nature can form a habit contrary to its nature. For instance the stone which by nature moves downwards cannot be habituated to move upwards, not even if one tries to train it by throwing it up ten thousand times; nor can fire be habituated to move downwards, nor can anything else that by nature behaves in one way be trained to behave in another. Neither by nature, then, nor contrary to nature do the virtues arise in us; rather we are adapted by nature to receive them, and are made perfect by habit.

Again, of all the things that come to us by nature we first acquire the potentiality and later exhibit the activity (this is plain in the case of the senses; for it was not by often seeing or often hearing that we got these senses, but on the contrary we had them before we used them, and did not come to have them by using them); but the virtues we get by first exercising them, as also happens in the case of the arts as well. For the things we have to learn before we can do them, we learn by doing them, e.g., men become builders by building and lyre-players by playing the lyre; so too we become just by doing just acts, temperate by doing temperate acts, brave by doing brave acts.

This is confirmed by what happens in states; for legislators make the citizens good by forming habits in them, and this is the wish of every legislator, and those who do not effect it miss their mark, and it is in this that a good constitution differs from a bad one.

Again, it is from the same causes and by the same means that every virtue is both produced and destroyed, and similarly every art; for it is from playing the lyre that both good and bad lyre-players are produced. And the corresponding statement is true of builders and of all the rest; men will be good or bad builders as a result of building well or badly. For if this were not so, there would have been no need of a teacher, but all men would have been born good or bad at their craft. This, then, is the case with the virtues also; by doing the acts that we do in our transactions with other men we become just or unjust, and by doing the acts that we do in the presence of danger, and being habituated to feel fear or confidence, we become brave or cowardly. The same is true of appetites and feelings of anger; some men become temperate and good-tempered, others self-indulgent and irascible, by behaving in one way or the other in the appropriate circumstances. Thus, in one word, states of character arise out of like activities. This is why the activities we exhibit must be of a certain kind; it is because the states of character correspond to the differences between these. It makes no small difference, then, whether we form habits of one kind or of another from our very youth; it makes a very great difference, or rather *all* the difference.

2. Since, then, the present inquiry does not aim at theoretical knowledge like the others (for we are inquiring not in order to know what virtue is, but in order to become good, since otherwise our inquiry would have been of no use), we must examine the nature of actions, namely how we ought to do them; for these determine also the nature of the states of character that are produced, as we have said. Now, that we must act according to the right rule is a common principle and must be assumed—it will be discussed later, i.e., both what the right rule is, and how it is related to the other virtues. But this must be agreed upon beforehand, that the whole account of matters of conduct must be given in outline and not precisely, as we said at the very beginning that the accounts we demand must be in accordance with the subject-matter; matters concerned with conduct and questions of what is good for us have no fixity, any more than matters of health. The general account being of this nature, the account of particular cases is yet more lacking in exactness; for they do not fall under any art or precept but the agents themselves must in each case consider what is appropriate to the occasion, as happens also in the art of medicine or of navigation.

But though our present account is of this nature we must give what help we can. First, then, let us consider this, that it is the nature of such things to be destroyed by defect and excess, as we see in the case of strength and of health (for to gain light on things imperceptible we must use the evidence of sensible things); both excessive and defective exercise destroys the strength, and similarly drink or food which is above or below a certain amount destroys the health, while that which is proportionate both produces and increases and preserves it. So too is it, then, in the case of temperance and courage and the other virtues. For the man who flies from and fears everything and does not stand his ground against anything becomes a coward, and the man who fears nothing at all but goes to meet every danger becomes rash; and similarly the man who indulges in every pleasure and abstains from none becomes self-indulgent, while the man who shuns every pleasure, as boors do, becomes in a way insensible; temperance and courage, then, are destroyed by excess and defect, and preserved by the mean.

But not only are the sources and causes of their origination and growth the same as those of their destruction, but also the sphere of their actualization will be the same; for this is also true of the things which are more evident to sense, e.g., of strength; it is produced by taking much food and undergoing much exertion, and it is the strong man that will be most able to do these things. So too is it with the virtues; by abstaining from pleasures we become temperate, and it is when we have become so that we are most able to abstain from them; and similarly too in the case of courage; for by being habituated to despise things that are terrible and to stand our ground against them we become brave, and it is when we have become so that we shall be most able to stand our ground against them.

3. We must take as a sign of states of character the pleasure or pain that ensues on acts; for the man who abstains from bodily pleasures and delights in this very fact is temperate, while the man who is annoyed at it is self-indulgent, and he who stands his ground against things that are terrible and delights in this or at least is not pained is brave, while the man who is pained is a coward. For moral excellence is concerned with pleasures and pains; it is on account of the pleasure that we do bad things, and on account of the pain that we abstain from noble ones. Hence we ought to have been

brought up in a particular way from our very youth, as Plato says, so as both to delight in and to be pained by the things that we ought; for this is the right education.

Again, if the virtues are concerned with actions and passions, and every passion and every action is accompanied by pleasure and pain, for this reason also virtue will be concerned with pleasures and pains. This is indicated also by the fact that punishment is inflicted by these means; for it is a kind of cure, and it is the nature of cures to be effected by contraries.

Again, as we said but lately, every state of soul has a nature relative to and concerned with the kind of things by which it tends to be made worse or better; but it is by reason of pleasures and pains that men become bad, by pursuing and avoiding these—either the pleasures and pains they ought not or when they ought not or as they ought not, or by going wrong in one of the other similar ways that may be distinguished. Hence men even define the virtues as certain states of impassivity and rest; not well, however, because they speak absolutely, and do not say 'as one ought' and 'as one ought not' and 'when one ought or ought not,' and the other things that may be added. We assume, then, that this kind of excellence tends to do what is best with regard to pleasures and pains, and vice does the contrary.

The following facts also may show us that virtue and vice are concerned with these same things. There being three objects of choice and three of avoidance, the noble, the advantageous, the pleasant, and their contraries, the base, the injurious, the painful, about all of these the good man tends to go right and the bad man to go wrong, and especially about pleasure; for this is common to the animals, and also it accompanies all objects of choice; for even the noble and the advantageous appear pleasant.

Again, it has grown up with us all from our infancy; this is why it is difficult to rub off this passion, engrained as it is in our life. And we measure even our actions, some of us more and others less, by the rule of pleasure and pain. For this reason, then, our whole inquiry must be about these; for to feel delight and pain rightly or wrongly has no small effect on our actions.

Again, it is harder to fight with pleasure than with anger, to use Heraclitus' phrase, but both art and virtue are always concerned with what is harder; for even the good is better when it is harder. Therefore for this reason also the whole concern both of virtue and of political science is with pleasures and pains; for the man who uses these well will be good, he who uses them badly bad.

That virtue, then, is concerned with pleasures and pains, and that by the acts from which it arises it is both increased and, if they are done differently, destroyed, and that the acts from which it arose are those in which it actualizes itself—let this be taken as said.

———

1. Here Aristotle discusses the relationship with being just and performing just actions. It is not enough to perform the proper action. What else is required of a moral person?

———

4. The question might be asked, what we mean by saying that we must become just by doing just acts, and temperate by doing temperate acts; for if men do just and temperate acts, they are already just and temperate, exactly as, if they do what is in accordance with the laws of grammar and of music, they are grammarians and musicians.

Or is this not true even of the arts? It is possible to do something that is in accordance with the laws of grammar, either by chance or at the suggestion of another. A man will be a grammarian, then, only when he has both done something grammatical and done it grammatically; and this means doing it in accordance with the grammatical knowledge in himself.

Again, the case of the arts and that of the virtues are not similar; for the products of the arts have their goodness in themselves, so that it is enough that they should have a certain character, but if the acts that are in accordance with the virtues have themselves a certain character it does not follow that they are done justly or temperately. The agent also must be in a certain condition when he does them; in the first place he must have knowledge, secondly he must choose the acts, and choose them for their own sakes, and thirdly his action must proceed from a firm and unchangeable character. These are not reckoned in as conditions of the possession of the arts, except the bare knowledge; but as a condition of the possession of the virtues knowledge has little or no weight, while the other conditions count not for a little but for everything, i.e., the very conditions which result from often doing just and temperate acts.

Actions, then, are called just and temperate when they are such as the just or the temperate man would do; but it is not the man who does these that is just and temperate, but the man who also does them *as* just and temperate men do them. It is well said, then, that it is by doing just acts that the just man is produced, and by doing temperate acts the temperate man; without doing these no one would have even a prospect of becoming good.

But most people do not do these, but take refuge in theory and think they are being philosophers and will become good in this way, behaving somewhat like patients who listen attentively to their doctors, but do none of the things they are ordered to do. As the latter will not be made well in body by such a course of treatment, the former will not be made well in soul by such a course of philosophy.

5. Next we must consider what virtue is. Since things that are found in the soul are of three kinds—passions, faculties, states of character, virtue must be one of these. By passions I mean appetite, anger, fear, confidence, envy, joy, friendly feeling, hatred, longing, emulation, pity, and in general the feelings that are accompanied by pleasure or pain; by faculties the things in virtue of which we are said to be capable of feeling these, e.g., of becoming angry or being pained or feeling pity; by states of character the things in virtue of which we stand well or badly with reference to the passions, e.g., with reference to anger we stand badly if we feel it violently or too weakly, and well if we feel it moderately; and similarly with reference to the other passions.

Now neither the virtues nor the vices are *passions,* because we are not called good or bad on the ground of our passions, but are so called on the ground of our virtues and our vices, and because we are neither praised nor blamed for our passions (for the man who feels fear or anger is not praised, nor is the man who simply feels anger blamed, but the man who feels it in a certain way), but for our virtues and our vices we *are* praised or blamed.

Again, we feel anger and fear without choice, but the virtues are modes of choice or involve choice. Further, in respect of the passions we are said to be moved, but in respect of the virtues and the vices we are said not to be moved but to be disposed in a particular way.

For these reasons also they are not *faculties;* for we are neither called good nor bad, nor praised nor blamed, for the simple capacity of feeling the passions; again, we have the faculties by nature, but we are not made good or bad by nature; we have spoken of this before.

If, then, the virtues are neither passions nor faculties, all that remains is that they should be *states of character.*

Thus we have stated what virtue is in respect of its genus.

6. We must, however, not only describe virtue as a state of character, but also say what sort of state it is. We may remark, then, that every virtue or excellence both brings into good condition the thing of which it is the excellence and makes the work of that thing be done well; e.g., the excellence of the eye makes both the eye and its work good; for it is by the excellence of the eye that we see well. Similarly the excellence of the horse makes a horse both good in itself and good at running and at carrying its rider and at awaiting the attack of the enemy. Therefore, if this is true in every case, the virtue of man also will be the state of character which makes a man good and which makes him do his own work well.

How this is to happen we have stated already, but it will be made plain also by the following consideration of the specific nature of virtue. In everything that is continuous and divisible it is possible to take more, less, or an equal amount, and that either in terms of the thing itself or relatively to us; and the equal is an intermediate between excess and defect. By the intermediate in the object I mean that which is equidistant from each of the extremes, which is one and the same for all men; by the intermediate relatively to us that which is neither too much nor too little—and this is not one, nor the same for all. For instance, if ten is many and two is few, six is the intermediate, taken in terms of the object; for it exceeds and is exceeded by an equal amount; this is intermediate according to arithmetical proportion. But the intermediate relatively to us is not to be taken so; if ten pounds are too much for a particular person to eat and two too little, it does not follow that the trainer will order six pounds; for this also is perhaps too much for the person who is to take it, or too little—too little for Milo, too much for the beginner in athletic exercises. The same is true of running and wrestling. Thus a master of any art avoids excess and defect, but seeks the intermediate and chooses this—the intermediate not in the object but relatively to us.

————

2. Aristotle discusses excess, defect, and the intermediate. How do these three categories relate to virtue? Why is virtue described as a kind of mean?

————

If it is thus, then, that every art does its work well—by looking to the intermediate and judging its works by this standard (so that we often say of good works of art that it is not possible either to take away or to add anything, implying that excess and defect destroy the goodness of works of art, while the mean preserves it; and good artists, as we say, look to this in their work), and if, further, virtue is more exact and better than any art, as nature also is, then virtue must have the quality of aiming at the intermediate. I mean moral virtue; for it is this that is concerned with passions and actions, and in these there is excess, defect, and the intermediate. For instance, both fear and confidence and appetite and anger and pity and in general pleasure and pain may be felt both too much and too little, and in both cases not well; but to feel them at the right times, with reference to the right objects, towards the right people, with the right motive, and in the right way, is what is both intermediate and best, and this is characteristic of virtue. Similarly with regard to actions also there is excess, defect, and the intermediate. Now virtue is concerned with passions and actions, in which excess is a form of failure, and so is defect, while the intermediate is praised and is a form of success; and being praised and being successful are both characteristics of virtue. Therefore virtue is a kind of mean, since, as we have seen, it aims at what is intermediate.

Again, it is possible to fail in many ways (for evil belongs to the class of the unlimited, as the Pythagoreans conjectured, and good to that of the limited), while to succeed is possible only in one way (for which reason also one is easy and the other difficult—to miss the mark easy, to hit it difficult); for these reasons also, then, excess and defect are characteristic of vice, and the mean of virtue;

For men are good in but one way, but bad in many.

Virtue, then, is a state of character concerned with choice, lying in a mean, i.e., the mean relative to us, this being determined by a rational principle, and by that principle by which the man of practical wisdom would determine it. Now it is a mean between two vices, that which depends on excess and that which depends on defect; and again it is a mean because the vices respectively fall short of or exceed what is right in both passions and actions, while virtue both finds and chooses that which is intermediate. Hence in respect of its substance and the definition which states its essence virtue is a mean, with regard to what is best and right an extreme.

But not every action nor every passion admits of a mean; for some have names that already imply badness, e.g., spite, shamelessness, envy, and in the case of actions adultery, theft, murder; for all of these and suchlike things imply by their names that they are themselves bad, and not the excesses or deficiencies of them. It is not possible, then, ever to be right with regard to them; one must always be wrong. Nor does goodness or badness with regard to such things depend on committing adultery with the right woman, at the right time, and in the right way, but simply to do any of them is to go wrong. It would be equally absurd, then, to expect that in unjust, cowardly, and voluptuous action there should be a mean, an excess, and a deficiency; for at that rate there would be a mean of excess and of deficiency, an excess of excess, and a deficiency of deficiency. But as there is no excess and deficiency of temperance and courage because what is intermediate is in a sense an extreme, so too of the actions we have mentioned there is no mean nor any excess and deficiency, but however they are done they are wrong; for in general there is neither a mean of excess and deficiency, nor excess and deficiency of a mean.

---

3. Aristotle describes the mean as it pertains to numerous virtues. See if you can discuss bravery or anger in terms of excess, defect, and the intermediate.

---

7. We must, however, not only make this general statement, but also apply it to the individual facts. For among statements about conduct those which are general apply more widely, but those which are particular are more genuine, since conduct has to do with individual cases, and our statements must harmonize with the facts in these cases. We may take these cases from our table. With regard to feelings of fear and confidence courage is the mean; of the people who exceed, he who exceeds

in fearlessness has no name (many of the states have no name), while the man who exceeds in confidence is rash, and he who exceeds in fear and falls short in confidence is a coward. With regard to pleasures and pains—not all of them, and not so much with regard to the pains—the mean is temperance, the excess self-indulgence. Persons deficient with regard to the pleasures are not often found; hence such persons also have received no name. But let us call them 'insensible.'

With regard to giving and taking of money the mean is liberality, the excess and the defect prodigality and meanness. In these actions people exceed and fall short in contrary ways; the prodigal exceeds in spending and falls short in taking, while the mean man exceeds in taking and falls short in spending. (At present we are giving a mere outline or summary, and are satisfied with this; later these states will be more exactly determined.) With regard to money there are also other dispositions—a mean, magnificence (for the magnificent man differs from the liberal man; the former deals with large sums, the latter with small ones), an excess, tastelessness and vulgarity, and a deficiency, niggardliness; these differ from the states opposed to liberality, and the mode of their difference will be stated later.

With regard to honor and dishonor the mean is proper pride, the excess is known as a sort of 'empty vanity,' and the deficiency is undue humility; and as we said liberality was related to magnificence, differing from it by dealing with small sums, so there is a state similarly related to proper pride, being concerned with small honors while that is concerned with great. For it is possible to desire honor as one ought, and more than one ought, and less, and the man who exceeds in his desires is called ambitious, the man who falls short unambitious, while the intermediate person has no name. The dispositions also are nameless, except that that of the ambitious man is called ambition. Hence the people who are at the extremes lay claim to the middle place; and we ourselves sometimes call the intermediate person ambitious and sometimes unambitious, and sometimes praise the ambitious man and sometimes the unambitious. The reason of our doing this will be stated in what follows; but now let us speak of the remaining states according to the method which has been indicated.

With regard to anger also there is an excess, a deficiency, and a mean. Although they can scarcely be said to have names, yet since we call the intermediate person good-tempered let us call the mean good temper; of the persons at the extremes let the one who exceeds be called irascible, and his vice irascibility, and the man who falls short an inirascible sort of person, and the deficiency inirascibility.

There are also three other means, which have a certain likeness to one another, but differ from one another: for they are all concerned with intercourse in words and actions, but differ in that one is concerned with truth in this sphere, the other two with pleasantness; and of this one kind is exhibited in giving amusement, the other in all the circumstances of life. We must therefore speak of these too, that we may the better see that in all things the mean is praiseworthy, and the extremes neither praiseworthy nor right, but worthy of blame. Now most of these states also have no names, but we must try, as in the other cases, to invent names ourselves so that we may be clear and easy to follow. With regard to truth, then, the intermediate is a truthful sort of person and the mean may be called truthfulness, while the pretense which exaggerates is boastfulness and the person characterized by it a boaster, and that which understates is mock modesty and the person characterized by it mock-modest. With regard to pleasantness in the giving of amusement the intermediate person is ready-witted and the disposition ready wit, the excess is buffoonery and the person characterized by it a buffoon, while the man who falls short is a sort of boor and his state is boorishness. With regard to the remaining kind of pleasantness, that which is exhibited in life in general, the man who is pleasant in the right way is friendly and the mean is friendliness, while the man who exceeds is an obsequious person if he has no end in view, a flatterer if he is aiming at his own advantage, and the man who falls short and is unpleasant in all circumstances is a quarrelsome and surly sort of person.

There are also means in the passions and concerned with the passions; since shame is not a virtue, and yet praise is extended to the modest man. For even in these matters one man is said to be intermediate, and another to exceed, as for instance the bashful man who is ashamed of everything; while he who falls short or is not ashamed of anything at all is shameless, and the intermediate person is modest. Righteous indignation is a mean between envy and spite, and these states are concerned with the pain and pleasure that are felt at the fortunes of our neighbors; the man who is characterized by righteous indignation is pained at undeserved good fortune, the envious man, going beyond him, is pained at all good fortune, and the spiteful man falls so far short of being pained that he even rejoices. But these states there will be an opportunity of describing elsewhere; with regard to justice, since it has not one simple meaning, we shall, after describing the other states, distinguish its two kinds and say how each of them is a mean; and similarly we shall treat also of the rational virtues.

8. There are three kinds of disposition, then, two of them vices, involving excess and deficiency respectively, and one a virtue, viz. the mean, and all are in a sense opposed to all; for the extreme states are contrary both to the intermediate state and to each other, and the intermediate to the extremes; as the equal is greater relatively to the less, less relatively to the greater, so the middle states are excessive relatively to the deficiencies, deficient relatively to the excesses, both in passions and in actions. For the brave man appears rash relatively to the coward, and cowardly relatively to the rash man; and similarly the temperate man appears self-indulgent relatively to the insensible man, insensible relatively to the self-indulgent, and the liberal man prodigal relatively to the mean man, mean relatively to the prodigal. Hence also the people at the extremes push the intermediate man each over to the other, and the brave man is called rash by the coward, cowardly by the rash man, and correspondingly in the other cases.

These states being thus opposed to one another, the greatest contrariety is that of the extremes to each other, rather than to the intermediate; for these are further from each other than from the intermediate, as the great is further from the small and the small from the great than both are from the equal. Again, to the intermediate some extremes show a certain likeness, as that of rashness to courage and that of prodigality to liberality; but the extremes show the greatest unlikeness to each other; now contraries are defined as the things that are furthest from each other, so that things that are further apart are more contrary.

To the mean in some cases the deficiency, in some the excess is more opposed; e.g., it is not rashness, which is an excess, but cowardice, which is a deficiency, that is more opposed to courage, and not insensibility, which is a deficiency, but self-indulgence, which is an excess, that is more opposed to temperance. This happens

from two reasons, one being drawn from the thing itself; for because one extreme is
nearer and liker to the intermediate, we oppose not this but rather its contrary to
the intermediate. E.g., since rashness is thought liker and nearer to courage, and
cowardice more unlike, we oppose rather the latter to courage; for things that are
further from the intermediate are thought more contrary to it. This, then, is one
cause, drawn from the thing itself; another is drawn from ourselves; for the things
to which we ourselves more naturally tend seem more contrary to the intermediate.
For instance, we ourselves tend more naturally to pleasures, and hence are more easily carried away towards self-indulgence than towards propriety. We describe as
contrary to the mean, then, rather the directions in which we more often go to great
lengths; and therefore self-indulgence, which is an excess, is the more contrary to
temperance.

9. That moral virtue is a mean, then, and in what sense it is so, and that it is a
mean between two vices, the one involving excess, the other deficiency, and that it
is such because its character is to aim at what is intermediate in passions and in actions, has been sufficiently stated. Hence also it is no easy task to be good. For in
everything it is no easy task to find the middle, e.g., to find the middle of a circle is
not for every one but for him who knows; so, too, any one can get angry—that is
easy—or give or spend money; but to do this to the right person, to the right extent,
at the right time, with the right motive, and in the right way, *that* is not for every
one, nor is it easy; wherefore goodness is both rare and laudable and noble.

Hence he who aims at the intermediate must first depart from what is the more
contrary to it, as Calypso advises—

Hold the ship out beyond that surf and spray.

For of the extremes one is more erroneous, one less so; therefore, since to hit the
mean is hard in the extreme, we must as a second best, as people say, take the least
of the evils; and this will be done best in the way we describe.

But we must consider the things towards which we ourselves also are easily carried away; for some of us tend to one thing, some to another; and this will be recognizable from the pleasure and the pain we feel. We must drag ourselves away to
the contrary extreme; for we shall get into the intermediate state by drawing well
away from error, as people do in straightening sticks that are bent.

Now in everything the pleasant or pleasure is most to be guarded against; for
we do not judge it impartially. We ought, then, to feel towards pleasure as the elders
of the people felt towards Helen, and in all circumstances repeat their saying; for if
we dismiss pleasure thus we are less likely to go astray. It is by doing this, then, (to
sum the matter up) that we shall best be able to hit the mean.

But this is no doubt difficult, and especially in individual cases; for it is not easy
to determine both how and with whom and on what provocation and how long one
should be angry; for we too sometimes praise those who fall short and call them
good-tempered, but sometimes we praise those who get angry and call them manly.
The man, however, who deviates little from goodness is not blamed, whether he do
so in the direction of the more or of the less, but only the man who deviates more
widely; for *he* does not fail to be noticed. But up to what point and to what extent
a man must deviate before he becomes blameworthy it is not easy to determine by
reasoning, any more than anything else that is perceived by the senses; such things

depend on particular facts, and the decision rests with perception. So much, then, is plain, that the intermediate state is in all things to be praised, but that we must incline sometimes towards the excess, sometimes towards the deficiency; for so shall we most easily hit the mean and what is right.

READING QUESTIONS

1. What are the two kinds of virtue?
2. Give Aristotle's two reasons that we must not be born with moral virtues.
3. What does Aristotle mean when he says that courage, temperance, and the other virtues are "destroyed by defect and excess"? Can you give an example where this might happen?
4. If virtue is a mean, what is it relative to?

Epicurus

By the time Aristotle died, in 322 B.C., the golden age of the Greek city-state had ended forever. By the middle of the fourth century B.C., weakened by a series of conflicts among themselves, the cities of Greece were brought under the yoke of the Macedonian Empire and their conquering leader, Alexander the Great. By the time of his death in 323 B.C., his empire included what is now Greece and Turkey and stretched from India in the east to Egypt in the west. His death brought on fifty years of fighting between his generals, who each sought to control the vast empire. Finally, the empire was split into three regions, each governed by one of three ruling families descended from Alexander's generals. The Ptolemy family ruled Egypt and Palestine, the Seluecids ruled Syria and Asia Minor, and the Antigonids ruled Greece and Macedonia. The freedom the Greeks had enjoyed in the age of the *polis* depended now on the whim of the Macedonian ruler. In time, Greece was to become but a province of Rome.

The changes in the political and social world of the Greeks affected the intellectual world. Plato and Aristotle were people of the *polis* and, as such, considered a person's role in the politics of the nation to be of uppermost concern. Their primary concerns were with their fellow Greeks; all others were barbarians and, therefore, strictly inferior to Greeks in every way. Political and cultural stability had fostered a climate of intellectual interest in which speculative and theoretical philosophy flourished.

With the end of the city-state and the increasing chaos that resulted from the power vacuum left by Alexander, philosophers mirrored the concerns of the common people and turned their attention to questions of ethics. Questions such as "What is the good life, and how can anyone attain it?" began to replace questions such as "What is reality?" and "What is knowledge?" In an age of uncertainty, people, including philosophers, sought certainty.

The **Hellenic Age** is that period of Greek cultural greatness in the original Greek territories. The period that begins with the deaths of Alexander and Aristotle is known to philosophers as the **Hellenistic Age.** During this period, Greek ideas and Greek influence extended throughout the Macedonian Empire. But influence tends to flow in many directions at once; the homogeneous Greek world became exposed to Eastern thought and Eastern culture. By the time the Roman Empire controlled most of the Western world, Western culture was a mixture of many different cultures. Beginning in Greece in the fourth century B.C., the focus on the *polis* was replaced by the focus on the *cosmopolis,* the people of the world.

Philosophy during the five hundred or so years between the death of Aristotle and the rise of Christianity is dominated by the philosophical descendants of Socrates. Two main schools predominated: the **Stoics,** with philosophical beginnings in the philosophy of the **Cynics,** founded by Socrates' follower Antisthenes; and the **Epicureans,** influenced by the philosophy of the **Cyrenaics,** begun by Socrates' follower Aristippus. Students of Plato and Aristotle, and the generations of subsequent followers, were also active, but no other philosophy dominated this period like that of the Stoics and Epicureans. Here we will investigate the moral philosophy of Epicurus, reserving study of the Stoics until later.

Epicurus, the founder of the philosophical movement that bears his name, was born in 341 B.C. He arrived in Athens from his native Samos, an Athenian colony, and set up a school known as "The Garden" in 306 B.C. In this tranquil setting, Epicurus taught his followers the secret to the good life: pursue pleasure and you will be happy. His message was not entirely original. Like the moral philosophy of the Cyrenaics, Epicureanism is a form of philosophical **hedonism**—the view that the pursuit of personal pleasure is the proper aim of all action. Like the Cyrenaics, Epicurus exhorted his followers to choose the more pleasurable alternative action except when the consequences of doing so will be more painful. For example, it may be more pleasurable to leave work and spend the day on the beach, but when you are fired and no longer able to buy food, your pain will be greater than the pleasure of the day. So, even though the momentary pleasure of the beach is tempting, one should not succumb to the temptation, as great pain will surely follow. Further, the Cyrenaics and Epicureans agreed that pain should never be chosen except when doing so will lead to greater pleasure. Having a cavity filled may cause some pain, but it prevents further, and much worse, pain later on. However, unlike the Cyrenaics, Epicurus did not promote a merely sensualist hedonism. True pleasure he defined as *ataraxia,* or tranquility, the result of ridding ourselves of wants by the simplest means.

Even though all hedonistic moral philosophies consider pleasure to be the highest, or even the sole, good, they do not all define pleasure in the same way. The extreme view, "if it feels good, do it," can be easily criticized: This is not a moral system but a rationale for short-sighted self-indulgence. If what is good is what makes *me* happy, who cares about the harm that comes to you? The point is often made, too, that pleasures of the moment seldom have lasting results. Drinking tequila may be fun, but hangovers are not. But Epicurus did not ascribe to the view that pleasure is merely whatever feels good. As you will see in the following reading, pleasure for Epicurus is the absence of pain. And the primary source of pain, taught Epicurus, is anxiety. It is unfortunate that many critics of the Epicurean movement, including the early Christians, characterized his philosophy as shallow and selfish. His critics characterized Epicureanism as a moral theory that led to a lack of civic responsibility and a life of libertine pleasures. Though such Epicureans doubtless existed, the philosophy of Epicurus was highly principled: much was made in his day of the saintly nature of Epicurus's life.

The impact of Epicurus and his philosophy was enormous. Generation after generation of disciples—an appropriate word since Epicurus was accorded nearly divine status by his followers, and his words were committed to memory as unvarnished truths—lived in Epicurean communities over half a millennium. Later hedonistic philosophies such as **utilitarianism** demonstrate the influence of Epicurus.

Letter to Menoeceus; Principal Doctrines

Scholars believe that Epicurus wrote some three hundred works, almost nothing of which remains. Much of the writing that philosophers consider to be consistent with the thought of Epicurus, if not the exact words,

From *Epicurus: The Extant Remains,* translated by Cyril Bailey, Clarendon Press, 1926. Reprinted by permission from Oxford University Press.

comes from two sources: letters that were quoted by a later writer, Diogenes Laertius, and a series of maxims or aphorisms collected by some of his followers and distributed to the faithful in a form that they could commit to memory, here titled the *Principal Doctrines.*

Of the three letters, the *Letter to Menoeceus,* reprinted here, contains Epicurean thoughts on moral philosophy. Epicureanism begins with the observation that all creatures, humans included, pursue what feels good to them and avoid what hurts. This fact appears undeniable. Yet just what constitutes pleasure and pain is open to dispute. Sleeping feels good when you're tired, but something more active is preferable when you're not. Some pleasures are easy to acquire, such as a drink of cool water when you're thirsty, and others difficult: a milkshake takes ice cream, milk, and flavorings—and it costs money. Also, if pleasure is my goal, how am I ever satisfied? It would seem that I would never be satisfied with pleasures that end, since it would always be better to have the pleasure continue forever. We should notice a further problem here that did not really take on philosophical importance until it was raised by G. E. Moore some two thousand years later: Just because we naturally pursue pleasure and avoid pain, how can we say that this is what we *ought* to do?

Epicurus describes the greatest obstacle to the life of pleasure in these writings: Anxiety about the future causes pain and prevents the enjoyment of attainable pleasures. His theory, that identifying anxiety as the source of human pain and giving the means to overcome anxiety, is sometimes described in the words of one of his later followers as the "four-part cure."

As you read these words from Epicurus, notice just how far the English word *epicurean* (one who is indulgent in food and drink) is from Epicurus's philosophy. He writes that pleasure comes from satisfying one's natural desires by the simplest means possible. Caviar may taste good, but it is expensive and may upset your stomach. Simple foods rid us of hunger just as well and do not lead to pain in the long run.   ✒

Epicurus to Menoeceus

Let no one when young delay to study philosophy, nor when he is old grow weary of his study. For no one can come too early or too late to secure the health of his soul. And the man who says that the age for philosophy has either not yet come or has gone by is like the man who says that the age for happiness is not yet come to him, or has passed away. Wherefore both when young and old a man must study philosophy, that as he grows old he may be young in blessings through the grateful recollection of what has been, and that in youth he may be old as well, since he will know no fear of what is to come. We must then meditate on the things that make our happiness, seeing that when that is with us we have all, but when it is absent we do all to win it.

The things which I used unceasingly to commend to you, these do and practice, considering them to be the first principles of the good life. First of all believe that god is a being immortal and blessed, even as the common idea of a god is engraved on men's minds, and do not assign to him anything alien to his immortality or ill-suited to his blessedness: but believe about him everything that can uphold his blessedness and immortality. For gods there are, since the knowledge of them is by clear vision. But they are not such as the many believe them to be: for indeed they do not consistently represent them as they believe them to be. And the impious man is not he who denies the gods of the many, but he who attaches to the gods the beliefs of the many. For the statements of the many about the gods are not conceptions derived from sensation, but false suppositions, according to which the greatest misfortunes befall the wicked and the greatest blessings the good by the gift of the gods. For men being accustomed always to their own virtues welcome those like themselves, but regard all that is not of their nature as alien.

------

1. A central focus of Epicurean philosophy is fear of death. Here Epicurus gives reasons that we should not fear death.

Become accustomed to the belief that death is nothing to us. For all good and evil consists in sensation, but death is deprivation of sensation. And therefore a right understanding that death is nothing to us makes the mortality of life enjoyable, not because it adds to it an infinite span of time, but because it takes away the craving for immortality. For there is nothing terrible in life for the man who has truly comprehended that there is nothing terrible in not living. So that the man speaks but idly who says that he fears death not because it will be painful when it comes, but because it is painful in anticipation. For that which gives no trouble when it comes, is but an empty pain in anticipation. So death, the most terrifying of ills, is nothing to us, since so long as we exist death is not with us; but when death comes, then we do not exist. It does not then concern either the living or the dead, since for the former it is not, and the latter are no more.

But the many at one moment shun death as the greatest of evils, at another yearn for it as a respite from the evils in life. But the wise man neither seeks to escape life nor fears the cessation of life, for neither does life offend him nor does the absence of life seem to be any evil. And just as with food he does not seek simply the larger share and nothing else, but rather the most pleasant, so he seeks to enjoy not the longest period of time, but the most pleasant.

And he who counsels the young man to live well, but the old man to make a good end, is foolish, not merely because of the desirability of life, but also because it is the same training which teaches to live well and to die well. Yet much worse still is the man who says it is good not to be born, but

'once born make haste to pass the gates of Death.' (Theognis, 427)

For if he says this from conviction why does he not pass away out of life? For it is open to him to do so, if he had firmly made up his mind to this. But if he speaks in jest, his words are idle among men who cannot receive them.

We must then bear in mind that the future is neither ours, nor yet wholly not ours, so that we may not altogether expect it as sure to come, nor abandon hope of it, as if it will certainly not come.

---

2. Epicurus makes some important distinctions about desires that will allow us to make the choices that will lead to a life of blessedness. Can you chart the types of desires he distinguishes? Here also he defines the life of blessedness.

We must consider that of desires some are natural, others vain, and of the natural some are necessary and others merely natural; and of the necessary some are necessary for happiness, others for the repose of the body, and others for very life. The right understanding of these facts enables us to refer all choice and avoidance to the health of the body and the soul's freedom from disturbance, since this is the aim of the life of blessedness. For it is to obtain this end that we always act, namely, to avoid pain and fear. And when this is once secured for us, all the tempest of the soul is dispersed, since the living creature has not to wander as though in search of something that is missing, and to look for some other thing by which he can fulfill the good of the soul and the good of the body. For it is then that we have need of pleasure, when we feel pain owing to the absence of pleasure; but when we do not feel pain, we no longer need pleasure. And for this cause we call pleasure the beginning and end of the blessed life. For we recognize pleasure as the first good innate in us, and from pleasure we begin every act of choice and avoidance, and to pleasure we return again, using the feeling as the standard by which we judge every good.

And since pleasure is the first good and natural to us, for this very reason we do not choose every pleasure, but sometimes we pass over many pleasures, when greater discomfort accrues to us as the result of them: and similarly we think many pains better than pleasures, since a greater pleasure comes to us when we have endured pains for a long time. Every pleasure then because of its natural kinship to us is good, yet not every pleasure is to be chosen: even as every pain also is an evil, yet not all are always of a nature to be avoided. Yet by a scale of comparison and by the consideration of advantages and disadvantages we must form our judgment on all these matters. For the good on certain occasions we treat as bad, and conversely the bad as good.

And again independence of desire we think a great good—not that we may at all times enjoy but a few things, but that, if we do not possess many, we may enjoy the few in the genuine persuasion that those have the sweetest pleasure in luxury who least need it, and that all that is natural is easy to be obtained, but that which is superfluous is hard. And so plain savors bring us a pleasure equal to a luxurious diet, when all the pain due to want is removed; and bread and water produce the highest pleasure, when one who needs them puts them to his lips. To grow accustomed therefore to simple and not luxurious diet gives us health to the full, and makes a man alert for the needful employments of life, and when after long intervals we approach luxuries, disposes us better towards them, and fits us to be fearless of fortune.

When, therefore, we maintain that pleasure is the end, we do not mean the pleasures of profligates and those that consist in sensuality, as is supposed by some who are either ignorant or disagree with us or do not understand, but freedom from pain in the body and from trouble in the mind. For it is not continuous drinkings and revelings, nor the satisfaction of lusts, nor the enjoyment of fish and other luxuries of the wealthy table, which produce a pleasant life, but sober reasoning, searching out the motives for all choice and avoidance, and banishing mere opinions, to which are due the greatest disturbance of the spirit.

Of all this the beginning and the greatest good is prudence. Wherefore prudence is a more precious thing even than philosophy: for from prudence are sprung all the other virtues, and it teaches us that it is not possible to live pleasantly without living prudently and honorably and justly, nor, again, to live a life of prudence, honor, and justice without living pleasantly. For the virtues are by nature bound up with the pleasant life, and the pleasant life is inseparable from them. For indeed who, think you, is a better man than he who holds reverent opinions concerning the gods, and is at all times free from fear of death, and has reasoned out the end ordained by nature? He understands that the limit of good things is easy to fulfill and easy to attain, whereas the course of ills is either short in time or slight in pain: he laughs at destiny, whom some have introduced as the mistress of all things. He thinks that with us lies the chief power in determining events, some of which happen by necessity and some by chance, and some are within our control; for while necessity cannot be called to account, he sees that chance is inconstant, but that which is in our control is subject to no master, and to it are naturally attached praise and blame. For, indeed, it were better to follow the myths about the gods than to become a slave to the destiny of the natural philosophers; for the former suggests a hope of placating the gods by worship, whereas the latter involves a necessity which knows no placation. As to chance, he does not regard it as a god as most men do (for in god's acts there is no disorder), nor as an uncertain cause of all things: for he does not believe that good and evil are given by chance to man for the framing of a blessed life, but that opportunities for great good and great evil are afforded by it. He therefore thinks it better to be unfortunate in reasonable action than to prosper in unreason. For it is better in a man's actions that what is well chosen should fail, rather than that what is ill chosen should be successful owing to chance.

Meditate therefore on these things and things akin to them night and day by yourself, and with a companion like to yourself, and never shall you be disturbed waking or asleep, but you shall live like a god among men. For a man who lives among immortal blessings is not like to a mortal being.

Principal Doctrines

3. These short maxims were meant to be memorized by Epicurus's followers. You will find few arguments here, but you will find some ideas repeated from the letter you just read. Can you identify two of them?

I. The blessed and immortal nature knows no trouble itself nor causes trouble to any other, so that it is never constrained by anger or favor. For all such things exist only in the weak.

II. Death is nothing to us: for that which is dissolved is without sensation; and that which lacks sensation is nothing to us.

III. The limit of quantity in pleasures is the removal of all that is painful. Wherever pleasure is present, as long as it is there, there is neither pain of body nor of mind, nor of both at once.

IV. Pain does not last continuously in the flesh, but the acutest pain is there for a very short time, and even that which just exceeds the pleasure in the flesh does not continue for many days at once. But chronic illnesses permit a predominance of pleasure over pain in the flesh.

V. It is not possible to live pleasantly without living prudently and honorably and justly, nor again to live a life of prudence, honor, and justice without living pleasantly. And the man who does not possess the pleasant life, is not living prudently and honorably and justly, and the man who does not possess the virtuous life, cannot possibly live pleasantly.

VI. To secure protection from men anything is a natural good, by which you may be able to attain this end.

VII. Some men wished to become famous and conspicuous, thinking that they would thus win for themselves safety from other men. Wherefore if the life of such men is safe, they have obtained the good which nature craves; but if it is not safe, they do not possess that for which they strove at first by the instinct of nature.

VIII. No pleasure is a bad thing in itself; but the means which produce some pleasures bring with them disturbances many times greater than the pleasures.

IX. If every pleasure could be intensified so that it lasted and influenced the whole organism or the most essential parts of our nature, pleasures would never differ from one another.

X. If the things that produce the pleasures of profligates could dispel the fears of the mind about the phenomena of the sky and death and its pains, and also teach the limits of desires and of pains, we should never have cause to blame them: for they would be filling themselves full with pleasures from every source and never have pain of body or mind, which is the evil of life.

XI. If we were not troubled by our suspicions of the phenomena of the sky and about death, fearing that it concerns us, and also by our failure to grasp the limits of pains and desires, we should have no need of natural science.

XII. A man cannot dispel his fear about the most important matters if he does not know what is the nature of the universe but suspects the truth of some mythical story. So that without natural science it is not possible to attain our pleasures unalloyed.

XIII. There is no profit in securing protection in relation to men, if things above and things beneath the earth and indeed all in the boundless universe remain matters of suspicion.

XIV. The most unalloyed source of protection from men, which is secured to some extent by a certain force of expulsion, is in fact the immunity which results from a quiet life and the retirement from the world.

XV. The wealth demanded by nature is both limited and easily procured; that demanded by idle imaginings stretches on to infinity.

XVI. In but few things chance hinders a wise man, but the greatest and most important matters reason has ordained and throughout the whole period of life does and will ordain.

XVII. The just man is most free from trouble, the unjust most full of trouble.

XVIII. The pleasure in the flesh is not increased, when once the pain due to want is removed, but is only varied: and the limit as regards pleasure in the mind is begotten by the reasoned understanding of these very pleasures and of the emotions akin to them, which used to cause the greatest fear to the mind.

XIX. Infinite time contains no greater pleasure than limited time, if one measures by reason the limits of pleasure.

XX. The flesh perceives the limits of pleasure as unlimited and unlimited time is required to supply it. But the mind, having attained a reasoned understanding of the ultimate good of the flesh and its limits and having dissipated the fears concerning the time to come, supplies us with the complete life, and we have no further need of infinite time: but neither does the mind shun pleasure, nor, when circumstances begin to bring about the departure from life, does it approach its end as though it fell short in any way of the best life.

XXI. He who has learned the limits of life knows that that which removes the pain due to want and makes the whole of life complete is easy to obtain; so that there is no need of actions which involve competition.

XXII. We must consider both the real purpose and all the evidence of direct perception, to which we always refer the conclusions of opinion; otherwise, all will be full of doubt and confusion.

XXIII. If you fight against all sensations, you will have no standard by which to judge even those of them which you say are false.

XXIV. If you reject any single sensation and fail to distinguish between the conclusion of opinion as to the appearance awaiting confirmation and that which is actually given by the sensation or feeling, or each intuitive apprehension of the mind, you will confound all other sensations as well with the same groundless opinion, so that you will reject every standard of judgment. And if among the mental images created by your opinion you affirm both that which awaits confirmation and that which does not, you will not escape error, since you will have preserved the whole cause of doubt in every judgment between what is right and what is wrong.

XXV. If on each occasion instead of referring your actions to the end of nature, you turn to some other nearer standard when you are making a choice or an avoidance, your actions will not be consistent with your principles.

XXVI. Of desires, all that do not lead to a sense of pain, if they are not satisfied, are not necessary, but involve a craving which is easily dispelled, when the object is hard to procure or they seem likely to produce harm.

XXVII. Of all the things which wisdom acquires to produce the blessedness of the complete life, far the greatest is the possession of friendship.

XXVIII. The same conviction which has given us confidence that there is nothing terrible that lasts forever or even for long, has also seen the protection of friendship most fully completed in the limited evils of this life.

XXIX. Among desires some are natural and necessary, some natural but not necessary, and others neither natural nor necessary, but due to idle imagination.

XXX. Wherever in the case of desires which are physical, but do not lead to a sense of pain, if they are not fulfilled, the effort is intense, such pleasures are due to idle imagination, and it is not owing to their own nature that they fail to be dispelled, but owing to the empty imaginings of the man.

XXXI. The justice which arises from nature is a pledge of mutual advantage to restrain men from harming one another and save them from being harmed.

XXXII. For all living things which have not been able to make compacts not to harm one another or be harmed, nothing ever is either just or unjust; and likewise too for all tribes of men which have been unable or unwilling to make compacts not to harm or be harmed.

XXXIII. Justice never is anything in itself, but in the dealings of men with one another in any place whatever and at any time it is a kind of compact not to harm or be harmed.

XXXIV. Injustice is not an evil in itself, but only in consequence of the fear which attaches to the apprehension of being unable to escape those appointed to punish such actions.

XXXV. It is not possible for one who acts in secret contravention of the terms of the compact not to harm or be harmed, to be confident that he will escape detection, even if at present he escapes a thousand times. For up to the time of death it cannot be certain that he will indeed escape.

XXXVI. In its general aspect justice is the same for all, for it is a kind of mutual advantage in the dealings of men with one another: but with reference to the individual peculiarities of a country or any other circumstances the same thing does not turn out to be just for all.

XXXVII. Among actions which are sanctioned as just by law, that which is proved on examination to be of advantage in the requirements of men's dealings with one another, has the guarantee of justice, whether it is the same for all or not. But if a man makes a law and it does not turn out to lead to advantage in men's dealings with each other, then it no longer has the essential nature of justice. And even if the advantage in the matter of justice shifts from one side to the other, but for a while accords with the general concept, it is none the less just for that period in the eyes of those who do not confound themselves with empty sounds but look to the actual facts.

XXXVIII. Where, provided the circumstances have not been altered, actions which were considered just, have been shown not to accord with the general concept in actual practice, then they are not just. But where, when circumstances have changed, the same actions which were sanctioned as just no longer lead to advantage, there they were just at the time when they were of advantage for the dealings of fellow-citizens with one another; but subsequently they are no longer just, when no longer of advantage.

XXXIX. The man who has best ordered the element of disquiet arising from external circumstances has made those things that he could akin to himself and the rest at least no alien: but with all to which he could not do even this, he has refrained from mixing, and has expelled from his life all which it was of advantage to treat thus.

XL. As many as possess the power to procure complete immunity from their neighbors, these also live most pleasantly with one another, since they have the most certain pledge of security, and after they have enjoyed the fullest intimacy, they do not lament the previous departure of a dead friend, as though he were to be pitied.

READING QUESTIONS

1. How does Epicurus characterize "the gods"?
2. What does Epicurus mean when he says that "death is nothing to us"?
3. What does he say is the goal of "the life of blessedness"?

4. State the different kinds of desires described by Epicurus.

5. Why is prudence better than even philosophy?

6. What are the implications of the following saying of Epicurus: "The wealth demanded by nature is both limited and easily procured; that demanded by idle imaginings stretches on to infinity"?

7. How does Epicurus define "justice"?

Epictetus

Moral philosophy in the Hellenistic Age, the period stretching from the death of Aristotle, in 322 B.C., to the rise of Christianity in the Roman Empire some 500 years later, was dominated by two philosophical movements: the Epicureans and the Stoics. As we read in the previous chapter, Greek political and social life underwent numerous changes during the Hellenistic Age, so it was natural for philosophers to direct their attention to ethics. The Epicureans offered an approach to ethics that appealed to many people, as generation after generation of followers of Epicurus attest. Arguably, however, the most important philosophical movement of the period was that of the Stoics. Founded in Athens by Zeno of Cyprus in 300 B.C., the Stoics (named after the porch, or *stoa,* from which Zeno taught) developed a system of philosophy that tied together psychology, natural science, logic, and moral philosophy. Stoic moral philosophy was similar to that of the Cynics, and because the Cynics based their own philosophy on that of Socrates, Stoic moral philosophy, like that of the Epicureans, ultimately derived from the moral teachings of Socrates.

Ethics formed the central theme in Stoic philosophy, but Stoic ethics rested on a foundation of physics and logic. They likened logic to a fence that surrounds and protects a farm, physics to the soil needed to grow the crops, and ethics to the fruit that the farm produces. The ethics they taught differed dramatically from that of their rivals, the Epicureans. It is not pleasure that is good, said the Stoics, but virtue. If we think that pleasure leads to the good life, we will always be disappointed since our desires can never be completely satisfied. The proper approach to life for the Stoic is not to try to change the world to get what you want; rather, it is to like whatever you get. Strive to desire what you have been given; do not strive to obtain what you desire.

The perfectly virtuous being—the ideal of Stoic philosophy—was known as the Sage. A Sage had acquired the one true virtue, wisdom of the good. Since rationality is a divine feature of the universe, acting morally is merely a matter of acting according to reason. Because the Stoics equated the universe with God, whatever occurred in the universe was good. Acting according to reason, then, is acting according to nature. When we choose to live in harmony with the orderliness and benevolence of the universe, we adapt ourselves to its order and fulfill our purpose. The contemporary meaning of the word *stoic* reveals one aspect of the life of the Stoic Sage. When we praise someone as "stoical," we mean that they face danger and endure suffering without complaint. Our usage of the word reflects the belief of the Stoic philosophers that emotions or passions are inferior to reason and thus not in harmony with the cosmos. If we succumb to emotions, whether those of sorrow and pity or even joy and happiness, we turn away from rationality, order, and virtue.

For the Stoic, the universe is perfectly ordered, and all events occur according to universal law. This philosophical position, the view that every event has a cause, is known as **determinism.** The ethical implications of determinism are enormous: If every event comes about according to unvarying laws, then nothing could happen any differently than it does. In a determined universe, free will and free choice appear to have no place. If so, what is the Stoic to make of moral responsibility? If all outcomes are determined, how can anyone be morally responsible for what happens? The Stoics answered with characteristic aplomb. We may not be able to change what happens, but we can choose how we react to it. Even though we cannot govern what does occur, we can control the way we feel about it. For this reason, the Stoic strove for complete indifference (*apatheia*) to everything but the wisdom of the law of nature. The aim of the Stoic was to accept the universe as it is and find it to be perfect.

Epictetus (c. A.D. 50–130), whose ethics we will study in this chapter, belongs to the Roman period of Stoicism. Along with other Roman Stoics, such as Seneca and Marcus Aurelius, Epictetus helped spread the Stoic teaching throughout the Roman world, where it eventually grew into the semiofficial philosophy of the establishment. Epictetus, born a slave, gained his freedom sometime after the death of Nero in A.D. 68. His life modeled the philosophy he advocated. He lived a disciplined, materialistically simple life and became widely admired for his loving and humble nature. Although he was not active politically, Epictetus was a moral activist, urging his followers to examine the morality of their actions since responsibility for one's choices rests on the individual alone. The ability to choose our response to what happens, granted to humans in an otherwise completely determined universe, is so powerful that not even Zeus could interfere with it. The virtuous Sage understands this fact and lives accordingly.

Like Socrates, Epictetus published nothing himself. For his teachings we must rely on the notes of Flavius Arrianus, one of his pupils. Perhaps more influential than his words, however, was the model of the good life that Epictetus both lived and preached. Epictetus helped promote a philosophy that thrived for over 500 years, one that was to have a profound influence on the Christian ethics that eventually replaced both it and Epicureanism throughout most of the Western world.

Encheiridion

The notes compiled by Epictetus's student Flavius Arrianus are collected together as the *Discourses*. What is given here, the *Encheiridion*, consists of extracts from the *Discourses*. You will find in them inspirational maxims and passages designed to appeal to the common people and to help them live more satisfying lives. Also included in this work are more philosophical parts in which Epictetus attempts to defend the notion of the Stoic ideal. Together they give a comprehensive view of both sides of the Stoic program: philosophical attention to argumentation and rational thought on the one hand, and a practical program for better living on the other.

As you read, keep in mind the dual purpose of this writing. At first glance, the Stoic program may sound unreachable and austere to the point of unfeeling. For example, Epictetus's advice to consider a child that has

From *The Encheiridion,* translated by G. Long, London, 1877.

died as one on loan that has been "restored" may seem too harsh to many of us; as we better understand the general thrust of the Stoic philosophy, however, we may see a measure of comfort in such a view. After all, if we continue to bemoan that which we must inevitably encounter, we will surely be miserable.   ✍

I

Of things some are in our power, and others are not. In our power are opinion, movement toward a thing, desire, aversion (turning from a thing); and in a word, whatever are our own acts: not in our power are the body, property, reputation, offices (magisterial power), and in a word, whatever are not our own acts. And the things in our power are by nature free, not subject to restraint nor hindrance: but the things not in our power are weak, slavish, subject to restraint, in the power of others. Remember then that if you think the things which are by nature slavish to be free, and the things which are in the power of others to be your own, you will be hindered, you will lament, you will be disturbed, you will blame both gods and men: but if you think that only which is your own to be your own, and if you think that what is another's, as it really is, belongs to another, no man will ever compel you, no man will hinder you, you will never blame any man, you will accuse no man, you will do nothing involuntarily (against your will), no man will harm you, you will have no enemy, for you will not suffer any harm.

If then you desire (aim at) such great things, remember that you must not (attempt to) lay hold of them with a small effort; but you must leave alone some things entirely, and postpone others for the present. But if you wish for these things also (such great things), and power (office) and wealth, perhaps you will not gain even these very things (power and wealth) because you aim also at those former things (such great things): certainly you will fail in those things through which alone happiness and freedom are secured. Straightway then practice saying to every harsh appearance, You are an appearance, and in no manner what you appear to be. Then examine it by the rules which you possess, and by this first and chiefly, whether it relates to the things which are in our power or to the things which are not in our power: and if it relates to anything which is not in our power, be ready to say, that it does not concern you.

II

Remember that desire contains in it the profession (hope) of obtaining that which you desire; and the profession (hope) in aversion (turning from a thing) is that you will not fall into that which you attempt to avoid: and he who fails in his desire is unfortunate; and he who falls into that which he would avoid, is unhappy. If then you attempt to avoid only the things contrary to nature which are within your power, you will not be involved in any of the things which you would avoid. But if you attempt to avoid disease or death or poverty, you will be unhappy. Take away then aversion from all things which are not in our power, and transfer it to the things contrary to nature which are in our power. But destroy desire completely for the present. For if you desire anything which is not in our power, you must be unfortunate: but of the things in our power, and which it would be good to desire, nothing yet is before you. But employ only the power of moving toward an object and retiring from it; and these powers indeed only slightly and with exceptions and with remission.

III

----

1. Epictetus says that it is possible to be undisturbed at the death of a spouse or of a child. What reasons does he give for saying this? How does this relate to his warnings about desires?

In everything which pleases the soul, or supplies a want, or is loved, remember to add this to the (description, notion); what is the nature of each thing, beginning from the smallest? If you love an earthen vessel, say it is an earthen vessel which you love; for when it has been broken, you will not be disturbed. If you are kissing your child or wife, say that it is a human being whom you are kissing, for when the wife or child dies, you will not be disturbed.

IV

When you are going to take in hand any act, remind yourself what kind of an act it is. If you are going to bathe, place before yourself what happens in the bath: some splashing the water, others pushing against one another, others abusing one another, and some stealing: and thus with more safety you will undertake the matter, if you say to yourself, I now intend to bathe, and to maintain my will in a manner comfortable to nature. And so you will do in every act: for thus if any hindrance to bathing shall happen, let this thought be ready; it was not this only that I intended, but I intended also to maintain my will in a way comfortable to nature; but I shall not maintain it so, if I am vexed at what happens.

V

Men are disturbed not by the things which happen, but by the opinions about the things: for example, death is nothing terrible, for if it were, it would have seemed so to Socrates; for the opinion about death, that it is terrible, is the terrible thing. When then we are impeded or disturbed or grieved, let us never blame others, but ourselves, that is, our opinions. It is the act of an ill-instructed man to blame others for his own bad condition; it is the act of one who has begun to be instructed, to lay the blame on himself; and of one whose instruction is completed, neither to blame another, nor himself.

VI

Be not elated at any advantage (excellence), which belongs to another. If a horse when he is elated should say, I am beautiful, one might endure it. But when you are elated, and say, I have a beautiful horse, you must know that you are elated at having a good horse. What then is your own? The use of appearances. Consequently when in the use of appearances you are conformable to nature, then be elated, for then you will be elated at something good which is your own.

VII

As on a voyage when the vessel has reached a port, if you go out to get water, it is an amusement by the way to pick up a shell-fish or some bulb, but your thoughts ought to be directed to the ship, and you ought to be constantly watching if the captain should call, and then you must throw away all those things, that you may not be bound and pitched into the ship like sheep: so in life also, if there be given to you instead of a little bulb and a shell a wife and child, there will be nothing to prevent (you from taking them). But if the captain should call, run to the ship, and leave all those things without regard to them. But if you are old, do not even go far from the ship, lest when you are called you make default.

VIII

---

2. Epictetus gives advice for a tranquil life. Notice how proper desires (wishes) are central to tranquility.

Seek not that the things which happen should happen as you wish; but wish the things which happen to be as they are, and you will have a tranquil flow of life.

IX

Disease is an impediment to the body, but not to the will, unless the will itself chooses. Lameness is an impediment to the leg, but not to the will. And add this reflection on the occasion of everything that happens; for you will find it an impediment to something else, but not to yourself.

X

On the occasion of every accident (event) that befalls you, remember to turn to yourself and inquire what power you have for turning it to use. If you see a fair man or a fair woman, you will find that the power to resist is temperance (continence). If labor (pain) be presented to you, you will find that it is endurance. If it be abusive words, you will find it to be patience. And if you have been thus formed to the (proper) habit, the appearances will not carry you along with them.

XI

Never say about anything, I have lost it, but say I have restored it. Is your child dead? It has been restored. Is your wife dead? She has been restored. Has your estate been taken from you? Has not then this also been restored? But he who has taken it from me is a bad man. But what is it to you, by whose hands the giver demanded it back? So long as he may allow you, take care of it as a thing which belongs to another, as travelers do with their inn.

XII

If you intend to improve, throw away such thoughts as these: if I neglect my affairs, I shall not have the means of living: unless I chastise my slave, he will be bad. For it is better to die of hunger and so be released from grief and fear than to live in abundance with perturbation; and it is better for your slave to be bad than for you to be unhappy. Begin then from little things. Is the oil spilled? Is a little wine stolen? Say on the occasion, at such price is sold freedom from perturbation; at such price is sold tranquility, but nothing is got for nothing. And when you call your slave, consider that it is possible that he does not hear; and if he does hear, that he will do nothing which you wish. But matters are not so well with him, but altogether well with you, that it should be in his power for you to be not disturbed.

XIII

If you would improve, submit to be considered without sense and foolish with respect to externals. Wish to be considered to know nothing: and if you shall seem to some to be a person of importance, distrust yourself. For you should know that it is not easy both to keep your will in a condition conformable to nature and (to secure) external things; but if a man is careful about the one, it is an absolute necessity that he will neglect the other.

XIV

If you would have your children and your wife and your friends to live forever, you are silly; for you would have the things which are not in your power to be in your power, and the things which belong to others to be yours. So if you would have your slave to be free from faults, you are a fool; for you would have badness not to be badness, but something else. But if you wish not to fail in your desires, you are able to do that. Practice then this which you are able to do. He is the master of every man who has the power over the things, which another person wishes or does not wish, the power to confer them on him or to take them away. Whoever then wishes to be free, let him neither wish for anything nor avoid anything which depends on others: if he does not observe this rule, he must be a slave.

XV

Remember that in life you ought to behave as at a banquet. Suppose that something is carried round and is opposite to you. Stretch out your hand and take a portion with decency. Suppose that it passes by you. Do not detain it. Suppose that it is not yet come to you. Do not send your desire forward to it, but wait till it is opposite to you. Do so with respect to children, so with respect to a wife, so with respect to magisterial offices, so with respect to wealth, and you will be some time a worthy partner of the banquets of the gods. But if you take none of the things which are set before you, and even despise them, then you will be not only a fellow-banqueter with the gods, but also a partner with them in power. For by acting thus Diogenes and Heracleitus and those like them were deservedly divine, and were so called.

XVI

When you see a person weeping in sorrow either when a child goes abroad or when he is dead, or when the man has lost his property, take care that the appearance do not hurry you away with it, as if he were suffering in external things. But straightway make a distinction in your own mind, and be in readiness to say, it is not that which has happened that afflicts this man, for it does not afflict another, but it is the opinion about this thing which afflicts the man. So far as words then do not be unwilling to show him sympathy, and even if it happens so, to lament with him. But take care that you do not lament internally also.

XVII

> *3. Another important notion is mentioned here—that all things happen as they are supposed to. Do you see how this relates to being an actor in a play?*

Remember that thou art an actor in a play of such a kind as the teacher (author) may choose; if short, of a short one; if long, of a long one: if he wishes you to act the part of a poor man, see that you act the part naturally; if the part of a lame man, of a magistrate, of a private person, (do the same). For this is your duty, to act well the part that is given to you; but to select the part, belongs to another.

XVIII

When a raven has croaked inauspiciously, let not the appearance hurry you away with it: but straightway make a distinction in your mind and say, None of these things is signified to me, but either to my poor body, or to my small property, or to my reputation, or to my children or to my wife: but to me all significations are auspicious if I choose. For whatever of these things results, it is in my power to derive benefit from it.

XIX

You can be invincible, if you enter into no contest in which it is not in your power to conquer. Take care then when you observe a man honored before others or possessed of great power or highly esteemed for any reason, not to suppose him happy, and be not carried away by the appearance. For if the nature of the good is in our power, neither envy nor jealousy will have a place in us. But you yourself will not wish to be a general or senator or consul, but a free man: and there is only one way to this, to despise (care not for) the things which are not in our power.

XX

Remember that it is not he who reviles you or strikes you, who insults you, but it is your opinion about these things as being insulting. When then a man irritates you, you must know that it is your own opinion which has irritated you. Therefore especially try not to be carried away by the appearance. For if you once gain time and delay, you will more easily master yourself.

XXI

Let death and exile and every other thing which appears dreadful be daily before your eyes; but most of all death: and you will never think of anything mean nor will you desire anything extravagantly.

XXII

If you desire philosophy, prepare yourself from the beginning to be ridiculed, to expect that many will sneer at you, and say, He has all at once returned to us as a philosopher; and whence does he get this supercilious look for us? Do you not show a supercilious look; but hold on to the things which seem to you best as one appointed by God to this station. And remember that if you abide in the same principles, these men who first ridiculed will afterward admire you: but if you shall have been overpowered by them, you will bring on yourself double ridicule.

XXIII

If it should ever happen to you to be turned to externals in order to please some person, you must know that you have lost your purpose in life. Be satisfied then in everything with being a philosopher; and if you wish to seem also to any person to be a philosopher, appear so to yourself, and you will be able to do this.

XXIV

Let not these thoughts afflict you, I shall live unhonored and be nobody nowhere. For if want of honor is an evil, you cannot be in evil through the means (fault) of another any more than you can be involved in anything base. Is it then your business to obtain the rank of magistrate, or to be received at a banquet? By no means. How then can this be want of honor (dishonor)? And how will you be nobody nowhere, when you ought to be somebody in those things only which are in your power, in which indeed it is permitted to you to be a man of the greatest worth? But your friends will be without assistance! What do you mean by being without assistance? They will not receive money from you, nor will you make them Roman citizens. Who then told you that these are among the things which are in our power, and not in the power of others? And who can give to another what he has not himself? Acquire money then, your friends say, that we also may have something. If I can acquire money and also keep myself modest, and faithful and magnanimous, point out the way, and I will acquire it. But if you ask me to lose the things which are good and my own, in order that you may gain the things which are not good, see how unfair and silly you are. Besides, which would you rather have, money or a faithful and modest friend? For this end then rather help me to be such a man, and do not ask me to do this by which I shall lose that character. But my country, you say, as far as it depends on me, will be without my help. I ask again, what help do you mean? It will not have porticoes or baths through you. And what does this mean? For it is not furnished with shoes by means of a smith, nor with arms by means of a shoemaker. But it is enough if every man fully discharges the work that is his own: and if you provided it with another citizen faithful and modest, would you not be useful to it? Yes. Then you also cannot be useless to it. What place then, you say, shall I hold in the city? Whatever you can, if you maintain at the same time your fidelity and modesty. But if when you wish to be useful to the state, you shall lose these qualities, what profit could you be to it, if you were made shameless and faithless?

XXV

Has any man been preferred before you at a banquet, or in being saluted, or in being invited to a consultation? If these things are good, you ought to rejoice that he has obtained them: but if bad, be not grieved because you have not obtained them; and remember that you cannot, if you do not the same things in order to obtain what is not in our power, be considered worthy of the same (equal) things. For how can a man obtain an equal share with another when he does not visit a man's doors as that other man does, when he does not attend him when he goes abroad, as the other man does; when he does not praise (flatter) him as another does? You will be unjust then and insatiable, if you do not part with the price, in return for which those things are sold, and if you wish to obtain them for nothing. Well, what is the price of lettuces? An obolus perhaps. If then a man gives up the obolus, and receives the lettuces, and if you do not give up the obolus and do not obtain the lettuces, do not suppose that you receive less than he who has got the lettuces; for as he has the lettuces, so you have the obolus which you did not give. In the same way then in the other matter also you have not been invited to a man's feast, for you did not give to the host the price at which the supper is sold; but he sells it for praise (flattery), he sells it for personal attention. Give then the price, if it is for your interest, for which it is sold. But if you wish both not to give the price and to obtain the things, you are insatiable and silly. Have you nothing then in place of the supper? You have indeed, you have the not flattering of him, whom you did not choose to flatter; you have the not enduring of the man when he enters the room.

XXVI

We may learn the wish (will) of nature from the things in which we do not differ from one another; for instance, when your neighbor's slave has broken his cup, or anything else, we are ready to say forthwith, that it is one of the things which happen. You must know then that when your cup also is broken, you ought to think as you did when your neighbor's cup was broken. Transfer this reflection to greater things also. Is another man's child or wife dead? There is no one who would not say, this is an event incident to man. But when a man's own child or wife is dead, forthwith he calls out, Woe to me, how wretched I am. But we ought to remember how we feel when we hear that it has happened to others.

XXVII

As a mark is not set up for the purpose of missing the aim, so neither does the nature of evil exist in the world.

XXVIII

If any person was intending to put your body in the power of any man whom you fell in with on the way, you would be vexed: but that you put your understanding in the power of any man whom you meet, so that if he should revile you, it is disturbed and troubled, are you not ashamed at this?

XXIX

In every act observe the things which come first, and those which follow it; and so proceed to the act. If you do not, at first you will approach it with alacrity, without having thought of the things which will follow; but afterward, when certain base (ugly) things have shown themselves, you will be ashamed. A man wishes to conquer at the Olympic games. I also wish indeed, for it is a fine thing. But observe both the things which come first, and the things which follow; and then begin the act. You must do everything according to rule, eat according to strict orders, abstain from delicacies, exercise yourself as you are bid at appointed times, in heat, in cold, you must not drink cold water, nor wine as you choose; in a word, you must deliver yourself up to the exercise master as you do to the physician, and then proceed to the contest. And sometimes you will strain the hand, put the ankle out of joint, swallow much dust, sometimes be flogged, and after all this be defeated. When you have considered all this, if you still choose, go to the contest: if you do not, you will behave like children, who at one time play at wrestlers, another time as flute players, again as gladiators, then as trumpeters, then as tragic actors: so you also will be at one time an athlete, at another a gladiator, then a rhetorician, then a philosopher, but with your whole soul you will be nothing at all; but like an ape you imitate everything that you see, and one thing after another pleases you. For you have not undertaken anything with consideration, nor have you surveyed it well; but carelessly and with cold desire. Thus some who have seen a philosopher and having heard one speak, as Euphrates speaks,—and who can speak as he does?—they wish to be philosophers themselves also. My man, first of all consider what kind of thing it is: and then examine your own nature, if you are able to sustain the character. Do you wish to be a pentathlete or a wrestler? Look at your arms, your thighs, examine your loins. For different men are formed by nature for different things. Do you think that if you do these things, you can eat in the same manner, drink in the same manner, and in the same manner loathe certain things? You must pass sleepless nights, endure toil, go away from your kinsmen, be despised by a slave, in everything have the inferior part, in honor, in office, in the courts of justice, in every little matter. Consider these things, if you would exchange for them, freedom from passions, liberty, tranquility. If not, take care that, like little children, you be not now a philosopher, then a servant of the publicani, then a rhetorician, then a procurator (manager) for Caesar. These things are not consistent. You must be one man, either good or bad. You must either cultivate your own ruling faculty, or external things; you must either exercise your skill on internal things or on external things; that is you must either maintain the position of a philosopher or that of a common person.

XXX

Duties are universally measured by relations. Is a man a father? The precept is to take care of him, to yield to him in all things, to submit when he is reproachful, when he inflicts blows. But suppose that he is a bad father. Were you then by nature made akin to a good father? No; but to a father. Does a brother wrong you? Maintain then your own position toward him, and do not examine what he is doing, but what you must do that your will shall be conformable to nature. For another will not damage you, unless you choose: but you will be damaged then when you shall think that you are damaged. In this way then you will discover your duty from the relation of a neighbor, from that of a citizen, from that of a general, if you are accustomed to contemplate the relations.

XXXI

———

4. Epictetus explains the relationship between humans and the Gods. Do you see how this supports his previous claims about good and evil being a product of our own acts?

———

As to piety toward the Gods you must know that this is the chief thing, to have right opinions about them, to think that they exist, and that they administer the All well and justly; and you must fix yourself in this principle (duty), to obey them, and yield to them in everything which happens, and voluntarily to follow it as being accomplished by the wisest intelligence. For if you do so, you will never either blame the Gods, nor will you accuse them of neglecting you. And it is not possible for this to be done in any other way than by withdrawing from the things which are not in our power, and by placing the good and the evil only in those things which are in our power. For if you think that any of the things which are not in our power is good or bad, it is absolutely necessary that, when you do not obtain what you wish, and when you fall into those things which you do not wish, you will find fault and hate those who are the cause of them; for every animal is formed by nature to this, to fly from and to turn from the things which appear harmful and the things which are the cause of the harm, but to follow and admire the things which are useful and the causes of the useful. It is impossible then for a person who thinks that he is harmed to be delighted with that which he thinks to be the cause of the harm, as it is also impossible to be pleased with the harm itself. For this reason also a father is reviled by his son, when he gives no part to his son of the things which are considered to be good: and it was this which made Polynices and Eteocles enemies, the opinion that royal power was a good. It is for this reason that the cultivator of the earth reviles the Gods, for this reason the sailor does, and the merchant, and for this reason those who lose their wives and their children. For where the useful (your interest) is, there also piety is. Consequently he who takes care to desire as he ought and to avoid as he ought, at the same time also cares after piety. But to make libations and to sacrifice and to offer first fruits according to the custom of our fathers, purely and not meanly nor carelessly nor scantily nor above our ability, is a thing which belongs to all to do.

XXXII

When you have recourse to divination, remember that you do not know how it will turn out, but that you are come to inquire from the diviner. But of what kind it is, you know when you come, if indeed you are a philosopher. For if it is any of the things which are not in our power, it is absolutely necessary that it must be neither good nor bad. Do not then bring to the diviner desire or aversion: if you do, you will approach him with fear. But having determined in your mind that everything which shall turn out (result) is indifferent, and does not concern you, and whatever it may be, for it will be in your power to use it well, and no man will hinder this, come then with confidence to the Gods as your advisers. And then when any advice shall have been given, remember whom you have taken as advisers, and whom you will have neglected, if you do not obey them. And go to divination, as Socrates said that you ought, about those matters in which all the inquiry has reference to the result, and in which means are not given either by reason nor by any other art for knowing the thing which is the subject of the inquiry. Wherefore when we ought to share a friend's danger or that of our country, you must not consult the diviner whether you ought to share it. For even if the diviner shall tell you that the signs of the victims are unlucky, it is plain that this is a token of death or mutilation of part of the body or of exile. But reason prevails that even with these risks we should share the dangers of our friend and of our country. Therefore attend to the greater diviner, the Pythian God, who ejected from the temple him who did not assist his friend when he was being murdered.

XXXIII

Immediately prescribe some character and some form to yourself, which you shall observe both when you are alone and when you meet with men.

And let silence be the general rule, or let only what is necessary be said, and in few words. And rarely and when the occasion calls we shall say something; but about none of the common subjects, nor about gladiators, nor horse-races, nor about athletes, nor about eating or drinking, which are the usual subjects; and especially not about men, as blaming them or praising them, or comparing them. If then you are able, bring over by your conversation the conversation of your associates to that which is proper; but if you should happen to be confined to the company of strangers, be silent.

Let not your laughter be much, nor on many occasions, nor excessive.

Refuse altogether to take an oath, if it is possible: if it is not, refuse as far as you are able.

Avoid banquets which are given by strangers and by ignorant persons. But if ever there is occasion to join in them, let your attention be carefully fixed, that you slip not into the manners of the vulgar (the uninstructed). For you must know, that if your companion be impure, he also who keeps company with him must become impure, though he should happen to be pure.

Take (apply) the things which relate to the body as far as the bare use, as food, drink, clothing, house, and slaves: but exclude everything which is for show or luxury.

As to pleasure with women, abstain as far as you can before marriage: but if you do indulge in it, do it in the way which is conformable to custom. Do not however be disagreeable to those who indulge in these pleasures, or reprove them; and do not often boast that you do not indulge in them yourself.

If a man has reported to you, that a certain person speaks ill of you, do not make any defense (answer) to what has been told you: but reply, The man did not know the rest of my faults, for he would not have mentioned these only.

It is not necessary to go to the theaters often: but if there is ever a proper occasion for going, do not show yourself as being a partisan of any man except yourself, that is, desire only that to be done which is done, and for him only to gain the prize who gains the prize; for in this way you will meet with no hindrance. But abstain entirely from shouts and laughter at any (thing or person), or violent emotions. And when you are come away, do not talk much about what has passed on the stage, except about that which may lead to your own improvement. For it is plain, if you do talk much that you admired the spectacle (more than you ought).

Do not go to the hearing of certain persons' recitations nor visit them readily. But if you do attend, observe gravity and sedateness, and also avoid making yourself disagreeable.

When you are going to meet with any person, and particularly one of those who are considered to be in a superior condition, place before yourself what Socrates or Zeno would have done in such circumstances, and you will have no difficulty in making a proper use of the occasion.

When you are going to any of those who are in great power, place before your-self that you will not find the man at home, that you will be excluded, that the door will not be opened to you, that the man will not care about you. And if with all this it is your duty to visit him, bear what happens, and never say to yourself that it was not worth the trouble. For this is silly, and marks the character of a man who is of-fended by externals.

In company take care not to speak much and excessively about your own acts or dangers: for as it is pleasant to you to make mention of your dangers, it is not so pleasant to others to hear what has happened to you. Take care also not to pro-voke laughter; for this is a slippery way toward vulgar habits, and is also adapted to diminish the respect of your neighbors. It is a dangerous habit also to approach obscene talk. When then anything of this kind happens, if there is a good oppor-tunity, rebuke the man who has proceeded to this talk: but if there is not an op-portunity, by your silence at least, and blushing and expression of dissatisfaction by your countenance, show plainly that you are displeased at such talk.

XXXIV

If you have received the impression of any pleasure, guard yourself against being carried away by it; but let the thing wait for you, and allow yourself a certain delay on your own part. Then think of both times, of the time when you will enjoy the pleasure, and of the time after the enjoyment of the pleasure when you will repent and will reproach yourself. And set against these things how you will rejoice if you have abstained from the pleasure, and how you will commend yourself. But if it seem to you seasonable to undertake (do) the thing, take care that the charm of it, and the pleasure, and the attraction of it shall not conquer you: but set on the other side the consideration how much better it is to be conscious that you have gained this victory.

XXXV

When you have decided that a thing ought to be done and are doing it, never avoid being seen doing it, though the many shall form an unfavorable opinion about it. For if it is not right to do it, avoid doing the thing; but if it is right, why are you afraid of those who shall find fault wrongly?

XXXVI

As the proposition it is either day or it is night is of great importance for the dis-junctive argument, but for the conjunctive is of no value, so in a symposium (en-tertainment) to select the larger share is of great value for the body, but for the maintenance of the social feeling is worth nothing. When then you are eating with another, remember to look not only to the value for the body of the things set be-fore you, but also to the value of the behavior toward the host which ought to be observed.

XXXVII

If you have assumed a character above your strength, you have both acted in this matter in an unbecoming way, and you have neglected that which you might have fulfilled.

XXXVIII

In walking about as you take care not to step on a nail or to sprain your foot, so take care not to damage your own ruling faculty: and if we observe this rule in every act, we shall undertake the act with more security.

XXXIX

The measure of possession (property) is to every man the body, as the foot is of the shoe. If then you stand on this rule (the demands of the body), you will maintain the measure: but if you pass beyond it, you must then of necessity be hurried as it were down a precipice. As also in the matter of the shoe, if you go beyond the (necessities of the) foot, the shoe is gilded, then of a purple color, then embroidered: for there is no limit to that which has once passed the true measure.

XL

Women forthwith from the age of fourteen are called by the men mistresses (dominae). Therefore since they see that there is nothing else that they can obtain, but only the power of lying with men, they begin to decorate themselves, and to place all their hopes in this. It is worth our while then to take care that they may know that they are valued (by men) for nothing else than appearing (being) decent and modest and discreet.

XLI

It is a mark of a mean capacity to spend much time on the things which concern the body, such as much exercise, much eating, much drinking, much easing of the body, much copulation. But these things should be done as subordinate things: and let all your care be directed to the mind.

XLII

When any person treats you ill or speaks ill of you, remember that he does this or says this because he thinks that it is his duty. It is not possible then for him to follow that which seems right to you, but that which seems right to himself. Accordingly if he is wrong in his opinion, he is the person who is hurt, for he is the person who has been deceived; for if a man shall suppose the true conjunction to be false, it is not the conjunction which is hindered, but the man who has been deceived about it. If you proceed then from these opinions, you will be mild in temper to him who reviles you: for say on each occasion, It seemed so to him.

XLIII

Everything has two handles, the one by which it may be borne, the other by which it may not. If your brother acts unjustly, do not lay hold of the act by that handle wherein he acts unjustly, for this is the handle which cannot be borne; but lay hold of the other, that he is your brother, that he was nurtured with you, and you will lay hold of the thing by that handle by which it can be borne.

XLIV

These reasonings do not cohere: I am richer than you, therefore I am better than you; I am more eloquent than you, therefore I am better than you. On the contrary these rather cohere. I am richer than you, therefore my possessions are greater than yours. I am more eloquent than you, therefore my speech is superior to yours. But you are neither possession nor speech.

XLV

Does a man bathe quickly (early)? do not say that he bathes badly, but that he bathes quickly. Does a man drink much wine? do not say that he does this badly, but say that he drinks much. For before you shall have determined the opinion, how do you know whether he is acting wrong? Thus it will not happen to you to comprehend some appearances which are capable of being comprehended, but to assent to others.

XLVI

On no occasion call yourself a philosopher, and do not speak much among the uninstructed about theorems (philosophical rules, precepts): but do that which follows from them. For example at a banquet do not say how a man ought to eat, but eat as you ought to eat. For remember that in this way Socrates also altogether avoided ostentation: persons used to come to him and ask to be recommended by him to philosophers, and he used to take them to philosophers: so easily did he submit to being overlooked. Accordingly if any conversation should arise among uninstructed persons about any theorem, generally be silent; for there is great danger that you will immediately vomit up what you have not digested. And when a man shall say to you, that you know nothing, and you are not vexed, then be sure that you have begun the work (of philosophy). For even sheep do not vomit up their grass and show to the shepherds how much they have eaten; but when they have internally digested the pasture, they produce externally wool and milk. Do you also show not your theorems to the uninstructed, but show the acts which come from their digestion.

XLVII

When at a small cost you are supplied with everything for the body, do not be proud of this; nor, if you drink water, say on every occasion, I drink water. But consider first how much more frugal the poor are than we, and how much more enduring of labor. And if you ever wish to exercise yourself in labor and endurance, do it for yourself, and not for others: do not embrace statues. But if you are ever very thirsty, take a draught of cold water, and spit it out, and tell no man.

XLVIII

The condition and characteristic of an uninstructed person is this: he never expects from himself profit (advantage) nor harm, but from externals. The condition and characteristic of a philosopher is this: he expects all advantage and all harm from himself. The signs (marks) of one who is making progress are these: he censures no man, he praises no man, he blames no man, he accuses no man, he says nothing about himself as if he were somebody or knew something; when he is impeded at all or hindered, he blames himself: if a man praises him, he ridicules the praiser to himself: if a man censures him, he makes no defense: he goes about like weak persons, being careful not to move any of the things which are placed, before they are firmly fixed: he removes all desire from himself, and he transfers aversion to those things only of the things within our power which are contrary to nature: he employs a moderate movement toward everything: whether he is considered foolish or ignorant, he cares not: and in a word he watches himself as if he were an enemy and lying in ambush.

XLIX

When a man is proud because he can understand and explain the writings of Chrysippus, say to yourself, If Chrysippus had not written obscurely, this man would have had nothing to be proud of. But what is it that I wish? To understand Nature and to follow it. I inquire therefore who is the interpreter: and when I have heard that it is Chrysippus, I come to him (the interpreter). But I do not understand what is written, and therefore I seek the interpreter. And so far there is yet nothing to be proud of. But when I shall have found the interpreter, the thing that remains is to use the precepts (the lessons). This itself is the only thing to be proud of. But if I shall admire the exposition, what else have I been made unless a grammarian instead of a philosopher? except in one thing, that I am explaining Chrysippus instead of Homer. When then any man says to me, Read Chrysippus to me, I rather blush, when I cannot show my acts like to and consistent with his words.

L

Whatever things (rules) are proposed to you (for the conduct of life) abide by them, as if they were laws, as if you would be guilty of impiety if you transgressed any of them. And whatever any man shall say about you, do not attend to it: for this is no affair of yours. How long will you then still defer thinking yourself worthy of the best things, and in no matter transgressing the distinctive reason? Have you accepted the theorems (rules), which it was your duty to agree to, and have you agreed to them? what teacher then do you still expect that you defer to him the correction of yourself? You are no longer a youth, but already a full-grown man. If then you are negligent and slothful, and are continually making procrastination after procrastination, and proposal (intention) after proposal, and fixing day after day, after which you will attend to yourself, you will not know that you are not making improvement, but you will continue ignorant (uninstructed) both while you live and till you die. Immediately then think it right to live as a full-grown man, and one who is making proficiency, and let everything which appears to you to be the best be to you a law which must not be transgressed. And if anything laborious, or pleasant or glorious or inglorious be presented to you, remember that now is the contest, now are the Olympic games, and they cannot be deferred; and that it depends on one defeat and one giving way that progress is either lost or maintained. Socrates in this way became perfect, in all things improving himself, attending to nothing except to reason. But you, though you are not yet a Socrates, ought to live as one who wishes to be a Socrates.

LI

The first and most necessary place (part) in philosophy is the use of theorems (precepts), for instance, that we must not lie: the second part is that of demonstrations, for instance, How is it proved that we ought not to lie: the third is that which is confirmatory of these two and explanatory, for example, How is this a demonstration? For what is demonstration, what is consequence, what is contradiction, what is truth, what is falsehood? The third part (topic) is necessary on account of the second, and the second on account of the first; but the most necessary and that on which we ought to rest is the first. But we do the contrary. For we spend our time on the third topic, and all our earnestness is about it: but we entirely neglect the first. Therefore we lie; but the demonstration that we ought not to lie we have ready to hand.

LII

In every thing (circumstance) we should hold these maxims ready to hand:

> Lead me, O Zeus, and thou O Destiny,
> The way that I am bid by you to go:
> To follow I am ready. If I choose not,
> I make myself a wretch, and still must follow.

But whoso nobly yields unto necessity,
We hold him wise, and skilled in things divine.

And the third also: O Crito, if so it pleases the Gods, so let it be; Anytus and Melitus are able indeed to kill me, but they cannot harm me.

READING QUESTIONS

1. According to Epictetus, what will happen if you attempt to avoid "disease or death or poverty"?

2. What does Epictetus say is wrong with proclaiming such a thing as "I have a beautiful horse"?

3. Why does he think that you should have death "daily before your eyes"?

4. Based on your response to question 3, what do you think is the point he is trying to make?

5. Describe the different ways in which the Stoic should consider the body and consider the mind.

St. Augustine

U ndoubtedly the most important influence on moral philosophy in the West since the fall of Rome has been the Christian religion. During the Middle Ages, that period beginning around the time of the sacking of Rome by the Visigoths in 410 and dissolving by degree during the European Renaissance of the fourteenth and fifteenth centuries, the division between theology and philosophy was not as pronounced as it is today. Theologians philosophize, yet the topics remain those of theology. But even with the enormous and continued influence of Christianity on Western philosophy, the influence of philosophy on Christianity was every bit as pronounced. This two-way influence is seen clearly in the work of St. Augustine (354–430), who most effectively wedded the moral philosophy of the classical world to Christian ethics in the early church—a marriage of reason and faith.

From the second to fourth centuries, Christianity spread throughout the Roman Empire, offering hope of otherworldly happiness for vast numbers of oppressed people. By the fourth century, the masses were largely won over, and it fell to the early church fathers such as Augustine, Clement of Alexandria, Origen, and Tertullian to interpret the Christian message for the intellectuals. Since Christianity arose in the homeland of the Jewish people, which was then part of the Roman Empire, the resulting ethics in the early Christian religion was a combination of Judaism and Greco-Roman philosophies. Christianity brought together two divergent sources of moral command—divine will and human reason. The first belongs to theology, the second to philosophy.

Aurelius Augustinus, later St. Augustine, was born in the Roman province of Numidia, near Carthage, in North Africa. His mother was a Christian (later canonized as St. Monica) and his father was a pagan (a non-Christian). In his *Confessions*, Augustine famously relates his intellectual search for truth amidst a life of sin, finally abandoned with a conversion to Christianity in 386. It is said that he had many times tried and failed to alter his sinful ways, but that it was the words of a child that awakened him to God. Weeping one day with helplessness, he heard in the distance a child chanting, "Take and read. Take and read." Believing this to be a sign from God, he opened the New Testament and his eyes fell on a passage from Romans (13:13–14): "Let us conduct ourselves becomingly as in the day, not in reveling and drunkenness, not in debauchery and licentiousness, not in quarreling and jealousy. But put on the Lord Jesus Christ, and make no provision for the flesh, to gratify its desires." At last he had found the strength to turn away from his evil life and to embrace the path of God. Embrace the path of God he did, eventually rising in the church to the office of bishop of Hippo.

Morality is a central concern in the works of St. Augustine. This is because he saw happiness as the goal of human life, yet he contended that happiness attained only in an earthly sphere was not true happiness. What actually brings happiness is following the will of God—and this depends on both proper thinking and proper acting. Augustine's ethics was, in large part, under the influence of the tradition of the Christian (i.e., Roman Catholic) church. What makes his thinking so important for philosophy is the way he interpreted the classical philosophers, particularly Plato, from the viewpoint of the Christian tradition. For example, he saw Plato as identifying the supreme good as God. Classical philosophy thus influenced, and was influenced by, Christian theology.

Because St. Augustine blends the worlds of Christianity and philosophy, it is not surprising to find parallels between the two. He accepted and advocated the four cardinal virtues put forward by Plato: temperance, justice, wisdom, and courage. Like the philosophers of Greece and Rome, he believed that people are responsible for their actions and have the freedom to choose between alternative courses. Yet he differs from his classical predecessors in crucial respects. The cardinal virtues are to be admired, but unless they are inspired by a faith in Christ, they are of no worth. Yes, people are responsible for their actions, but for Augustine people are rewarded or punished by their motives—whether they move in their actions toward God or away from God. And free will operates in a being who is a complex mix of different desires, drives, and impulses. Due to the sin of Adam and the fall of man, these impulses are disordered and out of harmony with the universe. If we act morally, we use our will to harmonize those impulses and make possible an eternal life of blessedness guided by the divine order of creation.

Augustine's major works are the *Confessions, The City of God, Enchiridion,* and *On Freedom of the Will.* His influence on Christian thought was enormous. His writings not only provided the cornerstones of the Catholic faith, but were influential in the formation of later Protestantism as well. In Western moral philosophy he remains, along with St. Thomas Aquinas (the subject of the next discussion), one of the two most influential minds of the Middle Ages.

The City of God

Many people, if asked about the origins of their own moral values, would point to their religion or to God. Society may dictate laws and customs, but morality is a product of a higher power. Augustine's writings in his great work *The City of God* exemplify a very early Christian version of this notion that a division exists between the concerns of this world and the concerns of the next.

In *The City of God,* Augustine compared the secular state, in his case the Roman Empire, to the heavenly state. Christianity had become the official religion of the Roman Empire in the third century, but the sack of Rome by the Visigoths in 410 led Augustine to reconsider the relation of worldly politics (the earthly city) and the heavenly realm (the heavenly city). In this work he reconsiders the place of the empire in the divine plan. His view that those who live according to man (citizens of the earthly city) are destined to eternal torment, and that those who live according to God (citizens of the heavenly city) are destined to eternal glory, helped undermine the close relationship of the Roman Empire and the Christian religion.

From *The Works of Aurelius Augustine,* translated by Marcus Dods, Edinburgh, T. & T. Clark, 1892.

5. That in all natures, of every kind and rank, God is glorified

All natures, then, inasmuch as they are, and have therefore a rank and species of their own, and a kind of internal harmony, are certainly good. And when they are in the places assigned to them by the order of their nature, they preserve such being as they have received. And those things which have not received everlasting being, are altered for better or for worse, so as to suit the wants and motions of those things to which the Creator's law has made them subservient; and thus they tend in the divine providence to that end which is embraced in the general scheme of the government of the universe. So that, though the corruption of transitory and perishable things brings them to utter destruction, it does not prevent their producing that which was designed to be their result. And this being so, God, who supremely is, and who therefore created every being which has not supreme existence (for that which was made of nothing could not be equal to Him, and indeed could not be at all had He not made it), is not to be found fault with on account of the creature's faults, but is to be praised in view of the natures He has made.

6. What the cause of the blessedness of the good angels is, and what the cause of the misery of the wicked

Thus the true cause of the blessedness of the good angels is found to be this, that they cleave to Him who supremely is. And if we ask the cause of the misery of the bad, it occurs to us, and not unreasonably, that they are miserable because they have forsaken Him who supremely is, and have turned to themselves who have no such essence. And this vice, what else is it called than pride? For "pride is the beginning of sin." They were unwilling, then, to preserve their strength for God; and as adherence to God was the condition of their enjoying an ampler being, they diminished it by preferring themselves to Him. This was the first defect, and the first impoverishment, and the first flaw of their nature, which was created, not indeed supremely existent, but finding its blessedness in the enjoyment of the Supreme Being; whilst by abandoning Him it should become, not indeed no nature at all, but a nature with a less ample existence, and therefore wretched.

If the further question be asked, What was the efficient cause of their evil will? there is none. For what is it which makes the will bad, when it is the will itself which makes the action bad? And consequently the bad will is the cause of the bad action, but nothing is the efficient cause of the bad will. For if anything is the cause, this thing either has or has not a will. If it has, the will is either good or bad. If good, who is so left to himself as to say that a good will makes a will bad? For in this case a good will would be the cause of sin; a most absurd supposition. On the other hand, if this hypothetical thing has a bad will, I wish to know what made it so; and that we may not go on forever, I ask at once, what made the *first* evil will bad? For that is not the first which was itself corrupted by an evil will, but that is the first which was made evil by no other will. For if it were preceded by that which made it evil, that will was first which made the other evil. But if it is replied, "Nothing made it evil; it always was evil," I ask if it has been existing in some nature. For if not, then it did not exist at all; and if it did exist in some nature, then it vitiated and corrupted it, and injured it, and consequently deprived it of good. And therefore the evil will could not exist in an evil nature, but in a nature at once good and mutable, which this vice could injure. For if it did no injury, it was no vice; and consequently the will in which it was, could not be called evil. But if it did injury, it did it by taking away or diminishing good. And therefore there could not be from eternity, as was suggested, an evil will in that thing in which there had been previously a natural good, which the evil will was able to diminish by corrupting it. If, then, it was not from eternity, who, I ask, made it? The only thing that can be suggested in reply is, that something which itself had no will, made the will evil. I ask, then, whether this thing was superior, inferior, or equal to it? If superior, then it is better. How, then, has it no will, and not rather a good will? The same reasoning applies if it was equal; for so long as two things have equally a good will, the one cannot produce in the other an evil will. Then remains the supposition that that which corrupted the will of the angelic nature which first sinned, was itself an inferior thing without a will. But that thing, be it of the lowest and most earthly kind, is certainly itself good, since it is a nature and being, with a form and rank of its own in its own kind and order. How, then, can a good thing be the efficient cause of an evil will? How, I say, can good be the cause of evil? For when the will abandons what is above itself, and turns to what is lower, it becomes evil—not because that is evil to which it turns, but because the turning itself is wicked. Therefore it is not an inferior thing which has made the will evil, but it is itself which has become so by wickedly and inordinately desiring an inferior thing. For if two men, alike in physical and moral constitution, see the same corporal beauty, and one of them is excited by the sight to desire an illicit enjoyment, while the other steadfastly maintains a modest restraint of his will, what do we suppose brings it about, that there is an evil will in the one and not in the other? What produces it in the man in whom it exists? Not the bodily beauty, for that was presented equally to the gaze of both, and yet did not produce in both an evil will. Did the flesh of the one cause the desire as he looked? But why did not the flesh of the other? Or was it the disposition? But why not the disposition of both? For we are supposing that both were of a like temperament of body and soul. Must we, then, say that the one was tempted by a secret suggestion of the evil spirit? As if it was not by his own will that he consented to this suggestion and to any inducement whatever! This consent, then, this evil will which he presented to the evil suasive influence—what was the cause of it, we ask? For, not to delay on such a difficulty as this, if both are tempted equally, and one yields and consents to the temptation, while the other remains unmoved by it, what other account can we give of the matter than this, that the one is willing, the other unwilling, to fall away from chastity? And what causes this but their own wills, in cases at least such as we are supposing, where the temperament is identical? The same beauty was equally obvious to the eyes of both; the same secret temptation pressed on both with equal violence. However minutely we examine the case, therefore, we can discern nothing which caused the will of the one to be evil. For if we say that the man himself made his will evil, what was the man himself before his will was evil but a good nature created by God, the unchangeable good? Here are two men who, before the temptation, were alike in body and soul, and of whom one yielded to the tempter who persuaded him, while the other could not be persuaded to desire that lovely body which was equally before the eyes of both. Shall we say of the successfully tempted man that he corrupted his own will, since he was certainly good before his will became bad? Then, why did he do so? Was it because his will was a nature, or because it was made of nothing? We shall find that the latter is the case. For if a nature is the cause of an evil will, what else can we say than that evil arises from good, or that good is the cause of evil? And how can it come to pass that a nature, good though mutable, should produce any evil—that is to say, should make the will itself wicked?

---

1. Augustine has been inquiring after the cause of evil in the world. After ruling out various possible answers, he gives here the conclusion of his argument.

---

7. That we ought not to expect to find any efficient cause of the evil will

Let no one, therefore, look for an efficient cause of the evil will; for it is not efficient, but deficient, as the will itself is not an effecting of something, but a defect. For defection from that which supremely is, to that which has less of being—this is to begin to have an evil will. Now, to seek to discover the causes of these defections—causes, as I have said, not efficient, but deficient—is as if some one sought to see darkness, or hear silence. Yet both of these are known by us, and the former by means only of the eye, the latter only by the ear; but not by their positive actuality, but by their want of it. Let no one, then, seek to know from me what I know that I do not know; unless he perhaps wishes to learn to be ignorant of that of which all we know is, that it cannot be known. For those things which are known not by their actuality, but by their want of it, are known, if our expression may be allowed and understood, by not knowing them, that by knowing them they may be not known. For when the eyesight surveys objects that strike the sense, it nowhere sees darkness but where it begins not to see. And so no other sense but the ear can perceive silence, and yet it is only perceived by not hearing. Thus, too, our mind perceives intelligible forms by understanding them; but when they are deficient, it knows them by not knowing them; for "who can understand defects?"

---

2. Here are important implications concerning blame and punishment that follow from his conclusion about the cause of an evil will. Why is the defection of the will evil?

---

8. Of the misdirected love whereby the will fell away from the immutable to the mutable good

This I do know, that the nature of God can never, nowhere, nowise be defective, and that natures made of nothing can. These latter, however, the more being they have, and the more good they do (for then they do something positive), the more they have efficient causes; but in so far as they are defective in being, and consequently do evil (for then what is their work but vanity?), they have deficient causes. And I know likewise, that the will could not become evil, were it unwilling to become so; and therefore its failings are justly punished, being not necessary, but voluntary. For its defections are not to evil things, but are themselves evil; that is to say, are not towards things that are naturally and in themselves evil, but the defection of the will is evil, because it is contrary to the order of nature, and an abandonment of that which has supreme being for that which has less. For avarice is not a fault inherent in gold, but in the man who inordinately loves gold, to the detriment of justice, which ought to be held in incomparably higher regard than gold. Neither is luxury the fault of lovely and charming objects, but of the heart that inordinately loves sensual pleasures, to the neglect of temperance, which attaches us to objects more lovely in their spirituality, and more delectable by their incorruptibility. Nor yet is boasting the fault of human praise, but of the soul that is inordinately fond of the applause of men, and that makes light of the voice of conscience. Pride, too, is not the fault of him who delegates power, nor of power itself, but of the soul that is inordinately enamored of its own power, and despises the more just dominion of a higher authority. Consequently he who inordinately loves the good which any nature possesses, even though he obtain it, himself becomes evil in the good, and wretched because deprived of a greater good.

---

3. Augustine presents an argument about the properly lived (blessed) life and eternity. What implications follow from this argument concerning the relative value of life on earth and immortal life?

---

25. Of true blessedness, which this present life cannot enjoy

However, if we look at this a little more closely, we see that no one lives as he wishes but the blessed, and that no one is blessed but the righteous. But even the righteous himself does not live as he wishes, until he has arrived where he cannot die, be deceived, or injured, and until he is assured that this shall be his eternal condition. For this nature demands; and nature is not fully and perfectly blessed till it attains what it seeks. But what man is at present able to live as he wishes, when it is not in his power so much as to live? He wishes to live, he is compelled to die. How, then, does he live as he wishes who does not live as long as he wishes? or if he wishes to die, how can he live as he wishes, since he does not wish even to live? Or if he wishes to die, not because he dislikes life, but that after death he may live better, still he is not yet living as he wishes, but only has the prospect of so living when, through death, he reaches that which he wishes. But admit that he lives as he wishes, because he has done violence to himself, and forced himself not to wish what he cannot obtain, and to wish only what he can (as Terence has it, "Since you cannot do what you will, will what you can"), is he therefore blessed because he is patiently wretched? For a blessed life is possessed only by the man who loves it. If it is loved and possessed, it must necessarily be more ardently loved than all besides; for whatever else is loved must be loved for the sake of the blessed life. And if it is loved as it deserves to be—and the man is not blessed who does not love the blessed life as it deserves—then he who so loves it cannot but wish it to be eternal. Therefore it shall then only be blessed when it is eternal.

28. Of the nature of the two cities, the earthly and the heavenly

Accordingly, two cities have been formed by two loves: the earthly by the love of self, even to the contempt of God; the heavenly by the love of God, even to the contempt of self. The former, in a word, glories in itself, the latter in the Lord. For the one seeks glory from men; but the greatest glory of the other is God, the witness of conscience. The one lifts up its head in its own glory; the other says to its God, "Thou art my glory, and the lifter up of mine head." In the one, the princes and the nations it subdues are ruled by the love of ruling; in the other, the princes and the subjects serve one another in love, the latter obeying, while the former take thought for all. The one delights in its own strength, represented in the persons of its rulers; the other says to its God, "I will love Thee, O Lord, my strength." And therefore the wise men of the one city, living according to man, have sought for profit to their own bodies or souls, or both, and those who have known God "glorified Him not as God, neither were thankful, but became vain in their imaginations, and their foolish heart was darkened; professing themselves to be wise"—that is, glorying in their own wisdom, and being possessed by pride—"they became fools, and changed the glory of the incorruptible God into an image made like to corruptible man, and to birds, and four-footed beasts, and creeping things." For they were either leaders or followers of the people in adoring images, "and worshipped and served the creature more than the Creator, who is blessed for ever." But in the other city there is no human wisdom, but only godliness, which offers due worship to the true God, and looks for its reward in the society of the saints, of holy angels as well as holy men, "that God may be all in all."

---

4. Augustine presents arguments for the power and necessity of faith. He argues against the philosophical view that humankind can determine the proper moral life without God's help.

---

4. What the Christians believe regarding the supreme good and evil, in opposition to the philosophers, who have maintained that the supreme good is in themselves

If, then, we be asked what the city of God has to say upon these points, and, in the first place, what its opinion regarding the supreme good and evil is, it will reply that life eternal is the supreme good, death eternal the supreme evil, and that to obtain the one and escape the other we must live rightly. And thus it is written, "The just lives by faith," for we do not as yet see our good, and must therefore live by faith; neither have we in ourselves power to live rightly, but can do so only if He who has given us faith to believe in His help do help us when we believe and pray. As for those who have supposed that the sovereign good and evil are to be found in this life, and have placed it either in the soul or the body, or in both, or, to speak more explicitly, either in pleasure or in virtue, or in both; in repose or in virtue, or in both; in pleasure and repose, or in virtue, or in all combined; in the primary objects of nature, or in virtue, or in both—all these have, with a marvelous shallowness, sought to find their blessedness in this life and in themselves. Contempt has been poured upon such ideas by the Truth, saying by the prophet, "The Lord knoweth the thoughts of men" (or, as the Apostle Paul cites the passage, "The Lord knoweth the thoughts of the *wise*") "that they are vain."

For what flood of eloquence can suffice to detail the miseries of this life? Cicero, in the *Consolation* on the death of his daughter, has spent all his ability in lamentation;

but how inadequate was even his ability here? For when, where, how, in this life can these primary objects of nature be possessed so that they may not be assailed by unforeseen accident? Is the body of the wise man exempt from any pain which may dispel pleasure, from any disquietude which may banish repose? The amputation or decay of the members of the body puts an end to its integrity, deformity blights its beauty, weakness its health, lassitude its vigor, sleepiness or sluggishness its activity— and which of these is it that may not assail the flesh of the wise man? Comely and fitting attitudes and movements of the body are numbered among the prime natural blessings; but what if some sickness makes the members tremble? what if a man suffers from curvature of the spine to such an extent that his hands reach the ground, and he goes upon all-fours like a quadruped? Does not this destroy all beauty and grace in the body, whether at rest or in motion? What shall I say of the fundamental blessings of the soul, sense and intellect, of which the one is given for the perception, and the other for the comprehension of truth? But what kind of sense is it that remains when a man becomes deaf and blind? where are reason and intellect when disease makes a man delirious? We can scarcely, or not at all, refrain from tears, when we think of or see the actions and words of such frantic persons, and consider how different from and even opposed to their own sober judgment and ordinary conduct their present demeanor is. And what shall I say of those who suffer from demoniacal possession? Where is their own intelligence hidden and buried while the malignant spirit is using their body and soul according to his own will? And who is quite sure that no such thing can happen to the wise man in this life? Then, as to the perception of truth, what can we hope for even in this way while in the body, as we read in the true book of Wisdom, "The corruptible body weigheth down the soul, and the earthly tabernacle presseth down the mind that museth upon many things"? And eagerness, or desire of action, if this is the right meaning to put upon the Greek ὁρμή, is also reckoned among the primary advantages of nature; and yet is it not this which produces those pitiable movements of the insane, and those actions which we shudder to see, when sense is deceived and reason deranged?

In fine, virtue itself, which is not among the primary objects of nature, but succeeds to them as the result of learning, though it holds the highest place among human good things, what is its occupation save to wage perpetual war with vices— not those that are outside of us, but within; not other men's, but our own—a war which is waged especially by that virtue which the Greeks call σωφροσύνη, and we temperance, and which bridles carnal lusts, and prevents them from winning the consent of the spirit to wicked deeds? For we must not fancy that there is no vice in us, when, as the apostle says, "The flesh lusteth against the spirit;" for to this vice there is a contrary virtue, when, as the same writer says, "The spirit lusteth against the flesh." "For these two," he says, "are contrary one to the other, so that you cannot do the things which you would." But what is it we wish to do when we seek to attain the supreme good, unless that the flesh should cease to lust against the spirit, and that there be no vice in us against which the spirit may lust? And as we cannot attain to this in the present life, however ardently we desire it, let us by God's help accomplish at least this, to preserve the soul from succumbing and yielding to the flesh that lusts against it, and to refuse our consent to the perpetration of sin. Far be it from us, then, to fancy that while we are still engaged in this intestine war, we have already found the happiness which we seek to reach by victory. And who is there so wise that he has no conflict at all to maintain against his vices?

What shall I say of that virtue which is called prudence? Is not all its vigilance spent in the discernment of good from evil things, so that no mistake may be admitted about what we should desire and what avoid? And thus it is itself a proof that we are in the midst of evils, or that evils are in us; for it teaches us that it is an evil to consent to sin, and a good to refuse this consent. And yet this evil, to which prudence teaches and temperance enables us not to consent, is removed from this life neither by prudence nor by temperance. And justice, whose office it is to render to every man his due, whereby there is in man himself a certain just order of nature, so that the soul is subjected to God, and the flesh to the soul, and consequently both soul and flesh to God—does not this virtue demonstrate that it is as yet rather laboring towards its end than resting in its finished work? For the soul is so much the less subjected to God as it is less occupied with the thought of God; and the flesh is so much the less subjected to the spirit as it lusts more vehemently against the spirit. So long, therefore, as we are beset by this weakness, this plague, this disease, how shall we dare to say that we are safe? and if not safe, then how can we be already enjoying our final beatitude? Then that virtue which goes by the name of fortitude is the plainest proof of the ills of life, for it is these ills which it is compelled to bear patiently. And this holds good, no matter though the ripest wisdom co-exists with it. And I am at a loss to understand how the Stoic philosophers can presume to say that these are no ills, though at the same time they allow the wise man to commit suicide and pass out of this life if they become so grievous that he cannot or ought not to endure them. But such is the stupid pride of these men who fancy that the supreme good can be found in this life, and that they can become happy by their own resources, that their wise man, or at least the man whom they fancifully depict as such, is always happy, even though he become blind, deaf, dumb, mutilated, racked with pains, or suffer any conceivable calamity such as may compel him to make away with himself; and they are not ashamed to call the life that is beset with these evils happy. O happy life, which seeks the aid of death to end it! If it is happy, let the wise man remain in it; but if these ills drive him out of it, in what sense is it happy? Or how can they say that these are not evils which conquer the virtue of fortitude, and force it not only to yield, but so to rave that it in one breath calls life happy and recommends it to be given up? For who is so blind as not to see that if it were happy it would not be fled from? And if they say we should flee from it on account of the infirmities that beset it, why then do they not lower their pride and acknowledge that it is miserable? Was it, I would ask, fortitude or weakness which prompted Cato to kill himself? for he would not have done so had he not been too weak to endure Cæsar's victory. Where, then, is his fortitude? It has yielded, it has succumbed, it has been so thoroughly overcome as to abandon, forsake, flee this happy life. Or was it no longer happy? Then it was miserable. How, then, were these not evils which made life miserable, and a thing to be escaped from?

And therefore those who admit that these are evils, as the Peripatetics do, and the Old Academy, the sect with Varro advocates, express a more intelligible doctrine; but theirs also is a surprising mistake, for they contend that this is a happy life which is beset by these evils, even though they be so great that he who endures them should commit suicide to escape them. "Pains and anguish of body," says Varro, "are evils, and so much the worse in proportion to their severity; and to escape them you must quit this life." What life, I pray? This life, he says, which is oppressed by such evils.

Then it is happy in the midst of these very evils on account of which you say we must quit it? Or do you call it happy because you are at liberty to escape these evils by death? What, then, if by some secret judgment of God you were held fast and not permitted to die, nor suffered to live without these evils? In that case, at least, you would say that such a life was miserable. It is soon relinquished, no doubt, but this does not make it not miserable; for were it eternal, you yourself would pronounce it miserable. Its brevity, therefore, does not clear it of misery; neither ought it to be called happiness because it is a brief misery. Certainly there is a mighty force in these evils which compel a man—according to them, even a wise man—to cease to be a man that he may escape them, though they say, and say truly, that it is as it were the first and strongest demand of nature that a man cherish himself, and naturally there-fore avoid death, and should so stand his own friend as to wish and vehemently aim at continuing to exist as a living creature, and subsisting in this union of soul and body. There is a mighty force in these evils to overcome this natural instinct by which death is by every means and with all a man's efforts avoided, and to overcome it so completely that what was avoided is desired, sought after, and if it cannot in any other way be obtained, is inflicted by the man on himself. There is a mighty force in these evils which make fortitude a homicide—if, indeed, that is to be called fortitude which is so thoroughly overcome by these evils, that it not only cannot preserve by patience the man whom it undertook to govern and defend, but is itself obliged to kill him. The wise man, I admit, ought to bear death with patience, but when it is in-flicted by another. If, then, as these men maintain, he is obliged to inflict it on him-self, certainly it must be owned that the ills which compel him to this are not only evils, but intolerable evils. The life, then, which is either subject to accidents, or en-vironed with evils so considerable and grievous, could never have been called happy, if the men who give it this name had condescended to yield to the truth, and to be conquered by valid arguments, when they inquired after the happy life, as they yield to unhappiness, and are overcome by overwhelming evils, when they put themselves to death, and if they had not fancied that the supreme good was to be found in this mortal life; for the very virtues of this life, which are certainly its best and most use-ful possessions, are all the more telling proofs of its miseries in proportion as they are helpful against the violence of its dangers, toils, and woes. For if these are true virtues—and such cannot exist save in those who have true piety—they do not pro-fess to be able to deliver the men who possess them from all miseries; for true virtues tell no such lies, but they profess that by the hope of the future world this life, which is miserably involved in the many and great evils of this world, is happy as it is also safe. For if not yet safe, how could it be happy? And therefore the Apostle Paul, speaking not of men without prudence, temperance, fortitude, and justice, but of those whose lives were regulated by true piety, and whose virtues were therefore true, says, "For we are saved by hope: now hope which is seen is not hope; for what a man seeth, why doth he yet hope for? But if we hope for that we see not, then do we with patience wait for it." As, therefore, we are saved, so we are made happy by hope. And as we do not as yet possess a present, but look for a future salvation, so is it with our happiness, and this "with patience"; for we are encompassed with evils, which we ought patiently to endure, until we come to the ineffable enjoyment of unmixed good; for there shall be no longer anything to endure. Salvation, such as it shall be in the world to come, shall itself be our final happiness. And this happiness these philosophers refuse to believe in, because they do not see it, and attempt to fabricate for themselves a happiness in this life, based upon a virtue which is as deceitful as it is proud.

READING QUESTIONS

1. According to Augustine, what is the cause of misery?
2. Why does Augustine deny that the cause of an evil will is an efficient cause and instead call it "deficient"?
3. Why is the defection of the will evil?
4. What are the two cities that Augustine speaks of, and how was each formed?
5. What can hope give us that the virtues of temperance, fortitude, and justice cannot?

St. Thomas Aquinas

The third main period in the history of Western philosophy—the **Middle Ages**—extends about one thousand years, roughly from the fall of Rome in A.D. 476 to the Renaissance of the fifteenth century. During this period, the dominant force in Western culture was religion, in particular the Christian religion. Since its designation (by Constantine, c. A.D. 320) as the official religion of Rome, the Western Christian Church (which eventually became known as Roman Catholicism) exerted a greater and greater influence on all aspects of culture until it became the single most powerful entity in the Western world. It is therefore not surprising that moral philosophy came under the Church's influence, too.

Even though philosophers and religious thinkers study similar topics—the nature of reality, the characteristics of a good human life—they employ quite different methods for finding what is true. Philosophy, as we have seen, relies on logic and argumentation as the method of attaining knowledge. **Theology** (the study of religion), on the other hand, uses a combination of authority, scripture, revelation, and sometimes mystical experience to attain knowledge. The reason we may identify some medieval ethical writings as philosophy and not exclusively theology is that many of the religious thinkers of the Middle Ages were influenced by the pagan philosophers of Greece and Rome, and combined the methods of philosophy and theology.

Many of the earliest Christian thinkers scorned both the philosophies and religions of Greece and Rome because they believed that all pagan works had been annulled by the life of Christ. But when Constantine (c. 320) declared Christianity the official religion of the Roman Empire, Christian thinkers returned to the philosophies of the ancient world as a way to make converts of the intellectuals. Since Platonism in its various forms was the dominant philosophy of the time, the philosophical influence on early Christianity was mostly Platonic. This can be seen especially in the writings of **St. Augustine** (354–430), the pivotal figure who stood squarely in the culture of classical Greek and Rome, into which he was born, but who, as a convert to the religion, provided much of the intellectual foundation of Christianity.

As influential as Christianity was, not all of the important philosophical work of the period belongs to Christians. Both Islamic and Jewish scholars contributed to the progress of philosophy. Such Islamic thinkers as **Avicenna** (born 980), **Algazali** (born 1058), and **Averroes** (born 1126) and Jewish thinkers such as **Saadia** (born 882) and **Maimonides** (born 1135) influenced Western ethical philosophy and continue to be the subject of study today. Still, the primary figures in medieval moral philosophy were Christians: **Boethius, Peter Abelard,** and **St. Anselm** are three important Christian philosophers of whom you may have heard. None of these thinkers, however, whether Jewish, Muslim, or Christian, was to have the tremendous impact on either Christianity or Western philosophy as the quiet, studious Dominican friar **St. Thomas Aquinas.**

Thomas Aquinas (c. 1224–1274) was born in Roccasecca, Italy, near Aquino, into an aristocratic family. His education took him to the University of Paris, where he eventually attained a professorship. In 1244 he entered the Dominican order of the Roman Catholic Church. It was natural that he should turn his brilliant mind to the work of Aristotle; Aquinas studied under a Dominican scholar named Albert (later St. Albert the Great), whose commentaries on Aristotle helped bring the Greek thinker to the attention of Christendom.

The writings of Aristotle (as well as many other Greek writers) had long been lost to the Christian world. Yet Jewish and Islamic scholars had preserved and elaborated on many of them. By the middle of the thirteenth century, most of the work of Aristotle was available in Latin, the language of the Christian philosophers.

Because Aristotle's ideas appeared to differ so from orthodox Christianity and the philosophy of St. Augustine, his newly translated works presented a dilemma for Christian thinkers. Whose ideas should they choose—those of Aristotle or those of Augustine? Responses to the dilemma differed among members of the two dominant Catholic orders. Franciscans, members of the order founded by St. Francis of Assisi, declared Aristotle's teachings to be a combination of half-truths and outright false-hoods. Since, in their view, Aristotle opposed Augustine, the Franciscan stance toward his work was critical. Yet the Dominicans, and especially Thomas Aquinas, took a different view. They thought the philosophy of Aristotle could be reconciled with the teachings of Catholicism. In fact, Aquinas revered the thought of Aristotle so much that he referred to him as *the* Philosopher.

Aquinas spent his intellectual life attempting to prove the compatibility of Aristotle's philosophy and Church theology. He did this by constructing a unified view of man, nature, and God. By reworking into a coherent whole the philosophies of his predecessors Aristotle, Augustine, and the **Neoplatonists** (who combined Platonic doctrines with other classical ideas), Aquinas's writings show both the stamp of his own intelligence and the influence of his religious commitment.

Aquinas reconciled the ethics of Aristotle with the ethics of the Church by making room for two kinds of ethical principles and concepts. For Aquinas two kinds of virtues exist: **natural virtues** and **theological virtues**. Natural virtues are attained by reason and training; theological virtues require faith and God's grace. The natural virtues lead to worldly happiness, the theological virtues to eternal happiness.

At the center of Aquinas's ethics is the concept of **natural law**. According to Aquinas, natural law is God's law (the law of the cosmos), which can be discovered by human intelligence. It is through our powers of reason that we understand natural moral law and what it demands of us. Yet knowing that human reason is not always reliable, God spelled out His law in two forms: the Law given to Moses, and the New Law taught by Christ. With this characterization of natural law—a moral law available to human reason yet also revealed by the Christian religion—Aquinas demonstrated that the power of human reason is consistent with the truths of Christianity. The ethics of Augustine and the ethics of Aristotle no longer had to be considered as competing standards of moral conduct. Instead, they could be seen as complementary. Aquinas's optimistic view of the power of knowledge and intelligent action to improve human life was to contribute to the rebirth of natural science in the thirteenth century.

The writings of Aquinas fill twenty-five volumes in their original Latin. Along with commentaries, letters, sermons, devotionals, and other writings, Aquinas produced two great comprehensive treatises: *Summa Contra Gentiles* and the *Summa Theologica* (the traditional misspelling of the original title, *Summa Theologiae*). The

Summa Contra Gentiles is a synthesis of theology and philosophy designed to guide Dominican missionaries in arguing against the Muslims. The *Summa Theologica,* begun around 1264, runs to five volumes but was never completed; in it Aquinas aimed to systematize theology for beginners in the subject. It is from the latter work that our excerpts are taken.

Summa Theologica

In Plato's *Euthyphro* we were presented with two different possible relationships between God and morality. As you will recall, Plato, through his character Socrates, asked whether an action is good because God commands it, or whether that action is good and that is the reason God commands it. The difference amounts to this: Either whatever God commands us to do is right, or certain things are right, and those things God commands us to do. Plato's dialogue closes with Euthyphro befuddled and unable to answer this question adequately. Christian thinkers have traditionally given two different responses to Plato's question. The first, given by Augustine, emphasizes the view that morality begins and ends with God's commands. The second, represented here by Aquinas, deemphasizes God's commands as the origin of morality, and instead places morality's origins in the law of the cosmos, the natural law. The difference was important for the emerging scientific view at the end of the Middle Ages; the proper job for humans became not merely understanding God's commands, but understanding the world in which we live.

The format of the *Summa Theologica* requires some explanation. This monumental work consists of 512 "Questions." Each question introduces an issue that is then broken down into more specific topics called "Articles." Each article begins with a question. Then Aquinas lists several "Objections" (with which he will disagree) and a contrasting position, which begins with "On the contrary." What follows then is Aquinas's own view of the matter, beginning with the words "I answer that." Finally, he presents a "reply" to each of the prior "objections." It is important to remember that what Aquinas says first is the opposite side of the issue from the one he will subsequently defend.

The Basic Writings of Saint Thomas Aquinas, translated by Anton C. Pegis, Random House, 1945, Vol. II, pp. 772–785. Reprinted by permission of Hackett Publishing Company.

Question XCIV: The Natural Law *(in Six Articles)*

We must now consider the natural law, concerning which there are six points of inquiry: (1) What is the natural law? (2) What are the precepts of the natural law? (3) Whether all the acts of the virtues are prescribed by the natural law? (4) Whether the natural law is the same in all? (5) Whether it is changeable? (6) Whether it can be abolished from the mind of man?

First Article: Whether the Natural Law Is a Habit?

We proceed thus to the First Article:—

Objection 1. It would seem that the natural law is a habit. For, as the Philosopher says, *there are three things in the soul, power, habit and passion.* But the natural law is not one of the soul's powers, nor is it one of the passions, as we may see by going through them one by one. Therefore the natural law is a habit.

Obj. 2. Further, Basil says that the *conscience or synderesis is the law of our mind;* which can apply only to the natural law. But *synderesis* is a habit, as was shown in the First Part. Therefore the natural law is a habit.

Obj. 3. Further, the natural law abides in man always, as will be shown further on. But man's reason, which the law regards, does not always think about the natural law. Therefore the natural law is not an act, but a habit.

On the contrary, Augustine says that *a habit is that whereby something is done when necessary.* But such is not the natural law, since it is in infants and in the damned who cannot act by it. Therefore the natural law is not a habit.

I answer that, A thing may be called a habit in two ways. First, properly and essentially, and thus the natural law is not a habit. For it has been stated above that the natural law is something appointed by reason, just as a proposition is a work of reason. Now that which a man does is not the same as that whereby he does it, for he makes a becoming speech by the habit of grammar. Since, then, a habit is that by which we act, a law cannot be a habit properly and essentially.

Secondly, the term habit may be applied to that which we hold by a habit. Thus *faith* may mean *that which we hold by faith.* Accordingly, since the precepts of the natural law are sometimes considered by reason actually, while sometimes they are in the reason only habitually, in this way the natural law may be called a habit. So, too, in speculative matters, the indemonstrable principles are not the habit itself whereby we hold these principles; they are rather the principles of which we possess the habit.

Reply Obj. 1. The Philosopher proposes there to discover the genus of virtue; and since it is evident that virtue is a principle of action, he mentions only those things which are principles of human acts, viz., powers, habits and passions. But there are other things in the soul besides these three: e.g., acts, as *to will* is in the one that wills; again, there are things known in the knower; moreover its own natural properties are in the soul, such as immortality and the like.

Reply Obj. 2. *Synderesis* is said to be the law of our intellect because it is a habit containing the precepts of the natural law, which are the first principles of human actions.

Reply Obj. 3. This argument proves that the natural law is held habitually; and this is granted.

To the argument advanced in the contrary sense we reply that sometimes a man is unable to make use of that which is in him habitually, because of some impediment. Thus, because of sleep, a man is unable to use the habit of science. In like manner, through the deficiency of his age, a child cannot use the habit of the understanding of principles, or the natural law, which is in him habitually.

Second Article: Whether the Natural Law Contains Several Precepts, or Only One?

We proceed thus to the Second Article:—

Objection 1. It would seem that the natural law contains, not several precepts, but only one. For law is a kind of precept, as was stated above. If therefore there were many precepts of the natural law, it would follow that there are also many natural laws.

Obj. 2. Further, the natural law is consequent upon human nature. But human nature, as a whole, is one, though, as to its parts, it is manifold. Therefore, either there is but one precept of the law of nature because of the unity of nature as a whole, or there are many by reason of the number of parts of human nature. The result would be that even things relating to the inclination of the concupiscible power would belong to the natural law.

Obj. 3. Further, law is something pertaining to reason, as was stated above. Now reason is but one in man. Therefore there is only one precept of the natural law.

On the contrary, The precepts of the natural law in man stand in relation to operable matters as first principles do to matters of demonstration. But there are several first indemonstrable principles. Therefore there are also several precepts of the natural law.

I answer that, As was stated above, the precepts of the natural law are to the practical reason what the first principles of demonstrations are to the speculative reason, because both are self-evident principles. Now a thing is said to be self-evident in two ways: first, in itself; secondly, in relation to us. Any proposition is said to be self-evident in itself, if its predicate is contained in the notion of the subject; even though it may happen that to one who does not know the definition of the subject, such a proposition is not self-evident. For instance, this proposition, *Man is a rational being,* is, in its very nature, self-evident, since he who says *man,* says *a rational being;* and yet to one who does not know what a man is, this proposition is not self-evident. Hence it is that, as Boethius says, certain axioms or propositions are universally self-evident to all; and such are the propositions whose terms are known to all, as, *Every whole is greater than its part,* and, *Things equal to one and the same are equal to one another.* But some propositions are self-evident only to the wise, who understand the meaning of the terms of such propositions. Thus to one who understands that an angel is not a body, it is self-evident that an angel is not circumscriptively in a place. But this is not evident to the unlearned, for they cannot grasp it.

---

1. Aquinas gives an argument that results in a statement about the first precept of the natural law. Can you state his main conclusion?

Now a certain order is to be found in those things that are apprehended by men. For that which first falls under apprehension is *being,* the understanding of which is included in all things whatsoever a man apprehends. Therefore the first indemonstrable principle is that *the same thing cannot be affirmed and denied at the same time,* which is based on the notion of *being* and *not-being:* and on this principle all others are based, as is stated in *Metaph.* iv. Now as *being* is the first thing that falls under the apprehension absolutely, so *good* is the first thing that falls under the apprehension of the practical reason, which is directed to action (since every agent acts for an end, which has the nature of good). Consequently, the first principle in the practical reason is one founded on the nature of good, viz., that *good is that which all things seek after.* Hence this is the first precept of law, that *good is to be done and promoted, and evil is to be avoided.* All other precepts of the natural law are based upon this; so that all the things which the practical reason naturally apprehends as man's good belong to the precepts of the natural law under the form of things to be done or avoided.

Since, however, good has the nature of an end, and evil, the nature of the contrary, hence it is that all those things to which man has a natural inclination are naturally apprehended by reason as being good, and consequently as objects of pursuit, and their contraries as evil, and objects of avoidance. Therefore, the order of the precepts of the natural law is according to the order of natural inclinations. For there is in man, first of all, an inclination to good in accordance with the nature which he has in common with all substances, inasmuch, namely, as every substance seeks the preservation of its own being, according to its nature; and by reason of this inclination, whatever is a means of preserving human life, and of warding off its obstacles, belongs to the natural law. Secondly, there is in man an inclination to things that pertain to him more specially, according to that nature which he has in common with other animals; and in virtue of this inclination, those things are said to belong to the natural law *which nature has taught to all animals,* such as sexual intercourse, the education of offspring and so forth. Thirdly, there is in man an inclination to good according to the nature of his reason, which nature is proper to him. Thus man has a natural inclination to know the truth about God, and to live in society; and in this respect, whatever pertains to this inclination belongs to the natural law: e.g., to shun ignorance, to avoid offending those among whom one has to live, and other such things regarding the above inclination.

Reply Obj. 1. All these precepts of the law of nature have the character of one natural law, inasmuch as they flow from one first precept.

Reply Obj. 2. All the inclinations of any parts whatsoever of human nature, e.g., of the concupiscible and irascible parts, in so far as they are ruled by reason, belong to the natural law, and are reduced to one first precept, as was stated above. And thus the precepts of the natural law are many in themselves, but they are based on one common foundation.

Reply Obj. 3. Although reason is one in itself, yet it directs all things regarding man; so that whatever can be ruled by reason is contained under the law of reason.

Third Article: Whether All the Acts of the Virtues Are Prescribed by the Natural Law?

We proceed thus to the Third Article:—

Objection 1. It would seem that not all the acts of the virtues are prescribed by the natural law. For, as was stated above, it is of the nature of law that it be ordained to the common good. But some acts of the virtues are ordained to the private good of the individual, as is evident especially in regard to acts of temperance. Therefore, not all the acts of the virtues are the subject of natural law.

Obj. 2. Further, every sin is opposed to some virtuous act. If therefore all the acts of the virtues are prescribed by the natural law, it seems to follow that all sins are against nature; whereas this applies to certain special sins.

Obj. 3. Further, those things which are according to nature are common to all. But the acts of the virtues are not common to all, since a thing is virtuous in one, and vicious in another. Therefore, not all the acts of the virtues are prescribed by the natural law.

On the contrary, Damascene says that *virtues are natural.* Therefore virtuous acts also are subject to the natural law.

I answer that, We may speak of virtuous acts in two ways: first, in so far as they are virtuous; secondly, as such and such acts considered in their proper species. If, then, we are speaking of the acts of the virtues in so far as they are virtuous, thus all virtuous acts belong to the natural law. For it has been stated that to the natural law belongs everything to which a man is inclined according to his nature. Now each thing is inclined naturally to an operation that is suitable to it according to its form: e.g., fire is inclined to give heat. Therefore, since the rational soul is the proper form of man, there is in every man a natural inclination to act according to reason; and this is to act according to virtue. Consequently, considered thus, all the acts of the virtues are prescribed by the natural law, since each one's reason naturally dictates to him to act virtuously. But if we speak of virtuous acts, considered in themselves, i.e., in their proper species, thus not all virtuous acts are prescribed by the natural law. For many things are done virtuously, to which nature does not primarily incline, but which, through the inquiry of reason, have been found by men to be conducive to well-living.

Reply Obj. 1. Temperance is about the natural concupiscences of food, drink and sexual matters, which are indeed ordained to the common good of nature, just as other matters of law are ordained to the moral common good.

Reply Obj. 2. By human nature we may mean either that which is proper to man, and in this sense all sins, as being against reason, are also against nature, as Damascene states; or we may mean that nature which is common to man and other animals, and in this sense, certain special sins are said to be against nature: e.g., contrary to sexual intercourse, which is natural to all animals, is unisexual lust, which has received the special name of the unnatural crime.

Reply Obj. 3. This argument considers acts in themselves. For it is owing to the various conditions of men that certain acts are virtuous for some, as being proportioned and becoming to them, while they are vicious for others, as not being proportioned to them.

Fourth Article: *Whether the Natural Law Is the Same in All Men?*

---

2. The three objections include the view of the Church (Decretals, *or official decrees of the Church*), *then Aristotle's position* (Ethics), *and finally observations that any of us could make.*

We proceed thus to the Fourth Article:—

Objection 1. It would seem that the natural law is not the same in all. For it is stated in the *Decretals* that *the natural law is that which is contained in the Law and the Gospel*. But this is not common to all men, because, as it is written (*Rom.* x. 16), *all do not obey the gospel*. Therefore the natural law is not the same in all men.

Obj. 2. Further, *Things which are according to the law are said to be just,* as is stated in *Ethics* v. But it is stated in the same book that nothing is so just for all as not to be subject to change in regard to some men. Therefore even the natural law is not the same in all men.

Obj. 3. Further, as was stated above, to the natural law belongs everything to which a man is inclined according to his nature. Now different men are naturally inclined to different things,—some to the desire of pleasures, others to the desire of honors, and other men to other things. Therefore, there is not one natural law for all.

On the contrary, Isidore says: *The natural law is common to all nations.*

I answer that, As we have stated above, to the natural law belong those things to which a man is inclined naturally; and among these it is proper to man to be inclined to act according to reason. Now it belongs to the reason to proceed from what is common to what is proper, as is stated in *Physics* i. The speculative reason, however, is differently situated, in this matter, from the practical reason. For, since the speculative reason is concerned chiefly with necessary things, which cannot be otherwise than they are, its proper conclusions, like the universal principles, contain the truth without fail. The practical reason, on the other hand, is concerned with contingent matters, which is the domain of human actions; and, consequently, although there is necessity in the common principles, the more we descend towards the particular, the more frequently we encounter defects. Accordingly, then, in speculative matters truth is the same in all men, both as to principles and as to conclusions; although the truth is not known to all as regards the conclusions, but only as regards the principles which are called *common notions*. But in matters of action, truth or practical rectitude is not the same for all as to what is particular, but only as to the common principles; and where there is the same rectitude in relation to particulars, it is not equally known to all.

It is therefore evident that, as regards the common principles whether of speculative or of practical reason, truth or rectitude is the same for all, and is equally known by all. But as to the proper conclusions of the speculative reason, the truth is the same for all, but it is not equally known to all. Thus, it is true for all that the three angles of a triangle are together equal to two right angles, although it is not known to all. But as to the proper conclusions of the practical reason, neither is the truth or rectitude the same for all, nor, where it is the same, is it equally known by all. Thus, it is right and true for all to act according to reason, and from this principle it follows, as a proper conclusion, that goods entrusted to another should be restored to their owner. Now this is true for the majority of cases. But it may happen in a particular case that it would be injurious, and therefore unreasonable, to restore goods held in trust; for instance, if they are claimed for the purpose of fighting against one's country. And this principle will be found to fail the more, according as we descend further towards the particular, e.g., if one were to say that goods held in trust should be restored with such and such a guarantee, or in such and such a way; because the greater the number of conditions added, the greater the number of ways in which the principle may fail, so that it be not right to restore or not to restore.

Consequently, we must say that the natural law, as to the first common principles, is the same for all, both as to rectitude and as to knowledge. But as to certain more particular aspects, which are conclusions, as it were, of those common principles, it is the same for all in the majority of cases, both as to rectitude and as to knowledge; and yet in some few cases it may fail, both as to rectitude, by reason of certain obstacles (just as natures subject to generation and corruption fail in some few cases because of some obstacle), and as to knowledge, since in some the reason is perverted by passion, or evil habit, or an evil disposition of nature. Thus at one time theft, although it is expressly contrary to the natural law, was not considered wrong among the Germans, as Julius Cæsar relates.

Reply Obj. 1. The meaning of the sentence quoted is not that whatever is contained in the Law and the Gospel belongs to the natural law, since they contain many things that are above nature; but that whatever belongs to the natural law is fully contained in them. Therefore Gratian, after saying that *the natural law is what is contained in the Law and the Gospel,* adds at once, by way of example, *by which everyone is commanded to do to others as he would be done by.*

Reply Obj. 2. The saying of the Philosopher is to be understood of things that are naturally just, not as common principles, but as conclusions drawn from them, having rectitude in the majority of cases, but failing in a few.

Reply Obj. 3: Just as in man reason rules and commands the other powers, so all the natural inclinations belonging to the other powers must needs be directed according to reason. Therefore it is universally right for all men that all their inclinations should be directed according to reason.

Fifth Article: Whether the Natural Law Can Be Changed?

We proceed thus to the Fifth Article:—

Objection 1. It would seem that the natural law can be changed. For on *Ecclus.* xvii. 9 (*He gave them instructions, and the law of life*) the *Gloss* says: *He wished the law of the letter to be written, in order to correct the law of nature.* But that which is corrected is changed. Therefore the natural law can be changed.

Obj. 2. Further, the slaying of the innocent, adultery and theft are against the natural law. But we find these things changed by God: as when God commanded Abraham to slay his innocent son (*Gen.* xxii. 2); and when He ordered the Jews to borrow and purloin the vessels of the Egyptians (*Exod.* xii. 35); and when He commanded Osee to take to himself *a wife of fornications* (*Osee* i. 2). Therefore the natural law can be changed.

Obj. 3. Further, Isidore says that *the possession of all things in common, and universal freedom, are matters of natural law.* But these things are seen to be changed by human laws. Therefore it seems that the natural law is subject to change.

On the contrary, It is said in the *Decretals: The natural law dates from the creation of the rational creature. It does not vary according to time, but remains unchangeable.*

I answer that, A change in the natural law may be understood in two ways. First, by way of addition. In this sense, nothing hinders the natural law from being changed, since many things for the benefit of human life have been added over and above the natural law, both by the divine law and by human laws.

Secondly, a change in the natural law may be understood by way of subtraction, so that what previously was according to the natural law, ceases to be so. In this sense, the natural law is altogether unchangeable in its first principles. But in its secondary principles, which, as we have said, are certain detailed proximate conclusions drawn from the first principles, the natural law is not changed so that what it prescribes be not right in most cases. But it may be changed in some particular cases of rare occurrence, through some special causes hindering the observance of such precepts, as was stated above.

Reply Obj. 1. The written law is said to be given for the correction of the natural law, either because it supplies what was wanting to the natural law, or because the natural law was so perverted in the hearts of some men, as to certain matters, that they esteemed those things good which are naturally evil; which perversion stood in need of correction.

Reply Obj. 2. All men alike, both guilty and innocent, die the death of nature; which death of nature is inflicted by the power of God because of original sin, according to *I Kings* ii. 6: *The Lord killeth and maketh alive.* Consequently, by the command of God, death can be inflicted on any man, guilty or innocent, without any injustice whatever.—In like manner, adultery is intercourse with another's wife; who is allotted to him by the law emanating from God. Consequently intercourse with any woman, by the command of God, is neither adultery nor fornication.—The same applies to theft, which is the taking of another's property. For whatever is taken by the command of God, to Whom all things belong, is not taken against the will of its owner, whereas it is in this that theft consists.—Nor is it only in human things that whatever is commanded by God is right; but also in natural things, whatever is done by God is, in some way, natural, as was stated in the First Part.

Reply Obj. 3. A thing is said to belong to the natural law in two ways. First, because nature inclines thereto: e.g., that one should not do harm to another. Secondly, because nature did not bring with it the contrary. Thus, we might say that for man to be naked is of the natural law, because nature did not give him clothes, but art invented them. In this sense, *the possession of all things in common and universal freedom* are said to be of the natural law, because, namely, the distinction of possessions and slavery were not brought in by nature, but devised by human reason for the benefit of human life. Accordingly, the law of nature was not changed in this respect, except by addition.

Sixth Article: Whether the Natural Law Can Be Abolished from the Heart of Man?

---

3. How do we account for the existence of people who perform terrible, wicked acts? Aquinas considers whether the sinner "blots out" the law of nature when he or she sins, or whether some other factor accounts for sin.

We proceed thus to the Sixth Article:—

Objection 1. It would seem that the natural law can be abolished from the heart of man. For on *Rom.* ii. 14 (*When the Gentiles who have not the law,* etc.) the *Gloss* says that *the law of justice, which sin had blotted out, is graven on the heart of man when he is restored by grace.* But the law of justice is the law of nature. Therefore the law of nature can be blotted out.

Obj. 2. Further, the law of grace is more efficacious than the law of nature. But the law of grace is blotted out by sin. Much more, therefore, can the law of nature be blotted out.

Obj. 3. Further, that which is established by law is proposed as something just. But many things are enacted by men which are contrary to the law of nature. Therefore the law of nature can be abolished from the heart of man.

On the contrary, Augustine says: *Thy law is written in the hearts of men, which iniquity itself effaces not.* But the law which is written in men's hearts is the natural law. Therefore the natural law cannot be blotted out.

I answer that, As we have stated above, there belong to the natural law, first, certain most common precepts that are known to all; and secondly, certain secondary and more particular precepts, which are, as it were, conclusions following closely from first principles. As to the common principles, the natural law, in its universal meaning, cannot in any way be blotted out from men's hearts. But it is blotted out in the case of a particular action, in so far as reason is hindered from applying the common principle to the particular action because of concupiscence or some other passion, as was stated above.—But as to the other, i.e., the secondary precepts, the natural law can be blotted out from the human heart, either by evil persuasions, just as in speculative matters errors occur in respect of necessary conclusions; or by vicious customs and corrupt habits, as, among some men, theft, and even unnatural vices, as the Apostle states (*Rom.* i. 24), were not esteemed sinful.

Reply Obj. 1. Sin blots out the law of nature in particular cases, not universally, except perchance in regard to the secondary precepts of the natural law, in the way stated above.

Reply Obj. 2. Although grace is more efficacious than nature, yet nature is more essential to man, and therefore more enduring.

Reply Obj. 3. This argument is true of the secondary precepts of the natural law, against which some legislators have framed certain enactments which are unjust.

Question XCV: Human Law *(in Four Articles)*

We must now consider human law, and (1) concerning this law considered in itself; (2) its power; (3) its mutability. Under the first head there are four points of inquiry: (1) Its utility. (2) Its origin. (3) Its quality. (4) Its division.

First Article: *Whether It Was Useful for Laws to Be Framed by Men?*

We proceed thus to the First Article:—

Objection 1. It would seem that it was not useful for laws to be framed by men. For the purpose of every law is that man be made good thereby, as was stated above. But men are more to be induced to be good willingly by means of admonitions, than against their will, by means of laws. Therefore there was no need to frame laws.

Obj. 2. Further, As the Philosopher says, *men have recourse to a judge as to animate justice.* But animate justice is better than inanimate justice, which is contained in laws. Therefore it would have been better for the execution of justice to be entrusted to the decision of judges than to frame laws in addition.

Obj. 3. Further, every law is framed for the direction of human actions, as is evident from what has been stated above. But since human actions are about singulars, which are infinite in number, matters pertaining to the direction of human actions cannot be taken into sufficient consideration except by a wise man, who looks into each one of them. Therefore it would have been better for human acts to be directed by the judgment of wise men, than by the framing of laws. Therefore there was no need of human laws.

On the contrary, Isidore says: *Laws were made that in fear thereof human audacity might be held in check, that innocence might be safeguarded in the midst of wickedness, and that the dread of punishment might prevent the wicked from doing harm.* But these things are most necessary to mankind. Therefore it was necessary that human laws should be made.

---

4. Aquinas explores the connection between human laws and the perfection of virtue. He has to account for the necessity of human laws in addition to natural laws. Why do we need to be afraid of punishment?

I answer that, As we have stated above, man has a natural aptitude for virtue; but the perfection of virtue must be acquired by man by means of some kind of training. Thus we observe that a man is helped by diligence in his necessities, for instance, in food and clothing. Certain beginnings of these he has from nature, viz., his reason and his hands; but he has not the full complement, as other animals have, to whom nature has given sufficiently of clothing and food. Now it is difficult to see how man could suffice for himself in the matter of this training, since the perfection of virtue consists chiefly in withdrawing man from undue pleasures, to which above all man is inclined, and especially the young, who are more capable of being trained. Consequently a man needs to receive this training from another, whereby to arrive at the perfection of virtue. And as to those young people who are inclined to acts of virtue by their good natural disposition, or by custom, or rather by the gift of God, paternal training suffices, which is by admonitions. But since some are found to be dissolute and prone to vice, and not easily amenable to words, it was necessary for such to be restrained from evil by force and fear, in order that, at least, they might desist from evil-doing, and leave others in peace, and that they themselves, by being habituated in this way, might be brought to do willingly what hitherto they did from fear, and thus become virtuous. Now this kind of training, which compels through fear of punishment, is the discipline of laws. Therefore, in order that man might have peace and virtue, it was necessary for laws to be framed; for, as the Philosopher says, *as man is the most noble of animals if he be perfect in virtue, so he is the lowest of all, if he be severed from law and justice.* For man can use his reason to devise means of satisfying his lusts and evil passions, which other animals are unable to do.

Reply Obj. 1. Men who are well disposed are led willingly to virtue by being admonished better than by coercion; but men whose disposition is evil are not led to virtue unless they are compelled.

Reply Obj. 2. As the Philosopher says, *it is better that all things be regulated by law, than left to be decided by judges.* And this for three reasons. First, because it is easier to find a few wise men competent to frame right laws, than to find the many who would be necessary to judge rightly of each single case.—Secondly, because those who make laws consider long beforehand what laws to make, whereas judgment on each single case has to be pronounced as soon as it arises; and it is easier for man to see what is right, by taking many instances into consideration, than by considering one solitary instance.— Thirdly, because lawgivers judge universally and about future events, whereas those who sit in judgment judge of things present, towards which they are affected by love, hatred, or some kind of cupidity; and thus their judgment becomes perverted.

Since, then, the animated justice of the judge is not found in every man, and since it can be bent, therefore it was necessary, whenever possible, for the law to determine how to judge, and for very few matters to be left to the decision of men.

Reply Obj. 3. Certain individual facts which cannot be covered by the law *have necessarily to be committed to judges,* as the Philosopher says in the same passage: e.g., *concerning something that has happened or not happened,* and the like.

Second Article: *Whether Every Human Law Is Derived from the Natural Law?*

We proceed thus to the Second Article:—

Objection 1. It would seem that not every human law is derived from the natural law. For the Philosopher says that *the legal just is that which originally was a matter of indifference.* But those things which arise from the natural law are not matters of indifference. Therefore the enactments of human laws are not all derived from the natural law.

Obj. 2. Further, positive law is divided against natural law, as is stated by Isidore and the Philosopher. But those things which flow as conclusions from the common principles of the natural law belong to the natural law, as was stated above. Therefore that which is established by human law is not derived from the natural law.

Obj. 3. Further, the law of nature is the same for all, since the Philosopher says that *the natural just is that which is equally valid everywhere.* If therefore human laws were derived from the natural law, it would follow that they too are the same for all; which is clearly false.

Obj. 4. Further, it is possible to give a reason for things which are derived from the natural law. But *it is not possible to give the reason for all the legal enactments of the lawgivers,* as the Jurist says. Therefore not all human laws are derived from the natural law.

On the contrary, Tully says: *Things which emanated from nature, and were approved by custom, were sanctioned by fear and reverence for the laws.*

I answer that, As Augustine says, *that which is not just seems to be no law at all.* Hence the force of a law depends on the extent of its justice. Now in human affairs a thing is said to be just from being right, according to the rule of reason. But the first rule of reason is the law of nature, as is clear from what has been stated above. Consequently, every human law has just so much of the nature of law as it is derived from the law of nature. But if in any point it departs from the law of nature, it is no longer a law but a perversion of law.

But it must be noted that something may be derived from the natural law in two ways: first, as a conclusion from principles; secondly, by way of a determination of certain common notions. The first way is like to that by which, in the sciences, demonstrated conclusions are drawn from the principles; while the second is likened to that whereby, in the arts, common forms are determined to some particular. Thus, the craftsman needs to determine the common form of a house to the shape of this or that particular house. Some things are therefore derived from the common principles of the natural law by way of conclusions: e.g., that *one must not kill* may be derived as a conclusion from the principle that *one should do harm to no man;* while some are derived therefrom by way of determination: e.g., the law of nature has it that the evil-doer should be punished, but that he be punished in this or that way is a determination of the law of nature.

Accordingly, both modes of derivation are found in the human law. But those things which are derived in the first way are contained in human law, not as emanating therefrom exclusively, but as having some force from the natural law also. But those things which are derived in the second way have no other force than that of human law.

Reply Obj. 1. The Philosopher is speaking of those enactments which are by way of determination or specification of the precepts of the natural law.

Reply Obj. 2. This argument holds for those things that are derived from the natural law by way of conclusion.

Reply Obj. 3. The common principles of the natural law cannot be applied to all men in the same way because of the great variety of human affairs; and hence arises the diversity of positive laws among various people.

Reply Obj. 4. These words of the Jurist are to be understood as referring to the decisions of rulers in determining particular points of the natural law; and to these determinations the judgment of expert and prudent men is related as to its principles, in so far, namely, as they see at once what is the best thing to decide. Hence the Philosopher says that, in such matters, *we ought to pay as much attention to the undemonstrated sayings and opinions of persons who surpass us in experience, age and prudence, as to their demonstrations.*

READING QUESTIONS

1. According to Aquinas, how does the Philosopher (Aristotle) arrive at the conclusion that the natural law is a habit?

2. What are the two ways in which a thing can be self-evident?

3. What is the first precept of the natural law?

4. What argument does Aquinas give for his conclusion that everyone has a natural inclination to act according to reason?

5. According to Aquinas, what is the purpose of human laws?

6. What does Aquinas consider laws that depart from the law of nature?

Thomas Hobbes

The philosophy of Thomas Hobbes is one of the earliest and most important contributions to what we call the **Modern** period in moral philosophy, spanning the years 1600–1800. Hobbes was born in England in 1588, the year England fought off invasion by Spain's Invincible Armada and established itself as the ruler of the world's seas. The period into which he was born was one of intense social and political upheaval. As we have seen, such periods typically bring about an increase in philosophical activity as traditional beliefs and traditional values become subject to question. During the sixteenth and seventeenth centuries, both the teachings of the Catholic Church and the ideas of Aristotle, which had become such an integral part of those teachings, were under fire from all sides: the **Galilean** and **Copernican** revolutions in science, the **Reformation,** and the rise of industrial democracy all threatened the established order.

As the old ideas of morality seemed less and less able to respond to the changes taking place all around, Hobbes undertook a search for an ethical method that could be universally accepted. Even though he was educated under the Aristotelian system, he was largely unimpressed by it. When, in 1610, he made his first visit to the Continent, he discovered for himself the diminishing influence of Aristotle's teachings. The new scientific method, being employed by such people as **Kepler, Descartes, Galileo,** and **Francis Bacon,** appeared to offer a more reliable way to understand how the world worked. At the same time, Hobbes admired the way in which the geometric method could arrive at mathematical conclusions that could not be doubted. Determined to adapt these insights to his interest in philosophy, Hobbes combined the scientific and geometric methods in the search for truths about humanity and society.

The concept of **natural law,** with its divinely sanctioned objective truths of the universe discoverable by reason, bore the brunt of Hobbes's criticism. Hobbes proposed a new understanding of natural law, one that was not divine but inherent in the nature of the human race. This form of natural law has as its cornerstone the inherent desire we all possess for self-preservation.

Hobbes defined the "good" as the object of any human desire. Therefore, that which humans naturally most desire (which he found to be self-preservation) must be the primary good. Moral rules, then, for Hobbes, are merely invented by societies in order to discourage those actions that lead to personal destruction or that threaten the means to self-preservation. However, Hobbes's innovation in moral philosophy lies not in his equating good with pleasure (a **hedonistic** view of ethics); this was merely a modern version of **Epicureanism.** Rather, Hobbes was important for insisting that the only means for ensuring that people follow these moral rules is a strong government. Societies adopt moral rules because rational people recognize that without such rules society gives way to a war of all against all, in which everyone is bound to suffer. What ensures that each person's tendencies toward greed, envy, and aggression are brought under control is the power of the state. Each person obeys the law because he or she knows that punishment by the state will be the cost of disobedience. People are willing to accept the power of the state because the alternative is so grim.

Leviathan, from which the following textual selections are excerpted, is Hobbes's major work. He was at the center of a number of philosophical and theological disputes in his day and by the time of his death, at the age of 91, was a veritable English institution. His influence on ethical theory was enormous. By rejecting ethics' reliance on revealed theology, Hobbes returned philosophy to the concerns that had engaged **Socrates** and the **Sophists.** But these concerns were raised to a higher level by Hobbes, who profited from both the Christian insights into the force of moral principles and the refinements of the scientific method.

What has become the mainstream of English ethics begins with Hobbes and the replies and criticisms he provoked. A whole group of English philosophers collectively known as the **British Moralists** criticized the pessimistic view of humanity that Hobbes gave, contending instead that benevolence was just as primary an emotion for humans as selfishness. We can trace the threads of Hobbesian thought to our own day. It exists most clearly in hedonistic theories such as **utilitarianism** and **ethical egoism,** and in the ethical theory of **contractarianism** (or social contract theory), discussed by Plato in the *Crito* and influential today in the ethics of John Rawls and others.

Leviathan

What do you suppose would happen if a group of people were stranded in a lifeboat with a limited amount of food and fresh water? At first, maybe you would expect them to ration out portions of food and drink as they tried to sustain themselves until they could be rescued. But what would happen as time went on and hope for an early rescue faded, with the store of food and drink shrinking day by day? It's not hard to imagine that at some point, since no one wants to die of thirst or starvation, each person would begin plotting to attain enough food and water to survive even if it meant that others must die. Fighting over scarce resources that are the means of life seems to many as just a part of human nature. The fight to live is not limited to human nature, you might say; it characterizes life itself. Birds may share their worms with their chicks, but not with other birds. Lions may all get a piece of the kill, but only after the strongest have eaten their fill.

Hobbes, in *Leviathan,* defends the view that self-preservation and self-interest are natural human desires and that the satisfaction of these desires is what we mean by "good." The only means to prevent the strong from taking anything and everything from the weak is a powerful government. Hobbes is famous for saying that life for primitive people, who lacked such a powerful keeper of the moral law, was "solitary, poor, nasty, brutish, and short."

Thomas Hobbes, *Leviathan,* Part I, Chs. 6, 13, 14, 15, Molesworth edition, London, 1841.

The notion that what is good is the satisfaction of a person's desires is advocated by Hobbes, but not original to him. We saw an earlier version of this view advanced by the Epicureans. Two other ideas prominent in these excerpts from *Leviathan* had their origins in Greek philosophy. First, the notion that morality is a system based on contracts constitutes a crucial part of the Hobbesian moral philosophy. We read about such a notion of contract in Plato's dialogue *Crito*. Our reading from Plato's *Republic* presented another idea that received renewed treatment by Hobbes—the notion that moral terms such as good and bad, right and wrong, are given their meanings by society. Morality, in this view, is relative to the society in which it arises. All three of these ideas—the equating of good with pleasure and satisfaction of desires, the notion of a system of contract underlying morality, and morality as social convention—all play a part in subsequent moral philosophy. These ideas remain as exciting and contentious today as they were in Hobbes's time.   ✒

Chapter VI
Of the Interior Beginnings of Voluntary Motions; Commonly Called the Passions; and the Speeches by Which They Are Expressed

There be in animals, two sorts of *motions* peculiar to them: one called *vital*; begun in generation, and continued without interruption through their whole life; such as are the *course* of the *blood,* the *pulse,* the *breathing,* the *concoction, nutrition, excretion,* etc., to which motions there needs no help of imagination: the other is *animal motion,* otherwise called *voluntary motion*; as to *go,* to *speak,* to *move* any of our limbs, in such manner as is first fancied in our minds. That sense is motion in the organs and interior parts of man's body, caused by the action of the things we see, hear, etc.; and that fancy is but the relics of the same motion, remaining after sense, has been already said in the first and second chapters. And because *going, speaking,* and the like voluntary motions, depend always upon a precedent thought of *whither, which way,* and *what*; it is evident, that the imagination is the first internal beginning of all voluntary motion. And although unstudied men do not conceive any motion at all to be there, where the thing moved is invisible; or the space it is moved in is, for the shortness of it, insensible; yet that does not hinder, but that such motions are. For let a space be never so little, that which is moved over a greater space, whereof that little one is part, must first be moved over that. These small beginnings of motion, within the body of man, before they appear in walking, speaking, striking, and other visible actions, are commonly called ENDEAVOR.

This endeavor, when it is toward something which causes it, is called APPETITE, or DESIRE; the latter, being the general name; and the other oftentimes restrained to signify the desire of food, namely *hunger* and *thirst*. And when the endeavor is fromward something, it is generally called AVERSION. These words, *appetite* and *aversion,* we have from the Latins; and they both of them signify the motions, one of approaching, the other of retiring. So also do the Greek words for the same, which are ὁρμή and ἀφορμή. For nature itself does often press upon men those truths, which afterwards, when they look for somewhat beyond nature, they stumble at. For the Schools find in mere appetite to go, or move, no actual motion at all: but because some motion they must acknowledge, they call it metaphorical motion; which is but an absurd speech: for though words may be called metaphorical; bodies and motions cannot.

That which men desire, they are also said to LOVE: and to HATE those things for which they have aversion. So that desire and love are the same thing; save that by desire, we always signify the absence of the object; by love, most commonly the presence of the same. So also by aversion, we signify the absence; and by hate, the presence of the object.

Of appetites and aversions, some are born with men; as appetite of food, appetite of excretion, and exoneration, which may also and more properly be called aversions, from somewhat they feel in their bodies; and some other appetites, not many. The rest, which are appetites of particular things, proceed from experience, and trial of their effects upon themselves or other men. For of things we know not at all, or believe not to be, we can have no further desire, than to taste and try. But aversion we have for things, not only which we know have hurt us, but also that we do not know whether they will hurt us, or not.

Those things which we neither desire, nor hate, we are said to *contemn;* CON-TEMPT being nothing else but an immobility, or contumacy of the heart, in resisting the action of certain things; and proceeding from that the heart is already moved otherwise, by other more potent objects; or from want of experience of them.

And because the constitution of a man's body is in continual mutation, it is impossible that all the same things should always cause in him the same appetites, and aversions: much less can all men consent, in the desire of almost any one and the same object.

---

1. Here Hobbes makes an important statement about what "good" means.

But whatsoever is the object of any man's appetite or desire, that is it which he for his part calleth *good:* and the object of his hate and aversion, evil; and of his contempt, *vile* and *inconsiderable.* For these words of good, evil, and contemptible, are ever used with relation to the person that uses them: there being nothing simply and absolutely so; nor any common rule of good and evil, to be taken from the nature of the objects themselves; but from the person of the man, where there is no commonwealth; or, in a commonwealth, from the person that represents it; or from an arbitrator or judge, whom men disagreeing shall by consent set up, and make his sentence the rule thereof.

The Latin tongue has two words, whose significations approach to those of good and evil; but are not precisely the same; and those are *pulchrum* and *turpe.* Whereof the former signifies that, which by some apparent signs promises good; and the latter, that which promises evil. But in our tongue we have not so general names to express them by. But for *pulchrum* we say in some things, *fair;* in others, *beautiful,* or *handsome,* or *gallant,* or *honorable,* or *comely,* or *amiable;* and for *turpe, foul, deformed, ugly, base, nauseous,* and the like, as the subject shall require; all which words, in their proper places, signify nothing else but the *mien,* or countenance, that promises good and evil. So that of good there be three kinds; good in the promise, that is *pulchrum;* good in effect, as the end desired, which is called *jucundum, delightful;* and good as the means, which is called *utile, profitable;* and as many of evil: for *evil* in promise, is that they call *turpe;* evil in effect, and end, is *molestum, unpleasant, troublesome;* and evil in the means, *inutile, unprofitable, hurtful.*

As, in sense, that which is really within us, is, as I have said before, only motion, caused by the action of external objects, but in appearance; to the sight, light and color; to the ear, sound; to the nostril, odor, etc.: so, when the action of the same object is continued from the eyes, ears, and other organs to the heart, the real effect there is nothing but motion, or endeavor; which consists in appetite, or aversion, to or from the object moving. But the appearance, or sense of that motion, is that we either call *delight,* or *trouble of mind.*

This motion, which is called appetite, and for the appearance of it *delight,* and *pleasure,* seems to be a corroboration of vital motion, and a help thereunto; and therefore such things as caused delight, were not improperly called *jucunda, a juvando,* from helping or fortifying; and the contrary, *molesta, offensive,* from hindering, and troubling the motion vital.

Pleasure therefore, or *delight,* is the appearance, or sense of good; and *molestation,* or *displeasure,* the appearance, or sense of evil. And consequently all appetite, desire, and love, is accompanied with some delight more or less; and all hatred and aversion, with more or less displeasure and offense.

Of pleasures or delights, some arise from the sense of an object present; and those may be called *pleasure of sense;* the word *sensual,* as it is used by those only that condemn them, having no place till there be laws. Of this kind are all onerations and exonerations of the body; as also all that is pleasant, in the *sight, hearing, smell, taste,* or *touch.* Others arise from the expectation, that proceeds from foresight of the end, or consequence of things; whether those things in the sense please or displease. And these are *pleasures of the mind* of him that draws those consequences, and are generally called JOY. In the like manner, displeasures are some in the sense, and called PAIN; others in the expectation of consequences, and are called GRIEF.

Chapter XIII
Of the Natural Condition of Mankind as Concerning
Their Felicity, and Misery

Nature has made men so equal, in the faculties of the body, and mind; as that though there be found one man sometimes manifestly stronger in body, or of quicker mind than another; yet when all is reckoned together, the difference between man, and man, is not so considerable, as that one man can thereupon claim to himself any benefit, to which another may not pretend, as well as he. For as to the strength of body, the weakest has strength enough to kill the strongest, either by secret machination, or by confederacy with others, that are in the same danger with himself.

And as to the faculties of the mind, setting aside the arts grounded upon words, and especially that skill of proceeding upon general, and infallible rules, called science; which very few have, and but in few things; as being not a native faculty, born with us; nor attained, as prudence, while we look after somewhat else, I find yet a greater equality amongst men, than that of strength. For prudence, is but experience; which equal time, equally bestows on all men, in those things they equally apply themselves unto. That which may perhaps make such equality incredible, is but a vain conceit of one's own wisdom, which almost all men think they have in a greater degree, than the vulgar; that is, than all men but themselves, and a few others, whom by fame, or for concurring with themselves, they approve. For such is the nature of men, that howsoever they may acknowledge many others to be more witty, or more eloquent, or more learned; yet they will hardly believe there be many so wise as themselves; for they see their own wit at hand, and other men's at a distance. But this proves rather that men are in that point equal, than unequal. For there is not ordinarily a greater sign of the equal distribution of any thing, than that every man is contented with his share.

From this equality of ability, arises equality of hope in the attaining of our ends. And therefore if any two men desire the same thing, which nevertheless they cannot both enjoy, they become enemies; and in the way to their end, which is principally their own conservation, and sometimes their delectation only, endeavor to destroy, or subdue one another. And from hence it comes to pass, that where an invader has no more to fear, than another man's single power; if one plant, sow, build, or possess a convenient seat, others may probably be expected to come prepared with forces united, to dispossess, and deprive him, not only of the fruit of his labor, but also of his life, or liberty. And the invader again is in the like danger of another.

And from this diffidence of one another, there is no way for any man to secure himself, so reasonable, as anticipation; that is, by force, or wiles, to master the persons of all men he can, so long, till he see no other power great enough to endanger him: and this is no more than his own conservation requires, and is generally allowed. Also because there be some, that taking pleasure in contemplating their own power in the acts of conquest, which they pursue farther than their security requires; if others, that otherwise would be glad to be at ease within modest bounds, should not by invasion increase their power, they would not be able, long time, by standing only on their defense, to subsist. And by consequence, such augmentation of dominion over men being necessary to a man's conservation, it ought to be allowed him.

Again, men have no pleasure, but on the contrary a great deal of grief, in keeping company, where there is no power able to over-awe them all. For every man looks that his companion should value him, at the same rate he sets upon himself: and upon all signs of contempt, or undervaluing, naturally endeavors, as far as he dares, (which amongst them that have no common power to keep them in quiet, is far enough to make them destroy each other), to extort a greater value from his contemners, by damage; and from others, by the example.

---

2. Hobbes distinguishes different causes of disputes between people. Because quarreling is part of our nature, Hobbes arrives at his famous conclusion about the plight of humankind if they lack a "common power." What do you think that common power might be?

So that in the nature of man, we find three principal causes of quarrel. First, competition; second, diffidence; thirdly, glory.

The first, makes men invade for gain; the second, for safety; and the third, for reputation. The first use violence, to make themselves masters of other men's persons, wives, children, and cattle; the second, to defend them; the third, for trifles, as a word, a smile, a different opinion, and any other sign of undervalue, either direct in their persons, or by reflection in their kindred, their friends, their nation, their profession, or their name.

Hereby it is manifest, that during the time men live without a common power to keep them all in awe, they are in that condition which is called war; and such a war, as is of every man, against every man. For WAR, consists not in battle only, or the act of fighting; but in a tract of time, wherein the will to contend by battle is sufficiently known: and therefore the notion of *time,* is to be considered in the nature of war; as it is in the nature of weather. For as the nature of foul weather, lies not in a shower or two of rain; but in an inclination thereto of many days together: so the nature of war, consists not in actual fighting; but in the known disposition thereto, during all the time there is no assurance to the contrary. All other time is PEACE.

Whatsoever therefore is consequent to a time of war, where every man is enemy to every man; the same is consequent to the time, wherein men live without other security, than what their own strength, and their own invention shall furnish them withal. In such condition, there is no place for industry; because the fruit thereof is uncertain: and consequently no culture of the earth; no navigation, nor use of the commodities that may be imported by sea; no commodious building; no instruments of moving, and removing, such things as require much force; no knowledge of the face of the earth; no account of time; no arts; no letters; no society; and which is worst of all, continual fear, and danger of violent death; and the life of man, solitary, poor, nasty, brutish, and short.

It may seem strange to some man, that has not well weighed these things; that nature should thus dissociate, and render men apt to invade, and destroy one another: and he may therefore, not trusting to this inference, made from the passions, desire perhaps to have the same confirmed by experience. Let him therefore consider with himself, when taking a journey, he arms himself, and seeks to go well accompanied; when going to sleep, he locks his doors; when even in his house he locks his chests; and this when he knows there be laws, and public officers, armed, to revenge all injuries shall be done him; what opinion he has of his fellow-subjects, when he rides armed; of his fellow citizens, when he locks his doors; and of his children, and servants, when he locks his chests. Does he not there as much accuse mankind by his actions, as I do by my words? But neither of us accuse man's nature in it. The desires, and other passions of man, are in themselves no sin. No more are the actions, that proceed from those passions, till they know a law that forbids them: which till laws be made they cannot know: nor can any law be made, till they have agreed upon the person that shall make it.

It may peradventure be thought, there was never such a time, nor condition of war as this; and I believe it was never generally so, over all the world: but there are many places, where they live so now. For the savage people in many places of America, except the government of small families, the concord whereof depends on natural lust, have no government at all; and live at this day in that brutish manner, as I said before. Howsoever, it may be perceived what manner of life there would be, where there were no common power to fear, by the manner of life, which men that have formerly lived under a peaceful government, use to degenerate into, in a civil war.

But though there had never been any time, wherein particular men were in a condition of war one against another; yet in all times, kings, and persons of sovereign authority, because of their independency, are in continual jealousies, and in the state and posture of gladiators; having their weapons pointing, and their eyes fixed on one another; that is, their forts, garrisons, and guns upon the frontiers of their kingdoms; and continual spies upon their neighbors; which is a posture of war. But because they uphold thereby, the industry of their subjects; there does not follow from it, that misery, which accompanies the liberty of particular men.

---

3. With war of all against all the natural state of humankind, Hobbes draws important conclusions about the relationship of a "common power" and morality. What is the origin of morality according to Hobbes?

To this war of every man, against every man, this also is consequent; that nothing can be unjust. The notions of right and wrong, justice and injustice have there no place. Where there is no common power, there is no law: where no law, no injustice. Force, and fraud, are in war the two cardinal virtues. Justice, and injustice are none of the faculties neither of the body, nor mind. If they were, they might be in a man that were alone in the world, as well as his senses, and passions. They are qualities, that relate to men in society, not in solitude. It is consequent also to the same condition, that there be no propriety, no dominion, no *mine* and *thine* distinct; but only that to be every man's, that he can get; and for so long, as he can keep it. And thus much for the ill condition, which man by mere nature is actually placed in; though with a possibility to come out of it, consisting partly in the passions, partly in his reason.

The passions that incline men to peace, are fear of death; desire of such things as are necessary to commodious living; and a hope by their industry to obtain them. And reason suggests convenient articles of peace, upon which men may be drawn to agreement. These articles, are they, which otherwise are called the Laws of Nature: whereof I shall speak more particularly, in the two following chapters.

Chapter XIV
Of the First and Second Natural Laws, and of Contracts

The RIGHT OF NATURE, which writers commonly call *jus naturale,* is the liberty each man has, to use his own power, as he will himself, for the preservation of his own nature; that is to say, of his own life; and consequently, of doing anything, which in his own judgment, and reason, he shall conceive to be the aptest means thereunto.

By LIBERTY, is understood, according to the proper signification of the word, the absence of external impediments: which impediments, may oft take away part of a man's power to do what he would; but cannot hinder him from using the power left him, according as his judgment, and reason shall dictate to him.

A LAW OF NATURE, *lex naturalis,* is a precept or general rule, found out by reason, by which a man is forbidden to do that, which is destructive of his life, or takes away the means of preserving the same; and to omit that, by which he thinks it may be best preserved. For though they that speak of this subject, use to confound *jus,* and *lex,* *right* and *law:* yet they ought to be distinguished; because RIGHT, consists in liberty to do, or to forbear; whereas LAW, determines, and binds to one of them: so that law, and right, differ as much, as obligation, and liberty; which in one and the same matter are inconsistent.

And because the condition of man, as has been declared in the precedent chapter, is a condition of war of every one against every one; in which case every one is governed by his own reason; and there is nothing he can make use of, that may not be a help unto him, in preserving his life against his enemies; it follows, that in such a condition, every man has a right to every thing; even to one another's body. And therefore, as long as this natural right of every man to every thing endures, there can be no security to any man, how strong or wise so ever he be, of living out the time, which nature ordinarily allows men to live. And consequently it is a precept, or general rule of reason, *that every man, ought to endeavor peace, as far as he has hope of obtaining it; and when he cannot obtain it, that he may seek, and use, all helps, and advantages of war.* The first branch of which rule, contains the first, and fundamental law of nature; which is, *to seek peace, and follow it.* The second, the sum of the right of nature; which is, *by all means we can, to defend ourselves.*

From this fundamental law of nature, by which men are commanded to endeavor peace, is derived this second law; *that a man be willing, when others are so too, as far forth, as for peace, and defense of himself he shall think it necessary, to lay down this right to all things; and be contented with so much liberty against other men, as he would allow other men against himself.* For as long as every man holds this right, of doing any thing he likes; so long are all men in the condition of war. But if other men will not lay down their right, as well as he; then there is no reason for anyone, to divest himself of his: for that were to expose himself to prey, which no man is bound to, rather than to dispose himself to peace. This is that law of the Gospel; *whatsoever you require that others should do to you, that do ye to them.* And that law of all men, *quod tibi fieri non vis, alteri ne feceris.*

---

4. Taking as his starting point that, in a state of war, each person has the right to everything, rights can only be given up voluntarily. Why would a person give up a right? What does he call the action of a person voluntarily giving up his or her right to something?

To *lay down* a man's *right* to any thing, is to *divest* himself of the *liberty,* of hindering another of the benefit of his own right to the same. For he that renounces, or passes away his right, gives not to any other man a right which he had not before; because there is nothing to which every man had not right by nature: but only stands out of his way, that he may enjoy his own original right, without hindrance from him; not without hindrance from another. So that the effect which redounds to one man, by another man's defect of right, is but so much diminution of impediments to the use of his own right original.

Right is laid aside, either by simply renouncing it; or by transferring it to another. By *simply* RENOUNCING; when he cares not to whom the benefit thereof redounds. By TRANSFERRING; when he intends the benefit thereof to some certain person, or persons. And when a man has in either manner abandoned, or granted away his right; then is he said to be OBLIGED, or BOUND, not to hinder those, to whom such right is granted, or abandoned, from the benefit of it: and that he *ought,* and it is his DUTY, not to make void that voluntary act of his own: and that such hindrance is INJUSTICE, and INJURY, as being *sine jure;* the right being before renounced, or transferred. So that *injury,* or *injustice,* in the controversies of the world, is somewhat like to that, which in the disputations of scholars is called *absurdity.* For as it is there called an absurdity, to contradict what one maintained in the beginning: so in the world, it is called injustice, and injury, voluntarily to undo that, which from the beginning he had voluntarily done. The way by which a man either simply renounces, or transfers his right, is a declaration, or signification, by some voluntary and sufficient sign, or signs, that he does so renounce, or transfer; or has so renounced, or transferred the same, to him that accepts it. And these signs are either words only, or actions only; or, as it happens most often, both words, and actions. And the same are the BONDS, by which men are bound, and obliged: bonds, that have their strength, not from their own nature, for nothing is more easily broken than a man's word, but from fear of some evil consequence upon the rupture.

Whensoever a man transfers his right, or renounces it; it is either in consideration of some right reciprocally transferred to himself; or for some other good he hopes for thereby. For it is a voluntary act: and of the voluntary acts of every man, the object is some *good to himself.* And therefore there be some rights, which no man can be understood by any words, or other signs, to have abandoned, or transferred. As first a man cannot lay down the right of resisting them, that assault him by force, to take away his life; because he cannot be understood to aim thereby, at any good to himself. The same may be said of wounds, and chains, and imprisonment; both because there is no benefit consequent to such patience; as there is to the patience of suffering another to be wounded, or imprisoned: as also because a man cannot tell, when he sees men proceed against him by violence, whether they intend his death or not. And lastly the motive, and end for which this renouncing, and transferring of right is introduced, is nothing else but the security of a man's person, in his life, and in the means of so preserving life, as not to be weary of it. And therefore if a man by words, or other signs, seem to despoil himself of the end, for which those signs were intended; he is not to be understood as if he meant it, or that it was his will; but that he was ignorant of how such words and actions were to be interpreted.

The mutual transferring of right, is that which men call CONTRACT.

Chapter XV
Of Other Laws of Nature

From that law of nature, by which we are obliged to transfer to another, such rights, as being retained, hinder the peace of mankind, there follows a third; which is this, *that men perform their covenants made:* without which, covenants are in vain, and but empty words; and the right of all men to all things remaining, we are still in the condition of war.

And in this law of nature, consists the fountain and original of JUSTICE. For where no covenant has preceded, there has no right being transferred, and every man has right to every thing; and consequently, no action can be unjust. But when a covenant is made, then to break it is *unjust:* and the definition of INJUSTICE, is no other than *the not performance of covenant.* And whatsoever is not unjust, is *just.*

But because covenants of mutual trust, where there is a fear of not performance on either part, as has been said in the former chapter, are invalid; though the original of justice be the making of covenants; yet injustice actually there can be none, till the cause of such fear be taken away; which while men are in the natural condition of war, cannot be done. Therefore before the names of just, and unjust can have place, there must be some coercive power, to compel men equally to the performance of their covenants, by the terror of some punishment, greater than the benefit they expect by the breach of their covenant; and to make good that propriety, which by mutual contract men acquire, in recompense of the universal right they abandon: and such power there is none before the erection of a commonwealth. And this is also to be gathered out of the ordinary definition of justice in the Schools: for they say, that *justice is the constant will of giving to every man his own.* And therefore where there is no *own,* that is no propriety, there is no injustice; and where is no coercive power erected, that is, where there is no commonwealth, there is no propriety; all men having right to all things: therefore where there is no commonwealth, there nothing is unjust. So that the nature of justice, consists in keeping of valid covenants: but the validity of covenants begins not but with the constitution of a civil power, sufficient to compel men to keep them: and then it is also that propriety begins.

The fool has said in his heart, there is no such thing as justice; and sometimes also with his tongue; seriously alleging, that every man's conservation, and contentment, being committed to his own care, there could be no reason, why every man might not do what he thought conduced thereunto: and therefore also to make, or not make; keep, or not keep covenants, was not against reason, when it conduced to one's benefit. He does not therein deny, that there be covenants; and that they are sometimes broken, sometimes kept; and that such breach of them may be called injustice, and the observance of them justice: but he questions, whether injustice, taking away the fear of God, for the same fool has said in his heart there is no God, may not sometimes stand with that reason, which dictates to every man his own good; and particularly then, when it conduces to such a benefit, as shall put a man in a condition, to neglect not only the dispraise, and revilings, but also the power of other men. The kingdom of God is gotten by violence: but what if it could be gotten by unjust violence? were it against reason so to get it, when it is impossible to receive hurt by it? and if it be not against reason, it is not against justice; or else justice is not to be approved for good. From such reasoning as this, successful wickedness has obtained the name of virtue: and some that in all other things have disallowed the violation of faith; yet have allowed it, when it is for the getting of a kingdom. And the heathen that believed, that Saturn was deposed by his son Jupiter, believed nevertheless the same Jupiter to be the avenger of injustice: somewhat like to a piece of law in Coke's *Commentaries on Littleton;* where he says, if the right heir of the crown be attainted of treason; yet the crown shall descend to him, and *eo instante* the attainder be void: from which instances a man will be very prone to infer; that when the heir apparent of a kingdom, shall kill him that is in possession, though his father; you may call it injustice, or by what other name you will; yet it can never be against reason, seeing all the voluntary actions of men tend to the benefit of themselves; and those actions are most reasonable, that conduce most to their ends. This specious reasoning is nevertheless false.

----

5. Here Hobbes argues for the reasonableness of keeping covenants. Notice how alone a person is who breaks a covenant.

For the question is not of promises mutual, where there is no security of performance on either side; as when there is no civil power erected over the parties promising; for such promises are no covenants: but either where one of the parties has performed already; or where there is a power to make him perform; there is the question whether it be against reason, that is, against the benefit of the other to perform, or not. And I say it is not against reason. For the manifestation whereof, we are to consider; first, that when a man does a thing, which notwithstanding anything can be foreseen, and reckoned on, tends to his own destruction, howsoever some accident which he could not expect, arriving may turn it to his benefit; yet such events do not make it reasonably or wisely done. Secondly, that in a condition of war, wherein every man to every man, for want of a common power to keep them all in awe, is an enemy, there is no man who can hope by his own strength, or wit, to defend himself from destruction, without the help of confederates; where everyone expects the same defense by the confederation, that any one else does: and therefore he which declares he thinks it reason to deceive those that help him, can in reason expect no other means of safety, than what can be had from his own single power. He therefore that breaks his covenant, and consequently declares that he thinks he may with reason do so, cannot be received into any society, that unite themselves for peace and defense, but by the error of them that receive him; nor when he is received, be retained in it, without seeing the danger of their error; which errors a man cannot reasonably reckon upon as the means of his security: and therefore if he be left, or cast out of society, he perishes; and if he live in society, it is by the errors of other men, which he could not foresee, nor reckon upon; and consequently against the reason of his preservation; and so, as all men that contribute not to his destruction, forbear him only out of ignorance of what is good for themselves.

As for the instance of gaining the secure and perpetual felicity of heaven, by any way; it is frivolous: there being but one way imaginable; and that is not breaking, but keeping of covenant.

And for the other instance of attaining sovereignty by rebellion; it is manifest, that though the event follow, yet because it cannot reasonably be expected, but rather the contrary; and because by gaining it so, others are taught to gain the same in like manner, the attempt thereof is against reason. Justice therefore, that is to say, keeping of covenant, is a rule of reason, by which we are forbidden to do any thing destructive to our life; and consequently a law of nature.

There be some that proceed further; and will not have the law of nature, to be those rules which conduce to the preservation of man's life on earth; but to the attaining of an eternal felicity after death; to which they think the breach of covenant may conduce; and consequently be just and reasonable; such are they that think it a work of merit to kill, or depose, or rebel against, the sovereign power constituted over them by their own consent. But because there is no natural knowledge of man's estate after death; much less of the reward that is then to be given to breach of faith; but only a belief grounded upon other men's saying, that they know it supernaturally, or that they know those, that knew them, that knew others, that knew it supernaturally; breach of faith cannot be called a precept of reason, or nature.

Others, that allow for a law of nature, the keeping of faith, do nevertheless make exception of certain persons; as heretics, and such as use not to perform their covenant to others: and this also is against reason. For if any fault of a man, be sufficient to discharge our covenant made; the same ought in reason to have been sufficient to have hindered the making of it.

The names of just, and unjust, when they are attributed to men, signify one thing; and when they are attributed to actions, another. When they are attributed to men, they signify conformity, or inconformity of manners, to reason. But when they are attributed to actions, they signify the conformity, or inconformity to reason, not of manners, or manner of life, but of particular actions. A just man therefore, is he that takes all the care he can, that his actions may be all just: and an unjust man, is he that neglects it. And such men are more often in our language styled by the names of righteous, and unrighteous; than just, and unjust; though the meaning be the same. Therefore a righteous man, does not lose that title, by one, or a few unjust actions, that proceed from sudden passion, or mistake of things, or persons: nor does an unrighteous man, lose his character, for such actions, as he does, or forbears to do, for fear: because his will is not framed by the justice, but by the apparent benefit of what he is to do. That which gives to human actions the relish of justice, is a certain nobleness or gallantness of courage, rarely found, by which a man scorns to be beholden for the contentment of his life, to fraud, or breach of promise. This justice of the manners, is that which is meant, where justice is called a virtue; and injustice a vice.

But the justice of actions denominates men, not just, but *guiltless;* and the injustice of the same, which is also called injury, gives them but the name of *guilty.*

Again, the injustice of manners, is the disposition, or aptitude to do injury; and is injustice before it proceed to act; and without supposing any individual person injured. But the injustice of an action, that is to say injury, supposes an individual person injured; namely him, to whom the covenant was made: and therefore many times the injury is received by one man, when the damage redounds to another. As when the master commands his servant to give money to a stranger; if it be not done, the injury is done to the master, whom he had before covenanted to obey; but the damage redounds to the stranger, to whom he had no obligation; and therefore could not injure him. And so also in commonwealths, private men may remit to one another their debts; but not robberies or other violences, whereby they are endamaged; because the detaining of debt, is an injury to themselves; but robbery and violence, are injuries to the person of the commonwealth.

Whatsoever is done to a man, conformable to his own will signified to the doer, is no injury to him. For if he that does it, has not passed away his original right to do what he please, by some antecedent covenant, there is no breach of covenant; and therefore no injury done him. And if he have: then his will to have it done being signified, is a release of that covenant: and so again there is no injury done him.

Justice of actions, is by writers divided into *commutative,* and *distributive:* and the former they say consists in proportion arithmetical; the latter in proportion geometrical. Commutative therefore, they place in the equality of value of the things contracted for; and distributive, in the distribution of equal benefit, to men of equal merit. As if it were injustice to sell dearer than we buy; or to give more to a man than he merits. The value of all things contracted for, is measured by the appetite of the contractors: and therefore the just value, is that which they be contented to give. And merit, besides that which is by covenant, where the performance on one part, merits the performance of the other part, and falls under justice commutative, not distributive, is not due by justice; but is rewarded of grace only. And therefore this distinction, in the sense wherein it uses to be expounded, is not right. To speak properly, commutative justice, is the justice, of a contractor; that is, a performance of covenant, in buying, and selling; hiring, and letting to hire; lending, and borrowing; exchanging, bartering, and other acts of contract.

And distributive justice, the justice of an arbitrator; that is to say, the act of defining what is just. Wherein, being trusted by them that make him arbitrator, if he perform his trust, he is said to distribute to every man his own: and this is indeed just distribution, and may be called, though improperly, distributive justice; but more properly equity; which also is a law of nature, as shall be shown in due place.

As justice depends on antecedent covenant; so does GRATITUDE depend on antecedent grace; that is to say, antecedent free gift: and is the fourth law of nature; which may be conceived in this form, *that a man which receives benefit from another of mere grace, endeavor that he which gives it, have no reasonable cause to repent him of his good will.* For no man gives, but with intention of good to himself; because gift is voluntary; and of all voluntary acts, the object is to every man his own good; of which if men see they shall be frustrated, there will be no beginning of benevolence, or trust; nor consequently of mutual help; nor of reconciliation of one man to another; and therefore they are to remain still in the condition of *war;* which is contrary to the first and fundamental law of nature, which commands men to *seek peace.* The breach of this law, is called *ingratitude;* and has the same relation to grace, that injustice has to obligation by covenant.

A fifth law of nature, is COMPLAISANCE; that is to say, *that every man strive to accommodate himself to the rest.* For the understanding whereof, we may consider, that there is in men's aptness to society, a diversity of nature, rising from their diversity of affections; not unlike to that we see in stones brought together for building of an edifice. For as that stone which by the asperity, and irregularity of figure, takes more room from others, than itself fills; and for the hardness, cannot be easily made plain, and thereby hinders the building, is by the builders cast away as unprofitable, and troublesome: so also, a man that by asperity of nature, will strive to retain those things which to himself are superfluous, and to others necessary; and for the stubbornness of his passions, cannot be corrected, is to be left, or cast out of society, as cumbersome thereunto. For seeing every man, not only by right, but also by necessity of nature, is supposed to endeavor all he can, to obtain that which is necessary for his conservation; he that shall oppose himself against it, for things superfluous, is guilty of the war that thereupon is to follow; and therefore does that, which is contrary to the fundamental law of nature, which commands *to seek peace.* The observers of this law, may be called SOCIABLE, the Latins call them *commodi;* the contrary, *stubborn, insociable, froward, intractable.*

A sixth law of nature, is this, *that upon caution of the future time, a man ought to pardon the offenses past of them that repenting, desire it.* For PARDON, is nothing but granting of peace; which though granted to them that persevere in their hostility, be not peace, but fear; yet not granted to them that give caution of the future time, is sign of an aversion to peace; and therefore contrary to the law of nature.

A seventh is, *that in revenges,* that is, retribution of evil for evil, *men look not at the greatness of the evil past, but the greatness of the good to follow.* Whereby we are forbidden to inflict punishment with any other design, than for correction of the offender, or direction of others. For this law is consequent to the next before it, that commands pardon, upon security of the future time. Besides, revenge without respect to the example, and profit to come, is a triumph, or glorying in the hurt of another, tending to no end; for the end is always somewhat to come; and glorying to no end, is vainglory, and contrary to reason, and to hurt without reason, tends to the introduction of war; which is against the law of nature; and is commonly styled by the name of *cruelty*.

READING QUESTIONS

1. What do appetite and aversion have in common? How do they differ?
2. What are the two sources of human appetites?
3. What reason does Hobbes give for people becoming enemies of one another?
4. Hobbes gives an analogy between the nature of war and the nature of weather with regard to time. What is the analogy?
5. According to Hobbes, what is the relation of law and justice?
6. What reasons does Hobbes give for declaring that people have the right to everything, "even to one another's body"?
7. What does justice have to do with contracts or covenants?

Mary Astell

A typical list of historically prominent Western moral philosophers would consist entirely of males. The impression this leaves is that either women were not interested in ethics or they did not write and publish philosophy equal in value to that of men. Although the value of the writings by women authors may remain a matter of contention, it certainly is false that no women were interested in moral philosophy. In the past, a number of women have published philosophical work, although not a great deal of it has survived the years. One of the main reasons for the scarcity of philosophy written by women is the denial of education to women, a subject of intense interest to Mary Astell.

Mary Astell (1666–1731) has been called the first English feminist. In an age when women were expected either to be married or about to be married, when an intelligent woman was treated with the same scorn as a spinster, Mary Astell was both unmarried and educated. It is hard to imagine the immense personal courage required for her to act so contrary to her entire society.

The person deemed responsible for her education was her uncle, who is believed to have instructed her in philosophy, mathematics, logic, and French (and possibly Latin). She read widely on her own without the advantage of a formal education. However, the lack of formal schooling did not prevent her from entering into debates with many well-known figures of her day concerning a variety of political, philosophical, and theological issues. Evidence of her interest in philosophical issues exists in the form of letters, which were later published, that she exchanged with John Norris, one of the last philosophers aligned with the Cambridge Platonist school of philosophy. In her day she was both widely admired and widely criticized. Most of all, she was widely read.

She is best known today as a powerful and passionate champion for women's education. Although she wrote and published poetry, political tracts, pamphlets, and letters, her most influential writings were her two books. The first, published in 1694, called *A Serious Proposal to the Ladies,* ran through four editions by 1701. In 1697 a second part was added to the work. (This offered a "Religious Retirement" where women could temporarily withdraw from the world for spiritual renewal.) Her second book, *Some Reflections upon Marriage,* appeared in 1700 and ran through four editions by 1730. People may have differed in their opinions toward her ideas—she had numerous supporters as well as critics—but we can see by the numerous editions of these books that great numbers read her work.

A Serious Proposal to the Ladies

Most of you who are taking a class in ethics probably believe that education, in general, is good. People with an education are more likely to get good jobs doing interesting work and making good money. In this sense,

From Mary Astell, *A Serious Proposal to the Ladies,* Fourth Edition, London, 1701.

an education has practical benefit. Also, most of you probably believe that people educated in a particular subject such as medicine, architecture, or carpentry have more skills in that department than people who are not educated. Again, the benefit of education is practical. But is education important for your life in any other way? Perhaps you think that educated people lead more fulfilling, happier lives. But have you ever considered educated people to be more moral than uneducated people?

In this selection, Mary Astell addresses the relation between knowledge and virtue as it pertains to women. If you can, imagine a time when females were taught that being beautiful was more important than being wise or good. Now suppose that these same people were criticized because they were preoccupied with appearance, vain about their looks, ignorant about practical matters, and generally bad people. In this selection, Mary Astell directs the reader's attention to the connection between women's ignorance and women's vices.

---

1. Astell begins this book by attempting to persuade the reader that what follows will be in her best interest. Notice that the thrust of the argument is to downplay outward beauty and focus instead on inward beauty. Do you think that this same kind of argument would be applicable to men?

Ladies,

Since the profitable adventures that have gone abroad in the world have met with so great encouragement, though the highest advantage they can propose, is an uncertain lot for such matters as opinion, not real worth, gives a value to; things which if obtained are as flitting and fickle as that chance which is to dispose of them; I therefore persuade myself, you will not be less kind to a proposition that comes attended with more certain and substantial gain; whose only design is to improve your charms and heighten your value, by suffering you no longer to be cheap and contemptible. Its aim is to fix that beauty, to make it lasting and permanent, which nature with all the helps of art cannot secure, and to place it out of the reach of sickness and old age, by transferring it from a corruptible body to an immortal mind. An obliging design, which would procure them *inward* beauty, to whom nature has unkindly denied the *outward,* and not permit those ladies who have comely bodies, to tarnish their glory with deformed souls. Would have you all be wits, or what is better, wise. Raise you above the vulgar by something more truly illustrious, than a sounding title or a great estate. Would excite in you a generous emulation to excel in the best things, and not in such trifles as every mean person who has but money enough may purchase as well as you. Not suffer you to take up with the low thought of distinguishing yourselves by anything that is not truly valuable, and procure you such ornaments as all the treasures of the Indies are not able to purchase. Would help you to surpass the men as much in virtue and ingenuity, as you do in beauty, that you may not only be as lovely, but as wise as angels. Exalt and establish your fame, more than the best wrought poems and loudest panegyrics, by ennobling your minds with such graces as really deserve it. And instead of the fustian compliments and fulsome flatteries of your admirers, obtain for you the plaudit of good men and angels, and the approbation of Him who cannot err. In a word, render you the glory and blessing of the present age, and the admiration and pattern of the next. And sure, I shall not need many words to persuade you to close with this proposal. The very offer is a sufficient inducement, nor does it need the set-offs of rhetoric to recommend it, were I capable, which yet I am not, of applying them with the greatest force. Since you can't be so unkind to yourselves, as to refuse you *real* interest, I only entreat you to be so wise as to examine wherein it consists; for nothing is of worse consequence than to be deceived in a matter of so great concern. It is as little beneath your grandeur as your prudence, to examine curiously what is in this case offered you, and to take care that cheating hucksters don't impose upon you with deceitful ware. This is a matter infinitely more worthy your debates, than what colors are most agreeable, or what's the dress becomes you best. Your glass will not do you half so much service as a serious reflection on your own minds, which will discover irregularities more worthy your correction, and keep you from being either too much elated or depressed by the representations of the other. It will not be near so advantageous to consult with your dancing master as with your own thoughts, how you may with greatest exactness tread in the paths of virtue, which has certainly the most attractive *air,* and wisdom the most graceful and becoming *mien:* Let these attend you, and your carriage will be always well composed, and every thing you do will carry its charm with it. No solicitude in the adornation of yourselves is discommended, provided you employ your care about that which is really your *self,* and do not neglect that particle of divinity within you, which must survive, and may (if you please) be happy and perfect, when its unsuitable and much inferior companion is mouldering into dust. Neither will any pleasure be denied you, who are only desired not to catch at the shadow and let the substance go. You may be as ambitious as you please, so you aspire to the best things, and contend with your neighbors as much as you can, that they may not outdo you in any commendable quality. Let it never be said, that they to whom pre-eminence is so very agreeable, can be tamely content that others should surpass them in *this,* and precede them in a *better* world! Remember, I pray you, the famous women of former Ages, the Orinda's of late, and the more modern heroines, and blush to think how much is now, and will hereafter be said of them, when you yourselves (as great a figure as you make) must be buried in silence and forgetfulness! Shall your emulation fail *there only* where it is commendable? Why are you so preposterously humble, as not to contend for one of the highest mansions in the court of heaven? Believe me, ladies, this is the only *place* worth contending for, you are neither better nor worse in yourselves for going before, or coming after *now,* but you are really so much the better, by how much the higher your station is in an orb of glory. How can you be content to be in the world like tulips in a garden, to make a fine *show* and be good for nothing; have all your glories set in the grave, or perhaps much sooner! What your own sentiments are I know not, but I can't without pity and resentment reflect, that those glorious temples on which your kind Creator has bestowed such exquisite workmanship, should enshrine no better than Egyptian deities; be like a garnished sepulchre, which for all its glittering, has nothing within but emptiness or putrefaction! What a pity it is, that whilst your beauty casts a luster all around you, your souls which are infinitely more bright and radiant, (of which if you had but a clear idea, as lovely as it is, and as much as you now value it, you would then despise and neglect the mean *case* that encloses it) should be suffered to over-run with weeds, lie fallow and neglected, unadorned with any grace! Although the beauty of the mind is necessary to secure those conquests which your eyes have gained, and time that mortal enemy to handsome faces, has no influence on a lovely soul, but to better and improve it. For shame let's abandon that *old,* and therefore one would think, unfashionable employment of pursuing butter-flies and trifles! No longer drudge on in the dull beaten road of vanity and folly which so many have gone before us, but dare to break the enchanted circle that custom has placed us in, and scorn the vulgar way of imitating all the impertinencies of our neigh-bors. Let us learn to pride ourselves in something more excellent than the invention of a fashion, and not entertain such a degrading thought of our own worth, as to imag-ine that our souls were given us only for the service of our bodies, and that the best improvement we can make of these, is to attract the eyes of men. We value *them* too much, and *ourselves* too little, if we place any part of our desert in their opinion, and don't think ourselves capable of nobler things than the pitiful conquest of some worth-less heart. She who has opportunities of making an interest in heaven, of obtaining the love and admiration of God and angels, is too prodigal of her time, and injurious to her charms, to throw them away on vain insignificant men. She need not make herself so cheap as to descend to court their applauses, for at the greater distance she keeps, and the more she is above them, the more effectually she secures their esteem and won-der. Be so generous then, ladies, as to do nothing unworthy of you; so true to your in-terest, as not to lessen your empire and depreciate your charms. Let not your thoughts be wholly busied in observing what respect is paid you, but a part of them at least, in studying to deserve it. And after all, remember that goodness is the truest greatness; to be wise for yourselves the greatest wit; and *that* beauty the most desirable which will endure to eternity.

---

2. Astell wants to make clear that she does not intend to blame women for their attention to physical beauty, but instead endeavors to rescue them from their dependence upon the opinions of men.

Pardon me the seeming rudeness of this proposal, which goes upon a supposition that there's something amiss in you, which it is intended to amend. My design is not to expose, but to rectify your failures. To be exempt from mistake, is a privilege few can pretend to, the greatest is to be past conviction and too obstinate to reform. Even the men, as exact as they would seem, and as much as they divert themselves with our miscarriages, are very often guilty of greater faults, and such, as considering the ad-vantages they enjoy, are much more inexcusable. But I will not pretend to correct their errors, who either are, or at least *think* themselves too wise to receive instruction from a woman's pen. My earnest desire is, that you ladies, would be as perfect and happy as it is possible to be in this imperfect state; for I love you too well to endure a spot upon your beauties, if I can be any means remove and wipe it off. I would have you live up to the dignity of your nature, and express your thankfulness to God for the benefits you enjoy by a due improvement of them: As I know very many of you do, who countenance that piety which the men decry, and are the brightest patterns of re-ligion that the age affords, it is my grief that all the rest of our sex do not imitate such illustrious examples, and therefore I would have them increased and rendered more conspicuous, that vice being put out of countenance, (because virtue is the only thing in fashion) may sneak out of the world, and its darkness be dispelled by the confluence of so many shining graces. The men perhaps will cry out that I teach you false doctrine, for because by their deductions some amongst us are become very mean and contemptible, they would fain persuade the rest to be as despicable and forlorn as they. We're indeed obliged to them for their management, in endeavoring to make us so, who use all the artifice they can to spoil, and deny us the means of improvement. So that instead of inquiring why all women are not wise and good, we have reason to wonder that there are any so. Were the men as much neglected, and as little care taken to cultivate and improve them, perhaps they would be so far from surpassing those whom they now despise, that they themselves would sink into the greatest stupidity and brutality. The preposterous returns that the most of them make, to all the care and pains that is bestowed on them, renders this no uncharitable, nor improbable conjecture. One would therefore almost think, that the wise disposer of all things, foreseeing how unjustly women are denied opportunities of improvement from *without*, has therefore by way of compensation endowed them with greater propensities to virtue and a natural goodness of temper *within*, which if duly managed would raise them to the most eminent pitch of heroic virtue. Hither, ladies, I desire you would aspire, it is a noble and becoming ambition, and to remove such obstacles as lie in your way is the design of this paper. We will therefore inquire what it is that stops your flight, that keeps you groveling here below, like Domitian catching flies when you should be busied in obtaining empires.

Although it has been said by men of more wit than wisdom, and perhaps of more malice than either, that women are naturally incapable of acting prudently, or that they are necessarily determined to folly, I must by no means grant it; that hypothesis would render my endeavors impertinent, for then it would be in vain to advise the one, or endeavor the reformation of the other. Besides, there are examples in all ages, which sufficiently confute the ignorance and malice of this assertion.

The incapacity, if there be any, is acquired not natural, and none of their follies are so necessary, but that they might avoid them if they pleased themselves. Some disadvantages indeed they labor under, and what these are we shall see by and by and endeavor to surmount; but women need not take up with mean things, since (if they are not wanting to themselves) they are capable of the best. Neither God nor nature has excluded them from being ornaments to their families and useful in their generation; there is therefore no reason they should be content to be ciphers in the world, useless at the best, and in a little time a burden and nuisance to all about them. And it is a very great pity that they who are so apt to overrate themselves in smaller matters, should, where it most concerns them to know and stand upon their value, be so insensible of their own worth. The cause therefore of the defects we labor under is, if not wholly, yet at least in the first place, to be ascribed to the mistakes of our education, which like an error in the first concoction, spreads its ill influence through all our lives.

The soil is rich and would if well cultivated produce a noble harvest, if then the unskillful managers, not only permit, but encourage noxious weeds, though we shall suffer by the neglect, yet they ought not in justice to blame any but themselves, if they reap the fruit of this their foolish conduct. Women are from their very infancy debarred those advantages, with the want of which they are afterwards reproached, and nursed up in those vices which will hereafter be upbraided to them. So partial are men as to expect brick where they afford no straw; and so abundantly civil as to take care we should make good that obliging epithet of *ignorant,* which out of an excess of good manners, they are pleased to bestow on us!

———————

3. Education is of supreme importance for women as well as men. Why is it in the interests of the parents to educate all children, girls as well as boys?

———————

One would be apt to think indeed, that parents should take all possible care of their children's education, not only for *their* sakes, but even for their *own.* And though the son convey the name to posterity, yet certainly a great part of the honor of their families depends on their daughters. It is the kindness of education that binds our duty fastest on us: For the being instrumental to the bringing of us into the world, is no matter of choice and therefore the less obliging; But to procure that we may live wisely and happily in it, and be capable of endless joys hereafter, is a benefit we can never sufficiently acknowledge. To introduce poor children into the world and neglect to fence them against the temptations of it, and so leave them exposed to temporal and eternal miseries, is a wickedness for which I want a name; it is beneath brutality; the beasts are better natured, for they take care of their offspring, till they are capable of caring for themselves. And if mothers had a due regard to their posterity, how *great* soever they are, they would not think themselves too *good* to perform what nature requires, nor through pride and delicacy remit the poor little one to the care of a foster parent. Or if necessity enforce them to depute another to perform *their* duty, they would be as choice at least, in the manners and inclinations, as they are in the complexions of their nurses, lest with their milk they transfuse their vices, and form in the child such evil habits as will not easily be eradicated.

Nature as bad as it is and as much as it is complained of, is so far improvable by the grace of God, upon our honest and hearty endeavors, that if we are not wanting to ourselves, we may all in *some,* though not in an *equal* measure, be instruments of his glory, blessings to this world, and capable of eternal blessedness in that to come. But if our nature is spoiled, instead of being improved, at first; if from our infancy we are nursed up in ignorance and vanity; are taught to be proud and petulant, delicate and fantastic, humorous and inconstant, it is not strange that the ill effects of this conduct appear in all the future actions of our lives. And seeing it is ignorance, either habitual or actual, which is the cause of all sin, how are they like to escape *this,* who are bred up in *that?* That therefore women are unprofitable to most, and a plague and dishonor to some men is not much to be regretted on account of the *men,* because it is the product of their own folly, in denying them the benefits of an ingenuous and liberal education, the most effectual means to direct them into, and to secure their progress in the ways of virtue.

For that ignorance is the cause of most feminine vices, may be instanced in that pride and vanity which is usually imputed to us, and which I suppose if thoroughly sifted, will appear to be some way or other, the rise and original of all the rest. These, though very bad weeds, are the product of a good soil, they are nothing else but generosity degenerated and corrupted. A desire to advance and perfect its being, is planted by God in all rational natures, to excite them hereby to every worthy and becoming action; for certainly next to the grace of God, nothing does so powerfully restrain people from evil and stir them up to good, as a generous temper. And therefore to be ambitious of perfections is no fault, though to assume the glory of our excellencies to ourselves, or to glory in such as we really have not, are. And were women's haughtiness expressed in disdaining to do a mean and evil thing, would they pride themselves in somewhat truly perfective of a rational nature, there were no hurt in it. But then they ought not to be denied the means of examining and judging what is so; they should not be imposed on with tinsel ware. If by reason of a false light, or undue medium, they choose amiss, theirs is the loss, but the crime is the deceiver's. She who rightly understands wherein the perfection of her nature consists, will lay out her thoughts and industry in the acquisition of such perfections: But she who is kept ignorant of the matter, will take up with such objects as first offer themselves, and bear any plausible resemblance to what she desires; a show of advantage being sufficient to render them agreeable baits to her who wants judgment and skill to discern between reality and pretense. From whence it easily follows, that she who has nothing else to value herself upon, will be proud of her beauty, or money and what that can purchase, and think herself mightily obliged to him, who tells her she has those perfections which she naturally longs for. Her inbred self-esteem and desire of good, which are degenerated into pride and mistaken self-love, will easily open her ears to whatever goes about to nourish and delight them; and when a cunning designed enemy from without, has drawn over to his party these traitors within, he has the poor unhappy person at his mercy, who now very glibly swallows down his poison, because it is presented in a golden cup, and credulously hearkens to the most disadvantageous proposals, because they come attended with a seeming esteem. She whose vanity makes her swallow praises by the whole sale, without examining whether she deserves them, or from what hand they come, will reckon it but gratitude to think well of him who values her so much, and think she must needs be merciful to the poor despairing lover whom her charms have reduced to die at her feet. Love and honor are what every one of us naturally esteem, they are excellent things in themselves and very worthy our regard, and by how much the readier we are to embrace whatever resembles them, by so much the more dangerous it is that these venerable names should be wretchedly abused and affixed to their direct contraries, yet this is the custom of the world: And how can she possibly detect the fallacy, who has no better notion of either than what she derives from plays and romances? How can she be furnished with any solid principles whose very instructors are froth and emptiness? Whereas women were they rightly educated, had they obtained a well-informed and discerning mind, they would be proof against all those batteries, see through and scorn those little silly artifices which are used to ensnare and deceive them. Such a one would value herself only on her virtue, and consequently be most chary of what she esteems so much. She would know, that not what others *say,* but what she herself *does,* is the true commendation and the only thing that exalts her; the loudest encomiums being not half so satisfactory, as the calm and secret plaudit of her own mind, which moving on true principles of honor and virtue, would not fail on a review of itself to anticipate that delightful eulogy she shall one day hear.

Whence is it but from ignorance, from a want of understanding to compare and judge of things, to choose a right end, to proportion the means to the end, and to rate everything according to its proper value, that we quit the substance for the shadow, reality for appearance, and embrace those very things which if we understood we should hate and fly, but now are reconciled to, merely because they usurp the name, though they have nothing of the nature of those venerable objects we desire and seek? Were it not for this delusion, is it probable a lady who passionately desires to be admired, should ever consent to such actions as render her base and contemptible? Would she be so absurd as to think either to get love, or to keep it, by those methods which occasion loathing and consequently end in hatred? Would she reckon it a piece of her grandeur, or hope to gain esteem by such excesses as really lessen her in the eyes of all considerate and judicious persons? Would she be so silly as to look big and think herself the better person because she has more money to bestow profusely, or the good luck to have a more ingenious tailor or milliner than her neighbor? Would she, who by the regard she pays to wit, seems to make some pretenses to it, undervalue her judgment so much as to admit the scurrility and profane noisy nonsense of men, whose foreheads are better than their brains, to pass under that character? Would she be so weak as to imagine that a few airy fancies joined with a great deal of impudence and ill-nature (the right definition of modern wit) can bespeak him a man of sense, who runs counter to all the sense and reason that ever appeared in the world? than which nothing can be an argument of greater shallowness, unless it be to regard and esteem him for it. Would a woman, if she truly understood herself, be affected either with the praises or calumnies of those worthless persons, whose lives are a direct contradiction to reason, a very sink of corruption, by whom one would blush to be commended, lest they should be mistaken for partners in or connivers at their crimes? Will she who has a jot of discernment think to satisfy her greedy desire of pleasure, with those promising nothings that have again and again deluded her? Or will she to obtain such bubbles, run the risk of forfeiting joys infinitely satisfying and eternal? In sum, did not ignorance impose on us, we would never lavish out the greatest part of our time and care, on the decoration of a tenement, in which our lease is so very short, and which for all our industry, may lose its beauty ere that lease be out, and in the meanwhile neglect a more glorious and durable mansion! We would never be so curious of the house and so careless of the inhabitant, whose beauty is capable of great improvement and will endure forever without diminution or decay!

Thus ignorance and a narrow education lay the foundation of vice, and imitation and custom rear it up. Custom, that merciless torrent that carries all before it, and which indeed can be stemmed by none but such as have a great deal of prudence and a rooted virtue. For it is but decorous that she who is not capable of giving better rules, should follow those she sees before her, lest she only change the instance and retain the absurdity. It would puzzle a considerate person to account for all that sin and folly that is in the world (which certainly has nothing in itself to recommend it) did not custom help to solve the difficulty. For virtue without question has on all accounts the preeminence of vice, it is abundantly more pleasant in the *act,* as well as more advantageous in the *consequences,* as any one who will but rightly use her reason, in a serious reflection on herself and the nature of things, may easily perceive. It is custom, therefore, that tyrant custom, which is the grand motive to all those irrational choices which we daily see made in the world, so very contrary to our *present* interest and pleasure, as well as to our future. We think it an unpardonable mistake not to do as our neighbors do, and part with our peace and pleasure as well as our innocence and virtue, merely in compliance with an unreasonable fashion, and having inured ourselves to folly, we know not how to quit it; we go on in vice, not because we find satisfaction in it, but because we are unacquainted with the joys of virtue.

Add to this the hurry and noise of the world, which does generally so busy and pre-engage us, that we have little time and less inclination to stand still and reflect on our own minds. Those impertinent amusements which have seized us, keep their hold so well and so constantly buzz about our ears, that we cannot attend to the dictates of our reason, nor to the soft whispers and winning persuasives of the divine spirit, by whose assistance were we disposed to make use of it, we might shake off these follies and regain our freedom. But alas! to complete our misfortunes, by a continual application to vanity and folly, we quite spoil the contexture and frame of our minds, so loosen and dissipate, that nothing solid and substantial will stay in them. By an habitual inadvertency we render ourselves incapable of any serious and improving thought, till our minds themselves become as light and frothy as those things they are conversant about. To all which if we further add the great industry that bad people use to corrupt the good, and that unaccountable backwardness that appears in too many good persons, to stand up for and propagate the piety they profess; (so strangely are things transposed, that virtue puts on the blushes which belong to vice, and vice insults with the authority of virtue!) and we have a pretty fair account of the causes of our non-improvement.

READING QUESTIONS

1. What is the analogy that Astell makes at the beginning of this passage about tulips and weeds?
2. Which beauty endures to eternity?
3. What reason of self-interest does Astell give for parents to take care of their children's education?
4. According to Astell, what provides the foundation for vice?
5. What part does custom play in vice?

A Serious Proposal to the Ladies, Second Part

In the previous reading, Astell addressed the issue of women's education. In this passage, from the second part of the *Proposal*, she addresses the relationship between knowledge and morality in a more abstract, philosophical manner. The relationship between knowledge and morality is a philosophical topic as old as ethics itself. For Socrates and Plato, knowledge was both a necessary and sufficient condition for acting morally. One could not do good without knowledge of the good, and one could not knowingly choose to do bad. Astell puts forward a similar position, but one that takes on a new importance when we realize that the author

From Mary Astell, *A Serious Proposal to the Ladies,* Fourth Edition, London, 1701.

was a woman, a member of that half of the population unable to attain a formal education.   ✒

Chap. I
Of the Mutual Relation between Ignorance and Vice, and Knowledge and Purity

What are ignorance and vice but diseases of the mind contracted in its two principal faculties the understanding and will? And such too as like many bodily distempers do mutually foment each other. Ignorance disposes to vice, and wickedness reciprocally keeps us ignorant, so that we cannot be free from the one unless we cure the other; the former part of this proposition has been already shown, and the latter may easily be made apparent; for as every plant does naturally draw such juices towards it as serve for its nutrition, as every creature has an aptness to take such courses as tend to its preservation; so vice that spawn of the devil, that *ignis fatuus* which can't subsist but in the dark night of ignorance, casts forth vapors and mists to darken the soul and eclipse the clear light of knowledge from her view. And though a wicked man may pretend to wit, though he have never so much acumen and facetiousness of humor, yet his impiety proclaims his folly; he may have a lively fancy, an intriguing cunning and contrivance, and so may an ape or a fox, who probably if they had but speech, though destitute of reason, would outdo him in his own way; but he wants the ingenuity of a man, he's a fool to all rational intents and purposes. She then who desires a clear head must have a pure heart; and she who has the first in any measure will never allow her self to be deficient in the other. But you will say what degrees of purity are requisite in order to knowledge, and how much must we know to the end we may heartily endeavor to purify?

Now in order to satisfy this demand I consider, that there are certain notices which we may call the rudiments of knowledge, which none who are rational are without however they came by them. It may happen indeed that a habit of vice or a long disuse has so obscured them that they seem to be extinguished, but it does only *seem* so, for were they really extinguished the person would be no longer rational, and no better than the shade and picture of a man. Because as irrational creatures act only by the will of him who made them, and according to the power of that mechanism by which they are formed, so every one who pretends to reason, who is a voluntary agent and therefore worthy of praise or blame, reward or punishment, must *choose* his actions and determine his will to that choice by some reasonings or principles either true or false, and in proportion to his principles and the consequences he deduces from them he is to be accounted, if they are right and conclusive a wise man, if evil, rash and injudicious a fool. If then it be the property of rational creatures, and essential to their very natures to choose their actions, and to determine their wills to that choice by such principles and reasonings as their understandings are furnished with, they who are desirous to be ranked in that order of beings must conduct their lives by these measures, begin with their intellectuals, inform themselves what are the plain and first principles of action and act accordingly.

_____

1. Having shown the connection between knowledge and purity, Astell investigates one possible principle for human action.

_____

By which it appears that there are some degrees of knowledge necessary before there can be *any* human acts, for till we are capable of choosing our own actions and directing them by some principle, though we move and speak and do many such like things, we live not the life of a rational creature but only of an animal. If it be farther demanded what these principles are? Not to dispute the number of them here, nobody I suppose will deny us one, which is, *that we ought as much as we can to endeavor the perfecting of our beings, and that we be as happy as possibly we may.* For this we see is natural to every creature of what sort soever, which endeavors to be in as good condition as its nature and circumstances will permit. And now we have got a principle which one would think were sufficient for the conduct of our actions through the whole course of our lives and so indeed it were, could we as easily discern wherein our happiness consists as it is natural to wish and desire it. But herein lies our real mistake and misfortune; for although we all pursue the same end, yet the means we take to obtain it are indefinite: There needs no other proof of this than the looking abroad into the world, which will convince us of the truth and raise our wonder at the absurdity that creatures of the same make should take not only so many different, but even contrary ways to accomplish the same end! We all agree that it's fit to be as happy as we can, and we need no instructor to teach us this knowledge, it is born with us, and is inseparable from our being, but we very much need to be informed what is the true way to happiness. When the will comes to ask the understanding this question, What must I do to fill up my vacuities, to accomplish my nature? Our reason is at first too weak, and afterwards too often too much sophisticated to return a proper answer, though it be the most important concern of our lives, for according as the understanding replies to it so is the moral conduct of the will, pure and right if the first be well informed, irregular and vicious if the other be weak and deluded. Indeed our power of willing exerts itself much sooner than that rational faculty which is to govern it, and therefore it will either be left to its own range, or to the reason of another to direct it; whence it comes that we generally take that course in our search after happiness, which education, example or custom puts us in, and though not always, yet most commonly, we cast of our first seasoning; which should teach us to take all the care we can that it be good, and likewise that how good soever it appear, we be not too much wedded to and biased by it. Well then, the first light of our understanding must be borrowed, we must take it on trust till we're furnished with a stock of our own, which we cannot long be without if we do but employ what was lent us in the purifying of our will, for as this grows more regular the other will enlarge, if it clear up, that will brighten and shine forth with diffusive rays.

Indeed if we search to the bottom I believe we shall find, that the corruption of the heart contributes *more* to the cloudiness of the head, than the clearness of our light does to the regularity of our affections, and it is oftener seen that our vicious inclinations keep us ignorant, than that our knowledge makes us good. For it must be confessed that purity is not *always* the product of knowledge; though the understanding be appointed by the author of nature to direct and govern the will, yet many times its head-strong and rebellious subject rushes on precipitately, without its directions. When a truth comes thwart our passions, when it dares contradict our mistaken pleasures and supposed interests, let the light shine never so clear we shut our eyes against it, will not be convinced, not because there's any want of evidence, but because we're *unwilling* to obey. This is the rise of all that infidelity that appears in the world; it is not the head but the heart that is the seat of atheism. No man without a brow of brass, and an impudence as strong as his arguments are weak, could demur to the convincing proofs of Christianity, had not he contracted such diseases in his passions as make him believe it is his interest to oppose *those* that he may gratify *these*. Yet this is no objection against what we have been proving, it rather confirms what was said concerning the mutual relation between the understanding and the will, and shows how necessary it is to take care of both, if we would improve and advance either.

The result of all then, and what gives a satisfactory answer to the question where we must begin is this; that some clearness of head, some lower degrees of knowledge, so much at least as will put us an endeavoring after more, is necessary to the obtaining purity of heart. For though some persons whom we vulgarly call ignorant may be honest and virtuous, yet they are not so in these particulars in which they are ignorant, but their integrity in practicing what they know, though it be but little, causes us to overlook that wherein they ignorantly transgress. But then any eminent degree of knowledge, especially of moral and divine knowledge, which is most excellent because most necessary and useful, can never be obtained without considerable degrees of purity: And afterwards when we have procured a competent measure of both, they mutually assist each other; the more pure we are the clearer will our knowledge be, and the more we know the more we shall purify. Accordingly therefore we shall first apply ourselves to the understanding, endeavoring to inform and put it right, and in the next place address to the will, when we have touched upon a few preliminaries, and endeavored to remove obstructions that are prejudicial to both.

READING QUESTIONS

1. What does Astell contend is the relation between ignorance and vice?
2. What must a person have who wants "a clear head"?
3. Why are humans worthy of praise or blame, reward or punishment?
4. What does she mean when she contends that there must be some degree of knowledge before there can be *any* human acts?
5. What is the "end" she says that we all pursue?
6. What is her response to the view that someone who is ignorant can be virtuous?

Catherine Trotter Cockburn

Catherine Trotter Cockburn (1679–1749) has fallen into obscurity over the last two and one-half centuries, her name hardly known today. Yet in the early eighteenth century she was a highly successful English writer whose talents were recognized by some of the finest minds of the day. She wrote her first successful play before she turned seventeen. By the age of nineteen she had written another, which earned her lavish praise and was performed for years. Besides writing plays, she was the author of well-received poetry.

Cockburn's serious interest, however, was reserved for philosophy and religion. She gained a degree of renown at the time for her tenacious defense of the philosophy of John Locke, the first of the famous English empiricists and one of the most talented thinkers of all time. In *A Defense of the Essay of Human Understanding* (1701), she argues that Locke's epistemology represents an adequate foundation for morality. Her collected works include a letter from Locke in which he praises her bold defense of his ideas and expresses his gratitude that she had become his "protectress."

In addition to the *Defense,* Cockburn's collected works include numerous letters, pamphlets, and short essays on theological and philosophical topics. The selection in this chapter is one such short essay, reprinted here in its entirety.

On Moral Virtue, and Its Natural Tendency to Happiness

In this short essay, Cockburn attacks an argument made by Hobbes, that what is right is what the society (or government) says is right. Hobbes's argument implies that good and bad are relative to humankind, a view that moral philosophers refer to as **ethical relativism.** The argument that Cockburn makes supports **ethical absolutism,** the position that ethical standards are objective (not the product of human social conventions). She argues for the "unalterable nature of moral good and evil."

A second theme occurs in the third paragraph, where Cockburn discusses what motivates a person to do good rather than evil. Hobbes, and others, declare the motivation to be merely self-interest: I don't harm you because I know that you will strike back or have me arrested if I do. As you read, notice how Cockburn uses our ordinary moral attitudes, what we praise and what we blame, to argue that our motivation is not so morally meager as simple self-interest.

Catherine Trotter Cockburn, *The Works of Mrs. Catherine Cockburn,* London, 1751.

The practice of moral virtue does so naturally tend to the happiness of men, that some of the ancient philosophers have placed their *summum bonum* [highest good] in it; and certainly they came very near the truth, since heaven itself, the reward, which revelation has proposed to those, who endeavor to perfect themselves in virtue here, is described to be a city, wherein dwelleth righteousness.

But this natural tendency of moral virtue to the happiness of mankind has, on the other hand, tempted some perverse minds to decry it, as a mere invention of politicians, to keep the several societies of men in good order; though this, by which they intended to deny, does in reality evidence, the unalterable nature of moral good and evil; for no laws of politicians could make virtue serve to promote the public good, if it did not so of its own nature, that is, from its suitableness to the nature of mankind, and from the unalterable relations of things, established by the rectitude of the divine nature. And where can we find a foundation more solid, more sacred, more unchangeable! Let the most artful *Machiavellian* try, if he can make injustice, cruelty, treachery, and ingratitude, by any laws in their favor, serve to promote the good of society: and if he cannot (as I believe no one will suppose that he can) let then such perverse reasoners confess, that moral good is not made so by the laws of men; and that those laws only give their sanction to that, which it itself is unalterably good, and necessary to the happiness of mankind.

———

1. Cockburn considers an important objection to moral theories that identify morality with happiness: If we act morally because it brings happiness, are we not acting merely out of self-interest?

———

But such is the ingenuity of depraved man to draw evil out of good, that because the practice of moral virtue does indeed generally advance the happiness of particular men, as well as of societies; therefore a late author has maintained, that man has no disposition to virtue, no motives to it, or sense of it, but from self-love and self-interest. If one, who argues thus, belies his own sentiments, to vilify or depreciate this greatest excellence of man, his capacity for the most generous heights of virtue, how ought he to be abhorred? If he speaks from what he feels in himself, if he is of that wretched frame of mind, never to have felt the pleasure of a benevolent disposition, the delight of doing good without any thought of advantage from it, how is he to be pitied? But were all mankind of the same sordid make, from whence could come that joy, that transport, which we find on the bare hearing of some noble beneficent action, done many ages ago, or at the greatest distance from us? If no man found in himself any other principle of action from self-interest, how could we have any notion of a generous benevolence? How could we expect any one to act from a public spirit? Whence could come that contempt, which we have even of beneficial actions, when we perceive them to be done on views of self-interest; and on the contrary, that high esteem, which we find for such, as are done solely for the good of others, without any prospect of advantage to the actors? And what rational account can we give of the conduct of those worthy *Romans* we so much admire, who sacrificed every private advantage and despised their own lives for the good of their country? Could an action so heroically virtuous, as that of *Regulus,* be performed on motives of self-love, and self-interest, without any sense of, or satisfaction in the good he was doing? How inconsistent is this with the very nature of the action itself?

We may then conclude, that virtue or moral good has a real excellence in itself, and suitableness to the very frame of our nature, which makes it lovely and eligible, even when we are sufferers by it. And though we cannot boast, as the *Stoics* did, of our wise man, that he is absolutely master of his own happiness, since the vices of others, and the evil of pain, from which he cannot exempt himself, will often disturb him in a state not intended for perfect happiness; yet this we may say, that virtue will make a man pass his time with the greatest tranquility here, and give him the most certain prospect of complete felicity hereafter. Some indeed are so nice, as to think the rewards of heaven too mercenary an end for heroic virtue to propose: but this can be only from a mistake of the nature of those rewards, which, as an excellent divine has observed, are themselves the perfection of virtue.

READING QUESTIONS

1. What does Cockburn claim is the relation between human virtue and happiness?
2. What is her challenge to "Machiavellians"?
3. What point is she making about our regard for "noble beneficent action" that was done in the past?

David Hume

O ne of the most important philosophers of all time, who lived during the Modern period, is David Hume (1711–1776). It would be difficult to overestimate his importance to the history of Western philosophy. His legacy is broad and enduring, with a great deal of current philosophical attention still focused on his ideas. Born in Edinburgh, Scotland, David Hume was the youngest of three children, whose father owned a small estate and whose mother came from a family of lawyers. Although his family intended him to study law, his interests lay elsewhere, and he pursued a literary career instead. He found his calling at an early age. By the time he reached eighteen years of age, he was convinced that he had a momentous idea for a major work in philosophy.

This idea took years of study and writing to make it reading for public consumption, and in 1739 his thoughts were published in his first book, *A Treatise of Human Nature*. Hume hoped that this book, on which he had labored so long, would ignite the interest of the book-reading population. In his day, educated people of all kinds were expected to be able to read and understand books on a wide variety of topics that today are limited mostly to specialists. Educated people eagerly read and discussed the latest ideas in economics, science, religion, and philosophy. Alas, to his bitter disappointment, the book failed to arouse the philosophical controversy he had imagined. In fact, it went almost completely unnoticed.

Convinced that the work's failure was due to its literary style rather than its content, Hume revised the *Treatise*. In 1748 he published the reworked first part as *An Enquiry Concerning Human Understanding* and the revised third part (on morality and politics) three years later as *An Enquiry Concerning the Principles of Morals*. These books did receive the notice he had so eagerly sought. The publication of these two works, along with some essays on politics and morals, secured fame and a degree of fortune for Hume. Hume declared at the end of his life that the second *Enquiry* was by far his best work, and it is from that work that the selections in the present text are chosen.

Hume's philosophy accurately reflected his time. The seventeenth and eighteenth centuries, often referred to as the **Age of Enlightenment,** were a period of intense interest in the development of the scientific method and the wondrous scientific discoveries to which it led. At the same time, philosophical interest in religion and metaphysics waned. Hume's philosophical writings reflect both the move toward science and the move away from religion and metaphysics. He wrote in opposition to the great **rationalistic metaphysics** of **Descartes, Spinoza,** and **Leibniz,** preferring instead the **empiricist** philosophy advocated by **Locke, Hutcheson,** and **Joseph Butler,** which he found so much more compatible with science.

Hume's main goal in the *Enquiry* was to understand both human nature and the world without reference to religious doctrine. A truly experimental science of human nature was what Hume sought. This science would combine an empirical investigation into the principles of the human mind with the experimental method employed by **Sir Isaac Newton,** whose monumental work *Principia* had been published in 1689.

When he directed the scientific method of Newton to the study of human moral life, Hume became convinced of the severe limitations of the power of human reason. Moral judgments are not decided by reason alone, he argued, but are the result of sentiment, or feeling. When we evaluate an action as good or bad, right or wrong, we are merely indicating how we *feel* about it. What pleases me or is useful to me I call good; what displeases me I consider bad.

Hume's ideas influenced later philosophy in different ways. For example, Hume's emphasis on the importance of feeling to morality influenced the subjectivist turn in ethics, especially in the twentieth-century theory known as **emotivism.** Also, by defining good in terms of usefulness (or utility), we can see in Hume's thought the beginnings of **utilitarianism,** a moral philosophy later formulated in detail by **Jeremy Bentham** and **John Stuart Mill.**

An Enquiry Concerning the Principles of Morals

Philosophy, as a discipline, seems devoted to the view that reason is the best means for solving important issues. After all, careful analysis and argumentation have continued to be the primary tools employed by philosophers since the days of the ancient Greeks. And philosophers who study morality are no different in this regard from other philosophers. Therefore, it seems plausible that moral philosophers would think that morality is deeply dependent on reason. Yet David Hume brings that dependence into question in the pages you are about to read: Is morality ultimately a matter of **feeling** rather than a matter of **reason?** The importance of the **moral sentiments** is a central theme in Hume's moral philosophy.

Utility, or usefulness, provides a second interesting theme in this reading. What is the connection between the actions that we applaud as good and the usefulness of these actions? When we inquire closely, he says, we find that the moral sentiments are brought about only by those actions we consider useful or pleasant. Think about the last time you did something to help someone else: Did it make you feel good?

Section I—Of the General Principles of Morals

Disputes with men, pertinaciously obstinate in their principles, are, of all others, the most irksome; except, perhaps, those with persons, entirely disingenuous, who really do not believe the opinions they defend, but engage in the controversy, from affectation, from a spirit of opposition, or from a desire of showing wit and ingenuity, superior to

David Hume, *An Enquiry Concerning the Principles of Morals,* 1777.

the rest of mankind. The same blind adherence to their own arguments is to be expected in both; the same contempt of their antagonists; and the same passionate vehemence, in enforcing sophistry and falsehood. And as reasoning is not the source, whence either disputant derives his tenets; it is in vain to expect, that any logic, which speaks not to the affections, will ever engage him to embrace sounder principles.

Those who have denied the reality of moral distinctions, may be ranked among the disingenuous disputants; nor is it conceivable, that any human creature could ever seriously believe, that all characters and actions were alike entitled to the affection and regard of everyone. The difference, which nature has placed between one man and another, is so wide, and this difference is still so much farther widened, by education, example, and habit, that, where the opposite extremes come at once under our apprehension, there is no skepticism so scrupulous, and scarce any assurance so determined, as absolutely to deny all distinction between them. Let a man's insensibility be ever so great, he must often be touched with the images of RIGHT and WRONG; and let his prejudices be ever so obstinate, he must observe, that others are susceptible of like impressions. The only way, therefore, of converting an antagonist of this kind, is to leave him to himself. For, finding that nobody keeps up the controversy with him, it is probable he will, at last, of himself, from mere weariness, come over to the side of common sense and reason.

There has been a controversy started of late, much better worth examination, concerning the general foundation of MORALS; whether they be derived from REASON, or from SENTIMENT; whether we attain the knowledge of them by a chain of argument and induction, or by an immediate feeling and finer internal sense; whether, like all sound judgment of truth and falsehood, they should be the same to every rational intelligent being; or whether, like the perception of beauty and deformity, they be founded entirely on the particular fabric and constitution of the human species.

The ancient philosophers, though they often affirm, that virtue is nothing but conformity to reason, yet, in general, seem to consider morals as deriving their existence from taste and sentiment. On the other hand, our modern enquirers, though they also talk much of the beauty of virtue, and deformity of vice, yet have commonly endeavored to account for these distinctions by metaphysical reasonings, and by deductions from the most abstract principles of the understanding. Such confusion reigned in these subjects, that an opposition of the greatest consequence could prevail between one system and another, and even in the parts of almost each individual system; and yet nobody, till very lately, was ever sensible of it. The elegant Lord Shaftesbury, who first gave occasion to remark this distinction, and who, in general, adhered to the principles of the ancients, is not, himself, entirely free from the same confusion.

It must be acknowledged, that both sides of the question are susceptible of specious arguments. Moral distinctions, it may be said, are discernible by pure *reason:* Else, whence the many disputes that reign in common life, as well as in philosophy, with regard to this subject: the long chain of proofs often produced on both sides; the examples cited, the authorities appealed to, the analogies employed, the fallacies detected, the inferences drawn, and the several conclusions adjusted to their proper principles. Truth is disputable; not taste: What exists in the nature of things is the standard of our judgment; what each man feels within himself is the standard of sentiment. Propositions in geometry may be proved, systems in physics may be controverted; but the harmony of verse, the tenderness of passion, the brilliancy of wit, must give immediate pleasure. No man reasons concerning another's beauty; but frequently concerning the justice or injustice of his actions. In every criminal trial the first object of the prisoner is to disprove the facts alleged, and deny the actions imputed to him: The second to prove, that, even if these actions were real, they might be justified, as innocent and lawful. It is confessedly by deductions of the understanding, that the first point is ascertained: How can we suppose that a different faculty of the mind is employed in fixing the other?

On the other hand, those who would resolve all moral determinations into *sentiment,* may endeavor to show, that it is impossible for reason ever to draw conclusions of this nature. To virtue, say they, it belongs to be *amiable,* and vice *odious.* This forms their very nature or essence. But can reason or argumentation distribute these different epithets to any subjects, and pronounce beforehand, that this must produce love, and that hatred? Or what other reason can we ever assign for these affections, but the original fabric and formation of the human mind, which is naturally adapted to receive them?

The end of all moral speculations is to teach us our duty; and, by proper representations of the deformity of vice and beauty of virtue, beget correspondent habits, and engage us to avoid the one, and embrace the other. But is this ever to be expected from inferences and conclusions of the understanding, which of themselves have no hold of the affections or set in motion the active powers of men? They discover truths: But where the truths which they discover are indifferent, and beget no desire or aversion, they can have no influence on conduct and behavior. What is honorable, what is fair, what is becoming, what is noble, what is generous, takes possession of the heart, and animates us to embrace and maintain it. What is intelligible, what is evident, what is probable, what is true, procures only the cool assent of the understanding; and gratifying a speculative curiosity, puts an end to our researches.

Extinguish all the warm feelings and prepossessions in favor of virtue, and all disgust or aversion to vice: Render men totally indifferent towards these distinctions; and morality is no longer a practical study, nor has any tendency to regulate our lives and actions.

These arguments on each side (and many more might be produced) are so plausible, that I am apt to suspect, they may, the one as well as the other, be solid and satisfactory, and that *reason* and *sentiment* concur in almost all moral determinations and conclusions. The final sentence, it is probable, which pronounces characters and actions amiable or odious, praiseworthy or blameable; that which stamps on them the mark of honor or infamy, approbation or censure; that which renders morality an active principle, and constitutes virtue our happiness, and vice our misery: It is probable, I say, that this final sentence depends on some internal sense or feeling, which nature has made universal in the whole species. For what else can have an influence of this nature? But in order to pave the way for such a sentiment, and give a proper discernment of its object, it is often necessary, we find, that much reasoning should precede, that nice distinctions be made, just conclusions drawn, distant comparisons formed, complicated relations examined, and general facts fixed and ascertained. Some species of beauty, especially the natural kinds, on their first appearance, command our affection and approbation; and where they fail of this effect, it is impossible for any reasoning to redress their influence, or adapt them better to our taste and sentiment. But in many orders of beauty, particularly those of the finer arts, it is requisite to employ much reasoning, in order to feel the proper sentiment; and a false relish may frequently be corrected by argument and reflection. There are just grounds to conclude, that moral beauty partakes much of this latter species, and demands the assistance of our intellectual faculties, in order to give it a suitable influence on the human mind.

———

1. After setting out the subject of his inquiry, Hume explains the method he will use.

———

But though this question, concerning the general principles of morals, be curious and important, it is needless for us, at present, to employ farther care in our researches concerning it. For if we can be so happy, in the course of this enquiry, as to discover the true origin of morals, it will then easily appear how far either sentiment or reason enters into all determinations of this nature. In order to attain this purpose, we shall endeavor to follow a very simple method: We shall analyze that complication of mental qualities, which form what, in common life, we call Personal Merit: We shall consider every attribute of the mind, which renders a man an object either of esteem and affection, or of hatred and contempt; every habit or sentiment or faculty, which, if ascribed to any person, implies either praise or blame, and may enter into any panegyric or satire of his character and manners. The quick sensibility, which, on this head, is so universal among mankind, gives a philosopher sufficient assurance, that he can never be considerably mistaken in framing the catalogue, or incur any danger of misplacing the objects of his contemplation: He needs only enter into his own breast for a moment, and consider whether or not he should desire to have this or that quality ascribed to him, and whether such or such an imputation would proceed from a friend or an enemy. The very nature of language guides us almost infallibly in forming a judgment of this nature; and as every tongue possesses one set of words which are taken in a good sense, and another in the opposite, the least acquaintance with the idiom suffices, without any reasoning, to direct us in collecting and arranging the estimable or blameable qualities of men. The only object of reasoning is to discover the circumstances on both sides, which are common to these qualities; to observe that particular in which the estimable qualities agree on the one hand, and the blameable on the other; and thence to reach the foundation of ethics, and find those universal principles, from which all censure or approbation is ultimately derived. As this is a question of fact, not of abstract science, we can only expect success, by following the experimental method, and deducing general maxims from a comparison of particular instances. The other scientifical method, where a general abstract principle is first established, and is afterwards branched out into a variety of inferences and conclusions, may be more perfect in itself, but suits less the imperfection of human nature, and is a common source of illusion and mistake in this as well as in other subjects. Men are now cured of their passion for hypotheses and systems in natural philosophy, and will hearken to no arguments but those which are derived from experience. It is full time they should attempt a like reformation in all moral disquisitions; and reject every system of ethics, however subtile or ingenious, which is not founded on fact and observation.

We shall begin our enquiry on this head by the consideration of social virtues, benevolence and justice. The explication of them will probably give us an opening by which others may be accounted for.

Section II—Of Benevolence

Part I

It may be esteemed, perhaps, a superfluous task to prove, that the benevolent or softer affections are ESTIMABLE; and wherever they appear, engage the approbation, and good-will of mankind. The epithets *sociable, good-natured, humane, merciful, grateful, friendly, generous, beneficent,* or their equivalents, are known in all languages, and universally express the highest merit, which *human nature* is capable of attaining. Where these amiable qualities are attended with birth and power and eminent abilities, and display themselves in the good government or useful instruction of mankind, they seem even to raise the possessors of them above the rank of *human nature,* and make them approach in some measure to the divine. Exalted capacity, undaunted courage, prosperous success; these may only expose a hero or politician to the envy or ill-will of the public: But as soon as the praises are added of humane and beneficent; when instances are displayed of lenity, tenderness, or friendship: envy itself is silent, or joins the general voice of approbation and applause.

When Pericles, the great Athenian statesman and general, was on his death-bed, his surrounding friends, deeming him now insensible, began to indulge their sorrow for their expiring patron, by enumerating his great qualities and successes, his conquests and victories, the unusual length of his administration, and his nine trophies erected over the enemies of the republic. *You forget,* cries the dying hero, who had heard all, *you forget the most eminent of my praises, while you dwell so much on those vulgar advantages, in which fortune had a principal share. You have not observed, that no citizen has ever yet worne mourning on my account.*

In men of more ordinary talents and capacity, the social virtues become, if possible, still more essentially requisite; there being nothing eminent, in that case, to compensate for the want of them, or preserve the person from our severest hatred, as well as contempt. A high ambition, an elevated courage, is apt, says Cicero, in less perfect characters, to degenerate into a turbulent ferocity. The more social and softer virtues are there chiefly to be regarded. These are always good and amiable.

The principal advantage, which Juvenal discovers in the extensive capacity of the human species is, that it renders our benevolence also more extensive, and gives us larger opportunities of spreading our kindly influence than what are indulged to the inferior creation. It must, indeed, be confessed, that by doing good only, can a man truly enjoy the advantages of being eminent. His exalted station, of itself, but the more exposes him to danger and tempest. His sole prerogative is to afford shelter to inferiors, who repose themselves under his cover and protection.

But I forget, that it is not my present business to recommend generosity and benevolence, or to paint, in their true colors, all the genuine charms of the social virtues. These, indeed, sufficiently engage every heart, on the first apprehension of them; and it is difficult to abstain from some sally of panegyric, as often as they occur in discourse or reasoning. But our object here being more the speculative, than the practical part of morals, it will suffice to remark, (what will readily, I believe, be allowed) that no qualities are more entitled to the general good-will and approbation of mankind than benevolence and humanity, friendship and gratitude, natural affection and public spirit, or whatever proceeds from a tender sympathy with others, and a generous concern for our kind and species. These, wherever they appear, seem to transfuse themselves, in a manner, into each beholder, and to call forth, in their own behalf, the same favorable and affectionate sentiments, which they exert on all around.

Part II

We may observe, that, in displaying the praises of any humane, beneficent man, there is one circumstance which never fails to be amply insisted on, namely, the happiness and satisfaction, derived to society from his intercourse and good offices. To his parents, we are apt to say, he endears himself by his pious attachment and duteous care, still more than by the connections of nature. His children never feel his authority, but when employed for their advantage. With him, the ties of love are consolidated by beneficence and friendship. The ties of friendship approach, in a fond observance of each obliging office, to those of love and inclination. His domestics and dependants have in him a sure resource; and no longer dread the power of fortune, but so far as she exercises it over him. From him the hungry receive food, the naked clothing, the ignorant and slothful skill and industry. Like the sun, an inferior minister of providence, he cheers, invigorates, and sustains the surrounding world.

If confined to private life, the sphere of his activity is narrower; but his influence is all benign and gentle. If exalted into a higher station, mankind and posterity reap the fruit of his labors.

----

2. Hume finds a common thread in actions for which people are praised.

As these topics of praise never fail to be employed, and with success, where we would inspire esteem for anyone; may it not thence be concluded, that the UTILITY, resulting from the social virtues, forms, at least, a *part* of their merit, and is one source of that approbation and regard so universally paid to them?

When we recommend even an animal or a plant as *useful* and *beneficial,* we give it an applause and recommendation suited to its nature. As, on the other hand, reflection on the baneful influence of any of these inferior beings always inspires us with the sentiment of aversion. The eye is pleased with the prospect of corn-fields and loaded vineyards; horses grazing, and flocks pasturing: But flies the view of briars and brambles, affording shelter to wolves and serpents.

A machine, a piece of furniture, a vestment, a house well contrived for use and conveniency, is so far beautiful, and is contemplated with pleasure and approbation. An experienced eye is here sensible to many excellencies, which escape persons ignorant and uninstructed.

Can anything stronger be said in praise of a profession, such as merchandise or manufacture, than to observe the advantages which it procures to society? And is not a monk and inquisitor enraged when we treat his order as useless or pernicious to mankind?

The historian exults in displaying the benefit arising from his labors. The writer of romance alleviates or denies the bad consequences ascribed to his manner of composition.

In general, what praise is implied in the simple epithet *useful!* What reproach in the contrary!

Your Gods, says Cicero, in opposition to the Epicureans, cannot justly claim any worship or adoration, with whatever imaginary perfections you may suppose them endowed. They are totally useless and unactive. Even the Egyptians, whom you so much ridicule, never consecrated any animal but on account of its utility.

The skeptics assert, though absurdly, that the origin of all religious worship was derived from the utility of inanimate objects, as the sun and moon, to the support and well-being of mankind. This is also the common reason assigned by historians, for the deification of eminent heroes and legislators.

To plant a tree, to cultivate a field, to beget children; meritorious acts, according to the religion of Zoroaster.

In all determinations of morality, this circumstance of public utility is ever principally in view; and wherever disputes arise, either in philosophy or common life, concerning the bounds of duty, the question cannot, by any means, be decided with greater certainty, than by ascertaining, on any side, the true interests of mankind. If any false opinion, embraced from appearances, has been found to prevail; as soon as farther experience and sounder reasoning have given us juster notions of human affairs; we retract our first sentiment, and adjust anew the boundaries of moral good and evil.

Giving alms to common beggars is naturally praised; because it seems to carry relief to the distressed and indigent: But when we observe the encouragement thence arising to idleness and debauchery, we regard that species of charity rather as a weakness than a virtue.

Tyrannicide, or the assassination of usurpers and oppressive princes, was highly extolled in ancient times; because it both freed mankind from many of these monsters, and seemed to keep the others in awe, whom the sword or poinard could not reach. But history and experience having since convinced us, that this practice increases the jealousy and cruelty of princes, a Timoleon and a Brutus, though treated with indulgence on account of the prejudices of their times, are now considered as very improper models for imitation.

Liberality in princes is regarded as a mark of beneficence: But when it occurs, that the homely bread of the honest and industrious is often thereby converted into delicious cates for the idle and the prodigal, we soon retract our heedless praises. The regrets of a prince, for having lost a day, were noble and generous: But had he intended to have spent it in acts of generosity to his greedy courtiers, it was better lost than misemployed after that manner.

Luxury, or a refinement on the pleasures and conveniencies of life, had long been supposed the source of every corruption in government, and the immediate cause of faction, sedition, civil wars, and the total loss of liberty. It was, therefore, universally regarded as a vice, and was an object of declamation to all satirists, and severe moralists. Those, who prove, or attempt to prove, that such refinements rather tend to the increase of industry, civility, and arts, regulate anew our *moral* as well as *political* sentiments, and represent, as laudable or innocent, what had formerly been regarded as pernicious and blameable.

---

3. Here Hume draws the conclusion from his investigation of praise and blame.

Upon the whole, then, it seems undeniable, *that* nothing can bestow more merit on any human creature than the sentiment of benevolence in an eminent degree; and *that* a *part,* at least, of its merit arises from its tendency to promote the interests of our species, and bestow happiness on human society. We carry our view into the salutary consequences of such a character and disposition; and whatever has so benign an influence, and forwards so desirable an end, is beheld with complacency and pleasure. The social virtues are never regarded without their beneficial tendencies, nor viewed as barren and unfruitful. The happiness of mankind, the order of society, the harmony of families, the mutual support of friends, are always considered as the result of their gentle dominion over the breasts of men.

How considerable a *part* of their merit we ought to ascribe to their utility, will better appear from future disquisitions; as well as the reason, why this circumstance has such a command over our esteem and approbation.

Section V—Why Utility Pleases

Part I

It seems so natural a thought to ascribe to their utility the praise, which we bestow on the social virtues, that one would expect to meet with this principle every where in moral writers, as the chief foundation of their reasoning and enquiry. In common life, we may observe, that the circumstance of utility is always appealed to; nor is it supposed, that a greater eulogy can be given to any man, than to display his usefulness to the public, and enumerate the services, which he has performed to mankind and society. What praise, even of an inanimate form, if the regularity and elegance of its parts destroy not its fitness for any useful purpose! And how satisfactory an apology for any disproportion or seeming deformity, if we can show the necessity of that particular construction for the use intended! A ship appears more beautiful to an artist, or one moderately skilled in navigation, where its prow is wide and swelling beyond its poop, than if it were framed with a precise geometrical regularity, in contradiction to all the laws of mechanics. A building, whose doors and windows were exact squares, would hurt the eye by that very proportion; as ill adapted to the figure of a human creature, for whose service the fabric was intended. What wonder then, that a man, whose habits and conduct are hurtful to society, and dangerous or pernicious to everyone who has an intercourse with him, should, on that account, be an object of disapprobation, and communicate to every spectator the strongest sentiment of disgust and hatred.

But perhaps the difficulty of accounting for these effects of usefulness, or its contrary, has kept philosophers from admitting them into their systems of ethics, and has induced them rather to employ any other principle, in explaining the origin of moral good and evil. But it is no just reason for rejecting any principle, confirmed by experience, that we cannot give a satisfactory account of its origin, nor are able to resolve it into other more general principles. And if we would employ a little thought on the present subject, we need be at no loss to account for the influence of utility, and to deduce it from principles, the most known and avowed in human nature.

----

4. Hume is here interested in whether all morality is merely an invention of humanity. Does he think it is?

From the apparent usefulness of the social virtues, it has readily been inferred by skeptics, both ancient and modern, that all moral distinctions arise from education, and were, at first, invented, and afterwards encouraged, by the art of politicians, in order to render men tractable, and subdue their natural ferocity and self-ishness, which incapacitated them for society. This principle, indeed, of precept and education, must so far be owned to have a powerful influence, that it may frequently increase or diminish, beyond their natural standard, the sentiments of approbation or dislike; and may even, in particular instances, create, without any natural princi-ple, a new sentiment of this kind; as is evident in all superstitious practices and ob-servances: But that *all* moral affection or dislike arises from this origin, will never surely be allowed by any judicious enquirer. Had nature made no such distinction, founded on the original constitution of the mind, the words, *honorable* and *shame-ful, lovely* and *odious, noble* and *despicable,* had never had place in any language; nor could politicians, had they invented these terms, ever have been able to render them intelligible, or make them convey any idea to the audience. So that nothing can be more superficial than this paradox of the skeptics; and it were well, if, in the ab-struser studies of logic and metaphysics, we could as easily obviate the cavils of that sect, as in the practical and more intelligible sciences of politics and morals.

The social virtues must, therefore, be allowed to have a natural beauty and ami-ableness, which, at first, antecedent to all precept or education, recommends them to the esteem of uninstructed mankind, and engages their affections. And as the public utility of these virtues is the chief circumstance, whence they derive their merit, it follows, that the end, which they have a tendency to promote, must be some way agreeable to us, and take hold of some natural affection. It must please, either from considerations of self-interest, or from more generous motives and regards.

It has often been asserted, that, as every man has a strong connection with so-ciety, and perceives the impossibility of his solitary subsistence, he becomes, on that account, favorable to all those habits or principles, which promote order in society, and insure to him the quiet possession of so inestimable a blessing. As much as we value our own happiness and welfare, as much must we applaud the practice of jus-tice and humanity, by which alone the social confederacy can be maintained, and every man reap the fruits of mutual protection and assistance.

This deduction of morals from self-love, or a regard to private interest, is an ob-vious thought, and has not arisen wholly from the wanton sallies and sportive as-saults of the skeptics. To mention no others, Polybius, one of the gravest and most judicious, as well as most moral writers of antiquity, has assigned this selfish origin to all our sentiments of virtue. But though the solid, practical sense of that author, and his aversion to all vain subtleties, render his authority on the present subject very considerable; yet is not this an affair to be decided by authority, and the voice of nature and experience seems plainly to oppose the selfish theory.

---

5. Hume has drawn a conclusion concerning the selfish origin of virtuous senti-ments. He now gives some examples. What are they intended to demonstrate?

We frequently bestow praise on virtuous actions, performed in very distant ages and remote countries; where the utmost subtlety of imagination would not discover any appearance of self-interest, or find any connection of our present happiness and security with events so widely separated from us.

A generous, a brave, a noble deed, performed by an adversary, commands our approbation; while in its consequences it may be acknowledged prejudicial to our particular interest.

Where private advantage concurs with general affection for virtue, we readily perceive and avow the mixture of these distinct sentiments, which have a very different feeling and influence on the mind. We praise, perhaps, with more alacrity, where the generous, humane action contributes to our particular interest: But the topics of praise, which we insist on, are very wide of this circumstance. And we may attempt to bring over others to our sentiments, without endeavoring to convince them, that they reap any advantage from the actions which we recommend to their approbation and applause.

Frame the model of a praiseworthy character, consisting of all the most amiable moral virtues: Give instances, in which these display themselves after an eminent and extraordinary manner: You readily engage the esteem and approbation of all your audience, who never so much as enquire in what age and country the person lived, who possessed these noble qualities: A circumstance, however, of all others, the most material to self-love, or a concern for our own individual happiness.

Once on a time, a statesman, in the shock and contest of parties, prevailed so far as to procure, by his eloquence, the banishment of an able adversary; whom he secretly followed, offering him money for his support during his exile, and soothing him with topics of consolation in his misfortunes. *Alas!* cries the banished statesman, *with what regret must I leave my friends in this city, where even enemies are so generous!* Virtue, though in an enemy, here pleased him: And we also give it the just tribute of praise and approbation; nor do we retract these sentiments, when we hear, that the action passed at Athens, about two thousand years ago, and that the persons' names were Eschines and Demosthenes.

What is that to me? There are few occasions, when this question is not pertinent: And had it that universal, infallible influence supposed, it would turn into ridicule every composition, and almost every conversation, which contain any praise or censure of men and manners.

It is but a weak subterfuge, when pressed by these facts and arguments, to say, that we transport ourselves, by the force of imagination, into distant ages and countries, and consider the advantage, which we should have reaped from these characters, had we been contemporaries, and had any commerce with the persons. It is not conceivable, how a *real* sentiment or passion can ever arise from a known *imaginary* interest; especially when our *real* interest is still kept in view, and is often acknowledged to be entirely distinct from the imaginary, and even sometimes opposite to it.

A man, brought to the brink of a precipice, cannot look down without trembling; and the sentiment of *imaginary* danger actuates him, in opposition to the opinion and belief of *real* safety. But the imagination is here assisted by the presence of a striking object; and yet prevails not, except it be also aided by novelty, and the unusual appearance of the object. Custom soon reconciles us to heights and precipices, and wears off these false and delusive terrors. The reverse is observable in the estimates, which we form of characters and manners; and the more we habituate ourselves to an accurate scrutiny of morals, the more delicate feeling do we acquire of the most minute distinctions between vice and virtue. Such frequent occasion, indeed, have we, in common life, to pronounce all kinds of moral determinations, that no object of this kind can be new or unusual to us; nor could any *false* views or prepossessions maintain their ground against an experience, so common and familiar. Experience being chiefly what forms the association of ideas, it is impossible, that any association could establish and support itself, in direct opposition to that principle.

Usefulness is agreeable, and engages our approbation. This is a matter of fact, confirmed by daily observation. But, *useful?* For what? For some body's interest, surely. Whose interest then? Not our own only: For our approbation frequently extends farther. It must, therefore, be the interest of those, who are served by the character or action approved of; and these we may conclude, however remote, are not totally indifferent to us. By opening up this principle, we shall discover one great source of moral distinctions.

Part II

Self-love is a principle in human nature of such extensive energy, and the interest of each individual is, in general, so closely connected with that of the community, that those philosophers were excusable, who fancied, that all our concern for the public might be resolved into a concern for our own happiness and preservation. They saw every moment, instances of approbation or blame, satisfaction or displeasure towards characters and actions; they denominated the objects of these sentiments, *virtues,* or *vices;* they observed, that the former had a tendency to increase the happiness, and the latter the misery of mankind; they asked, whether it were possible that we could have any general concern for society, or any disinterested resentment of the welfare or injury of others; they found it simpler to consider all these sentiments as modifications of self-love; and they discovered a pretense, at least, for this unity of principle, in that close union of interest, which is so observable between the public and each individual.

But notwithstanding this frequent confusion of interests, it is easy to attain what natural philosophers, after Lord Bacon, have affected to call the *experimentum crucis,* or that experiment, which points out the right way in any doubt or ambiguity. We have found instances, in which private interest was separate from public; in which it was even contrary: And yet we observed the moral sentiment to continue, notwithstanding this disjunction of interests. And wherever these distinct interests sensibly concurred, we always found a sensible increase of the sentiment, and a more warm affection to virtue, and detestation of vice, or what we properly call, *gratitude* and *revenge.* Compelled by these instances, we must renounce the theory, which accounts for every moral sentiment by the principle of self-love. We must adopt a more public affection, and allow, that the interests of society are not, even on their own account, entirely indifferent to us. Usefulness is only a tendency to a certain end; and it is a contradiction in terms, that any thing pleases as means to an end, where the end itself no wise affects us. If usefulness, therefore, be a source of moral sentiment, and if this usefulness be not always considered with a reference to self; it follows, that every thing, which contributes to the happiness of society, recommends itself directly to our approbation and goodwill. Here is a principle, which accounts, in great part, for the origin of morality: And what need we seek for abstruse and remote systems, when there occurs one so obvious and natural?

Have we any difficulty to comprehend the force of humanity and benevolence? Or to conceive, that the very aspect of happiness, joy, prosperity, gives pleasure; that of pain, suffering, sorrow, communicates uneasiness? The human countenance, says Horace, borrows smiles or tears from the human countenance. Reduce a person to solitude, and he loses all enjoyment, except either of the sensual or speculative kind; and that because the movements of his heart are not forwarded by correspondent movements in his fellow-creatures. The signs of sorrow and mourning, though arbitrary, affect us with melancholy; but the natural symptoms, tears and cries and groans, never fail to infuse compassion and uneasiness. And if the effects of misery touch us in so lively a manner; can we be supposed altogether insensible or indifferent towards its causes; when a malicious or treacherous character and behavior are presented to us?

———

6. After describing the way in which we feel emotions like those expressed by the people we encounter, Hume goes on to give a series of examples. What do they illustrate?

———

We enter, I shall suppose, into a convenient, warm, well-contrived apartment: We necessarily receive a pleasure from its very survey; because it presents us with the pleasing ideas of ease, satisfaction, and enjoyment. The hospitable, good-humored, humane landlord appears. This circumstance surely must embellish the whole: nor can we easily forbear reflecting, with pleasure, on the satisfaction which results to every one from his intercourse and good-offices.

His whole family, by the freedom, ease, confidence, and calm enjoyment, diffused over their countenances, sufficiently express their happiness. I have a pleasing sympathy in the prospect of so much joy, and can never consider the source of it, without the most agreeable emotions.

He tells me, that an oppressive and powerful neighbor had attempted to dispossess him of his inheritance, and had long disturbed all his innocent and social pleasures. I feel an immediate indignation arise in me against such violence and injury.

But it is no wonder, he adds, that a private wrong should proceed from a man, who had enslaved provinces, depopulated cities, and made the field and scaffold stream with human blood. I am struck with horror at the prospect of so much misery, and am actuated by the strongest antipathy against its author.

In general, it is certain, that, wherever we go, whatever we reflect on or converse about, every thing still presents us with the view of human happiness or misery, and excites in our breast a sympathetic movement of pleasure or uneasiness. In our serious occupations, in our careless amusements, this principle still exerts its active energy.

A man, who enters the theatre, is immediately struck with the view of so great a multitude participating of one common amusement; and experiences, from their very aspect, a superior sensibility or disposition of being affected with every sentiment, which he shares with his fellow-creatures.

He observes the actors to be animated by the appearance of a full audience, and raised to a degree of enthusiasm, which they cannot command in any solitary or calm moment.

Every movement of the theatre, by a skillful poet, is communicated, as it were by magic, to the spectators; who weep, tremble, resent, rejoice, and are enflamed with all the variety of passions, which actuate the several personages of the drama.

Where any event crosses our wishes, and interrupts the happiness of the favorite characters, we feel a sensible anxiety and concern. But where their sufferings proceed from the treachery, cruelty, or tyranny of an enemy, our breasts are affected with the liveliest resentment against the author of these calamities.

It is here esteemed contrary to the rules of art to represent anything cool and indifferent. A distant friend, or a confidant, who has no immediate interest in the catastrophe, ought, if possible, to be avoided by the poet; as communicating a like indifference to the audience, and checking the progress of the passions.

Few species of poetry are more entertaining than *pastoral;* and every one is sensible, that the chief source of its pleasure arises from those images of a gentle and tender tranquility, which it represents in its personages, and of which it communicates a like sentiment to the reader. Sannazarius, who transferred the scene to the sea-shore, though he presented the most magnificent object in nature, is confessed to have erred in his choice. The idea of toil, labor, and danger, suffered by the fishermen, is painful; by an unavoidable sympathy, which attends every conception of human happiness or misery.

When I was twenty, says a French poet, Ovid was my favorite: Now I am forty, I declare for Horace. We enter, to be sure, more readily into sentiments, which resemble those we feel every day: But no passion, when well represented, can be entirely indifferent to us; because there is none, of which every man has not, within him, at least the seeds and first principles. It is the business of poetry to bring every affection near to us by lively imagery and representation, and make it look like truth and reality: A certain proof, that, wherever that reality is found, our minds are disposed to be strongly affected by it.

Any recent event or piece of news, by which the fate of states, provinces, or many individuals is affected, is extremely interesting even to those whose welfare is not immediately engaged. Such intelligence is propagated with celerity, heard with avidity, and inquired into with attention and concern. The interest of society appears, on this occasion, to be, in some degree, the interest of each individual. The imagination is sure to be affected; though the passions excited may not always be so strong and steady as to have great influence on the conduct and behavior.

The perusal of a history seems a calm entertainment; but would be no entertainment at all, did not our hearts beat with correspondent movements to those which are described by the historian.

Thucydides and Guicciardin support with difficulty our attention; while the former describes the trivial rencontres of the small cities of Greece, and the latter the harmless wars of Pisa. The few persons interested, and the small interest fill not the imagination, and engage not the affections. The deep distress of the numerous Athenian army before Syracuse; the danger which so nearly threatens Venice; these excite compassion; these move terror and anxiety.

The indifferent, uninteresting style of Suetonius, equally with the masterly pencil of Tacitus, may convince us of the cruel depravity of Nero or Tiberius: But what a difference of sentiment! While the former coldly relates the facts; and the latter sets before our eyes the venerable figures of a Soranus and a Thrasea, intrepid in their fate, and only moved by the melting sorrows of their friends and kindred. What sympathy then touches every human heart! What indignation against the tyrant, whose causeless fear or unprovoked malice gave rise to such detestable barbarity!

If we bring these subjects nearer: If we remove all suspicion of fiction and deceit: What powerful concern is excited, and how much superior, in many instances, to the narrow attachments of self-love and private interest! Popular sedition, party zeal, a devoted obedience to factious leaders; these are some of the most visible, though less laudable effects of this social sympathy in human nature.

The frivolousness of the subject too, we may observe, is not able to detach us entirely from what carries an image of human sentiment and affection.

When a person stutters, and pronounces with difficulty, we even sympathize with this trivial uneasiness, and suffer for him. And it is a rule in criticism, that every combination of syllables or letters, which gives pain to the organs of speech in the recital, appears also, from a species of sympathy, harsh and disagreeable to the ear. Nay, when we run over a book with our eye, we are sensible of such unharmonious composition; because we still imagine, that a person recites it to us, and suffers from the pronunciation of these jarring sounds. So delicate is our sympathy!

Easy and unconstrained postures and motions are always beautiful: An air of health and vigor is agreeable: Clothes which warm, without burdening the body; which cover, without imprisoning the limbs, are well-fashioned. In every judgment of beauty, the feelings of the person affected enter into consideration, and communicate to the spectator similar touches of pain or pleasure. What wonder, then, if we can pronounce no judgment concerning the character and conduct of men, without considering the tendencies of their actions, and the happiness or misery which thence arises to society? What association of ideas would ever operate, were that principle here totally unactive.

If any man from a cold insensibility, or narrow selfishness of temper, is unaffected with the images of human happiness or misery, he must be equally indifferent to the images of vice and virtue: As, on the other hand, it is always found, that a warm concern for the interests of our species is attended with a delicate feeling of all moral distinctions; a strong resentment of injury done to men; a lively approbation of their welfare. In this particular, though great superiority is observable of one man above another; yet none are so entirely indifferent to the interest of their fellow-creatures, as to perceive no distinctions of moral good and evil, in consequence of the different tendencies of actions and principles. How, indeed, can we suppose it possible in anyone, who wears a human heart, that if there be subjected to his censure, one character or system of conduct, which is beneficial, and another, which is pernicious, to his species or community, he will not so much as give a cool preference to the former, or ascribe to it the smallest merit or regard? Let us suppose such a person ever so selfish; let private interest have engrossed ever so much his attention; yet in instances, where that is not concerned, he must unavoidably feel *some* propensity to the good of mankind, and make it an object of choice, if everything else be equal. Would any man, who is walking along, tread as willingly on another's gouty toes, whom he has no quarrel with, as on the hard flint and pavement? There is here surely a difference in the case. We surely take into consideration the happiness and misery of others, in weighing the several motives of action, and incline to the former, where no private regards draw us to seek our own promotion or advantage by the injury of our fellow-creatures. And if the principles of humanity are capable, in many instances, of influencing our actions, they must, at all times, have *some* authority over our sentiments, and give us a general approbation of what is useful to society, and blame of what is dangerous or pernicious. The degrees of these sentiments may be the subject of controversy; but the reality of their existence, one should think, must be admitted, in every theory or system.

A creature, absolutely malicious and spiteful, were there any such in nature, must be worse than indifferent to the images of vice and virtue. All his sentiments must be inverted, and directly opposite to those, which prevail in the human species.

Whatever contributes to the good of mankind as it crosses the constant bent of his wishes and desires, must produce uneasiness and disapprobation; and on the contrary, whatever is the source of disorder and misery in society, must, for the same reason, be regarded with pleasure and complacency. Timon, who, probably from his affected spleen, more than any inveterate malice, was denominated the man-hater, embraced Alcibiades, with great fondness. *Go on my boy!* cried he, *acquire the confidence of the people: You will one day, I foresee, be the cause of great calamities to them:* Could we admit the two principles of the Manicheans, it is an infallible consequence, that their sentiments of human actions, as well as of every thing else, must be totally opposite, and that every instance of justice and humanity, from its necessary tendency, must please the one deity and displease the other. All mankind so far resemble the good principle, that, where interest or revenge or envy perverts not our disposition, we are always inclined, from our natural philanthropy, to give the preference to the happiness of society, and consequently to virtue, above its opposite. Absolute, unprovoked, disinterested malice has never, perhaps, place in any human breast; or if it had, must there pervert all the sentiments of morals, as well as the feelings of humanity. If the cruelty of Nero be allowed entirely voluntary, and not rather the effect of constant fear and resentment; it is evident, that Tigellinus, preferably to Seneca or Burrhus, must have possessed his steady and uniform approbation.

A statesman or patriot, who serves our own country, in our own time, has always a more passionate regard paid to him, than one whose beneficial influence operated on distant ages or remote nations; where the good, resulting from his generous humanity, being less connected with us, seems more obscure, and affects us with a less lively sympathy. We may own the merit to be equally great, though our sentiments are not raised to an equal height, in both cases. The judgment here corrects the inequalities of our internal emotions and perceptions; in like manner, as it preserves us from error, in the several variations of images, presented to our external senses. The same object, at a double distance, really throws on the eye a picture of but half the bulk; yet we imagine that it appears of the same size in both situations; because we know, that, on our approach to it, its image would expand on the eye, and that the difference consists not in the object itself, but in our position with regard to it. And, indeed, without such a correction of appearances, both in internal and external sentiment, men could never think or talk steadily on any subject; while their fluctuating situations produce a continual variation on objects, and throw them into such different and contrary lights and positions.

The more we converse with mankind, and the greater social intercourse we maintain, the more shall we be familiarized to these general preferences and distinctions, without which our conversation and discourse could scarcely be rendered intelligible to each other. Every man's interest is peculiar to himself, and the aversions and desires, which result from it, cannot be supposed to affect others in a like degree. General language, therefore, being formed for general use, must be molded on some more general views, and must affix the epithets of praise or blame, in conformity to sentiments, which arise from the general interests of the community. And if these sentiments, in most men, be not so strong as those, which have a reference to private good; yet still they must make some distinction, even in persons the most depraved and selfish; and must attach the notion of good to a beneficent conduct, and of evil to the contrary. Sympathy, we shall allow, is much fainter than our concern for ourselves, and sympathy with persons remote from us, much fainter than that with persons near and contiguous; but for this very reason, it is necessary for us, in our calm judgments and discourse concerning the characters of men, to neglect all these differences, and render our sentiments more public and social. Besides, that we ourselves often change our situation in this particular, we every day meet with persons, who are in a situation different from us, and who could never converse with us, were we to remain constantly in that position and point of view, which is peculiar to ourselves. The intercourse of sentiments, therefore, in society and conversation, makes us form some general unalterable standard, by which we may approve or disapprove of characters and manners. And though the heart takes not part with those general notions, nor regulates all its love and hatred, by the universal, abstract differences of vice and virtue, without regard to self, or the persons with whom we are more intimately connected; yet have these moral differences a considerable influence, and being sufficient, at least, for discourse, serve all our purposes in company, in the pulpit, on the theatre, and in the schools.

Thus, in whatever light we take this subject, the merit, ascribed to the social virtues, appears still uniform, and arises chiefly from that regard, which the natural sentiment of benevolence engages us to pay to the interests of mankind and society. If we consider the principles of the human make, such as they appear to daily experience and observation, we must, *à priori*, conclude it impossible for such a creature as man to be totally indifferent to the well or ill-being of his fellow-creatures, and not readily, of himself, to pronounce, where nothing gives him any particular bias, that what promotes their happiness is good, what tends to their misery is evil, without any farther regard or consideration. Here then are the faint rudiments, at least, or outlines, of a *general* distinction between actions; and in proportion as the humanity of the person is supposed to increase, his connection with those who are injured or benefited, and his lively conception of their misery or happiness; his consequent censure or approbation acquires proportionable vigor. There is no necessity, that a generous action, barely mentioned in an old history or remote gazette, should communicate any strong feelings of applause and admiration. Virtue, placed at such a distance, is liked a fixed star, which, though to the eye of reason, it may appear as luminous as the sun in his meridian, is so infinitely removed, as to affect the senses, neither with light nor heat. Bring this virtue nearer, by our acquaintance or connection with the persons, or even by an eloquent recital of the case; our hearts are immediately caught, our sympathy enlivened, and our cool approbation converted into the warmest sentiments of friendship and regard. These seem necessary and infallible consequences of the general principles of human nature, as discovered in common life and practice.

Again; reverse these views and reasonings: Consider the matter *à posteriori;* and weighing the consequences, inquire if the merit of social virtue be not, in a great measure, derived from the feelings of humanity, with which it affects the spectators. It appears to be matter of fact, that the circumstance of *utility,* in all subjects, is a source of praise and approbation: That it is constantly appealed to in all moral decisions concerning the merit and demerit of actions: That it is the *sole* source of that high regard paid to justice, fidelity, honor, allegiance, and chastity: That it is inseparable from all the other social virtues, humanity, generosity, charity, affability, lenity, mercy, and moderation: And, in a word, that it is a foundation of the chief part of morals, which has a reference to mankind and our fellow-creatures.

It appears also, that in our general approbation of characters and manners, the useful tendency of the social virtues moves us not by any regards to self-interest, but has an influence much more universal and extensive. It appears, that a tendency to public good, and to the promoting of peace, harmony, and order in society, does always, by affecting the benevolent principles of our frame, engage us on the side of the social virtues. And it appears, as an additional confirmation, that these principles of humanity and sympathy enter so deeply into all our sentiments, and have so powerful an influence, as may enable them to excite the strongest censure and applause. The present theory is the simple result of all these inferences, each of which seems founded on uniform experience and observation.

Were it doubtful, whether there were any such principle in our nature as humanity or a concern for others, yet when we see, in numberless instances, that whatever has a tendency to promote the interests of society, is so highly approved of, we ought thence to learn the force of the benevolent principle; since it is impossible for any thing to please as means to an end, where the end is totally indifferent. On the other hand, were it doubtful, whether there were, implanted in our nature, any general principle of moral blame and approbation, yet when we see, in numberless instances, the influence of humanity, we ought thence to conclude, that it is impossible, but that everything, which promotes the interest of society, must communicate pleasure, and what is pernicious give uneasiness. But when these different reflections and observations concur in establishing the same conclusion, must they not bestow an undisputed evidence upon it?

It is however hoped, that the progress of this argument will bring a farther confirmation of the present theory, by showing the rise of other sentiments of esteem and regard from the same or like principles.

READING QUESTIONS

1. Name the two possible foundations of morality given by Hume.

2. Hume finds benevolent acts praiseworthy, but only when they have one other important feature. What is that feature? Why is it essential?

3. What reasons does Hume give for believing that selfishness is not the origin of our moral sentiments?

4. What does Hume say is the reaction of theater spectators to treachery or cruelty exhibited on the stage? Why?

5. What enters into every judgment of beauty? Why?

6. Why must we attempt to turn our sentiments toward public and social interests?

Immanuel Kant

The Modern period in moral philosophy (1600–1800) saw the inception of the two ethical theories that would come to dominate ethical debate in the West. In England, intense interest in moral philosophy during this period led to **utilitarianism,** the ethical theory that was developed fully only in the nineteenth century by John Stuart Mill. According to utilitarianism, what determines the rightness or wrongness of an action are the consequences of that action. An act is right if (and only if) it maximizes happiness for all concerned and wrong if it does not. The rival theory put forward by Immanuel Kant (1724–1804), the German who was to become one of the premier figures in philosophy, was decidedly nonutilitarian. Kantian theory (often called **duty theory**) is **deontological** because it holds that some acts are obligatory regardless of their consequences. The consequences of an act do not determine the act's rightness or wrongness. An act is right, according to Kant, only if it is done from a sense of duty. These two theories, utilitarianism and Kant's duty theory, formed the crux of the debate that was to dominate moral philosophy in the nineteenth century, a debate that is still provocative and very much alive today.

Born in Königsberg, in East Prussia, Kant attended the university there. He stayed on at the university to become a lecturer and eventually a professor, making him the first major philosopher since the days of the Greeks and Romans to earn his living as a teacher of philosophy. Kant was a man of conservative habit who never married and lived always in the town of his birth.

Kant's initial academic duties lay in teaching such subjects as physics and mathematics as well as philosophy. His early published work mostly concerned natural science, but he turned his full attention to philosophical issues after 1760. His varied early interests were later to enliven his philosophical lectures, delivered to audiences filled with students and others who frequently traveled from distant parts of Germany just to hear the great thinker. It may come as a surprise to many who have experienced Kant's cumbersome writing style that he was considered a most entertaining lecturer. His writing style appears unimaginative because of the scholastic style common in his day, not because of his own dullness.

Kant's philosophical writings are usually separated into two periods: the precritical period, prior to 1770, and the "critical period," after 1770. His primary written work of the critical period begins with the publication in 1780 of his magnum opus, the eagerly awaited *Critique of Pure Reason*. Even though Kant had an established reputation by the time this book was published, its arrival was met mostly with bewilderment and confusion. Few could understand his ideas, due in part to his formal argumentation style and in part to the highly abstract nature of his subject matter. In an effort to dispel this confusion, he restated the main arguments more simply in a short work, the *Prolegomena to Every Future Metaphysics,* published in 1783. His major contributions to ethical theory appeared soon after. By 1785 he had published the *Fundamental Principles of the Metaphysics of Morals,* followed by the *Critique of Practical Reason* in 1788 and the *Critique of Judgment* in 1790.

Like many of his contemporaries, Kant embraced the Enlightenment belief in the power of reason over authority and tradition, especially in its respect for the advances of science. But he was mostly alone in recognizing the challenge that the **determinism** implicit in Newtonian physics creates for ethics. The problem is this: The doctrine of determinism states that every event has a cause, which is demonstrably true for physics. However, morality presumes that human beings are able to choose which acts (right ones or wrong ones) they perform, and that such free choice seems necessary if we are to praise or blame people for their actions. But what happens to human freedom of choice if the choice itself is merely the result of past events? If our choices are not really free, then the whole idea of moral responsibility seems undermined, and the very possibility of ethics becomes imperiled. This debate, **free will versus determinism,** has remained at the center of moral philosophy. What Kant attempted to do in his ethical writings, beginning with *Fundamental Principles,* was to combine the insights of science while retaining the presumption of human free will (or **autonomy**).

If Kant had published nothing other than his *Fundamental Principles,* he would have ensured himself a place in the history of ethics. His sole aim in this work, as he states in the preface, is "to seek out and establish the supreme principle of morality." This he does by investigating the special features of moral decisions. What are the unique features of those decisions? According to Kant, humans are creatures with rationality as well as feelings. Although our feelings determine many of our actions, and in these actions reason assumes, as **Hume** said, the role of "handmaiden," not all acts are determined by feelings.

In moral actions, the roles of reason and feeling are reversed. We act morally when we act not out of an interest in the consequences of that act (as the utilitarians would have it), but out of respect for moral principle. We may not be able to choose our inclinations and desires, yet we can choose between acting from inclination and acting from duty. It is in this choice that morality lies.

Kant's deontological ethical theory is one of the primary theories in the moral philosophy of our day, and even his opponents must acknowledge the powerful influence of his thought. Utilitarians, for example, still must address the challenge of Kant's theory. Yet large numbers of moral philosophers continue to analyze, promote, and, where necessary, amend Kant's ethical theory; others see his ideas as, at least in part, the root of their own. One example of an influential ethical theory inspired by Kantian principles (covered in the present volume) is the **contractarian theory** of **John Rawls.**

Fundamental Principles of the Metaphysics of Morals

Trying to decide on the right thing to do can be a bewildering experience. We are often torn between what we think we *ought* to do and what we *want* to do. For instance, you may feel that you ought to visit your ill grandmother

Immanuel Kant, *Fundamental Principles of the Metaphysics of Morals,* translated by Thomas Abbot, London, Longmans, Green and Co., 1898.

but also have been invited to go out with friends, which would probably be more fun. Should we do what we think we have to do, or should we do what we want to do? When we look closely at such situations to give a thoughtful answer, we may be confused about the proper place to focus our attention: Should we decide which action is best by considering which outcome will be most enjoyable for you? If so, you'd probably be happier going with your friends. Or perhaps we should decide what to do based on the punishment or reward we think will occur? If so, then maybe you should visit your grand-mother because your family may be angry if you don't, and they may do something nice for you if you do. Which part of the situation do we look at in order to decide? In these pages from Kant, he turns the focus of the moral philosophy debate away from the consequences, or effects, of an action and toward the motivation of the person doing the act. Is it enough to do the right thing, or must we do the right thing for some particular reason?

Suppose that you decide to visit your grandmother, but only because you think that you may inherit money from her if you visit regularly. It appears as if you are doing the right thing—visiting grandma, even though you really do not want to. But your reasoning for going is suspect: It appears that your decision is based only on concerns about your own advantage. In such a case, you seem to be doing the right thing, but you are doing it for a selfish motive. Are you being moral?   ✍

First Section

Transition from the Common Rational Knowledge of Morality to the Philosophical

Nothing can possibly be conceived in the world, or even out of it, which can be called good without qualification, except a Good Will. Intelligence, wit, judgment, and the other talents of the mind, however they may be named, or courage, resolution, per-severance, as qualities of temperament, are undoubtedly good and desirable in many respects; but these gifts of nature may also become extremely bad and mischievous if the will which is to make use of them, and which, therefore, constitutes what is called *character*, is not good. It is the same with the *gifts of fortune*. Power, riches, honor, even health, and the general well-being and contentment with one's condition which is called *happiness,* inspire pride, and often presumption, if there is not a good will to correct the influence of these on the mind, and with this also to rectify the whole principle of acting, and adapt it to its end. The sight of a being who is not adorned with a single feature of a pure and good will, enjoying unbroken prosperity, can never give pleasure to an impartial rational spectator. Thus a good will appears to consti-tute the indispensable condition even of being worthy of happiness.

There are even some qualities which are of service to this good will itself, and may facilitate its action, yet which have no intrinsic unconditional value, but always presuppose a good will, and this qualifies the esteem that we justly have for them, and does not permit us to regard them as absolutely good. Moderation in the affections and passions, self-control and calm deliberation are not only good in many respects, but even seem to constitute part of the intrinsic worth of the person; but they are far from deserving to be called good without qualification, although they have been so unconditionally praised by the ancients. For without the principles of a good will, they may become extremely bad, and the coolness of a villain not only makes him far more dangerous, but also directly makes him more abominable in our eyes than he would have been without it.

A good will is good not because of what it performs or effects, not by its aptness for the attainment of some proposed end, but simply by virtue of the volition, that is, it is good in itself, and considered by itself is to be esteemed much higher than all that can be brought about by it in favor of any inclination, nay, even of the sum total of all inclinations. Even if it should happen that, owing to special disfavor of fortune, or the niggardly provision of a step-motherly nature, this will should wholly lack power to accomplish its purpose, if with its greatest efforts it should yet achieve nothing, and there should remain only the good will (not, to be sure, a mere wish, but the summoning of all means in our power), then, like a jewel, it would still shine by its own light, as a thing which has its whole value in itself. Its usefulness or fruitlessness can neither add to nor take away anything from this value. It would be, as it were, only the setting to enable us to handle it the more conveniently in common commerce or to attract to it the attention of those who are not yet connoisseurs, but not to recommend it to true connoisseurs, or to determine its value.

There is, however, something so strange in this idea of the absolute value of the mere will, in which no account is taken of its utility, that notwithstanding the thorough assent of even common reason to the idea, yet a suspicion must arise that it may perhaps really be the product of mere high-flown fancy, and that we may have misunderstood the purpose of nature in assigning reason as the governor of our will. Therefore we will examine this idea from this point of view.

---

1. Kant discusses the relationship of reason to happiness. If reason does not give us happiness, what does Kant think its purpose is?

In the physical constitution of an organized being, that is, a being adapted suitably to the purposes of life, we assume it as a fundamental principle that no organ for any purpose will be found but what is also the fittest and best adapted for that purpose. Now in a being which has reason and a will, if the proper object of nature were its *conservation*, its *welfare*, in a word, its *happiness*, then nature would have hit upon a very bad arrangement in selecting the reason of the creature to carry out this purpose. For all the actions which the creature has to perform with a view to this purpose, and the whole rule of its conduct, would be far more surely prescribed to it by instinct, and that end would have been attained thereby much more certainly than it ever can be by reason. Should reason have been communicated to this favored creature over and above, it must only have served it to contemplate the happy constitution of its nature, to admire it, to congratulate itself thereon, and to feel thankful for it to the beneficent cause, but not that it should subject its desires to that weak and delusive guidance, and meddle bunglingly with the purpose of nature. In a word, nature would have taken care that reason should not break forth into *practical exercise,* nor have the presumption, with its weak insight, to think out for itself the plan of happiness, and of the means of attaining it. Nature would not only have taken on herself the choice of the ends, but also of the means, and with wise foresight would have entrusted both to instinct.

And, in fact, we find that the more a cultivated reason applies itself with deliberate purpose to the enjoyment of life and happiness, so much the more does the man fail of true satisfaction. And from this circumstance there arises in many, if they are candid enough to confess it, a certain degree of *misology,* that is, hatred of reason, especially in the case of those who are most experienced in the use of it, because after calculating all the advantages they derive, I do not say from the invention of all the arts of common luxury, but even from the sciences (which seem to them to be after all only a luxury of the understanding), they find that they have, in fact, only brought more trouble on their shoulders, rather than gained in happiness; and they end by envying, rather than despising, the more common stamp of men who keep closer to the guidance of mere instinct, and do not allow their reason much influence on their conduct. And this we must admit, that the judgment of those who would very much lower the lofty eulogies of the advantages which reason gives us in regard to the happiness and satisfaction of life, or who would even reduce them below zero, is by no means morose or ungrateful to the goodness with which the world is governed, but that there lies at the root of these judgments the idea that our existence has a different and far nobler end, for which, and not for happiness, reason is properly intended, and which must, therefore, be regarded as the supreme condition to which the private ends of man must, for the most part, be postponed.

For as reason is not competent to guide the will with certainty in regard to its objects and the satisfaction of all our wants (which it to some extent even multiplies), this being an end to which an implanted instinct would have led with much greater certainty; and since, nevertheless, reason is imparted to us as a practical faculty, i.e., as one which is to have influence on the *will,* therefore, admitting that nature generally in the distribution of her capacities has adapted the means to the end, its true destination must be to produce a *will,* not merely good as a *means* to something else, but *good in itself,* for which reason was absolutely necessary. This will then, though not indeed the sole and complete good, must be the supreme good and the condition of every other, even of the desire of happiness. Under these circumstances, there is nothing inconsistent with the wisdom of nature in the fact that the cultivation of the reason, which is requisite for the first and unconditional purpose, does in many ways interfere, at least in this life, with the attainment of the second, which is always conditional, namely, happiness. Nay, it may even reduce it to nothing, without nature thereby failing of her purpose. For reason recognizes the establishment of a good will as its highest practical destination, and in attaining this purpose is capable only of a satisfaction of its own proper kind, namely, that from the attainment of an end, which end again is determined by reason only, notwithstanding that this may involve many a disappointment to the ends of inclination.

We have then to develop the notion of a will which deserves to be highly esteemed for itself, and is good without a view to anything further, a notion which exists already in the sound natural understanding, requiring rather to be cleared up than to be taught, and which in estimating the value of our actions always takes the first place, and constitutes the condition of all the rest. In order to do this we will take the notion of duty, which includes that of a good will, although implying certain subjective restrictions and hindrances. These, however, far from concealing it, or rendering it unrecognizable, rather bring it out by contrast, and make it shine forth so much the brighter.

----

2. The subject is duty. Kant distinguishes actions done from duty *from other types of actions. Can you think of an instance in which you did your duty for some self-serving reason (such as avoiding punishment)?*

I omit here all actions which are already recognized as inconsistent with duty, although they may be useful for this or that purpose, for with these the question whether they are done *from duty* cannot arise at all, since they even conflict with it. I also set aside those actions which really conform to duty, but to which men have *no* direct *inclination,* performing them because they are impelled thereto by some other inclination. For in this case we can readily distinguish whether the action which agrees with duty is done *from duty,* or from a selfish view. It is much harder to make this distinction when the action accords with duty, and the subject has besides a *direct* inclination to it. For example, it is always a matter of duty that a dealer should not overcharge an inexperienced purchaser, and wherever there is much commerce the prudent tradesman does not overcharge, but keeps a fixed price for everyone, so that a child buys of him as well as any other. Men are thus *honestly* served; but this is not enough to make us believe that the tradesman has so acted from duty and from principles of honesty: his own advantage required it; it is out of the question in this case to suppose that he might besides have a direct inclination in favor of the buyers, so that, as it were, from love he should give no advantage to one over another. Accordingly the action was done neither from duty nor from direct inclination, but merely with a selfish view.

On the other hand, it is a duty to maintain one's life; and, in addition, every one has also a direct inclination to do so. But on this account the often anxious care which most men take for it has no intrinsic worth, and their maxim has no moral import. They preserve their life *as duty requires,* no doubt, but not *because duty requires.* On the other hand, if adversity and hopeless sorrow have completely taken away the relish for life; if the unfortunate one, strong in mind, indignant at his fate rather than desponding or dejected, wishes for death, and yet preserves his life without loving it—not from inclination or fear, but from duty—then his maxim has a moral worth.

To be beneficent when we can is a duty; and besides this, there are many minds so sympathetically constituted that, without any other motive of vanity or self-interest, they find a pleasure in spreading joy around them, and can take delight in the satisfaction of others so far as it is their own work. But I maintain that in such a case an action of this kind, however proper, however amiable it may be, has nevertheless no true moral worth, but is on a level with other inclinations, e.g., the inclination to honor, which, if it is happily directed to that which is in fact of public utility and accordant with duty, and consequently honorable, deserves praise and encouragement, but not esteem. For the maxim lacks the moral import, namely, that such actions be done *from duty,* not from inclination. Put the case that the mind of that philanthropist were clouded by sorrow of his own extinguishing all sympathy with the lot of others, and that while he still has the power to benefit others in distress, he is not touched by their trouble because he is absorbed with his own; and now suppose that he tears himself out of this dead insensibility, and performs the action without any inclination to it, but simply from duty, then first has his action its genuine moral worth. Further still; if nature has put little sympathy in the heart of this or that man; if he, supposed to be an upright man, is by temperament cold and indifferent to the sufferings of others, perhaps because in respect of his own he is provided with the special gift of patience and fortitude, and supposes, or even requires, that others should have the same—and such a man would certainly not be the meanest product of nature—but if nature had not specially framed him for a philanthropist, would he not still find in himself a source from whence to give himself a far higher worth than that of a good-natured temperament could be? Unquestionably. It is just in this that the moral worth of the character is brought out which is incomparably the highest of all, namely, that he is beneficent, not from inclination, but from duty.

To secure one's own happiness is a duty, at least indirectly; for discontent with one's condition, under a pressure of many anxieties and amidst unsatisfied wants, might easily become a great *temptation to transgression of duty*. But here again, without looking to duty, all men have already the strongest and most intimate inclination to happiness, because it is just in this idea that all inclinations are combined in one total. But the precept of happiness is often of such a sort that it greatly interferes with some inclinations, and yet a man cannot form any definite and certain conception of the sum of satisfaction of all of them which is called happiness. It is not then to be wondered at that a single inclination, definite both as to what it promises and as to the time within which it can be gratified, is often able to overcome such a fluctuating idea, and that a gouty patient, for instance, can choose to enjoy what he likes, and to suffer what he may, since, according to his calculation, on this occasion at least, he has [only] not sacrificed the enjoyment of the present moment to a possibly mistaken expectation of a happiness which is supposed to be found in health. But even in this case, if the general desire for happiness did not influence his will, and supposing that in his particular case health was not a necessary element in this calculation, there yet remains in this, as in all other cases, this law, namely, that he should promote his happiness not from inclination but from duty, and by this would his conduct first acquire true moral worth.

It is in this manner, undoubtedly, that we are to understand those passages of Scripture also in which we are commanded to love our neighbor, even our enemy. For love, as an affection, cannot be commanded, but beneficence for duty's sake may; even though we are not impelled to it by any inclination—nay, are even repelled by a natural and unconquerable aversion. This is *practical* love, and not *pathological*—a love which is seated in the will, and not in the propensities of sense—in principles of action and not of tender sympathy; and it is this love alone which can be commanded.

The second[1] proposition is: That an action done from duty derives its moral worth, *not from the purpose* which is to be attained by it, but from the maxim by which it is determined, and therefore does not depend on the realization of the object of the action, but merely on the *principle of volition* by which the action has taken place, without regard to any object of desire. It is clear from what precedes that

---

[1] The first proposition was that, to have moral worth, an action must be done from duty.

the purposes which we may have in view in our actions, or their effects regarded as ends and springs of the will, cannot give to actions any unconditional or moral worth. In what, then, can their worth lie, if it is not to consist in the will and in reference to its expected effect? It cannot lie anywhere but in the *principle of the will* without regard to the ends which can be attained by the action. For the will stands between its *à priori* principle, which is formal, and its *à posteriori* spring, which is material, as between two roads, and as it must be determined by something, it follows that it must be determined by the formal principle of volition when an action is done from duty, in which case every material principle has been withdrawn from it.

The third proposition, which is a consequence of the two preceding, I would express thus: *Duty is the necessity of acting from respect for the law.* I may have *inclination* for an object as the effect of my proposed action, but I cannot have *respect* for it, just for this reason, that it is an effect and not an energy of will. Similarly, I cannot have respect for inclination, whether my own or another's; I can at most, if my own, approve it; if another's, sometimes even love it; i.e., look on it as favorable to my own interest. It is only what is connected with my will as a principle, by no means as an effect—what does not subserve my inclination, but overpowers it, or at least in case of choice excludes it from its calculation—in other words, simply the law of itself which can be an object of respect, and hence a command. Now an action done from duty must wholly exclude the influence of inclination, and with it every object of the will, so that nothing remains which can determine the will except objectively the *law*, and subjectively *pure respect* for this practical law, and consequently the maxim[2] that I should follow this law even to the thwarting of all my inclinations.

Thus the moral worth of an action does not lie in the effect expected from it, nor in any principle of action which requires to borrow its motive from this expected effect. For all these effects—agreeableness of one's condition, and even the promotion of the happiness of others—could have been also brought about by other causes, so that for this there would have been no need of the will of a rational being; whereas it is in this alone that the supreme and unconditional good can be found. The pre-eminent good which we call moral can therefore consist in nothing else than *the conception of law* in itself, *which certainly is only possible in a rational being*, in so far as this conception, and not the expected effect, determines the will. This is a good which is already present in the person who acts accordingly, and we have not to wait for it to appear first in the result.

3. In this paragraph Kant gives the first formulation of the conception of the law that he just discussed. Notice the example he uses of the person who is tempted to break a promise: Can breaking a promise be morally right?

But what sort of law can that be, the conception of which must determine the will, even without paying any regard to the effect expected from it, in order that this will may be called good absolutely and without qualification? As I have deprived the will of every impulse which could arise to it from obedience to any law, there

---

[2] A *maxim* is the subjective principle of volition. The objective principle (i.e., that which would also serve subjectively as a practical principle to all rational beings if reason had full power over the faculty of desire) is the practical *law*.

remains nothing but the universal conformity of its actions to law in general, which alone is to serve the will as a principle, i.e., I am never to act otherwise than so *that I could also will that my maxim should become a universal law.* Here now, it is the simple conformity to law in general, without assuming any particular law applicable to certain actions, that serves the will as its principle, and must so serve it, if duty is not to be a vain delusion and a chimerical notion. The common reason of men in its practical judgments perfectly coincides with this, and always has in view the principle here suggested. Let the question be, for example: May I when in distress make a promise with the intention not to keep it? I readily distinguish here between the two significations which the question may have: Whether it is prudent, or whether it is right, to make a false promise. The former may undoubtedly often be the case. I see clearly indeed that it is not enough to extricate myself from a present difficulty by means of this subterfuge, but it must be well considered whether there may not hereafter spring from this lie much greater inconvenience than that from which I now free myself, and as, with all my supposed *cunning,* the consequences cannot be so easily foreseen but that credit once lost may be much more injurious to me than any mischief which I seek to avoid at present, it should be considered whether it would not be more *prudent* to act herein according to a universal maxim, and to make it a habit to promise nothing except with the intention of keeping it. But it is soon clear to me that such a maxim will still only be based on the fear of consequences. Now it is a wholly different thing to be truthful from duty, and to be so from apprehension of injurious consequences. In the first case, the very notion of the action already implies a law for me; in the second case, I must first look about elsewhere to see what results may be combined with it which would affect myself. For to deviate from the principle of duty is beyond all doubt wicked; but to be unfaithful to my maxim of prudence may often be very advantageous to me, although to abide by it is certainly safer. The shortest way, however, and an unerring one, to discover the answer to this question whether a lying promise is consistent with duty, is to ask myself, Should I be content that my maxim (to extricate myself from difficulty by a false promise) should hold good as a universal law, for myself as well as for others? and should I be able to say to myself, "Everyone may make a deceitful promise when he finds himself in a difficulty from which he cannot otherwise extricate himself"? Then I presently become aware that while I can will the lie, I can by no means will that lying should be a universal law. For with such a law there would be no promises at all, since it would be in vain to allege my intention in regard to my future actions to those who would not believe this allegation, or if they over-hastily did so would pay me back in my own coin. Hence my maxim, as soon as it should be made a universal law, would necessarily destroy itself.

---

4. Many of Kant's main points are presented here in condensed form. You should pay particular attention to the connection that he says holds between duty, practical respect for the law, and the good will.

I do not, therefore, need any far-reaching penetration to discern what I have to do in order that my will may be morally good. Inexperienced in the course of the world, incapable of being prepared for all its contingencies, I only ask myself: Canst thou also will that thy maxim should be a universal law? If not, then it must be rejected, and that not because of a disadvantage accruing from it to myself or even to others, but because it cannot enter as a principle into a possible universal legislation, and reason extorts from me immediate respect for such legislation. I do not indeed as yet *discern* on what this respect is based (this the philosopher may inquire), but at least I understand this, that it is an estimation of the worth which far outweighs all worth of what is recommended by inclination, and that the necessity of acting from *pure* respect for the practical law is what constitutes duty, to which every other motive must give place, because it is the condition of a will being good *in itself,* and the worth of such a will is above everything.

Thus, then, without quitting the moral knowledge of common human reason, we have arrived at its principle. And although, no doubt, common men do not conceive it in such an abstract and universal form, yet they always have it really before their eyes, and use it as the standard of their decision. Here it would be easy to show how, with this compass in hand, men are well able to distinguish, in every case that occurs, what is good, what bad, conformably to duty or inconsistent with it, if, without in the least teaching them anything new, we only, like Socrates, direct their attention to the principle they themselves employ; and that therefore we do not need science and philosophy to know what we should do to be honest and good, yea, even wise and virtuous. Indeed we might well have conjectured beforehand that the knowledge of what every man is bound to do, and therefore also to know, would be within the reach of every man, even the commonest. Here we cannot forbear admiration when we see how great an advantage the practical judgment has over the theoretical in the common understanding of men. In the latter, if common reason ventures to depart from the laws of experience and from the perceptions of the senses it falls into mere inconceivabilities and self-contradictions, at least into a chaos of uncertainty, obscurity, and instability. But in the practical sphere it is just when the common understanding excludes all sensible springs from practical laws that its power of judgment begins to show itself to advantage. It then becomes even subtle, whether it be that it chicanes with its own conscience or with other claims respecting what is to be called right, or whether it desires for its own instruction to determine honestly the worth of actions; and, in the latter case, it may even have as good a hope of hitting the mark as any philosopher whatever can promise himself. Nay, it is almost more sure of doing so, because the philosopher cannot have any other principle, while he may easily perplex his judgment by a multitude of considerations foreign to the matter, and so turn aside from the right way. Would it not therefore be wiser in moral concerns to acquiesce in the judgment of common reason, or at most only to call in philosophy for the purpose of rendering the system of morals more complete and intelligible, and its rules more convenient for use (especially for disputation), but not so as to draw off the common understanding from its happy simplicity, or to bring it by means of philosophy into a new path of inquiry and instruction?

Innocence is indeed a glorious thing, only, on the other hand, it is very sad that it cannot well maintain itself, and is easily seduced. On this account even wisdom—which otherwise consists more in conduct than in knowledge—yet has need of science, not in order to learn from it, but to secure for its precepts admission and permanence. Against all the commands of duty which reason represents to man as so deserving of respect, he feels in himself a powerful counterpoise in his wants and inclinations, the entire satisfaction of which he sums up under the name of happiness. Now reason issues its commands unyieldingly, without promising anything to the inclinations, and, as it were, with disregard and contempt for these claims, which are so impetuous, and at the same time so plausible, and which will not allow themselves to be suppressed by any command. Hence there arises a natural *dialectic,* i.e., a disposition to argue against these strict laws of duty and to question their validity, or at least their purity and strictness; and, if possible, to make them more accordant with our wishes and inclinations, that is to say, to corrupt them at their very source, and entirely to destroy their worth—a thing which even common practical reason cannot ultimately call good.

Thus is the *common reason of man* compelled to go out of its sphere, and to take a step into the field of a *practical philosophy,* not to satisfy any speculative want (which never occurs to it as long as it is content to be mere sound reason), but even on practical grounds, in order to attain in it information and clear instruction respecting the source of its principle, and the correct determination of it in opposition to the maxims which are based on wants and inclinations, so that it may escape from the perplexity of opposite claims, and not run the risk of losing all genuine moral principles through the equivocation into which it easily falls. Thus, when practical reason cultivates itself, there insensibly arises in it a dialectic which forces it to seek aid in philosophy, just as happens to it in its theoretic use; and in this case, therefore, as well as in the other, it will find rest nowhere but in a thorough critical examination of our reason.

Second Section

Transition from Popular Moral Philosophy to the Metaphysics of Morals

Everything in nature works according to laws. Rational beings alone have the faculty of acting according *to the conception* of laws, that is according to principles, i.e., have a *will.* Since the deduction of actions from principles requires *reason,* the will is nothing but practical reason. If reason infallibly determines the will, then the actions of such a being which are recognized as objectively necessary are subjectively necessary also, i.e., the will is a faculty to choose *that only* which reason independent on inclination recognizes as practically necessary, i.e., as good. But if reason of itself does not sufficiently determine the will, if the latter is subject also to subjective conditions (particular impulses) which do not always coincide with the objective conditions; in a word, if the will does not *in itself* completely accord with reason (which is actually the case with men), then the actions which objectively are recognized as necessary are subjectively contingent, and the determination of such a will according to objective laws is *obligation,* that is to say, the relation of the objective laws to a will that is not thoroughly good is conceived as the determination of the will of a rational being by principles of reason, but which the will from its nature does not of necessity follow.

The conception of an objective principle, in so far as it is obligatory for a will, is called a command (of reason), and the formula of the command is called an imperative.

All imperatives are expressed by the word *ought* [or *shall*], and thereby indicate the relation of an objective law of reason to a will, which from its subjective constitution is not necessarily determined by it (an obligation). They say that something would be good to do or to forbear, but they say it to a will which does not always do a thing because it is conceived to be good to do it. That is practically *good,* however, which determines the will by means of the conceptions of reason, and consequently not from subjective causes, but objectively, that is on principles which are valid for every rational being as such. It is distinguished from the *pleasant,* as that which influences the will only by means of sensation from merely subjective causes, valid only for the sense of this or that one, and not as a principle of reason, which holds for every one.

A perfectly good will would therefore be equally subject to objective laws (viz. laws of good), but could not be conceived as *obliged* thereby to act lawfully, because of itself from its subjective constitution it can only be determined by the conception of good. Therefore no imperatives hold for the Divine will, or in general for a *holy* will; *ought* is here out of place, because the volition is already of itself necessarily in unison with the law. Therefore imperatives are only formulae to express the relation of objective laws of all volition to the subjective imperfection of the will of this or that rational being, e.g., the human will.

------

5. The important distinction between hypothetical and categorical imperatives is the subject of the next several paragraphs. Can you think of an illustration of a hypothetical imperative?

Now all *imperatives* command either *hypothetically* or *categorically*. The former represent the practical necessity of a possible action as means to something else that is willed (or at least which one might possibly will). The categorical imperative would be that which represented an action as necessary of itself without reference to another end, i.e., as objectively necessary.

Since every practical law represents a possible action as good, and on this account, for a subject who is practically determinable by reason, necessary, all imperatives are formulae determining an action which is necessary according to the principle of a will good in some respects. If now the action is good only as a means *to something else,* then the imperative is *hypothetical*; if it is conceived as good *in itself* and consequently as being necessarily the principle of a will which of itself conforms to reason, then it is *categorical.*

Thus the imperative declares what action possible by me would be good, and presents the practical rule in relation to a will which does not forthwith perform an action simply because it is good, whether because the subject does not always know that it is good, or because, even if it know this, yet its maxims might be opposed to the objective principles of practical reason.

Accordingly the hypothetical imperative only says that the action is good for some purpose, *possible* or *actual.* In the first case it is a problematical, in the second an assertorial practical principle. The categorical imperative which declares an action to be objectively necessary in itself without reference to any purpose, i.e., without any other end, is valid as a (practical) Apodictic principle.

------

6. Kant articulates the one categorical imperative. In the following paragraphs he gives four examples of the imperative in operation. Remember that with these examples he is trying to use the categorical imperative to determine whether or not these acts are right.

In this problem we will first inquire whether the mere conception of a categorical imperative may not perhaps supply us also with the formula of it, containing the proposition which alone can be a categorical imperative; for even if we know the tenor of such an absolute command, yet how it is possible will require further special and laborious study, which we postpone to the last section.

When I conceive a hypothetical imperative in general I do not know beforehand what it will contain until I am given the condition. But when I conceive a categorical imperative I know at once what it contains. For as the imperative contains besides the law only the necessity that the maxims shall conform to this law, while the law contains no conditions restricting it, there remains nothing but the general statement that the maxim of the action should conform to a universal law, and it is this conformity alone that the imperative properly represents as necessary.

There is therefore but one categorical imperative, namely this: *Act only on that maxim whereby thou canst at the same time will that it should become a universal law.*

Now if all imperatives of duty can be deduced from this one imperative as from their principle, then, although it should remain undecided whether what is called duty is not merely a vain notion, yet at least we shall be able to show what we understand by it and what this notion means.

Since the universality of the law according to which effects are produced constitutes what is properly called *nature* in the most general sense (as to form), that is, the existence of things so far as it is determined by general laws, the imperative of duty may be expressed thus: *Act as if the maxim of thy action were to become by thy will a universal law of nature.*

We will now enumerate a few duties, adopting the usual division of them into duties to ourselves and to others, and into perfect and imperfect duties.

1. A man reduced to despair by a series of misfortunes feels wearied of life, but is still so far in possession of his reason that he can ask himself whether it would not be contrary to his duty to himself to take his own life. Now he inquires whether the maxim of his action could become a universal law of nature. His maxim is: From self-love I adopt it as a principle to shorten my life when its longer duration is likely to bring more evil than satisfaction. It is asked then simply whether this principle founded on self-love can become a universal law of nature. Now we see at once that a system of nature of which it should be a law to destroy life by means of the very feeling whose special nature it is to impel to the improvement of life would contradict itself, and therefore could not exist as a system of nature; hence that maxim cannot possibly exist as a universal law of nature, and consequently would be wholly inconsistent with the supreme principle of all duty.

2. Another finds himself forced by necessity to borrow money. He knows that he will not be able to repay it, but sees also that nothing will be lent to him, unless he promises stoutly to repay it in a definite time. He desires to make this promise, but he has still so much conscience as to ask himself: Is it not unlawful and inconsistent with duty to get out of a difficulty in this way? Suppose however that he resolves to do so, then the maxim of his action would be expressed thus: When I think myself in want of money, I will borrow money and promise to repay it, although I know that I never can do so. Now this principle of self-love or of one's own advantage may perhaps be consistent with my whole future welfare; but the question now is, is it right? I change then the suggestion of self-love into a universal law, and state the question thus: How would it be if my maxim were a universal law? Then I see at once that it could never hold as a universal law of nature but would necessarily contradict itself. For supposing it to be a universal law that everyone when he thinks himself in a difficulty should be able to promise whatever he pleases, with the purpose of not keeping his promise, the promise itself would become impossible, as well

as the end that one might have in view in it, since no one would consider that any-thing was promised to him, but would ridicule all such statements as vain pretenses.

3. A third finds in himself a talent which with the help of some culture might make him a useful man in many respects. But he finds himself in comfortable circum-stances, and prefers to indulge in pleasure rather than to take pains in enlarging and improving his happy natural capacities. He asks, however, whether his maxim of neg-lect of his natural gifts, besides agreeing with his inclination to indulgence, agrees also with what is called duty. He sees then that a system of nature could indeed subsist with such a universal law although men (like the South Sea islanders) should let their tal-ents rust, and resolve to devote their lives merely to idleness, amusement, and propa-gation of their species—in a word, to enjoyment; but he cannot possibly *will* that this should be a universal law of nature, or be implanted in us as such by a natural instinct. For, as a rational being, he necessarily wills that his faculties be developed, since they serve him, and have been given him, for all sorts of possible purposes.

4. A fourth, who is in prosperity, while he sees that others have to contend with great wretchedness and that he could help them, thinks: What concern is it of mine? Let everyone be as happy as heaven pleases, or as he can make himself; I will take nothing from him nor even envy him, only I do not wish to contribute anything to his welfare or to his assistance in distress! Now no doubt if such a mode of thinking were a universal law, the human race might very well subsist, and doubtless even better than in a state in which every one talks of sympathy and good-will, or even takes care occasionally to put it into practice, but on the other side, also cheats when he can, betrays the rights of men, or otherwise violates them. But although it is possible that a universal law of nature might exist in accordance with that maxim, it is impossible to *will* that such a principle should have the universal validity of a law of nature. For a will which resolved this would contradict itself, inasmuch as many cases might occur in which one would have need of the love and sympathy of others, and in which, by such a law of nature, sprung from his own will, he would deprive himself of all hope of the aid he desires.

These are a few of the many actual duties, or at least what we regard as such, which obviously fall into two classes on the one principle that we have laid down. We must be *able to will* that a maxim of our action should be a universal law. This is the canon of the moral appreciation of the action generally. Some actions are of such a character that their maxim cannot without contradiction be even *conceived* as a uni-versal law of nature, far from it being possible that we should *will* that it *should* be so. In others this intrinsic impossibility is not found, but still it is impossible to *will* that their maxim should be raised to the universality of a law of nature, since such a will would contradict itself. It is easily seen that the former violate strict or rigorous (inflexible) duty; the latter only laxer (meritorious) duty. Thus it has been completely shown by these examples how all duties depend as regards the nature of the obliga-tion (not the object of the action) on the same principle.

If now we attend to ourselves on occasion of any transgression of duty, we shall find that we in fact do not will that our maxim should be a universal law, for that is impossible for us; on the contrary we will that the opposite should remain a uni-versal law, only we assume the liberty of making an *exception* in our own favor or (just for this time only) in favor of our inclination. Consequently if we considered all cases from one and the same point of view, namely, that of reason, we should find a contradiction in our own will, namely, that a certain principle should be ob-jectively necessary as a universal law, and yet subjectively should not be universal, but admit of exceptions. As however we at one moment regard our action from the point of view of a will wholly conformed to reason, and then again look at the same action from the point of view of a will affected by inclination, there is not really any contradiction, but an antagonism of inclination to the precept of reason, whereby the universality of the principle is changed into a mere generality, so that the practical principle of reason shall meet the maxim half way. Now, although this cannot be justified in our own impartial judgment, yet it proves that we do really recognize the validity of the categorical imperative and (with all respect for it) only allow ourselves a few exceptions, which we think unimportant and forced from us.

We have thus established at least this much, that if duty is a conception which is to have any import and real legislative authority for our actions, it can only be expressed in categorical, and not at all in hypothetical imperatives. We have also, which is of great importance, exhibited clearly and definitely for every practical application the content of the categorical imperative, which must contain the principle of all duty if there is such a thing at all. We have not yet, however, advanced so far as to prove *à priori* that there actually is such an imperative, that there is a practical law which commands absolutely of itself, and without any other impulse, and that the following of this law is duty.

READING QUESTIONS

1. What must a person have to be worthy of happiness?
2. What does Kant use "the coolness of a villain" to illustrate?
3. How does Kant define happiness?
4. Why isn't the shopkeeper who treats you honestly not necessarily an example of a person acting *from duty*?
5. What is the difference between practical love and pathological love, according to Kant?
6. According to Kant, how can a person be sure that breaking a promise is wrong?
7. What kind of command is an imperative?
8. What are the two ways that imperatives can command?
9. State the reasoning behind Kant's claim that suicide is always immoral, even for a person who is "weary of life."

Mary Wollstonecraft

Mary Wollstonecraft contributed a strong voice for women's rights before it was possible for many women to be heard on this issue. She was born in England in 1757, the second of seven children. Her father had inherited a sizable fortune before Mary was born, which allowed him to pursue the life of the gentleman farmer. For a variety of reasons, some entirely out of his control, each of his repeated attempts at farming resulted in failure. As failure followed failure, the family moved often and her father began to ease his worries with frequent drinking bouts. More and more often, he flew into rages at his wife and children. Neither the children, his wife, nor even their hunting dogs were safe from his attacks. So much concern did Mary have for the safety of her mother, that she often would sleep outside her door to protect her. Mary's miserable existence would have destroyed most people—but it served to make Mary strong, an irrepressible foe of oppression in any form with the unbounded courage to fight it.

Because of her tumultuous family life, Wollstonecraft early on assumed adult responsibilities. She began writing at the urging of friends and in 1786 published her first book, *Thoughts on the Education of Daughters.* Among her writings was a novel (at least loosely autobiographical), *Mary, a Fiction,* published two years later. In 1790, as a champion of liberty and an enemy of tyranny, she boldly wrote *A Vindication of the Rights of Men,* a critical reply to Edmund Burke's *Reflections on the Revolution in France* (1790). But the work that brought her the most attention, and that has secured her place as an early champion of women's rights, is *A Vindication of the Rights of Woman,* published in 1792.

By the time of Wollstonecraft's writing, the notion that certain "inalienable rights" belong to all *men* was an idea whose time had come. The American colonies had just fought for, and won, their independence from England with the "rights of man" as one of the foundations of the new society. So, too, in France, the French revolution had championed the "rights of man" and had excited those people throughout Europe who dreamed of a society free of oppression and governmental abuse. In the first *Vindication,* Wollstonecraft passionately argued for the extension of rights to all men. In the second *Vindication,* Wollstonecraft wrote to demand for women the human rights accorded men. She contended that the notion of human rights must not be based on gender: rights belong equally to men and women.

Mary Wollstonecraft's life was not long; she died during the birth of her second daughter, in 1797. This daughter, also named Mary, went on to achieve literary fame as the author of the classic horror story *Frankenstein* and as the wife of the British poet Percy Bysshe Shelley.

Wollstonecraft's legacy in moral and political philosophy was neither extensive nor long lasting. In fact, after her death, opponents of her views on human rights vilified her in a manner that would be shameful if directed toward a person who was able to defend herself, but absolutely unforgivable when directed toward the dead. By the end of the nineteenth century, however, her ideas enjoyed a renewed interest with the publication of the first full-length biography of her and the resultant reissue of *A Vindication of the Rights of Woman.* Recently she has attracted increased scholarly attention mostly as an early and ardent feminist. Her words will likely become known to the readers of yet another century.

A Vindication of the Rights of Men
A Letter to the Right Honorable Edmund Burke

The existence of basic, universal human rights might seem obvious to people born and raised in the United States in the twentieth century. To be sure, in many countries human rights are ignored or abused, but the existence of human rights seems to many to be a foregone conclusion. However, the notion of a universal human right is a relatively recent innovation, a product of the Age of Enlightenment.

In the late eighteenth century, two revolutions were at least partly fought over the issue of human rights: the American Revolution and the French Revolution. But the degree to which human rights should be extended was a contentious issue. In England in 1790, Mary Wollstonecraft joined a raging battle over human rights that was being carried out in books, pamphlets, and sermons. Her target was Edmund Burke's book *Reflections on the Revolution in France*. Burke condemned the French Revolution and passionately pleaded with the English citizens to maintain the institutions that time had proven sound. Wollstonecraft believed that Burke, once an ardent supporter of the American Revolution, was now a supporter of tyranny and oppression. In *A Vindication of the Rights of Men* she assails both the character and political ideas of Burke. As you read, note how the anger she feels for him personally cannot be contained.

Sir,

It is not necessary, with courtly insincerity, to apologize to you for thus intruding on your precious time, not to profess that I think it an honor to discuss an important subject with a man whose literary abilities have raised him to notice in the state. I have not yet learned to twist my periods, nor, in the equivocal idiom of politeness, to disguise my sentiments, and imply what I should be afraid to utter: if, therefore, in the course of this epistle, I chance to express contempt, and even indignation, with some emphasis, I beseech you to believe that it is not a flight of fancy; for truth, in morals, has ever appeared to me the essence of the sublime; and, in taste, simplicity the only criterion of the beautiful. But I war not with an individual when I contend for the *rights of men* and the liberty of reason. You see I do not condescend to cull my words to avoid the invidious phrase, nor shall I be prevented from giving a manly definition of it, by the flimsy ridicule which a lively fancy has interwoven with the present acceptation of the term. Reverencing the rights of humanity, I shall

From Mary Wollstonecraft, *A Vindication of the Rights of Men*, London, Joseph Johnson, 1796.

dare to assert them; not intimidated by the horse laugh that you have raised, or waiting till time has wiped away the compassionate tears which you have elaborately labored to excite.

From the many just sentiments interspersed through the letter before me, and from the whole tendency of it, I should believe you to be a good, though a vain man, if some circumstances in your conduct did not render the inflexibility of your integrity doubtful; and for this vanity a knowledge of human nature enables me to discover such extenuating circumstances, in the very texture of your mind, that I am ready to call it amiable, and separate the public from the private character.

I know that a lively imagination renders a man particularly calculated to shine in conversation and in those desultory productions where method is disregarded; and the instantaneous applause which his eloquence extorts is at once a reward and a spur. Once a wit and always a wit, is an aphorism that has received the sanction of experience; yet I am apt to conclude that the man who with scrupulous anxiety endeavors to support that shining character, can never nourish by reflection any profound, or, if you please, metaphysical passion. Ambition becomes only the tool of vanity, and his reason, the weather-cock of unrestrained feelings, is only employed to varnish over the faults which it ought to have corrected.

Sacred, however, would the infirmities and errors of a good man be, in my eyes, if they were only displayed in a private circle; if the venial fault only rendered the wit anxious, like a celebrated beauty, to raise admiration on every occasion, and excite emotion, instead of the calm reciprocation of mutual esteem and unimpassioned respect. Such vanity enlivens social intercourse, and forces the little great man to be always on his guard to secure his throne; and an ingenious man, who is ever on the watch for conquest, will, in his eagerness to exhibit his whole store of knowledge, furnish an attentive observer with some useful information, calcined by fancy and formed by taste.

And though some dry reasoner might whisper that the arguments were superficial, and should even add, that the feelings which are thus ostentatiously displayed are often the cold declamation of the head, and not the effusions of the heart—what will these shrewd remarks avail, when the witty arguments and ornamental feelings are on a level with the comprehension of the fashionable world, and a book is found very amusing? Even the Ladies, Sir, may repeat your sprightly sallies, and retail in theatrical attitudes many of your sentimental exclamations. Sensibility is the *manie* of the day, and compassion the virtue which is to cover a multitude of vices, whilst justice is left to mourn in sullen silence, and balance truth in vain.

In life, an honest man with a confined understanding is frequently the slave of his habits and the dupe of his feelings, whilst the man with a clearer head and colder heart makes the passions of others bend to his interest; but truly sublime is the character that acts from principle, and governs the inferior springs of activity without slackening their vigor; whose feelings give vital heat to his resolves, but never hurry him into feverish eccentricities.

However, as you have informed us that respect chills love, it is natural to conclude, that all your pretty flights arise from your pampered sensibility; and that, vain of this fancied pre-eminence of organs, you foster every emotion till the fumes, mounting to your brain, dispel the sober suggestions of reason. It is not in this view surprising, that when you should argue you become impassioned, and that reflection inflames your imagination, instead of enlightening your understanding.

Quitting now the flowers of rhetoric, let us, Sir, reason together; and, believe me, I should not have meddled with these troubled waters, in order to point out your inconsistencies, if your wit had not burnished up some rusty, baneful opinions, and swelled the shallow current of ridicule till it resembled the flow of reason, and presumed to be the test of truth.

I shall not attempt to follow you through 'horse-way and foot-path'; but, attacking the foundation of your opinions, I shall leave the superstructure to find a center of gravity on which it may lean till some strong blast puffs it into the air; or your teeming fancy, which the ripening judgment of sixty years has not tamed, produces another Chinese erection, to stare, at every turn, the plain country people in the face, who bluntly call such an airy edifice—a folly.

1. Wollstonecraft defines a "birthright." What do you think of this definition?

The birthright of man, to give you, Sir, a short definition of this disputed right, is such a degree of liberty, civil and religious, as is compatible with the liberty of every other individual with whom he is united in a social compact, and the continued existence of that compact.

Liberty, in this simple, unsophisticated sense, I acknowledge, is a fair idea that has never yet received a form in the various governments that have been established on our beauteous globe; the demon of property has ever been at hand to encroach on the sacred rights of men, and to fence round with awful pomp laws that war with justice. But that it results from the eternal foundation of right—from immutable truth—who will presume to deny, that pretends to rationality—if reason has led them to build their morality[1] and religion on an everlasting foundation—the attributes of God?

I glow with indignation when I attempt, methodically, to unravel your slavish paradoxes, in which I can find no fixed first principle to refute; I shall not, therefore, condescend to show where you affirm in one page what you deny in another; and how frequently you draw conclusions without any previous premises:—it would be something like cowardice to fight with a man who had never exercised the weapons with which his opponent chose to combat, and irksome to refute sentence after sentence in which the latent spirit of tyranny appeared.

I perceive, from the whole tenor of your Reflections, that you have a mortal antipathy to reason; but, if there is any thing like argument, or first principles, in your wild declamation, behold the result:—that we are to reverence the rust of antiquity, and term the unnatural customs, which ignorance and mistaken self-interest have consolidated, the sage fruit of experience: nay, that, if we do discover some errors, our *feelings* should lead us to excuse, with blind love, or unprincipled filial affection, the venerable vestiges of ancient days. These are gothic notions of beauty—the ivy is beautiful, but, when it insidiously destroys the trunk from which it receives support, who would not grub it up?

---

[1] As religion is included in my idea of morality, I should not have mentioned the term without specifying all the simple ideas which that comprehensive word generalizes; but as the charge of atheism has been very freely banded about in the letter I am considering, I wish to guard against misrepresentation.

Further, that we ought cautiously to remain forever in frozen inactivity, because a thaw, whilst it nourishes the soil, spreads a temporary inundation; and the fear of risking any personal present convenience should prevent a struggle for the most estimable advantages. This is sound reasoning, I grant, in the mouth of the rich and short-sighted.

Yes, Sir, the strong gained riches, the few have sacrificed the many to their vices; and, to be able to pamper their appetites, and supinely exist without exercising mind or body, they have ceased to be men.—Lost to the relish of true pleasure, such beings would, indeed, deserve compassion, if injustice was not softened by the tyrant's plea—necessity; if prescription was not raised as an immortal boundary against innovation. Their minds, in fact, instead of being cultivated, have been so warped by education, that it may require some ages to bring them back to nature, and enable them to see their true interest, with that degree of conviction which is necessary to influence their conduct.

---

2. Notice where Wollstonecraft places the blame for inequality in European civilization.

The civilization which has taken place in Europe has been very partial, and, like every custom that an arbitrary point of honor has established, refines the manners at the expense of morals, by making sentiments and opinions current in conversation that have no root in the heart, or weight in the cooler resolves of the mind.—And what has stopped its progress?—hereditary property—hereditary honors. The man has been changed into an artificial monster by the station in which he was born, and the consequent homage that benumbed his faculties like the torpedo's touch;—or a being, with a capacity of reasoning, would not have failed to discover, as his faculties unfolded, that true happiness arose from the friendship and intimacy which can only be enjoyed by equals; and that charity is not a condescending distribution of alms, but an intercourse of good offices and mutual benefits, founded on respect for justice and humanity.

Governed by these principles, the poor wretch, whose *inelegant* distress extorted from a mixed feeling of disgust and animal sympathy present relief, would have been considered as a man, whose misery demanded a part of his birthright, supposing him to be industrious; but should his vices have reduced him to poverty, he could only have addressed his fellow-men as weak beings, subject to like passions, who ought to forgive, because they expect to be forgiven, for suffering the impulse of the moment to silence the suggestions of conscience, or reason, which you will; for, in my view of things, they are synonymous terms.

Will Mr. Burke be at the trouble to inform us, how far we are to go back to discover the rights of men, since the light of reason is such a fallacious guide that none but fools trust to its cold investigation?

In the infancy of society, confining our view to our own country, customs were established by the lawless power of an ambitious individual; or a weak prince was obliged to comply with every demand of the licentious barbarous insurgents, who disputed his authority with irrefragable arguments at the point of their swords; or the more specious requests of the Parliament, who only allowed him conditional supplies.

Are these the venerable pillars of our constitution? And is Magna Charta to rest for its chief support on a former grant, which reverts to another, till chaos becomes the base of the mighty structure—or we cannot tell what?—for coherence, without some pervading principle of order, is a solecism.

Speaking of Edward III Hume observes, that "he was a prince of great capacity, not governed by favorites, not led astray by any unruly passion, sensible that nothing could be more essential to his interests than to keep on good terms with his people: yet, on the whole, it appears that the government, at best, was only a barbarous monarchy, not regulated by any fixed maxims, or bounded by any certain or undisputed rights, which in practice were regularly observed. The King conducted himself by one set of principles; the Barons by another; the Commons by a third; the Clergy by a fourth. All these systems of government were opposite and incompatible: each of them prevailed in its turn, as incidents were favorable to it: a great prince rendered the monarchical power predominant: the weakness of a king gave reins to the aristocracy: a superstitious age saw the clergy triumphant: the people, for whom chiefly government was instituted, and who chiefly deserve consideration, were the weakest of the whole."

And just before that most auspicious era, the fourteenth century, during the reign of Richard II, whose total incapacity to manage the reins of power, and keep in subjection his haughty Barons, rendered him a mere cipher; the House of Commons, to whom he was obliged frequently to apply, not only for subsidies but assistance to quell the insurrections that the contempt in which he was held naturally produced, gradually rose into power; for whenever they granted supplies to the King, they demanded in return, though it bore the name of petition, a confirmation, or the renewal of former charters, which had been infringed, and even utterly disregarded by the King and his seditious Barons, who principally held their independence of the crown by force of arms, and the encouragement which they gave to robbers and villains, who infested the country, and lived by rapine and violence.

To what dreadful extremities were the poorer sort reduced, their property, the fruit of their industry, being entirely at the disposal of their lords, who were so many petty tyrants!

In return for the supplies and assistance which the king received from the commons, they demanded privileges, which Edward, in his distress for money to prosecute the numerous wars in which he was engaged during the greater part of his reign, was constrained to grant them; so that by degrees they rose to power, and became a check on both king and nobles. Thus was the foundation of our liberty established, chiefly through the pressing necessities of the king, who was more intent on being supplied for the moment, in order to carry on his wars and ambitious projects, than aware of the blow he gave to kingly power, by thus making a body of men feel their importance, who afterwards might strenuously oppose tyranny and oppression, and effectually guard the subject's property from seizure and confiscation. Richard's weakness completed what Edward's ambition began.

At this period, it is true, Wickliffe opened a vista for reason by attacking some of the most pernicious tenets of the church of Rome; still the prospect was sufficiently misty to authorize the question—Where was the dignity of thinking of the fourteenth century?

A Roman Catholic, it is true, enlightened by the reformation, might, with singular propriety, celebrate the epoch that preceded it, to turn our thoughts from former atrocious enormities; but a Protestant must acknowledge that this faint dawn of liberty only made the subsiding darkness more visible; and that the boasted virtues of that century all bear the stamp of stupid pride and headstrong barbarism. Civility was then called condescension, and ostentatious almsgiving humanity; and men were content to borrow their virtues, or, to speak with more propriety, their consequence, from posterity, rather than undertake the arduous task of acquiring it for themselves.

The imperfection of all modern governments must, without waiting to repeat the trite remark, that all human institutions are unavoidably imperfect, in a great measure have arisen from this simple circumstance, that the constitution, if such an heterogeneous mass deserve that name, was settled in the dark days of ignorance, when the minds of men were shackled by the grossest prejudices and most immoral superstition. And do you, Sir, a sagacious philosopher, recommend night as the fittest time to analyze a ray of light?

------

3. *Are power and right the same? We saw this question taken up in Plato's* Republic.

Are we to seek for the rights of men in the ages when a few marks were the only penalty imposed for the life of a man, and death for death when the property of the rich was touched? when—I blush to discover the depravity of our nature—when a deer was killed! Are these the laws that it is natural to love, and sacrilegious to invade?—Were the rights of men understood when the law authorized or tolerated murder?—or is power and right the same in your creed?

But in fact all your declamation leads so directly to this conclusion, that I beseech you to ask your own heart, when you call yourself a friend of liberty, whether it would not be more consistent to style yourself the champion of property, the adorer of the golden image which power has set up?—And, when you are examining your heart, if it would not be too much like mathematical drudgery, to which a fine imagination very reluctantly stoops, inquire further, how it is consistent with the vulgar notions of honesty, and the foundation of morality—truth; for a man to boast of his virtue and independence, when he cannot forget that he is at the moment enjoying the wages of falsehood; and that, in a skulking, unmanly way, he has secured himself a pension of fifteen hundred pounds per annum on the Irish establishment? Do honest men, Sir, for I am not rising to the refined principle of honor, ever receive the reward of their public services, or secret assistance, in the name of *another?*

But to return from a digression which you will more perfectly understand than any of my readers—on what principle you, Sir, can justify the reformation, which tore up by the roots an old establishment, I cannot guess—but, I beg your pardon, perhaps you do not wish to justify it—and have some mental reservation to excuse you, to yourself, for not openly avowing your reverence. Or, to go further back;— had you been a Jew—you would have joined in the cry, crucify him!—crucify him! The promulgator of a new doctrine, and the violator of old laws and customs, that not melting, like ours, into darkness and ignorance, rested on Divine authority, must have been a dangerous innovator, in your eyes, particularly if you had not been informed that the Carpenter's Son was of the stock and lineage of David. But there is no end to the arguments which might be deduced to combat such palpable absurdities, by showing the manifest inconsistencies which are necessarily involved in a direful train of false opinions.

———

4. The topic again is birthrights. In the next paragraph, she gives an example that may be helpful.

———

It is necessary emphatically to repeat, that there are rights which men inherit at their birth, as rational creatures, who were raised above the brute creation by their improvable faculties; and that, in receiving these, not from their forefathers but, from God, prescription can never undermine natural rights.

A father may dissipate his property without his child having any right to complain;—but should he attempt to sell him for a slave, or fetter him with laws contrary to reason; nature, in enabling him to discern good from evil, teaches him to break the ignoble chain, and not to believe that bread becomes flesh, and wine blood, because his parents swallowed the Eucharist with this blind persuasion.

There is no end to this implicit submission to authority—some where it must stop, or we return to barbarism; and the capacity of improvement, which gives us a natural scepter on earth, is a cheat, an ignis-fatuus, that leads us from inviting meadows into bogs and dung-hills. And if it be allowed that many of the precautions, with which any alteration was made, in our government, were prudent, it rather proves its weakness than substantiates an opinion of the soundness of the stamina, or the excellence of the constitution.

But on what principle Mr. Burke could defend American independence, I cannot conceive; for the whole tenor of his plausible arguments settles slavery on an everlasting foundation. Allowing his servile reverence for antiquity, and prudent attention to self-interest, to have the force which he insists on, the slave trade ought never to be abolished; and, because our ignorant forefathers, not understanding the native dignity of man, sanctioned a traffic that outrages every suggestion of reason and religion, we are to submit to the inhuman custom, and term an atrocious insult to humanity the love of our country, and a proper submission to the laws by which our property is secured.—Security of property! Behold, in a few words, the definition of English liberty. And to this selfish principle every nobler one is sacrificed.—The Briton takes place of the man, and the image of God is lost in the citizen! But it is not that enthusiastic flame which in Greece and Rome consumed every sordid passion: no, self is the focus; and the disparting rays rise not above our foggy atmosphere. But softly—it is only the property of the rich that is secure; the man who lives by the sweat of his brow has no asylum from oppression; the strong man may enter—when was the castle of the poor sacred? and the base informer steal him from the family that depend on his industry for subsistence.

Fully sensible as you must be of the baneful consequences that inevitably follow this notorious infringement on the dearest rights of men, and that it is an infernal blot on the very face of our immaculate constitution, I cannot avoid expressing my surprise that when you recommended our form of government as a model, you did not caution the French against the arbitrary custom of pressing men for the sea service. You should have hinted to them, that property in England is much more secure than liberty, and not have concealed that the liberty of an honest mechanic—his all—is often sacrificed to secure the property of the rich. For it is a farce to pretend that a man fights for *his country, his hearth, or his altars,* when he has neither liberty nor property.—His property is in his nervous arms—and they are compelled to pull a strange rope at the surly command of a tyrannic boy, who probably obtained his rank on account of his family connections, or the prostituted vote of his father, whose interest in a borough, or voice as a senator, was acceptable to the minister.

Our penal laws punish with death the thief who steals a few pounds; but to take by violence, or trepan, a man, is no such heinous offense. —For who shall dare to complain of the venerable vestige of the law that rendered the life of a deer more sacred than that of a man? But it was the poor man with only his native dignity who was thus oppressed—and only metaphysical sophists and cold mathematicians can discern this insubstantial form; it is a work of abstraction—and a *gentleman* of lively imagination must borrow some drapery from fancy before he can love or pity a *man.* Misery, to reach your heart, I perceive, must have its cap and bells; your tears are reserved, very *naturally* considering your character, for the declamation of the theatre, or for the downfall of queens, whose rank alters the nature of folly, and throws a graceful veil over vices that degrade humanity; whilst the distress of many industrious mothers, whose *helpmates* have been torn from them, and the hungry cry of helpless babes, were vulgar sorrows that could not move your commiseration, though they might extort an alms. "The tears that are shed for fictitious sorrow are admirably adapted," says Rousseau, "to make us proud of all the virtues which we do not possess."

The baneful effects of the despotic practice of pressing we shall, in all probability, soon feel; for a number of men, who have been taken from their daily employments, will shortly be let loose on society, now that there is no longer any apprehension of a war.

The vulgar, and by this epithet I mean not only to describe a class of people, who, working to support the body, have not had time to cultivate their minds; but likewise those who, born in the lap of affluence, have never had their invention sharpened by a necessity are, nine out of ten, the creatures of habit and impulse.

If I were not afraid to derange your nervous system by the bare mention of a metaphysical inquiry, I should observe, Sir, that self-preservation is, literally speaking, the first law of nature; and that the care necessary to support and guard the body is the first step to unfold the mind, and inspire a manly spirit of independence. The mewing babe in a swaddling-clothes, who is treated like a superior being, may perchance become a gentleman; but nature must have given him uncommon faculties if, when pleasure hangs on every bough, he has sufficient fortitude either to exercise his mind or body in order to acquire personal merit. The passions are necessary auxiliaries of reason: a present impulse pushes us forward, and when we discover that the game did not deserve the chase, we find that we have gone over much ground, and not only gained many new ideas, but a habit of thinking. The exercise of our faculties is the great end, though not the goal we had in view when we started with such eagerness.

It would be straying still further into metaphysics to add, that this is one of the strongest arguments for the natural immortality of the soul.—Everything looks like a means, nothing like an end, or point of rest, when we can say, now let us sit down and enjoy the present moment; our faculties and wishes are proportioned to the present scene; we may return without repining to our sister clod. And, if no conscious dignity whisper that we are capable of relishing more refined pleasures, the thirst of truth appears to be allayed; and thought, the faint type of an immaterial energy, no longer bounding it knows not where, is confined to the tenement that affords it sufficient variety.—The rich man may then thank his God that he is not like other men—but when is retribution to be made to the miserable, who cry day and night for help, and there is no one at hand to help them? And not only misery but immorality proceeds from this stretch of arbitrary authority. The vulgar have not the power of emptying their mind of the only ideas they imbibed whilst their hands were employed; they cannot quickly turn from one kind of life to another. Pressing them entirely unhinges their minds; they acquire new habits, and cannot return to their old occupations with their former readiness; consequently they fall into idleness, drunkenness, and the whole train of vices which you stigmatize as gross.

A government that acts in this manner cannot be called a good parent, nor inspire natural (habitual is the proper word) affection, in the breasts of children who are thus disregarded.

READING QUESTIONS

1. What does Wollstonecraft charge is the primary obstruction to liberty?
2. To what does Wollstonecraft attribute the "imperfection of all modern governments"?
3. From whom do men receive the rights Wollstonecraft is discussing?

A Vindication of the Rights of Woman

If all *men* are accorded rights, why aren't those same rights accorded to *women*? In this chapter, Wollstonecraft attacks a particular sort of argument used to defend the inferior status of women. Men must be the leaders and women the followers, because women do not have the depth of understanding, the strength of mind, to be virtuous. The proper kind of education, argues Wollstonecraft, will overcome this deficiency.

The two primary targets of her criticism are Dr. John Gregory and Jean Jacques Rousseau. In his best-selling book *Father's Legacy to His Daughters* (1774), Dr. Gregory told young women how to make themselves pleasing to men. One way to do that? Conceal your intelligence, he advises. Rousseau, the famous French philosopher, enraged Wollstonecraft by his account of women and their proper, subservient, role in his novel *Emile.*

From Mary Wollstonecraft, *A Vindication of the Rights of Woman*, London, Joseph Johnson, 1790.

Chapter II
The Prevailing Opinion of a Sexual Character Discussed

---

1. In this opening paragraph, Wollstonecraft describes the argument to which she is opposed. Notice the connection between reason and virtue, and between passion and vice.

To account for, and excuse the tyranny of man, many ingenious arguments have been brought forward to prove, that the two sexes, in the acquirement of virtue, ought to aim at attaining a very different character; or, to speak explicitly, women are not allowed to have sufficient strength of mind to acquire what really deserves the name of virtue. Yet it should seem, allowing them to have souls, that there is but one way appointed by Providence to lead *mankind* to either virtue or happiness.

If then women are not a swarm of ephemeron triflers, why should they be kept in ignorance under the specious name of innocence? Men complain, and with reason, of the follies and caprices of our sex, when they do not keenly satirize our headstrong passions and groveling vices. Behold, I should answer, the natural effect of ignorance! The mind will ever be unstable that has only prejudices to rest on, and the current will run with destructive fury when there are no barriers to break its force. Women are told from their infancy, and taught by the example of their mothers, that a little knowledge of human weakness, justly termed cunning, softness of temper, *outward* obedience, and a scrupulous attention to a puerile kind of propriety, will obtain for them the protection of man; and should they be beautiful, everything else is needless, for, at least, twenty years of their lives.

Thus Milton describes our first frail mother; though when he tells us that women are formed for softness and sweet attractive grace, I cannot comprehend his meaning, unless, in the true Mahometan strain, he meant to deprive us of souls, and insinuate that we were beings only designed by sweet attractive grace, and docile blind obedience, to gratify the senses of man when he can no longer soar on the wing of contemplation.

How grossly do they insult us who thus advise us only to render ourselves gentle, domestic brutes! For instance, the winning softness so warmly, and frequently, recommended, that governs by obeying. What childish expressions, and how insignificant is the being—can it be an immortal one? who will condescend to govern by such sinister methods! "Certainly," says Lord Bacon, "man is of kin to the beasts by his body; and if he be not of kin to God by his spirit, he is a base and ignoble creature!" Men, indeed, appear to me to act in a very unphilosophical manner when they try to secure the good conduct of women by attempting to keep them always in a state of childhood. Rousseau was more consistent when he wished to stop the progress of reason in both sexes, for if men eat of the tree of knowledge, women will come in for a taste; but, from the imperfect cultivation which their understandings now receive, they only attain a knowledge of evil.

Children, I grant, should be innocent; but when the epithet is applied to men, or women, it is but a civil term for weakness. For if it be allowed that women were destined by Providence to acquire human virtues, and by the exercise of their understandings, that stability of character which is the firmest ground to rest our future hopes upon, they must be permitted to turn to the fountain of light, and not forced to shape their course by the twinkling of a mere satellite. Milton, I grant, was of a very different opinion; for he only bends to the indefeasible right of beauty, though it would be difficult to render two passages which I now mean to contrast, consistent. But into similar inconsistencies are great men often led by their senses.

> To whom thus Eve with *perfect beauty* adorn'd.
> My Author and Disposer, what thou bidst
> *Unargued* I obey; so God ordains;
> God is *thy law, thou mine:* to know no more
> Is Woman's *happiest* knowledge and her *praise.*

These are exactly the arguments that I have used to children; but I have added, your reason is now gaining strength, and, till it arrives at some degree of maturity, you must look up to me for advice—then you ought to *think,* and only rely on God.

Yet in the following lines Milton seems to coincide with me; when he makes Adam thus expostulate with his Maker.

> Hast thou not made me here thy substitute,
> And these inferior far beneath me set?
> Among *unequals* what society
> Can sort, what harmony or true delight?
> Which must be mutual, in proportion due
> Giv'n and receiv'd; but in *disparity*
> The one intense, the other still remiss
> Cannot well suit with either, but soon prove
> Tedious alike: of *fellowship* I speak
> Such as I seek, fit to participate
> All Rational delight—

In treating, therefore, of the manners of women, let us, disregarding sensual arguments, trace what we should endeavor to make them in order to cooperate, if the expression be not too bold, with the supreme Being.

------

2. Her topic here is education. She carefully distinguishes the kind of education she has in mind from a typical education.

By individual education, I mean, for the sense of the word is not precisely defined, such an attention to a child as will slowly sharpen the senses, form the temper, regulate the passions as they begin to ferment, and set the understanding to work before the body arrives at maturity; so that the man may only have to proceed, not to begin, the important task of learning to think and reason.

To prevent any misconstruction, I must add, that I do not believe that a private education can work the wonders which some sanguine writers have attributed to it. Men and women must be educated, in a great degree, by the opinions and manners of the society they live in. In every age there has been a stream of popular opinion that has carried all before it, and given a family character, as it were, to the century. It may then fairly be inferred, that, till society be differently constituted, much cannot be expected from education. It is, however, sufficient for my present purpose to assert, that, whatever effect circumstances have on the abilities, every being may become virtuous by the exercise of its own reason; for if but one being was created with vicious inclinations, that is positively bad, what can save us from atheism? Or if we worship a God, is not that God a devil?

Consequently, the most perfect education, in my opinion, is such an exercise of the understanding as is best calculated to strengthen the body and form the heart. Or, in other words, to enable the individual to attain such habits of virtue as will render it independent. In fact, it is a farce to call any being virtuous whose virtues do not result from the exercise of its own reason. This was Rousseau's opinion respecting men: I extend it to women, and confidently assert that they have been drawn out of their sphere by false refinement, and not by an endeavor to acquire masculine qualities. Still the regal homage which they receive is so intoxicating, that till the manners of the times are changed, and formed on more reasonable principles, it may be impossible to convince them that the illegitimate power, which they obtain, by degrading themselves, is a curse, and that they must return to nature and equality, if they wish to secure the placid satisfaction that unsophisticated affections impart. But for this epoch we must wait—wait, perhaps, till kings and nobles, enlightened by reason, and, preferring the real dignity of man to childish state, throw off their gaudy hereditary trappings: and if then women do not resign the arbitrary power of beauty—they will prove that they have *less* mind than man.

I may be accused of arrogance; still I must declare what I firmly believe, that all the writers who have written on the subject of female education and manners, from Rousseau to Dr. Gregory, have contributed to render women more artificial, weak characters, than they would otherwise have been; and consequently, more useless members of society. I might have expressed this conviction in a lower key; but I am afraid it would have been the whine of affectation, and not the faithful expression of my feelings, of the clear result which experience and reflection have led me to draw. When I come to that division of the subject, I shall advert to the passages that I more particularly disapprove of, in the works of the authors I have just alluded to; but it is first necessary to observe, that my objection extends to the whole purport of those books, which tend, in my opinion, to degrade one half of the human species, and render women pleasing at the expense of every solid virtue.

Though, to reason on Rousseau's ground, if man did attain a degree of perfection of mind when his body arrived at maturity, it might be proper, in order to make a man and his wife *one,* that she should rely entirely on his understanding; and the graceful ivy, clasping the oak that supported it, would form a whole in which strength and beauty would be equally conspicuous. But, alas! husbands, as well as their helpmates, are often only overgrown children; nay, thanks to early debauchery, scarcely men in their outward form—and if the blind lead the blind, one need not come from heaven to tell us the consequence.

3. One cause that contributes to the oppression of women is here discussed. In the following paragraphs she will discuss the repercussions.

Many are the causes that, in the present corrupt state of society, contribute to enslave women by cramping their understandings and sharpening their senses. One, perhaps, that silently does more mischief than all the rest, is their disregard of order.

To do everything in an orderly manner, is a most important precept, which women, who, generally speaking, receive only a disorderly kind of education, seldom attend to with that degree of exactness that men, who from their infancy are broken into method, observe. This negligent kind of guess-work, for what other epithet can be used to point out the random exertions of a sort of instinctive common sense, never brought to the test of reason? prevents their generalizing matters of fact—so they do today, what they did yesterday, merely because they did it yesterday.

This contempt of the understanding in early life has more baneful consequences than is commonly supposed; for the little knowledge which women of strong minds attain, is, from various circumstances, of a more desultory kind than the knowledge of men, and it is acquired more by sheer observations on real life, than from comparing what has been individually observed with the results of experience generalized by speculation. Led by their dependent situation and domestic employments more into society, what they learn is rather by snatches; and as learning is with them, in general, only a secondary thing, they do not pursue any one branch with that persevering ardor necessary to give vigor to the faculties, and clearness to the judgment. In the present state of society, a little learning is required to support the character of a gentleman; and boys are obliged to submit to a few years of discipline. But in the education of women, the cultivation of the understanding is always subordinate to the acquirement of some corporeal accomplishment; even while enervated by confinement and false notions of modesty, the body is prevented from attaining that grace and beauty which relaxed half-formed limbs never exhibit. Besides, in youth their faculties are not brought forward by emulation; and having no serious scientific study, if they have natural sagacity it is turned too soon on life and manners. They dwell on effects, and modifications, without tracing them back to causes; and complicated rules to adjust behavior are a weak substitute for simple principles.

As a proof that education gives this appearance of weakness to females, we may instance the example of military men, who are, like them, sent into the world before their minds have been stored with knowledge or fortified by principles. The consequences are similar; soldiers acquire a little superficial knowledge, snatched from the muddy current of conversation, and, from continually mixing with society, they gain, what is termed a knowledge of the world; and this acquaintance with manners and customs has frequently been confounded with a knowledge of the human heart. But can the crude fruit of casual observation, never brought to the test of judgment, formed by comparing speculation and experience, deserve such a distinction? Soldiers, as well as women, practice the minor virtues with punctilious politeness. Where is then the sexual difference, when the education has been the same? All the difference that I can discern, arises from the superior advantage of liberty, which enables the former to see more of life.

It is wandering from my present subject, perhaps, to make a political remark; but, as it was produced naturally by the train of my reflections, I shall not pass it silently over.

———

4. She compares women's understanding to that of military men.

———

Standing armies can never consist of resolute robust men; they may be well disciplined machines, but they will seldom contain men under the influence of strong passions, or with very vigorous faculties. And as for any depth of understanding, I will venture to affirm, that it is as rarely to be found in the army as amongst women;

and the cause, I maintain, is the same. It may be further observed, that officers are also particularly attentive to their persons, fond of dancing, crowded rooms, adventures, and ridicule.[1] Like the *fair* sex, the business of their lives is gallantry. They were taught to please, and they only live to please. Yet they do not lose their rank in the distinction of sexes, for they are still reckoned superior to women, though in what their superiority consists, beyond what I have just mentioned, it is difficult to discover.

The great misfortune is this, that they both acquire manners before morals, and a knowledge of life before they have, from reflection, any acquaintance with the grand ideal outline of human nature. The consequence is natural; satisfied with common nature, they become a prey to prejudices, and taking all their opinions on credit, they blindly submit to authority. So that, if they have any sense, it is a kind of instinctive glance, that catches proportions, and decides with respect to manners; but fails when arguments are to be pursued below the surface, or opinions analyzed.

5. Wollstonecraft argues that civilized life leads to the oppression of women.

May not the same remark be applied to women? Nay, the argument may be carried still further, for they are both thrown out of a useful station by the unnatural distinctions established in civilized life. Riches and hereditary honors have made ciphers of women to give consequence to the numerical figure; and idleness has produced a mixture of gallantry and despotism into society, which leads the very men who are the slaves of their mistresses to tyrannize over their sisters, wives, and daughters. This is only keeping them in rank and file, it is true. Strengthen the female mind by enlarging it, and there will be an end to blind obedience; but, as blind obedience is ever sought for by power, tyrants and sensualists are in the right when they endeavor to keep women in the dark, because the former only want slaves, and the latter a plaything. The sensualist, indeed, has been the most dangerous of tyrants, and women have been duped by their lovers, as princes by their ministers, whilst dreaming that they reigned over them.

I now principally allude to Rousseau, for his character of Sophia is, undoubtedly, a captivating one, though it appears to me grossly unnatural; however it is not the superstructure, but the foundation of her character, the principles on which her education was built, that I mean to attack; nay, warmly as I admire the genius of that able writer, whose opinions I shall often have occasion to cite, indignation always takes place of admiration, and the rigid frown of insulted virtue effaces the smile of complacency, which his eloquent periods are wont to raise, when I read his voluptuous reveries. Is this the man, who, in his ardor for virtue, would banish all the soft arts of peace, and almost carry us back to Spartan discipline? Is this the man who delights to paint the useful struggles of passion, the triumphs of good dispositions, and the heroic flights which carry the glowing soul out of itself?—How are these mighty sentiments lowered when he describes the pretty foot and enticing airs of his little favorite! But, for the present, I waive the subject, and, instead of severely reprehending the transient effusions of overweening sensibility, I shall only observe,

---

[1] Why should women be censured with petulant acrimony, because they seem to have a passion for a scarlet coat? Has not education placed them more on a level with soldiers than any other class of men?

that whoever has cast a benevolent eye on society, must often have been gratified by the sight of humble mutual love, not dignified by sentiment, or strengthened by a union in intellectual pursuits. The domestic trifles of the day have afforded matters for cheerful converse, and innocent caresses have softened toils which did not require great exercise of mind or stretch of thought: yet, has not the sight of this moderate felicity excited more tenderness than respect? An emotion similar to what we feel when children are playing, or animals sporting[2] while the contemplation of the noble struggles of suffering merit has raised admiration, and carried our thoughts to that world where sensation will give place to reason.

Women are, therefore, to be considered either as moral beings, or so weak that they must be entirely subjected to the superior faculties of men.

Let us examine this question. Rousseau declares that a woman should never, for a moment, feel herself independent, that she should be governed by fear to exercise her *natural* cunning, and made a coquettish slave in order to render her a more alluring object of desire, a *sweeter* companion to man, whenever he chooses to relax himself. He carries the arguments, which he pretends to draw from the indications of nature, still further, and insinuates that truth and fortitude, the corner stones of all human virtue, should be cultivated with certain restrictions, because, with respect to the female character, obedience is the grand lesson which ought to be impressed with unrelenting rigor.

What nonsense! when will a great man arise with sufficient strength of mind to puff away the fumes which pride and sensuality have thus spread over the subject! If women are by nature inferior to men, their virtues must be the same in quality, if not in degree, or virtue is a relative idea; consequently, their conduct should be founded on the same principles, and have the same aim.

Connected with man as daughters, wives, and mothers, their moral character may be estimated by their manner of fulfilling those simple duties; but the end, the grand end of their exertions should be to unfold their own faculties and acquire the dignity of conscious virtue. They may try to render their road pleasant; but ought never to forget, in common with man, that life yields not the felicity which can satisfy an immortal soul. I do not mean to insinuate that either sex should be so lost in abstract reflections or distant views, as to forget the affections and duties that lie before them, and are, in truth, the means appointed to produce the fruit of life; on the contrary, I would warmly recommend them, even while I assert, that they afford most satisfaction when they are considered in their true, sober light.

Probably the prevailing opinion, that woman was created for man, may have taken its rise from Moses's poetical story; yet, as very few, it is presumed, who have bestowed any serious thought on the subject, ever supposed that Eve was, literally speaking, one of Adam's ribs, the deduction must be allowed to fall to the ground; or, only be so far admitted as it proves that man, from the remotest antiquity, found it convenient to exert his strength to subjugate his companion, and his invention to

---

[2] Similar feelings has Milton's pleasing picture of paradisaical happiness ever raised in my mind; yet, instead of envying the lovely pair, I have, with conscious dignity, or Satanic pride, turned to hell for sublimer objects. In the same style, when viewing some noble monument of human art, I have traced the emanation of the Deity in the order I admired, till, descending from that giddy height, I have caught myself contemplating the grandest of all human sights;—for fancy quickly placed, in some solitary recess, an outcast of fortune, rising superior to passion and discontent.

show that she ought to have her neck bent under the yoke, because the whole creation was only created for his convenience or pleasure.

Let it not be concluded that I wish to invert the order of things; I have already granted, that, from the constitution of their bodies, men seem to be designed by Providence to attain a greater degree of virtue. I speak collectively of the whole sex; but I see not the shadow of a reason to conclude that their virtues should differ in respect to their nature. In fact, how can they, if virtue has only one eternal standard? I must therefore, if I reason consequentially, as strenuously maintain that they have the same simple direction, as that there is a God.

It follows then that cunning should not be opposed to wisdom, little cares to great exertions, or insipid softness, varnished over with the name of gentleness, to that fortitude which grand views alone can inspire.

READING QUESTIONS

1. What are women told will obtain for them the protection of a man?
2. What must change before education can change?
3. What is the most perfect education?
4. What does Wollstonecraft say is one of the main causes of women's lack of understanding?
5. What great misfortune befalls both women and military men as a result of their education?

John Stuart Mill

John Stuart Mill (1806–1873), philosopher and fervent champion of social reform in the nineteenth century, was born in London, the son of the Scottish philosopher James Mill. Young Mill was given an extraordinary education by his father. By the age of three he had begun reading Greek; he was studying Latin by the age of eight. By the age of fourteen, Mill had read most of the Greek and Latin classics, was well versed in history, and had carried out extensive work in logic and mathematics. At fifteen, he came upon a political treatise by Jeremy Bentham that seized him with all the power of a religious revelation. Having discovered his life's work, Mill set out to reform the world.

Mill became an enthusiastic member of the radical social reform movement that took its inspiration from Bentham and James Mill. Progress in reshaping society and its institutions, Mill thought, would best be achieved by making the ideas of the reformers appeal to as wide a population as possible. Mill was a dynamic propagandist for radical ideas through his frequent contributions to the *Westminster Review,* numerous debates at the London Debating Society, and establishment of the Utilitarian Society. Mill has been criticized by subsequent philosophers for being a mediocre thinker who merely popularized the philosophical ideas of others while offering few new thoughts of his own. This perception followed from Mill's efforts to provide a philosophy both tolerant and inclusive enough to appeal to many kinds of people across all levels of society. Philosophical critics have pointed out numerous flaws in his theories, but these might be expected when a theory is meant to please a wide audience. Mill's guiding thought was that successful social reform required a larger audience, and it was that goal, not his lack of mental acuity, that dictated the form of his philosophical works.

Mill wrote many articles, essays, and tracts on a wide variety of subjects. His *System of Logic,* published in 1843, achieved rapid and wide success, and was adopted as a text at both Oxford and Cambridge. He felt his book *On Liberty* (1859) to be the work of most enduring value. But it is in his essay *Utilitarianism* (1863) that he most clearly articulates his ethical views.

Mill discerned in his own time the first signs of the widespread weakening of the Christian moral view that had been so deeply entrenched in Western civilization from the Middle Ages onward. A society that lacked a fundamental, widely embraced system of moral values, he thought, would descend into chaos. The task he gave himself, therefore, was to provide a system of moral values that would appeal to both those who still adhered to the institutions and values of Christianity and to those seeking new ideas and new values. The moral system that was to unify society under the banner of shared moral values was **utilitarianism.**

Utilitarianism is a moral theory in which the consequences of an action determine whether the act is a morally right one or not. In utilitarianism, because good is equated with an internal state called pleasure, or happiness, actions are right if they produce the maximum amount of pleasure, or happiness, and the minimum amount of pain, or unhappiness, for all people concerned. Thus, no act, whether stealing, lying, or killing innocent people, is wrong in and of itself: acts are wrong because of the unhappiness and pain that they cause.

Many of Mill's philosophical predecessors had laid the foundation for utilitarianism. Even among the ancient Greeks, the Epicureans had developed an ethical theory equating good with pleasure. But credit for creating the first articulation of utilitarianism is typically given to Jeremy Bentham. Bentham's version of the theory, unfortunately, contained serious defects that opponents seized upon. Mill attempted to remedy these defects in his essay *Utilitarianism*. For example, Mill correctly observed that Bentham's view that pleasures were all equal in quality, that "pushpin [a simple children's game] was as good as philosophy" (to use Bentham's phrase), reduces the notion of pleasure to that of mere bodily feelings. As an alternative, Mill argued that some pleasures were more valuable than others. In Mill's famous words, "It is better to be Socrates dissatisfied than a fool satisfied."

Mill was largely successful in his efforts to make the moral theory of utilitarianism appeal to a wide audience. It is mostly due to his efforts that utilitarianism has continued to have a powerful influence to this day. Many current philosophers promote this ethical theory, preserve it from attack by opponents, and stretch it to encompass advances in moral philosophy made since Mill's time. Later in this volume, a recent attack on utilitarianism by the British philosopher Bernard Williams is included to demonstrate some of the recent interest in this theory.

Utilitarianism

When we think before we act, we usually are considering the effects of the act. If I skip class, then I will have fun with my friends. If I go to class, I may not have as much fun, but I will do better on the exam. Considering the consequences of our actions is natural, and many moral philosophers have contended that weighing consequences is the way we should determine whether our actions are right or wrong. Such a theory is considered a **consequentialist** theory, and utilitarianism is a type of consequentialism. Since we quite naturally ponder outcomes before we choose which course of action to take, a theory that uses outcomes to determine whether an act is moral makes good sense to many people. And the fact that utilitarianism determines the right action by the amount of happiness it brings about, may also be quite appealing to most of us. Don't we often do things for people because it will make them happy? Aren't many of our social institutions, from hospitals to homeless shelters, meant to help people who are suffering in one way or another?

Yet utilitarianism has its detractors. What is happiness but a fleeting moment? And aren't many pleasures really self-indulgent and decadent,

John Stuart Mill, *Utilitarianism,* London, 1863.

more suited to animals than to rational human beings? These and many other criticisms have been leveled at utilitarians, and in this reading Mill provides both a careful articulation of the principles of utilitarianism and a spirited defense against its critics. Most criticism, he thinks, results from misrepresentation of the theory, and here his aim is to set out the principles of the theory correctly and clearly. ✍

Chapter 1
General Remarks

There are few circumstances among those which make up the present condition of human knowledge more unlike what might have been expected, or more significant of the backward state in which speculation on the most important subjects still lingers, than the little progress which has been made in the decision of the controversy respecting the criterion of right and wrong. From the dawn of philosophy, the question concerning the *summum bonum,* or, what is the same thing, concerning the foundation of morality, has been accounted the main problem in speculative thought, has occupied the most gifted intellects and divided them into sects and schools, carrying on a vigorous warfare against one another. And after more than two thousand years the same discussions continue, philosophers are still ranged under the same contending banners, and neither thinkers nor mankind at large seem nearer to being unanimous on the subject than when the youth Socrates listened to the old Protagoras, and asserted (if Plato's dialogue be grounded on a real conversation) the theory of utilitarianism against the popular morality of the so-called sophist.

It is true that similar confusion and uncertainty and, in some cases, similar discordance exist respecting the first principles of all the sciences, not excepting that which is deemed the most certain of them—mathematics, without much impairing, generally indeed without impairing at all, the trustworthiness of the conclusions of those sciences. An apparent anomaly, the explanation of which is that the detailed doctrines of a science are not usually deduced from, nor depend for their evidence upon, what are called its first principles. Were it not so, there would be no science more precarious, or whose conclusions were more insufficiently made out, than algebra, which derives none of its certainty from what are commonly taught to learners as its elements, since these, as laid down by some of its most eminent teachers, are as full of fictions as English law, and of mysteries as theology. The truths which are ultimately accepted as the first principles of a science are really the last results of metaphysical analysis, practiced on the elementary notions with which the science is conversant; and their relation to the science is not that of foundations to an edifice, but of roots to a tree, which may perform their office equally well though they be never dug down to and exposed to light. But though in science the particular truths precede the general theory, the contrary might be expected to be the case with a practical art, such as morals or legislation. All action is for the sake of some end, and rules of action, it seems natural to suppose, must take their whole character and color from the end to which they are subservient. When we engage in a pursuit, a clear and precise conception of what we are pursuing would seem to be the first thing we need, instead of the last we are to look forward to. A test of right and wrong must be the means, one would think, of ascertaining what is right or wrong, and not a consequence of having already ascertained it.

1. Mill's topic is the foundations of morality, the first principles, and this is evident in his criticism of intuitionist and inductive theories of ethics.

The difficulty is not avoided by having recourse to the popular theory of a natural faculty, a sense or instinct, informing us of right and wrong. For—besides that the existence of such a moral instinct is itself one of the matters in dispute—those believers in it who have any pretensions to philosophy have been obliged to abandon the idea that it discerns what is right or wrong in the particular case in hand, as our other senses discern the sight or sound actually present. Our moral faculty, according to all those of its interpreters who are entitled to the name of thinkers, supplies us only with the general principles of moral judgments; it is a branch of our reason, not of our sensitive faculty; and must be looked to for the abstract doctrines of morality, not for perception of it in the concrete. The intuitive, no less than what may be termed the inductive, school of ethics insists on the necessity of general laws. They both agree that the morality of an individual action is not a question of direct perception, but of the application of a law to an individual case. They recognize also, to a great extent, the same moral laws, but differ as to their evidence and the source from which they derive their authority. According to the one opinion, the principles of morals are evident *a priori*, requiring nothing to command assent except that the meaning of the terms be understood. According to the other doctrine, right and wrong, as well as truth and falsehood, are questions of observation and experience. But both hold equally that morality must be deduced from principles; and the intuitive school affirm as strongly as the inductive that there is a science of morals. Yet they seldom attempt to make out a list of the *a priori* principles which are to serve as the premises of the science; still more rarely do they make any effort to reduce those various principles to one first principle, or common ground of obligation. They either assume the ordinary precepts of morals as of *a priori* authority, or they lay down as the common groundwork of those maxims, some generality much less obviously authoritative than the maxims themselves, and which has never succeeded in gaining popular acceptance. Yet to support their pretensions there ought either to be some one fundamental principle or law at the root of all morality, or, if there be several, there should be a determinate order of precedence among them; and the one principle, or the rule for deciding between the various principles when they conflict, ought to be self-evident.

To inquire how far the bad effects of this deficiency have been mitigated in practice, or to what extent the moral beliefs of mankind have been vitiated or made uncertain by the absence of any distinct recognition of an ultimate standard, would imply a complete survey and criticism of past and present ethical doctrine. It would, however, be easy to show that whatever steadiness or consistency these moral beliefs have attained has been mainly due to the tacit influence of a standard not recognized. Although the non-existence of an acknowledged first principle has made ethics not so much a guide as a consecration of men's actual sentiments, still, as men's sentiments, both in favor and of aversion, are greatly influenced by what they suppose to be the effect of things upon their happiness, the principle of utility, or, as Bentham latterly called it, the greatest happiness principle, has had a large share in forming the moral doctrines even of those who most scornfully reject its authority. Nor is there any school of thought which refuses to admit that the influence of actions on happiness is a most material and even predominant consideration in many of the details of morals, however unwilling to acknowledge it as the fundamental principle of morality and the source of moral obligation. I might go much further and say that to all those *a priori* moralists who deem it necessary to argue at all, utilitarian arguments are indispensable. It is not my present purpose to criticize these thinkers; but I cannot help referring, for illustration, to a systematic treatise by one of the most illustrious of them, the *Metaphysics of Ethics* by Kant. This remarkable man, whose system of thought will long remain one of the landmarks in the history of philosophical speculation, does, in the treatise in question, lay down a universal first principle as the origin and ground of moral obligation; it is this: "So act that the rule on which thou actest would admit of being adopted as a law by all rational beings." But when he begins to deduce from this precept any of the actual duties of morality, he fails, almost grotesquely, to show that there would be any contradiction, any logical (not to say physical) impossibility, in the adoption by all rational beings of the most outrageously immoral rules of conduct. All he knows is that the *consequences* of their universal adoption would be such as no one would choose to incur.

———

2. Before Mill proceeds to present his own theory, he gives a detailed account of the kind of "proof" that is possible for ultimate ends. This discussion helps explain why people still disagree so often about the way to determine what is right and wrong.

———

On the present occasion, I shall, without further discussion of the other theories, attempt to contribute something towards the understanding and appreciation of the "utilitarian" or "happiness" theory, and towards such proof as it is susceptible of. It is evident that this cannot be proof in the ordinary and popular meaning of the term. Questions of ultimate ends are not amenable to direct proof. Whatever can be proved to be good must be so by being shown to be a means to something admitted to be good without proof. The medical art is proved to be good by its conducing to health; but how is it possible to prove that health is good? The art of music is good, for the reason, among others, that it produces pleasure; but what proof is it possible to give that pleasure is good? If, then, it is asserted that there is a comprehensive formula, including all things which are in themselves good, and that whatever else is good is not so as an end but as a means, the formula may be accepted or rejected, but is not a subject of what is commonly understood by proof. We are not, however, to infer that its acceptance or rejection must depend on blind impulse, or arbitrary choice. There is a larger meaning of the word "proof," in which this question is as amenable to it as any other of the disputed questions of philosophy. The subject is within the cognizance of the rational faculty; and neither does that faculty deal with it solely in the way of intuition. Considerations may be presented capable of determining the intellect either to give or withhold its assent to the doctrine; and this is equivalent to proof.

We shall examine presently of what nature are these considerations; in what manner they apply to the case, and what rational grounds, therefore, can be given for accepting or rejecting the utilitarian formula. But it is a preliminary condition of rational acceptance or rejection that the formula should be correctly understood. I believe that the very imperfect notion ordinarily formed of its meaning is the chief obstacle which impedes its reception, and that, could it be cleared even from only the grosser misconceptions the question would be greatly simplified and a large proportion of its difficulties removed. Before, therefore, I attempt to enter into the philosophical grounds which can be given for assenting to the utilitarian standard, I shall offer some illustrations of the doctrine itself, with the view of showing more clearly what it is, distinguishing it from what it is not, and disposing of such of the practical objections to it as either originate in, or are closely connected with, mistaken interpretation of its meaning. Having thus prepared the ground, I shall afterwards endeavor to throw such light as I can call upon the question considered as one of philosophical theory.

Chapter 2
What Utilitarianism Is

A passing remark is all that needs be given to the ignorant blunder of supposing that those who stand up for utility as the test of right and wrong use the term in that restricted and merely colloquial sense in which utility is opposed to pleasure. An apology is due to the philosophical opponents of utilitarianism, for even the momentary appearance of confounding them with anyone capable of so absurd a misconception; which is the more extraordinary, inasmuch as the contrary accusation, of referring everything to pleasure, and that, too, in its grossest form, is another of the common charges against utilitarianism: and, as has been pointedly remarked by an able writer, the same sort of persons, and often the very same persons, denounce the theory "as impracticably dry when the word 'utility' precedes the word 'pleasure,' and as too practically voluptuous when the word 'pleasure' precedes the word 'utility.'" Those who know anything about the matter are aware that every writer, from Epicurus to Bentham, who maintained the theory of utility, meant by it, not something to be contradistinguished from pleasure, but pleasure itself, together with exemption from pain; and instead of opposing the useful to the agreeable or the ornamental, have always declared that the useful means these, among other things. Yet the common herd, including the herd of writers, not only in newspapers and periodicals, but in books of weight and pretension, are perpetually falling into this shallow mistake. Having caught up the word "utilitarian," while knowing nothing whatever about it but its sound, they habitually express by it the rejection or the neglect of pleasure in some of its forms: of beauty, of ornament, or of amusement. Nor is the term thus ignorantly misapplied solely in disparagement, but occasionally in compliment, as though it implied superiority to frivolity and the mere pleasures of the moment. And this perverted use is the only one in which the word is popularly known, and the one from which the new generation are acquiring their sole notion of its meaning. Those who introduced the word, but who had for many years discontinued it as a distinctive appellation, may well feel themselves called upon to resume it if by doing so they can hope to contribute anything towards rescuing it from this utter degradation.[1]

---

3. After denouncing those who misrepresent the utilitarian position, Mill begins to lay out the theory of utilitarianism. He begins by defining this "creed."

The creed which accepts as the foundation of morals "utility" or the "greatest happiness principle" holds that actions are right in proportion as they tend to promote happiness, wrong as they tend to produce the reverse of happiness. By happiness is intended pleasure, and the absence of pain; by unhappiness, pain, and the privation of pleasure. To give a clear view of the moral standard set up by the theory, much more requires to be said; in particular, what things it includes in the ideas of pain and pleasure; and to what extent this is left an open question. But these supplementary explanations do not affect the theory of life on which this theory of morality is grounded—namely, that pleasure and freedom from pain are the only things desirable as ends; and that all desirable things (which are as numerous in the utilitarian as in any other scheme) are desirable either for the pleasure inherent in themselves, or as means to the promotion of pleasure and the prevention of pain.

Now such a theory of life excites in many minds, and among them in some of the most estimable in feeling and purpose, inveterate dislike. To suppose that life has (as they express it) no higher end than pleasure—no better and nobler object of desire and pursuit—they designate as utterly mean and groveling; as a doctrine worthy only of swine, to whom the followers of Epicurus were, at a very early period, contemptuously likened; and modern holders of the doctrine are occasionally made the subject of equally polite comparisons by its German, French, and English assailants.

When thus attacked, the Epicureans have always answered that it is not they, but their accusers, who represent human nature in a degrading light, since the accusation supposes human beings to be capable of no pleasures except those of which swine are capable. If this supposition were true, the charge could not be gainsaid, but would then be no longer an imputation; for if the sources of pleasure were precisely the same to human beings and to swine, the rule of life which is good enough for the one would be good enough for the other. The comparison of the Epicurean life to that of beasts is felt as degrading, precisely because a beast's pleasures do not satisfy a human being's conceptions of happiness. Human beings have faculties more elevated than the animal appetites and, when once made conscious of them, do not regard anything as happiness which does not include their gratification. I do not, indeed, consider the Epicureans to have been by any means faultless in drawing out their scheme of consequences from the utilitarian principle. To do this in any sufficient manner, many Stoic, as well as Christian, elements require to be included.

---

[1] The author of this essay has reason for believing himself to be the first person who brought the word "utilitarian" into use. He did not invent it, but adopted it from a passing expression in Mr. Galt's *Annals of the Parish.* After using it as a designation for several years, he and others abandoned it from a growing dislike to anything resembling a badge or watchword of sectarian distinction. But as a name for one single opinion, not a set of opinions—to denote the recognition of utility as a standard, not any particular way of applying it—the term supplies a want in the language, and offers, in many cases, a convenient mode of avoiding tiresome circumlocution.

But there is no known Epicurean theory of life which does not assign to the pleasures of the intellect, of the feelings and imagination, and of the moral sentiments,
a much higher value of pleasures than to those of mere sensation. It must be admitted, however, that utilitarian writers in general have placed the superiority of mental over bodily pleasures chiefly in the greater permanency, safety, uncostliness, etc.,
of the former—that is, in their circumstantial advantages rather than in their intrinsic nature. And on all these points utilitarians have fully proved their case; but they
might have taken the other and, as it may be called, higher ground with entire consistency. It is quite compatible with the principle of utility to recognize the fact that
some kinds of pleasure are more desirable and more valuable than others. It would
be absurd that, while, in estimating all other things, quality is considered as well as
quantity, the estimation of pleasures should be supposed to depend on quantity
alone.

*4. Mill makes an important distinction between kinds of pleasure. Notice that
he is using this to refute those who charge utilitarians (and the ancient hedonistic philosopher Epicurus) with advocating "swinish" or decadent pleasures.
How does Mill's distinction protect against that kind of criticism?*

If I am asked what I mean by difference of quality in pleasures, or what makes
one pleasure more valuable than another, merely as a pleasure, except its being
greater in amount, there is but one possible answer. Of two pleasures, if there be one
to which all or almost all who have experience of both give a decided preference, irrespective of a feeling of moral obligation to prefer it, that is the more desirable
pleasure. If one of the two is, by those who are competently acquainted with both,
placed so far above the other that they prefer it, even though knowing it to be attended with a greater amount of discontent, and would not resign it for any quantity of the other pleasure which their nature is capable of, we are justified in
ascribing to the preferred enjoyment a superiority in quality so far outweighing
quantity as to render it, in comparison, of small account.

*5. At the end of this paragraph is Mill's famous line about Socrates. What does
he mean?*

Now it is an unquestionable fact that those who are equally acquainted with
and equally capable of appreciating and enjoying both, do give a most marked preference to the manner of existence which employs their higher faculties. Few human
creatures would consent to be changed into any of the lower animals for a promise
of the fullest allowance of a beast's pleasures; no intelligent human being would consent to be a fool, no instructed person would be an ignoramus, no person of feeling
and conscience would be selfish and base, even though they should be persuaded
that the fool, the dunce, or the rascal is better satisfied with his lot than they are
with theirs. They would not resign what they possess more than he for the most
complete satisfaction of all the desires which they have in common with him. If they
ever fancy they would, it is only in cases of unhappiness so extreme that to escape
from it they would exchange their lot for almost any other, however undesirable in
their own eyes. A being of higher faculties requires more to make him happy, is capable probably of more acute suffering, and certainly accessible to it at more points,

than one of an inferior type; but in spite of these liabilities, he can never really wish to sink into what he feels to be a lower grade of existence. We may give what explanation we please of this unwillingness; we may attribute it to pride, a name which is given indiscriminately to some of the most and to some of the least estimable feelings of which mankind are capable: we may refer it to the love of liberty and personal independence, an appeal to which was with the Stoics one of the most effective means for the inculcation of it; to the love of power or to the love of excitement, both of which do really enter into and contribute to it; but its most appropriate appellation is a sense of dignity, which all human beings possess in one form or other, and in some, though by no means in exact, proportion to their higher faculties, and which is so essential a part of the happiness of those in whom it is strong that nothing which conflicts with it could be otherwise than momentarily an object of desire to them. Whoever supposes that this preference takes place at a sacrifice of happiness—that the superior being, in anything like equal circumstances, is not happier than the inferior—confounds the two very different ideas of happiness and content. It is indisputable that the being whose capacities of enjoyment are low has the greatest chance of having them fully satisfied; and a highly endowed being will always feel that any happiness which he can look for, as the world is constituted, is imperfect. But he can learn to bear its imperfections, if they are at all bearable; and they will not make him envy the being who is indeed unconscious of the imperfections, but only because he feels not at all the good which those imperfections qualify. It is better to be a human being dissatisfied than a pig satisfied; better to be Socrates dissatisfied than a fool satisfied. And if the fool, or the pig, are of a different opinion, it is because they only know their own side of the question. The other party to the comparison knows both sides.

It may be objected that many who are capable of the higher pleasures occasionally, under the influence of temptation, postpone them to the lower. But this is quite compatible with a full appreciation of the intrinsic superiority of the higher. Men often, from infirmity of character, make their election for the nearer good, though they know it to be the less valuable; and this no less when the choice is between two bodily pleasures than when it is between bodily and mental. They pursue sensual indulgences to the injury of health, though perfectly aware that health is the greater good. It may be further objected that many who begin with youthful enthusiasm for everything noble, as they advance in years, sink into indolence and selfishness. But I do not believe that those who undergo this very common change voluntarily choose the lower description of pleasures in preference to the higher. I believe that, before they devote themselves exclusively to the one, they have already become incapable of the other. Capacity for the nobler feelings is in most natures a very tender plant, easily killed, not only by hostile influences, but by mere want of sustenance; and in the majority of young persons it speedily dies away if the occupations to which their position in life has devoted them, and the society into which it has thrown them, are not favorable to keeping that higher capacity in exercise. Men lose their high aspirations as they lose their intellectual tastes, because they have not time or opportunity for indulging them; and they addict themselves to inferior pleasures, not because they deliberately prefer them, but because they are either the only ones to which they have access, or the only ones which they are any longer capable of enjoying. It may be questioned whether anyone who has remained equally susceptible to both classes of pleasures, ever knowingly and calmly preferred the lower, though many, in all ages, have broken down in an ineffectual attempt to combine both.

From this verdict of the only competent judges, I apprehend there can be no appeal. On a question which is the best worth having of two pleasures, or which of two modes of existence is the most grateful to the feelings, apart from its moral attributes and from its consequences, the judgment of those who are qualified by knowledge of both, or, if they differ, that of the majority of them, must be admitted as final. And there needs be the less hesitation to accept this judgment respecting the quality of pleasures, since there is no other tribunal to be referred to even on the question of quantity. What means are there of determining which is the acutest of two pains, or the intensest of two pleasurable sensations, except the general suffrage of those who are familiar with both? Neither pains nor pleasures are homogeneous, and pain is always heterogeneous with pleasure. What is there to decide whether a particular pleasure is worth purchasing at the cost of a particular pain, except the feelings and judgment of the experienced? When, therefore, those feelings and judgment declare the pleasures derived from the higher faculties to be preferable *in kind,* apart from the question of intensity, to those of which the animal nature, disjoined from the higher faculties, is susceptible, they are entitled on this subject to the same regard.

---

6. Mill reminds the reader that utilitarianism is a theory that is concerned with happiness for all, not just with happiness for oneself. He extends our moral concern to "the whole sentient creation." What does this include that other theories often ignore?

I have dwelt on this point, as being a necessary part of a perfectly just conception of utility or happiness considered as the directive rule of human conduct. But it is by no means an indispensable condition to the acceptance of the utilitarian standard; for that standard is not the agent's own greatest happiness, but the greatest amount of happiness altogether; and if it may possibly be doubted whether a noble character is always the happier for its nobleness, there can be no doubt that it makes other people happier, and that the world in general is immensely a gainer by it. Utilitarianism, therefore, could only attain its end by the general cultivation of nobleness of character, even if each individual were only benefited by the nobleness of others, and his own, so far as happiness is concerned, were a sheer deduction from the benefit. But the bare enunciation of such an absurdity as this last renders refutation superfluous.

According to the greatest happiness principle, as above explained, the ultimate end, with reference to and for the sake of which all other things are desirable— whether we are considering our own good or that of other people—is an existence exempt as far as possible from pain, and as rich as possible in enjoyments, both in point of quantity and quality; the test of quality and the rule for measuring it against quantity being the preference felt by those who, in their opportunities of experience, to which must be added their habits of self-consciousness and self-observation, are best furnished with the means of comparison. This, being, according to the utilitarian opinion, the end of human action, is necessarily also the standard of morality, which may accordingly be defined "the rules and precepts for human conduct," by the observance of which an existence such as has been described might be, to the greatest extent possible, secured to all mankind; and not to them only, but, so far as the nature of things admits, to the whole sentient creation.

Against this doctrine, however, arises another class of objectors who say that happiness, in any form, cannot be the rational purpose of human life and action; because, in the first place, it is unattainable; and they contemptuously ask, What right hast thou to be happy?—a question which Mr. Carlyle clenches by the addition, What right, a short time ago, hadst thou even *to be?* Next they say that men can do *without* happiness; that all noble human beings have felt this, and could not have become noble but by learning the lesson of *Entsagen,* or renunciation; which lesson, thoroughly learnt and submitted to, they affirm to be the beginning and necessary condition of all virtue.

The first of these objections would go to the root of the matter were it well founded; for if no happiness is to be had at all by human beings, the attainment of it cannot be the end of morality or of any rational conduct. Though, even in that case, something might still be said for the utilitarian theory, since utility includes not solely the pursuit of happiness, but the prevention or mitigation of unhappiness; and if the former aim be chimerical, there will be all the greater scope and more imperative need for the latter, so long at least as mankind think fit to live, and do not take refuge in the simultaneous act of suicide recommended under certain conditions by Novalis. When, however, it is thus positively asserted to be impossible that human life should be happy, the assertion, if not something like a verbal quibble, is at least an exaggeration. If by happiness be meant a continuity of highly pleasurable excitement, it is evident enough that this is impossible. A state of exalted pleasure lasts only moments or in some cases, and with some intermissions, hours or days, and is the occasional brilliant flash of enjoyment, not its permanent and steady flame. Of this the philosophers who have taught that happiness is the end of life were as fully aware as those who taunt them. The happiness which they meant was not a life of rapture; but moments of such, in an existence made up of few and transitory pains, many and various pleasures, with a decided predominance of the active over the passive, and having as the foundation of the whole not to expect more from life than it is capable of bestowing. A life thus composed, to those who have been fortunate enough to obtain it, has always appeared worthy of the name of happiness. And such an existence is even now the lot of many, during some considerable portion of their lives. The present wretched education and wretched social arrangements are the only real hindrance to its being attainable by almost all.

The objectors perhaps may doubt whether human beings, if taught to consider happiness as the end of life, would be satisfied with such a moderate share of it. But great numbers of mankind have been satisfied with much less. The main constituents of a satisfied life appear to be two, either of which by itself is often found sufficient for the purpose: tranquility and excitement. With much tranquility, many find that they can be content with very little pleasure; with much excitement, many can reconcile themselves to a considerable quantity of pain. There is assuredly no inherent impossibility of enabling even the mass of mankind to unite both, since the two are so far from being incompatible that they are in natural alliance, the prolongation of either being a preparation for, and exciting a wish for, the other. It is only those in whom indolence amounts to a vice that do not desire excitement after an interval of repose; it is only those in whom the need of excitement is a disease that feel the tranquility which follows excitement dull and insipid, instead of plea-surable in direct proportion to the excitement which preceded it. When people who are tolerably fortunate in their outward lot do not find in life sufficient enjoyment to make it valuable to them, the cause generally is caring for nobody but themselves. To those who have neither public nor private affections, the excitements of life are much curtailed, and in any case dwindle in value as the time approaches when all selfish interests must be terminated by death; while those who leave after them ob-jects of personal affection, and especially those who have also cultivated a fellow-feeling with the collective interests of mankind, retain as lively an interest in life on the eve of death as in the vigor of youth and health. Next to selfishness, the princi-pal cause which makes life unsatisfactory is want of mental cultivation. A cultivated mind—I do not mean that of a philosopher, but any mind to which the fountains of knowledge have been opened, and which has been taught, in any tolerable degree, to exercise its faculties—finds sources of inexhaustible interest in all that surrounds it: in the objects of nature, the achievements of art, the imaginations of poetry, the incidents of history, the ways of mankind, past and present, and their prospects in the future. It is possible, indeed, to become indifferent to all this, and that too with-out having exhausted a thousandth part of it, but only when one has had from the beginning no moral or human interest in these things, and has sought in them only the gratification of curiosity.

7. We can see in these words what a passionate social reformer Mill is. The happiness he has spoken of in the previous passages, he ardently wishes for everyone. Why should a utilitarian be so interested in education?

Now there is absolutely no reason in the nature of things why an amount of mental culture sufficient to give an intelligent interest in these objects of contem-plation should not be the inheritance of every one born in a civilized country. As lit-tle is there an inherent necessity that any human being should be a selfish egotist, devoid of every feeling or care but those which center in his own miserable individ-uality. Something far superior to this is sufficiently common even now, to give ample earnest of what the human species may be made. Genuine private affections and a sincere interest in the public good are possible, though in unequal degrees, to every rightly brought up human being. In a world in which there is so much to interest, so much to enjoy, and so much also to correct and improve, every one who has this moderate amount of moral and intellectual requisites is capable of an existence which may be called enviable; and unless such a person, through bad laws or sub-jection to the will of others, is denied the liberty to use the sources of happiness within his reach, he will not fail to find this enviable existence, if he escape the pos-itive evils of life, the great sources of physical and mental suffering—such as indi-gence, disease, and the unkindness, worthlessness, or premature loss of objects of affection. The main stress of the problem lies, therefore, in the contest with these calamities from which it is a rare good fortune entirely to escape; which, as things now are, cannot be obviated, and often cannot be in any material degree mitigated. Yet no one whose opinion deserves a moment's consideration can doubt that most of the great positive evils of the world are in themselves removable, and will, if human affairs continue to improve, be in the end reduced within narrow limits. Poverty, in any sense implying suffering, may be completely extinguished by the wisdom of society combined with the good sense and providence of individuals. Even that most intractable of enemies, disease, may be indefinitely reduced in dimensions by good physical and moral education and proper control of noxious influences, while the progress of science holds out a promise for the future of still more direct conquests over this detestable foe. And every advance in that direction relieves us from some, not only of the chances which cut short our own lives, but, what concerns us still more, which deprive us of those in whom our happiness is wrapt up. As for vicissitudes of fortune and other disappointments connected with worldly circumstances, these are principally the effect either of gross imprudence, of ill-regulated desires, or of bad or imperfect social institutions. All the grand sources, in short, of human suffering are in a great degree, many of them almost entirely, conquerable by human care and effort; and though their removal is grievously slow—though a long succession of generations will perish in the breach before the conquest is completed, and this world becomes all that, if will and knowledge were not wanting, it might easily be made—yet every mind sufficiently intelligent and generous to bear a part, however small and inconspicuous, in the endeavor will draw a noble enjoyment from the contest itself, which he would not for any bribe in the form of selfish indulgence consent to be without.

And this leads to the true estimation of what is said by the objectors concerning the possibility and the obligation of learning to do without happiness. Unquestionably it is possible to do without happiness; it is done involuntarily by nineteen-twentieths of mankind, even in those parts of our present world which are least deep in barbarism; and it often has to be done voluntarily by the hero or the martyr, for the sake of something which he prizes more than his individual happiness. But this something, what is it, unless the happiness of others or some of the requisites of happiness? It is noble to be capable of resigning entirely one's own portion of happiness, or chances of it; but, after all, this self-sacrifice must be for some end; it is not its own end; and if we are told that its end is not happiness but virtue, which is better than happiness, I ask, would the sacrifice be made if the hero or martyr did not believe that it would earn for others immunity from similar sacrifices? Would it be made if he thought that his renunciation of happiness for himself would produce no fruit for any of his fellow creatures, but to make their lot like his, and place them also in the condition of persons who have renounced happiness? All honor to those who can abnegate for themselves the personal enjoyment of life when by such renunciation they contribute worthily to increase the amount of happiness in the world; but he who does it or professes to do it for any other purpose is no more deserving of admiration than the ascetic mounted on his pillar. He may be an inspiriting proof of what men *can* do, but assuredly not an example of what they *should*.

Though it is only in a very imperfect state of the world's arrangements that any one can best serve the happiness of others by the absolute sacrifice of his own, yet, so long as the world is in that imperfect state, I fully acknowledge that the readiness to make such a sacrifice is the highest virtue which can be found in man. I will add that in this condition of the world, paradoxical as the assertion may be, the conscious ability to do without happiness gives the best prospect of realizing such happiness as is attainable. For nothing except that consciousness can raise a person above the chances of life, by making him feel that, let fate and fortune do their worst, they have not power to subdue him; which, once felt, frees him from excess of anxiety concerning the evils of life, and enables him, like many a Stoic in the worst times of the Roman Empire, to cultivate in tranquility the sources of satisfaction accessible to him, without concerning himself about the uncertainty of their duration any more than about their inevitable end.

Meanwhile, let utilitarians never cease to claim the morality of self-devotion as a possession which belongs by as good a right to them as either to the Stoic or to the Transcendentalist. The utilitarian morality does recognize in human beings the power of sacrificing their own greatest good for the good of others. It only refuses to admit that the sacrifice is itself a good. A sacrifice which does not increase or tend to increase the sum total of happiness, it considers as wasted. The only self-renunciation which it applauds is devotion to the happiness, or to some of the means of happiness, of others, either of mankind collectively or of individuals within the limits imposed by the collective interests of mankind.

I must again repeat what the assailants of utilitarianism seldom have the justice to acknowledge, that the happiness which forms the utilitarian standard of what is right in conduct is not the agent's own happiness but that of all concerned. As between his own happiness and that of others, utilitarianism requires him to be as strictly impartial as a disinterested and benevolent spectator. In the golden rule of Jesus of Nazareth, we read the complete spirit of the ethics of utility. "To do as you would be done by," and "to love your neighbor as yourself," constitute the ideal perfection of utilitarian morality. As the means of making the nearest approach to this ideal, utility would enjoin, first, that laws and social arrangements should place the happiness or (as, speaking practically, it may be called) the interest of every individual as nearly as possible in harmony with the interest of the whole; and, secondly, that education and opinion, which have so vast a power over human character, should so use that power as to establish in the mind of every individual an indissoluble association between his own happiness and the good of the whole, especially between his own happiness and the practice of such modes of conduct, negative and positive, as regard for the universal happiness prescribes; so that not only he may be able to conceive the possibility of happiness to himself, consistently with conduct opposed to the general good, but also that a direct impulse to promote the general good may be in every individual one of the habitual motives of action, and the sentiments connected therewith may fill a large and prominent place in every human being's sentient existence. If the impugners of the utilitarian morality represented it to their own minds in this its true character, I know not what recommendation possessed by any other morality they could possibly affirm to be wanting to it; what more beautiful or more exalted developments of human nature any other ethical system can be supposed to foster, or what springs of action, not accessible to the utilitarian, such systems rely on for giving effect to their mandates.

READING QUESTIONS

1. Mill provides an analogy between the first principles of science and a tree. What is that analogy?
2. What does Mill call the principle of utility?
3. What is Mill's criticism of Kant concerning consequences?

4. What does Mill mean by "happiness"?

5. What is better than a satisfied pig? Why?

6. Mill responds to critics who contend that happiness is not possible in human lives. He agrees that "exalted pleasure" cannot be maintained throughout life, but he maintains that a happy life is attainable. What constitutes a happy life?

7. What is the real hindrance to happiness, according to Mill?

Karl Marx

Karl Marx (1818–1883), social activist, economist, philosopher, and revolution-ary theorist, remains one of the most influential thinkers of the nineteenth cen-tury. Unlike most philosophers, his words and ideas brought action: his blistering criticism of capitalism inspired the leaders of communist revolutions in Russia, China, Vietnam, Cuba, and numerous other countries during the twentieth century. Yet despite his reputation for revolutionary theory and rhetoric, Marx's ideas are pertinent to moral philosophy as well. Born in Trier, Prussia (in today's Germany), Marx's education was in law and philosophy. He attended German universities in Bonn, where he studied law; Berlin, where he studied philosophy and history; and Jena, where he earned a doctorate in 1841. His doctoral thesis was on the ancient Greek philosophers Democritus and Epicurus.

A university position under the Prussian government of the day was impossible because Marx was an outspoken, militant atheist. So Marx took a position as the editor of a businessman's newspaper in Cologne. In 1843 the paper was subjected to such severe censorship by the government that Marx resigned his position. He in-tended to join the fight against the oppressive Prussian government but would be most effective, he thought, working from outside the country. Thus, he moved to Paris, where he met and began what turned out to be a lifelong collaboration with a successful businessman who had socialist interests, Friedrich Engels. Banished from Paris in 1844, Marx moved to Brussels, where he was soon joined by Engels. During the next two years he and Engels wrote; together they completed *The German Ideology* while Marx, on his own, wrote *The Poverty of Philosophy* (1847). While living in Brussels, Marx and Engels were asked by a group of German radicals, who lived in Paris and called themselves the Communist League, to write a manifesto on behalf of their group. This piece, the *Communist Manifesto,* was first published in London in 1848. By 1850, Marx had moved to London and had begun studying economics in the British Museum. Engels took a position with a firm in Manchester to help support himself as well as Marx.

Marx wrote extensively; this output included articles for newspapers, speeches, and books. Yet through all of his major works sounded a consistent, and relatively simple, theme. Even though Europe had progressed through the Reformation to the Enlightenment, and had even begun its Industrial Revolution, the plight of the com-mon person had not improved. In fact, from all appearances it had never been worse. For Marx, history was driven by class conflict. In the capitalist society of the nineteenth century, this conflict was between two opposing forces: the capitalist owners of production, the **bourgeoisie,** and the exploited workers, the **proletariat.** The only way, argued Marx, that the common people, the proletariat, could im-prove their position was by overthrowing the capitalist society. Out of the ashes of the capitalist society would arise a classless socialist society and the end of oppres-sion. The bourgeois system of private ownership would be replaced by a communist system.

Marx is not generally thought of as an ethicist, yet an ethical concern is ever present in his political and economic writings. For Marx, a society's values are mere products of the economic system under which they arose. Thus, European society in the nineteenth century reflected the values of the bourgeoisie. He could not support either of the two dominant theories of moral philosophy of the nineteenth century, utilitarianism or Kantian duty theory, because they merely reflected the marketplace values of the bourgeoisie. Class lines drew exclusive ethical boundaries; the morality of the capitalist class could not be used to judge the lives of the oppressed laborers. For Marx, therefore, no moral absolutes exist; moral values are relative to the class and the class system that produces them. Yet it is interesting to note that in the *Manifesto* he relentlessly charges the bourgeoisie with moral failure according to their own standards. However, the moral gulf that exists between these two disparate groups in society does not mean that values will always remain relative. After the revolution, which he thought to be inevitable, when the oppressed working people of the world would unite and throw off their chains, the classless society that followed would bring about flourishing lives for all. It is clear that his utopian ideals were never quite realized.

The radical ideas of Karl Marx have influenced philosophers as well as revolutionaries up to the present time. With the downfall of communist governments in the Soviet Union and elsewhere, less public attention has been given to Marx and Marxism. Yet this zealous German produced work that sparked controversy, debate, and revolution for more than a century and a half. His most famous works are the *Communist Manifesto* and *Capital*.

Communist Manifesto

Most moral philosophers investigate questions about how to determine what is right and what is wrong. They look to find a foundation for societal or personal values. They argue about whether character is more important than rules, whether pleasure means the same thing as happiness, and whether one set of values is applicable to all people or only to particular societies at particular times. Sometimes, though, moral philosophers question the whole system of ethical values. That is exactly the strategy of Karl Marx.

In this excerpt from his famous work, Marx does not directly address moral philosophy. The main topic of his interest is the justification and promotion of revolution against the existing society, not a change in its value system. But as you read this text, notice the crucial role played by ethical issues. While not written as a piece of philosophy, Marx does offer reasons to justify his passionate assertions. For example, he justifies communist policy because capitalism exploits the laborer. This he clearly believes is wrong. Thus, these kinds of reasons can be evaluated in the same manner in which the reasons that constitute any philosophical argument can be evaluated.

Karl Marx, "Manifesto of the Communist Party," from *The Marx-Engels Reader*, Second Edition, by Robert C. Tucker. Copyright © 1978, 1972 by W. W. Norton & Company, Inc. Reprinted by permission of W. W. Norton & Company, Inc.

But aside from the argument he gives, notice the tone of the writing. Marx suggests a moral appraisal of the despised bourgeois movement in two mutually supporting ways. On the one hand, he gives reasons to justify his conclusions; on the other hand, his passionate, angry tone may inflame the reader as much as, or more than, his reasons do.   ✍

A specter is haunting Europe—the specter of Communism. All the Powers of old Europe have entered into a holy alliance to exorcise this specter: Pope and Czar, Metternich and Guizot, French Radicals and German police-spies.

Where is the party in opposition that has not been decried as Communistic by its opponents in power? Where the Opposition that has not hurled back the branding reproach of Communism, against the more advanced opposition parties, as well as against its reactionary adversaries?

Two things result from this fact.

I. Communism is already acknowledged by all European Powers to be itself a Power.

II. It is high time that Communists should openly, in the face of the whole world, publish their views, their aims, their tendencies, and meet this nursery tale of the Specter of Communism with a Manifesto of the party itself.

To this end, Communists of various nationalities have assembled in London, and sketched the following Manifesto, to be published in the English, French, German, Italian, Flemish and Danish languages.

I. Bourgeois and Proletarians[1]

The history of all hitherto existing society[2] is the history of class struggles.

Freeman and slave, patrician and plebeian, lord and serf, guild-master[3] and journeyman, in a word, oppressor and oppressed, stood in constant opposition to one another, carried on an uninterrupted, now hidden, now open fight, a fight that each

---

[1] By bourgeoisie is meant the class of modern Capitalists, owners of the means of social production and employers of wage-labor. By proletariat, the class of modern wage-laborers who, having no means of production of their own, are reduced to selling their labor-power in order to live. [*Engels, English edition of 1888*]

[2] That is, all *written* history. In 1847, the pre-history of society, the social organization existing previous to recorded history, was all but unknown. Since then, Haxthausen discovered common ownership of land in Russia, Maurer proved it to be the social foundation from which all Teutonic races started in history, and by and by village communities were found to be, or to have been the primitive form of society everywhere from India to Ireland. The inner organization of this primitive Communistic society was laid bare, in its typical form, by Morgan's crowning discovery of the true nature of the *gens* and its relation to the *tribe*. With the dissolution of these primeval communities society begins to be differentiated into separate and finally antagonistic classes. I have attempted to retrace this process of dissolution in: "Der Ursprung der Familie, des Privateigenthums und des Staats" [*The Origin of the Family, Private Property and the State*], 2nd edition, Stuttgart 1886. [*Engels, English edition of 1888*].

[3] Guild-master, that is, a full member of a guild, a master within, not a head of a guild. [*Engels, English edition of 1888*]

time ended, either in a revolutionary reconstitution of society at large, or in the common ruin of the contending classes.

In the earlier epochs of history, we find almost everywhere a complicated arrangement of society into various orders, a manifold gradation of social rank. In ancient Rome we have patricians, knights, plebeians, slaves; in the Middle Ages, feudal lords, vassals, guild-masters, journeymen, apprentices, serfs; in almost all of these classes, again, subordinate gradations.

The modern bourgeois society that has sprouted from the ruins of feudal society has not done away with class antagonisms. It has but established new classes, new conditions of oppression, new forms of struggle in place of the old ones.

Our epoch, the epoch of the bourgeoisie, possesses, however, this distinctive feature: it has simplified the class antagonisms: Society as a whole is more and more splitting up into two great hostile camps, into two great classes directly facing each other: Bourgeoisie and Proletariat.

From the serfs of the Middle Ages sprang the chartered burghers of the earliest towns. From these burgesses the first elements of the bourgeoisie were developed.

The discovery of America, the rounding of the Cape, opened up fresh ground for the rising bourgeoisie. The East-Indian and Chinese markets, the colonization of America, trade with the colonies, the increase in the means of exchange and in commodities generally, gave to commerce, to navigation, to industry, an impulse never before known, and thereby, to the revolutionary element in the tottering feudal society, a rapid development.

The feudal system of industry, under which industrial production was monopolized by closed guilds, now no longer sufficed for the growing wants of the new markets. The manufacturing system took its place. The guild-masters were pushed on one side by the manufacturing middle class; division of labor between the different corporate guilds vanished in the face of division of labor in each single workshop.

Meantime the markets kept ever growing, the demand ever rising. Even manufacture no longer sufficed. Thereupon, steam and machinery revolutionized industrial production. The place of manufacture was taken by the giant, Modern Industry, the place of the industrial middle class, by industrial millionaires, the leaders of whole industrial armies, the modern bourgeois.

Modern industry has established the world-market, for which the discovery of America paved the way. This market has given an immense development to commerce, to navigation, to communication by land. This development has, in its turn, reacted on the extension of industry; and in proportion as industry, commerce, navigation, railways extended, in the same proportion the bourgeoisie developed, increased its capital, and pushed into the background every class handed down from the Middle Ages.

---

1. Marx draws his conclusion from the preceding paragraphs.

We see, therefore, how the modern bourgeoisie is itself the product of a long course of development, of a series of revolutions in the modes of production and of exchange.

Each step in the development of the bourgeoisie was accompanied by a corresponding political advance of that class. An oppressed class under the sway of the feudal nobility, an armed and self-governing association in the medieval commune;[4] here independent urban republic (as in Italy and Germany), there taxable "third estate" of the monarchy (as in France), afterwards, in the period of manufacture proper, serving either the semi-feudal or the absolute monarchy as a counterpoise against the nobility, and, in fact, corner-stone of the great monarchies in general, the bourgeoisie has at last, since the establishment of Modern Industry and of the world-market, conquered for itself, in the modern representative State, exclusive political sway. The executive of the modern State is but a committee for managing the common affairs of the whole bourgeoisie.

---

2. Details of the impact of the development of the bourgeoisie are listed in the remaining paragraphs. Is Marx's antagonism apparent even in his tone?

The bourgeoisie, historically, has played a most revolutionary part.

The bourgeoisie, wherever it has got the upper hand, has put an end to all feudal, patriarchal, idyllic relations. It has pitilessly torn asunder the motley feudal ties that bound man to his "natural superiors," and has left remaining no other nexus between man and man than naked self-interest, than callous "cash payment." It has drowned the most heavenly ecstasies of religious fervor, of chivalrous enthusiasm, of philistine sentimentalism, in the icy water of egotistical calculation. It has resolved personal worth into exchange value, and in place of the numberless indefeasible chartered freedoms, has set up that single, unconscionable freedom—Free Trade. In one word, for exploitation, veiled by religious and political illusions, it has substituted naked, shameless, direct, brutal exploitation.

The bourgeoisie has stripped of its halo every occupation hitherto honored and looked up to with reverent awe. It has converted the physician, the lawyer, the priest, the poet, the man of science, into its paid wage-laborers.

The bourgeoisie has torn away from the family its sentimental veil, and has reduced the family relation to a mere money relation.

The bourgeoisie has disclosed how it came to pass that the brutal display of vigor in the Middle Ages, which Reactionists so much admire, found its fitting complement in the most slothful indolence. It has been the first to show what man's activity can bring about. It has accomplished wonders far surpassing Egyptian pyramids, Roman aqueducts, and Gothic cathedrals; it has conducted expeditions that put in the shade all former Exoduses of nations and crusades.

The bourgeoisie cannot exist without constantly revolutionizing the instruments of production, and thereby the relations of production, and with them the whole relations of society. Conservation of the old modes of production in unaltered form, was, on the contrary, the first condition of existence for all earlier industrial classes. Constant revolutionizing of production, uninterrupted disturbance

---

[4]"Commune" was the name taken, in France, by the nascent towns even before they had conquered from their feudal lords and masters local self-government and political rights as the "Third Estate." Generally speaking, for the economical development of the bourgeoisie, England is here taken as the typical country; for its political development, France. [*Engels, English edition of 1888*].

This was the name given their urban communities by the townsmen of Italy and France, after they had purchased or wrested their initial rights of self-government from their feudal lords. [*Engels, German edition of 1890*].

of all social conditions, everlasting uncertainty and agitation distinguish the bourgeois epoch from all earlier ones. All fixed, fast-frozen relations, with their train of ancient and venerable prejudices and opinions, are swept away, all new-formed ones become antiquated before they can ossify. All that is solid melts into air, all that is holy is profaned, and man is at last compelled to face with sober senses, his real conditions of life, and his relations with his kind.

The need of a constantly expanding market for its products chases the bourgeoisie over the whole surface of the globe. It must nestle everywhere, settle everywhere, establish connections everywhere.

The bourgeoisie has through its exploitation of the world-market given a cosmopolitan character to production and consumption in every country. To the great chagrin of Reactionists, it has drawn from under the feet of industry the national ground on which it stood. All old-established national industries have been destroyed or are daily being destroyed. They are dislodged by new industries, whose introduction becomes a life and death question for all civilized nations, by industries that no longer work up indigenous raw material, but raw material drawn from the remotest zones; industries whose products are consumed, not only at home, but in every quarter of the globe. In place of the old wants, satisfied by the productions of the country, we find new wants, requiring for their satisfaction the products of distant lands and climes. In place of the old local and national seclusion and self-sufficiency, we have intercourse in every direction, universal interdependence of nations. And as in material, so also in intellectual production. The intellectual creations of individual nations become common property. National one-sidedness and narrow-mindedness become more and more impossible, and from the numerous national and local literatures, there arises a world literature.

The bourgeoisie, by the rapid improvement of all instruments of production, by the immensely facilitated means of communication, draws all, even the most barbarian, nations into civilization. The cheap prices of its commodities are the heavy artillery with which it batters down all Chinese walls, with which it forces the barbarians' intensely obstinate hatred of foreigners to capitulate. It compels all nations, on pain of extinction, to adopt the bourgeois mode of production; it compels them to introduce what it calls civilization into their midst, i.e., to become bourgeois themselves. In one word, it creates a world after its own image.

II. Proletarians and Communists

In what relation do the Communists stand to the proletarians as a whole?

The Communists do not form a separate party opposed to other working-class parties.

They have no interests separate and apart from those of the proletariat as a whole.

The do not set up any sectarian principles of their own, by which to shape and mold the proletarian movement.

The Communists are distinguished from the other working-class parties by this only: (1) In the national struggles of the proletarians of the different countries, they point out and bring to the front the common interests of the entire proletariat, independently of all nationality. (2) In the various stages of development which the struggle of the working class against the bourgeoisie has to pass through, they always and everywhere represent the interests of the movement as a whole.

The Communists, therefore, are on the one hand, practically, the most advanced and resolute section of the working-class parties of every country, that section which pushes forward all others; on the other hand, theoretically, they have over the great mass of the proletariat the advantage of clearly understanding the line of march, the conditions, and the ultimate general results of the proletarian movement.

The immediate aim of the Communists is the same as that of all the other proletarian parties: formation of the proletariat into a class, overthrow of the bourgeois supremacy, conquest of political power by the proletariat.

The theoretical conclusions of the Communists are in no way based on ideas or principles that have been invented, or discovered, by this or that would-be universal reformer.

They merely express, in general terms, actual relations springing from an existing class struggle, from a historical movement going on under our very eyes. The abolition of existing property relations is not at all a distinctive feature of Communism.

All property relations in the past have continually been subject to historical change consequent upon the change in historical conditions.

The French Revolution, for example, abolished feudal property in favor of bourgeois property.

The distinguishing feature of Communism is not the abolition of property generally, but the abolition of bourgeois property. But modern bourgeois private property is the final and most complete expression of the system of producing and appropriating products, that is based on class antagonisms, on the exploitation of the many by the few.

3. A summation of the theory of the communists.

In this sense, the theory of the Communists may be summed up in the single sentence: Abolition of private property.

We Communists have been reproached with the desire of abolishing the right of personally acquiring property as the fruit of a man's own labor, which property is alleged to be the groundwork of all personal freedom, activity and independence.

Hard-won, self-acquired, self-earned property! Do you mean the property of the petty artisan and of the small peasant, a form of property that preceded the bourgeois form? There is no need to abolish that; the development of industry has to a great extent already destroyed it, and is still destroying it daily.

Or do you mean modern bourgeois private property?

But does wage-labor create any property for the laborer? Not a bit. It creates capital, i.e., that kind of property which exploits wage-labor, and which cannot increase except upon condition of begetting a new supply of wage-labor for fresh exploitation. Property, in its present form, is based on the antagonism of capital and wage-labor. Let us examine both sides of this antagonism.

To be a capitalist, is to have not only a purely personal, but a social *status* in production. Capital is a collective product, and only by the united action of many members, nay, in the last resort, only by the united action of all members of society, can it be set in motion.

Capital is, therefore, not a personal, it is a social power.

When, therefore, capital is converted into common property, into the property of all members of society, personal property is not thereby transformed into social property. It is only the social character of the property that is changed. It loses its class-character.

Let us now take wage-labor.

The average price of wage-labor is the minimum wage, i.e., that quantum of the means of subsistence, which is absolutely requisite to keep the laborer in bare existence as a laborer. What, therefore, the wage-laborer appropriates by means of his labor, merely suffices to prolong and reproduce a bare existence. We by no means intend to abolish this personal appropriation of the products of labor, an appropriation that is made for the maintenance and reproduction of human life, and that leaves no surplus wherewith to command the labor of others. All that we want to do away with, is the miserable character of this appropriation, under which the laborer lives merely to increase capital, and is allowed to live only in so far as the interest of the ruling class requires it.

In bourgeois society, living labor is but a means to increase accumulated labor. In Communist society, accumulated labor is but a means to widen, to enrich, to promote the existence of the laborer.

In bourgeois society, therefore, the past dominates the present; in Communist society, the present dominates the past. In bourgeois society capital is independent and has individuality, while the living person is dependent and has no individuality.

---

4. Two different views of freedom are presented. Notice the underlying moral nature of Marx's attack on the bourgeoisie.

And the abolition of this state of things is called by the bourgeois, abolition of individuality and freedom! And rightly so. The abolition of bourgeois individuality, bourgeois independence, and bourgeois freedom is undoubtedly aimed at.

By freedom is meant, under the present bourgeois conditions of production, free trade, free selling and buying.

But if selling and buying disappears, free selling and buying disappears also. This talk about free selling and buying, and all the other "brave words" of our bourgeoisie about freedom in general, have a meaning, if any, only in contrast with restricted selling and buying, with the fettered traders of the Middle Ages, but have no meaning when opposed to the Communistic abolition of buying and selling, of the bourgeois conditions of production, and of the bourgeoisie itself.

You are horrified at our intending to do away with private property. But in your existing society, private property is already done away with for nine-tenths of the population; its existence for the few is solely due to its nonexistence in the hands of those nine-tenths. You reproach us, therefore, with intending to do away with a form of property, the necessary condition for whose existence is the nonexistence of any property for the immense majority of society.

---

5. Marx admits that the communists are out to do just what they are accused of. But he has given reasons for their actions in the preceding paragraph.

In one word, you reproach us with intending to do away with your property. Precisely so; that is just what we intend.

From the moment when labor can no longer be converted into capital, money, or rent, into a social power capable of being monopolized, i.e., from the moment when individual property can no longer be transformed into bourgeois property, into capital, from that moment, you say, individuality vanishes.

You must, therefore, confess that by "individual" you mean no other person than the bourgeois, than the middle-class owner of property. This person must, indeed, be swept out of the way, and made impossible.

Communism deprives no man of the power to appropriate the products of society; all that it does is to deprive him of the power to subjugate the labor of others by means of such appropriation.

___

6. He responds to another criticism in a different manner. In the following paragraphs he responds to criticism after criticism. How many different topics can you find?

___

It has been objected that upon the abolition of private property all work will cease, and universal laziness will overtake us.

According to this, bourgeois society ought long ago to have gone to the dogs through sheer idleness; for those of its members who work, acquire nothing, and those who acquire anything, do not work. The whole of this objection is but another expression of the tautology: that there can no longer be any wage-labor when there is no longer any capital.

All objections urged against the Communistic mode of producing and appropriating material products, have, in the same way, been urged against the Communistic modes of producing and appropriating intellectual products. Just as, to the bourgeois, the disappearance of class property is the disappearance of production itself, so the disappearance of class culture is to him identical with the disappearance of all culture.

That culture, the loss of which he laments, is, for the enormous majority, a mere training to act as a machine.

But don't wrangle with us so long as you apply, to our intended abolition of bourgeois property, the standard of your bourgeois notions of freedom, culture, law, etc. Your very ideas are but the outgrowth of the conditions of your bourgeois production and bourgeois property, just as your jurisprudence is but the will of your class made into a law for all, a will, whose essential character and direction are determined by the economical conditions of existence of your class.

The selfish misconception that induces you to transform into eternal laws of nature and of reason, the social forms springing from your present mode of production and form of property—historical relations that rise and disappear in the progress of production—this misconception you share with every ruling class that has preceded you. What you see clearly in the case of ancient property, what you admit in the case of feudal property, you are of course forbidden to admit in the case of your own bourgeois form of property.

Abolition of the family! Even the most radical flare up at this infamous proposal of the Communists.

On what foundation is the present family, the bourgeois family, based? On capital, on private gain. In its completely developed form this family exists only among the bourgeoisie. But this state of things finds its complement in the practical absence of the family among the proletarians, and in public prostitution.

The bourgeois family will vanish as a matter of course when its complement vanishes, and both will vanish with the vanishing of capital.

Do you charge us with wanting to stop the exploitation of children by their parents? To this crime we plead guilty.

But, you will say, we destroy the most hallowed of relations, when we replace home education by social.

And your education! Is not that also social, and determined by the social conditions under which you educate, by the intervention, direct or indirect, of society, by means of schools, etc.? The Communists have not invented the intervention of society in education; they do but seek to alter the character of that intervention, and to rescue education from the influence of the ruling class.

The bourgeois clap-trap about the family and education, about the hallowed co-relation of parent and child, becomes all the more disgusting, the more, by the action of Modern Industry, all family ties among the proletarians are torn asunder, and their children transformed into simple articles of commerce and instruments of labor.

-----

7. The communists are accused of introducing a community of women. Marx has a powerful response at the ready.

But you Communists would introduce community of women, screams the whole bourgeoisie in chorus.

The bourgeois sees in his wife a mere instrument of production. He hears that the instruments of production are to be exploited in common, and naturally, can come to no other conclusion than that the lot of being common to all will likewise fall to the women.

He has not even a suspicion that the real point aimed at is to do away with the status of women as mere instruments of production.

For the rest, nothing is more ridiculous than the virtuous indignation of our bourgeois at the community of women which, they pretend, is to be openly and officially established by the Communists. The Communists have no need to introduce community of women; it has existed almost from time immemorial.

Our bourgeois, not content with having the wives and daughters of their proletarians at their disposal, not to speak of common prostitutes, take the greatest pleasure in seducing each other's wives.

Bourgeois marriage is in reality a system of wives in common and thus, at the most, what the Communists might possibly be reproached with, is that they desire to introduce, in substitution for a hypocritically concealed, an openly legalized community of women. For the rest, it is self-evident that the abolition of the present system of production must bring with it the abolition of the community of women springing from that system, i.e., of prostitution both public and private.

The Communists are further reproached with desiring to abolish countries and nationality.

The working men have no country. We cannot take from them what they have not got. Since the proletariat must first of all acquire political supremacy, must rise to be the leading class of the nation, must constitute itself *the* nation, it is, so far, itself national, though not in the bourgeois sense of the word.

National differences and antagonisms between peoples are daily more and more vanishing, owing to the development of the bourgeoisie, to freedom of commerce, to the world-market, to uniformity in the mode of production and in the conditions of life corresponding thereto.

The supremacy of the proletariat will cause them to vanish still faster. United action, of the leading civilized countries at least, is one of the first conditions for the emancipation of the proletariat.

In proportion as the exploitation of one individual by another is put an end to, the exploitation of one nation by another will also be put an end to. In proportion as the antagonism between classes within the nation vanishes, the hostility of one nation to another will come to an end.

The charges against Communism made from a religious, a philosophical, and, generally, from an ideological standpoint, are not deserving of serious examination.

Does it require deep intuition to comprehend that man's ideas, views and conceptions, in one word, man's consciousness, changes with every change in the conditions of his material existence, in his social relations and in his social life?

What else does the history of ideas prove, than that intellectual production changes its character in proportion as material production is changed? The ruling ideas of each age have ever been the ideas of its ruling class.

When people speak of ideas that revolutionize society, they do but express the fact, that within the old society, the elements of a new one have been created, and that the dissolution of the old ideas keeps even pace with the dissolution of the old conditions of existence.

When the ancient world was in its last throes, the ancient religions were overcome by Christianity. When Christian ideas succumbed in the 18th century to rationalist ideas, feudal society fought its death battle with the then revolutionary bourgeoisie. The ideas of religious liberty and freedom of conscience merely gave expression to the sway of free competition within the domain of knowledge.

"Undoubtedly," it will be said, "religious, moral, philosophical and juridical ideas have been modified in the course of historical development. But religion, morality, philosophy, political science, and law, constantly survived this change."

---

8. Marx specifically discusses morality here. Can you see how he disparages all previous moral systems? What do they have in common?

"There are, besides, eternal truths, such as Freedom, Justice, etc., that are common to all states of society. But Communism abolishes eternal truths, it abolishes all religion, and all morality, instead of constituting them on a new basis; it therefore acts in contradiction to all past historical experience."

What does this accusation reduce itself to? The history of all past society has consisted in the development of class antagonisms, antagonisms that assumed different forms at different epochs.

But whatever form they may have taken, one fact is common to all past ages, *viz.*, the exploitation of one part of society by the other. No wonder, then, that the social consciousness of past ages, despite all the multiplicity and variety it displays, moves within certain common forms, or general ideas, which cannot completely vanish except with the total disappearance of class antagonisms.

The Communist revolution is the most radical rupture with traditional property relations; no wonder that its development involves the most radical rupture with traditional ideas.

But let us have done with the bourgeois objections to Communism.

We have seen above, that the first step in the revolution by the working class, is to raise the proletariat to the position of ruling class, to win the battle of democracy.

The proletariat will use its political supremacy to wrest, by degrees, all capital from the bourgeoisie, to centralize all instruments of production in the hands of the State, i.e., of the proletariat organized as the ruling class; and to increase the total of productive forces as rapidly as possible.

Of course, in the beginning, this cannot be effected except by means of despotic inroads on the rights of property, and on the conditions of bourgeois production; by means of measures, therefore, which appear economically insufficient and untenable, but which, in the course of the movement, outstrip themselves, necessitate further inroads upon the old social order, and are unavoidable as a means of entirely revolutionizing the mode of production.

These measures will of course be different in different countries.

Nevertheless in the most advanced countries, the following will be pretty generally applicable.

1. Abolition of property in land and application of all rents of land to public purposes.

2. A heavy progressive or graduated income tax.

3. Abolition of all right of inheritance.

4. Confiscation of the property of all emigrants and rebels.

5. Centralization of credit in the hands of the State, by means of a national bank with State capital and an exclusive monopoly.

6. Centralization of the means of communication and transport in the hands of the State.

7. Extension of factories and instruments of production owned by the State; the bringing into cultivation of waste-lands, and the improvement of the soil generally in accordance with a common plan.

8. Equal liability of all to labor. Establishment of industrial armies, especially for agriculture.

9. Combination of agriculture with manufacturing industries; gradual abolition of the distinction between town and country, by a more equable distribution of the population over the country.

10. Free education for all children in public schools. Abolition of children's factory labor in its present form. Combination of education with industrial production, etc., etc.

When, in the course of development, class distinctions have disappeared, and all production has been concentrated in the hands of a vast association of the whole nation, the public power will lose its political character. Political power, properly so called, is merely the organized power of one class for oppressing another. If the proletariat during its contest with the bourgeoisie is compelled, by the force of circumstances, to organize itself as a class, if, by means of a revolution, it makes itself the ruling class, and, as such, sweeps away by force the old conditions of production, then it will, along with these conditions, have swept away the conditions for the existence of class antagonisms and of classes generally, and will thereby have abolished its own supremacy as a class.

In place of the old bourgeois society, with its classes and class antagonisms, we shall have an association, in which the free development of each is the condition for the free development of all.

READING QUESTIONS

1. What name does Marx use for "our" epoch? What distinctive feature does it have?
2. What single freedom has been set up by the bourgeoisie?
3. What need has forced the bourgeoisie to settle over the whole surface of the globe?
4. Why isn't the abolition of existing property relations a distinctive feature of communism?
5. According to Marx, what is the basis for the modern, bourgeois family?
6. What is the first step in the revolution by the working class?

Friedrich Nietzsche

O ne of the most notorious philosophers of all time, Friedrich Nietzsche was born in Rocken, Prussia, in 1844. He was born into a religious family: both grandfathers and his father were Lutheran ministers. Although his family expected him to follow in his father's occupation, Nietzsche instead became one of his century's most vocal critics of the Christian faith into which he was born. He abandoned the religion and the patriotism of his family, yet he and his father did share a similar fate. Both men were to die insane.

As a young man, Nietzsche excelled in his studies. He began his university education studying theology and classical philology at the University of Bonn, later transferring to the University of Leipzig. While enrolled at Leipzig, he published some pamphlets that drew the attention of the classics department at the University of Basel, in Switzerland. When, in 1868, they asked Nietzsche's mentor at Leipzig whether he could recommend the author of the pamphlets for a professor's position in their department, he praised Nietzsche so unhesitatingly that Basel appointed him to a chair in their university even though Nietzsche had not yet received his doctorate. In 1869 Leipzig awarded him his doctorate, without Nietzsche's writing a thesis or taking an examination.

Nietzsche's first published book, *The Birth of Tragedy* (1872), upset the world of classical studies by arguing that the culture and spirit of ancient Greece were more complex than prevailing wisdom acknowledged. He identified two contrary tendencies, which he called the **Apollonian** (the tendency for restraint and harmony praised by classical scholars) and the **Dionysian** (a cruel and excessive exuberance), which together made up the Greek spirit. As was to occur with his following books, this initial work was met with withering scorn and disparagement from other classical scholars, since it went counter to established notions. Yet his ideas were to outshine and outlive those of his critics, eventually changing the prevalent understanding of Greece.

The will to power, the central and most prominent concept in Nietzsche's philosophy, developed out of his study of classical Greece. Nietzsche claimed that what all people want is power, and power is the goal for which everything else is done. All relationships are power relationships. Like Hobbes, Nietzsche regarded altruism as contrary to human nature because concern for the welfare of others led to a devaluation of oneself. Although his concept of the will to power was, and still is, often regarded as the foundation of fascism (especially since the Nazis claimed him as their inspiration), most serious interpreters of his thought resist such a conclusion. But this charge, along with accusations of anti-Semitism, his infamous pronouncement that God is dead, and his promotion of a new, superior man—the Superman—have all contributed to a certain mystique surrounding the philosophy of Nietzsche, even to this day.

Adding to this aura of menace and mystery is the manner in which Nietzsche presented his ideas. Much of his work is in the form of **aphorisms** (briefly stated proverbs), which can often be interpreted in a variety of ways. And he enjoyed being outrageous and controversial. As he declared in a subtitle to one of his later works, he "philosophized with a hammer." In this text are excerpts from two books, *Beyond Good and Evil* (1886), two hundred pages of numbered aphorisms, and *A*

Genealogy of Morals (1887), a collection of three essays. These two works are usually considered his most philosophical.

Nietzsche's philosophy dismissed ethical theories such as utilitarianism and Kant's duty theory as examples of moral codes meant to protect mediocre people from people with creative genius and real individuality. It is in *Beyond Good and Evil* that he famously articulates his idea of **master and slave morality.** Morality is a mixture of both types, yet the differences between them are critical. In the morality of the master (or aristocratic morality), "good" and "bad" mean something like "noble" and "ignoble." One can picture the master as the "lord of the manor," ordering his servants about. But slave morality does not consider most noble actions good. Instead, it praises ignoble actions when they are beneficial to the weak and powerless. The person who is good by the standards of master morality is regarded as evil by the standards of slave morality (which Nietzsche disparagingly calls the morality of the herd). In *A Genealogy of Morals* he continues the same theme, but adds the concept of resentment. Because they fear the powerful, the weak and powerless feel resentment, and this becomes their only real weapon. The history of morality is the conflict between master and slave moralities.

Nietzsche's pronouncements still excite great numbers of followers both within and without philosophy. However, his ideas have exerted the most influence on twentieth-century **existentialists** such as **Albert Camus, Jean-Paul Sartre** (discussed in this volume), **Paul Tillich,** and **Max Scheler.** Yet even his detractors have to acknowledge the power of his ideas, which went largely unrecognized until after his death. This rebellious philosopher went insane in January 1889. His last years were spent in a vegetative state, unaware of the approach of the tumultuous modern era about which he was so prophetic. He died in 1900.

A Genealogy of Morals;
Beyond Good and Evil

As soon as you enter this reading from Nietzsche, you will most likely find many of your long-cherished notions of morality under assault. That is exactly what Nietzsche would wish. The sense of morality that most people hold, Nietzsche clearly despises. Yet before you assume that you are reading the rantings of a madman, ask yourself these questions: Don't we value the strong even when we feel pity for the weak; don't we value courage even when we sympathize with the coward? Perhaps our everyday sense of morality is not as different from Nietzsche's as we first thought.

From Friedrich Nietzsche, *Beyond Good and Evil,* translated by Helen Zimmern, and *Genealogy of Morals,* translated by Horace B. Samuel, George Allen & Unwin Publishers.

Genealogy of Morals
10

1. This initial section gives a real flavor of the writing of Nietzsche. In it, he distinguishes two types of morality, master and slave. Notice how they differ in the way they develop their values.

The revolt of the slaves in morals begins in the very principle of *resentment* becoming creative and giving birth to values—a resentment experienced by creatures who, deprived as they are of the proper outlet of action, are forced to find their compensation in an imaginary revenge. While every aristocratic morality springs from a triumphant affirmation of its own demands, the slave morality says "no" from the very outset to what is "outside itself," "different from itself," and "not itself": and this "no" is its creative deed. This volte-face of the valuing standpoint—this *inevitable* gravitation to the objective instead of back to the subjective—is typical of "resentment": the slave-morality requires as the condition of its existence an external and objective world, to employ physiological terminology, it requires objective stimuli to be capable of action at all—its action is fundamentally a reaction. The contrary is the case when we come to the aristocrat's system of values: it acts and grows spontaneously, it merely seeks its antithesis in order to pronounce a more grateful and exultant "yes" to its own self;—its negative conception, "low," "vulgar," "bad," is merely a pale late-born foil in comparison with its positive and fundamental conception (saturated as it is with life and passion), of "we aristocrats, we good ones, we beautiful ones, we happy ones."

2. The two moralities establish different values. Nietzsche's preference is obvious by his disdainful tone.

When the aristocratic morality goes astray and commits sacrilege on reality, this is limited to that particular sphere with which it is *not* sufficiently acquainted—a sphere, in fact, from the real knowledge of which it disdainfully defends itself. It misjudges, in some cases, the sphere which it despises, the sphere of the common vulgar man and the low people: on the other hand, due weight should be given to the consideration that in any case the mood of contempt, of disdain, of superciliousness, even on the supposition that it *falsely* portrays the object of its contempt, will always be far removed from that degree of falsity which will always characterize the attacks—in effigy, of course—of the vindictive hatred and revengefulness of the weak in onslaughts on their enemies. In point of fact, there is in contempt too strong an admixture of nonchalance, of casualness, of boredom, of impatience, even of personal exultation, for it to be capable of distorting its victim into a real caricature or a real monstrosity. Attention again should be paid to the almost benevolent *nuances* which, for instance, the Greek nobility imports into all the words by which it distinguishes the common people from itself; note how continuously a kind of pity, care, and consideration imparts its honeyed *flavor*, until at last almost all the words which are applied to the vulgar man survive finally as expressions for "unhappy," "worthy of pity"—and how, conversely, "bad," "low," "unhappy" have never ceased to ring in the Greek ear with a tone in which "unhappy" is the predominant note: this is a heritage of the old noble aristocratic morality, which remains true to itself even in contempt. The "well-born" simply *felt* themselves the "happy"; they did not have to manufacture their happiness artificially through looking at their enemies, or in cases to talk and lie themselves into happiness (as is the custom with all resentful men); and similarly, complete men as they were, exuberant with strength, and consequently *necessarily* energetic, they were too wise to dissociate happiness from action—activity becomes in their minds necessarily counted as happiness (that is the etymology of εὐπράττειν)— all in sharp contrast to the "happiness" of the weak and the oppressed, with their festering venom and malignity, among whom happiness appears essentially as a narcotic, a deadening, a quietude, a peace, a "Sabbath," an enervation of the mind and relaxation of the limbs,—in short, a purely *passive* phenomenon. While the aristocratic man lived in confidence and openness with himself (γενναῖος, "noble-born," emphasizes the nuance "sincere," and perhaps also "naive"), the resentful man, on the other hand, is neither sincere nor naive, nor honest and candid with himself. His soul *squints;* his mind loves hidden crannies, tortuous paths and backdoors, everything secret appeals to him as *his* world, *his* safety, *his* balm; he is past master in silence, in not forgetting, in waiting, in provisional self-depreciation and self-abasement. A race of such *resentful* men will of necessity eventually prove more *prudent* than any aristocratic race, it will honor prudence on quite a distinct scale, as, in fact, a paramount condition of existence, while prudence among aristocratic men is apt to be tinged with a delicate flavor of luxury and refinement; so among them it plays nothing like so integral a part as that complete certainty of function of the governing *unconscious* instincts, or as indeed a certain lack of prudence, such as a vehement and valiant charge, whether against danger or the enemy, or as those ecstatic bursts of rage, love, reverence, gratitude, by which at all times noble souls have recognized each other. When the resentment of the aristocratic man manifests itself, it fulfills and exhausts itself in an immediate reaction, and consequently instills no *venom:* on the other hand, it never manifests itself at all in countless instances, when in the case of the feeble and weak it would be inevitable. An inability to take seriously for any length of time their enemies, their disasters, their *misdeeds*—that is the sign of the full strong natures who possess a superfluity of molding plastic force, that heals completely and produces forgetfulness: a good example of this in the modern world is Mirabeau, who had no memory for any insults and meannesses which were practiced on him, and who was only incapable of forgiving because he forgot. Such a man indeed shakes off with a shrug many a worm which would have buried itself in another; it is only in characters like these that we see the possibility (supposing, of course, that there is such a possibility in the world) of the real "*love* of one's enemies." What respect for his enemies is found, forsooth, in an aristocratic man—and such a reverence is already a bridge to love! He insists on having his enemy to himself as his distinction. He tolerates no other enemy but a man in whose character there is nothing to despise and *much* to honor! On the other hand, imagine the "enemy" as the resentful man conceives him— and it is here exactly that we see his work, his creativeness; he has conceived "the evil enemy," the "evil one," and indeed that is the root idea from which he now evolves as a contrasting and corresponding figure a "good one," himself—his very self!

11

3. Nietzsche's praise of the aristocratic "beast of prey" is shocking—yet by the end of the paragraph he gives reasons for his preference.

The method of this man is quite contrary to that of the aristocratic man, who conceives the root idea "good" spontaneously and straight away, that is to say, out of himself, and from that material then creates for himself a concept of "bad"! This "bad" of aristocratic origin and that "evil" out of the cauldron of unsatisfied hatred—the former an imitation, an "extra," an additional nuance; the latter, on the other hand, the original, the beginning, the essential act in the conception of a slave-morality—these two words "bad" and "evil," how great a difference do they mark, in spite of the fact that they have an identical contrary in the idea "good." But the idea "good" is *not* the same: much rather let the question be asked, "Who is really evil according to the meaning of the morality of resentment?" In all sternness let it be answered thus:—*just* the good man of the other morality, just the aristocrat, the powerful one, the one who rules, but who is distorted by the venomous eye of resentfulness, into a new color, a new signification, a new appearance. This particular point we would be the last to deny: the man who learned to know those "good" ones only as enemies, learned at the same time not to know them only as *"evil enemies,"* and the same men who *inter pares* were kept so rigorously in bounds through convention, respect, custom, and gratitude, though much more through mutual vigilance and jealousy *inter pares,* these men who in their relations with each other find so many new ways of manifesting consideration, self-control, delicacy, loyalty, pride, and friendship, these men are in reference to what is outside their circle (where the foreign element, a *foreign* country, begins), not much better than beasts of prey, which have been let loose. They enjoy there freedom from all social control, they feel that in the wilderness they can give vent with impunity to that tension which is produced by enclosure and imprisonment in the peace of society, they *revert* to the innocence of the beast-of-prey conscience, like jubilant monsters, who perhaps come from a ghostly bout of murder, arson, rape, and torture, with bravado and a moral equanimity, as though merely some wild student's prank had been played, perfectly convinced that the poets have now an ample theme to sing and celebrate. It is impossible not to recognize at the core of all these aristocratic races the beast of prey; the magnificent *blonde brute,* avidly rampant for spoil and victory; this hidden core needed an outlet from time to time, the beast must get loose again, must return into the wilderness—the Roman, Arabic, German, and Japanese nobility, the Homeric heroes, the Scandinavian Vikings, are all alike in this need. It is the aristocratic races who have left the idea "Barbarian" on all the tracks in which they have marched; nay, a consciousness of this very barbarianism, and even a pride in it, manifests itself even in their highest civilization (for example, when Pericles says to his Athenians in that celebrated funeral oration, "Our audacity has forced a way over every land and sea, rearing everywhere imperishable memorials of itself for *good* and for *evil*"). This audacity of aristocratic races, mad, absurd, and spasmodic as may be its expression; the incalculable and fantastic nature of their enterprises,—Pericles sets in special relief and glory the ραϑυμια of the Athenians, their nonchalance and contempt for safety, body, life, and comfort, their awful joy and intense delight in all destruction, in all the ecstasies of victory and cruelty,—all these features become crystallized, for those who suffered thereby in the picture of the "barbarian," of the "evil enemy," perhaps of the "Goth" and of the "Vandal." The profound, icy mistrust which the German provokes, as soon as he arrives at power,—even at the present time,—is always still an aftermath of that inextinguishable horror with which for whole centuries Europe has regarded the wrath of the blonde Teuton beast (although between the old Germans and ourselves there exists scarcely a psychological, let alone a physical, relationship). I have once called attention to the embarrassment of Hesiod, when he conceived the series of social ages, and endeavored to express them in gold, silver, and bronze. He could only dispose of the contradiction, with which he was confronted, by the Homeric world, an age magnificent indeed, but at the same time so awful and so violent, by making two ages out of one, which he henceforth placed one behind the other—first, the age of the heroes and demigods, as that world had remained in the memories of the aristocratic families, who found therein their own ancestors; secondly, the bronze age, as that corresponding age appeared to the descendants of the oppressed, spoiled, ill-treated, exiled, enslaved; namely, as an age of bronze, as I have said, hard, cold, terrible, without feelings and without conscience, crushing everything, and bespattering everything with blood. Granted the truth of the theory now believed to be true, that the very *essence of all civilization* is to *train* out of man, the beast of prey, a tame and civilized animal, a domesticated animal, it follows indubitably that we must regard as the real *tools of civilization* all those instincts of reaction and resentment, by the help of which the aristocratic races, together with their ideals, were finally degraded and overpowered; though that has not yet come to be synonymous with saying that the bearers of those tools also *represented* the civilization. It is rather the contrary that is not only probable—nay, it is *palpable* today; these bearers of vindictive instincts that have to be bottled up, these descendants of all European and non-European slavery, especially of the pre-Aryan population—these people, I say, represent the *decline* of humanity! These "tools of civilization" are a disgrace to humanity, and constitute in reality more of an argument against civilization, more of a reason why civilization should be suspected. One may be perfectly justified in being always afraid of the blonde beast that lies at the core of all aristocratic races, and in being on one's guard: but who would not a hundred times prefer to be afraid, when one at the same time admires, than to be immune from fear, at the cost of being perpetually obsessed with the loathsome spectacle of the distorted, the dwarfed, the stunted, the envenomed? And is that not our fate? What produces today our repulsion towards "man"?—for we *suffer* from "man," there is no doubt about it. It is not fear; it is rather that we have nothing more to fear from men; it is that the worm "man" is in the foreground and pullulates; it is that the "tame man," the wretched mediocre and unedifying creature, has learned to consider himself a goal and a pinnacle, an inner meaning, an historic principle, a "higher man"; yes, it is that he has a certain right so to consider himself, in so far as he feels that in contrast to that excess of deformity, disease, exhaustion, and effeteness whose odor is beginning to pollute present-day Europe, he at any rate has achieved a relative success, he at any rate still says "yes" to life.

12

I cannot refrain at this juncture from uttering a sigh and one last hope. What is it precisely which I find intolerable? That which I alone cannot get rid of, which makes me choke and faint? Bad air! Bad air! That something misbegotten comes near me; that I must inhale the odor of the entrails of a misbegotten soul!—That excepted, what can one not endure in the way of need, privation, bad weather, sickness, toil, solitude? In point of fact, one manages to get over everything, born as one is to a burrowing and battling existence; one always returns once again to the light, one always lives again one's golden hour of victory—and then one stands as one was born, unbreakable, tense, ready for something more difficult, for something more distant, like a bow stretched but the tauter by every strain. But from time to time do ye grant me—assuming that "beyond good and evil" there are goddesses who can grant—one glimpse, grant me but one glimpse only, of something perfect, fully realized, happy, mighty, triumphant, of something that still gives cause for fear! A glimpse of a man that justifies the existence of man, a glimpse of an incarnate human happiness that realizes and redeems, for the sake of which one may hold fast to *the belief in man!* For the position is this: in the dwarfing and leveling of the European man lurks *our* greatest peril, for it is this outlook which fatigues—we see today nothing which wishes to be greater, we surmise that the process is always still backwards, still backwards towards something more attenuated, more inoffensive, more cunning, more comfortable, more mediocre, more indifferent, more Chinese, more Christian—man, there is no doubt about it, grows always "better"—the destiny of Europe lies even in this—that in losing the fear of man, we have also lost the hope in man, yea, the will to be man. The sight of man now fatigues.—What is present-day Nihilism if it is not *that?*—We are tired of *man.*

13

---

4. A metaphor helps make clear the difference between the two moralities. Who are the lambs?

But let us come back to it; the problem of *another* origin of the good—of the good, as the resentful man has thought it out—demands its solution. It is not surprising that the lambs should bear a grudge against the great birds of prey, but that is no reason for blaming the great birds of prey for taking the little lambs. And when the lambs say among themselves, "Those birds of prey are evil, and he who is as far removed from being a bird of prey, who is rather its opposite, a lamb,—is he not good?" then there is nothing to cavil at in the setting up of this ideal, though it may also be that the birds of prey will regard it a little sneeringly, and perchance say to themselves, "*We* bear no grudge against them, these good lambs, we even like them: nothing is tastier than a tender lamb." To require of strength that it should *not* express itself as strength, that it should not be a wish to overpower, a wish to overthrow, a wish to become master, a thirst for enemies and antagonisms and triumphs, is just as absurd as to require of weakness that it should express itself as strength. A quantum of force is just such a quantum of movement, will, action—rather it is nothing else than just those very phenomena of moving, willing, acting, and can only appear otherwise in the misleading errors of language (and the fundamental fallacies of reason which have become petrified therein), which understands, and understands wrongly, all working as conditioned by a worker, by a "subject." And just exactly as the people separate the lightning from its flash, and interpret the latter as a thing done, as the working of a subject which is called lightning, so also does the popular morality separate strength from the expression of strength, as though behind the strong man there existed some indifferent neutral *substratum*, which enjoyed a *caprice and option* as to whether or not it should express strength. But there is no such *substratum*, there is no "being" behind doing, working, becoming; "the doer" is a mere appanage to the action. The action is everything. In point of fact, the people duplicate the doing, when they make the lightning lighten, that is a "doing-doing"; they make the same phenomenon first a cause, and then, secondly, the effect of that cause. The scientists fail to improve matters when they say, "Force moves, force causes," and so on. Our whole science is still, in spite of all its coldness, of all its freedom from passion, a dupe of the tricks of language, and has never succeeded in getting rid of that superstitious changeling "the subject" (the atom, to give another instance, is such a changeling, just as the Kantian "Thing-in-itself"). What wonder, if the suppressed and stealthily simmering passions of revenge and hatred exploit for their own advantage their belief, and indeed hold no belief with a more steadfast enthusiasm than this— "that the strong has the *option* of being weak, and the bird of prey of being a lamb." Thereby do they win for themselves the right of attributing to the birds of prey the *responsibility* for being birds of prey: when the oppressed, downtrodden, and overpowered say to themselves with the vindictive guile of weakness, "Let us be otherwise than the evil, namely, good! and good is every one who does not oppress, who hurts no one, who does not attack, who does not pay back, who hands over revenge to God, who holds himself, as we do, in hiding; who goes out of the way of evil, and demands, in short, little from life; like ourselves the patient, the meek, the just,"—yet all this, in its cold and unprejudiced interpretation, means nothing more than "once for all, the weak are weak; it is good to do *nothing for which we are not strong enough*"; but this dismal state of affairs, this prudence of the lowest order, which even insects possess (which in a great danger are fain to sham death so as to avoid doing "too much"), has, thanks to the counterfeiting and self-deception of weakness, come to masquerade in the pomp of an ascetic, mute, and expectant virtue, just as though the *very* weakness of the weak—that is, forsooth, its *being*, its working, its whole unique inevitable inseparable reality—were a voluntary result, something wished, chosen, a deed, an act of *merit*. This kind of man finds the belief in a neutral, free-choosing "subject" *necessary* from an instinct of self-preservation, of self-assertion, in which every lie is fain to sanctify itself. The subject (or, to use popular language, the *soul*) has perhaps proved itself the best dogma in the world simply because it rendered possible to the horde of mortal, weak, and oppressed individuals of every kind, that most sublime specimen of self-deception, the interpretation of weakness as freedom, of being this, or being that, as *merit*.

Beyond Good and Evil
Chapter IX
What Is Noble?

257

Every elevation of the type "man," has hitherto been the work of an aristocratic society and so it will always be—a society believing in a long scale of gradations of rank and differences of worth among human beings, and requiring slavery in some form or other. Without the *pathos of distance,* such as grows out of the incarnated difference of classes, out of the constant outlooking and downlooking of the ruling caste on subordinates and instruments, and out of their equally constant practice of obeying and commanding, of keeping down and keeping at a distance—that other more mysterious pathos could never have arisen, the longing for an ever new widening of distance within the soul itself, the formation of ever higher, rarer, further, more extended, more comprehensive states, in short, just the elevation of the type "man," the continued "self-surmounting of man," to use a moral formula in a supermoral sense. To be sure, one must not resign oneself to any humanitarian illusions about the history of the origin of an aristocratic society (that is to say, of the preliminary condition for the elevation of the type "man"): the truth is hard. Let us acknowledge unprejudicedly how every higher civilization hitherto has *originated!* Men with a still natural nature, barbarians in every terrible sense of the word, men of prey, still in possession of unbroken strength of will and desire for power, threw themselves upon weaker, more moral, more peaceful races (perhaps trading or cattle-rearing communities), or upon old mellow civilizations in which the final vital force was flickering out in brilliant fireworks of wit and depravity. At the commencement, the noble caste was always the barbarian caste: their superiority did not consist first of all in their physical, but their psychical power—they were more *complete* men (which at every point also implies the same as "more complete beasts").

258

Corruption—as the indication that anarchy threatens to break out among the instincts, and that the foundation of the emotions, called "life," is convulsed—is something radically different according to the organization in which it manifests itself. When, for instance, an aristocracy like that of France at the beginning of the Revolution, flung away its privileges with sublime disgust and sacrificed itself to an excess of its moral sentiments, it was corruption:—it was really only the closing act of the corruption which had existed for centuries, by virtue of which that aristocracy had abdicated step by step its lordly prerogatives and lowered itself to a *function* of royalty (in the end even to to its decoration and parade-dress). The essential thing, however, in a good and healthy aristocracy is that it should *not* regard itself as a function either of the kingship or the commonwealth, but as the *significance* and highest justification thereof—that it should therefore accept with a good conscience the sacrifice of a legion of individuals, who, *for its sake,* must be suppressed and reduced to imperfect men, to slaves and instruments. Its fundamental belief must be precisely that society is *not* allowed to exist for its own sake, but only as a foundation and scaffolding, by means of which a select class of beings may be able to elevate themselves to their higher duties, and in general to a higher *existence:* like those sun-seeking climbing plants in Java—they are called *Sipo Matador,*—which encircle an oak so long and so often with their arms, until at last, high above it, but supported by it, they can unfold their tops in the open light, and exhibit their happiness.

259

To refrain mutually from injury, from violence, from exploitation, and put one's will on a par with that of others: this may result in a certain rough sense in good conduct among individuals when the necessary conditions are given (namely, the actual similarity of the individuals in amount of force and degree of worth, and their co-relation within one organization). As soon, however, as one wished to take this principle more generally, and if possible even as *the fundamental principle of society,* it would immediately disclose what it really is—namely, a will to the *denial* of life, a principle of dissolution and decay. Here one must think profoundly to the very basis and resist all sentimental weakness: life itself is *essentially* appropriation, injury, conquest of the strange and weak, suppression, severity, obtrusion of peculiar forms, incorporation, and at the least, putting it mildest, exploitation;—but why should one for ever use precisely these words on which for ages a disparaging purpose has been stamped? Even the organization within which, as was previously supposed, the individuals treat each other as equal—it takes place in every healthy aristocracy—must itself, if it be a living and not a dying organization, do all that towards other bodies, which the individuals within it refrain from doing to each other: it will have to be the incarnated Will to Power, it will endeavor to grow, to gain ground, attract to itself and acquire ascendancy—not owing to any morality or immorality, but because it *lives*, and because life *is* precisely Will to Power. On no point, however, is the ordinary consciousness of Europeans more unwilling to be corrected than on this matter; people now rave everywhere, even under the guise of science, about coming conditions of society in which "the exploiting character" is to be absent:—that sounds to my ears as if they promised to invent a mode of life which should refrain from all organic functions. "Exploitation" does not belong to a depraved, or imperfect and primitive society: it belongs to the *nature* of the living being as a primary organic function; it is a consequence of the intrinsic Will to Power, which is precisely the Will to Life.— Granting that as a theory this is a novelty—as a reality it is the *fundamental fact* of all history: let us be so far honest towards ourselves!

260

5. *The fundamental values and attitudes of master and slave moralities are again contrasted. The contempt that Nietzsche feels toward the slave morality is made even more apparent in the passage near the end of this paragraph.*

In a tour through the many finer and coarser moralities which have hitherto prevailed or still prevail on the earth, I found certain traits recurring regularly together, and connected with one another, until finally two primary types revealed themselves to me, and a radical distinction was brought to light. There is *master-morality* and *slave-morality*;—I would at once add, however, that in all higher and mixed civilizations, there are also attempts at the reconciliation of the two moralities; but one finds still oftener the confusion and mutual misunderstanding of them, indeed, sometimes their close juxtaposition—even in the same man, within one soul. The distinctions of moral values have either originated in a ruling caste, pleasantly conscious of being different from the ruled—or among the ruled class, the slaves and dependents of all sorts. In the first case, when it is the rulers who determine the conception "good," it is the exalted, proud disposition which is regarded as the distinguishing feature, and that which determines the order of rank. The noble type of man separates from himself the beings in whom the opposite of this exalted, proud disposition displays itself: he despises them. Let it at once be noted that in this first kind of morality the antithesis "good" and "bad" means practically the same as "noble" and "despicable";—the antithesis "good" and "*evil*" is of a different origin. The cowardly, the timid, the insignificant, and those thinking merely of narrow utility are despised; moreover, also, the distrustful, with their constrained glances, the self-abasing, the dog-like kind of men who let themselves be abused, the mendicant flatterers, and above all the liars: it is a fundamental belief of all aristocrats that the common people are untruthful. "We truthful ones"—the nobility in ancient Greece called themselves. It is obvious that everywhere the designations of moral value were at first applied to *men*, and were only derivatively and at a later period applied to *actions;* it is a gross mistake, therefore, when historians of morals start with questions like, "Why have sympathetic actions been praised?" The noble type of man regards *himself* as a determiner of values; he does not require to be approved of; he passes the judgment: "What is injurious to me is injurious in itself"; he knows that it is he himself only who confers honor on things; he is a *creator of values.* He honors whatever he recognizes in himself: such morality is self-glorification. In the foreground there is the feeling of plenitude, of power, which seeks to overflow, the happiness of high tension, the consciousness of a wealth which would fain give and bestow:—the noble man also helps the unfortunate, but not—or scarcely—out of pity, but rather from an impulse generated by the super-abundance of power. The noble man honors in himself the powerful one, him also who has power over himself, who knows how to speak and how to keep silence, who takes pleasure in subjecting himself to severity and hardness, and has reverence for all that is severe and hard. "Wotan placed a hard heart in my breast," says an old Scandinavian Saga: it is thus rightly expressed from the soul of a proud Viking. Such a type of man is even proud of *not* being made for sympathy; the hero of the Saga therefore adds warningly: "He who has not a hard heart when young, will never have one." The noble and brave who think thus are the furthest removed from the morality which sees precisely in sympathy, or in acting for the good of others, or in *désintéressement,* the characteristic of the moral; faith in oneself, pride in oneself, a radical enmity and irony towards "selflessness," belong as definitely to noble morality, as do a careless scorn and precaution in presence of sympathy and the "warm heart."—It is the powerful who *know* how to honor, it is their art, their domain for invention. The profound reverence for age and for tradition—all law rests on this double reverence,—the belief and prejudice in favor of ancestors and unfavorable to newcomers, is typical in the morality of the powerful; and if, reversely, men of "modern ideas" believe almost instinctively in "progress" and the "future," and are more and more lacking in respect for old age, the ignoble origin of these "ideas" has complacently betrayed itself thereby. A morality of the ruling class, however, is more especially foreign and irritating to present-day taste in the sternness of its principle that one has duties only to one's equals; that one may act towards beings of a lower rank, towards all that is foreign, just as seems good to one, or "as the heart desires," and in any case "beyond good and evil": it is here that sympathy and similar sentiments can have a place. The ability and obligation to exercise prolonged gratitude and prolonged revenge—both only within the circle of equals,—artfulness in retaliation, *raffinement* of the idea in friendship, a certain necessity to have enemies (as outlets for the emotions of envy, quarrelsomeness, arrogance—in fact, in order to be a good *friend*): all these are typical characteristics of the noble morality, which, as has been pointed out, is not the morality of "modern ideas," and is therefore at present difficult to realize and also to unearth and disclose.—It is otherwise with the second type of morality, *slave-morality*. Supposing that the abused, the oppressed, the suffering, the unemancipated, the weary, and those uncertain of themselves, should moralize, what will be the common element in their moral estimates? Probably a pessimistic suspicion with regard to the entire situation of man will find expression, perhaps a condemnation of man, together with his situation. The slave has an unfavorable eye for the virtues of the powerful; he has a skepticism and distrust, a *refinement* of distrust of everything "good" that is there honored—he would fain persuade himself that the very happiness there is not genuine. On the other hand, *those* qualities which serve to alleviate the existence of sufferers are brought into prominence and flooded with light; it is here that sympathy, the kind, helping hand, the warm heart, patience, diligence, humility, and friendliness attain to honor; for here these are the most useful qualities, and almost the only means of supporting the burden of existence. Slave-morality is essentially the morality of utility. Here is the seat of the origin of the famous antithesis "good" and "evil":—power and danger-ousness are assumed to reside in the evil, a certain dreadfulness, subtlety, and strength, which do not admit of being despised. According to slave-morality, there-fore, the "evil" man arouses fear; according to master-morality, it is precisely the "good" man who arouses fear and seeks to arouse it, while the bad man is regarded as the despicable being. The contrast attains its maximum when, in accordance with the logical consequences of slave-morality, a shade of depreciation—it may be slight and well-intentioned—at last attaches itself to the "good" man of this morality; be-cause, according to the servile mode of thought, the good man must in any case be the *safe* man: he is good-natured, easily deceived, perhaps a little stupid, *un bon-homme*. Everywhere that slave-morality gains the ascendancy, language shows a tendency to approximate the significations of the words "good" and "stupid."—A last fundamental difference: the desire for *freedom,* the instinct for happiness and the refinements of the feeling of liberty belong as necessarily to slave-morals and morality, as artifice and enthusiasm in reverence and devotion are the regular symp-toms of an aristocratic mode of thinking and estimating.—Hence we can understand without further detail why love *as a passion*—it is our European specialty—must ab-solutely be of noble origin; as is well known, its invention is due to the Provençal poet-cavaliers, those brilliant, ingenious men of the *"gai saber,"* to whom Europe owes so much, and almost owes itself.

261

Vanity is one of the things which are perhaps most difficult for a noble man to un-derstand: he will be tempted to deny it, where another kind of man thinks he sees it self-evidently. The problem for him is to represent to his mind beings who seek to arouse a good opinion of themselves which they themselves do not possess—and con-sequently also do not "deserve,"—and who yet *believe* in this good opinion after-wards. This seems to him on the one hand such bad taste and so self-disrespectful, and on the other hand so grotesquely unreasonable, that he would like to consider vanity an exception, and is doubtful about it in most cases when it is spoken of. He will say, for instance: "I may be mistaken about my value, and on the other hand may nevertheless demand that my value should be acknowledged by others precisely as I rate it:—that, however, is not vanity (but self-conceit, or, in most cases, that which is called 'humility,' and also 'modesty')." Or he will even say: "For many reasons I can delight in the good opinion of others, perhaps because I love and honor them, and rejoice in all their joys, perhaps also because their good opinion endorses and strengthens my belief in my own good opinion, perhaps because the good opinion of others, even in cases where I do not share it, is useful to me, or gives promise of use-fulness:—all this, however, is not vanity." The man of noble character must first bring it home forcibly to his mind, especially with the aid of history, that, from time im-memorial, in all social strata in any way dependent, the ordinary man *was* only that which he *passed for:*—not being at all accustomed to fix values, he did not assign even to himself any other value than that which his master assigned to him (it is the peculiar *right of masters* to create values). It may be looked upon as the result of an extraordinary atavism, that the ordinary man, even at present, is still always *waiting* for an opinion about himself, and then instinctively submitting himself to it; yet by no means only to a "good" opinion, but also to a bad and unjust one (think, for instance, of the greater part of the self-appreciations and self-depreciations which believing women learn from their confessors, and which in general the believing Christian learns from his Church). In fact, conformably to the slow rise of the democratic social order (and its cause, the blending of the blood of masters and slaves), the originally noble and rare impulse of the masters to assign a value to themselves and to "think well" of themselves, will now be more and more encouraged and extended; but it has at all times an older, ampler, and more radically ingrained propensity opposed to it—and in the phenomenon of "vanity" this older propensity overmasters the younger. The vain person rejoices over *every* good opinion which he hears about himself (quite apart from the point of view of its usefulness, and equally regardless of its truth or falsehood), just as he suffers from every bad opinion: for he subjects himself to both, he *feels* himself subjected to both, by that oldest instinct of subjection which breaks forth in him.—It is "the slave" in the vain man's blood, the remains of the slave's craftiness—and how much of the "slave" is still left in woman, for instance!—which seeks to *seduce* to good opinions of itself; it is the slave, too, who immediately afterwards falls prostrate himself before these opinions, as though he had not called them forth.—And to repeat it again: vanity is an atavism.

READING QUESTIONS

1. Describe the two ways that Nietzsche portrays happiness as it is differently associated in each of the two moralities.

2. Who is really capable of loving his enemies? Why?

3. Who is really evil in the morality of resentment?

4. What does Nietzsche say is the essence of civilization?

5. What follows from the belief that the strong have the option of being weak?

6. What does Nietzsche call the "fundamental fact" of all history?

7. In the aristocratic, or noble, morality, who creates values?

8. Why is it necessary for the noble person to have enemies?

G. E. Moore

George Edward Moore (1873–1958) is a transitional figure in the history of moral philosophy. Even though other philosophers of his era were more influential on the Continent and in the Americas, many moral philosophers use the 1903 publication of Moore's major work, the *Principia Ethica,* to indicate the beginning of contemporary ethical theory.

Moore was born near London in 1873. His family was relatively prosperous: his father was a physician, and his mother's family were prominent Quaker merchants. In 1892 he enrolled in Trinity College, Cambridge, to study classics. He turned his attention to philosophy two years later and studied under a renowned English moral philosopher of the day, Henry Sidgwick. After Moore completed a dissertation on Kant's ethics, he earned a fellowship at Cambridge and taught there from 1898 to 1904 amid lively philosophical discussion with his colleague Bertrand Russell, one of the most popular philosophers during the first half of the twentieth century. When his fellowship expired, Moore continued to write philosophy, living on an inheritance until, in 1911, he was invited back to Cambridge. There he remained until 1939, when he reached the mandatory age of retirement. Even after his retirement from the university, Moore continued his philosophical activities, writing and discussing problems with students and friends until his death at the age of 85. His life outside of philosophy was relatively uneventful, but his effect on moral philosophy has been profound.

While Moore was on his fellowship at Cambridge, he published several articles and what was to become a most important book, the *Principia Ethica.* In this now famous work, Moore charges previous moral philosophers with a failure to begin their work at the beginning. Before we can decide which actions are good, we must define what the concept of "good" means. Moore claims that previous philosophers failed to make a distinction between two important questions in ethics: What kinds of actions ought we to perform, and what kinds of things ought to exist for their own sake? The answer to the first question for Moore is simply those actions that bring about the most good. But attempts to answer the second question, that is, attempts to define "good," commit what Moore labeled the "naturalistic fallacy," so called because they define ethical terms by means of nonethical (or natural) concepts. Moore makes the radical claim that good, like the property yellow, is a simple, unanalyzable, nonnatural characteristic. It cannot be defined in terms of any other properties that are more fundamental. We may know goodness (or yellowness) when we see it, but we cannot define it in such a way as to make it intelligible to someone not already directly aware of it.

The primary object of Moore's attack is **ethical naturalism,** a kind of moral theory that stresses an empirical or scientific attitude in which ethics is merely a part of the natural world. Two theories that he considers representative of ethical naturalism and singled out by Moore for criticism are those of **John Stuart Mill** and of **Herbert Spencer.** As we have seen, for **utilitarians** such as Mill, good is defined in terms of happiness (or pleasure). If "good" means "happiness," then Mill is *identifying* good with happiness. But, says Moore, happiness cannot be identical to good because one can always ask whether happiness itself is good. Moore charges that Mill has failed to define "good"; instead, he has merely given an example of something that is good. Moore criticizes the famous nineteenth-century philosopher of evolution Herbert Spencer similarly. "Good," according to Spencer, means "more evolved." Yet good cannot be identical to more evolved since we can always ask whether being more evolved is necessarily good. Even though it is debatable whether Moore fairly characterized either of these two eminent philosophers, his influence in ethical theory was, and remains, widely felt.

If he denies that we are able to define what good is, what does Moore offer as a remedy? Moore's positive ethical philosophy is a kind of **intuitionism.** For Moore, we cannot define goodness, but we know what goodness is by a special faculty—intuition. It is through intuition that we are able to identify and appreciate the good things in life such as friendship and aesthetic pleasures.

Moore's arguments against ethical naturalism have generated a great deal of controversy in contemporary moral philosophy, and this is largely the reason he is considered the starting point for contemporary ethics. Some subsequent philosophers supported Moore's nonnaturalism but promoted quite different alternative theories. Two such nonnaturalists included in this volume are **W. D. Ross** and **A. J. Ayer.** Other philosophers support naturalistic theories of various kinds. One of the early attempts to justify a naturalistic ethics (also covered in this volume) is the moral philosophy of **John Dewey.** In the latter half of the twentieth century, interest in naturalistic theories such as evolutionary ethics has exploded.

Principia Ethica
ᴇᴙ ᴊᴇ

Sometimes when children want permission to go somewhere or do something and the parents resist, they plead by saying, "Everybody else gets to do it." Usually, this does not influence the parents much, but that kind of reasoning is similar to the issue that Moore examines in this reading. Parents may refuse to be swayed by the appeal to everyone else's behavior by noting that everyone's doing something does not make it *right* to act this way. We can discover facts about the world, but where in those facts are the *values* that we associate with them?   ᴊᴇ

Chapter I
The Subject-Matter of Ethics

1. It is very easy to point out some among our everyday judgments, with the truth of which Ethics is undoubtedly concerned. Whenever we say, "So and so is a good man," or "That fellow is a villain"; whenever we ask, "What ought I to do?" or "Is it wrong for me to do like this?"; whenever we hazard such remarks as "Temperance is a virtue and drunkenness a vice"—it is undoubtedly the business of Ethics to dis-

---

From G. E. Moore, *Principia Ethica*, Revised Edition, edited by Thomas Baldwin. Reprinted with the permission of Cambridge University Press.

cuss such questions and such statements; to argue what is the true answer when we ask what it is right to do, and to give reasons for thinking that our statements about the character of persons or the morality of actions are true or false. In the vast majority of cases, where we make statements involving any of the terms 'virtue,' 'vice,' 'duty,' 'right,' 'ought,' 'good,' 'bad,' we are making ethical judgments; and if we wish to discuss their truth, we shall be discussing a point of Ethics.

So much as this is not disputed; but it falls very far short of defining the province of Ethics. That province may indeed be defined as the whole truth about that which is at the same time common to all such judgments and peculiar to them. But we have still to ask the question: What is it that is thus common and peculiar? And this is a question to which very different answers have been given by ethical philosophers of acknowledged reputation, and none of them, perhaps, completely satisfactory.

---

1. Moore begins by explicating definitions of "ethics." Notice his emphasis on conduct. He gives his definition. Does it involve conduct?

---

2. If we take such examples as those given above, we shall not be far wrong in saying that they are all of them concerned with the question of 'conduct'—with the question, what, in the conduct of us, human beings, is good, and what is bad, what is right, and what is wrong. For when we say that a man is good, we commonly mean that he acts rightly; when we say that drunkenness is a vice, we commonly mean that to get drunk is a wrong or wicked action. And this discussion of human conduct is, in fact, that with which the name 'Ethics' is most intimately associated. It is so associated by derivation; and conduct is undoubtedly by far the commonest and most generally interesting object of ethical judgments.

Accordingly, we find that many ethical philosophers are disposed to accept as an adequate definition of 'Ethics' the statement that it deals with the question what is good or bad in human conduct. They hold that its inquiries are properly confined to 'conduct' or to 'practice'; they hold that the name 'practical philosophy' covers all the matter with which it has to do. Now, without discussing the proper meaning of the word (for verbal questions are properly left to the writers of dictionaries and other persons interested in literature; philosophy, as we shall see, has no concern with them), I may say that I intend to use 'Ethics' to cover more than this—a usage, for which there is, I think, quite sufficient authority. I am using it to cover an inquiry for which, at all events, there is no other word: the general inquiry into what is good.

---

2. What must moral philosophers do to start at the beginning?

Ethics is undoubtedly concerned with the question what good conduct is; but, being concerned with this, it obviously does not start at the beginning, unless it is prepared to tell us what is good as well as what is conduct. For 'good conduct' is a complex notion: all conduct is not good; for some is certainly bad and some may be indifferent. And on the other hand, other things, beside conduct, may be good; and if they are so, then, 'good' denotes some property, that is common to them and conduct; and if we examine good conduct alone of all good things, then we shall be in danger of mistaking for this property, some property which is not shared by those other things: and thus we shall have made a mistake about Ethics even in this limited sense; for we shall not know what good conduct really is. This is a mistake which many writers have actually made, from limiting their inquiry to conduct. And hence I shall try to avoid it by considering first what is good in general; hoping, that if we can arrive at any certainty about this, it will be much easier to settle the question of good conduct: for we all know pretty well what 'conduct' is. This, then, is our first question: What is good? and What is bad? and to the discussion of this question (or these questions) I give the name of Ethics, since that science must, at all events, include it.

3. But this is a question which may have many meanings. If, for example, each of us were to say "I am doing good now" or "I had a good dinner yesterday," these statements would each of them be some sort of answer to our question, although perhaps a false one. So, too, when A asks B what school he ought to send his son to, B's answer will certainly be an ethical judgment. And similarly all distribution of praise or blame to any personage or thing that has existed, now exists, or will exist, does give some answer to the question "What is good?" In all such cases some particular thing is judged to be good or bad: the question "What?" is answered by "This." But this is not the sense in which a scientific Ethics asks the question. Not one, of all the many million answers of this kind, which must be true, can form a part of an ethical system; although that science must contain reasons and principles sufficient for deciding on the truth of all of them. There are far too many persons, things and events in the world, past, present, or to come, for a discussion of their individual merits to be embraced in any science. Ethics, therefore, does not deal at all with facts of this nature, facts that are unique, individual, absolutely particular; facts with which such studies as history, geography, astronomy, are compelled, in part at least, to deal. And, for this reason, it is not the business of the ethical philosopher to give personal advice or exhortation.

4. But there is another meaning which may be given to the question "What is good?" "Books are good" would be an answer to it, though an answer obviously false; for some books are very bad indeed. And ethical judgments of this kind do indeed belong to Ethics; though I shall not deal with many of them. Such is the judgment "Pleasure is good"—a judgment, of which Ethics should discuss the truth, although it is not nearly as important as that other judgment, with which we shall be much occupied presently—"Pleasure *alone* is good." It is judgments of this sort, which are made in such books on Ethics as contain a list of 'virtues'—in Aristotle's 'Ethics' for example. But it is judgments of precisely the same kind, which form the substance of what is commonly supposed to be a study different from Ethics, and one much less respectable—the study of Casuistry. We may be told that Casuistry differs from Ethics, in that it is much more detailed and particular, Ethics much more general. But it is most important to notice that Casuistry does not deal with anything that is absolutely particular—particular in the only sense in which a perfectly precise line can be drawn between it and what is general. It is not particular in the sense just noticed, the sense in which this book is a particular book, and A's friend's advice particular advice. Casuistry may indeed be *more* particular and Ethics *more* general; but that means that they differ only in degree and not in kind.

And this is universally true of 'particular' and 'general,' when used in this common, but inaccurate, sense. So far as Ethics allows itself to give lists of virtues or even to name constituents of the Ideal, it is indistinguishable from Casuistry. Both alike deal with what is general, in the sense in which physics and chemistry deal with what is general. Just as chemistry aims at discovering what are the properties of oxygen, *wherever it occurs*, and not only of this or that particular specimen of oxygen; so Casuistry aims at discovering what actions are good, *whenever they occur*. In this respect Ethics and Casuistry alike are to be classed with such sciences as physics, chemistry and physiology, in their absolute distinction from those of which history and geography are instances. And it is to be noted that, owing to their detailed nature, casuistical investigations are actually nearer to physics and to chemistry than are the investigations usually assigned to Ethics. For just as physics cannot rest content with the discovery that light is propagated by waves of ether, but must go on to discover the particular nature of the ether-waves corresponding to each several color; so Casuistry, not content with the general law that charity is a virtue must attempt to discover the relative merits of every different form of charity. Casuistry forms, therefore, part of the ideal of ethical science: Ethics cannot be complete without it. The defects of Casuistry are not defects of principle; no objection can be taken to its aim and object. It has failed only because it is far too difficult a subject to be treated adequately in our present state of knowledge. The casuist has been unable to distinguish, in the cases which he treats, those elements upon which their value depends. Hence he often thinks two cases to be alike in respect of value, when in reality they are alike only in some other respect. It is to mistakes of this kind that the pernicious influence of such investigations has been due. For Casuistry is the goal of ethical investigation. It cannot be safely attempted at the beginning of our studies, but only at the end.

————

3. Here Moore shows the main thrust of his inquiry and why he thinks it so vital to moral philosophy.

————

5. But our question "What is good?" may have still another meaning. We may, in the third place, mean to ask, not what thing or things are good, but how "good"is to be defined. This is an inquiry which belongs only to Ethics, not to Casuistry; and this is the inquiry which will occupy us first.

It is an inquiry to which most special attention should be directed; since this question, how 'good' is to be defined, is the most fundamental question in all Ethics. That which is meant by 'good' is, in fact, except its converse 'bad,' the *only* simple object of thought which is peculiar to Ethics. Its definition is, therefore, the most essential point in the definition of Ethics; and moreover a mistake with regard to it entails a far larger number of erroneous ethical judgments than any other. Unless this first question be fully understood, and its true answer clearly recognized, the rest of Ethics is as good as useless from the point of view of systematic knowledge. True ethical judgments, of the two kinds last dealt with, may indeed be made by those who do not know the answer to this question as well as by those who do; and it goes without saying that the two classes of people may lead equally good lives. But it is extremely unlikely that the *most general* ethical judgments will be equally valid, in the absence of a true answer to this question: I shall presently try to show that the gravest errors have been largely due to beliefs in a false answer. And, in any case, it is impossible that, till the answer to this question be known, any one should know *what is the evidence* for any ethical judgment whatsoever. But the main object of Ethics, as a systematic science, is to give correct *reasons* for thinking that this or that is good; and, unless this question be answered, such reasons cannot be given. Even, therefore, apart from the fact that a false answer leads to false conclusions, the present inquiry is a most necessary and important part of the science of Ethics.

6. What, then, is good? How is good to be defined? Now, it may be thought that this is a verbal question. A definition does indeed often mean the expressing of one word's meaning in other words. But this is not the sort of definition I am asking for. Such a definition can never be of ultimate importance in any study except lexicography. If I wanted that kind of definition I should have to consider in the first place how people generally used the word 'good'; but my business is not with its proper usage, as established by custom. I should, indeed, be foolish, if I tried to use it for something which it did not usually denote: if, for instance, I were to announce that, whenever I used the word 'good,' I must be understood to be thinking of that object which is usually denoted by the word 'table.' I shall, therefore, use the word in the sense in which I think it is ordinarily used; but at the same time I am not anxious to discuss whether I am right in thinking that it is so used. My business is solely with that object or idea, which I hold, rightly or wrongly, that the word is generally used to stand for. What I want to discover is the nature of that object or idea, and about this I am extremely anxious to arrive at an agreement.

But, if we understand the question in this sense, my answer to it may seem a very disappointing one. If I am asked "What is good?" my answer is that good is good, and that is the end of the matter. Or if I am asked "How is good to be defined?" my answer is that it cannot be defined, and that is all I have to say about it. But disappointing as these answers may appear, they are of the very last importance. To readers who are familiar with philosophic terminology, I can express their importance by saying that they amount to this: That propositions about the good are all of them synthetic and never analytic; and that is plainly no trivial matter. And the same thing may be expressed more popularly, by saying that, if I am right, then nobody can foist upon us such an axiom as that "Pleasure is the only good" or that "The good is the desired" on the pretense that this is "the very meaning of the word."

---

4. Moore is famous for what he says in this paragraph. Can you see how "good" is related to "yellow"?

---

7. Let us, then, consider this position. My point is that 'good' is a simple notion, just as 'yellow' is a simple notion; that, just as you cannot, by any manner of means, explain to any one who does not already know it, what yellow is, so you cannot explain what good is. Definitions of the kind that I was asking for, definitions which describe the real nature of the object or notion denoted by a word, and which do not merely tell us what the word is used to mean, are only possible when the object or notion in question is something complex. You can give a definition of a horse, because a horse has many different properties and qualities, all of which you can enumerate. But when you have enumerated them all, when you have re-

duced a horse to his simplest terms, then you can no longer define those terms. They are simply something which you think of or perceive, and to anyone who cannot think of or perceive them, you can never, by any definition, make their nature known. It may perhaps be objected to this that we are able to describe to others, objects which they have never seen or thought of. We can, for instance, make a man understand what a chimera is, although he has never heard of one or seen one. You can tell him that it is an animal with a lioness's head and body, with a goat's head growing from the middle of its back, and with a snake in place of a tail. But here the object which you are describing is a complex object; it is entirely composed of parts, with which we are all perfectly familiar—a snake, a goat, a lioness; and we know, too, the manner in which those parts are to be put together, because we know what is meant by the middle of a lioness's back, and where her tail is wont to grow. And so it is with all objects, not previously known, which we are able to define: they are all complex; all composed of parts, which may themselves, in the first instance, be capable of similar definition, but which must in the end be reducible to simplest parts, which can no longer be defined. But yellow and good, we say, are not complex: they are notions of that simple kind, out of which definitions are composed and with which the power of further defining ceases.

---

5. *Definitions can have different senses, as Moore distinguishes here.*

---

8. When we say, as Webster says, "The definition of horse is 'a hoofed quadruped of the genus Equus,'" we may, in fact, mean three different things. (1) We may mean merely: "When I say 'horse,' you are to understand that I am talking about a hoofed quadruped of the genus Equus." This might be called the arbitrary verbal definition: and I do not mean that good is indefinable in that sense. (2) We may mean, as Webster ought to mean: "When most English people say 'horse,' they mean a hoofed quadruped of the genus Equus." This may be called the verbal definition proper, and I do not say that good is indefinable in this sense either; for it is certainly possible to discover how people use a word: otherwise, we could never have known that 'good' may be translated by 'gut' in German and by 'bon' in French. But (3) we may, when we define horse, mean something much more important. We may mean that a certain object, which we all of us know, is composed in a certain manner: that it has four legs, a head, a heart, a liver, etc., etc., all of them arranged in definite relations to one another. It is in this sense that I deny good to be definable. I say that it is not composed of any parts, which we can substitute for it in our minds when we are thinking of it. We might think just as clearly and correctly about a horse, if we thought of all its parts and their arrangement instead of thinking of the whole: we could, I say, think how a horse differed from a donkey just as well, just as truly, in this way, as now we do, only not so easily; but there is nothing whatsoever which we could so substitute for good; and that is what I mean, when I say that good is indefinable.

9. But I am afraid I have still not removed the chief difficulty which may prevent acceptance of the proposition that good is indefinable. I do not mean to say that *the* good, that which is good, is thus indefinable; if I did think so, I should not be writing on Ethics, for my main object is to help towards discovering that definition. It is just because I think there will be less risk of error in our search for a definition of 'the good,' that I am now insisting that *good* is indefinable. I must try to explain the difference between these two. I suppose it may be granted that 'good'

is an adjective. Well 'the good,' 'that which is good,' must therefore be the sub-stantive to which the adjective 'good' will apply: it must be the whole of that to which the adjective will apply, and the adjective must *always* truly apply to it. But if it is that to which the adjective will apply, it must be something different from that adjective itself; and the whole of that something different, whatever it is, will be our definition of *the* good. Now it may be that this something will have other adjectives, beside 'good,' that will apply to it. It may be full of pleasure, for exam-ple; it may be intelligent: and if these two adjectives are really part of its definition, then it will certainly be true, that pleasure and intelligence are good. And many people appear to think that, if we say "Pleasure and intelligence are good," or if we say "Only pleasure and intelligence are good," we are defining 'good.' Well, I cannot deny that propositions of this nature may sometimes be called definitions; I do not know well enough how the word is generally used to decide upon this point. I only wish it to be understood that that is not what I mean when I say there is no possible definition of good, and that I shall not mean this if I use the word again. I do most fully believe that some true proposition of the form "Intelligence is good and intelligence alone is good" can be found; if none could be found, our definition of *the* good would be impossible. As it is, I believe *the* good to be defin-able; and yet I still say that good itself is indefinable.

10. 'Good,' then, if we mean by it that quality which we assert to belong to a thing, when we say that the thing is good, is incapable of any definition, in the most important sense of that word. The most important sense of 'definition' is that in which a definition states what are the parts which invariably compose a certain whole; and in this sense 'good' has no definition because it is simple and has no parts. It is one of those innumerable objects of thought which are themselves incapable of definition, because they are the ultimate terms by reference to which whatever *is* capable of definition must be defined. That there must be an indefinite number of such terms is obvious, on re-flection; since we cannot define anything except by an analysis, which, when carried as far as it will go, refers us to something, which is simply different from anything else, and which by that ultimate difference explains the peculiarity of the whole which we are defining: for every whole contains some parts which are common to other wholes also. There is, therefore, no intrinsic difficulty in the contention that 'good' denotes a simple and indefinable quality. There are many other instances of such qualities.

---

6. Moore explains why "yellow" is indefinable. He will then make an analogy with "good." At the end of this section is a famous fallacy associated with Moore.

Consider yellow, for example. We may try to define it, by describing its physi-cal equivalent; we may state what kind of light-vibrations must stimulate the nor-mal eye, in order that we may perceive it. But a moment's reflection is sufficient to show that those light-vibrations are not themselves what we mean by yellow. *They* are not what we perceive. Indeed we should never have been able to discover their existence, unless we had first been struck by the patent difference of quality between the different colors. The most we can be entitled to say of those vibrations is that they are what corresponds in space to the yellow which we actually perceive.

Yet a mistake of this simple kind has commonly been made about 'good.' It may be true that all things which are good are *also* something else, just as it is true that all things which are yellow produce a certain kind of vibration in the light. And it is a fact, that Ethics aims at discovering what are those other properties belonging to all things which are good. But far too many philosophers have thought that when they named those other properties they were actually defining good; that these properties, in fact, were simply not 'other,' but absolutely and entirely the same with goodness. This view I propose to call the 'naturalistic fallacy' and of it I shall now endeavor to dispose.

11. Let us consider what it is such philosophers say. And first it is to be noticed that they do not agree among themselves. They not only say that they are right as to what good is, but they endeavor to prove that other people who say that it is something else, are wrong. One, for instance, will affirm that good is pleasure, another, perhaps, that good is that which is desired; and each of these will argue eagerly to prove that the other is wrong. But how is that possible? One of them says that good is nothing but the object of desire, and at the same time tries to prove that it is not pleasure. But from his first assertion, that good just means the object of desire, one of two things must follow as regards his proof:

(1) He may be trying to prove that the object of desire is not pleasure. But, if this be all, where is his Ethics? The position he is maintaining is merely a psychological one. Desire is something which occurs in our minds, and pleasure is something else which so occurs; and our would-be ethical philosopher is merely holding that the latter is not the object of the former. But what has that to do with the question in dispute? His opponent held the ethical proposition that pleasure was the good, and although he should prove a million times over the psychological proposition that pleasure is not the object of desire, he is no nearer proving his opponent to be wrong. The position is like this. One man says a triangle is a circle: another replies "A triangle is a straight line, and I will prove to you that I am right: *for*" (this is the only argument) "a straight line is not a circle." "That is quite true," the other may reply; "but nevertheless a triangle is a circle, and you have said nothing whatever to prove the contrary. What is proved is that one of us is wrong, for we agree that a triangle cannot be both a straight line and a circle: but which is wrong, there can be no earthly means of proving, since you define triangle as straight line and I define it as circle."—Well, that is one alternative which any naturalistic Ethics has to face; if good is *defined* as something else, it is then impossible either to prove that any other definition is wrong or even to deny such definition.

(2) The other alternative will scarcely be more welcome. It is that the discussion is after all a verbal one. When A says "Good means pleasant" and B says "Good means desired," they may merely wish to assert that most people have used the word for what is pleasant and for what is desired respectively. And this is quite an interesting subject for discussion: only it is not a whit more an ethical discussion than the last was. Nor do I think that any exponent of naturalistic Ethics would be willing to allow that this was all he meant. They are all so anxious to persuade us that what they call the good is what we really ought to do. "Do, pray, act so, because the word 'good' is generally used to denote actions of this nature": such, on this view, would be the substance of their teaching. And in so far as they tell us how we ought to act, their teaching is truly ethical, as they mean it to be. But how perfectly absurd is the reason they would give for it! "You are to do this, because most people use a certain word to denote conduct such as this." "You are to say the thing which is not, because

most people call it lying." That is an argument just as good!—My dear sirs, what we want to know from you as ethical teachers, is not how people use a word; it is not even, what kind of actions they approve, which the use of this word 'good' may certainly imply: what we want to know is simply what *is* good. We may indeed agree that what most people do think good, is actually so; we shall at all events be glad to know their opinions: but when we say their opinions about what *is* good, we do mean what we say; we do not care whether they call that thing which they mean 'horse' or 'table' or 'chair,' 'gut' or 'bon' or 'ἀγαθός'; we want to know what it is that they so call. When they say "Pleasure is good," we cannot believe that they merely mean "Pleasure is pleasure" and nothing more than that.

12. Suppose a man says "I am pleased"; and suppose that is not a lie or a mistake but the truth. Well, if it is true, what does that mean? It means that his mind, a certain definite mind, distinguished by certain definite marks from all others, has at this moment a certain definite feeling called pleasure. 'Pleased' *means* nothing but having pleasure, and though we may be more pleased or less pleased, and even, we may admit for the present, have one or another kind of pleasure; yet in so far as it is pleasure we have, whether there be more or less of it, and whether it be of one kind or another, what we have is one definite thing, absolutely indefinable, some one thing that is the same in all the various degrees and in all the various kinds of it that there may be. We may be able to say how it is related to other things: that, for example, it is in the mind, that it causes desire, that we are conscious of it, etc., etc. We can, I say, describe its relations to other things, but define it we can *not*. And if anybody tried to define pleasure for us as being any other natural object; if anybody were to say, for instance, that pleasure *means* the sensation of red, and were to proceed to deduce from that that pleasure is a color, we should be entitled to laugh at him and to distrust his future statements about pleasure. Well, that would be the same fallacy which I have called the naturalistic fallacy. That 'pleased' does not mean 'having the sensation of red,' or anything else whatever, does not prevent us from understanding what it does mean. It is enough for us to know that 'pleased' does mean 'having the sensation of pleasure,' and though pleasure is absolutely indefinable, though pleasure is pleasure and nothing else whatever, yet we feel no difficulty in saying that we are pleased. The reason is, of course, that when I say "I am pleased," I do not mean that 'I' am the same thing as 'having pleasure.' And similarly no difficulty need be found in my saying that "pleasure is good" and yet not meaning that 'pleasure' is the same thing as 'good,' that pleasure *means* good, and that good *means* pleasure. If I were to imagine that when I said "I am pleased," I meant that I was exactly the same thing as 'pleased,' I should not indeed call that a naturalistic fallacy, although it would be the same fallacy as I have called naturalistic with reference to Ethics. The reason of this is obvious enough. When a man confuses two natural objects with one another, defining the one by the other, if for instance, he confuses himself, who is one natural object, with 'pleased' or with 'pleasure' which are others, then there is no reason to call the fallacy naturalistic. But if he confuses 'good,' which is not in the same sense a natural object, with any natural object whatever, then there is a reason for calling that a naturalistic fallacy; its being made with regard to 'good' marks it as something quite specific, and this specific mistake deserves a name because it is so common. As for the reasons why good is not to be considered a natural object, they may be reserved for discussion in another place. But, for the present, it is sufficient to notice this: Even if it were a nat-

ural object, that would not alter the nature of the fallacy nor diminish its importance one whit. All that I have said about it would remain quite equally true: only the name which I have called it would not be so appropriate as I think it is. And I do not care about the name: what I do care about is the fallacy. It does not matter what we call it, provided we recognize it when we meet with it. It is to be met with in almost every book on Ethics; and yet it is not recognized: and that is why it is necessary to multiply illustrations of it, and convenient to give it a name. It is a very simple fallacy indeed. When we say that an orange is yellow, we do not think our statement binds us to hold that 'orange' means nothing else than 'yellow,' or that nothing can be yellow but an orange. Supposing the orange is also sweet! Does that bind us to say that 'sweet' is exactly the same thing as 'yellow,' that 'sweet' must be defined as 'yellow'? And supposing it be recognized that 'yellow' just means 'yellow' and nothing else whatever, does that make it any more difficult to hold that oranges are yellow? Most certainly it does not: on the contrary, it would be absolutely meaningless to say that oranges were yellow, unless yellow did in the end mean just 'yellow' and nothing else whatever—unless it was absolutely indefinable. We should not get any very clear notion about things, which are yellow—we should not get very far with our science, if we were bound to hold that everything which was yellow, *meant* exactly the same thing as yellow. We should find we had to hold that an orange was exactly the same thing as a stool, a piece of paper, a lemon, anything you like. We could prove any number of absurdities; but should we be the nearer to the truth? Why, then, should it be different with 'good'? Why, if good is good and indefinable, should I be held to deny that pleasure is good? Is there any difficulty in holding both to be true at once? On the contrary, there is no meaning in saying that pleasure is good, unless good is something different from pleasure. It is absolutely useless, so far as Ethics is concerned, to prove, as Mr. Spencer tries to do, that increase of pleasure coincides with increase of life, unless good *means* something different from either life or pleasure. He might just as well try to prove that an orange is yellow by showing that it always is wrapped up in paper.

READING QUESTIONS

1. What is the definition of "ethics" that Moore prefers?

2. Give an example where "good" is employed that is not an ethical judgment.

3. What does Moore say is the most fundamental question in all ethics? What makes it fundamental?

4. What does Moore mean when he says that "good is a simple notion"?

5. What fallacy does he say results from attempts to define good in terms of something else?

John Dewey

John Dewey (1859–1952) is the first American philosopher in our readings. In his moral philosophy he is representative of a number of ethical naturalists who were (and still are) unconvinced by the critique of naturalism made by G. E. Moore. Born in Burlington, Vermont, the young Dewey was merely an adequate student who seemed unlikely to become one of America's premier philosophers and social reformers. He entered the University of Vermont in 1875 and taught high school upon graduation. After a time, he followed up his interest in philosophy by enrolling in the graduate program at Johns Hopkins University. Among his teachers at Johns Hopkins was Charles Peirce, one of the founders of **pragmatism,** a philosophical movement that considered ideas to have meaning only insofar as they are practical or useful. Pragmatism became the philosophy with which Dewey is most often associated.

Dewey's career was spent teaching and writing in a variety of areas of philosophy, including ethics, aesthetics (the philosophy of art), philosophy of education, and social criticism. His first teaching appointment was at the University of Michigan, where he stayed for ten years. During this period he became less interested in abstract theory and instead sought to make philosophy a useful tool to improve people's lives. In 1894 he left Michigan for the University of Chicago, where he founded the laboratory school known as the Dewey School, a place to test his philosophical and psychological hypotheses. Because of problems with the administration, he left Chicago in 1904 to take an appointment at Columbia University, where he stayed until his retirement in 1930. Although Dewey is an important figure in American twentieth-century philosophy, his influence is primarily confined to America. His only real importance abroad was indirect, in his response to problems in ethics generated by G. E. Moore.

Dewey advocated a form of **ethical naturalism,** a kind of moral theory that stresses an empirical or scientific view of the world. He felt that the traditional philosophical view, reflected in the ideas of Moore, wrongly distinguished between scientific knowledge and moral knowledge. Dewey reflects the pragmatic philosophy that holds that all knowledge is practical knowledge, and the only way of attaining that knowledge is through the experimental method. According to Dewey, we should use the scientific method to solve problems in moral philosophy, just as we do to solve problems in science.

Along with his work in moral philosophy, Dewey wrote and carried out extensive research in the philosophy of education and social theory. In fact, he is probably best known for his work in the philosophy of education, although all of his philosophical interests were connected. For Dewey, philosophy of education is not a separate area of philosophy but incorporates all areas of philosophy. Nor did his social philosophy stand alone; he considered it to be entwined with ethics. For Dewey, the purpose of social philosophy is to point the way to the societal conditions that will bring about the kind of life that enables people to make the intelligent decisions morality requires. Although many of his ideas were innovative—even radical—his role throughout his life was that of reformer, not revolutionary. He remained skeptical of grand schemes and quick fixes but embraced the power of philosophy to improve society. The work excerpted here, *The Quest for Certainty,* was published in 1929 and helped point the way for current biological, sociobiological, evolutionary, and other naturalist theories of ethics.

The Quest for Certainty

Many, perhaps most, people believe that a necessary connection exists between values and religion. That is, religion determines values (or communicates values that God determines), and society is left in a kind of value vacuum without religion. This perceived connection leads to the modern predicament that results from the ever-increasing respect for, and reliance on, science and technology. Science seems to undermine religion, in many people's minds. And if religion is undermined, so are values.

Many moral philosophers deny the necessary connection between religion and values. These philosophers stress the importance of scientific investigation in all areas of human inquiry. If science can discover the truth about the world, it can discover the truth about values, about good and bad, as well. This selection from John Dewey looks seriously at the supposed gulf between morality and science and proposes the empirical method to be the proper means to establish values.

Chapter X
The Construction of Good

We saw at the outset of our discussion that insecurity generates the quest for certainty. Consequences issue from every experience, and they are the source of our interest in what is present. Absence of arts of regulation diverted the search for security into irrelevant modes of practice, into rite and cult; thought was devoted to discovery of omens rather than of signs of what is to occur. Gradually there was differentiation of two realms, one higher, consisting of the powers which determine human destiny in all important affairs. With this religion was concerned. The other consisted of the prosaic matters in which man relied upon his own skill and his matter-of-fact insight. Philosophy inherited the idea of this division. Meanwhile in Greece many of the arts had attained a state of development which raised them above a merely routine state; there were intimations of measure, order and regularity in materials dealt with which give intimations of underlying rationality. Because of the growth of mathematics, there arose also the ideal of a purely rational knowledge, intrinsically solid and worthy and the means by which the intimations of rationality within changing phenomena could be comprehended within science. For the intellectual class the stay and consolation, the warrant of certainty, provided by religion was henceforth found in intellectual demonstration of the reality of the objects of an ideal realm.

With the expansion of Christianity, ethico-religious traits came to dominate the purely rational ones. The ultimate authoritative standards for regulation of the dispositions and purposes of the human will were fused with those which satisfied the demands for necessary and universal truth. The authority of ultimate Being was, moreover, represented on earth by the Church; that which in its nature transcended intellect was made known by a revelation of which the Church was the interpreter and guardian. The system endured for centuries. While it endured, it provided an integration of belief and conduct for the western world. Unity of thought and practice extended down to every detail of the management of life; efficacy of its operation did not depend upon thought. It was guaranteed by the most powerful and authoritative of all social institutions.

---

1. In this paragraph, we see the problem announced, its importance shown, and the goal of philosophy articulated.

Its seemingly solid foundation was, however, undermined by the conclusions of modern science. They effected, both in themselves and even more in the new interests and activities they generated, a breach between what man is concerned with here and now and the faith concerning ultimate reality which, in determining his ultimate and eternal destiny, had previously given regulation to his present life. The problem of restoring integration and cooperation between man's beliefs about the world in which he lives and his beliefs about the values and purposes that should direct his conduct is the deepest problem of modern life. It is the problem of any philosophy that is not isolated from that life.

The attention which has been given to the fact that in its experimental procedure science has surrendered the separation between knowing and doing has its source in the fact that there is now provided within a limited, specialized and technical field the possibility and earnest, as far as theory is concerned, of effecting the needed integration in the wider field of collective human experience. Philosophy is called upon to be the theory of the practice, through ideas sufficiently definite to be operative in experimental endeavor, by which the integration may be made secure in actual experience. Its central problem is the relation that exists between the beliefs about the nature of things due to natural science and beliefs about values— using that word to designate whatever is taken to have rightful authority in the direction of conduct. A philosophy which should take up this problem is struck first of all by the fact that beliefs about values are pretty much in the position in which beliefs about nature were before the scientific revolution. There is either a basic distrust of the capacity of experience to develop its own regulative standards, and an appeal to what philosophers call eternal values, in order to ensure regulation of belief and action; or there is acceptance of enjoyments actually experienced irrespective of the method or operation by which they are brought into existence. Complete bifurcation between rationalistic method and an empirical method has its final and most deeply human significance in the ways in which good and bad are thought of and acted for and upon.

As far as technical philosophy reflects this situation, there is division of theories of values into two kinds. On the one hand, goods and evils, in every region of life, as they are concretely experienced, are regarded as characteristic of an inferior order of Being—intrinsically inferior. Just because they are things of human experience, their worth must be estimated by reference to standards and ideals derived from ul-timate reality. Their defects and perversion are attributed to the same fact; they are to be corrected and controlled through adoption of methods of conduct derived from loyalty to the requirements of Supreme Being. This philosophic formulation gets actuality and force from the fact that it is a rendering of the beliefs of men in general as far as they have come under the influence of institutional religion. Just as rational conceptions were once superimposed upon observed and temporal phe-nomena, so eternal values are superimposed upon experienced goods. In one case as in the other, the alternative is supposed to be confusion and lawlessness. Phil-osophers suppose these eternal values are known by reason; the mass of persons that they are divinely revealed.

Nevertheless, with the expansion of secular interests, temporal values have enormously multiplied; they absorb more and more attention and energy. The sense of transcendent values has become enfeebled; instead of permeating all things in life, it is more and more restricted to special times and acts. The authority of the church to declare and impose divine will and purpose has narrowed. Whatever men say and profess, their tendency in the presence of actual evils is to resort to natural and empirical means to remedy them. But in formal belief, the old doctrine of the inherently disturbed and unworthy character of the goods and standards of ordinary experience persists. This divergence between what men do and what they nominally profess is closely connected with the confusions and conflicts of modern thought.

It is not meant to assert that no attempts have been made to replace the older theory regarding the authority of immutable and transcendent values by concep-tions more congruous with the practices of daily life. The contrary is the case. The utilitarian theory, to take one instance, has had great power. The idealistic school is the only one in contemporary philosophies, with the exception of one form of neo-realism, that makes much of the notion of a reality which is all one with ultimate moral and religious values. But this school is also the one most concerned with the conservation of "spiritual" life. Equally significant is the fact that empirical theories retain the notion that thought and judgment are concerned with values that are ex-perienced independently of them. For these theories, emotional satisfactions occupy the same place that sensations hold in traditional empiricism. Values are constituted by liking and enjoyment; to be enjoyed and to be a value are two names for one and the same fact. Since science has extruded values from its objects, these empirical the-ories do everything possible to emphasize their purely subjective character of value. A psychological theory of desire and liking is supposed to cover the whole ground of the theory of values; in it, immediate feeling is the counterpart of immediate sen-sation.

I shall not object to this empirical theory as far as it connects the theory of values with concrete experiences of desire and satisfaction. The idea that there is such a connection is the only way known to me by which the pallid remoteness of the rationalistic theory, and the only too glaring presence of the institutional the-ory of transcendental values can be escaped. The objection is that the theory in question holds down value to objects *antecedently* enjoyed, apart from reference to the method by which they come into existence; it takes enjoyments which are casual because unregulated by intelligent operations to be values in and of them-selves. Operational thinking needs to be applied to the judgment of values just as it has now finally been applied in conceptions of physical objects. Experimental empiricism in the field of ideas of good and bad is demanded to meet the conditions of the present situation.

The scientific revolution came about when material of direct and uncontrolled experience was taken as problematic; as supplying material to be transformed by reflective operations into known objects. The contrast between experienced and known objects was found to be a temporal one; namely, one between empirical subject matters which were had or "given" prior to the acts of experimental variation and redisposition and those which succeeded these acts and issued from them. The notion of an act whether of sense or thought which supplied a valid measure of thought in immediate knowledge was discredited. Consequences of operations became the important thing. The suggestion almost imperatively follows that escape from the defects of transcendental absolutism is not to be had by setting up as values enjoyments that happen anyhow, but in defining value by enjoyments which are the consequences of intelligent action. Without the intervention of thought, enjoyments are not values but problematic goods, becoming values when they re-issue in a changed form from intelligent behavior. The fundamental trouble with the current empirical theory of values is that it merely formulates and justifies the socially prevailing habit of regarding enjoyments as they are actually experienced as values in and of themselves. It completely side-steps the question of regulation of these enjoyments. This issue involves nothing less than the problem of the directed reconstruction of economic, political and religious institutions.

There was seemingly a paradox involved in the notion that if we turned our backs upon the immediately perceived qualities of things, we should be enabled to form valid conceptions of objects, and that these conceptions could be used to bring about a more secure and more significant experience of them. But the method terminated in disclosing the connections or interactions upon which perceived objects, viewed as events, depend. Formal analogy suggests that we regard our direct and original experience of things liked and enjoyed as only *possibilities* of values to be achieved; that enjoyment becomes a value when we discover the relations upon which its presence depends. Such a causal and operational definition gives only a conception of a value, not a value itself. But the utilization of the conception in action results in an object having secure and significant value.

---

2. Dewey is stressing the distinction between certain kinds of statements of fact and statements of value. He gives several instructive examples.

The formal statement may be given concrete content by pointing to the difference between the enjoyed and the enjoyable, the desired and the desirable, the satis*fying* and the satis*factory*. To say that something is enjoyed is to make a statement about a fact, something already in existence; it is not to judge the value of that fact. There is no difference between such a proposition and one which says that something is sweet or sour, red or black. It is just correct or incorrect and that is the end of the matter. But to call an object a value is to assert that it satisfies or fulfills certain conditions. Function and status in meeting conditions is a different matter from bare existence. The fact that something is desired only raises the *question* of its desirability; it does not settle it. Only a child in the degree of his immaturity thinks to settle the question of desirability by reiterated proclamation: "I want it, I want it, I want it." What is objected to in the current empirical theory of values is not connection of them with desire and enjoyment but failure to distinguish between enjoyments of radically different sorts. There are many common expressions in which the difference of the two kinds is clearly recognized. Take for example the difference between the ideas of "satisfying" and "satisfactory." To say that something satisfies is to report something as an isolated finality. To assert that it is satis*factory* is to define it in its connections and interactions. The fact that it pleases or is immediately congenial poses a problem to judgment. How shall the satisfaction be rated? Is it a value or is it not? Is it something to be prized and cherished, *to be* enjoyed? Not stern moralists alone but everyday experience informs us that finding satisfaction in a thing may be a warning, a summons to be on the lookout for consequences. To declare something satis*factory* is to assert that it meets specifiable conditions. It is in effect, a judgment that the thing "will do." It involves a prediction; it contemplates a future in which the thing will continue to serve; it *will* do. It asserts a consequence the thing will actively institute; it will *do*. That it is satisfying is the content of a proposition of fact; that it is satisfactory is a judgment, an estimate, an appraisal. It denotes an attitude *to be* taken, that of striving to perpetuate and to make secure.

It is worth notice that besides the instances given, there are many other recognitions in ordinary speech of the distinction. The endings "able," "worthy," and "ful" are cases in point. Noted and notable, noteworthy; remarked and remarkable; advised and advisable; wondered at and wonderful; pleasing and beautiful; loved and lovable; blamed and blameable, blameworthy; objected to and objectionable; esteemed and estimable; admired and admirable; shamed and shameful; honored and honorable; approved and approvable, worthy of approbation, etc. The multiplication of words adds nothing to the force of the distinction. But it aids in conveying a sense of the fundamental character of the distinction; of the difference between mere report of an already existent fact and judgment as to the importance and need of bringing a fact into existence; or, if it is already there, of sustaining it in existence. The latter is a genuine practical judgment, and marks the only type of judgment that has to do with the direction of action. Whether or no we reserve the term "value" for the latter, (as seems to me proper) is a minor matter; that the distinction be acknowledged as the key to understanding the relation of values to the direction of conduct is the important thing.

This element of direction by an idea of value applies to science as well as anywhere else. For in every scientific undertaking, there is passed a constant succession of estimates; such as "it is worth treating these facts as data or evidence; it is advisable to try this experiment; to make that observation; to entertain such and such a hypothesis; to perform this calculation," etc.

---

3. By defining "taste" in a special way, Dewey helps clarify his point about values and their relation to experience.

The word "taste" has perhaps got too completely associated with arbitrary liking to express the nature of judgments of value. But if the word be used in the sense of an appreciation at once cultivated and active, one may say that the formation of taste is the chief matter wherever values enter in, whether intellectual, esthetic or moral. Relatively immediate judgments, which we call tact or to which we give the name of intuition, do not precede reflective inquiry, but are the funded products of much thoughtful experience. Expertness of taste is at once the result and the reward of constant exercise of thinking. Instead of there being no disputing about tastes, they are the one thing worth disputing about, if by "dispute" is signified discussion involving reflective inquiry. Taste, if we use the word in its best sense, is the outcome of experience brought cumulatively to bear on the intelligent appreciation of the real worth of likings and enjoyments. There is nothing in which a person so completely reveals himself as in the things which he judges enjoyable and desirable. Such judgments are the sole alternative to the domination of belief by impulse, chance, blind habit and self-interest. The formation of a cultivated and effectively operative good judgment or taste with respect to what is esthetically admirable, intellectually acceptable and morally approvable is the supreme task set to human beings by the incidents of experience.

Propositions about what is or has been liked are of instrumental value in reaching judgments of value, in as far as the conditions and consequences of the thing liked are thought about. In themselves they make no claims; they put forth no demand upon subsequent attitudes and acts; they profess no authority to direct. If one likes a thing he likes it; that *is* a point about which there can be no dispute:—although it is not so easy to state just *what* is liked as is frequently assumed. A judgment about what is *to be* desired and enjoyed is, on the other hand, a claim on future action; it possesses *de jure* and not merely *de facto* quality. It is a matter of frequent experience that likings and enjoyments are of all kinds, and that many are such as reflective judgments condemn. By way of self-justification and "rationalization," an enjoyment creates a tendency to assert that the thing enjoyed is a value. This assertion of validity adds authority to the fact. It is a decision that the object has a right to exist and hence a claim upon action to further its existence.

The analogy between the status of the theory of values and the theory of ideas about natural objects before the rise of experimental inquiry may be carried further. The sensationalistic theory of the origin and test of thought evoked, by way of reaction, the transcendental theory of *a priori* ideas. For it failed utterly to account for objective connection, order and regularity in objects observed. Similarly, any doctrine that identifies the mere fact of being liked with the value of the object liked so fails to give direction to conduct when direction is needed that it automatically calls forth the assertion that there are values eternally in Being that are the standards of all judgments and the obligatory ends of all action. Without the introduction of operational thinking, we oscillate between a theory that, in order to save the objectivity of judgments of values, isolates them from experience and nature, and a theory that, in order to save their concrete and human significance, reduces them to mere statements about our own feelings.

Not even the most devoted adherents of the notion that enjoyment and value are equivalent facts would venture to assert that because we have once liked a thing we should go on liking it; they are compelled to introduce the idea that *some* tastes are to be cultivated. Logically, there is no ground for introducing the idea of cultivation; liking is liking, and one is as good as another. If enjoyments *are* values, the judgment of value cannot regulate the form which liking takes; it cannot regulate its own conditions. Desire and purpose, and hence action, are left without guidance, although the question of regulation of their formation is the supreme problem of practical life. Values (to sum up) may be connected inherently with liking, and yet not with *every* liking but only with those that judgment has approved, after examination of the relation upon which the object liked depends. A casual liking is one that happens without knowledge of how it occurs nor to what effect. The difference between it and one which is sought because of a judgment that it is worth having and is to be striven for, makes just the difference between enjoyments which are accidental and enjoyments that have value and hence a claim upon our attitude and conduct.

In any case, the alternative rationalistic theory does not afford the guidance for the sake of which eternal and immutable norms are appealed to. The scientist finds no help in determining the probable truth of some proposed theory by comparing it with a standard of absolute truth and immutable being. He has to rely upon definite operations undertaken under definite conditions—upon method. We can hardly imagine an architect getting aid in the construction of a building from an ideal at large, though we can understand his framing an ideal on the basis of knowledge of actual conditions and needs. Nor does the ideal of perfect beauty in antecedent Being give direction to a painter in producing a particular work of art. In morals, absolute perfection does not seem to be more than a generalized hypostatization of the recognition that there is a good to be sought, an obligation to be met—both being concrete matters. Nor is the defect in this respect merely negative. An examination of history would reveal, I am confident, that these general and remote schemes of value actually obtain a content definite enough and near enough to concrete situations as to afford guidance in action only by consecrating some institution or dogma already having social currency. Concreteness is gained, but it is by protecting from inquiry some accepted standard which perhaps is outworn and in need of criticism.

---

4. Here Dewey articulates his main proposition. Can you see how it is related to the preceding discussion?

When theories of values do not afford intellectual assistance in framing ideas and beliefs about values that are adequate to direct action, the gap must be filled by other means. If intelligent method is lacking, prejudice, the pressure of immediate circumstance, self-interest and class-interest, traditional customs, institutions of accidental historic origin, are *not* lacking, and they tend to take the place of intelligence. Thus we are led to our main proposition: *Judgments about values are judgments about the conditions and the results of experienced objects; judgments about that which should regulate the formation of our desires, affections and enjoyments.* For whatever decides their formation will determine the main course of our conduct, personal and social.

If it sounds strange to hear that we should frame our judgments as to what has value by considering the connections in existence of what we like and enjoy, the reply is not far to seek. As long as we do not engage in this inquiry enjoyments (values if we choose to apply that term) are casual; they are given by "nature," not constructed by art. Like natural objects in their qualitative existence, they at most only supply material for elaboration in rational discourse. A *feeling* of good or excellence is as far removed from goodness in fact as a feeling that objects are intellectually thus and so is removed from their being actually so. To recognize that the truth of natural objects can be reached only by the greatest care in selecting and arranging directed operations, and then to suppose that values can be truly determined by the mere fact of liking seems to leave us in an incredible position. All the serious perplexities of life come back to the genuine difficulty of forming a judgment as to the values of the situation; they come back to a conflict of goods. Only dogmatism can suppose that serious moral conflict is between something clearly bad and something known to be good, and that uncertainty lies wholly in the will of the one choosing. Most conflicts of importance are conflicts between things which are or have been satisfying, not between good and evil. And to suppose that we can make a hierarchical table of values at large once for all, a kind of catalogue in which they are arranged in an order of ascending or descending worth, is to indulge in a gloss on our inability to frame intelligent judgments in the concrete. Or else it is to dignify customary choice and prejudice by a title of honor.

———

5. The important distinction between what is desired and what is desirable is shown in an analogy.

———

The alternative to definition, classification and systematization of satisfactions just as they happen to occur is judgment of them by means of the relations under which they occur. If we know the conditions under which the act of liking, of desire and enjoyment, takes place, we are in a position to know what are the consequences of that act. The difference between the desired and the desirable, admired and the admirable, becomes effective at just this point. Consider the difference between the proposition "That thing has been eaten," and the judgment "That thing is edible." The former statement involves no knowledge of any relation except the one stated; while we are able to judge of the edibility of anything only when we have a knowledge of its interactions with other things sufficient to enable us to foresee its probable effects when it is taken into the organism and produces effects there.

To assume that anything can be known in isolation from its connections with other things is to identify knowing with merely having some object before perception or in feeling, and is thus to lose the key to the traits that distinguish an object as known. It is futile, even silly, to suppose that some quality that is directly present constitutes the whole of the thing presenting the quality. It does not do so when the quality is that of being hot or fluid or heavy, and it does not when the quality is that of giving pleasure, or being enjoyed. Such qualities are, once more, effects, ends in the sense of closing termini of processes involving causal connections. They are something to be investigated, challenges to inquiry and judgment. The more connections and interactions we ascertain, the more we *know* the object in question. Thinking is search for these connections. Heat experienced as a consequence of directed operations has a meaning quite different from the heat that is casually experienced without knowledge of how it came about. The same is true of enjoyments. Enjoyments that issue from conduct directed by insight into relations have a meaning and a validity due to the way in which they are experienced. Such enjoyments are not repented of; they generate no after-taste of bitterness. Even in the midst of direct enjoyment, there is a sense of validity, of authorization, which intensifies the enjoyment. There is solicitude for perpetuation of the *object* having value which is radically different from mere anxiety to perpetuate the *feeling* of enjoyment.

———

6. Consider the parallel cases Dewey presents about enjoyment and value, on the one hand, and knowledge and perception, on the other.

———

Such statements as we have been making are, therefore, far from implying that there are values apart from things actually enjoyed as good. To find a thing enjoy*able* is, so to say, a *plus* enjoyment. We saw that it was foolish to treat the scientific ob-

ject as a rival to or substitute for the perceived object, since the former is intermediate between uncertain and settled situations and those experienced under conditions
of greater control. In the same way, judgment of the value of an object to be experienced is instrumental to appreciation of it when it is realized. But the notion that
every object that happens to satisfy has an equal claim with every other to be a value
is like supposing that every object of perception has the same cognitive force as every
other. There is no knowledge without perception; but objects perceived are *known*
only when they are determined as consequences of connective operations. There is no
value except where there is satisfaction, but there have to be certain conditions fulfilled to transform a satisfaction into a value.

The time will come when it will be found passing strange that we of this age
should take such pains to control by every means at command the formation of
ideas of physical things, even those most remote from human concern, and yet are
content with haphazard beliefs about the qualities of objects that regulate our deepest interests; that we are scrupulous as to methods of forming ideas of natural objects, and either dogmatic or else driven by immediate conditions in framing those
about values. There is, by implication, if not explicitly, a prevalent notion that values are already well known and that all which is lacking is the will to cultivate them
in the order of their worth. In fact the most profound lack is not the will to act upon
goods already known but the will to know what they are.

It is not a dream that it is possible to exercise some degree of regulation of the
occurrence of enjoyments which are of value. Realization of the possibility is exemplified, for example, in the technologies and arts of industrial life—that is, up to a
definite limit. Men desired heat, light, and speed of transit and of communication
beyond what nature provides of itself. These things have been attained not by laud-
ing the enjoyment of these things and preaching their desirability, but by study of
the conditions of their manifestation. Knowledge of relations having been obtained,
ability to produce followed, and enjoyment ensued as a matter of course. It is, however, an old story that enjoyment of these things as goods is no warrant of their
bringing only good in their train. As Plato was given to pointing out, the physician
knows how to heal and the orator to persuade, but the ulterior knowledge of
whether it is better for a man to be healed or to be persuaded to the orator's opinion remains unsettled. Here there appears the split between what are traditionally
and conventionally called the values of the baser arts and the higher values of the
truly personal and humane arts.

---

*7. Dewey has just distinguished two kinds of traditional values and now dis-
cusses the differences between them. Notice the signs indicating that he is critical of the distinction.*

With respect to the former, there is no assumption that they can be had and enjoyed without definite operative knowledge. With respect to them it is also clear that
the degree in which we value them is measurable by the pains taken to control the
conditions of their occurrence. With respect to the latter, it is assumed that no one
who is honest can be in doubt what they are; that by revelation, or conscience, or
the instruction of others, or immediate feeling, they are clear beyond question. And
instead of action in their behalf being taken to be a measure of the extent to which
things *are* values to us, it is assumed that the difficulty is to persuade men to act

upon what they already know to be good. Knowledge of conditions and consequences is regarded as wholly indifferent to judging what is of serious value, though it is useful in a prudential way in trying to actualize it. In consequence, the existence of values that are by common consent of a secondary and technical sort are under a fair degree of control, while those denominated supreme and imperative are subject to all the winds of impulse, custom and arbitrary authority.

This distinction between higher and lower types of value is itself something to be looked into. Why should there be a sharp division made between some goods as physical and material and others as ideal and "spiritual"? The question touches the whole dualism of the material and the ideal at its root. To denominate anything "matter" or "material" is not in truth to disparage it. It is, if the designation is correctly applied, a way of indicating that the thing in question is a condition or means of the existence of something else. And disparagement of effective means is practically synonymous with disregard of the things that are termed, in eulogistic fashion, ideal and spiritual. For the latter terms if they have any concrete application at all signify something which is a desirable consummation of conditions, a cherished fulfillment of means. The sharp separation between material and ideal good thus deprives the latter of the underpinning of effective support while it opens the way for treating things which should be employed as means as ends in themselves. For since men cannot after all live without some measure of possession of such matters as health and wealth, the latter things will be viewed as values and ends in isolation unless they are treated as integral constituents of the goods that are deemed supreme and final.

The relations that determine the occurrence of what human beings experience, especially when social connections are taken into account, are indefinitely wider and more complex than those that determine the events termed physical; the latter are the outcome of definite selective operations. This is the reason why we know something about remote objects like the stars better than we know significantly characteristic things about our own bodies and minds. We forget the infinite number of things we do not know about the stars, or rather that what we call a star is itself the product of the elimination, enforced and deliberate, of most of the traits that belong to an actual existence. The amount of knowledge we possess about stars would not seem very great or very important if it were carried over to human beings and exhausted our knowledge of them. It is inevitable that genuine knowledge of man and society should lag far behind physical knowledge.

But this difference is not a ground for making a sharp division between the two, nor does it account for the fact that we make so little use of the experimental method of forming our ideas and beliefs about the concerns of man in his characteristic social relations. For this separation religions and philosophies must admit some responsibility. They have erected a distinction between a narrower scope of relations and a wider and fuller one into a difference of kind, naming one kind material, and the other mental and moral. They have charged themselves gratuitously with the office of diffusing belief in the necessity of the division, and with instilling contempt for the material as something inferior in kind in its intrinsic nature and worth. Formal philosophies undergo evaporation of their technical solid contents; in a thinner and more viable form they find their way into the minds of those who know nothing of their original forms. When these diffuse and, so to say, airy emanations re-crystallize in the popular mind they form a hard deposit of opinion that alters slowly and with great difficulty.

What difference would it actually make in the arts of conduct, personal and social, if the experimental theory were adopted not as a mere theory, but as a part of the working equipment of habitual attitudes on the part of everyone? It would be impossible, even were time given, to answer the question in adequate detail, just as men could not foretell in advance the consequences for knowledge of adopting the experimental method. It is the nature of the method that it has to be tried. But there are generic lines of difference which, within the limits of time at disposal, may be sketched.

Change from forming ideas and judgments of value on the basis of conformity to antecedent objects, to constructing enjoyable objects directed by knowledge of consequences, is a change from looking to the past to looking to the future. I do not for a moment suppose that the experiences of the past, personal and social, are of no importance. For without them we should not be able to frame any ideas whatever of the conditions under which objects are enjoyed nor any estimate of the consequences of esteeming and liking them. But past experiences are significant in giving us intellectual instrumentalities of judging just these points. They are tools, not finalities. Reflection upon what we have liked and have enjoyed is a necessity. But it tells us nothing about the *value* of these things until enjoyments are themselves reflectively controlled, or, until, as they are recalled, we form the best judgment possible about what led us to like this sort of thing and what has issued from the fact that we liked it.

------

8. Dewey wonders what the effects on morality will be if we adopt the experimental theory.

We are not, then, to get away from enjoyments experienced in the past and from recall of them, but from the notion that they are the arbiters of things to be further enjoyed. At present, the arbiter is found in the past, although there are many ways of interpreting what in the past is authoritative. Nominally, the most influential conception doubtless is that of a revelation once had or a perfect life once lived. Reliance upon precedent, upon institutions created in the past, especially in law, upon rules of morals that have come to us through unexamined customs, upon uncriticized tradition, are other forms of dependence. It is not for a moment suggested that we can get away from customs and established institutions. A mere break would doubtless result simply in chaos. But there is no danger of such a break. Mankind is too inertly conservative both by constitution and by education to give the idea of this danger actuality. What there is genuine danger of is that the force of new conditions will produce disruption externally and mechanically: this is an ever-present danger. The prospect is increased, not mitigated, by that conservatism which insists upon the adequacy of old standards to meet new conditions. What is needed is intelligent examination of the consequences that are actually effected by inherited institutions and customs, in order that there may be intelligent consideration of the ways in which they are to be intentionally modified in behalf of generation of different consequences.

This is the significant meaning of transfer of experimental method from the technical field of physical experience to the wider field of human life. We trust the method in forming our beliefs about things not directly connected with human life. In effect, we distrust it in moral, political and economic affairs. In the fine arts, there are many signs of a change. In the past, such a change has often been an omen and precursor of changes in other human attitudes. But, generally speaking, the idea of actively adopting experimental method in social affairs, in the matters deemed of most enduring and ultimate worth, strikes most persons as a surrender of all standards and regulative authority. But in principle, experimental method does not signify random and aimless action; it implies direction by ideas and knowledge. The question at issue is a practical one. Are there in existence the ideas and the knowledge that permit experimental method to be effectively used in social interests and affairs?

Where will regulation come from if we surrender familiar and traditionally prized values as our directive standards? Very largely from the findings of the natural sciences. For one of the effects of the separation drawn between knowledge and action is to deprive scientific knowledge of its proper service as a guide of conduct—except once more in those technological fields which have been degraded to an inferior rank. Of course, the complexity of the conditions upon which objects of human and liberal value depend is a great obstacle, and it would be too optimistic to say that we have as yet enough knowledge of the scientific type to enable us to regulate our judgments of value very extensively. But we have more knowledge than we try to put to use, and until we try more systematically we shall not know what are the important gaps in our sciences judged from the point of view of their moral and humane use.

For moralists usually draw a sharp line between the field of the natural sciences and the conduct that is regarded as moral. But a moral that frames its judgments of value on the basis of consequences must depend in a most intimate manner upon the conclusions of science. For the knowledge of the relations between changes which enable us to connect things as antecedents and consequences *is* science. The narrow scope which moralists often give to morals, their isolation of some conduct as virtuous and vicious from other large ranges of conduct, those having to do with health and vigor, business, education, with all the affairs in which desires and affection are implicated, is perpetuated by this habit of exclusion of the subject-matter of natural science from a role in formation of moral standards and ideals. The same attitude operates in the other direction to keep natural science a technical specialty, and it works unconsciously to encourage its use exclusively in regions where it can be turned to personal and class advantage, as in war and trade.

Another great difference to be made by carrying the experimental habit into all matter of practice is that it cuts the roots of what is often called subjectivism, but which is better termed egoism. The subjective attitude is much more widespread than would be inferred from the philosophies which have that label attached. It is as rampant in realistic philosophies as in any others, sometimes even more so, although disguised from those who hold these philosophies under the cover of reverence for and enjoyment of ultimate values. For the implication of placing the standard of thought and knowledge in antecedent existence is that our thought makes no difference in what is significantly real. It then affects only our own attitude toward it.

This constant throwing of emphasis back upon a change made in ourselves instead of one made in the world in which we live seems to me the essence of what is objectionable in "subjectivism." Its taint hangs about even Platonic realism with its insistent evangelical dwelling upon the change made within the mind by contemplation of the realm of essence, and its depreciation of action as transient and all but sordid—a concession to the necessities of organic existence. All the theories which put conversion "of the eye of the soul" in the place of a conversion of natural and social objects that modifies goods actually experienced, is a retreat and escape from existence—and this retraction into self is, once more, the heart of subjective ego-isms. The typical example is perhaps the other-worldliness found in religions whose chief concern is with the salvation of the personal soul. But other-worldliness is found as well in estheticism and in all seclusion within ivory towers.

It is not in the least implied that change in personal attitudes, in the disposition of the "subject," is not of great importance. Such change, on the contrary, is involved in any attempt to modify the conditions of the environment. But there is a radical differ-ence between a change in the self that is cultivated and valued as an end, and one that is a means to alteration, through action, of objective conditions. The Aristotelian-medieval conviction that highest bliss is found in contemplative possession of ultimate Being presents an ideal attractive to some types of mind; it sets forth a refined sort of enjoyment. It is a doctrine congenial to minds that despair of the effort involved in cre-ation of a better world of daily experience. It is, apart from theological attachments, a doctrine sure to recur when social conditions are so troubled as to make actual en-deavor seem hopeless. But the subjectivism so externally marked in modern thought as compared with ancient is either a development of the old doctrine under new condi-tions or is of merely technical import. The medieval version of the doctrine at least had the active support of a great social institution by means of which man could be brought into the state of mind that prepared him for ultimate enjoyment of eternal Being. It had a certain solidity and depth which is lacking in modern theories that would attain the result by merely emotional or speculative procedures, or by any means not demanding a change in objective existence so as to render objects of value more empirically secure.

The nature in detail of the revolution that would be wrought by carrying into the region of values the principle now embodied in scientific practice cannot be told; to at-tempt it would violate the fundamental idea that we know only after we have acted and in consequences of the outcome of action. But it would surely effect a transfer of atten-tion and energy from the subjective to the objective. Men would think of themselves as agents not as ends; ends would be found in experienced enjoyment of the fruits of a transforming activity. In as far as the subjectivity of modern thought represents a dis-covery of the part played by personal responses, organic and acquired, in the causal pro-duction of the qualities and values of objects, it marks the possibility of a decisive gain. It puts us in possession of some of the conditions that control the occurrence of experi-enced objects, and thereby it supplies us with an instrument of regulation. There is some-thing querulous in the sweeping denial that things as experienced, as perceived and enjoyed, in any way depend upon interaction with human selves. The error of doctrines that have exploited the part played by personal and subjective reactions in determining what is perceived and enjoyed lies either in exaggerating this factor of constitution into the sole condition—as happens in subjective idealism—or else in treating it as a finality instead of, as with all knowledge, an instrument in direction of further action.

---

9. The third significant change that would follow from using the experimental method to study morality is the subject of this paragraph. Can you find the previous two changes he has mentioned?

A third significant change that would issue from carrying over experimental method from physics to man concerns the import of standards, principles, rules. With the transfer, these, and all tenets and creeds about good and goods, would be recognized to be hypotheses. Instead of being rigidly fixed, they would be treated as intellectual instruments to be tested and confirmed—and altered—through consequences effected by acting upon them. They would lose all pretense of finality—the ulterior source of dogmatism. It is both astonishing and depressing that so much of the energy of mankind has gone into fighting for (with weapons of the flesh as well as of the spirit) the truth of creeds, religious, moral and political, as distinct from what has gone into effort to try creeds by putting them to the test of acting upon them. The change would do away with the intolerance and fanaticism that attend the notion that beliefs and judgments are capable of inherent truth and authority; inherent in the sense of being independent of what they lead to when used as directive principles. The transformation does not imply merely that men are responsible for acting upon what they profess to believe; that is an old doctrine. It goes much further. Any belief as such is tentative, hypothetical; it is not just to be acted upon, but is to be *framed* with reference to its office as a guide to action. Consequently, it should be the last thing in the world to be picked up casually and then clung to rigidly. When it is apprehended as a tool and only a tool, an instrumentality of direction, the same scrupulous attention will go to its formation as now goes into the making of instruments of precision in technical fields. Men, instead of being proud of accepting and asserting beliefs and "principles" on the ground of loyalty, will be as ashamed of that procedure as they would now be to confess their assent to a scientific theory out of reverence for Newton or Helmholz or whomever, without regard to evidence.

If one stops to consider the matter, is there not something strange in the fact that men should consider loyalty to "laws," principles, standards, ideals to be an inherent virtue, accounted unto them for righteousness? It is as if they were making up for some secret sense of weakness by rigidity and intensity of insistent attachment. A moral law, like a law in physics, is not something to swear by and stick to at all hazards; it is a formula of the way to respond when specified conditions present themselves. Its soundness and pertinence are tested by what happens when it is acted upon. Its claim or authority rests finally upon the imperativeness of the situation that has to be dealt with, not upon its own intrinsic nature—as any tool achieves dignity in the measure of needs served by it. The idea that adherence to standards external to experienced objects is the only alternative to confusion and lawlessness was once held in science. But knowledge became steadily progressive when it was abandoned, and clues and tests found within concrete acts and objects were employed. The test of consequences is more exacting than that afforded by fixed general rules. In addition, it secures constant development, for when new acts are tried new results are experienced, while the lauded immutability of eternal ideals and norms is in itself a denial of the possibility of development and improvement.

10. The words "summed up" suggest that this paragraph is important.

The various modifications that would result from adoption in social and humane subjects of the experimental way of thinking are perhaps summed up in saying that it would place *method and means* upon the level of importance that has, in the past, been imputed exclusively to ends. Means have been regarded as menial, and the useful as the servile. Means have been treated as poor relations to be endured, but not inherently welcome. The very meaning of the word "ideals" is significant of the divorce which has obtained between means and ends. "Ideals" are thought to be remote and inaccessible of attainment; they are too high and fine to be sullied by realization. They serve vaguely to arouse "aspiration," but they do not evoke and direct strivings for embodiment in actual existence. They hover in an indefinite way over the actual scene; they are expiring ghosts of a once significant kingdom of divine reality whose rule penetrated to every detail of life.

It is impossible to form a just estimate of the paralysis of effort that has been produced by indifference to means. Logically, it is truistic that lack of consideration for means signifies that so-called ends are not taken seriously. It is as if one professed devotion to painting pictures conjoined with contempt for canvas, brush and paints; or love of music on condition that no instruments, whether the voice or something external, be used to make sounds. The good workman in the arts is known by his respect for his tools and by his interest in perfecting his technique. The glorification in the arts of ends at the expense of means would be taken to be a sign of complete insincerity or even insanity. Ends separated from means are either sentimental indulgences or if they happen to exist are merely accidental. The ineffectiveness in action of "ideals" is due precisely to the supposition that means and ends are not on exactly the same level with respect to the attention and care they demand.

It is, however, much easier to point out the formal contradiction implied in ideals that are professed without equal regard for the instruments and techniques of their realization, than it is to appreciate the concrete ways in which belief in their separation has found its way into life and borne corrupt and poisonous fruits. The separation marks the form in which the traditional divorce of theory and practice has expressed itself in actual life. It accounts for the relative impotency of arts concerned with enduring human welfare. Sentimental attachment and subjective eulogy take the place of action. For there is no art without tools and instrumental agencies. But it also explains the fact that in actual behavior, energies devoted to matters nominally thought to be inferior, material and sordid, engross attention and interest. After a polite and pious deference has been paid to "ideals," men feel free to devote themselves to matters which are more immediate and pressing.

It is usual to condemn the amount of attention paid by people in general to material ease, comfort, wealth, and success gained by competition, on the ground that they give to mere means the attention that ought to be given to ends, or that they have taken for ends things which in reality are only means. Criticisms of the place which economic interest and action occupy in present life are full of complaints that men allow lower aims to usurp the place that belongs to higher and ideal values. The final source of the trouble is, however, that moral and spiritual "leaders" have propagated the notion that ideal ends may be cultivated in isolation from "material" means, as if means and material were not synonymous. While they condemn men for giving to means the thought and energy that ought to go to ends, the condemnation should go to them. For they have not taught their followers to think of material and economic activities as *really* means. They have been unwilling to frame their conception of the values that should be regulative of human conduct on the basis of the actual conditions and operations by which alone values can be actualized.

Practical needs are imminent; with the mass of mankind they are imperative. Moreover, speaking generally, men are formed to act rather than to theorize. Since the ideal ends are so remotely and accidentally connected with immediate and urgent conditions that need attention, after lip service is given to them, men naturally devote themselves to the latter. If a bird in the hand is worth two in a neighboring bush, an actuality in hand is worth, for the direction of conduct, many ideals that are so remote as to be invisible and inaccessible. Men hoist the banner of the ideal, and then march in the direction that concrete conditions suggest and reward.

Deliberate insincerity and hypocrisy are rare. But the notion that action and sentiment are inherently unified in the constitution of human nature has nothing to justify it. Integration is something to be achieved. Division of attitudes and responses, compartmentalizing of interests, is easily acquired. It goes deep just because the acquisition is unconscious, a matter of habitual adaptation to conditions. Theory separated from concrete doing and making is empty and futile; practice then becomes an immediate seizure of opportunities and enjoyments which conditions afford without the direction which theory—knowledge and ideas—has power to supply. The problem of the relation of theory and practice is not a problem of theory alone; it is that, but it is also the most practical problem of life. For it is the question of how intelligence may inform action, and how action may bear the fruit of increased insight into meaning: a clear view of the values that are worth while and of the means by which they are to be made secure in experienced objects. Construction of ideals in general and their sentimental glorification are easy; the responsibilities both of studious thought and of action are shirked. Persons having the advantage of positions of leisure and who find pleasure in abstract theorizing— a most delightful indulgence to those to whom it appeals—have a large measure of liability for a cultivated diffusion of ideals and aims that are separated from the conditions which are the means of actualization. Then other persons who find themselves in positions of social power and authority readily claim to be the bearers and defenders of ideal ends in church and state. They then use the prestige and authority their representative capacity as guardians of the highest ends confers on them to cover actions taken in behalf of the harshest and narrowest of material ends.

The present state of industrial life seems to give a fair index of the existing separation of means and ends. Isolation of economics from ideal ends, whether of morals or of organized social life, was proclaimed by Aristotle. Certain things, he said, are conditions of a worthy life, personal and social, but are not constituents of it. The economic life of man, concerned with satisfaction of wants, is of this nature. Men have wants and they must be satisfied. But they are only prerequisites of a good life, not intrinsic elements in it. Most philosophers have not been so frank nor perhaps so logical. But upon the whole, economics has been treated as on a lower level than either morals or politics. Yet the life which men, women and children actually lead, the opportunities open to them, the values they are capable of enjoying, their education, their share in all the things of art and science, are mainly determined by economic conditions. Hence we can hardly expect a moral system which ignores economic conditions to be other than remote and empty.

Industrial life is correspondingly brutalized by failure to equate it as the means by which social and cultural values are realized. That the economic life, thus exiled from the pale of higher values, takes revenge by declaring that it is the only social reality, and by means of the doctrine of materialistic determination of institutions and conduct in all fields, denies to deliberate morals and politics any share of causal regulation, is not surprising.

When economists were told that their subject-matter was merely material, they naturally thought they could be "scientific" only by excluding all reference to distinctively human values. Material wants, efforts to satisfy them, even the scientifically regulated technologies highly developed in industrial activity, are then taken to form a complete and closed field. If any reference to social ends and values is introduced it is by way of an external addition, mainly hortatory. That economic life largely determines the conditions under which mankind has access to concrete values may be recognized or it may not be. In either case, the notion that it is the means to be utilized in order to secure significant values as the common and shared possession of mankind is alien and inoperative. To many persons, the idea that the ends professed by morals are impotent save as they are connected with the working machinery of economic life seems like deflowering the purity of moral values and obligations.

The social and moral effects of the separation of theory and practice have been merely hinted at. They are so manifold and so pervasive that an adequate consideration of them would involve nothing less than a survey of the whole field of morals, economics and politics. It cannot be justly stated that these effects are in fact direct consequences of the quest for certainty by thought and knowledge isolated from action. For, as we have seen, this quest was itself a reflex product of actual conditions. But it may be truly asserted that this quest, undertaken in religion and philosophy, has had results which have reinforced the conditions which originally brought it about. Moreover, search for safety and consolation amid the perils of life by means other than intelligent action, by feeling and thought alone, began when actual means of control were lacking, when arts were undeveloped. It had then a relative historic justification that is now lacking. The primary problem for thinking which lays claim to be philosophic in its breadth and depth is to assist in bringing about a reconstruction of all beliefs rooted in a basic separation of knowledge and action; to develop a system of operative ideas congruous with present knowledge and with present facilities of control over natural events and energies.

We have noted more than once how modern philosophy has been absorbed in the problem of affecting an adjustment between the conclusions of natural science and the beliefs and values that have authority in the direction of life. The genuine and poignant issue does not reside where philosophers for the most part have placed it. It does not consist in accommodation to each other of two realms, one physical and the other ideal and spiritual, nor in the reconciliation of the "categories" of theoretical and practical reason. It is found in that isolation of executive means and ideal interests which has grown up under the influence of the separation of theory and practice. For this, by nature, involves the separation of the material and the spiritual. Its solution, therefore, can be found only in action wherein the phenomena of material and economic life are equated with the purposes that command the loyalties of affection and purpose, and in which ends and ideals are framed in terms of the possibilities of actually experienced situations. But while the solution cannot be found in "thought" alone, it can be furthered by thinking which is operative—which frames and defines ideas in terms of what may be done, and which uses the conclusions of science and instrumentalities. William James was well within the bounds of moderation when he said that looking forward instead of backward, looking to what the world and life might become instead of to what they have been, is an alteration in the "seat of authority."

It was incidentally remarked earlier in our discussion that the serious defect in the current empirical philosophy of values, the one which identifies them with things actually enjoyed irrespective of the conditions upon which they depend, is that it formulates and in so far consecrates the conditions of our present social experience. Throughout these chapters, primary attention has perforce been given to the methods and statements of philosophic theories. But these statements are technical and specialized in formulation only. In origin, content and import they are reflections of some condition or some phase of concrete human experience. Just as the theory of the separation of theory and practice has a practical origin and a momentous practical consequence, so the empirical theory that values are identical with whatever men actually enjoy, no matter how or what, formulates an aspect, and an undesirable one, of the present social situation.

For while our discussion has given more attention to the other type of philosophical doctrine, that which holds that regulative and authoritative standards are found in transcendent eternal values, it has not passed in silence over the fact that actually the greater part of the activities of the greater number of human beings is spent in effort to seize upon and hold onto such enjoyments as the actual scene permits. Their energies and their enjoyments are controlled in fact, but they are controlled by external conditions rather than by intelligent judgment and endeavor. If philosophies have any influence over the thoughts and actions of men, it is a serious matter that the most widely held empirical theory should in effect justify this state of things by identifying values with the objects of any interest as such. As long as the only theories of value placed before us for intellectual assent alternate between sending us to a realm of eternal and fixed values and sending us to enjoyments such as actually obtain, the formulation, even as only a theory, of an experimental empiricism which finds values to be identical with goods that are the fruit of intelligently directed activity has its measure of practical significance.

READING QUESTIONS

1. What does Dewey mean by "taste"? Why can tastes be disputed?
2. Which values are inherently connected with liking?
3. Dewey denies that most conflicts are between good and evil. What does he say most conflict is about?
4. What is the difference between saying "That thing has been eaten" and saying "That thing is edible"?
5. Dewey says that a moral law is like a law in physics. How are they alike?
6. What does he say happens when theory and practice are separated?

W. D. Ross

Among those who followed G. E. Moore in his attack on **naturalism** were philosophers who are broadly categorized as **intuitionists**, such as Moore. Yet many were intuitionists of a different stripe. In general, intuitionists are **nonnaturalists** because they believe that it is impossible to produce an ethical theory from the facts of reality. Instead, people determine whether ethical judgments are true using proper insight, or intuition. However, whereas Moore advocated an ideal, nonnatural form of **utilitarianism**, others opposed any kind of **consequentialist** moral theory. Instead, these intuitionists advocated ethical theories that were **deontological.** (A deontological theory considers the value of an act intrinsic to some feature of the act itself, not to the consequences of the act.) The most extreme of these deontological intuitionists was H. A. Prichard, who argued in his landmark article "Does Moral Philosophy Rest on a Mistake?" that reasoning has no place in the determination of our obligations. When we are in a situation where we must make a moral decision, we are either immediately aware of our obligations or we are not. The philosopher whom we will read in this chapter, Sir David Ross, used the work of Prichard as a starting point and became the most influential of the deontological intuitionists.

William David Ross, Aristotle scholar and moral philosopher, was born in Scotland in 1877. Educated at Edinburgh University and Balliol College, Oxford, Ross became professor and later provost at Oriel College, Oxford. Ross was prominent in both academic and public life; he was awarded the Order of the British Empire for his contributions in World War I and was knighted in 1938. He died in 1971.

It was as an Aristotle scholar that Ross first made a significant contribution to philosophy. Ross edited the Oxford translations of Aristotle, published between 1908 and 1931, translating the *Metaphysics* and the *Ethics* himself. Apart from Aristotelian scholarship, his main contribution to philosophy was in moral philosophy. He argued the case for a deontological version of intuitionism in his classic work *The Right and the Good* (1930). In a following book, *Foundations of Ethics* (1939), he restated his case and replied to criticisms.

Ross accepted Prichard's view that we have an intuitive understanding of our obligations. Our duties, he went on, are of a special kind, what Ross called *prima facie* duties. A *prima facie* duty is, as the name implies, self-evident. When we examine our *prima facie* duties, argued Ross, we see that we should not always reason as the utilitarian recommends. That is, we should not always seek to maximize good but instead should recognize that some acts, such as keeping promises, are obligatory regardless of the goodness or badness that results from them. Although Ross's theory is deontological, he disputes the theory of the premier deontologist, Immanuel Kant, arguing that Kant errs in claiming that our moral obligations are **absolute.** An absolute moral duty can never be overridden by another duty. Ross argued that our various *prima facie* duties often conflict, and no duty takes precedence over another in all cases.

Even though Ross's ethical theory received harsh criticism from opponents of both deontological theories and intuitionist theories, his work has had a lasting impact on subsequent moral philosophy. *The Right and the Good* has come to be considered a classic work of moral philosophy after having been the center of controversy for many years. Even at the end of the twentieth century Ross's view of *prima facie* duties has many adherents who consider it a viable theory.

The Right and the Good

Even though the utilitarian view that we ought to bring about the maximum amount of happiness or pleasure in the world appeals to many people's sense of morality, people also believe that a sense of duty should play an important role in our moral lives. To many people, keeping a promise once it's been made seems right, just as does telling the truth even when it is painful. After all, who would say that we need to keep only convenient promises or that we need to be truthful only when it makes us look good? In this reading, Ross speaks to that sense of duty and introduces a new ethical concept, that of the *prima facie* duty. Relationships matter to our lives, and therefore they are important to our moral lives. With relationships come special duties to the other party or parties. Acting according to these special duties, or *prima facie* duties, is what Ross says makes a right act right.

II. What Makes Right Acts Right?

The real point at issue between hedonism and utilitarianism on the one hand and their opponents on the other is not whether 'right' means 'productive of so and so'; for it cannot with any plausibility be maintained that it does. The point at issue is that to which we now pass, viz. whether there is any general character which makes right acts right, and if so, what it is. Among the main historical attempts to state a single characteristic of all right actions which is the foundation of their rightness are those made by egoism and utilitarianism. But I do not propose to discuss these, not because the subject is unimportant, but because it has been dealt with so often and so well already, and because there has come to be so much agreement among moral philosophers that neither of these theories is satisfactory. A much more attractive theory has been put forward by Professor Moore: that what makes actions right is that they are productive of more *good* than could have been produced by any other action open to the agent.[1]

This theory is in fact the culmination of all the attempts to base rightness on productivity of some sort of result. The first form this attempt takes is the attempt to base rightness on conduciveness to the advantage or pleasure of the agent. This theory comes

---

From W. D. Ross, *The Right and the Good*, Clarendon Press, 1930. Reprinted by permission of Oxford University Press.
[1] I take the theory which, as I have tried to show, seems to be put forward in *Ethics* rather than the earlier and less plausible theory put forward in *Principia Ethica*. . . .

to grief over the fact, which stares us in the face, that a great part of duty consists in an observance of the rights and a furtherance of the interests of others, whatever the cost to ourselves may be. Plato and others may be right in holding that a regard for the rights of others never in the long run involves a loss of happiness for the agent, that "the just life profits a man." But this, even if true, is irrelevant to the rightness of the act. As soon as a man does an action *because* he thinks he will promote his own interests thereby, he is acting not from a sense of its rightness but from self-interest.

To the egoistic theory hedonistic utilitarianism supplies a much-needed amendment. It points out correctly that the fact that a certain pleasure will be enjoyed by the agent is no reason why he *ought* to bring it into being rather than an equal or greater pleasure to be enjoyed by another, though, human nature being what it is, it makes it not unlikely that he *will* try to bring it into being. But hedonistic utilitarianism in its turn needs a correction. On reflection it seems clear that pleasure is not the only thing in life that we think good in itself, that for instance we think the possession of a good character, or an intelligent understanding of the world, as good or better. A great advance is made by the substitution of "productive of the greatest good" for "productive of the greatest pleasure."

Not only is this theory more attractive than hedonistic utilitarianism, but its logical relation to that theory is such that the latter could not be true unless *it* were true, while it might be true though hedonistic utilitarianism were not. It is in fact one of the logical bases of hedonistic utilitarianism. For the view that what produces the maximum pleasure is right has for its bases the views (1) that what produces the maximum good is right, and (2) that pleasure is the only thing good in itself. If they were not assuming that what produces the maximum *good* is right, the utilitarians' attempt to show that pleasure is the only thing good in itself, which is in fact the point they take most pains to establish, would have been quite irrelevant to their attempt to prove that only what produces the maximum *pleasure* is right. If, therefore, it can be shown that productivity of the maximum good is not what makes all right actions right, we shall *a fortiori* have refuted hedonistic utilitarianism.

---

1. Ross gives an example that he thinks counts against utilitarianism. Why do you keep your promises?

When a plain man fulfills a promise because he thinks he ought to do so, it seems clear that he does so with no thought of its total consequences, still less with any opinion that these are likely to be the best possible. He thinks in fact much more of the past than of the future. What makes him think it right to act in a certain way is the fact that he has promised to do so—that and, usually, nothing more. That his act will produce the best possible consequences is not his reason for calling it right. What lends color to the theory we are examining, then, is not the actions (which form probably a great majority of our actions) in which some such reflection as "I have promised" is the only reason we give ourselves for thinking a certain action right, but the exceptional cases in which the consequences of fulfilling a promise (for instance) would be so disastrous to others that we judge it right not to do so. It must of course be admitted that such cases exist. If I have promised to meet a friend at a particular time for some trivial purpose, I should certainly think myself justified in breaking my engagement if by doing so I could prevent a serious accident or bring relief to the victims of one. And the supporters of the view we are examining hold that my thinking so is due to my thinking that I shall bring more good into existence by the one action than by the other. A different account may, however, be given of the matter, an account which will, I believe, show itself to be the true one. It may be said that besides the duty of fulfilling promises I have and recognize a duty of relieving distress,[2] and that when I think it right to do the latter at the cost of not doing the former, it is not because I think I shall produce more good thereby but because I think it the duty which is in the circumstances more of a duty. This account surely corresponds much more closely with what we really think in such a situation. If, so far as I can see, I could bring equal amounts of good into being by fulfilling my promise and by helping someone to whom I had made no promise, I should not hesitate to regard the former as my duty. Yet on the view that what is right is right because it is productive of the most good I should not so regard it.

There are two theories, each in its way simple, that offer a solution of such cases of conscience. One is the view of Kant, that there are certain duties of perfect obligation, such as those of fulfilling promises, of paying debts, of telling the truth, which admit of no exception whatever in favor of duties of imperfect obligation, such as that of relieving distress. The other is the view of, for instance, Professor Moore and Dr. Rashdall, that there is only the duty of producing good, and that all 'conflicts of duties' should be resolved by asking "by which action will most good be produced?" But it is more important that our theory fit the facts than that it be simple, and the account we have given above corresponds (it seems to me) better than either of the simpler theories with what we really think, viz. that normally promise-keeping, for example, should come before benevolence, but that when and only when the good to be produced by the benevolent act is very great and the promise comparatively trivial, the act of benevolence becomes our duty.

2. Ross introduces the concept of prima facie *duties. Notice how these duties depend upon certain relationships that exist between people.*

In fact the theory of 'ideal utilitarianism,' if I may for brevity refer so to the theory of Professor Moore, seems to simplify unduly our relations to our fellows. It says, in effect, that the only morally significant relation in which my neighbors stand to me is that of being possible beneficiaries by my action.[3] They do stand in this relation to me, and this relation is morally significant. But they may also stand to me in the relation of promisee to promiser, of creditor to debtor, of wife to husband, of child to parent, of friend to friend, of fellow countryman to fellow countryman, and the like; and each of these relations is the foundation of a *prima facie* duty, which is more or less incumbent on me according to the circumstances of the case. When I am in a situation, as perhaps I always am, in which more than one of these *prima facie* duties is incumbent on me, what I have to do is to study the situation as fully as I can until I form the considered opinion (it is never more) that in the circumstances one of them is more incumbent than any other; then I am bound to think that to do this *prima facie* duty is my duty *sans phrase* in the situation.

---

[2] These are not strictly speaking duties, but things that tend to be our duty, or *prima facie* duties. . . .

[3] Some will think it, apart from other considerations, a sufficient refutation of this view to point out that I also stand in that relation to myself, so that for this view the distinction of oneself from others is morally insignificant.

I suggest 'prima facie duty' or 'conditional duty' as a brief way of referring to the characteristic (quite distinct from that of being a duty proper) which an act has, in virtue of being of a certain kind (e.g., the keeping of a promise), of being an act which would be a duty proper if it were not at the same time of another kind which is morally significant. Whether an act is a duty proper or actual duty depends on *all* the morally significant kinds it is an instance of. The phrase 'prima facie duty' must be apologized for, since (1) it suggests that what we are speaking of is a certain kind of duty, whereas it is in fact not a duty, but something related in a special way to duty. Strictly speaking, we want not a phrase in which duty is qualified by an adjective, but a separate noun. (2) '*Prima*' *facie* suggests that one is speaking only of an appearance which a moral situation presents at first sight, and which may turn out to be illusory; whereas what I am speaking of is an objective fact involved in the nature of the situation, or more strictly in an element of its nature, though not, as duty proper does, arising from its *whole* nature. I can, however, think of no term which fully meets the case. 'Claim' has been suggested by Professor Prichard. The word 'claim' has the advantage of being quite a familiar one in this connection, and it seems to cover much of the ground. It would be quite natural to say, "a person to whom I have made a promise has a claim on me," and also, "a person whose distress I could relieve (at the cost of breaking the promise) has a claim on me." But (1) while 'claim' is appropriate from *their* point of view, we want a word to express the corresponding fact from the agent's point of view—the fact of his being subject to claims that can be made against him; and ordinary language provides us with no such correlative to 'claim.' And (2) (what is more important) 'claim' seems inevitably to suggest two persons, one of whom might make a claim on the other; and while this covers the ground of social duty, it is inappropriate in the case of that important part of duty which is the duty of cultivating a certain kind of character in oneself. It would be artificial, I think, and at any rate metaphorical, to say that one's character has a claim on oneself.

There is nothing arbitrary about these *prima facie* duties. Each rests on a definite circumstance which cannot seriously be held to be without moral significance. Of *prima facie* duties I suggest, without claiming completeness or finality for it, the following division.[4]

---

3. Here Ross describes the different types of prima facie *duties.*

---

(1) Some duties rest on previous acts of my own. These duties seem to include two kinds, (*a*) those resting on a promise or what may fairly be called an implicit promise, such as the implicit undertaking not to tell lies which seems to be implied

---

[4] I should make it plain at this stage that I am *assuming* the correctness of some of our main convictions as to *prima facie* duties, or, more strictly, am claiming that we *know* them to be true. To me it seems as self-evident as anything could be, that to make a promise, for instance, is to create a moral claim on us in someone else. Many readers will perhaps say that they do *not* know this to be true. If so, I certainly cannot prove it to them; I can only ask them to reflect again, in the hope that they will ultimately agree that they also know it to be true. The main moral convictions of the plain man seem to me to be, not opinions which it is for philosophy to prove or disprove, but knowledge from the start; and in my own case I seem to find little difficulty in distinguishing these essential convictions from other moral convictions which I also have, which are merely fallible opinions based on an imperfect study of the working for good or evil of certain institutions or types of action.

in the act of entering into conversation (at any rate by civilized men), or of writing books that purport to be history and not fiction. These may be called the duties of fidelity. (*b*) Those resting on a previous wrongful act. These may be called the duties of reparation. (2) Some rest on previous acts of other men, i.e., services done by them to me. These may be loosely described as the duties of gratitude. (3) Some rest on the fact or possibility of a distribution of pleasure or happiness (or of the means thereto) which is not in accordance with the merit of the persons concerned; in such cases there arises a duty to upset or prevent such a distribution. These are the duties of justice. (4) Some rest on the mere fact that there are other beings in the world whose condition we can make better in respect of virtue, or of intelligence, or of pleasure. These are the duties of beneficence. (5) Some rest on the fact that we can improve our own condition in respect of virtue or of intelligence. These are the duties of self-improvement. (6) I think that we should distinguish from (4) the duties that may be summed up under the title of 'not injuring others.' No doubt to injure others is incidentally to fail to do them good; but it seems to me clear that non-maleficence is apprehended as a duty distinct from that of beneficence, and as a duty of a more stringent character. It will be noticed that this alone among the types of duty has been stated in a negative way. An attempt might no doubt be made to state this duty, like the others, in a positive way. It might be said that it is really the duty to prevent ourselves from acting either from an inclination to harm others or from an inclination to seek our own pleasure, in doing which we should incidentally harm them. But on reflection it seems clear that the primary duty here is the duty not to harm others, this being a duty whether or not we have an inclination that if followed would lead to our harming them; and that when we have such an inclination the primary duty not to harm others gives rise to a consequential duty to resist the inclination. The recognition of this duty of non-maleficence is the first step on the way to the recognition of the duty of beneficence; and that accounts for the prominence of the commands "thou shalt not kill," "thou shalt not commit adultery," "thou shalt not steal," "thou shalt not bear false witness," in so early a code as the Decalogue. But even when we have come to recognize the duty of beneficence, it appears to me that the duty of non-maleficence is recognized as a distinct one, and as *prima facie* more binding. We should not in general consider it justifiable to kill one person in order to keep another alive, or to steal from one in order to give alms to another.

The essential defect of the 'ideal utilitarian' theory is that it ignores, or at least does not do full justice to, the highly personal character of duty. If the only duty is to produce the maximum of good, the question who is to have the good—whether it is myself, or my benefactor, or a person to whom I have made a promise to confer that good on him, or a mere fellow man to whom I stand in no such special relation—should make no difference to my having a duty to produce that good. But we are all in fact sure that it makes a vast difference.

One or two other comments must be made on this provisional list of the divisions of duty. (1) The nomenclature is not strictly correct. For by 'fidelity' or 'gratitude' we mean, strictly, certain states of motivation; and, as I have urged, it is not our duty to have certain motives, but to do certain acts. By 'fidelity,' for instance, is meant, strictly, the disposition to fulfill promises and implicit promises *because we have made them.* We have no general word to cover the actual fulfillment of promises and implicit promises *irrespective of motive;* and I use 'fidelity,' loosely but perhaps conveniently, to fill this gap. So too I use 'gratitude' for the returning of services, irrespective of motive. The term 'justice' is not so much confined, in ordinary usage, to a certain state of motivation, for we should often talk of a man as acting justly even when we did not think his motive was the wish to do what was just simply for the sake of doing so. Less apology is therefore needed for our use of 'justice' in this sense. And I have used the word 'beneficence' rather than 'benevolence,' in order to emphasize the fact that it is our duty to do certain things, and not to do them from certain motives.

(2) If the objection be made, that this catalogue of the main types of duty is an unsystematic one resting on no logical principle, it may be replied, first, that it makes no claim to being ultimate. It is a *prima facie* classification of the duties which reflection on our moral convictions seems actually to reveal. And if these convictions are, as I would claim that they are, of the nature of knowledge, and if I have not misstated them, the list will be a list of authentic conditional duties, correct as far as it goes though not necessarily complete. The list of *goods* put forward by the rival theory is reached by exactly the same method—the only sound one in the circumstances—viz. that of direct reflection on what we really think. Loyalty to the facts is worth more than a symmetrical architectonic or a hastily reached simplicity. If further reflection discovers a perfect logical basis for this or for a better classification, so much the better.

(3) It may, again, be objected that our theory that there are these various and often conflicting types of *prima facie* duty leaves us with no principle upon which to discern what is our actual duty in particular circumstances. But this objection is not one which the rival theory is in a position to bring forward. For when we have to choose between the production of two heterogeneous goods, say knowledge and pleasure, the 'ideal utilitarian' theory can only fall back on an opinion, for which no logical basis can be offered, that one of the goods is the greater; and this is no better than a similar opinion that one of two duties is the more urgent. And again, when we consider the infinite variety of the effects of our actions in the way of pleasure, it must surely be admitted that the claim which *hedonism* sometimes makes, that it offers a readily applicable criterion of right conduct, is quite illusory.

I am unwilling, however, to content myself with an *argumentum ad hominem*, and I would contend that in principle there is no reason to anticipate that every act that is our duty is so for one and the same reason. Why should two sets of circumstances, or one set of circumstances, *not* possess different characteristics, any one of which makes a certain act our *prima facie* duty? When I ask what it is that makes me in certain cases sure that I have a *prima facie* duty to do so and so, I find that it lies in the fact that I have made a promise; when I ask the same question in another case, I find the answer lies in the fact that I have done a wrong. And if on reflection I find (as I think I do) that neither of these reasons is reducible to the other, I must not on any *a priori* ground assume that such a reduction is possible.

---

4. In this and the following paragraphs, Ross discusses the various kinds of prima facie *duties that he set out earlier. The discussion of the duty we have to promote our own pleasure is especially interesting because, as he says, initially promoting our pleasure appears incompatible with doing our duty.*

An attempt may be made to arrange in a more systematic way the main types of duty which we have indicated. In the first place it seems self-evident that if there are things that are intrinsically good, it is *prima facie* a duty to bring them into existence rather than not to do so, and to bring as much of them into existence as possible. It will be argued in our fifth chapter that there are three main things that are intrinsically good—virtue, knowledge, and, with certain limitations, pleasure. And since a given virtuous disposition, for instance, is equally good whether it is realized in myself or in another, it seems to be my duty to bring it into existence whether in myself or in another. So too with a given piece of knowledge.

The case of pleasure is difficult; for while we clearly recognize a duty to produce pleasure for others, it is by no means so clear that we recognize a duty to produce pleasure for ourselves. This appears to arise from the following facts. The thought of an act as our duty is one that presupposes a certain amount of reflection about the act; and for that reason does not normally arise in connection with acts towards which we are already impelled by another strong impulse. So far, the cause of our not thinking of the promotion of our own pleasure as a duty is analogous to the cause which usually prevents a highly sympathetic person from thinking of the promotion of the pleasure of others as a duty. He is impelled so strongly by direct interest in the well-being of others towards promoting their pleasure that he does not stop to ask whether it is his duty to promote it; and we are all impelled so strongly towards the promotion of our own pleasure that we do not stop to ask whether it is a duty or not. But there is a further reason why even when we stop to think about the matter it does not usually present itself as a duty: viz. that, since the performance of most of our duties involves the giving up of some pleasure that we desire, the doing of duty and the getting of pleasure for ourselves come by a natural association of ideas to be thought of as incompatible things. This association of ideas is in the main salutary in its operation, since it puts a check on what but for it would be much too strong, the tendency to pursue one's own pleasure without thought of other considerations. Yet if pleasure is good, it seems in the long run clear that it is right to get it for ourselves as well as to produce it for others, when this does not involve the failure to discharge some more stringent *prima facie* duty. The question is a very difficult one, but it seems that this conclusion can be denied only on one or other of three grounds: (1) that pleasure is not *prima facie* good (i.e., good when it is neither the actualization of a bad disposition nor undeserved), (2) that there is no *prima facie* duty to produce as much that is good as we can, or (3) that though there is a *prima facie* duty to produce other things that are good, there is no *prima facie* duty to produce pleasure which will be enjoyed by ourselves. I give reasons later for not accepting the first contention. The second hardly admits of argument but seems to me plainly false. The third seems plausible only if we hold that an act that is pleasant or brings pleasure to ourselves must for that reason not be a duty; and this would lead to paradoxical consequences, such as that if a man enjoys giving pleasure to others or working for their moral improvement, it cannot be his duty to do so. Yet it seems to be a very stubborn fact, that in our ordinary consciousness we are not aware of a duty to get pleasure for ourselves; and by way of partial explanation of this I may add that though, as I think, one's own pleasure is a good and there is a duty to produce it, it is only if we *think* of our own pleasure not as simply our own pleasure, but as an objective good, something that an impartial spectator would approve, that we can think of the getting it as a duty; and we do not habitually think of it in this way.

If these contentions are right, what we have called the duty of beneficence and the duty of self-improvement rest on the same ground. No different principles of duty are involved in the two cases. If we feel a special responsibility for improving our own character rather than that of others, it is not because a special principle is involved, but because we are aware that the one is more under our control than the other. It was on this ground that Kant expressed the practical law of duty in the form 'seek to make yourself good and other people happy.' He was so persuaded of the internality of virtue that he regarded any attempt by one person to produce virtue in another as bound to produce, at most, only a counterfeit of virtue, the doing of externally right acts not from the true principle of virtuous action but out of regard to another person. It must be admitted that one man cannot compel another to be virtuous; compulsory virtue would just not be virtue. But experience clearly shows that Kant overshoots the mark when he contends that one man cannot do anything to *promote* virtue in another, to bring such influences to bear upon him that his own response to them is more likely to be virtuous than his response to other influences would have been. And our duty to do this is not different in kind from our duty to improve our own characters.

It is equally clear, and clear at an earlier stage of moral development, that if there are things that are bad in themselves we ought, *prima facie,* not to bring them upon others; and on this fact rests the duty of non-maleficence.

The duty of justice is particularly complicated, and the word is used to cover things which are really very different—things such as the payment of debts, the reparation of injuries done by oneself to another, and the bringing about of a distribution of happiness between other people in proportion to merit. I use the word to denote only the last of these three. In the fifth chapter I shall try to show that besides the three (comparatively) simple goods, virtue, knowledge, and pleasure, there is a more complex good, not reducible to these, consisting in the proportionment of happiness to virtue. The bringing of this about is a duty which we owe to all men alike, though it may be reinforced by special responsibilities that we have undertaken to particular men. This, therefore, with beneficence and self-improvement, comes under the general principle that we should produce as much good as possible, though the good here involved is different in kind from any other.

But besides this general obligation, there are special obligations. These may arise, in the first place, incidentally, from acts which were not essentially meant to create such an obligation, but which nevertheless create it. From the nature of the case such acts may be of two kinds—the infliction of injuries on others, and the acceptance of benefits from them. It seems clear that these put us under a special obligation to other men, and that only these acts can do so incidentally. From these arise the twin duties of reparation and gratitude.

And finally there are special obligations arising from acts the very intention of which, when they were done, was to put us under such an obligation. The name for such acts is 'promises'; the name is wide enough if we are willing to include under it implicit promises, i.e., modes of behavior in which without explicit verbal promise we intentionally create an expectation that we can be counted on to behave in a certain way in the interest of another person.

These seem to be, in principle, all the ways in which *prima facie* duties arise. In actual experience they are compounded together in highly complex ways. Thus, for example, the duty of obeying the laws of one's country arises partly (as Socrates contends in the *Crito*) from the duty of gratitude for the benefits one has received from it; partly from the implicit promise to obey which seems to be involved in permanent residence in a country whose laws we know we are *expected* to obey, and still more clearly involved when we ourselves invoke the protection of its laws (this is the truth underlying the doctrine of the social contract); and partly (if we are fortunate in our country) from the fact that its laws are potent instruments for the general good.

Or again, the sense of a general obligation to bring about (so far as we can) a just apportionment of happiness to merit is often greatly reinforced by the fact that many of the existing injustices are due to a social and economic system which we have, not indeed created, but taken part in and assented to; the duty of justice is then reinforced by the duty of reparation.

---

5. After describing the various kinds of prima facie *duties in detail, Ross explains the differences between these duties and actual or absolute duties.*

It is necessary to say something by way of clearing up the relation between *prima facie* duties and the actual or absolute duty to do one particular act in particular circumstances. If, as almost all moralists except Kant are agreed, and as most plain men think, it is sometimes right to tell a lie or to break a promise, it must be maintained that there is a difference between *prima facie* duty and actual or absolute duty. When we think ourselves justified in breaking, and indeed morally obliged to break, a promise in order to relieve some one's distress, we do not for a moment cease to recognize a *prima facie* duty to keep our promise, and this leads us to feel, not indeed shame or repentance, but certainly compunction, for behaving as we do; we recognize, further, that it is our duty to make up somehow to the promisee for the breaking of the promise. We have to distinguish from the characteristic of being our duty that of tending to be our duty. Any act that we do contains various elements in virtue of which it falls under various categories. In virtue of being the breaking of a promise, for instance, it tends to be wrong; in virtue of being an instance of relieving distress it tends to be right. Tendency to be one's duty may be called a parti-resultant attribute, i.e., one which belongs to an act in virtue of some one component in its nature. *Being* one's duty is a toti-resultant attribute, one which belongs to an act in virtue of its whole nature and of nothing less than this. This distinction between parti-resultant and toti-resultant attributes is one which we shall meet in another context also.

Another instance of the same distinction may be found in the operation of natural laws. *Qua* subject to the force of gravitation towards some other body, each body tends to move in a particular direction with a particular velocity; but its actual movement depends on *all* the forces to which it is subject. It is only by recognizing this distinction that we can preserve the absoluteness of laws of nature, and only by recognizing a corresponding distinction that we can preserve the absoluteness of the general principles of morality. But an important difference between the two cases must be pointed out. When we say that in virtue of gravitation a body tends to move in a certain way, we are referring to a causal influence actually exercised on it by another body or other bodies. When we say that in virtue of being deliberately untrue a certain remark tends to be wrong, we are referring to no causal relation, to no relation that involves succession in time, but to such a relation as connects the various attributes of a mathematical figure. And if the word 'tendency' is thought to suggest too much a causal relation, it is better to talk of certain types of act as being *prima facie* right or wrong (or of different persons as having different and possibly conflicting claims upon us), than of their tending to be right or wrong.

Something should be said of the relation between our apprehension of the *prima facie* rightness of certain types of act and our mental attitude towards particular acts. It is proper to use the word 'apprehension' in the former case and not in the latter. That an act, *qua* fulfilling a promise, or *qua* effecting a just distribution of good, or *qua* returning services rendered, or *qua* promoting the good of others, or *qua* promoting the virtue or insight of the agent, is *prima facie* right, is self-evident; not in the sense that it is evident from the beginning of our lives, or as soon as we attend to the proposition for the first time, but in the sense that when we have reached sufficient mental maturity and have given sufficient attention to the proposition it is evident without any need of proof, or of evidence beyond itself. It is self-evident just as a mathematical axiom, or the validity of a form of inference, is evident. The moral order expressed in these propositions is just as much part of the fundamental nature of the universe (and, we may add, of any possible universe in which there were moral agents at all) as is the spatial or numerical structure expressed in the axioms of geometry or arithmetic. In our confidence that these propositions are true there is involved the same trust in our reason that is involved in our confidence in mathematics; and we should have no justification for trusting it in the latter sphere and distrusting it in the former. In both cases we are dealing with propositions that cannot be proved, but that just as certainly need no proof.

Some of these general principles of *prima facie* duty may appear to be open to criticism. It may be thought, for example, that the principle of returning good for good is a falling off from the Christian principle, generally and rightly recognized as expressing the highest morality, of returning good for evil. To this it may be replied that I do not suggest that there is a principle commanding us to return good for good and forbidding us to return good for evil, and that I do suggest that there is a positive duty to seek the good of all men. What I maintain is that an act in which good is returned for good is recognized as *specially* binding on us just because it is of that character, and that *ceteris paribus* any one would think it his duty to help his benefactors rather than his enemies, if he could not do both; just as it is generally recognized that *ceteris paribus* we should pay our debts rather than give our money in charity, when we cannot do both. A benefactor is not only a man, calling for our effort on his behalf on that ground, but also our benefactor, calling for our *special* effort on *that* ground.

Our judgments about our actual duty in concrete situations have none of the certainty that attaches to our recognition of the general principles of duty. A statement is certain, i.e., is an expression of knowledge, only in one or other of two cases: when it is either self-evident, or a valid conclusion from self-evident premises. And our judgments about our particular duties have neither of these characters. (1) They are not self-evident. Where a possible act is seen to have two characteristics, in virtue of one of which it is *prima facie* right, and in virtue of the other *prima facie* wrong, we are (I think) well aware that we are not certain whether we ought or ought not to do it; that whether we do it or not, we are taking a moral risk. We come in the long run, after consideration, to think one duty more pressing than the other, but we do not feel certain that it is so. And though we do not always recognize that a possible act has two such characteristics, and though there *may* be cases in which it has not, we are never certain that any particular possible act has not, and therefore never certain that it is right, nor certain that it is wrong. For, to go no further in the analysis, it is enough to point out that any particular act will in all probability in the course of time contribute to the bringing about of good or of evil for many human beings, and thus have a *prima facie* rightness or wrongness of which we know nothing. (2) Again, our judgments about our particular duties are not logical conclusions from self-evident premises. The only possible premises would be the general principles stating their *prima facie* rightness or wrongness *qua* having the different characteristics they do have; and even if we could (as we cannot) apprehend the extent to which an act will tend on the one hand, for example, to bring about advantages for our benefactors, and on the other hand to bring about disadvantages for fellow men who are not our benefactors, there is no principle by which we can draw the conclusion that it is on the whole right or on the whole wrong. In this respect the judgment as to the rightness of a particular act is just like the judgment as to the beauty of a particular natural object or work of art. A poem is, for instance, in respect of certain qualities beautiful and in respect of certain others not beautiful; and our judgment as to the degree of beauty it possesses on the whole is never reached by logical reasoning from the apprehension of its particular beauties or particular defects. Both in this and in the moral case we have more or less probable opinions which are not logically justified conclusions from the general principles that are recognized as self-evident.

There is therefore much truth in the description of the right act as a fortunate act. If we cannot be certain that it is right, it is our good fortune if the act we do is the right act. This consideration does not, however, make the doing of our duty a mere matter of chance. There is a parallel here between the doing of duty and the doing of what will be to our personal advantage. We never *know* what act will in the long run be to our advantage. Yet it is certain that we are more likely in general to secure our advantage if we estimate to the best of our ability the probable tendencies of our actions in this respect, than if we act on caprice. And similarly we are more likely to do our duty if we reflect to the best of our ability on the *prima facie* rightness or wrongness of various possible acts in virtue of the characteristics we perceive them to have, than if we act without reflection. With this greater likelihood we must be content.

Many people would be inclined to say that the right act for me is not that whose general nature I have been describing, viz. that which if I were omniscient I should see to be my duty, but that which on all the evidence available to me I should think to be my duty. But suppose that from the state of partial knowledge in which I think act A to be my duty, I could pass to a state of perfect knowledge in which I saw act B to be my duty, should I not say "act B was the right act for me to do?" I should no doubt add "though I am not to be blamed for doing act A." But in adding this, am I not passing from the question "what is right" to the question "what is morally good"? At the same time I am not making the *full* passage from the one notion to the other; for in order that the act should be morally good, or an act I am not to be blamed for doing, it must not merely be the act which it is reasonable for me to think my duty; it must also be done for that reason, or from some other morally good motive. Thus the conception of the right act as the act which it is reasonable for me to think my duty is an unsatisfactory compromise between the true notion of the right act and the notion of the morally good action.

---

6. How do we come to know these self-evident principles? To answer, Ross provides an analogy with the way in which we learn the axioms of mathematics.

The general principles of duty are obviously not self-evident from the beginning of our lives. How do they come to be so? The answer is, that they come to be self-evident to us just as mathematical axioms do. We find by experience that this couple of matches and that couple make four matches, that this couple of balls on a wire and that couple make four balls: and by reflection on these and similar discoveries we come to see that it is of the nature of two and two to make four. In a precisely similar way, we see the *prima facie* rightness of an act which would be the fulfillment of a particular promise, and of another which would be the fulfillment of another promise, and when we have reached sufficient maturity to think in general terms, we apprehend *prima facie* rightness to belong to the nature of any fulfillment of promise. What comes first in time is the apprehension of the self-evident *prima facie* rightness of an individual act of a particular type. From this we come by reflection to apprehend the self-evident general principle of *prima facie* duty. From this, too, perhaps along with the apprehension of the self-evident *prima facie* rightness of the same act in virtue of its having another characteristic as well, and perhaps in spite of the apprehension of its *prima facie* wrongness in virtue of its having some third characteristic, we come to believe something not self-evident at all, but an object of probable opinion, viz. that this particular act is (not *prima facie* but) actually right.

In this respect there is an important difference between rightness and mathematical properties. A triangle which is isosceles necessarily has two of its angles equal, whatever other characteristics the triangle may have—whatever, for instance, be its area, or the size of its third angle. The equality of the two angles is a parti-resultant attribute. And the same is true of all mathematical attributes. It is true, I may add, of *prima facie* rightness. But no act is ever, in virtue of falling under some general description, necessarily actually right; its rightness depends on its whole nature[5] and not on any element in it. The reason is that no mathematical object (no figure, for instance, or angle) ever has two characteristics that tend to give it opposite resultant characteristics, while moral acts often (as every one knows) and indeed always (as on reflection we must admit) have different characteristics that tend to make them at the same time *prima facie* right and *prima facie* wrong; there is probably no act, for instance, which does good to any one without doing harm to some one else, and vice versa.

READING QUESTIONS

1. We keep promises, as Ross says, because we think that we ought to. If this is right, how does this work against the utilitarian view?
2. What is a *prima facie* duty?
3. How is a "claim" related to a "*prima facie* duty"?
4. Name three kinds of *prima facie* duties.
5. What does Ross consider to be the most important defect in "ideal utilitarianism"? Explain.
6. What are the three main things that are intrinsically good?
7. How does Ross defend his position from the charge that his theory falls short of the Christian principle that one should not only return good for good, but good for evil as well?

---

[5] To avoid complicating unduly the statement of the general view I am putting forward, I have here rather overstated it. Any act is the origination of a great variety of things many of which make no difference to its rightness or wrongness. But there are always many elements in its nature (i.e., in what it is the origination of) that make a difference to its rightness or wrongness, and no element in its nature can he dismissed without consideration as indifferent.

A. J. Ayer

B oth ethical naturalism (associated with John Dewey) and ethical nonnaturalism (as represented by Moore and Ross) are considered **cognitive moral theories.** A cognitive theory considers moral judgments to be statements of fact that are either true or false. For example, if you declare that stealing is wrong (as a Kantian might) or that good acts maximize happiness (as a utilitarian might), you are making a claim that is either true or false. However, an influential ethical theory arose in the early part of this century that is a **noncognitive ethical theory.**

This theory, now known as **emotivism** (or emotive theory), holds that moral judgments are not factual statements and, thus, are neither true nor false. Words like "good," "right," and "ought" are considered emotive terms—used either to indicate the attitude of the speaker (or writer) or to evoke a response in the hearer (or reader). Therefore, when you declare that stealing is wrong, it merely appears that you are making a standard declarative statement. According to emotivism, the actual purpose of these words is to show your disapproval of stealing or to indicate that you have a negative feeling toward stealing. The English philosophers I. A. Richards and Bertrand Russell introduced the theory (created by a Swedish philosopher named Axel Hagerstrom) to the English-speaking world. It was the later development of the theory by A. J. Ayer and C. L. Stevenson, however, that made the theory a force to be reckoned with in moral philosophy. A reading from Ayer represents emotivism in this text.

Alfred Jules Ayer was born in England in 1910 and was educated at Eton and Christ Church, Oxford. He began his teaching career in 1933 at Oxford, and as a young man of twenty-six wrote one of the most influential philosophical books of this century, *Language, Truth and Logic.* Published in 1936, this book clearly and vigorously presented the radical moral philosophy of the emotivists.

Ayer argued that since there are no moral facts, there can be no moral knowledge. Moral judgments do not state facts or assert truths but instead play a noncognitive role: they are used to express, or evoke, attitudes and emotions. This means that the role of moral philosophy is not the search for the rational foundations of morality or the systematic formulation of an ethical theory—the traditional goals of moral philosophers since the time of the ancient Greeks. Instead, emotivists declare moral philosophy to be merely the investigation of moral language.

Emotivism became an extremely powerful and popular ethical theory, quickly surpassing Moore's intuitionism. For many of its proponents, emotivism marked the completion of work in moral philosophy. It appeared to explain why moral philosophy was forever destined to be marked by dispute, controversy, and a lack of agreement about all principle matters. After all, if people are merely expressing their individual moral attitudes when they make moral judgments, the prospect of bringing an opponent over to your side in a moral dispute looks to be impossible. It would be much like trying to convince someone that vanilla ice cream tastes better than chocolate (or vice versa). Yet despite its popularity, many moral philosophers eventually came to believe that something was inherently wrong with this theory. Since emotivism denied the possibility of moral reasoning, its proponents were accused of trying to discredit ethics altogether. Eventually emotivism was repudiated by most subsequent writers on moral philosophy.

Language, Truth and Logic

You may have noticed that many of the most disputed and controversial issues, whether in the nation or between friends and family, are ethical issues. You may also have noticed that rarely, if ever, do these disputes get settled. Which particular controversial issues attract attention may change, "hot topics" come and go, but resolution of moral issues remains extremely rare. Sometimes the best that can be hoped for is that the disputants will "agree to disagree." What is it that makes ethical issues so tough to resolve? Some philosophers contend that ethical problems have not been settled, and will always remain unsettled, because ethical judgments are neither true nor false. If ethical judgments are neither true nor false, no ethical position can be shown to be better than another is. Each side is as right, or wrong, as the other.

In this chapter, Ayer focuses on the special features of ethical statements. He wants to demonstrate that they are not a special kind of empirical, or factual, statement like most moral philosophers have thought. If I declare that "stealing is wrong," I tell more about me than I do about stealing. And Ayer believes that once philosophers understand his argument and recognize, as he does, the actual function of moral judgments, they will also agree with him that the inquiry we call philosophy no longer has any need to inquire about ethics.

Chapter VI
Critique of Ethics and Theology

There is still one objection to be met before we can claim to have justified our view that all synthetic propositions are empirical hypotheses. This objection is based on the common supposition that our speculative knowledge is of two distinct kinds—that which relates to questions of empirical fact, and that which relates to questions of value. It will be said that "statements of value" are genuine synthetic propositions, but that they cannot with any show of justice be represented as hypotheses, which are used to predict the course of our sensations; and, accordingly, that the existence of ethics and aesthetics as branches of speculative knowledge presents an insuperable objection to our radical empiricist thesis.

In face of this objection, it is our business to give an account of "judgments of value" which is both satisfactory in itself and consistent with our general empiricist principles. We shall set ourselves to show that in so far as statements of

From A. J. Ayer, *Language, Truth and Logic*, 1935. Reprinted by permission of Dover Publications, Inc.

value are significant, they are ordinary "scientific" statements; and that in so far as they are not scientific, they are not in the literal sense significant, but are simply expressions of emotion which can be neither true nor false. In maintaining this view, we may confine ourselves for the present to the case of ethical statements. What is said about them will be found to apply, *mutatis mutandis*, to the case of aesthetic statements also.

The ordinary system of ethics, as elaborated in the works of ethical philosophers, is very far from being a homogeneous whole. Not only is it apt to contain pieces of metaphysics, and analyses of non-ethical concepts: its actual ethical contents are themselves of very different kinds. We may divide them, indeed, into four main classes. There are, first of all, propositions which express definitions of ethical terms, or judgments about the legitimacy or possibility of certain definitions. Secondly, there are propositions describing the phenomena of moral experience, and their causes. Thirdly, there are exhortations to moral virtue. And, lastly, there are actual ethical judgments. It is unfortunately the case that the distinction between these four classes, plain as it is, is commonly ignored by ethical philosophers; with the result that it is often very difficult to tell from their works what it is that they are seeking to discover or prove.

In fact, it is easy to see that only the first of our four classes, namely that which comprises the propositions relating to the definitions of ethical terms, can be said to constitute ethical philosophy. The propositions which describe the phenomena of moral experience, and their causes, must be assigned to the science of psychology, or sociology. The exhortations to moral virtue are not propositions at all, but ejaculations or commands which are designed to provoke the reader to action of a certain sort. Accordingly, they do not belong to any branch of philosophy or science. As for the expressions of ethical judgments, we have not yet determined how they should be classified. But inasmuch as they are certainly neither definitions nor comments upon definitions, nor quotations, we may say decisively that they do not belong to ethical philosophy. A strictly philosophical treatise on ethics should therefore make no ethical pronouncements. But it should, by giving an analysis of ethical terms, show what is the category to which all such pronouncements belong. And this is what we are now about to do.

A question which is often discussed by ethical philosophers is whether it is possible to find definitions which would reduce all ethical terms to one or two fundamental terms. But this question, though it undeniably belongs to ethical philosophy, is not relevant to our present enquiry. We are not now concerned to discover which term, within the sphere of ethical terms, is to be taken as fundamental; whether, for example, "good" can be defined in terms of "right" or "right" in terms of "good," or both in terms of "value." What we are interested in is the possibility of reducing the whole sphere of ethical terms to non-ethical terms. We are inquiring whether statements of ethical value can be translated into statements of empirical fact.

That they can be so translated is the contention of those ethical philosophers who are commonly called subjectivists, and of those who are known as utilitarians. For the utilitarian defines the rightness of actions, and the goodness of ends, in terms of the pleasure, or happiness, or satisfaction, to which they give rise; the subjectivist, in terms of the feelings of approval which a certain person, or group of people, has towards them. Each of these types of definition makes moral judgments into a sub-class of psychological or sociological judgments; and for this reason they are very attractive to us. For, if either was correct, it would follow that ethical assertions were not generically different from the factual assertions which are ordinarily contrasted with them; and the account which we have already given of empirical hypotheses would apply to them also.

---

1. Now that Ayer has identified two kinds of ethical philosophies that consider ethical statements to be a kind of factual assertion, he argues that both are incorrect. Why is he so concerned with self-contradiction?

Nevertheless we shall not adopt either a subjectivist or a utilitarian analysis of ethical terms. We reject the subjectivist view that to call an action right, or a thing good, is to say that it is generally approved of, because it is not self-contradictory to assert that some actions which are generally approved of are not right, or that some things which are generally approved of are not good. And we reject the alternative subjectivist view that a man who asserts that a certain action is right, or that a certain thing is good, is saying that he himself approves of it, on the ground that a man who confessed that he sometimes approved of what was bad or wrong would not be contradicting himself. And a similar argument is fatal to utilitarianism. We cannot agree that to call an action right is to say that of all the actions possible in the circumstances it would cause, or be likely to cause, the greatest happiness, or the greatest balance of pleasure over pain, or the greatest balance of satisfied over unsatisfied desire, because we find that it is not self-contradictory to say that it is sometimes wrong to perform the action which would actually or probably cause the greatest happiness, or the greatest balance of pleasure over pain, or of satisfied over unsatisfied desire. And since it is not self-contradictory to say that some pleasant things are not good, or that some bad things are desired, it cannot be the case that the sentence "x is good" is equivalent to "x is pleasant," or to "x is desired." And to every other variant of utilitarianism with which I am acquainted the same objection can be made. And therefore we should, I think, conclude that the validity of ethical judgments is not determined by the felicific tendencies of actions, any more than by the nature of people's feelings; but that it must be regarded as "absolute" or "intrinsic," and not empirically calculable.

If we say this, we are not, of course, denying that it is possible to invent a language in which all ethical symbols are definable in non-ethical terms, or even that it is desirable to invent such a language and adopt it in place of our own; what we are denying is that the suggested reduction of ethical to non-ethical statements is consistent with the conventions of our actual language. That is, we reject utilitarianism and subjectivism, not as proposals to replace our existing ethical notions by new ones, but as analyses of our existing ethical notions. Our contention is simply that, in our language, sentences which contain normative ethical symbols are not equivalent to sentences which express psychological propositions, or indeed empirical propositions of any kind.

It is advisable here to make it plain that it is only normative ethical symbols, and not descriptive ethical symbols, that are held by us to be indefinable in factual terms. There is a danger of confusing these two types of symbols, because they are commonly constituted by signs of the same sensible form. Thus a complex sign of the form "x is wrong" may constitute a sentence which expresses a moral judgment concerning a certain type of conduct, or it may constitute a sentence which states that a certain type of conduct is repugnant to the moral sense of a particular society. In the latter case, the symbol "wrong" is a descriptive ethical symbol, and the sentence in which it occurs expresses an ordinary sociological proposition; in the former case, the symbol "wrong" is a normative ethical symbol, and the sentence in which it occurs does not, we maintain, express an empirical proposition at all. It is only with normative ethics that we are at present concerned; so that whenever ethical symbols are used in the course of this argument without qualification, they are always to be interpreted as symbols of the normative type.

------

2. Ayer's attention turns to intuitionist moral philosophies, which claim that statements of value are not verifiable by observation, as other empirical claims are, but by intuition. Do you think he's right that people have, or could have, different moral intuitions?

In admitting that normative ethical concepts are irreducible to empirical concepts, we seem to be leaving the way clear for the "absolutist" view of ethics—that is, the view that statements of value are not controlled by observation, as ordinary empirical propositions are, but only by a "mysterious intellectual intuition." A feature of this theory, which is seldom recognized by its advocates, is that it makes statements of value unverifiable. For it is notorious that what seems intuitively certain to one person may seem doubtful, or even false, to another. So that unless it is possible to provide some criterion by which one may decide between conflicting intuitions, a mere appeal to intuition is worthless as a test of a proposition's validity. But in the case of moral judgments, no such criterion can be given. Some moralists claim to settle the matter by saying that they "know" that their own moral judgments are correct. But such an assertion is of purely psychological interest, and has not the slightest tendency to prove the validity of any moral judgment. For dissentient moralists may equally well "know" that their ethical views are correct. And, as far as subjective certainty goes, there will be nothing to choose between them. When such differences of opinion arise in connection with an ordinary empirical proposition, one may attempt to resolve them by referring to, or actually carrying out, some relevant empirical test. But with regard to ethical statements, there is, on the "absolutist" or "intuitionist" theory, no relevant empirical test. We are therefore justified in saying that on this theory ethical statements are held to be unverifiable. They are, of course, also held to be genuine synthetic propositions.

Considering the use which we have made of the principle that a synthetic proposition is significant only if it is empirically verifiable, it is clear that the acceptance of an "absolutist" theory of ethics would undermine the whole of our main argument. And as we have already rejected the "naturalistic" theories which are commonly supposed to provide the only alternative to "absolutism" in ethics, we seem to have reached a difficult position. We shall meet the difficulty by showing that the correct treatment of ethical statements is afforded by a third theory, which is wholly compatible with our radical empiricism.

------

3. Ayer starts to lay out his own view of ethical statements. He begins to make it clear why his theory is considered an "emotivist" theory. Do you see the reason?

We begin by admitting that the fundamental ethical concepts are unanalyzable, inasmuch as there is no criterion by which one can test the validity of the judgments in which they occur. So far we are in agreement with the absolutists. But, unlike the absolutists, we are able to give an explanation of this fact about ethical concepts. We say that the reason why they are unanalyzable is that they are mere pseudo-concepts. The presence of an ethical symbol in a proposition adds nothing to its factual content. Thus if I say to someone, "You acted wrongly in stealing that money," I am not stating anything more than if I had simply said, "You stole that money." In adding that this action is wrong I am not making any further statement about it. I am simply evincing my moral disapproval of it. It is as if I had said, "You stole that money," in a peculiar tone of horror, or written it with the addition of some special exclamation marks. The tone, or the exclamation marks, adds nothing to the literal meaning of the sentence. It merely serves to show that the expression of it is attended by certain feelings in the speaker.

If now I generalize my previous statement and say, "Stealing money is wrong," I produce a sentence which has no factual meaning—that is, expresses no proposition which can be either true or false. It is as if I had written "Stealing money!!"—where the shape and thickness of the exclamation marks show, by a suitable convention, that a special sort of moral disapproval is the feeling which is being expressed. It is clear that there is nothing said here which can be true or false. Another man may disagree with me about the wrongness of stealing, in the sense that he may not have the same feelings about stealing as I have, and he may quarrel with me on account of my moral sentiments. But he cannot, strictly speaking, contradict me. For in saying that a certain type of action is right or wrong, I am not making any factual statement, not even a statement about my own state of mind. I am merely expressing certain moral sentiments. And the man who is ostensibly contradicting me is merely expressing his moral sentiments. So that there is plainly no sense in asking which of us is in the right. For neither of us is asserting a genuine proposition.

What we have just been saying about the symbol "wrong" applies to all normative ethical symbols. Sometimes they occur in sentences which record ordinary empirical facts besides expressing ethical feeling about those facts: sometimes they occur in sentences which simply express ethical feeling about a certain type of action, or situation, without making any statement of fact. But in every case in which one would commonly be said to be making an ethical judgment, the function of the relevant ethical word is purely "emotive." It is used to express feeling about certain objects, but not to make any assertion about them.

It is worth mentioning that ethical terms do not serve only to express feeling. They are calculated also to arouse feeling, and so to stimulate action. Indeed some of them are used in such a way as to give the sentences in which they occur the effect of commands. Thus the sentence "It is your duty to tell the truth" may be regarded both as the expression of a certain sort of ethical feeling about truthfulness and as the expression of the command "Tell the truth." The sentence "You ought to tell the truth" also involves the command "Tell the truth," but here the tone of the command is less emphatic. In the sentence "It is good to tell the truth" the command has become little more than a suggestion. And thus the "meaning" of the word "good," in its ethical usage, is differentiated from that of the word "duty" or the word "ought." In fact we may define the meaning of the various ethical words in terms both of the different feelings they are ordinarily taken to express, and also the different responses which they are calculated to provoke.

We can now see why it is impossible to find a criterion for determining the validity of ethical judgments. It is not because they have an "absolute" validity which is mysteriously independent of ordinary sense-experience, but because they have no objective validity whatsoever. If a sentence makes no statement at all, there is obviously no sense in asking whether what it says is true or false. And we have seen that sentences which simply express moral judgments do not say anything. They are pure expressions of feeling and as such do not come under the category of truth and falsehood. They are unverifiable for the same reason as a cry of pain or a word of command is unverifiable—because they do not express genuine propositions.

Thus, although our theory of ethics might fairly be said to be radically subjectivist, it differs in a very important respect from the orthodox subjectivist theory. For the orthodox subjectivist does not deny, as we do, that the sentences of a moralizer express genuine propositions. All he denies is that they express propositions of a unique non-empirical character. His own view is that they express propositions about the speaker's feelings. If this were so, ethical judgments clearly would be capable of being true or false. They would be true if the speaker had the relevant feelings, and false if he had not. And this is a matter which is, in principle, empirically verifiable. Furthermore they could be significantly contradicted. For if I say, "Tolerance is a virtue," and someone answers, "You don't approve of it," he would, on the ordinary subjectivist theory, be contradicting me. On our theory, he would not be contradicting me, because, in saying that tolerance was a virtue, I should not be making any statement about my own feelings or about anything else. I should simply be evincing my feelings, which is not at all the same thing as saying that I have them.

The distinction between the expression of feeling and the assertion of feeling is complicated by the fact that the assertion that one has a certain feeling often accompanies the expression of that feeling, and is then, indeed, a factor in the expression of that feeling. Thus I may simultaneously express boredom and say that I am bored, and in that case my utterance of the words, "I am bored," is one of the circumstances which make it true to say that I am expressing or evincing boredom. But I can express boredom without actually saying that I am bored. I can express it by my tone and gestures, while making a statement about something wholly unconnected with it, or by an ejaculation, or without uttering any words at all. So that even if the assertion that one has a certain feeling always involves the expression of that feeling, the expression of a feeling assuredly does not always involve the assertion that one has it. And this is the important point to grasp in considering the distinction between our theory and the ordinary subjectivist theory. For whereas the subjectivist holds that ethical statements actually assert the existence of certain feelings, we hold that ethical statements are expressions and excitants of feeling which do not necessarily involve any assertions.

---

4. Now that he has distinguished his theory from other subjectivist theories, Ayer considers criticisms that have been leveled at the other subjectivist theories to determine whether his theory escapes the criticisms.

We have already remarked that the main objection to the ordinary subjectivist theory is that the validity of ethical judgments is not determined by the nature of their author's feelings. And this is an objection which our theory escapes. For it does not imply that the existence of any feelings is a necessary and sufficient condition of the validity of an ethical judgment. It implies, on the contrary, that ethical judgments have no validity.

There is, however, a celebrated argument against subjectivist theories which our theory does not escape. It has been pointed out by Moore that if ethical statements were simply statements about the speaker's feelings, it would be impossible to argue about questions of value. To take a typical example: if a man said that thrift was a virtue, and another replied that it was a vice, they would not, on this theory, be disputing with one another. One would be saying that he approved of thrift, and the other that *he* didn't; and there is no reason why both these statements should not be true. Now Moore held it to be obvious that we do dispute about questions of value, and accordingly concluded that the particular form of subjectivism which he was discussing was false.

It is plain that the conclusion that it is impossible to dispute about questions of value follows from our theory also. For as we hold that such sentences as "Thrift is a virtue" and "Thrift is a vice" do not express propositions at all, we clearly cannot hold that they express incompatible propositions. We must therefore admit that if Moore's argument really refutes the ordinary subjectivist theory, it also refutes ours. But, in fact, we deny that it does refute even the ordinary subjectivist theory. For we hold that one really never does dispute about questions of value.

This may seem, at first sight, to be a very paradoxical assertion. For we certainly do engage in disputes which are ordinarily regarded as disputes about questions of value. But, in all such cases, we find, if we consider the matter closely, that the dispute is not really about a question of value, but about a question of fact. When someone disagrees with us about the moral value of a certain action or type of action, we do admittedly resort to argument in order to win him over to our way of thinking. But we do not attempt to show by our arguments that he has the "wrong" ethical feeling towards a situation whose nature he has correctly apprehended. What we attempt to show is that he is mistaken about the facts of the case. We argue that he has misconceived the agent's motive: or that he has misjudged the effects of the action, or its probable effects in view of the agent's knowledge; or that he has failed to take into account the special circumstances in which the agent was placed. Or else we employ more general arguments about the effects which actions of a certain type tend to produce, or the qualities which are usually manifested in their performance. We do this in the hope that we have only to get our opponent to agree with us about the nature of the empirical facts for him to adopt the same moral attitude towards them as we do. And as the people with whom we argue have generally received the same moral education as ourselves, and live in the same social order, our expectation is usually justified. But if our opponent happens to have undergone a different process of moral "conditioning" from ourselves, so that, even when he acknowledges all the facts, he still disagrees with us about the moral value of the actions under discussion, then we abandon the attempt to convince him by argument. We say that it is impossible to argue with him because he has a distorted or undeveloped moral sense; which signifies merely that he employs a different set of values from our own. We feel that our own system of values is superior, and therefore speak in such derogatory terms of his. But we cannot bring forward any arguments to show that our system is superior. For our judgment that it is so is itself a judgment of value, and accordingly outside the scope of argument. It is because argument fails us when we come to deal with pure questions of value, as distinct from questions of fact, that we finally resort to mere abuse.

In short, we find that argument is possible on moral questions only if some system of values is presupposed. If our opponent concurs with us in expressing moral disapproval of all actions of a given type t, then we may get him to condemn a particular action A, by bringing forward arguments to show that A is of type t. For the question whether A does or does not belong to that type is a plain question of fact. Given that a man has certain moral principles, we argue that he must, in order to be consistent, react morally to certain things in a certain way. What we do not and cannot argue about is the validity of these moral principles. We merely praise or condemn them in the light of our own feelings.

If anyone doubts the accuracy of this account of moral disputes, let him try to construct even an imaginary argument on a question of value which does not reduce itself to an argument about a question of logic or about an empirical matter of fact. I am confident that he will not succeed in producing a single example. And if that is the case, he must allow that its involving the impossibility of purely ethical arguments is not, as Moore thought, a ground of objection to our theory, but rather a point in favor of it.

Having upheld our theory against the only criticism which appeared to threaten it, we may now use it to define the nature of all ethical inquiries. We find that ethical philosophy consists simply in saying that ethical concepts are pseudo-concepts and therefore unanalyzable. The further task of describing the different feelings that the different ethical terms are used to express, and the different reactions that they customarily provoke, is a task for the psychologist. There cannot be such a thing as ethical science, if by ethical science one means the elaboration of a "true" system of morals. For we have seen that, as ethical judgments are mere expressions of feeling, there can be no way of determining the validity of any ethical system, and, indeed, no sense in asking whether any such system is true. All that one may legitimately inquire in this connection is, What are the moral habits of a given person or group of people, and what causes them to have precisely those habits and feelings? And this inquiry falls wholly within the scope of the existing social sciences.

It appears, then, that ethics, as a branch of knowledge, is nothing more than a department of psychology and sociology. And in case anyone thinks that we are overlooking the existence of casuistry, we may remark that casuistry is not a science, but is a purely analytical investigation of the structure of a given moral system. In other words, it is an exercise in formal logic.

When one comes to pursue the psychological inquiries which constitute ethical science, one is immediately enabled to account for the Kantian and hedonistic theories of morals. For one finds that one of the chief causes of moral behavior is fear, both conscious and unconscious, of a god's displeasure, and fear of the enmity of society. And this, indeed, is the reason why moral precepts present themselves to some people as "categorical" commands. And one finds, also, that the moral code of a society is partly determined by the beliefs of that society concerning the conditions of its own happiness—or, in other words, that a society tends to encourage or discourage a given type of conduct by the use of moral sanctions according as it appears to promote or detract from the contentment of the society as a whole. And this is the reason why altruism is recommended in most moral codes and egotism condemned. It is from the observation of this connection between morality and happiness that hedonistic or eudaemonistic theories of morals ultimately spring, just as the moral theory of Kant is based on the fact, previously explained, that moral precepts have for some people the force of inexorable commands. As each of these theories ignores the fact which lies at the root of the other, both may be criticized as being one-sided; but this is not the main objection to either of them. Their essential defect is that they treat propositions which refer to the causes and attributes of our ethical feelings as if they were definitions of ethical concepts. And thus they fail to recognize that ethical concepts are pseudo-concepts and consequently indefinable.

---

5. Ayer has concluded his critique of ethical statements, and now he will apply many of the same criticisms to another kind of value statement, aesthetic statements.

As we have already said, our conclusions about the nature of ethics apply to aesthetics also. Aesthetic terms are used in exactly the same way as ethical terms. Such aesthetic words as "beautiful" and "hideous" are employed, as ethical words are employed, not to make statements of fact, but simply to express certain feelings and evoke a certain response. It follows, as in ethics, that there is no sense in attributing objective validity to aesthetic judgments, and no possibility of arguing about questions of value in aesthetics, but only about questions of fact. A scientific treatment of aesthetics would show us what in general were the causes of aesthetic feeling, why various societies produced and admired the works of art they did, why taste varies as it does within a given society, and so forth. And these are ordinary psychological or sociological questions. They have, of course, little or nothing to do with aesthetic criticism as we understand it. But that is because the purpose of aesthetic criticism is not so much to give knowledge as to communicate emotion. The critic, by calling attention to certain features of the work under review, and expressing his own feelings about them, endeavors to make us share his attitude towards the work as a whole. The only relevant propositions that he formulates are propositions describing the nature of the work. And these are plain records of fact. We conclude, therefore, that there is nothing in aesthetics, any more than there is in ethics, to justify the view that it embodies a unique type of knowledge.

It should now be clear that the only information which we can legitimately derive from the study of our aesthetic and moral experiences is information about our own mental and physical make-up. We take note of these experiences as providing data for our psychological and sociological generalizations. And this is the only way in which they serve to increase our knowledge. It follows that any attempt to make our use of ethical and aesthetic concepts the basis of a metaphysical theory concerning the existence of a world of values, as distinct from the world of facts, involves a false analysis of these concepts. Our own analysis has shown that the phenomena of moral experience cannot fairly be used to support any rationalist or metaphysical doctrine whatsoever. In particular, they cannot, as Kant hoped, be used to establish the existence of a transcendent god.

---

6. After disposing of ethics and aesthetics, Ayer now considers the possibility of religious knowledge. Not surprisingly, he finds religious statements to be on a par with ethical statements: neither kind is verifiable.

This mention of God brings us to the question of the possibility of religious knowledge. We shall see that this possibility has already been ruled out by our treatment of metaphysics. But, as this is a point of considerable interest, we may be permitted to discuss it at some length.

It is now generally admitted, at any rate by philosophers, that the existence of a being having the attributes which define the god of any non-animistic religion cannot be demonstratively proved. To see that this is so, we have only to ask ourselves what are the premises from which the existence of such a god could be deduced. If the conclusion that a god exists is to be demonstratively certain, then these premises must be certain; for, as the conclusion of a deductive argument is already contained in the premises, any uncertainty there may be about the truth of the premises is necessarily shared by it. But we know that no empirical proposition can ever be anything more than probable. It is only *a priori* propositions that are logically certain. But we cannot deduce the existence of a god from an *a priori* proposition. For we know that the reason why *a priori* propositions are certain is that they are tautologies. And from a set of tautologies nothing but a further tautology can be validly deduced. It follows that there is no possibility of demonstrating the existence of a god.

What is not so generally recognized is that there can be no way of proving that the existence of a god, such as the God of Christianity, is even probable. Yet this also is easily shown. For if the existence of such a god were probable, then the proposition that he existed would be an empirical hypothesis. And in that case it would be possible to deduce from it, and other empirical hypotheses, certain experiential propositions which were not deducible from those other hypotheses alone. But in fact this is not possible. It is sometimes claimed, indeed, that the existence of a certain sort of regularity in nature constitutes sufficient evidence for the existence of a god. But if the sentence "God exists" entails no more than that certain types of phenomena occur in certain sequences, then to assert the existence of a god will be simply equivalent to asserting that there is the requisite regularity in nature; and no religious man would admit that this was all he intended to assert in asserting the existence of a god. He would say that in talking about God, he was talking about a transcendent being who might be known through certain empirical manifestations, but certainly could not be defined in terms of those manifestations. But in that case the term "god" is a metaphysical term. And if "god" is a metaphysical term, then it cannot be even probable that a god exists. For to say that "God exists" is to make a metaphysical utterance which cannot be either true or false. And by the same criterion, no sentence which purports to describe the nature of a transcendent god can possess any literal significance.

It is important not to confuse this view of religious assertions with the view that is adopted by atheists, or agnostics.[1] For it is characteristic of an agnostic to hold that the existence of a god is a possibility in which there is no good reason either to believe or disbelieve; and it is characteristic of an atheist to hold that it is at least probable that no god exists. And our view that all utterances about the nature of God are nonsensical, so far from being identical with, or even lending any support to, either of these familiar contentions, is actually incompatible with them. For if the assertion that there is a god is nonsensical, then the atheist's assertion that there is no god is equally nonsensical, since it is only a significant proposition that can be significantly contradicted. As for the agnostic, although he refrains from saying either that there is or that there is not a god, he does not deny that the question whether a transcendent god exists is a genuine question. He does not deny that the two sentences "There is a transcendent god" and "There is no transcendent god" express propositions one of which is actually true and the other

---

[1] This point was suggested to me by Professor H. H. Price.

false. All he says is that we have no means of telling which of them is true, and therefore ought not to commit ourselves to either. But we have seen that the sentences in question do not express propositions at all. And this means that agnosticism also is ruled out.

Thus we offer the theist the same comfort as we gave to the moralist. His assertions cannot possibly be valid, but they cannot be invalid either. As he says nothing at all about the world, he cannot justly be accused of saying anything false, or anything for which he has insufficient grounds. It is only when the theist claims that in asserting the existence of a transcendent god he is expressing a genuine proposition that we are entitled to disagree with him.

It is to be remarked that in cases where deities are identified with natural objects, assertions concerning them may be allowed to be significant. If, for example, a man tells me that the occurrence of thunder is alone both necessary and sufficient to establish the truth of the proposition that Jehovah is angry, I may conclude that, in his usage of words, the sentence "Jehovah is angry" is equivalent to "It is thundering." But in sophisticated religions, though they may be to some extent based on men's awe of natural process which they cannot sufficiently understand, the "person" who is supposed to control the empirical world is not himself located in it; he is held to be superior to the empirical world, and so outside it; and he is endowed with super-empirical attributes. But the notion of a person whose essential attributes are non-empirical is not an intelligible notion at all. We may have a word which is used as if it named this "person," but, unless the sentences in which it occurs express propositions which are empirically verifiable, it cannot be said to symbolize anything. And this is the case with regard to the word "god," in the usage in which it is intended to refer to a transcendent object. The mere existence of the noun is enough to foster the illusion that there is a real, or at any rate a possible entity corresponding to it. It is only when we inquire what God's attributes are that we discover that "God," in this usage, is not a genuine name.

It is common to find belief in a transcendent god conjoined with belief in an after-life. But, in the form which it usually takes, the content of this belief is not a genuine hypothesis. To say that men do not ever die, or that the state of death is merely a state of prolonged insensibility, is indeed to express a significant proposition, though all the available evidence goes to show that it is false. But to say that there is something imperceptible inside a man, which is his soul or his real self, and that it goes on living after he is dead, is to make a metaphysical assertion which has no more factual content than the assertion that there is a transcendent god.

It is worth mentioning that, according to the account which we have given of religious assertions, there is no logical ground for antagonism between religion and natural science. As far as the question of truth or falsehood is concerned, there is no opposition between the natural scientist and the theist who believes in a transcendent god. For since the religious utterances of the theist are not genuine propositions at all, they cannot stand in any logical relation to the propositions of science. Such antagonism as there is between religion and science appears to consist in the fact that science takes away one of the motives which make men religious. For it is acknowledged that one of the ultimate sources of religious feeling lies in the inability of men to determine their own destiny; and science tends to destroy the feeling of awe with which men regard an alien world, by making them believe that they can understand and anticipate the course of natural phenomena, and even to some extent control it. The fact that it has recently become fashionable for physicists themselves to be sympathetic towards religion is a point in favor of this hypothesis. For this sympathy towards religion marks the physicists' own lack of confidence in the validity of their hypotheses, which is a reaction on their part from the anti-religious dogmatism of nineteenth-century scientists, and a natural outcome of the crisis through which physics has just passed.

It is not within the scope of this inquiry to enter more deeply into the causes of religious feeling, or to discuss the probability of the continuance of religious belief. We are concerned only to answer those questions which arise out of our discussion of the possibility of religious knowledge. The point which we wish to establish is that there cannot be any transcendent truths of religion. For the sentences which the theist uses to express such "truths" are not literally significant.

An interesting feature of this conclusion is that it accords with what many theists are accustomed to say themselves. For we are often told that the nature of God is a mystery which transcends the human understanding. But to say that something transcends the human understanding is to say that it is unintelligible. And what is unintelligible cannot significantly be described. Again, we are told that God is not an object of reason but an object of faith. This may be nothing more than an admission that the existence of God must be taken on trust, since it cannot be proved. But it may also be an assertion that God is the object of a purely mystical intuition, and cannot therefore be defined in terms which are intelligible to the reason. And I think there are many theists who would assert this. But if one allows that it is impossible to define God in intelligible terms, then one is allowing that it is impossible for a sentence both to be significant and to be about God. If a mystic admits that the object of his vision is something which cannot be described, then he must also admit that he is bound to talk nonsense when he describes it.

For his part, the mystic may protest that his intuition does reveal truths to him, even though he can not explain to others what these truths are; and that we who do not possess this faculty of intuition can have no ground for denying that it is a cognitive faculty. For we can hardly maintain *a priori* that there are no ways of discovering true propositions except those which we ourselves employ. The answer is that we set no limit to the number of ways in which one may come to formulate a true proposition. We do not in any way deny that a synthetic truth may be discovered by purely intuitive methods as well as by the rational method of induction. But we do say that every synthetic proposition, however it may have been arrived at, must be subject to the test of actual experience. We do not deny *a priori* that the mystic is able to discover truths by his own special methods. We wait to hear what are the propositions which embody his discoveries, in order to see whether they are verified or confuted by our empirical observations. But the mystic, so far from producing propositions which are empirically verified, is unable to produce any intelligible propositions at all. And therefore we say that his intuition has not revealed to him any facts. It is no use his saying that he has apprehended facts but is unable to express them. For we know that if he really had acquired any information, he would be able to express it. He would be able to indicate in some way or other how the genuineness of his discovery might be empirically determined. The fact that he cannot reveal what he "knows," or even himself devise an empirical test to validate his "knowledge," shows that his state of mystical intuition is not a genuinely cognitive state. So that in describing his vision the mystic does not give us any information about the external world; he merely gives us indirect information about the condition of his own mind.

These considerations dispose of the argument from religious experience, which many philosophers still regard as a valid argument in favor of the existence of a god. They say that it is logically possible for men to be immediately acquainted with God, as they are immediately acquainted with a sense-content, and that there is no reason why one should be prepared to believe a man when he says that he is seeing a yellow patch, and refuse to believe him when he says that he is seeing God. The answer to this is that if the man who asserts that he is seeing God is merely asserting that he is experiencing a peculiar kind of sense-content, then we do not for a moment deny that his assertion may be true. But, ordinarily, the man who says that he is seeing God is saying not merely that he is experiencing a religious emotion, but also that there exists a transcendent being who is the object of this emotion; just as the man who says that he sees a yellow patch is ordinarily saying not merely that his visual sense-field contains a yellow sense-content, but also that there exists a yellow object to which the sense-content belongs. And it is not irrational to be prepared to believe a man when he asserts the existence of a yellow object, and to refuse to believe him when he asserts the existence of a transcendent god. For whereas the sentence "There exists here a yellow-colored material thing" expresses a genuine synthetic proposition which could be empirically verified, the sentence "There exists a transcendent god" has, as we have seen, no literal significance.

We conclude, therefore, that the argument from religious experience is altogether fallacious. The fact that people have religious experiences is interesting from the psychological point of view, but it does not in any way imply that there is such a thing as religious knowledge, any more than our having moral experiences implies that there is such a thing as moral knowledge. The theist, like the moralist, may believe that his experiences are cognitive experiences, but, unless you can formulate his "knowledge" in propositions that are empirically verifiable, we may be sure that he is deceiving himself. It follows that those philosophers who fill their books with assertions that they intuitively "know" this or that moral or religious "truth" are merely providing material for the psycho-analyst. For no act of intuition can be said to reveal a truth about any matter of fact unless it issues in verifiable propositions. And all such propositions are to be incorporated in the system of empirical propositions which constitutes science.

READING QUESTIONS

1. What follows, according to Ayer, from the utilitarian assertion that ethical statements of value are a subclass of psychological or sociological judgments?

2. Ayer charges that absolutist theories, which claim that ethical statements are "controlled" not by observation but by intuition, imply that such statements are "unverifiable." How does he substantiate his charge?

3. Why is the charge of unverifiability of ethical statements potentially damaging to these intuitionist theories?

4. According to Ayer, what is the actual function of ethical terms?

5. Why is it impossible to determine a criterion for determining the validity of ethical judgments?

6. In what cases does Ayer think that moral argument is possible?

Jean-Paul Sartre

A bold, innovative approach to ethics, with its roots in French and German philosophy, thrust itself into the popular spotlight after World War II. This alternative view of ethics was the product of a philosophical movement known as **existentialism**. Although a number of philosophers are usually considered existentialist—Kierkegaard, Nietzsche, Camus, Merleau-Ponty, and Jaspers are some examples—the French philosopher Jean-Paul Sartre was one of the first to label himself an existentialist.

Born in Paris in 1905, Sartre studied philosophy in both France and Germany. After leaving school he taught in a number of French schools, and he wrote novels, plays, and philosophy, beginning before World War II. During the war he was a soldier in the French army and was captured and imprisoned by the Nazis in 1940. Later he became active in the French Resistance. As the war ended, Sartre became the dominant figure in the existentialism movement. This philosophical and literary movement was causing a sensation in postwar Europe and America, in part because people were excited by its bohemian associations, and also because they longed for meaning in a world that seemed to have lost all meaning.

Sartre wrote a great variety of material, including serious philosophy, reviews, plays, and stories, all of which attempted to communicate his existential view of the human condition. Some of his most successful literary works are *No Exit* (1947), *The Flies* (1947), and *Nausea* (1938). His most important philosophical work, completed during the German occupation of Paris, was *Being and Nothingness* (1943). *Existentialism Is a Humanism* (1946), from which the following excerpt is taken, originated as a lecture in which Sartre attempted to lay out in a clear and unambiguous way the fundamentals of existentialism first presented in *Being and Nothingness*.

Although much of Sartre's writing covers a variety of important, traditional philosophical topics such as **epistemology** (the study of knowledge) and **ontology** (the study of the nature of existence), everything Sartre wrote can be considered to be primarily about ethics. All of his work displays his profoundly moral and humanistic interests. This is because the existentialist movement, especially the atheistic existentialism advocated by Sartre, is at base a study of human *being*. In fact, his greatest philosophical importance lies in his drawing out of the implications of atheism, the belief that God does not exist.

Not all existentialists are atheists, but atheism is central to Sartre's definition. Existentialism, as defined by Sartre, is the philosophical movement that insists that for human beings, existence precedes essence. This means that among all of creation, only humans have no innate purpose or function. Created objects have a purpose, determined by their creator. But, for an atheist like Sartre, people have no creator to predetermine their purpose or to give meaning to their lives. Instead, people unavoidably define themselves and give themselves purpose through their choices. Without God, neither the universe nor anything in it has objective value. Values are created only by human beings, through their choices.

The legacy of existentialism for moral philosophy is mixed. Most moral philosophers in the English-speaking world, recipients of a tradition based on the English philosophers from Hobbes onward, have dismissed existentialism as an insupportable philosophy. However, the influence of existentialism has been much stronger on subsequent philosophy on the Continent and in Latin America. Even though many people consider existentialism depressing or gloomy in its view of the predicament of human beings in a godless world, with its emphasis on alienation, anxiety, and death, many others find in it a philosophy that captures aspects of real human lives ignored by other philosophical movements.

Existentialism Is a Humanism

Existentialism struck a real chord among large numbers of people immediately following World War II. Existential artists, writers, and intellectuals were everywhere the rage. Yet, the philosophical movement known by that name was (and in some quarters remains) a serious challenge to the reigning orthodoxy of scientific and analytic philosophy. In this essay, Sartre attempts to defend the philosophical integrity of existentialism while addressing his ideas to a wide audience, which would include non-philosophers.

Much of the discussion centers around emotional terms that have special meaning for existentialism. Many people find that these emotions characterize something with which they are familiar, even if they are unable to articulate what they are feeling. Even if these emotions do not seem to correspond to your own experience, if you can imagine yourself with the atheistic beliefs of the existentialist that Sartre describes, you may better understand the reason he thinks these emotional states are so important.

What is meant by the term *existentialism*?

Most people who use the word would be rather embarrassed if they had to explain it, since, now that the word is all the rage, even the work of a musician or painter is being called existentialist. A gossip columnist in *Clartés* signs himself *The Existentialist,* so that by this time the word has been so stretched and has taken on so broad a meaning, that it no longer means anything at all. It seems that for want of an advance-guard doctrine analogous to surrealism, the kind of people who are eager for scandal and flurry turn to this philosophy which in other respects does not at all serve their purposes in this sphere.

1. Sartre distinguishes the two types of existentialists and also states what they have in common. Next, he will explain what he means.

Actually, it is the least scandalous, the most austere of doctrines. It is intended strictly for specialists and philosophers. Yet it can be defined easily. What complicates matters is that there are two kinds of existentialist: first, those who are Christian, among whom I would include Jaspers and Gabriel Marcel, both Catholic; and on the

From Jean-Paul Sartre, *Existentialism Is a Humanism,* 1946. Reprinted by permission from Philosophical Library, New York.

other hand the atheistic existentialists, among whom I class Heidegger, and then the French existentialists and myself. What they have in common is that they think that existence precedes essence, or, if you prefer, that subjectivity must be the starting point.

Just what does that mean? Let us consider some object that is manufactured, for example, a book or a paper-cutter: here is an object which has been made by an artisan whose inspiration came from a concept. He referred to the concept of what a paper-cutter is and likewise to a known method of production, which is part of the concept, something which is, by and large, a routine. Thus, the paper-cutter is at once an object produced in a certain way and, on the other hand, one having a specific use; and one cannot postulate a man who produces a paper-cutter but does not know what it is used for. Therefore, let us say that, for the paper-cutter, essence—that is, the ensemble of both the production routines and the properties which enable it to be both produced and defined—precedes existence. Thus, the presence of the paper-cutter or book in front of me is determined. Therefore, we have here a technical view of the world whereby it can be said that production precedes existence.

When we conceive God as the Creator, He is generally thought of as a superior sort of artisan. Whatever doctrine we may be considering, whether one like that of Descartes or that of Leibnitz, we always grant that will more or less follows understanding or, at the very least, accompanies it, and that when God creates He knows exactly what He is creating. Thus, the concept of man in the mind of God is comparable to the concept of paper-cutter in the mind of the manufacturer, and, following certain techniques and a conception, God produces man, just as the artisan, following a definition and a technique, makes a paper-cutter. Thus, the individual man is the realization of a certain concept in the divine intelligence.

In the eighteenth century, the atheism of the *philosophes* discarded the idea of God, but not so much for the notion that essence precedes existence. To a certain extent, this idea is found everywhere; we find it in Diderot, in Voltaire, and even in Kant. Man has a human nature; this human nature, which is the concept of the human, is found in all men, which means that each man is a particular example of a universal concept, man. In Kant, the result of this universality is that the wild-man, the natural man, as well as the bourgeois, are circumscribed by the same definition and have the same basic qualities. Thus, here too the essence of man precedes the historical existence that we find in nature.

Atheistic existentialism, which I represent, is more coherent. It states that if God does not exist, there is at least one being in whom existence precedes essence, a being who exists before he can be defined by any concept, and that this being is man, or, as Heidegger says, human reality. What is meant here by saying that existence precedes essence? It means that, first of all, man exists, turns up, appears on the scene, and, only afterwards, defines himself. If man, as the existentialist conceives him, is indefinable, it is because at first he is nothing. Only afterward will he be something, and he himself will have made what he will be. Thus, there is no human nature, since there is no God to conceive it. Not only is man what he conceives himself to be, but he is also only what he wills himself to be after this thrust toward existence.

---

2. For existentialists, human beings are different from other things that exist, and this difference leads to an enormous burden of responsibility. In the following paragraphs, Sartre presents an argument for his extended notion of responsibility.

Man is nothing else but what he makes of himself. Such is the first principle of existentialism. It is also what is called subjectivity, the name we are labeled with when charges are brought against us. But what do we mean by this, if not that man has a greater dignity than a stone or table? For we mean that man first exists, that is, that man first of all is the being who hurls himself toward a future and who is conscious of imagining himself as being in the future. Man is at the start a plan which is aware of itself, rather than a patch of moss, a piece of garbage, or a cauliflower; nothing exists prior to this plan; there is nothing in heaven; man will be what he will have planned to be. Not what he will want to be. Because by the word "will" we generally mean a conscious decision, which is subsequent to what we have already made of ourselves. I may want to belong to a political party, write a book, get married; but all that is only a manifestation of an earlier, more spontaneous choice that is called "will." But if existence really does precede essence, man is responsible for what he is. Thus, existentialism's first move is to make every man aware of what he is and to make the full responsibility of his existence rest on him. And when we say that a man is responsible for himself, we do not only mean that he is responsible for his own individuality, but that he is responsible for all men.

The word "subjectivism" has two meanings, and our opponents play on the two. Subjectivism means, on the one hand, that an individual chooses and makes himself; and, on the other, that it is impossible for man to transcend human subjectivity. The second of these is the essential meaning of existentialism. When we say that man chooses his own self, we mean that every one of us does likewise; but we also mean by that that in making this choice he also chooses all men. In fact, in creating the man that we want to be, there is not a single one of our acts which does not at the same time create an image of man as we think he ought to be. To choose to be this or that is to affirm at the same time the value of what we choose, because we can never choose evil. We always choose the good, and nothing can be good for us without being good for all.

If, on the other hand, existence precedes essence, and if we grant that we exist and fashion our image at one and the same time, the image is valid for everybody and for our whole age. Thus, our responsibility is much greater than we might have supposed, because it involves all mankind. If I am a workingman and choose to join a Christian trade-union rather than be a communist, and if by being a member I want to show that the best thing for man is resignation, that the kingdom of man is not of this world, I am not only involving my own case—I want to be resigned for everyone. As a result, my action has involved all humanity. To take a more individual matter, if I want to marry, to have children; even if this marriage depends solely on my own circumstances or passion or wish, I am involving all humanity in monogamy and not merely myself. Therefore, I am responsible for myself and for everyone else. I am creating a certain image of man of my own choosing. In choosing myself, I choose man.

---

3. Sartre introduces, and then explains, three critical concepts of existentialism. Have you ever experienced these feelings as he describes them?

This helps us understand what the actual content is of such rather grandiloquent words as anguish, forlornness, despair. As you will see, it's all quite simple.

First, what is meant by anguish? The existentialists say at once that man is anguish. What that means is this: the man who involves himself and who realizes that he is not only the person he chooses to be, but also a law-maker who is, at the same time, choosing all mankind as well as himself, cannot help escape the feeling of his total and deep responsibility. Of course, there are many people who are not anxious; but we claim that they are hiding their anxiety, that they are fleeing from it. Certainly, many people believe that when they do something, they themselves are the only ones involved, and when someone says to them, "What if everyone acted that way?" they shrug their shoulders and answer, "Everyone doesn't act that way." But really, one should always ask himself, "What would happen if everybody looked at things that way?" There is no escaping this disturbing thought except by a kind of double-dealing. A man who lies and makes excuses for himself by saying "not everybody does that," is someone with an uneasy conscience, because the act of lying implies that a universal value is conferred upon the lie.

Anguish is evident even when it conceals itself. This is the anguish that Kierkegaard called the anguish of Abraham. You know the story: an angel has ordered Abraham to sacrifice his son; if it really were an angel who has come and said, "You are Abraham, you shall sacrifice your son," everything would be all right. But everyone might first wonder, "Is it really an angel, and am I really Abraham? What proof do I have?"

There was a madwoman who had hallucinations; someone used to speak to her on the telephone and give her orders. Her doctor asked her, "Who is it who talks to you?" She answered, "He says it's God." What proof did she really have that it was God? If an angel comes to me, what proof is there that it's an angel? And if I hear voices, what proof is there that they come from heaven and not from hell, or from the subconscious, or a pathological condition? What proves that they are addressed to me? What proof is there that I have been appointed to impose my choice and my conception of man on humanity? I'll never find any proof or sign to convince me of that. If a voice addresses me, it is always for me to decide that this is the angel's voice; if I consider that such an act is a good one, it is I who will choose to say that it is good rather than bad.

Now, I'm not being singled out as an Abraham, and yet at every moment I'm obliged to perform exemplary acts. For every man, everything happens as if all mankind had its eyes fixed on him and were guiding itself by what he does. And every man ought to say to himself, "Am I really the kind of man who has the right to act in such a way that humanity might guide itself by my actions?" And if he does not say that to himself, he is masking his anguish.

There is no question here of the kind of anguish which would lead to quietism, to inaction. It is a matter of a simple sort of anguish that anybody who has had responsibilities is familiar with. For example, when a military officer takes the responsibility for an attack and sends a certain number of men to death, he chooses to do so, and in the main he alone makes the choice. Doubtless, orders come from above, but they are too broad; he interprets them, and on this interpretation depend the lives of ten or fourteen or twenty men. In making a decision he cannot help having a certain anguish. All leaders know this anguish. That doesn't keep them from acting; on the contrary, it is the very condition of their action. For it implies that they envisage a number of possibilities, and when they choose one, they realize that it has value only because it is chosen. We shall see that this kind of anguish, which is the kind that existentialism describes, is explained, in addition, by a direct responsibility to the other men whom it involves. It is not a curtain separating us from action, but is part of action itself.

-----

4. As Sartre defines and explains forlornness, he argues against the idea that universal values exist even without God.

When we speak of forlornness, a term Heidegger was fond of, we mean only that God does not exist and that we have to face all the consequences of this. The existentialist is strongly opposed to a certain kind of secular ethics which would like to abolish God with the least possible expense. About 1880, some French teachers tried to set up a secular ethics which went something like this: God is a useless and costly hypothesis; we are discarding it; but, meanwhile, in order for there to be an ethics, a society, a civilization, it is essential that certain values be taken seriously and that they be considered as having an *a priori* existence. It must be obligatory, *a priori*, to be honest, not to lie, not to beat your wife, to have children, etc., etc. So we're going to try a little device which will make it possible to show that values exist all the same, inscribed in a heaven of ideas, though otherwise God does not exist. In other words—and this, I believe, is the tendency of everything called reformism in France—nothing will be changed if God does not exist. We shall find ourselves with the same norms of honesty, progress, and humanism, and we shall have made of God an outdated hypothesis which will peacefully die off by itself.

The existentialist, on the contrary, thinks it very distressing that God does not exist, because all possibility of finding values in a heaven of ideas disappears along with Him; there can no longer be an *a priori* Good, since there is no infinite and perfect consciousness to think it. Nowhere is it written that the Good exists, that we must be honest, that we must not lie; because the fact is we are on a plane where there are only men. Dostoyevsky said, "If God didn't exist, everything would be possible." That is the very starting point of existentialism. Indeed, everything is permissible if God does not exist, and as a result man is forlorn, because neither within him nor without does he find anything to cling to. He can't start making excuses for himself.

If existence really does precede essence, there is no explaining things away by reference to a fixed and given human nature. In other words, there is no determinism, man is free, man is freedom. On the other hand, if God does not exist, we find no values or commands to turn to which legitimize our conduct. So, in the bright realm of values, we have no excuse behind us, nor justification before us. We are alone, with no excuses.

That is the idea I shall try to convey when I say that man is condemned to be free. Condemned, because he did not create himself, yet, in other respects is free; because, once thrown into the world, he is responsible for everything he does. The existentialist does not believe in the power of passion. He will never agree that a sweeping passion is a ravaging torrent which fatally leads a man to certain acts and is therefore an excuse. He thinks that man is responsible for his passion.

The existentialist does not think that man is going to help himself by finding in the world some omen by which to orient himself. Because he thinks that man will interpret the omen to suit himself. Therefore, he thinks that man, with no support and no aid, is condemned every moment to invent man. Ponge, in a very fine article, has said, "Man is the future of man." That's exactly it. But if it is taken to mean that this future is recorded in heaven, that God sees it, then it is false, because it would really no longer be a future. If it is taken to mean that, whatever a man may be, there is a future to be forged, a virgin future before him, then this remark is sound. But then we are forlorn.

---

5. An example serves to illustrate, and dramatize, what Sartre means by forlornness. Notice how, in the example, the boy finds other systems of values (for example, Christianity and Kantianism) ineffective in helping him choose the right action.

To give you an example which will enable you to understand forlornness better, I shall cite the case of one of my students who came to see me under the following circumstances: his father was on bad terms with his mother, and, moreover, was inclined to be a collaborationist; his older brother had been killed in the German offensive of 1940, and the young man, with somewhat immature but generous feelings, wanted to avenge him. His mother lived alone with him, very much upset by the half-treason of her husband and the death of her older son; the boy was her only consolation.

The boy was faced with the choice of leaving for England and joining the Free French Forces—that is, leaving his mother behind—or remaining with his mother and helping her to carry on. He was fully aware that the woman lived only for him and that his going-off—and perhaps his death—would plunge her into despair. He was also aware that every act that he did for his mother's sake was a sure thing, in the sense that it was helping her to carry on, whereas every effort he made toward going off and fighting was an uncertain move which might run aground and prove completely useless; for example, on his way to England he might, while passing through Spain, be detained indefinitely in a Spanish camp; he might reach England or Algiers and be stuck in an office at a desk job. As a result, he was faced with two very different kinds of action: one, concrete, immediate, but concerning only one individual; the other concerned an incomparably vaster group, a national collectivity, but for that very reason was dubious, and might be interrupted en route. And, at the same time, he was wavering between two kinds of ethics. On the one hand, an ethics of sympathy, of personal devotion; on the other, a broader ethics, but one whose efficacy was more dubious. He had to choose between the two.

Who could help him choose? Christian doctrine? No. Christian doctrine says, "Be charitable, love your neighbor, take the more rugged path, etc., etc." But which is the more rugged path? Whom should he love as a brother? The fighting man or his mother? Which does the greater good, the vague act of fighting in a group, or the concrete one of helping a particular human being to go on living? Who can decide *a priori*? Nobody. No book of ethics can tell him. The Kantian ethics says, "Never treat any person as a means, but as an end." Very well, if I stay with my mother, I'll treat her as an end and not as a means; but by virtue of this very fact, I'm running the risk of treating the people around me who are fighting, as means; and, conversely, if I go to join those who are fighting, I'll be treating them as an end, and, by doing that, I run the risk of treating my mother as a means.

If values are vague, and if they are always too broad for the concrete and specific case that we are considering, the only thing left for us is to trust our instincts. That's what this young man tried to do; and when I saw him, he said, "In the end, feeling is what counts. I ought to choose whichever pushes me in one direction. If I feel that I love my mother enough to sacrifice everything else for her—my desire for vengeance, for action, for adventure—then I'll stay with her. If, on the contrary, I feel that my love for my mother isn't enough, I'll leave."

But how is the value of a feeling determined? What gives his feeling for his mother value? Precisely the fact that he remained with her. I may say that I like so-and-so well enough to sacrifice a certain amount of money for him, but I may say so only if I've done it. I may say, "I love my mother well enough to remain with her" if I have remained with her. The only way to determine the value of this affection is, precisely, to perform an act which confirms and defines it. But, since I require this affection to justify my act, I find myself caught in a vicious circle.

On the other hand, Gide has well said that a mock feeling and a true feeling are almost indistinguishable; to decide that I love my mother and will remain with her, or to remain with her by putting on an act, amount somewhat to the same thing. In other words, the feeling is formed by the acts one performs; so, I cannot refer to it in order to act upon it. Which means that I can neither seek within myself the true condition which will impel me to act, nor apply to a system of ethics for concepts which will permit me to act. You will say, "At least, he did go to a teacher for advice." But if you seek advice from a priest, for example, you have chosen this priest; you already knew, more or less, just about what advice he was going to give you. In other words, choosing your adviser is involving yourself. The proof of this is that if you are a Christian, you will say, "Consult a priest." But some priests are collaborating, some are just marking time, some are resisting. Which to choose? If the young man chooses a priest who is resisting or collaborating, he has already decided on the kind of advice he's going to get. Therefore, in coming to see me he knew the answer I was going to give him, and I had only one answer to give: "You're free, choose, that is, invent." No general ethics can show you what is to be done; there are no omens in the world. The Catholics will reply, "But there are." Granted—but, in any case, I myself choose the meaning they have.

When I was a prisoner, I knew a rather remarkable young man who was a Jesuit. He had entered the Jesuit order in the following way: he had had a number of very bad breaks; in childhood, his father died, leaving him in poverty, and he was a scholarship student at a religious institution where he was constantly made to feel that he was being kept out of charity; then, he failed to get any of the honors and distinctions that children like; later on, at about eighteen, he bungled a love affair; finally, at twenty-two, he failed in military training, a childish enough matter, but it was the last straw.

This young fellow might well have felt that he had botched everything. It was a sign of something, but of what? He might have taken refuge in bitterness or despair. But he very wisely looked upon all this as a sign that he was not made for secular triumphs, and that only the triumphs of religion, holiness, and faith were open to him. He saw the hand of God in all this, and so he entered the order. Who can help seeing that he alone decided what the sign meant?

Some other interpretation might have been drawn from this series of setbacks; for example, that he might have done better to turn carpenter or revolutionist. Therefore, he is fully responsible for the interpretation. Forlornness implies that we ourselves choose our being. Forlornness and anguish go together.

---

6. The last of the three key existentialist concepts, despair, is the subject of the following paragraphs. Why should despair be associated with these events, over which we have no control?

As for despair, the term has a very simple meaning. It means that we shall confine ourselves to reckoning only with what depends upon our will, or on the ensemble of probabilities which make our action possible. When we want something, we always have to reckon with probabilities. I may be counting on the arrival of a friend. The friend is coming by rail or street-car; this supposes that the train will arrive on schedule, or that the street-car will not jump the track. I am left in the realm of possibility; but possibilities are to be reckoned with only to the point where my action comports with the ensemble of these possibilities, and no further. The moment the possibilities I am considering are not rigorously involved by my action, I ought to disengage myself from them, because no God, no scheme, can adapt the world and its possibilities to my will. When Descartes said, "Conquer yourself rather than the world," he meant essentially the same thing.

The Marxists to whom I have spoken reply, "You can rely on the support of others in your action, which obviously has certain limits because you're not going to live forever. That means: rely on both what others are doing elsewhere to help you, in China, in Russia, and what they will do later on, after your death, to carry on the action and lead it to its fulfillment, which will be the revolution. You even *have* to rely upon that, otherwise you're immoral." I reply at once that I will always rely on fellow-fighters insofar as these comrades are involved with me in a common struggle, in the unity of a party or a group in which I can more or less make my weight felt; that is, one whose ranks I am in as a fighter and whose movements I am aware of at every moment. In such a situation, relying on the unity and will of the party is exactly like counting on the fact that the train will arrive on time or that the car won't jump the track. But, given that man is free and that there is no human nature for me to depend on, I cannot count on men whom I do not know by relying on human goodness or man's concern for the good of society. I don't know what will become of the Russian revolution; I may make an example of it to the extent that at the present time it is apparent that the proletariat plays a part in Russia that it plays in no other nation. But I can't swear that this will inevitably lead to a triumph of the proletariat. I've got to limit myself to what I see.

Given that men are free and that tomorrow they will freely decide what man will be, I cannot be sure that, after my death, fellow-fighters will carry on my work to bring it to its maximum perfection. Tomorrow, after my death, some men may decide to set up Fascism, and the others may be cowardly and muddled enough to let them do it. Fascism will then be the human reality, so much the worse for us.

Actually, things will be as man will have decided they are to be. Does that mean that I should abandon myself to quietism? No. First, I should involve myself; then, act on the old saw, "Nothing ventured, nothing gained." Nor does it mean that I shouldn't belong to a party, but rather that I shall have no illusions and shall do what I can. For example, suppose I ask myself, "Will socialization, as such, ever come about?" I know nothing about it. All I know is that I'm going to do everything in my power to bring it about. Beyond that, I can't count on anything. Quietism is the attitude of people who say, "Let others do what I can't do." The doctrine I am presenting is the very opposite of quietism, since it declares, "There is no reality except in action." Moreover, it goes further, since it adds, "Man is nothing else than his plan; he exists only to the extent that he fulfills himself; he is therefore nothing else than the ensemble of his acts, nothing else than his life."

According to this, we can understand why our doctrine horrifies certain people. Because often the only way they can bear their wretchedness is to think, "Circumstances have been against me. What I've been and done doesn't show my true worth. To be sure, I've had no great love, no great friendship, but that's because I haven't met a man or woman who was worthy. The books I've written haven't been very good because I haven't had the proper leisure. I haven't had children to devote myself to because I didn't find a man with whom I could have spent my life. So there remains within me, unused and quite viable, a host of propensities, inclinations, possibilities, that one wouldn't guess from the mere series of things I've done."

Now, for the existentialist there is really no love other than one which manifests itself in a person's being in love. There is no genius other than one which is expressed in works of art; the genius of Proust is the sum of Proust's works; the genius of Racine is his series of tragedies. Outside of that, there is nothing. Why say that Racine could have written another tragedy, when he didn't write it? A man is involved in life, leaves his impress on it, and outside of that there is nothing. To be sure, this may seem a harsh thought to someone whose life hasn't been a success. But, on the other hand, it prompts people to understand that reality alone is what counts, that dreams, expectations, and hopes warrant no more than to define a man as a disappointed dream, as miscarried hopes, as vain expectations. In other words, to define him negatively and not positively. However, when we say, "You are nothing else than your life," that does not imply that the artist will be judged solely on the basis of his works of art; a thousand other things will contribute toward summing him up. What we mean is that a man is nothing else than a series of undertakings, that he is the sum, the organization, the ensemble of the relationships which make up these undertakings.

READING QUESTIONS

1. What are the two types of existentialists?
2. What is the essence of a paper-cutter?
3. According to Sartre, why is there no human nature?
4. What is a human being responsible for, according to Sartre?
5. What emotional state characterizes the person who understands the totality of his or her responsibility?
6. What is "forlornness"?
7. What does Sartre mean when he says that people are "condemned to be free"?
8. Why doesn't the moral philosophy of Kant help the young man make the proper choice between staying with his mother and joining the Free French Forces?

G. E. M. Anscombe

The historical tradition of Western moral philosophy has been the search for a **normative ethical theory**. A normative ethical theory tries to set out the way we ought to live. Thus, its interests are the obligations people have to their fellow creatures, whether actions such as telling lies and keeping promises are right or wrong, and the details of a fair society. However, with the publication of G. E. Moore's *Principia Ethica* in 1903, the ability of philosophers to construct a normative ethical theory was seriously called into question. As a result, in the first half of the twentieth century, moral philosophy (especially in England and the United States) became increasingly concerned with the analysis of the language and logic of ethics, what philosophers call **metaethics**. The emotivism of A. J. Ayer is a good example of this kind of moral philosophy.

By mid-century, however, a renewed interest in normative ethics began to emerge. Although many metaethical issues are still of great interest to moral philosophers in the United States and elsewhere, recent work in normative ethics has built on and pushed forward the work of the great philosophers of the past.

"Modern Moral Philosophy" by G. E. M. Anscombe was the beginning point of a renewed interest in an approach to moral philosophy that had not received much attention for, literally, millennia. Many moral philosophers had grown dissatisfied with both of the predominant theories of normative ethics, **utilitarianism** and **Kant's duty theory**. They found themselves persuaded by Anscombe's call in this article to turn moral philosophy away from its discussions of moral obligation and right action. These concepts, Anscombe argued, belong to an ethical theory built on an earlier conception of ethics, one requiring a divine moral law that is not applicable to moral philosophy in the twentieth century. According to Anscombe, discussing what one ought to do— what is right and what is wrong—no longer contributed any benefit to moral philosophy. As an alternative, Anscombe encouraged moral philosophers to turn their attention to virtues, moral norms, and character.

Largely because of the influence of Anscombe's landmark article, moral philosophers revived an interest in the ethical writings of Aristotle, with their focus on virtues, norms, and character. The theory that has developed from this twentieth-century philosophical direction—typically called **virtue ethics**—emphasizes the *character* of the moral person rather than the rightness or wrongness of actions. For the virtue theorist, the question to be answered in moral philosophy is, What kind of person should I be? rather than, What kind of acts should I perform? For a more recent article that addresses concerns about the virtues and character, see "Moral Saints" by Susan Wolf later in this volume.

Modern Moral Philosophy

When people try to convince one another to act in some way rather than another, to carry out one action as opposed to an alternative, they often

From G. E. M. Anscombe, "Modern Moral Philosophy," *Philosophy,* Vol. 33 (January 1958), pp. 1–15. Reprinted with the permission of Cambridge University Press.

charge that the person "ought" to act in this way. We all know what this means. If I ought to do something, it means that I will be acting immorally if I don't do it. It is this sense of moral sanction hanging over our heads that makes people think that the things they *ought* to do are just those things that they never *want* to do. It all sounds so punitive and lawlike.

This is the notion that Anscombe investigates in this article. What is it that gives the "ought" such force? If it is to have force, then it must rely on some concept of law. And it is in this issue that Anscombe sees trouble for most theories of moral philosophy. They no longer have the concept of law serving as a foundation for their concept of moral sanction: the concept that a person "ought" to do some particular act or refrain from another act. This article raised serious questions for these theories and led a great number of philosophers to reappraise ethical theories that emphasized moral character. ✍

---

1. The three theses of this work are presented in the first paragraph.

I will begin by stating three theses which I present in this paper. The first is that it is not profitable for us at present to do moral philosophy; that should be laid aside at any rate until we have an adequate philosophy of psychology, in which we are conspicuously lacking. The second is that the concepts of obligation, and duty—*moral* obligation and *moral* duty, that is to say—and of what is *morally* right and wrong, and of the *moral* sense of "ought," ought to be jettisoned if this is psychologically possible; because they are survivals, or derivatives from survivals, from an earlier conception of ethics which no longer generally survives, and are only harmful without it. My third thesis is that the differences between the well-known English writers on moral philosophy from Sidgwick to the present day are of little importance.

Anyone who has read Aristotle's *Ethics* and has also read modern moral philosophy must have been struck by the great contrasts between them. The concepts which are prominent among the moderns seem to be lacking, or at any rate buried or far in the background, in Aristotle. Most noticeably, the term "moral" itself, which we have by direct inheritance from Aristotle, just doesn't seem to fit, in its modern sense, into an account of Aristotelian ethics. Aristotle distinguishes virtues as moral and intellectual. Have some of what he calls "intellectual" virtues what *we* should call a "moral" aspect? It would seem so; the criterion is presumably that a failure in an "intellectual" virtue—like that of having good judgment in calculating how to bring about something useful, say in municipal government—may be *blameworthy*. But—it may reasonably be asked—cannot *any* failure be made a matter of blame or reproach? Any derogatory criticism, say of the workmanship of a product or the design of a machine, can be called blame or reproach. So we want to put in the word "morally" again: sometimes such a failure may be *morally* blameworthy, sometimes not. Now has Aristotle got this idea of *moral* blame, as opposed to any other? If he has, why isn't it more central? There are some mistakes, he says, which are causes, not of involuntariness in actions, but of scoundrelism, and for which a man is blamed. Does this mean that there is a *moral* obligation not to make certain intellectual mistakes? Why doesn't he discuss obligation in general, and this obligation in particular? If someone professes to be expounding Aristotle and talks in a modern fashion about "moral" such-and-such, he must be very imperceptive if he does not constantly feel like someone whose jaws have somehow got out of alignment: the teeth don't come together in a proper bite.

We cannot, then, look to Aristotle for any elucidation of the modern way of talking about "moral" goodness, obligation, etc. And all the best-known writers on ethics in modern times, from Butler to Mill, appear to me to have faults as thinkers on the subject which make it impossible to hope for any direct light on it from them. I will state these objections with the brevity which their character makes possible.

Butler exalts conscience, but appears ignorant that a man's conscience may tell him to do the vilest things.

Hume defines "truth" in such a way as to exclude ethical judgments from it, and professes that he has proved that they are so excluded. He also implicitly defines "passion" in such a way that aiming at anything is having a passion. His objection to passing from "is" to "ought" would apply equally to passing from "is" to "owes" or from "is" to "needs." (However, because of the historical situation, he has a point here, which I shall return to.)

Kant introduces the idea of "legislating for oneself," which is as absurd as if in these days, when majority votes command great respect, one were to call each reflective decision a man made a *vote* resulting in a majority, which as a matter of proportion is overwhelming, for it is always 1–0. The concept of legislation requires superior power in the legislator. His own rigoristic convictions on the subject of lying were so intense that it never occurred to him that a lie could be relevantly described as anything but just a lie (e.g., as "a lie in such-and-such circumstances"). His rule about universalizable maxims is useless without stipulations as to what shall count as a relevant description of an action with a view to constructing a maxim about it.

Bentham and Mill do not notice the difficulty of the concept "pleasure." They are often said to have gone wrong through committing the "naturalistic fallacy"; but this charge does not impress me because I do not find accounts of it coherent. But the other point—about pleasure—seems to me a fatal objection from the very outset. The ancients found this concept pretty baffling. It reduced Aristotle to sheer babble about "the bloom on the cheek of youth" because, for good reasons, he wanted to make it out both identical with and different from the pleasurable activity. Generations of modern philosophers found this concept quite unperplexing, and it reappeared in the literature as a problematic one only a year or two ago when Ryle wrote about it. The reason is simple: since Locke, pleasure was taken to be some sort of internal impression. But it was superficial, if that was the right account of it, to make it the point of actions. One might adapt something Wittgenstein said about "meaning" and say, "Pleasure cannot be an internal impression, for no internal impression could have the consequences of pleasure."

Mill also, like Kant, fails to realize the necessity for stipulation as to relevant descriptions, if his theory is to have content. It did not occur to him that acts of murder and theft could be otherwise described. He holds that where a proposed action is of such a kind as to fall under some one principle established on grounds of utility, one must go by that; where it falls under none or several, the several suggesting contrary views of the action, the thing to do is to calculate particular consequences. But pretty well any action can be so described as to make it fall under a variety of principles of utility (as I shall say for short) if it falls under any.

---

2. After Anscombe has criticized earlier philosophers, she turns the focus to Hume. Anscombe gives an example of the importance of Hume's work.

I will now return to Hume. The features of Hume's philosophy which I have mentioned, like many other features of it, would incline me to think that Hume was a mere—brilliant—sophist; and his procedures are certainly sophistical. But I am forced, not to reverse, but to add to, this judgment by a peculiarity of Hume's philosophizing: namely that although he reaches his conclusions—with which he is in love—by sophistical methods, his considerations constantly open up very deep and important problems. It is often the case that in the act of exhibiting the sophistry one finds oneself noticing matters which deserve a lot of exploring: the obvious stands in need of investigation as a result of the points that Hume pretends to have made. In this, he is unlike, say, Butler. It was already well known that conscience could dictate vile actions; for Butler to have written disregarding this does not open up any new topics for us. But with Hume it is otherwise: hence he is a very profound and great philosopher, in spite of his sophistry. For example:

Suppose that I say to my grocer "Truth consists in *either* relations of ideas, as that 20s. = £1, or matters of fact, as that I ordered potatoes, you supplied them, and you sent me a bill. So it doesn't apply to such a proposition as that I *owe* you such-and-such a sum."

Now if one makes this comparison, it comes to light that the relation of the facts mentioned to the description "X owes Y so much money" is an interesting one, which I will call that of being "brute relative to" that description. Further, the "brute" facts mentioned here themselves have descriptions relatively to which *other* facts are "brute"—as, e.g., *he had potatoes carted to my house* and *they were left there* are brute facts relative to "he supplied me with potatoes." And the fact X *owes* Y *money* is in turn "brute" relative to other descriptions—e.g., "X is solvent." Now the relation of "relative bruteness" is a complicated one. To mention a few points: if xyz is a set of facts brute relative to a description A, then xyz is a set out of a range some set among which holds if A holds; but the holding of some set among these does not necessarily entail A, because exceptional circumstances can always make a difference; and what are exceptional circumstances relatively to A can generally only be explained by giving a few diverse examples, and *no* theoretically adequate provision can be made for exceptional circumstances, since a further special context can theoretically always be imagined that would reinterpret any special context. Further, though in normal circumstances, xyz would be a justification for A, that is not to say that A just comes to the same as "xyz"; and also there is apt to be an institutional context which gives its point to the description A, of which institution A is of course not itself a description. (E.g., the statement that I give someone a shilling is not a description of the institution of money or of the currency of this country.) Thus, though it would be ludicrous to pretend that there can be no such thing as a transition from, e.g., "is" to "owes," the character of the transition is in fact rather interesting and comes to light as a result of reflecting on Hume's arguments.

That I owe the grocer such-and-such a sum would be one of a set of facts which would be "brute" in relation to the description "I am a bilker." "Bilking" is of course a species of "dishonesty" or "injustice." (Naturally the consideration will not have any effect on my actions unless I want to commit or avoid acts of injustice.)

So far, in spite of their strong associations, I conceive "bilking," "injustice" and "dishonesty" in a merely "factual" way. That I can do this for "bilking" is obvious enough; "justice" I have no idea how to define, except that its sphere is that of actions which relate to someone else, but "injustice," its defect, can for the moment be offered as a generic name covering various species: e.g., "bilking," "theft" (which is relative to whatever property institutions exist), "slander," "adultery," "punishment of the innocent."

3. How do we connect "unjust" to "bad"?

In present-day philosophy an explanation is required how an unjust man is a bad man, or an unjust action a bad one; to give such an explanation belongs to ethics; but it cannot even be begun until we are equipped with a sound philosophy of psychology. For the proof that an unjust man is a bad man would require a positive account of justice as a "virtue." This part of the subject-matter of ethics is, however, completely closed to us until we have an account of what *type of characteristic* a virtue is—a problem, not of ethics, but of conceptual analysis—and how it relates to the actions in which it is instanced: a matter which I think Aristotle did not succeed in really making clear. For this we certainly need an account at least of what a human action is at all, and how its description as "doing such-and-such" is affected by its motive and by the intention or intentions in it; and for this an account of such concepts is required.

The terms "should" or "ought" or "needs" relate to good and bad: e.g., machinery needs oil, or should or ought to be oiled, in that running without oil is bad for it, or it runs badly without oil. According to this conception, of course, "should" and "ought" are not used in a special "moral" sense when one says that a man should not bilk. (In Aristotle's sense of the term "moral" (ἠθικός), they are being used in connection with a *moral* subject-matter: namely that of human passions and (non-technical) actions.) But they have now acquired a special so-called "moral" sense—i.e., a sense in which they imply some absolute verdict (like one of guilty/not guilty on a man) on what is described in the "ought" sentences used in certain types of context: not merely the contexts that *Aristotle* would call "moral"—passions and actions—but also some of the contexts that he would call "intellectual."

4. An important conclusion is being drawn. The origin of this connection with law will be discussed next.

The ordinary (and quite indispensable) terms "should," "needs," "ought," "must"—acquired this special sense by being equated in the relevant contexts with "is obliged," or "is bound," or "is required to," in the sense in which one can be obliged or bound by law, or something can be required by law.

How did this come about? The answer is in history: between Aristotle and us came Christianity, with its *law* conception of ethics. For Christianity derived its ethical notions from the Torah. (One might be inclined to think that a law conception of ethics could arise only among people who accepted an allegedly divine positive law; that this is not so is shown by the example of the Stoics, who also thought that whatever was involved in conformity to human virtues was required by divine law.)

In consequence of the dominance of Christianity for many centuries, the concepts of being bound, permitted, or excused became deeply embedded in our language and thought. The Greek word "ἁμαρτάνειν," the aptest to be turned to that use, acquired the sense "sin," from having meant "mistake," "missing the mark," "going wrong." The Latin *peccatum,* which roughly corresponded to ἁμάρτημα, was even apter for the sense "sin," because it was already associated with "culpa"—"guilt"—a juridical notion. The blanket term "illicit," "unlawful," meaning much the same as our blanket term "wrong," explains itself. It is interesting that Aristotle did not have such a blanket term. He has blanket terms for wickedness—"villain," "scoundrel"; but of course a man is not a villain or a scoundrel by the performance of one bad action, or a few bad actions. And he has terms like "disgraceful," "impious"; and specific terms signifying defect of the relevant virtue, like "unjust"; but no term corresponding to "illicit." The extension of this term (i.e., the range of its application) could be indicated in his terminology only by a quite lengthy sentence: that is "illicit" which, whether it is a thought or a consented-to passion or an action or an omission in thought or action, is something contrary to one of the virtues the lack of which shows a man to be bad *qua* man. That formulation would yield a concept co-extensive with the concept "illicit."

------

5. Here is a main point for the connection of "unjust" to "bad" begun earlier. Can you state in your own words how a law is required to connect those terms?

To have a *law* conception of ethics is to hold that what is needed for conformity with the virtues failure in which is the mark of being bad *qua* man (and not merely, say, *qua* craftsman or logician)—that what is needed for *this,* is required by divine law. Naturally it is not possible to have such a conception unless you believe in God as a lawgiver; like Jews, Stoics, and Christians. But if such a conception is dominant for many centuries, and then is given up, it is a natural result that the concepts of "obligation," of being bound or required as by a law, should remain though they had lost their root; and if the word "ought" has become invested in certain contexts with the sense of "obligation," it too will remain to be spoken with a special emphasis and a special feeling in these contexts.

It is as if the notion "criminal" were to remain when criminal law and criminal courts had been abolished and forgotten. A Hume discovering this situation might conclude that there was a special sentiment, expressed by "criminal," which alone gave the word its sense. So Hume discovered the situation in which the notion "obligation" survived, and the notion "ought" was invested with that peculiar force having which it is said to be used in a "moral" sense, but in which the belief in divine law had long since been abandoned: for it was substantially given up among Protestants at the time of the Reformation.[1] The situation, if I am right, was the interesting one of the survival of a concept outside the framework of thought that made it a really intelligible one.

------

[1]They did not deny the existence of divine law; but their most characteristic doctrine was that it was given, not to be obeyed, but to show man's incapacity to obey it, even by grace; and this applied not merely to the ramified prescriptions of the Torah, but to the requirements of "natural divine law." Cf. in this connection the decree of Trent against the teaching that Christ was only to be trusted in as mediator, not obeyed as legislator.

When Hume produced his famous remarks about the transition from "is" to "ought," he was, then, bringing together several quite different points. One I have tried to bring out by my remarks on the transition from "is" to "owes" and on the relative "bruteness" of facts. It would be possible to bring out a different point by enquiring about the transition from "is" to "needs"; from the characteristics of an organism to the environment that it needs, for example. To say that it needs that environment is not to say, e.g., that you want it to have that environment, but that it won't flourish unless it has it. Certainly, it all depends whether you *want* it to flourish! as Hume would say. But what "all depends" on whether you want it to flourish is whether the fact that it needs that environment, or won't flourish without it, has the slightest influence on your actions. Now *that* such-and-such "ought" to be or "is needed" is supposed to have an influence on your actions: from which it seemed natural to infer that to judge that it "ought to be" was in fact to grant what you judged "ought to be" influence on your actions. And no amount of truth as to what *is* the case could possibly have a logical claim to have influence on your actions. (It is not judgment as such that sets us in motion; but our judgment on how to get or do something we *want*.) Hence it *must* be impossible to infer "needs" or "ought to be" from "is." But in the case of a plant, let us say, the inference from "is" to "needs" is certainly not in the least dubious. It is interesting and worth examining; but not at all fishy. Its interest is similar to the interest of the relation between brute and less brute facts: these relations have been very little considered. And while you can contrast "what it needs" with "what it's got"—like contrasting *de facto* and *de jure*—that does not make its needing this environment less of a "truth."

Certainly in the case of what the plant needs, the thought of a need will only affect action if you want the plant to flourish. Here, then, there is no necessary connection between what you can judge the plant "needs" and what you want. But there is some sort of necessary connection between what you think *you* need, and what you want. The connection is a complicated one; it is possible *not* to want something that you judge you need. But, e.g., it is not possible never to want *anything* that you judge you need. This, however, is not a fact about the meaning of the word "to need," but about the phenomenon of *wanting*. Hume's reasoning, we might say, in effect, leads one to think it must be about the word "to need," or "to be good for."

Thus we find two problems already wrapped up in the remark about a transition from "is" to "ought"; now supposing that we had clarified the "relative bruteness" of facts on the one hand, and the notions involved in "needing," and "flourishing" on the other—there would *still* remain a third point. For, following Hume, someone might say: Perhaps you have made out your point about a transition from "is" to "owes" and from "is" to "needs": but only at the cost of showing "owes" and "needs" sentences to express a *kind* of truths, a *kind* of facts. And it remains impossible to infer *"morally ought"* from "is" sentences.

This comment, it seems to me, would be correct. This word "ought," having become a word of mere mesmeric force, could not, in the character of having that force, be inferred from anything whatever. It may be objected that it could be inferred from other "morally ought" sentences: but that cannot be true. The appearance that this is so is produced by the fact that we say "All men are φ" and "Socrates is a man" implies "Socrates is φ." But here "φ" is a dummy predicate. We mean that if you substitute a real predicate for "φ" the implication is valid. A real predicate is required; not just a word containing no intelligible thought: a word retaining the suggestion force, and apt to have a strong psychological effect, but which no longer signifies a real concept at all.

For its suggestion is one of a *verdict* on my action, according as agrees or disagrees with the description in the "ought" sentence. And where one does not think there is a judge or a law, the notion of verdict may retain its psychological effect, but not its meaning. Now imagine that just this word "verdict" *were* so used—with a characteristically solemn emphasis—as to retain its atmosphere but not its meaning, and someone were to say: "For a *verdict,* after all, you need a law and a judge." The reply might be made: "Not at all, for if there were a law and a judge who gave a verdict, the question for us would be whether accepting that verdict is something that there is a *Verdict* on." This is an analogue of an argument which is so frequently referred to as decisive: If someone does have a divine law conception of ethics, all the same, he has to agree that he has to have a judgment that he *ought* (morally ought) to obey the divine law; so his ethic is in exactly the same position as any other: he merely has a "practical major premise":[2] "Divine law ought to be obeyed" where someone else has, e.g., "The greatest happiness principle ought to be employed in all decisions."

I should judge that Hume and our present-day ethicists had done a considerable service by showing that no content could be found in the notion "morally ought"; if it were not that the latter philosophers try to find an alternative (very fishy) content and to retain the psychological force of the term. It would be most reasonable to drop it. It has no reasonable sense outside a law conception of ethics; they are not going to maintain such a conception; and you can do ethics without it, as is shown by the example of Aristotle. It would be a great improvement if, instead of "morally wrong," one always named a genus such as "untruthful," "unchaste," "unjust." We should no longer ask whether doing something was "wrong," passing directly from some description of an action to this notion; we should ask whether, e.g., it was unjust; and the answer would sometimes be clear at once.

---

6. Anscombe turns now to more modern English moral philosophy. Notice the point about consequentialist theories and the Hebrew-Christian ethic near the end of the paragraph. This relates back to her discussion about a divine lawgiver.

I now come to the epoch in modern English moral philosophy marked by Sidgwick. There is a startling change that seems to have taken place between Mill and Moore. Mill assumes, as we saw, that there is no question of calculating the particular consequences of an action such as murder or theft; and we saw too that his position was stupid, because it is not at all clear how an action *can* fall under just one principle of utility. In Moore and in subsequent academic moralists of England we find it taken to be pretty obvious that "the right action" is the action which produces the best possible consequences (reckoning among consequences the intrinsic values ascribed to certain kinds of act by some "Objectivists"[3]). Now it follows from this that a man does

---

[2]As it is absurdly called. Since major premise = premise containing the term which is predicate in the conclusion, it is a solecism to speak of it in the connection with practical reasoning.

[3]Oxford Objectivists of course distinguish between "consequences" and "intrinsic values" and so produce a misleading appearance of not being "consequentialists." But they do not hold—and Ross explicitly denies—that the gravity of, e.g., procuring the condemnation of the innocent is such that it cannot be outweighed by, e.g., national interest. Hence their distinction is of no importance.

short
even
long

well, subjectively speaking, if he acts for the best in the particular circumstances according to his judgment of the total consequences of this particular action. I say that this follows, not that any philosopher has said precisely that. For discussion of these questions can of course get extremely complicated: e.g. it can be doubted whether "such-and-such is the right action" is a satisfactory formulation, on the grounds that things have to exist to have predicates—so perhaps the best formulation is "I am obliged"; or again, a philosopher may deny that "right" is a "descriptive" term, and then take a roundabout route through linguistic analysis to reach a view which comes to the same thing as "the right action is the one productive of the best consequences" (e.g., the view that you frame your "principles" to effect the end you choose to pursue, the connection between "choice" and "best" being supposedly such that choosing reflectively means that you choose how to act so as to produce the best consequences); further, the roles of what are called "moral principles" and of the "motive of duty" have to be described; the differences between "good" and "morally good" and "right" need to be explored, the special characteristics of "ought" sentences investigated. Such discussions generate an appearance of significant diversity of views where what is really significant is an overall similarity. The overall similarity is made clear if you consider that every one of the best known English academic moral philosophers has put out a philosophy according to which, e.g., it is not possible to hold that it cannot be right to kill the innocent as a means to any end whatsoever and that someone who thinks otherwise is in error. (I have to mention both points; because Mr. Hare, for example, while teaching a philosophy which would encourage a person to judge that killing the innocent would be what he "ought" to choose for overriding purposes, would also teach, I think, that if a man chooses to make avoiding killing the innocent for any purpose his "supreme practical principle," he cannot be impugned for error: that just is his "principle." But with that qualification, I think it can be seen that the point I have mentioned holds good of every single English academic moral philosopher since Sidgwick.) Now this is a significant thing: for it means that all these philosophies are quite incompatible with the Hebrew-Christian ethic. For it has been characteristic of that ethic to teach that there are certain things forbidden whatever *consequences* threaten, such as: choosing to kill the innocent for any purpose, however good; vicarious punishment; treachery (by which I mean obtaining a man's confidence in a grave matter by promises of trustworthy friendship and then betraying him to his enemies); idolatry; sodomy; adultery; making a false profession of faith. The prohibition of certain things simply in virtue of their description as such-and-such identifiable kinds of action, regardless of any further consequences, is certainly not the whole of the Hebrew-Christian ethic; but it is a noteworthy feature of it; and if every academic philosopher since Sidgwick has written in such a way as to exclude this ethic, it would argue a certain provinciality of mind not to see this incompatibility as the most important fact about these philosophers, and the differences between them as somewhat trifling by comparison.

It is noticeable that none of these philosophers displays any consciousness that there is such an ethic, which he is contradicting: it is pretty well taken for obvious among them all that a prohibition such as that on murder does not operate in face of some consequences. But of course the strictness of the prohibition has as its point *that you are not to be tempted by fear or hope of consequences.*

If you notice the transition from Mill to Moore, you will suspect that it was made somewhere by someone; Sidgwick will come to mind as a likely name; and you will in fact find it going on, almost casually, in him. He is rather a dull author; and the important things in him occur in asides and footnotes and small bits of argument which are not concerned with his grand classification of the "methods of ethics." A divine law theory of ethics is reduced to an insignificant variety by a footnote telling us that "the best theologians" (God knows whom he meant) tell us that God is to be obeyed in his capacity of a *moral* being. ἤ φορτικός δ ἔπαινος; one seems to hear Aristotle saying: "Isn't the praise vulgar?"[4]—But Sidgwick *is* vulgar in that kind of way: he thinks, for example, that humility consists in underestimating your own merits—i.e., in a species of untruthfulness; and that the ground for having laws against blasphemy was that it was offensive to believers; and that to go accurately into the virtue of purity is to offend against its canons, a thing he reproves "medieval theologians" for not realizing.

From the point of view of the present enquiry, the most important thing about Sidgwick was his definition of intention. He defines intention in such a way that one must be said to intend any foreseen consequences of one's voluntary action. This definition is obviously incorrect, and I dare say that no one would be found to defend it now. He uses it to put forward an ethical thesis which would now be accepted by many people: the thesis that it does not make any difference to a man's responsibility for something that he foresaw, that he felt no desire for it, either as an end or as a means to an end. Using the language of intention more correctly, and avoiding Sidgwick's faulty conception, we may state the thesis thus: it does not make any difference to a man's responsibility for an effect of his action which he can foresee, that he does not intend it. Now this sounds rather edifying; it is I think quite characteristic of very bad degenerations of thought on such questions that they sound edifying. We can see what it amounts to by considering an example. Let us suppose that a man has a responsibility for the maintenance of some child. Therefore deliberately to withdraw support from it is a bad sort of thing for him to do. It would be bad for him to withdraw its maintenance because he didn't want to maintain it any longer; *and* also bad for him to withdraw it because by doing so he would, let us say, compel someone else to do something. (We may suppose for the sake of argument that compelling that person to do that thing is in itself quite admirable.) But now he has to choose between doing something disgraceful and going to prison; if he goes to prison, it will follow that he withdraws support from the child. By Sidgwick's doctrine, there is no difference in his responsibility for ceasing to maintain the child, between the case where he does it for its own sake or as a means to some other purpose, and when it happens as a foreseen and unavoidable consequence of his going to prison rather than do something disgraceful. It follows that he must weigh up the relative badness of withdrawing support from the child and of doing the disgraceful thing; and it may easily be that the disgraceful thing is in fact a less vicious action than intentionally withdrawing support from the child would be; if then the fact that withdrawing support from the child is a side effect of his going to prison does not make any difference to his responsibility, this consideration will incline him to do the disgraceful thing; which can still be pretty bad. And of course, once he has started to look at the matter in this light, the only reasonable thing for him to consider will be the consequences and not the intrinsic badness of this or that action. So that, given that he judges reasonably that no *great* harm will come of it, he can do a much more disgraceful thing than deliberately

---

[4]E.N. [*Ethica Nicomachea*] 1178b16.

short
even
long

withdrawing support from the child. And if his calculations turn out in fact wrong, it will appear that he was not responsible for the consequences, because he did not foresee them. For in fact Sidgwick's thesis leads to its being quite impossible to estimate the badness of an action except in the light of *expected* consequences. But if so, then *you* must estimate the badness in the light of the consequences *you* expect; and so it will follow that you can exculpate yourself from the *actual* consequences of the most disgraceful actions, so long as you can make out a case for not having foreseen them. Whereas I should contend that a man is responsible for the bad consequences of his bad actions, but gets no credit for the good ones; and contrariwise is not responsible for the bad consequences of good actions.

The denial of *any* distinction between foreseen and intended consequences, as far as responsibility is concerned, was not made by Sidgwick in developing any one "method of ethics"; he made this important move on behalf of everybody and just on its own account; and I think it plausible to suggest that *this* move on the part of Sidgwick explains the difference between old-fashioned Utilitarianism and that *consequentialism,* as I name it, which marks him and every English academic moral philosopher since him. By it, the kind of consideration which would formerly have been regarded as a temptation, the kind of consideration urged upon men by wives and flattering friends, was given a status by moral philosophers in their theories.

7. *Anscombe stresses a weakness of consequentialism.*

It is a necessary feature of consequentialism that it is a shallow philosophy. For there are always borderline cases in ethics. Now if you are either an Aristotelian, or a believer in divine law, you will deal with a borderline case by considering whether doing such-and-such in such-and-such circumstances is, say, murder, or is an act of injustice; and according as you decide it is or it isn't, you judge it to be a thing to do or not. This would be the method of casuistry; and while it may lead you to stretch a point on the circumference, it will not permit you to destroy the center. But if you are a consequentialist, the question "What is it right to do in such-and-such circumstances?" is a stupid one to raise. The casuist raises such a question only to ask "Would it be *permissible* to do so-and-so?" or "Would it be permissible *not* to do so-and-so?" Only if it would *not* be permissible *not* to do so-and-so could he say "*This* would be *the* thing to do."[5] Otherwise, though he may speak *against* some action, he cannot prescribe any—for in an *actual* case, the circumstances (beyond the ones imagined) might suggest all sorts of possibilities, and you can't know in advance what the possibilities are going to be. Now the consequentialist has no footing on which to say "This would be permissible, this not"; because by his own hypothesis, it is the consequences that are to decide, and he has no business to pretend that he can lay it down what possible twists a man could give doing this or that; the most he can say is: a man must not *bring about* this or that; he has no right to say he will, in an actual case, bring about such-and-such unless he does so-and-so. Further, the consequentialist, in order to be imagining borderline cases at all, has of course to assume some sort of law or standard according to which this is a borderline case, Where then does he get the standard from? In practice the answer in-

---

[5]Necessarily a rare case: for the positive precepts, e.g., "Honor your parents," hardly ever prescribe, and seldom even necessitate, any particular action.

variably is: from the standards current in his society or his circle. And it has in fact been the mark of all these philosophers that they have been extremely conventional; they have nothing in them by which to revolt against the conventional standards of their sort of people; it is impossible that they should be profound. But the chance that a whole range of conventional standards will be decent is small.—Finally, the point of considering hypothetical situations, perhaps very improbable ones, *seems* to be to elicit from yourself or someone else a hypothetical decision to do something of a bad kind. I don't doubt this has the effect of predisposing people—who will never get into the situations for which they have made hypothetical choices—to consent to similar bad actions, or to praise and flatter those who do them, so long as their crowd does so too, when the desperate circumstances imagined don't hold at all.

Those who recognize the origins of the notions of "obligation" and of the emphatic, "moral," *ought,* in the divine law conception of ethics, but who reject the notion of a divine legislator, sometimes look about for the possibility of retaining a law conception without a divine legislator. This search, I think, has some interest in it. Perhaps the first thing that suggests itself is the "norms" of a society. But just as one cannot be impressed by Butler when one reflects what conscience can tell people to do, so, I think, one cannot be impressed by this idea if one reflects what the "norms" of a society can be like. That legislation can be "for oneself" I reject as absurd; whatever you do "for yourself" may be admirable; but is not legislating. Once one sees this, one may say: I have to frame my own rules, and these are the best I can frame, and I shall go by them until I know something better: as a man might say "I shall go by the customs of my ancestors." Whether this leads to good or evil will depend on the *content* of the rules or of the customs of one's ancestors. If one is lucky it will lead to good. Such an attitude would be hopeful in this at any rate: it seems to have in it some Socratic doubt where, from having to fall back on such expedients, it should be clear that Socratic doubt is good; in fact rather generally it must be good for anyone to think "Perhaps in some way I can't see, I may be on a bad path, perhaps I am hopelessly wrong in some essential way."—The search for "norms" might lead someone to look for laws of nature, as if the universe were a legislator; but in the present day this is not likely to lead to good results: it might lead one to eat the weaker according to the laws of nature, but would hardly lead anyone nowadays to notions of justice; the pre-Socratic feeling about justice as comparable to the balance or harmony which kept things going is very remote to us.

8. The possibility of a contractual "ought" is examined.

There is another possibility here: "obligation" may be contractual. Just as we look at the law to find out what a man subject to it is required by it to do, so we look at a contract to find out what the man who has made it is required by it to do. Thinkers, admittedly remote from us, might have the idea of a *foedus rerum,* of the universe not as a legislator but as the embodiment of a contract. Then if you could find out what the contract was, you would learn your obligations under it. Now, you cannot be under a law unless it has been promulgated to you; and the thinkers who believed in "natural divine law" held that it was promulgated to every grown man in his knowledge of good and evil. Similarly you cannot be in a contract without having contracted, i.e., given signs of entering upon the contract. Just possibly, it might be argued that the use of language which one makes in the ordinary conduct of life amounts in some sense to

short
even
long

giving the signs of entering into various contracts. If anyone had this theory, we should want to see it worked out. I suspect that it would be largely formal; it might be possible to construct a system embodying the law (whose status might be compared to that of "laws" of logic): "what's sauce for the goose is sauce for the gander," but hardly one descending to such particularities as the prohibition on murder or sodomy. Also, while it is clear that you can be subject to a law that you do not acknowledge and have not thought of as law, it does not seem reasonable to say that you can enter upon a contract without knowing that you are doing so; such ignorance is usually held to be destructive of the nature of a contract.

It might remain to look for "norms" in human virtues: just as *man* has so many teeth, which is certainly not the average number of teeth men have, but is the number of teeth for the species, so perhaps the species *man*, regarded not just biologically, but from the point of view of the activity of thought and choice in regard to the various departments of life—powers and faculties and use of things needed—"has" such-and-such virtues: and this "man" with the complete set of virtues is the "norm," as "man" with, e.g., a complete set of teeth is a norm. But in *this* sense "norm" has ceased to be roughly equivalent to "law." In *this* sense the notion of a "norm" brings us nearer to an Aristotelian than a law conception of ethics. There is, I think, no harm in that; but if someone looked in this direction to give "norm" a sense, then he ought to recognize what has happened to the notion "norm," which he wanted to mean "law—without bringing God in"—it has ceased to mean "law" at all; and *so* the notions of "moral obligation," "the moral ought," and "duty" are best put on the Index, if he can manage it.

But meanwhile—is it not clear that there are several concepts that need investigating simply as part of the philosophy of psychology and,—as I should recommend—*banishing ethics totally* from our minds? Namely—to begin with: "action," "intention," "pleasure," "wanting." More will probably turn up if we start with these. Eventually it might be possible to advance to considering the concept "virtue"; with which, I suppose, we should be beginning some sort of a study of ethics.

---

9. Anscombe suggests some changes in our moral vocabulary.

I will end by describing the advantages of using the word "ought" in a nonemphatic fashion, and not in a special "moral" sense; of discarding the term "wrong" in a "moral" sense, and using such notions as "unjust."

It is possible, if one is allowed to proceed just by giving examples, to distinguish between the intrinsically unjust, and what is unjust given the circumstances. To arrange to get a man judicially punished for something which it can be clearly seen he has not done is intrinsically unjust. This might be done, of course, and often has been done, in all sorts of ways; by suborning false witnesses, by a rule of law by which something is "deemed" to be the case which is admittedly not the case as a matter of fact, and by open insolence on the part of the judges and powerful people when they more or less openly say: "A fig for the fact that you did not do it; we mean to sentence you for it all the same." What is unjust given, e.g., normal circumstances is to deprive people of their ostensible property without legal procedure, not to pay debts, not to keep contracts, and a host of other things of the kind. Now, the circumstances can clearly make a great deal of difference in estimating the justice or injustice of such procedures as these; and these circumstances may *sometimes* include expected consequences; for example, a man's claim to a bit of property can become a nullity when its seizure and use can avert some obvious disaster:

as, e.g., if you could use a machine of his to produce an explosion in which it would be destroyed, but by means of which you could divert a flood or make a gap which a fire could not jump. Now this certainly does not mean that what would ordinarily be an act of injustice, but is not intrinsically unjust, can always be rendered just by a reasonable calculation of better consequences; far from it; but the problems that would be raised in an attempt to draw a boundary line (or boundary area) here are obviously complicated. And while there are certainly some general remarks which ought to be made here, and some boundaries that can be drawn, the decision on particular cases would for the most part be determined κατὰ τὸν ὀρθὸν λόγον "according to what's reasonable."—E.g., that *such-and-such* a delay of payment of a *such-and-such* debt to a person *so* circumstanced, on the part of a person *so* circumstanced, would or would not be unjust, is really only to be decided "according to what's reasonable"; and for this there can *in principle* be no canon other than giving a few examples. That is to say, while it is because of a big gap in philosophy that we can give no general account of the concept of virtue and of the concept of justice, but have to proceed, using the concepts, only by giving examples; still there is an area where it is not because of any gap, but is in principle the case, that there is no account except by way of examples: and that is where the canon is "what's reasonable": which of course is *not* a canon.

That is all I wish to say about what is just in some circumstances, unjust in others; and about the way in which expected consequences can play a part in determining what is just. Returning to my example of the intrinsically unjust: if a procedure *is* one of judicially punishing a man for what he is clearly understood not to have done, there can be absolutely no argument about the description of this as unjust. No circumstances, and no expected consequences, which do *not* modify the description of the procedure as one of judicially punishing a man for what he is known not to have done can modify the description of it as unjust. Someone who attempted to dispute this would only be pretending not to know what "unjust" means: for this is a paradigm case of injustice.

And here we see the superiority of the term "unjust" over the terms "morally right" and "morally wrong." For in the context of English moral philosophy since Sidgwick it appears legitimate to discuss whether it *might* be "morally right" in some circumstances to adopt that procedure; but it cannot be argued that the procedure would in any circumstances be just.

Now I am not able to do the philosophy involved—and I think that no one in the present situation of English philosophy *can* do the philosophy involved—but it is clear that a good man is a just man; and a just man is a man who habitually refuses to commit or participate in any unjust actions for fear of any consequences, or to obtain any advantage, for himself or anyone else. Perhaps no one will disagree. But, it will be said, what *is* unjust is sometimes determined by expected consequences; and

---

[6]If he thinks it in the concrete situation, he is of course merely a normally tempted human being. In discussion when this paper was read, as was perhaps to be expected, this case was produced: a government is required to have an innocent man tried, sentenced and executed under threat of a "hydrogen bomb war." It would seem strange to me to have much hope of so averting a war threatened by such men as made this demand. But the most important thing about the way in which cases like this are invented in discussions, is the assumption that only two courses are open: here, compliance and open defiance. No one can say in advance of such a situation what the possibilities are going to be—e.g., that there is none of stalling by a feigned willingness to comply, accompanied by a skillfully arranged "escape" of the victim.

certainly that is true. But there are cases where it is not: now if someone says, "I agree, but all this wants a lot of explaining," then he is right, and, what is more, the situation at present is that we can't do the explaining; we lack the philosophic equipment. But if someone really thinks, *in advance*,[6] that it is open to question whether such an action as procuring the judicial execution of the innocent should be quite excluded from consideration—I do not want to argue with him; he shows a corrupt mind.

In such cases our moral philosophers seek to impose a dilemma upon us. "If we have a case where the term 'unjust' applies purely in virtue of a factual description, can't one raise the question whether one sometimes conceivably ought to do injustice? If 'what is unjust' is determined by consideration of whether it is *right* to do so-and-so in such-and-such circumstances, then the question whether it is 'right' to commit injustice can't arise, just because 'wrong' has been built into the definition of injustice. But if we have a case where the description 'unjust' applies purely in virtue of the facts, without bringing 'wrong' in, then the question can arise whether one 'ought' perhaps to commit an injustice, whether it might not be 'right' to? And of course 'ought' and 'right' are being used in their *moral* senses here. Now either you must decide what is 'morally right' in the light of certain *other* 'principles,' or you make a 'principle' about *this* and decide that an injustice is never 'right'; but even if you do the latter you are going beyond the facts; you are making a decision that you will not, or that it is wrong to, commit injustice. But in either case, *if* the term 'unjust' is determined simply by the facts, it is not the term 'unjust' that determines that the term 'wrong' applies, but a decision that injustice is *wrong*, together with the diagnosis of the 'factual' description as entailing injustice. But the man who makes an absolute decision that injustice is 'wrong' has no footing on which to criticize someone who does *not* make that decision as judging falsely."

In this argument "wrong" of course is explained as meaning "morally wrong," and all the atmosphere of the term is retained while its substance is guaranteed quite null. Now let us remember that "morally wrong" is the term which is the heir of the notion "illicit," or "what there is an obligation *not* to do"; which belongs in a divine law theory or ethics. Here it really does add something to the description "unjust" to say there is an obligation not to do it; for what obliges is the divine law—as rules oblige in a game. So if the divine law obliges not to commit injustice by forbidding injustice, it really does add something to the description "unjust" to say there is an obligation not to do it. And it is because "morally wrong" is the heir of this concept, but an heir that is cut off from the family of concepts from which it sprang, that "morally wrong" *both* goes beyond the mere factual description "unjust" *and* seems to have no discernible content except a certain compelling force, which I should call purely psychological. And such is the force of the term that philosophers actually suppose that the divine law notion can be dismissed as making no essential difference even if it is held—*because* they think that a "practical principle" running "I *ought* (i.e., am morally obliged) to obey divine laws" is required for the man who believes in divine laws. But actually this notion of obligation is a notion which only operates in the context of law. And I should be inclined to congratulate the present-day moral philosophers on depriving "morally ought" of its now delusive appearance of content, if only they did not manifest a detestable desire to retain the atmosphere of the term.

It may be possible, if we are resolute, to discard the notion "morally ought," and simply return to the ordinary "ought," which, we ought to notice, is such an extremely frequent term of human language that it is difficult to imagine getting on without it. Now if we do return to it, can't it reasonably be asked whether one might ever need to commit injustice, or whether it won't be the best thing to do? Of course it can. And the answers will be various. One man—a philosopher—may say that since justice is a virtue, and injustice a vice, and virtues and vices are built up by the performances of the action in which they are instanced, an act of injustice will tend to make a man bad; and essentially the flourishing of a man *qua* man consists in his being good (e.g., in virtues); but for any X to which such terms apply, X needs what makes it flourish, so a man needs, or ought to perform, only virtuous actions; and even if, as it must be admitted may happen, he flourishes less, or not at all, in inessentials, by avoiding injustice, his life is spoiled in essentials by not avoiding injustice—so he still needs to perform only just actions. That is roughly how Plato and Aristotle talk; but it can be seen that philosophically there is a huge gap, at present unfillable as far as we are concerned, which needs to be filled by an account of human nature, human action, the type of characteristic a virtue is, and above all of human "flourishing." And it is the last concept that appears the most doubtful. For it is a bit much to swallow that a man in pain and hunger and poor and friendless is "flourishing," as Aristotle himself admitted. Further, someone might say that one at least needed to stay alive to "flourish." Another man unimpressed by all that will say in a hard case "What we need is such-and-such, which we won't get without doing this (which is unjust)—so this is what we ought to do." Another man, who does not follow the rather elaborate reasoning of the philosophers, simply says "I know it is in any case a disgraceful thing to say that one had better commit this unjust action." The man who believes in divine laws will say perhaps "It is forbidden, and however it looks, it cannot be to anyone's profit to commit injustice"; he like the Greek philosophers can think in terms of "flourishing." If he is a Stoic, he is apt to have a decidedly strained notion of what "flourishing consists" in; if he is a Jew or Christian, he need not have any very distinct notion: the way it will profit him to abstain from injustice is something that he leaves it to God to determine, himself only saying "It can't do me any good to go against his law." (But he also hopes for a great reward in a new life later on, e.g., at the coming of Messiah; but in this he is relying on special promises.)

It is left to modern moral philosophy—the moral philosophy of all the well-known English ethicists since Sidgwick—to construct systems according to which the man who says "We need such-and-such, and will only get it this way" *may* be a virtuous character: that is to say, it is left open to debate whether such a procedure as the judicial punishment of the innocent may not in some circumstances be the "right" one to adopt; and though the present Oxford moral philosophers would accord a man *permission* to "make it his principle" not to do such a thing, they teach a philosophy according to which the particular consequences of such an action *could* "morally" be taken into account by a man who was debating what to do; and if they were such as to conflict with his "ends," it might be a step in his moral education to frame a moral principle under which he "managed" (to use Mr. Nowell-Smith's phrase[7]) to bring the

---

[7] *Ethics.*

action; or it might be a new "decision of principle," making which was an advance in the formation of his moral thinking (to adopt Mr. Hare's conception), to decide: in such-and-such circumstances one ought to procure the judicial condemnation of the innocent. And that is my complaint.

READING QUESTIONS

1. What does Butler fail to notice about a person's conscience?
2. Anscombe provides an example about machinery where concepts such as "needs" and "should" connect to the concepts of "bad" and "good." State the example.
3. What does Anscombe argue is necessary for a law conception of ethics?
4. What does Anscombe say is the most important thing about Sidgwick?
5. What moral theory does Anscombe associate with Sidgwick?
6. What does Anscombe say about the possibility of entering into a contract without knowing you are doing so?

John Rawls

In his long and distinguished publishing career, dating from the 1950s, John Rawls (born 1921) has produced a number of influential books and articles on moral philosophy. Yet one of his books stands out from the rest. It is difficult to overestimate the effect that his now classic book *A Theory of Justice* (1971) has had on current work in ethics. With this book, Rawls, a professor of philosophy at Harvard University, helped direct the attention of moral philosophers to the issues of justice and rights. What are the conditions for a just society and just social institutions? How should we balance the concerns of individual rights and equality within society? Answering these kinds of questions has taken on a new importance for moral philosophers as a result of Rawls's influential book.

In *A Theory of Justice,* Rawls is specifically interested in the way the basic organization of a just society should be determined. Social arrangements in an ideal, just society would not have been handed down from time immemorial, nor would they have been determined by the strongest people in the society. Rather, the rules that govern social transactions and social institutions would result from negotiations among all members of the society, but only if those negotiations take place under special circumstances. Negotiators must occupy what Rawls calls the "original position." In the original position, negotiations occur behind a "veil of ignorance," so called because the negotiators must choose rules and principles while ignorant of their own positions within the future society. For example, without first knowing his or her position in society, each negotiator must choose the principles of justice that will underline the basic social institutions. Since the negotiator's position is determined by access to what Rawls calls primary social goods, the principles chosen behind the veil of ignorance will be those that bring the most benefit to all members of society. Existing differences regarding primary social goods can be justified, he argues, only if those differences are beneficial to the least advantaged, not only the most advantaged. Thus, a just society will have rules that are as fair as possible to everyone in the society. Each person will have the most extensive liberty possible without infringing upon the liberty of others, and social goods will be distributed equally unless some inequality is to everyone's advantage.

Rawls's theory is an original, systematic ethical theory that attempts to present the conditions for a just society. Yet his theory is heavily influenced by ideas from the history of moral philosophy. For example, he draws upon **contractarianism,** or social contract theory, which has its main historical roots in the moral philosophy of Thomas Hobbes in the seventeenth century. (We also saw social contract themes in Plato's *Crito.*) For social contract theory, morality results from following the rules that are necessary for a society to function well. Therefore, the theory analyzes the interaction of social forces that could produce a justifiable system of rules within society.

The interest in contractarianism generated in the last three decades shows no sign of diminishing. The theory has taken its place alongside utilitarianism, Kantian duty theory, and virtue ethics as one of the prominent theories of moral philosophy in the latter half of this century.

A Theory of Justice

If moral philosophy concerns itself with rationally deciding how we ought to live, it makes sense that moral philosophers would concern themselves with the ways in which societies operate. After all, people are social creatures and always inhabit some kind of society. Why not look at the conditions that make ethics possible?

In his social contract theory, Rawls does just that. His concern here is not directly with the way that people ought to treat each other; rather, in this excerpt he discusses the way that a society should decide on its most basic principles. The rules that Rawls uses to determine the starting point of the negotiations in which the members of society will choose these fundamental principles might initially strike you as counterintuitive: Shouldn't I want to know as much as possible about my future situation? How can the situation be for the best if I am behind a veil of ignorance? Perhaps an analogy will help to make sense of the veil of ignorance. How would you organize a class, or an exam, if you didn't know whether you would be the teacher or the student when the class began? What kind of internal policies would you choose for a business if you did not know what job you would have in it? Presumably, you would want a class or business in which you would flourish no matter what your ultimate position.   ✒

The Main Idea of the Theory of Justice

1. The first paragraph sets out Rawls's agenda and also shows the historical roots of his theory.

My aim is to present a conception of justice which generalizes and carries to a higher level of abstraction the familiar theory of the social contract as found, say, in Locke, Rousseau, and Kant.[1] In order to do this we are not to think of the original contract as one to enter a particular society or to set up a particular form of government.

[1]As the text suggests, I shall regard Locke's *Second Treatise of Government,* Rousseau's *The Social Contract,* and Kant's ethical works beginning with *The Foundations of the Metaphysics of Morals* as definitive of the contract tradition. For all of its greatness, Hobbes's *Leviathan* raises special problems. A general historical survey is provided by J. W. Gough, *The Social Contract,* 2nd ed. (Oxford, The Clarendon Press, 1957), and Otto Gierke, *Natural Law and the Theory of Society,* trans. with an introduction by Ernest Barker (Cambridge, The University Press, 1934). A presentation of the contract view as primarily an ethical theory is to be found in G. R. Grice, *The Grounds of Moral Judgment* (Cambridge, The University Press, 1967).

Rather, the guiding idea is that the principles of justice for the basic structure of society are the object of the original agreement. They are the principles that free and rational persons concerned to further their own interests would accept in an initial position of equality as defining the fundamental terms of their association. These principles are to regulate all further agreements; they specify the kinds of social cooperation that can be entered into and the forms of government that can be established. This way of regarding the principles of justice I shall call justice as fairness.

Thus we are to imagine that those who engage in social cooperation choose together, in one joint act, the principles which are to assign basic rights and duties and to determine the division of social benefits. Men are to decide in advance how they are to regulate their claims against one another and what is to be the foundation charter of their society. Just as each person must decide by rational reflection what constitutes his good, that is, the system of ends which it is rational for him to pursue, so a group of persons must decide once and for all what is to count among them as just and unjust. The choice which rational men would make in this hypothetical situation of equal liberty, assuming for the present that this choice problem has a solution, determines the principles of justice.

In justice as fairness the original position of equality corresponds to the state of nature in the traditional theory of the social contract. This original position is not, of course, thought of as an actual historical state of affairs, much less as a primitive condition of culture. It is understood as a purely hypothetical situation characterized so as to lead to a certain conception of justice.[2] Among the essential features of this situation is that no one knows his place in society, his class position or social status, nor does any one know his fortune in the distribution of natural assets and abilities, his intelligence, strength, and the like. I shall even assume that the parties do not know their conceptions of the good or their special psychological propensities. The principles of justice are chosen behind a veil of ignorance. This ensures that no one is advantaged or disadvantaged in the choice of principles by the outcome of natural chance or the contingency of social circumstances. Since all are similarly situated and no one is able to design principles to favor his particular condition, the principles of justice are the result of a fair agreement or bargain. For given the circumstances of the original position, the symmetry of everyone's relations to each other, this initial situation is fair between individuals as moral persons, that is, as rational beings with their own ends and capable, I shall assume, of a sense of justice. The original position is, one might say, the appropriate initial status quo, and thus the fundamental agreements reached in it are fair. This explains the propriety of the name "justice as fairness": it conveys the idea that the principles of justice are agreed to in an initial situation that is fair. The name does not mean that the concepts of justice and fairness are the same, any more than the phrase "poetry as metaphor" means that the concepts of poetry and metaphor are the same.

Justice as fairness begins, as I have said, with one of the most general of all choices which persons might make together, namely, with the choice of the first principles of

---

[2]Kant is clear that the original agreement is hypothetical. See *The Metaphysics of Morals,* pt. I (*Rechtslehre*), especially §§47, 52; and pt. II of the essay "Concerning the Common Saying: This May Be True in Theory but It Does Not Apply in Practice," in *Kant's Political Writings,* ed. Hans Reiss and trans. by H. B. Nisbet (Cambridge, The University Press, 1970), pp. 73–87. See Georges Vlachos, *La Pensée politique de Kant* (Paris, Presses Universitaires de France, 1962), pp. 326–335; and J. G. Murphy, *Kant: The Philosophy of Right* (London, Macmillan, 1970), pp. 109–112, 133–136, for a further discussion.

a conception of justice which is to regulate all subsequent criticism and reform of institutions. Then, having chosen a conception of justice, we can suppose that they are to choose a constitution and a legislature to enact laws, and so on, all in accordance with the principles of justice initially agreed upon. Our social situation is just if it is such that by this sequence of hypothetical agreements we would have contracted into the general system of rules which defines it. Moreover, assuming that the original position does determine a set of principles (that is, that a particular conception of justice would be chosen), it will then be true that whenever social institutions satisfy these principles those engaged in them can say to one another that they are cooperating on terms to which they would agree if they were free and equal persons whose relations with respect to one another were fair. They could all view their arrangements as meeting the stipulations which they would acknowledge in an initial situation that embodies widely accepted and reasonable constraints on the choice of principles. The general recognition of this fact would provide the basis for a public acceptance of the corresponding principles of justice. No society can, of course, be a scheme of cooperation which men enter voluntarily in a literal sense; each person finds himself placed at birth in some particular position in some particular society, and the nature of this position materially affects his life prospects. Yet a society satisfying the principles of justice as fairness comes as close as a society can to being a voluntary scheme, for it meets the principles which free and equal persons would assent to under circumstances that are fair. In this sense its members are autonomous and the obligations they recognize self-imposed.

One feature of justice as fairness is to think of the parties in the initial situation as rational and mutually disinterested. This does not mean that the parties are egoists, that is, individuals with only certain kinds of interests, say in wealth, prestige, and domination. But they are conceived as not taking an interest in one another's interests. They are to presume that even their spiritual aims may be opposed, in the way that the aims of those of different religions may be opposed. Moreover, the concept of rationality must be interpreted as far as possible in the narrow sense, standard in economic theory, of taking the most effective means to given ends. I shall modify this concept to some extent, as explained later, but one must try to avoid introducing into it any controversial ethical elements. The initial situation must be characterized by stipulations that are widely accepted.

2. Now that he has outlined the basic features of his theory, Rawls discusses its compatibility with the principle of utility. If you read carefully, you will see that he explains, subtly, what the principle of utility is.

In working out the conception of justice as fairness one main task clearly is to determine which principles of justice would be chosen in the original position. To do this we must describe this situation in some detail and formulate with care the problem of choice which it presents. These matters I shall take up in the immediately succeeding chapters. It may be observed, however, that once the principles of justice are thought of as arising from an original agreement in a situation of equality, it is an open question whether the principle of utility would be acknowledged. Offhand it hardly seems likely that persons who view themselves as equals, entitled to press their claims upon one another, would agree to a principle which may require lesser life prospects for some simply for the sake of a greater sum of advantages enjoyed by others. Since each desires to protect his interests, his capacity to advance his conception of the good, no one has a reason to acquiesce in an enduring loss for himself in order to bring about a greater net balance of satisfaction. In the absence of strong and lasting benevolent impulses, a rational man would not accept a basic structure merely because it maximized the algebraic sum of advantages irrespective of its permanent effects on his own basic rights and interests. Thus it seems that the principle of utility is incompatible with the conception of social cooperation among equals for mutual advantage. It appears to be inconsistent with the idea of reciprocity implicit in the notion of a well-ordered society. Or, at any rate, so I shall argue.

I shall maintain instead that the persons in the initial situation would choose two rather different principles: the first requires equality in the assignment of basic rights and duties, while the second holds that social and economic inequalities, for example inequalities of wealth and authority, are just only if they result in compensating benefits for everyone, and in particular for the least advantaged members of society. These principles rule out justifying institutions on the grounds that the hardships of some are offset by a greater good in the aggregate. It may be expedient but it is not just that some should have less in order that others may prosper. But there is no injustice in the greater benefits earned by a few provided that the situation of persons not so fortunate is thereby improved. The intuitive idea is that since everyone's well-being depends upon a scheme of cooperation without which no one could have a satisfactory life, the division of advantages should be such as to draw forth the willing cooperation of everyone taking part in it, including those less well situated. Yet this can be expected only if reasonable terms are proposed. The two principles mentioned seem to be a fair agreement on the basis of which those better endowed, or more fortunate in their social position, neither of which we can be said to deserve, could expect the willing cooperation of others when some workable scheme is a necessary condition of the welfare of all.[3] Once we decide to look for a conception of justice that nullifies the accidents of natural endowment and the contingencies of social circumstance as counters in quest for political and economic advantage, we are led to these principles. They express the result of leaving aside those aspects of the social world that seem arbitrary from a moral point of view.

The problem of the choice of principles, however, is extremely difficult. I do not expect the answer I shall suggest to be convincing to everyone. It is, therefore, worth noting from the outset that justice as fairness, like other contract views, consists of two parts: (1) an interpretation of the initial situation and of the problem of choice posed there, and (2) a set of principles which, it is argued, would be agreed to. One may accept the first part of the theory (or some variant thereof), but not the other, and conversely. The concept of the initial contractual situation may seem reasonable although the particular principles proposed are rejected. To be sure, I want to maintain that the most appropriate conception of this situation does lead to principles of justice contrary to utilitarianism and perfectionism, and therefore that the contract doctrine provides an alternative to these views. Still, one may dispute this contention even though one grants that the contractarian method

---

[3]For the formulation of this intuitive idea I am indebted to Allan Gibbard.

is a useful way of studying ethical theories and of setting forth their underlying assumptions.

———

3. In this paragraph and the two following, Rawls discusses his theory as a kind of contract theory. Note his discussion of the advantages of considering it as a contract theory, particularly his acknowledgment of the historical roots of contract theory.

———

Justice as fairness is an example of what I have called a contract theory. Now there may be an objection to the term "contract" and related expressions, but I think it will serve reasonably well. Many words have misleading connotations which at first are likely to confuse. The terms "utility" and "utilitarianism" are surely no exception. They too have unfortunate suggestions which hostile critics have been willing to exploit; yet they are clear enough for those prepared to study utilitarian doctrine. The same should be true of the term "contract" applied to moral theories. As I have mentioned, to understand it one has to keep in mind that it implies a certain level of abstraction. In particular, the content of the relevant agreement is not to enter a given society or to adopt a given form of government, but to accept certain moral principles. Moreover, the undertakings referred to are purely hypothetical: a contract view holds that certain principles would be accepted in a well-defined initial situation.

The merit of the contract terminology is that it conveys the idea that principles of justice may be conceived as principles that would be chosen by rational persons, and that in this way conceptions of justice may be explained and justified. The theory of justice is a part, perhaps the most significant part, of the theory of rational choice. Furthermore, principles of justice deal with conflicting claims upon the advantages won by social cooperation; they apply to the relations among several persons or groups. The word "contract" suggests this plurality as well as the condition that the appropriate division of advantages must be in accordance with principles acceptable to all parties. The condition of publicity for principles of justice is also connoted by the contract phraseology. Thus, if these principles are the outcome of an agreement, citizens have a knowledge of the principles that others follow. It is characteristic of contract theories to stress the public nature of political principles. Finally there is the long tradition of the contract doctrine. Expressing the tie with this line of thought helps to define ideas and accords with natural piety. There are then several advantages in the use of the term "contract." With due precautions taken, it should not be misleading.

A final remark. Justice as fairness is not a complete contract theory. For it is clear that the contractarian idea can be extended to the choice of more or less an entire ethical system, that is, to a system including principles for all the virtues and not only for justice. Now for the most part I shall consider only principles of justice and others closely related to them; I make no attempt to discuss the virtues in a systematic way. Obviously if justice as fairness succeeds reasonably well, a next step would be to study the more general view suggested by the name "rightness as fairness." But even this wider theory fails to embrace all moral relationships, since it would seem to include only our relations with other persons and to leave out of account how we are to conduct ourselves toward animals and the rest of nature. I do not contend that the contract notion offers a way to approach these questions which are certainly of the first importance; and I shall have to put them aside. We must recognize the limited scope of justice as fairness and of the general type of view that it exemplifies. How far its conclusions must be revised once these other matters are understood cannot be decided in advance.

The Original Position and Justification

I have said that the original position is the appropriate initial status quo which ensures that the fundamental agreements reached in it are fair. This fact yields the name "justice as fairness." It is clear, then, that I want to say that one conception of justice is more reasonable than another, or justifiable with respect to it, if rational persons in the initial situation would choose its principles over those of the other for the role of justice. Conceptions of justice are to be ranked by their acceptability to persons so circumstanced. Understood in this way the question of justification is settled by working out a problem of deliberation: we have to ascertain which principles it would be rational to adopt given the contractual situation. This connects the theory of justice with the theory of rational choice.

If this view of the problem of justification is to succeed, we must, of course, describe in some detail the nature of this choice problem. A problem of rational decision has a definite answer only if we know the beliefs and interests of the parties, their relations with respect to one another, the alternatives between which they are to choose, the procedure whereby they make up their minds, and so on. As the circumstances are presented in different ways, correspondingly different principles are accepted. The concept of the original position, as I shall refer to it, is that of the most philosophically favored interpretation of this initial choice situation for the purposes of a theory of justice.

But how are we to decide what is the most favored interpretation? I assume, for one thing, that there is a broad measure of agreement that principles of justice should be chosen under certain conditions. To justify a particular description of the initial situation one shows that it incorporates these commonly shared presumptions. One argues from widely accepted but weak premises to more specific conclusions. Each of the presumptions should by itself be natural and plausible; some of them may seem innocuous or even trivial. The aim of the contract approach is to establish that taken together they impose significant bounds on acceptable principles of justice. The ideal outcome would be that these conditions determine a unique set of principles; but I shall be satisfied if they suffice to rank the main traditional conceptions of social justice.

-----

4. The purpose of the veil of ignorance is explained in greater detail. The example given here may assist the reader in understanding the need for the veil.

One should not be misled, then, by the somewhat unusual conditions which characterize the original position. The idea here is simply to make vivid to ourselves the restrictions that it seems reasonable to impose on arguments for principles of justice, and therefore on these principles themselves. Thus it seems reasonable and generally acceptable that no one should be advantaged or disadvantaged by natural fortune or social circumstances in the choice of principles. It also seems widely agreed that it should be impossible to tailor principles to the circumstances of one's own case. We should ensure further that particular inclinations and aspirations, and persons' conceptions of their good do not affect the principles adopted. The aim is to rule out those principles that it would be rational to propose for acceptance, however little the chance of success, only if one knew certain things that are irrelevant from the standpoint of justice. For example, if a man knew that he was wealthy, he might find it rational to advance the principle that various taxes for welfare measures be counted unjust; if he knew that he was poor, he would most likely propose the contrary principle. To represent the desired restrictions one imagines a situation in which everyone is deprived of this sort of information. One excludes the knowledge of those contingencies which sets men at odds and allows them to be guided by their prejudices. In this manner the veil of ignorance is arrived at in a natural way. This concept should cause no difficulty if we keep in mind the constraints on arguments that it is meant to express. At any time we can enter the original position, so to speak, simply by following a certain procedure, namely, by arguing for principles of justice in accordance with these restrictions.

It seems reasonable to suppose that the parties in the original position are equal. That is, all have the same rights in the procedure for choosing principles; each can make proposals, submit reasons for their acceptance, and so on. Obviously the purpose of these conditions is to represent equality between human beings as moral persons, as creatures having a conception of their good and capable of a sense of justice. The basis of equality is taken to be similarity in these two respects. Systems of ends are not ranked in value; and each man is presumed to have the requisite ability to understand and to act upon whatever principles are adopted. Together with the veil of ignorance, these conditions define the principles of justice as those which rational persons concerned to advance their interests would consent to as equals when none are known to be advantaged or disadvantaged by social and natural contingencies.

There is, however, another side to justifying a particular description of the original position. This is to see if the principles which would be chosen match our considered convictions of justice or extend them in an acceptable way. We can note whether applying these principles would lead us to make the same judgments about the basic structure of society which we now make intuitively and in which we have the greatest confidence; or whether, in cases where our present judgments are in doubt and given with hesitation, these principles offer a resolution which we can affirm on reflection. There are questions which we feel sure must be answered in a certain way. For example, we are confident that religious intolerance and racial discrimination are unjust. We think that we have examined these things with care and have reached what we believe is an impartial judgment not likely to be distorted by an excessive attention to our own interests. These convictions are provisional fixed points which we presume any conception of justice must fit. But we have much less assurance as to what is the correct distribution of wealth and authority. Here we may be looking for a way to remove our doubts. We can check an interpretation of the initial situation, then, by the capacity of its principles to accommodate our firmest convictions and to provide guidance where guidance is needed.

---

5. Reflective equilibrium is important in this theory. Note that he explains why it is reflective and why it is an equilibrium.

In searching for the most favored description of this situation we work from both ends. We begin by describing it so that it represents generally shared and preferably weak conditions. We then see if these conditions are strong enough to yield a significant set of principles. If not, we look for further premises equally reasonable. But if so, and these principles match our considered convictions of justice, then so far well and good. But presumably there will be discrepancies. In this case we have a choice. We can either modify the account of the initial situation or we can revise our existing judgments, for even the judgments we take provisionally as fixed points are liable to revision. By going back and forth, sometimes altering the conditions of the contractual circumstances, at others withdrawing our judgments and conforming them to principle, I assume that eventually we shall find a description of the initial situation that both expresses reasonable conditions and yields principles which match our considered judgments duly pruned and adjusted. This state of affairs I refer to as reflective equilibrium.[4] It is an equilibrium because at last our principles and judgments coincide; and it is reflective since we know to what principles our judgments conform and the premises of their derivation. At the moment everything is in order. But this equilibrium is not necessarily stable. It is liable to be upset by further examination of the conditions which should be imposed on the contractual situation and by particular cases which may lead us to revise our judgments. Yet for the time being we have done what we can to render coherent and to justify our convictions of social justice. We have reached a conception of the original position.

Two Principles of Justice

6. *He stated in the first section of this reading that all contract theories consist of two parts. The first part, describing the initial situation, has just been completed. In this section he describes the second part, the principles that would be arrived at from the initial situation.*

I shall now state in a provisional form the two principles of justice that I believe would be chosen in the original position. In this section I wish to make only the most general comments, and therefore the first formulation of these principles is tentative. As we go on I shall run through several formulations and approximate step by step the final statement to be given much later. I believe that doing this allows the exposition to proceed in a natural way.

The first statement of the two principles reads as follows.

First: each person is to have an equal right to the most extensive basic liberty compatible with a similar liberty for others.

Second: social and economic inequalities are to be arranged so that they are both (a) reasonably expected to be to everyone's advantage, and (b) attached to positions and offices open to all. There are two ambiguous phrases

---

[4]The process of mutual adjustment of principles and considered judgments is not peculiar to moral philosophy. See Nelson Goodman, *Fact, Fiction, and Forecast* (Cambridge, Mass., Harvard University Press, 1955), pp. 65–68, for parallel remarks concerning the justification of the principles of deductive and inductive inference.

in the second principle, namely "everyone's advantage" and "equally open to all." Determining their sense more exactly will lead to a second formulation of the principle. . . .

By way of general comment, these principles primarily apply, as I have said, to the basic structure of society. They are to govern the assignment of rights and duties and to regulate the distribution of social and economic advantages. As their formulation suggests, these principles presuppose that the social structure can be divided into two more or less distinct parts, the first principle applying to the one, the second to the other. They distinguish between those aspects of the social system that define and secure the equal liberties of citizenship and those that specify and establish social and economic inequalities. The basic liberties of citizens are, roughly speaking, political liberty (the right to vote and to be eligible for public office) together with freedom of speech and assembly; liberty of conscience and freedom of thought; freedom of the person along with the right to hold (personal) property; and freedom from arbitrary arrest and seizure as defined by the concept of the rule of law. These liberties are all required to be equal by the first principle, since citizens of a just society are to have the same basic rights.

The second principle applies, in the first approximation, to the distribution of income and wealth and to the design of organizations that make use of differences in authority and responsibility, or chains of command. While the distribution of wealth and income need not be equal, it must be to everyone's advantage, and at the same time, positions of authority and offices of command must be accessible to all. One applies the second principle by holding positions open, and then, subject to this constraint, arranges social and economic inequalities so that everyone benefits.

These principles are to be arranged in a serial order with the first principle prior to the second. This ordering means that a departure from the institutions of equal liberty required by the first principle cannot be justified by, or compensated for, by greater social and economic advantages. The distribution of wealth and income, and the hierarchies of authority, must be consistent with both the liberties of equal citizenship and equality of opportunity.

It is clear that these principles are rather specific in their content, and their acceptance rests on certain assumptions that I must eventually try to explain and justify. A theory of justice depends upon a theory of society in ways that will become evident as we proceed. For the present, it should be observed that the two principles (and this holds for all formulations) are a special case of a more general conception of justice that can be expressed as follows.

> All social values—liberty and opportunity, income and wealth, and the bases of self-respect—are to be distributed equally unless an unequal distribution of any, or all, of these values is to everyone's advantage.

Injustice, then, is simply inequalities that are not to the benefit of all. Of course, this conception is extremely vague and requires interpretation.

---

7. Primary goods are distributed evenly. Can you see the purpose this serves?

As a first step, suppose that the basic structure of society distributes certain primary goods, that is, things that every rational man is presumed to want. These goods normally have a use whatever a person's rational plan of life. For simplicity, assume that the chief primary goods at the disposition of society are rights and liberties, powers and opportunities, income and wealth. These are the social primary goods. Other primary goods such as health and vigor, intelligence and imagination, are natural goods; although their possession is influenced by the basic structure, they are not so directly under its control. Imagine, then, a hypothetical initial arrangement in which all the social primary goods are equally distributed: everyone has similar rights and duties, and income and wealth are evenly shared. This state of affairs provides a benchmark for judging improvements. If certain inequalities of wealth and organizational powers would make everyone better off than in this hypothetical starting situation, then they accord with the general conception.

Now it is possible, at least theoretically, that by giving up some of their fundamental liberties men are sufficiently compensated by the resulting social and economic gains. The general conception of justice imposes no restrictions on what sort of inequalities are permissible; it only requires that everyone's position be improved. We need not suppose anything so drastic as consenting to a condition of slavery. Imagine instead that men forgo certain political rights when the economic returns are significant and their capacity to influence the course of policy by the exercise of these rights would be marginal in any case. It is this kind of exchange which the two principles as stated rule out; being arranged in serial order they do not permit exchanges between basic liberties and economic and social gains. The serial ordering of principles expresses an underlying preference among primary social goods. When this preference is rational so likewise is the choice of these principles in this order.

In developing justice as fairness I shall, for the most part, leave aside the general conception of justice and examine instead the special case of the two principles in serial order. The advantage of this procedure is that from the first the matter of priorities is recognized and an effort made to find principles to deal with it. One is led to attend throughout to the conditions under which the acknowledgment of the absolute weight of liberty with respect to social and economic advantages, as defined by the lexical order of the two principles, would be reasonable. Offhand, this ranking appears extreme and too special a case to be of much interest; but there is more justification for it than would appear at first sight. Or at any rate, so I shall maintain. Furthermore, the distinction between fundamental rights and liberties and economic and social benefits marks a difference among primary social goods that one should try to exploit. It suggests an important division in the social system. Of course, the distinctions drawn and the ordering proposed are bound to be at best only approximations. There are surely circumstances in which they fail. But it is essential to depict clearly the main lines of a reasonable conception of justice; and under many conditions anyway, the two principles in serial order may serve well enough. When necessary we can fall back on the more general conception.

The fact that the two principles apply to institutions has certain consequences. Several points illustrate this. First of all, the rights and liberties referred to by these principles are those which are defined by the public rules of the basic structure. Whether men are free is determined by the rights and duties established by the major institutions of society. Liberty is a certain pattern of social forms. The first principle simply requires that certain sorts of rules, those defining basic liberties, apply to everyone equally and that they allow the most extensive liberty compatible with a like liberty for all. The only reason for circumscribing the rights defining liberty and making men's freedom less extensive than it might otherwise be is that these equal rights as institutionally defined would interfere with one another.

Another thing to bear in mind is that when principles mention persons, or require that everyone gain from an inequality, the reference is to representative persons holding the various social positions, or offices, or whatever, established by the basic structure. Thus in applying the second principle I assume that it is possible to assign an expectation of well-being to representative individuals holding these positions. This expectation indicates their life prospects as viewed from their social station. In general, the expectations of representative persons depend upon the distribution of rights and duties throughout the basic structure. When this changes, expectations change. I assume, then, that expectations are connected: by raising the prospects of the representative man in one position we presumably increase or decrease the prospects of representative men in other positions. Since it applies to institutional forms, the second principle (or rather the first part of it) refers to the expectations of representative individuals. As I shall discuss below, neither principle applies to distributions of particular goods to particular individuals who may be identified by their proper names. The situation where someone is considering how to allocate certain commodities to needy persons who are known to him is not within the scope of the principles. They are meant to regulate basic institutional arrangements. We must not assume that there is much similarity from the standpoint of justice between an administrative allotment of goods to specific persons and the appropriate design of society. Our commonsense intuitions for the former may be a poor guide to the latter.

Now the second principle insists that each person benefit from permissible inequalities in the basic structure. This means that it must be reasonable for each relevant representative man defined by this structure, when he views it as a going concern, to prefer his prospects with the inequality to his prospects without it. One is not allowed to justify differences in income or organizational powers on the ground that the disadvantages of those in one position are outweighed by the greater advantages of those in another. Much less can infringements of liberty be counterbalanced in this way. Applied to the basic structure, the principle of utility would have us maximize the sum of expectations of representative men (weighted by the number of persons they represent, on the classical view); and this would permit us to compensate for the losses of some by the gains of others. Instead, the two principles require that everyone benefit from economic and social inequalities.

READING QUESTIONS

1. What does Rawls call his way of regarding the principles of justice?

2. What aspect of the original position ensures that the fundamental agreements reached in it are fair?

3. What are the two parts of his, or any other, contract theory?

4. What purpose can our commonsense, or intuitive, convictions serve when compared with the principles arrived at from the original position?

5. Why is the "reflective equilibrium" an equilibrium?

6. How many principles of justice does Rawls think would be chosen in the original position? What is the first one?

7. What does he mean by "primary goods"? What are the two kinds of primary goods? Name two of each kind.

Bernard Williams

I n this reading from *Utilitarianism: For and Against* (1973), the prominent English
philosopher Bernard Williams puts forward a forceful criticism of **utilitarianism**.
Utilitarianism is the ethical theory proposed by Jeremy Bentham and John Stuart
Mill in which the rightness or wrongness of an act is determined by the good or bad
consequences of that act. Williams argues that utilitarianism fails to provide an adequate account of personal integrity. Therefore, it is possible that utilitarians may
find themselves in situations where they must compromise their personal integrity
or give up what Williams calls their "deeply held projects" in order to do what their
theory deems right. Williams gives as an example a case that has become famous in
recent moral philosophy. Imagine a situation, says Williams, where a tourist in
South America accidentally encounters some soldiers preparing to execute twenty
Indians in a small village. The Indians are being executed following some anti-
government protest, as a lesson to the other villagers. The captain of the soldiers offers this unfortunate tourist an "honored guest's" privilege: If he personally kills one
of the Indians, the other nineteen will be set free. If the tourist refuses, all twenty
will be shot.

Williams charges that in this case the moral decision is clear for the utilitarian.
If the tourist kills one Indian, less misery occurs than if the soldiers kill twenty.
Misery times twenty is worse than misery times one. Therefore, it is clear that the
right thing for the tourist to do is to kill the Indian. Of course, the utilitarian will
acknowledge that the tourist will suffer if he has to kill an innocent person, and that
suffering must be taken into account in determining the right thing to do. Yet even
when the tourist's revulsion to killing is included in the utilitarian calculation of
happiness and unhappiness, the only moral choice is to kill the Indian. His resistance to carrying out the murder suggests some form of moral cowardice, not integrity. Here is the point Williams wants to emphasize: Utilitarianism does not, and
cannot, place a value on a person's integrity or personal projects. To demand that
the tourist kill an innocent man, even to save nineteen others, is to attack his integrity, to alienate him from his own actions and convictions. Williams believes that
this example illuminates inherent flaws in utilitarianism that should be enough to
condemn it as a viable moral system.

Utilitarianism: For and Against

꿍 ꩜

Utilitarianism has been a popular, and a controversial, theory over the last
two centuries. At first glance, it impresses many people not only as quite
plausible, but as the source of many of the actions we see in society.
When a new freeway project requires that some people sell their homes

From Bernard Williams and J. J. C. Smart, *Utilitarianism: For and Against,* 1973. Reprinted with the
permission of Cambridge University Press.

and move to make room for the road, we may feel sorry for them, yet we believe it is for the best because so many people will benefit from the new road. Because utilitarianism determines what is right by calculating what will benefit the most people, this theory may even appear to be the antidote for selfishness: Think less about yourself and your own happiness, and more about the happiness, you can bring to others.

Yet utilitarianism has acquired a number of critics through the years. Worries about a majority imposing its will on a minority—for example, an obvious social injustice such as slavery could be justified because more people benefit than suffer under it—and other enormous problems with the theory have been voiced. In this article, Williams discusses a challenging question for the theory: How well does it take account of the value people attach to their own projects, actions, and integrity?

Negative Responsibility: and Two Examples

Consequentialism is basically indifferent to whether a state of affairs consists in what I do, or is produced by what I do, where that notion is itself wide enough to include, for instance, situations in which other people do things which I have made them do, or allowed them to do, or encouraged them to do, or given them a chance to do. All that consequentialism is interested in is the idea of these doings being *consequences* of what I do, and that is a relation broad enough to include the relations just mentioned, and many others.

Just what the relation is, is a different question, and at least as obscure as the nature of its relative, cause and effect. It is not a question I shall try to pursue; I will rely on cases where I suppose that any consequentialist would be bound to regard the situations in question as consequences of what the agent does. There are cases where the supposed consequences stand in a rather remote relation to the action, which are sometimes difficult to assess from a practical point of view, but which raise no very interesting question for the present enquiry. The more interesting points about consequentialism lie rather elsewhere. There are certain situations in which the causation of the situation, the relation it has to what I do, is in no way remote or problematic in itself, and entirely justifies the claim that the situation is a consequence of what I do: for instance, it is quite clear, or reasonably clear, that if I do a certain thing, this situation will come about, and if I do not, it will not. So from a consequentialist point of view it goes into the calculation of consequences along with any other state of affairs accessible to me. Yet from some, at least, non-consequentialist points of view, there is a vital difference between some such situations and others: namely, that in some a vital link in the production of the eventual outcome is provided by *someone else's* doing something. But for consequentialism, all causal connections are on the same level, and it makes no difference, so far as that goes, whether the causation of a given state of affairs lies through another agent, or not.

Correspondingly, there is no relevant difference which consists *just* in one state of affairs being brought about by me, without intervention of other agents, and another being brought about through the intervention of other agents; although some genuinely causal differences involving a difference of value may correspond to that (as when, for instance, the other agents derive pleasure or pain from the transaction), that kind of difference will already be included in the specification of the state of affairs to be produced. Granted that the states of affairs have been adequately described in causally and evaluatively relevant terms, it makes no further comprehensible difference who produces them. It is because consequentialism attaches value ultimately to states of affairs, and its concern is with what states of affairs the world contains, that it essentially involves the notion of *negative responsibility*: that if I am ever responsible for anything, then I must be just as much responsible for things that I allow or fail to prevent, as I am for things that I myself, in the more everyday restricted sense, bring about.[1] Those things also must enter my deliberations, as a responsible moral agent, on the same footing. What matters is what states of affairs the world contains, and so what matters with respect to a given action is what comes about if it is done, and what comes about if it is not done, and those are questions not intrinsically affected by the nature of the causal linkage, in particular by whether the outcome is partly produced by other agents.

The strong doctrine of negative responsibility flows directly from consequentialism's assignment of ultimate value to states of affairs. Looked at from another point of view, it can be seen also as a special application of something that is favored in many moral outlooks not themselves consequentialist—something which, indeed, some thinkers have been disposed to regard as the essence of morality itself: a principle of impartiality. Such a principle will claim that there can be no relevant difference from a moral point of view which consists just in the fact, not further explicable in general terms, that benefits or harms accrue to one person rather than to another— "it's me" can never in itself be a morally comprehensible reason.[2] This principle, familiar with regard to the reception of harms and benefits, we can see consequentialism as extending to their production: from the moral point of view, there is no comprehensible difference which consists just in my bringing about a certain outcome rather than someone else's producing it. That the doctrine of negative responsibility represents in this way the extreme of impartiality, and abstracts from the identity of the agent, leaving just a locus of causal intervention in the world—that fact is not merely a surface paradox. It helps to explain why consequentialism can seem to some to express a more serious attitude than non-consequentialist views, why part of its appeal is to a certain kind of high-mindedness. Indeed, that is part of what is wrong with it.

For a lot of the time so far we have been operating at an exceedingly abstract level. This has been necessary in order to get clearer in general terms about the differences between consequentialist and other outlooks, an aim which is important if we want to know what features of them lead to what results for our thought. Now, however, let us look more concretely at two examples, to see what utilitarianism might say about them, what we might say about utilitarianism and, most importantly of all, what

---

[1]This is a fairly modest sense of 'responsibility,' introduced merely by one's ability to reflect on, and decide, what one ought to do. . . .

[2]There is a tendency in some writers to suggest that it is not a comprehensible reason at all. But this, I suspect, is due to the overwhelming importance those writers ascribe to the moral point of view.

would be implied by certain ways of thinking about the situations. The examples are inevitably schematized, and they are open to the objection that they beg as many questions as they illuminate. There are two ways in particular in which examples in moral philosophy tend to beg important questions. One is that, as presented, they arbitrarily cut off and restrict the range of alternative courses of action—this objection might particularly be made against the first of my two examples. The second is that they inevitably present one with the situation as a going concern, and cut off questions about how the agent got into it, and correspondingly about moral considerations which might flow from that: this objection might perhaps specially arise with regard to the second of my two situations. These difficulties, however, just have to be accepted, and if anyone finds these examples cripplingly defective in this sort of respect, then he must in his own thought rework them in richer and less question-begging form. If he feels that no presentation of any imagined situation can ever be other than misleading in morality, and that there can never be any substitute for the concrete experienced complexity of actual moral situations, then this discussion, with him, must certainly grind to a halt: but then one may legitimately wonder whether every discussion with him about conduct will not grind to a halt, including any discussion about the actual situations, since discussion about how one would think and feel about situations somewhat different from the actual (that is to say, situations to that extent imaginary) plays an important role in discussion of the actual.

---

1. Having discussed how consequentialism considers the relationship between agent and the states of affairs that he or she either brings about directly or allows to come about indirectly, Williams now provides two examples. Concrete examples can help make his abstract claims more clear.

---

(1) George, who has just taken his Ph.D. in chemistry, finds it extremely difficult to get a job. He is not very robust in health, which cuts down the number of jobs he might be able to do satisfactorily. His wife has to go out to work to keep them, which itself causes a great deal of strain, since they have small children and there are severe problems about looking after them. The results of all this, especially on the children, are damaging. An older chemist, who knows about this situation, says that he can get George a decently paid job in a certain laboratory, which pursues research into chemical and biological warfare. George says that he cannot accept this, since he is opposed to chemical and biological warfare. The older man replies that he is not too keen on it himself, come to that, but after all George's refusal is not going to make the job or the laboratory go away; what is more, he happens to know that if George refuses the job, it will certainly go to a contemporary of George's who is not inhibited by any such scruples and is likely if appointed to push along the research with greater zeal than George would. Indeed, it is not merely concern for George and his family, but (to speak frankly and in confidence) some alarm about this other man's excess of zeal, which has led the older man to offer to use his influence to get George the job. . . . George's wife, to whom he is deeply attached, has views (the details of which need not concern us) from which it follows that at least there is nothing particularly wrong with research into CBW. What should he do?

(2) Jim finds himself in the central square of a small South American town. Tied up against the wall are a row of twenty Indians, most terrified, a few defiant,

in front of them several armed men in uniform. A heavy man in a sweat-stained khaki shirt turns out to be the captain in charge and, after a good deal of questioning of Jim which establishes that he got there by accident while on a botanical expedition, explains that the Indians are a random group of the inhabitants who, after recent acts of protest against the government, are just about to be killed to remind other possible protestors of the advantages of not protesting. However, since Jim is an honored visitor from another land, the captain is happy to offer him a guest's privilege of killing one of the Indians himself. If Jim accepts, then as a special mark of the occasion, the other Indians will be let off. Of course, if Jim refuses, then there is no special occasion, and Pedro here will do what he was about to do when Jim arrived, and kill them all. Jim, with some desperate recollection of schoolboy fiction, wonders whether if he got hold of a gun, he could hold the captain, Pedro and the rest of the soldiers to threat, but it is quite clear from the set-up that nothing of that kind is going to work: any attempt at that sort of thing will mean that all the Indians will be killed, and himself. The men against the wall, and the other villagers, understand the situation, and are obviously begging him to accept. What should he do?

To these dilemmas, it seems to me that utilitarianism replies, in the first case, that George should accept the job, and in the second, that Jim should kill the Indian. Not only does utilitarianism give these answers but, if the situations are essentially as described and there are no further special factors, it regards them, it seems to me, as *obviously* the right answers. But many of us would certainly wonder whether, in (1), that could possibly be the right answer at all; and in the case of (2), even one who came to think that perhaps that was the answer, might well wonder whether it was obviously the answer. Nor is it just a question of the rightness or obviousness of these answers. It is also a question of what sort of considerations come into finding the answer. A feature of utilitarianism is that it cuts out a kind of consideration which for some others makes a difference to what they feel about such cases: a consideration involving the idea, as we might first and very simply put it, that each of us is specially responsible for what *he* does, rather than for what other people do. This is an idea closely connected with the value of integrity. It is often suspected that utilitarianism, at least in its direct forms, makes integrity as a value more or less unintelligible. I shall try to show that this suspicion is correct. Of course, even if that is correct, it would not necessarily follow that we should reject utilitarianism; perhaps, as utilitarians sometimes suggest, we should just forget about integrity, in favor of such things as a concern for the general good. However, if I am right, we cannot merely do that, since the reason why utilitarianism cannot understand integrity is that it cannot coherently describe the relations between a man's projects and his actions.

Two Kinds of Remoter Effect

A lot of what we have to say about this question will be about the relations between my projects and other people's projects. But before we get on to that, we should first ask whether we are assuming too hastily what the utilitarian answers to the dilemmas will be. In terms of more direct effects of the possible decisions, there does not indeed seem much doubt about the answer in either case; but it might be said that in terms of more remote or less evident effects counterweights might be found to enter the utilitarian scales. Thus the effect on George of a decision to take the job might be invoked, or its effect on others who might know of his decision. The possibility of there being more beneficent labors in the future from which he might be barred or disqualified, might be mentioned; and so forth. Such effects—in particular, possible effects on the agent's character, and effects on the public at large—are often invoked by utilitarian writers dealing with problems about lying or promise-breaking, and some similar considerations might be invoked here.

There is one very general remark that is worth making about arguments of this sort. The certainty that attaches to these hypotheses about possible effects is usually pretty low; in some cases, indeed, the hypothesis invoked is so implausible that it would scarcely pass if it were not being used to deliver the respectable moral answer, as in the standard fantasy that one of the effects of one's telling a particular lie is to weaken the disposition of the world at large to tell the truth. The demands on the certainty or probability of these beliefs as beliefs about particular actions are much milder than they would be on beliefs favoring the unconventional course. It may be said that this is as it should be, since the presumption must be in favor of the conventional course: but that scarcely seems a *utilitarian* answer, unless utilitarianism has already taken off in the direction of not applying the consequences to the particular act at all.

Leaving aside that very general point, I want to consider now two types of effect that are often invoked by utilitarians, and which might be invoked in connection with these imaginary cases. The attitude or tone involved in invoking these effects may sometimes seem peculiar; but that sort of peculiarity soon becomes familiar in utilitarian discussions, and indeed it can be something of an achievement to retain a sense of it.

---

2. Williams discusses the way that the utilitarian takes account of the bad feelings that Jim and George will have about their actions. Utilitarians do weigh the effect that killing the Indian will have on Jim.

First, there is the psychological effect on the agent. Our descriptions of these situations have not so far taken account of how George or Jim will be after they have taken the one course or the other; and it might be said that if they take the course which seemed at first the utilitarian one, the effects on them will be in fact bad enough and extensive enough to cancel out the initial utilitarian advantages of that course. Now there is one version of this effect in which, for a utilitarian, some confusion must be involved, namely that in which the agent feels bad, his subsequent conduct and relations are crippled and so on, *because he thinks that he has done the wrong thing*—for if the balance of outcomes was as it appeared to be *before* invoking this effect, then he has not (from the utilitarian point of view) done the wrong thing. So that version of the effect, for a rational and utilitarian agent, could not possibly make any difference to the assessment of right and wrong. However, perhaps he is not a thoroughly rational agent, and is disposed to have bad feelings, whichever he decided to do. Now such feelings, which are from a strictly utilitarian point of view irrational—nothing, a utilitarian can point out, is advanced by having them—cannot, consistently, have any great weight in a utilitarian calculation. I shall consider in a moment an argument to suggest that they should have no weight at all in it. But short of that, the utilitarian could reasonably say that such feelings should not be encouraged, even if we accept their existence, and that to give them a lot of weight is to encourage them. Or, at the very best, even if they are straightforwardly and without any discount to be put into the calculation, their weight must be small: they are after all (and at best) one man's feelings.

That consideration might seem to have particular force in Jim's case. In George's case, his feelings represent a larger proportion of what is to be weighed, and are more commensurate in character with other items in the calculation. In Jim's case, however, his feelings might seem to be of very little weight compared with other things that are at stake. There is a powerful and recognizable appeal that can be made on this point: as that a refusal by Jim to do what he has been invited to do would be a kind of self-indulgent squeamishness. That is an appeal which can be made by other than utilitarians—indeed, there are some uses of it which cannot be consistently made by utilitarians, as when it essentially involves the idea that there is something dishonorable about such self-indulgence. But in some versions it is a familiar, and it must be said a powerful, weapon of utilitarianism. One must be clear, though, about what it can and cannot accomplish. The most it can do, so far as I can see, is to invite one to consider how seriously, and for what reasons, one feels that what one is invited to do is (in these circumstances) wrong, and in particular, to consider that question from the utilitarian point of view. When the agent is not seeing the situation from a utilitarian point of view, the appeal cannot force him to do so; and if he does come round to seeing it from a utilitarian point of view, there is virtually nothing left for the appeal to do. If he does not see it from a utilitarian point of view, he will not see his resistance to the invitation, and the unpleasant feelings he associates with accepting it, *just* as disagreeable experiences of his; they figure rather as emotional expressions of a thought that to accept would be wrong. He may be asked, as by the appeal, to consider whether he is right, and indeed whether he is fully serious, in thinking that. But the assertion of the appeal, that he is being self-indulgently squeamish, will not itself answer that question, or even help to answer it, since it essentially tells him to regard his feelings just as unpleasant experiences of his, and he cannot, by doing that, answer the question they pose when they are precisely not so regarded, but are regarded as indications[3] of what he thinks is right and wrong. If he does come round fully to the utilitarian point of view then of course he will regard these feelings just as unpleasant experiences of his. And once Jim—at least—has come to see them in that light, there is nothing left for the appeal to do, since *of course* his feelings, so regarded, are of virtually no weight at all in relation to the other things at stake. The 'squeamishness' appeal is not an argument which adds in a hitherto neglected consideration. Rather, it is an invitation to consider the situation, and one's own feelings, from a utilitarian point of view.

The reason why the squeamishness appeal can be very unsettling, and one can be unnerved by the suggestion of self-indulgence in going against utilitarian considerations,

---

[3]On the non-cognitivist meta-ethic in terms of which Smart presents his utilitarianism, the term 'indications' here would represent an understatement.

is not that we are utilitarians who are uncertain what utilitarian value to attach to our moral feelings, but that we are partially at least not utilitarians, and cannot regard our moral feelings merely as objects of utilitarian value. Because our moral relation to the world is partly given by such feelings, and by a sense of what we can or cannot 'live with,' to come to regard those feelings from a purely utilitarian point of view, that is to say, as happenings outside one's moral self, is to lose a sense of one's moral identity; to lose, in the most literal way, one's integrity. At this point utilitarianism alienates one from one's moral feelings; we shall see a little later how, more basically, it alienates one from one's actions as well.

If, then, one is really going to regard one's feelings from a strictly utilitarian point of view, Jim should give very little weight at all to his; it seems almost indecent, in fact, once one has taken that point of view, to suppose that he should give any at all. In George's case one might feel that things were slightly different. It is interesting, though, that one reason why one might think that—namely that one person principally affected is his wife—is very dubiously available to a utilitarian. George's wife has some reason to be interested in George's integrity and his sense of it; the Indians, quite properly, have no interest in Jim's. But it is not at all clear how utilitarianism would describe that difference.

There is an argument, and a strong one, that a strict utilitarian should give not merely small extra weight, in calculations of right and wrong, to feelings of this kind, but that he should give absolutely no weight to them at all. This is based on the point, which we have already seen, that if a course of action is, before taking these sorts of feelings into account, utilitarianly preferable, then bad feelings about that kind of action will be from a utilitarian point of view irrational. Now it might be thought that even if that is so, it would not mean that in a utilitarian calculation such feelings should not be taken into account; it is after all a well-known boast of utilitarianism that it is a realistic outlook which seeks the best in the world as it is, and takes any form of happiness or unhappiness into account. While a utilitarian will no doubt seek to diminish the incidence of feelings which are utilitarianly irrational—or at least of disagreeable feelings which are so—he might be expected to take them into account while they exist. This is without doubt classical utilitarian doctrine, but there is good reason to think that utilitarianism cannot stick to it without embracing results which are startlingly unacceptable and perhaps self-defeating.

Suppose that there is in a certain society a racial minority. Considering merely the ordinary interests of the other citizens, as opposed to their sentiments, this minority does no particular harm; we may suppose that it does not confer any very great benefits either. Its presence is in those terms neutral or mildly beneficial. However, the other citizens have such prejudices that they find the sight of this group, even the knowledge of its presence, very disagreeable. Proposals are made for removing in some way this minority. If we assume various quite plausible things (as that programs to change the majority sentiment are likely to be protracted and ineffective) then even if the removal would be unpleasant for the minority, a utilitarian calculation might well end up favoring this step, especially if the minority were a rather small minority and the majority were very severely prejudiced, that is to say, were made very severely uncomfortable by the presence of the minority.

A utilitarian might find that conclusion embarrassing; and not merely because of its nature, but because of the grounds on which it is reached. While a utilitarian might be expected to take into account certain other sorts of consequences of the prejudice, as that a majority prejudice is likely to be displayed in conduct disagreeable to the minority, and so forth, he might be made to wonder whether the unpleasant experiences of the prejudiced people should be allowed, *merely as such,* to count. If he does count them, merely as such, then he has once more separated himself from a body of ordinary moral thought which he might have hoped to accommodate; he may also have started on the path of defeating his own view of things. For one feature of these sentiments is that they are from the utilitarian point of view itself irrational, and a thoroughly utilitarian person would either not have them, or if he found that he did tend to have them, would himself seek to discount them. Since the sentiments in question are such that a rational utilitarian would discount them in himself, it is reasonable to suppose that he should discount them in his calculations about society; it does seem quite unreasonable for him to give just as much weight to feelings—considered just in themselves, one must recall, as experiences of those that have them—which are essentially based on views which are from a utilitarian point of view irrational, as to those which accord with utilitarian principles. Granted this idea, it seems reasonable for him to rejoin a body of moral thought in other respects congenial to him, and discount those sentiments, just considered in themselves, totally, on the principle that no pains or discomforts are to count in the utilitarian sum which their subjects have just because they hold views which are by utilitarian standards irrational. But if he accepts that, then in the cases we are at present considering no extra weight at all can be put in for bad feelings of George or Jim about their choices, if those choices are, leaving out those feelings, on the first round utilitarianly rational.

---

3. The discussion to this point has centered around the feelings of the agents, Jim and George, faced with a dilemma where they must do something they find abhorrent. He now considers a different effect in the two examples, what he calls the "precedent effect." The action that these agents take may affect future actions in similar circumstances.

The psychological effect on the agent was the first of two general effects considered by utilitarians, which had to be discussed. The second is in general a more substantial item, but it need not take so long, since it is both clearer and has little application to the present cases. This is the *precedent effect.* As Burke rightly emphasized, this effect can be important: that one morally *can* do what someone has actually done, is a psychologically effective principle, if not a deontically valid one. For the effect to operate, obviously some conditions must hold on the publicity of the act and on such things as the status of the agent (such considerations weighed importantly with Sir Thomas More); what these may be will vary evidently with circumstances.

In order for the precedent effect to make a difference to a utilitarian calculation, it must be based upon a confusion. For suppose that there is an act which would be the best in the circumstances, except that doing it will encourage by precedent other people to do things which will not be the best things to do. Then the situation of those other people must be relevantly different from that of the original agent; if it were not, then in doing the same as what would be the best course for the original agent, they would necessarily do the best thing themselves. But if the situations are in this way relevantly different, it must be a confused perception which takes the first situation, and the agent's course in it, as an adequate precedent for the second.

However, the fact that the precedent effect, if it really makes a difference, is in this sense based on a confusion, does not mean that it is not perfectly real, nor that it is to be discounted: social effects are by their nature confused in this sort of way. What it does emphasize is that calculations of the precedent effect have got to be realistic, involving considerations of how people are actually likely to be influenced. In the present examples, however, it is very implausible to think that the precedent effect could be invoked to make any difference to the calculation. Jim's case is extraordinary enough, and it is hard to imagine who the recipients of the effect might be supposed to be; while George is not in a sufficiently public situation or role for the question to arise in that form, and in any case one might suppose that the motivations of others on such an issue were quite likely to be fixed one way or another already.

No appeal, then, to these other effects is going to make a difference to what the utilitarian will decide about our examples. Let us now look more closely at the structure of those decisions.

Integrity

The situations have in common that if the agent does not do a certain disagreeable thing, someone else will, and in Jim's situation at least the result, the state of affairs after the other man has acted, if he does, will be worse than after Jim has acted, if Jim does. The same, on a smaller scale, is true of George's case. I have already suggested that it is inherent in consequentialism that it offers a strong doctrine of negative responsibility: if I know that if I do X, O_1 will eventuate, and if I refrain from doing X, O_2 will, and that O_2 is worse than O_1, then I am responsible for O_2 if I refrain voluntarily from doing X. "You could have prevented it," as will be said, and truly, to Jim, if he refuses, by the relatives of the other Indians. (I shall leave the important question, which is to the side of the present issue, of the obligations, if any, that nest round the word 'know': how far does one, under utilitarianism, have to research into the possibilities of maximally beneficent action, including prevention?)

---

4. Pedro says that he will kill twenty innocent Indians if Jim refuses to kill one. In that case, who would be responsible for the deaths, Jim or Pedro?

In the present cases, the situation of O_2 includes another agent bringing about results worse than O_1. So far as O_2 has been identified up to this point—merely as the worse outcome which will eventuate if I refrain from doing X—we might equally have said that what that other brings about is O_2; but that would be to underdescribe the situation. For what occurs if Jim refrains from action is not solely twenty Indians dead, but *Pedro's killing twenty Indians*, and that is not a result which Pedro brings about, though the death of the Indians is. We can say: what one does is not included in the outcome of what one does, while what another does can be included in the outcome of what one does. For that to be so, as the terms are now being used, only a very weak condition has to be satisfied: for Pedro's killing the Indians to be the outcome of Jim's refusal, it only has to be causally true that if Jim had not refused, Pedro would not have done it.

That may be enough for us to speak, in some sense, of Jim's responsibility for that outcome, if it occurs; but it is certainly not enough, it is worth noticing, for us to speak of Jim's *making* those things happen. For granted this way of their coming about, he could have made them happen only by making Pedro shoot, and there is no acceptable sense in which his refusal makes Pedro shoot. If the captain had said on Jim's refusal, "you leave me with no alternative," he would have been lying, like most who use that phrase. While the deaths, and the killing, may be the outcome of Jim's refusal, it is misleading to think, in such a case, of Jim having an *effect* on the world through the medium (as it happens) of Pedro's acts; for this is to leave Pedro out of the picture in his essential role of one who has intentions and projects, projects for realizing which Jim's refusal would leave an opportunity. Instead of thinking in terms of supposed effects of Jim's projects on Pedro, it is more revealing to think in terms of the effects of Pedro's projects on Jim's decision. This is the direction from which I want to criticize the notion of negative responsibility.

There are of course other ways in which this notion can be criticized. Many have hoped to discredit it by insisting on the basic moral relevance of the distinction between action and inaction, between intervening and letting things take their course. The distinction is certainly of great moral significance, and indeed it is not easy to think of any moral outlook which could get along without making some use of it. But it is unclear, both in itself and in its moral applications, and the unclarities are of a kind which precisely cause it to give way when, in very difficult cases, weight has to be put on it. There is much to be said in this area, but I doubt whether the sort of dilemma we are considering is going to be resolved by a simple use of this distinction. Again, the issue of negative responsibility can be pressed on the question of how limits are to be placed on one's apparently boundless obligation, implied by utilitarianism, to improve the world. Some answers are needed to that, too—and answers which stop short of relapsing into the bad faith of supposing that one's responsibilities could be adequately characterized just by appeal to one's roles.[4] But, once again, while that is a real question, it cannot be brought to bear directly on the present kind of case, since it is hard to think of anyone supposing that in Jim's case it would be an adequate response for him to say that it was none of his business.

What projects does a utilitarian agent have? As a utilitarian, he has the general project of bringing about maximally desirable outcomes; how he is to do this at any given moment is a question of what causal levers, so to speak, are at that moment within reach. The desirable outcomes, however, do not just consist of agents carrying out *that* project; there must be other more basic or lower-order projects which he and other agents have, and the desirable outcomes are going to consist, in part, of the maximally harmonious realization of those projects ('in part,' because one component of a utilitarianly desirable outcome may be the occurrence of agreeable experiences which are not the satisfaction of anybody's projects). Unless there were first-order projects, the general utilitarian project would have nothing to work on, and would be vacuous. What do the more basic or lower-order projects comprise? Many will be the obvious kinds of desires for things for oneself, one's family, one's

---

[4]For some remarks bearing on this, see *Morality,* the section on "Goodness and roles," and Cohen's article there cited.

friends, including basic necessities of life, and in more relaxed circumstances, objects of taste. Or there may be pursuits and interests of an intellectual, cultural or creative character. I introduce those as a separate class not because the objects of them lie in a separate class, and provide—as some utilitarians, in their churchy way, are fond of saying—'higher' pleasures. I introduce them separately because the agent's identification with them may be of a different order. It does not have to be: cultural and aesthetic interests just belong, for many, along with any other taste; but some people's commitment to these kinds of interests just is at once more thoroughgoing and serious than their pursuit of various objects of taste, while it is more individual and permeated with character than the desire for the necessities of life.

Beyond these, someone may have projects connected with his support of some cause: Zionism, for instance, or the abolition of chemical and biological warfare. Or there may be projects which flow from some more general disposition towards human conduct and character, such as a hatred of injustice, or of cruelty, or of killing.

It may be said that this last sort of disposition and its associated project do not count as (logically) 'lower-order' relative to the higher-order project of maximizing desirable outcomes; rather, it may be said, it is itself a 'higher-order' project. The vital question is not, however, how it is to be classified, but whether it and similar projects are to count among the projects whose satisfaction is to be included in the maximizing sum, and, correspondingly, as contributing to the agent's happiness. If the utilitarian says 'no' to that, then he is almost certainly committed to a version of utilitarianism as absurdly superficial and shallow as Benthamite versions have often been accused of being. For this project will be discounted, presumably, on the ground that it involves, in the specification of its object, the mention of other people's happiness or interests: thus it is the kind of project which (unlike the pursuit of food for myself) presupposes a reference to other people's projects. But that criterion would eliminate any desire at all which was not blankly and in the most straightforward sense egoistic.[5] Thus we should be reduced to frankly egoistic first-order projects, and—for all essential purposes—the one second-order utilitarian project of maximally satisfying first-order projects. Utilitarianism has a tendency to slide in this direction, and to leave a vast hole in the range of human desires, between egoistic inclinations and necessities at one end, and impersonally benevolent happiness-management at the other. But the utilitarianism which has to leave this hole is the most primitive form, which offers a quite rudimentary account of desire. Modern versions of the theory are supposed to be neutral with regard to what sorts of things make people happy or what their projects are. Utilitarianism would do well then to acknowledge the evident fact that among the things that make people happy is not only making other people happy, but being taken up or involved in any of a vast range of projects, or—if we waive the evangelical and moralizing associations of the word—commitments. One can be committed to such things as a person, a cause, an institution, a career, one's own genius, or the pursuit of danger.

Now none of these is itself the *pursuit of happiness:* by an exceedingly ancient platitude, it is not at all clear that there could be anything which was just that, or at least anything that had the slightest chance of being successful. Happiness, rather, requires being involved in, or at least content with, something else.[6] It is not im-

---

[5]On the subject of egoistic and non-egoistic desires, see "Egoism and altruism," in *Problems of the Self* (Cambridge University Press, London, 1973).

possible for utilitarianism to accept that point: it does not have to be saddled with a naïve and absurd philosophy of mind about the relation between desire and happiness. What it does have to say is that if such commitments are worthwhile, then pursuing the projects that flow from them, and realizing some of those projects, will make the person for whom they are worthwhile, happy. It may be that to claim that is still wrong: it may well be that a commitment can make sense to a man (can make sense of his life) without his supposing that it will make him *happy*.[7] But that is not the present point; let us grant to utilitarianism that all worthwhile human projects must conduce, one way or another, to happiness. The point is that even if that is true, it does not follow, nor could it possibly be true, that those projects are themselves projects of pursuing happiness. One has to believe in, or at least want, or quite minimally, be content with, other things, for there to be anywhere that happiness can come from.

Utilitarianism, then, should be willing to agree that its general aim of maximizing happiness does not imply that what everyone is doing is just pursuing happiness. On the contrary, people have to be pursuing other things. What those other things may be, utilitarianism, sticking to its professed empirical stance, should be prepared just to find out. No doubt some possible projects it will want to discourage, on the grounds that their being pursued involves a negative balance of happiness to others: though even there, the unblinking accountant's eye of the strict utilitarian will have something to put in the positive column, the satisfactions of the destructive agent. Beyond that, there will be a vast variety of generally beneficent or at least harmless projects; and some no doubt, will take the form not just of tastes or fancies, but of what I have called 'commitments.' It may even be that the utilitarian researcher will find that many of those with commitments, who have really identified themselves with objects outside themselves, who are thoroughly involved with other persons, or institutions, or activities or causes, are actually happier than those whose projects and wants are not like that. If so, that is an important piece of utilitarian empirical lore.

When I say 'happier' here, I have in mind the sort of consideration which any utilitarian would be committed to accepting: as for instance that such people are less likely to have a break-down or commit suicide. Of course that is not all that is actually involved, but the point in this argument is to use to the maximum degree utilitarian notions, in order to locate a breaking point in utilitarian thought. In appealing to this strictly utilitarian notion, I am being more consistent with utilitarianism than Smart is. In his struggles with the problem of the brain-electrode man, Smart commends the idea that 'happy' is a partly evaluative term, in the sense that we call 'happiness' those kinds of satisfaction which, as things are, we approve of. But *by what standard* is this surplus element of approval supposed, from a utilitarian point of view, to be allocated? There is no source for it, on a strictly utilitarian view, except further degrees of satisfaction, but there are none of those available, or the problem would not arise. Nor does it help to appeal to the fact that we dislike in prospect things which we like when we get there, for

---

[6]This does not imply that there is no such thing as the project of pursuing pleasure. Some writers who have correctly resisted the view that all desires are desires for pleasure, have given an account of pleasure so thoroughly adverbial as to leave it quite unclear how there could be a distinctively hedonist way of life at all. Some room has to be left for that, though there are important difficulties both in defining it and living it. Thus (particularly in the case of the very rich) it often has highly ritual aspects, apparently part of a strategy to counter boredom.

[7]For some remarks on this possibility, see *Morality*, section on "What is morality about?"

from a utilitarian point of view it would seem that the original dislike was merely irrational or based on an error. Smart's argument at this point seems to be embarrassed by a well-known utilitarian uneasiness, which comes from a feeling that it is not respectable to ignore the 'deep,' while not having anywhere left in human life to locate it.[8]

Let us now go back to the agent as utilitarian, and his higher-order project of maximizing desirable outcomes. At this level, he is committed only to that: what the outcome will actually consist of will depend entirely on the facts, on what persons with what projects and what potential satisfactions there are within calculable reach of the causal levers near which he finds himself. His own substantial projects and commitments come into it, but only as one lot among others—they potentially provide one set of satisfactions among those which he may be able to assist from where he happens to be. He is the agent of the satisfaction system who happens to be at a particular point at a particular time: in Jim's case, our man in South America. His own decisions as a utilitarian agent are a function of all the satisfactions which he can affect from where he is: and this means that the projects of others, to an indeterminately great extent, determine his decision.

This may be so either positively or negatively. It will be so positively if agents within the causal field of his decision have projects which are at any rate harmless, and so should be assisted. It will equally be so, but negatively, if there is an agent within the causal field whose projects are harmful, and have to be frustrated to maximize desirable outcomes. So it is with Jim and the soldier Pedro. On the utilitarian view, the undesirable projects of other people as much determine, in this negative way, one's decisions as the desirable ones do positively: if those people were not there, or had different projects, the causal nexus would be different, and it is the actual state of the causal nexus which determines the decision. The determination to an indefinite degree of my decisions by other people's projects is just another aspect of my unlimited responsibility to act for the best in a casual framework formed to a considerable extent by their projects.

The decision so determined is, for utilitarianism, the right decision. But what if it conflicts with some project of mine? This, the utilitarian will say, has already been dealt with: the satisfaction to you of fulfilling your project, and any satisfactions to others of your so doing, have already been through the calculating device and have been found inadequate. Now in the case of many sorts of projects, that is a perfectly reasonable sort of answer. But in the case of projects of the sort I have called 'commitments,' those with which one is more deeply and extensively involved and identified, this cannot just by itself be an adequate answer, and there may be no adequate answer at all. For, to take the extreme sort of case, how can a man, as a utilitarian agent, come to regard as one satisfaction among others, and a dispensable one, a project or attitude round which he has built his life, just because someone else's projects have so structured the causal scene that that is how the utilitarian sum comes out?

---

5. What is wrong with the utilitarian attitude toward Jim and his revulsion at killing a human being? It fails to take into account how such an act will change what his life is about.

The point here is not, as utilitarians may hasten to say, that if the project or attitude is that central to his life, then to abandon it will be very disagreeable to him

---

[8]One of many resemblances in spirit between utilitarianism and high-minded evangelical Christianity.

and great loss of utility will be involved. I have already argued . . . that it is not like that; on the contrary, once he is prepared to look at it like that, the argument in any serious case is over anyway. The point is that he is identified with his actions as flowing from projects and attitudes which in some cases he takes seriously at the deepest level, as what his life is about (or, in some cases, this section of his life—seriousness is not necessarily the same as persistence). It is absurd to demand of such a man, when the sums come in from the utility network which the projects of others have in part determined, that he should just step aside from his own project and decision and acknowledge the decision which utilitarian calculation requires. It is to alienate him in a real sense from his actions and the source of his action in his own convictions. It is to make him into a channel between the input of everyone's projects, including his own, and an output of optimific decision; but this is to neglect the extent to which *his* actions and *his* decisions have to be seen as the actions and decisions which flow from the projects and attitudes with which he is most closely identified. It is thus, in the most literal sense, an attack on his integrity.[9]

These sorts of considerations do not in themselves give solutions to practical dilemmas such as those provided by our examples; but I hope they help to provide other ways of thinking about them. In fact, it is not hard to see that in George's case, viewed from this perspective, the utilitarian solution would be wrong. Jim's case is different, and harder. But if (as I suppose) the utilitarian is probably right in this case, that is not to be found out just by asking the utilitarian's questions. Discussions of it—and I am not going to try to carry it further here—will have to take seriously the distinction between my killing someone, and its coming about because of what I do that someone else kills them: a distinction based, not so much on the distinction between action and inaction, as on the distinction between my projects and someone else's projects. At least it will have to start by taking that seriously, as utilitarianism does not; but then it will have to build out from there by asking why that distinction seems to have less, or a different, force in this case than it has in George's. One question here would be how far one's powerful objection to killing people just is, in fact, an application of a powerful objection to their being killed. Another dimension of that is the issue of how much it matters that the people at risk are actual, and there, as opposed to hypothetical, or future, or merely elsewhere.[10]

There are many other considerations that could come into such a question, but the immediate point of all this is to draw one particular contrast with utilitarianism: that to reach a grounded decision in such a case should not be regarded as a matter of just discounting one's reactions, impulses and deeply held projects in the face of the pattern of utilities, nor yet merely adding them in—but in the first instance of trying to understand them.

Of course, time and circumstances are unlikely to make a grounded decision, in Jim's case at least, possible. It might not even be decent. Instead of thinking in a rational

---

[9]Interestingly related to these notions is the Socratic idea that courage is a virtue particularly connected with keeping a clear sense of what one regards as most important. They also centrally raise questions about the value of pride. Humility, as something beyond the real demand of correct self-appraisal, was specially a Christian virtue because it involved subservience to God. In a secular context it can only represent subservience to other men and their projects.

[10]For a more general discussion of the issue see Charles Fried, *An Anatomy of Values* (Harvard University Press, Cambridge, Mass., 1970), Part Three.

and systematic way either about utilities or about the value of human life, the relevance of the people at risk being present, and so forth, the presence of the people at risk may just have its effect. The significance of the immediate should not be underestimated. Philosophers, not only utilitarian ones, repeatedly urge one to view the world *sub specie aeternitatis,* but for most human purposes that is not a good *species* to view it under. If we are not agents of the universal satisfaction system, we are not primarily janitors of any system of values, even our own: very often, we just act, as a possibly confused result of the situation in which we are engaged. That, I suspect, is very often an exceedingly good thing. To what extent utilitarians regard it as a good thing is an obscure question.

READING QUESTIONS

1. What does Williams mean by the notion of negative responsibility?
2. What will happen to the Indians if Jim fails to shoot one of them?
3. What does Williams say is the *obviously* right answer for the consequentialist to Jim's dilemma?
4. If Jim is a utilitarian, why shouldn't he think that he has done the wrong thing by killing someone?
5. According to Williams, how will Jim be alienated if he follows the utilitarian decision?

Thomas E. Hill, Jr.

K antian deontology has experienced a revival in the latter half of the twentieth century. Kant's ethical theory is considered **deontological** because it does not judge the rightness or wrongness of an action by considering the act's consequences, as does **utilitarianism**. Instead, for Kantian duty theory, morality is founded on absolute moral rules, and these can be determined by reason alone. To act morally, a person must follow these absolute rules out of regard for duty.

Although it is Kantian deontology that is experiencing renewed interest, Kant's is not the only deontological ethical theory. The ***prima facie* duty** theory of Ross, introduced earlier in this century, is also a deontological theory. But unlike Kant, Ross did not believe that our duties, known "at first glance," are absolute—that is, unconditional and without exception. Sometimes other considerations outweigh our *prima facie* duty, and sometimes our duties conflict with one another.

Among the authors who have written extensively in support of a Kantian ethical system is Thomas E. Hill, Jr., professor of philosophy at the University of North Carolina, Chapel Hill. In his 1973 article included here, Hill gives examples of servile characters—those who betray a lack of a certain kind of self-respect—and argues that utilitarianism fails to identify what is morally wrong about servility. For the utilitarian, servility is wrong if it leads to bad consequences, and we would expect the servile person to be less happy. Yet this need not be the case. The harm that accrues to the servile wife, argues Hill, may be overbalanced by the pleasure given the domineering husband. By utilitarian standards, servility in this case would be good, not bad, since by being servile, the wife brings about more pleasure and less pain overall. To account for the wrongness of servility, contends Hill, one must appeal to Kantian issues, not utilitarian ones. What is wrong with servility is that the servile person fails to treat himself or herself in a morally appropriate way because, according to Kantian theory, to respect the moral law one must respect oneself.

Servility and Self-Respect

Usually we think that morality requires us to act in particular ways toward other people. We need to treat each other fairly, we need to assist those in need, and we are sometimes asked to give up something we want in order to do our duty to someone else. However, many moral philosophers suggest that morality is also concerned with the way that we treat ourselves. Not only must we treat others in a morally appropriate way, but we must treat ourselves in a morally appropriate way. One way to demonstrate the proper moral attitude is to have a due measure of self-respect. Failure to prevent our own rights from being trampled indicates a lack of self-respect and, thus, a failure to treat oneself morally.

From Thomas E. Hill, Jr., "Servility and Self-Respect," *The Monist,* Vol. 57, No. 1 (January 1973), pp. 87–104. Copyright © 1973 The Monist, La Salle, IL 61301. Reprinted by permission.

In this article, Hill draws upon three kinds of individuals who he thinks fail to treat themselves morally. These are the Uncle Tom, the Self-Deprecator, and the Deferential Wife. In each of these examples we see a person who fails to show respect for himself or herself. Yet although our intuitions may suggest that acting in a servile manner is wrong, a Kantian theory explains why servility is immoral in ways not available to a utilitarian theory.   ✍

Several motives underlie this paper.[1] In the first place, I am curious to see if there is a legitimate source for the increasingly common feeling that servility can be as much a vice as arrogance. There seems to be something morally defective about the Uncle Tom and the submissive housewife; and yet, on the other hand, if the only interests they sacrifice are their own, it seems that we should have no right to complain. Secondly, I have some sympathy for the now unfashionable view that each person has duties to himself as well as to others. It does seem absurd to say that a person could literally violate his own rights or owe himself a debt of gratitude, but I suspect that the classic defenders of duties to oneself had something different in mind. If there are duties to oneself, it is natural to expect that a duty to avoid being servile would have a prominent place among them. Thirdly, I am interested in making sense of Kant's puzzling, but suggestive, remarks about respect for persons and respect for the moral law. On the usual reading, these remarks seem unduly moralistic; but, viewed in another way, they suggest an argument for a kind of self-respect which is incompatible with a servile attitude.

My procedure will not be to explicate Kant directly. Instead I shall try to isolate the defect of servility and sketch an argument to show why it is objectionable, noting only in passing how this relates to Kant and the controversy about duties to oneself. What I say about self-respect is far from the whole story. In particular, it is not concerned with esteem for one's special abilities and achievements or with the self-confidence which characterizes the especially autonomous person. Nor is my concern with the psychological antecedents and effects of self-respect. Nevertheless, my conclusions, if correct, should be of interest; for they imply that, given a common view of morality, there are nonutilitarian moral reasons for each person, regardless of his merits, to respect himself. To avoid servility to the extent that one can is not simply a right but a duty, not simply a duty to others but a duty to oneself.

I

1. To begin, Hill gives three examples of the kind of behavior he calls servility.

Three examples may give a preliminary idea of what I mean by *servility*. Consider, first, an extremely deferential black, whom I shall call the *Uncle Tom*. He always steps aside for white men; he does not complain when less qualified whites take over his job; he gratefully accepts whatever benefits his all-white government and employers allot

[1] An earlier version of this paper was presented at the meetings of the American Philosophical Association, Pacific Division. A number of revisions have been made as a result of the helpful comments of others, especially Norman Dahl, Sharon Hill, Herbert Morris, and Mary Mothersill.

him, and he would not think of protesting its insufficiency. He displays the symbols of deference to whites, and of contempt towards blacks: he faces the former with bowed stance and a ready "sir" and "Ma'am"; he reserves his strongest obscenities for the latter. Imagine, too, that he is not playing a game. He is not the shrewdly prudent calculator, who knows how to make the best of a bad lot and mocks his masters behind their backs. He accepts without question the idea that, as a black, he is owed less than whites. He may believe that blacks are mentally inferior and of less social utility, but that is not the crucial point. The attitude which he displays is that what he values, aspires for, and can demand is of less importance than what whites value, aspire for, and can demand. He is far from the picture book's carefree, happy servant, but he does not feel that he has a right to expect anything better.

Another pattern of servility is illustrated by a person I shall call the *Self-Deprecator*. Like the Uncle Tom, he is reluctant to make demands. He says nothing when others take unfair advantage of him. When asked for his preferences or opinions, he tends to shrink away as if what he said should make no difference. His problem, however, is not a sense of racial inferiority but rather an acute awareness of his own inadequacies and failures as an individual. These defects are not imaginary: he has in fact done poorly by his own standards and others'. But, unlike many of us in the same situation, he acts as if his failings warrant quite unrelated maltreatment even by strangers. His sense of shame and self-contempt make him content to be the instrument of others. He feels that nothing is owed him until he has earned it and that he has earned very little. He is not simply playing a masochist's game of winning sympathy by disparaging himself. On the contrary, he assesses his individual merits with painful accuracy.

A rather different case is that of the *Deferential Wife*. This is a woman who is utterly devoted to serving her husband. She buys the clothes *he* prefers, invites the guests *he* wants to entertain, and makes love whenever *he* is in the mood. She willingly moves to a new city in order for him to have a more attractive job, counting her own friendships and geographical preferences insignificant by comparison. She loves her husband, but her conduct is not simply an expression of love. She is happy, but she does not subordinate herself as a means to happiness. She does not simply defer to her husband in certain spheres as a trade-off for his deference in other spheres. On the contrary, she tends not to form her own interests, values, and ideals; and, when she does, she counts them as less important than her husband's. She readily responds to appeals from Women's Liberation that she agrees that women are mentally and physically equal, if not superior, to men. She just believes that the proper role for a woman is to serve her family. As a matter of fact, much of her happiness derives from her belief that she fulfills this role very well. No one is trampling on her rights, she says; for she is quite glad, and proud, to serve her husband as she does.

Each one of these cases reflects the attitude which I call servility.[2] It betrays the absence of a certain kind of self-respect. What I take this attitude to be, more specifically,

---

[2] Each of the cases is intended to represent only one possible pattern of servility. I make no claims about how often these patterns are exemplified, nor do I mean to imply that only these patterns could warrant the labels "Deferential Wife," "Uncle Tom," etc. All the more, I do not mean to imply any comparative judgments about the causes or relative magnitude of the problems of racial and sexual discrimination. One person, e.g., a self-contemptuous woman with a sense of racial inferiority, might exemplify features of several patterns at once; and, of course, a person might view her being a woman the way an Uncle Tom views his being black, etc.

will become clearer later on. It is important at the outset, however, not to confuse the three cases sketched above with other, superficially similar cases. In particular, the cases I have sketched are not simply cases in which someone refuses to press his rights, speaks disparagingly of himself, or devotes himself to another. A black, for example, is not necessarily servile because he does not demand a just wage; for, seeing that such a demand would result in his being fired, he might forbear for the sake of his children. A self-critical person is not necessarily servile by virtue of bemoaning his faults in public; for his behavior may be merely a complex way of satisfying his own inner needs quite independent of a willingness to accept abuse from others. A woman need not be servile whenever she works to make her husband happy and prosperous; for she might freely and knowingly choose to do so from love or from a desire to share the rewards of his success. If the effort did not require her to submit to humiliation or maltreatment, her choice would not mark her as servile. There may, of course, be grounds for objecting to the attitudes in these cases; but the defect is not servility of the sort I want to consider. It should also be noted that my cases of servility are not simply instances of deference to superior knowledge or judgment. To defer to an expert's judgment on matters of fact is not to be servile; to defer to his every wish and whim is. Similarly, the belief that one's talents and achievements are comparatively low does not, by itself, make one servile. It is no vice to acknowledge the truth, and one may in fact have achieved less, and have less ability, than others. To be servile is not simply to hold certain empirical beliefs but to have a certain attitude concerning one's rightful place in a moral community.

II

Are there grounds for regarding the attitudes of the Uncle Tom, the Self-Deprecator, and the Deferential Wife as morally objectionable? Are there moral arguments we could give them to show that they ought to have more self-respect? None of the more obvious replies is entirely satisfactory.

2. How does a utilitarian theory treat the case of servility?

One might, in the first place, adduce utilitarian considerations. Typically the servile person will be less happy than he might be. Moreover, he may be less prone to make the best of his own socially useful abilities. He may become a nuisance to others by being overly dependent. He will, in any case, lose the special contentment that comes from standing up for one's rights. A submissive attitude encourages exploitation, and exploitation spreads misery in a variety of ways. These considerations provide a prima facie case against the attitudes of the Uncle Tom, the Deferential Wife, and the Self-Deprecator, but they are hardly conclusive. Other utilities tend to counterbalance the ones just mentioned. When people refuse to press their rights, there are usually others who profit. There are undeniable pleasures in associating with those who are devoted, understanding, and grateful for whatever we see fit to give them—as our fondness for dogs attests. Even the servile person may find his attitude a source of happiness, as the case of the Deferential Wife illustrates. There may be comfort and security in thinking that the hard choices must be made by others, that what I would say has little to do with what ought to be done. Self-condemnation may bring relief from the pangs of guilt even if it is not deliberately used for that purpose. On balance, then, utilitarian considerations may turn out to favor servility as much as they oppose it.

For those who share my moral intuitions, there is another sort of reason for not trying to rest a case against servility on utilitarian considerations. Certain utilities seem irrelevant to the issue. The utilitarian must weigh them along with others, but to do so seems morally inappropriate. Suppose, for example, that the submissive attitudes of the Uncle Tom and the Deferential Wife result in positive utilities for those who dominate and exploit them. Do we need to tabulate *these* utilities before conceding that servility is objectionable? The Uncle Tom, it seems, is making an error, a moral error, quite apart from consideration of how much others in fact profit from his attitude. The Deferential Wife may be quite happy; but if her happiness turns out to be contingent on her distorted view of her own rights and worth as a person, then it carries little moral weight against the contention that she ought to change that view. Suppose I could cause a woman to find her happiness in denying all her rights and serving my every wish. No doubt I could do so only by nonrational manipulative techniques, which I ought not to use. But is this the only objection? My efforts would be wrong, it seems, not only because of the techniques they require but also because the resultant attitude is itself objectionable. When a person's happiness stems from a morally objectionable attitude, it ought to be discounted. That a sadist gets pleasure from seeing others suffer should not count even as a partial justification for his attitude. That a servile person derives pleasure from denying her moral status, for similar reasons, cannot make her attitude acceptable. These brief intuitive remarks are not intended as a refutation of utilitarianism, with all its many varieties; but they do suggest that it is well to look elsewhere for adequate grounds for rejecting the attitudes of the Uncle Tom, the Self-Deprecator, and the Deferential Wife.

One might try to appeal to meritarian considerations. That is, one might argue that the servile person *deserves* more than he allows himself. This line of argument, however, is no more adequate than the utilitarian one. It may be wrong to deny others what they deserve, but it is not so obviously wrong to demand less for oneself than one deserves. In any case, the Self-Deprecator's problem is not that he underestimates his merits. By hypothesis, he assesses his merits quite accurately. We cannot reasonably tell him to have more respect for himself because he *deserves* more respect; he knows that he has not *earned* better treatment. His problem, in fact, is that he thinks of his moral status with regard to others as entirely dependent upon his merits. His interests and choices are important, he feels, only if he has earned the right to make demands; or if he had rights by birth, they were forfeited by his subsequent failures and misdeeds. My Self-Deprecator is no doubt an atypical person, but nevertheless he illustrates an important point. Normally when we find a self-contemptuous person, we can plausibly argue that he is not so bad as he thinks, that his self-contempt is an overreaction prompted more by inner needs than by objective assessment of his merits. Because this argument cannot work with the Self-Deprecator, his case draws attention to a distinction, applicable in other cases as well, between saying that someone deserves respect for his merits and saying that he is owed respect as a person. On meritarian grounds we can only say "You deserve better than this," but the defect of the servile person is not merely failure to recognize his merits.

Other common arguments against the Uncle Tom, et al., may have some force but seem not to strike to the heart of the problem. For example, philosophers sometimes appeal to the value of human potentialities. As a human being, it is said, one at least has a capacity for rationality, morality, excellence, or autonomy, and this capacity is worthy of respect. Although such arguments have the merit of making respect independent of a person's actual deserts, they seem quite misplaced in some cases. There comes a time when we have sufficient evidence that a person is not ever going to *be* rational, moral, excellent, or autonomous even if he still has a capacity, in some sense, for being so. As a person approaches death with an atrocious record so far, the chances of his realizing his diminishing capacities become increasingly slim. To make these capacities the basis of his self-respect is to rest it on a shifting and unstable ground. We do, of course, respect persons for capacities which they are not exercising at the moment; for example, I might respect a person as a good philosopher even though he is just now blundering into gross confusion. In these cases, however, we respect the person for an active capacity, a ready disposition, which he has displayed on many occasions. On this analogy, a person should have respect for himself only when his capacities are developed and ready, needing only to be triggered by an appropriate occasion or the removal of some temporary obstacle. The Uncle Tom and the Deferential Wife, however, may in fact have quite limited capacities of this sort, and, since the Self-Deprecator is already overly concerned with his own inadequacies, drawing attention to his capacities seems a poor way to increase his self-respect. In any case, setting aside the Kantian nonempirical capacity for autonomy, the capacities of different persons vary widely; but what the servile person seems to overlook is something by virtue of which he is equal with every other person.

III

---

3. Hill looks more closely at the three cases and finds that the problem revolves around denial of one's own rights. A discussion of rights follows.

Why, then, is servility a moral defect? There is, I think, another sort of answer which is worth exploring. The first part of this answer must be an attempt to isolate the objectionable features of the servile person; later we can ask why these features are objectionable. As a step in this direction, let us examine again our three paradigm cases. The moral defect in each case, I suggest, is a failure to understand and acknowledge one's own moral rights. I assume, without argument here, that each person has moral rights.[3] Some of these rights may be basic human rights; that is, rights for which a person needs only to be human to qualify. Other rights will be derivative and contingent upon his special commitments, institutional affiliations, etc. Most rights will be prima facie ones; some may be absolute. Most can be waived under appropriate conditions; perhaps some cannot. Many rights can be forfeited; but some, presumably, cannot. The servile person does not, strictly speaking, violate his own rights. At

---

[3]As will become evident, I am also presupposing some form of cognitive or "naturalistic" interpretation of rights. If, to accommodate an emotivist or prescriptivist, we set aside talk of moral knowledge and ignorance, we might construct a somewhat analogous case against servility from the point of view of those who adopt principles ascribing rights to all; but the argument, I suspect, would be more complex and less persuasive.

least in our paradigm cases he fails to acknowledge fully his own moral status because he does not fully understand what his rights are, how they can be waived, and when they can be forfeited.

The defect of the Uncle Tom, for example, is that he displays an attitude that denies his moral equality with whites. He does not realize, or apprehend in an effective way, that he has as much right to a decent wage and a share of political power as any comparable white. His gratitude is misplaced; he accepts benefits which are his by right as if they were gifts. The Self-Deprecator is servile in a more complex way. He acts as if he has forfeited many important rights which in fact he has not. He does not understand, or fully realize in his own case, that certain rights to fair and decent treatment do not have to be earned. He sees his merits clearly enough, but he fails to see that what he can expect from others is not merely a function of his merits. The Deferential Wife *says* that she understands her rights vis-à-vis her husband, but what she fails to appreciate is that her consent to serve him is a valid waiver of her rights only under certain conditions. If her consent is coerced, say, by the lack of viable options for women in her society, then her consent is worth little. If socially fostered ignorance of her own talents and alternatives is responsible for her consent, then her consent should not count as a fully legitimate waiver of her right to equal consideration within the marriage. All the more, her consent to defer constantly to her husband is not a legitimate setting aside of her rights if it results from her mistaken belief that she has a moral duty to do so. (Recall: "The *proper* role for a woman is to serve her family.") If she believes that she has a *duty* to defer to her husband, then, whatever she may say, she cannot fully understand that she has a *right* not to defer to him. When she says that she freely gives up such a right, she is confused. Her confusion is rather like that of a person who has been persuaded by an unscrupulous lawyer that it is legally incumbent on him to refuse a jury trial but who nevertheless tells the judge that he understands that he has a right to a jury trial and freely waives it. He does not really understand what it is to have and freely give up the right if he thinks that it would be an offense for him to exercise it.

Insofar as servility results from moral ignorance or confusion, it need not be something for which a person is to blame. Even self-reproach may be inappropriate; for at the time a person is in ignorance he cannot feel guilty about his servility, and later he may conclude that his ignorance was unavoidable. In some cases, however, a person might reasonably believe that he should have known better. If, for example, the Deferential Wife's confusion about her rights resulted from a motivated resistance to drawing the implications of her own basic moral principles, then later she might find some ground for self-reproach. Whether blameworthy or not, servility could still be morally objectionable at least in the sense that it ought to be discouraged, that social conditions which nourish it should be reformed, and the like. Not all morally undesirable features of a person are ones for which he is responsible, but that does not mean that they are defects merely from an esthetic or prudential point of view.

In our paradigm cases, I have suggested, servility is a kind of deferential attitude towards others resulting from ignorance or misunderstanding of one's moral rights. A sufficient remedy, one might think, would be moral enlightenment. Suppose, however, that our servile persons come to know their rights but do not substantially alter their behavior. Are they not still servile in an objectionable way?

One might even think that reproach is more appropriate now because they know what they are doing.

The problem, unfortunately, is not as simple as it may appear. Much depends on what they tolerate and why. Let us set aside cases in which a person merely refuses to *fight* for his rights, chooses not to exercise certain rights, or freely waives many rights which he might have insisted upon. Our problem concerns the previously servile person who continues to display the same marks of deference even after he fully knows his rights. Imagine, for example, that even after enlightenment our Uncle Tom persists in his old pattern behavior, giving all the typical signs of believing that the injustices done to him are not really wrong. Suppose, too, that the newly enlightened Deferential Wife continues to defer to her husband, refusing to disturb the old way of life by introducing her new ideas. She acts as if she accepts the idea that she is merely doing her duty though actually she no longer believes it. Let us suppose, further, that the Uncle Tom and the Deferential Wife are not merely generous with their time and property; they also accept without protest, and even appear to sanction, treatment which is humiliating and degrading. That is, they do not simply consent to waive mutually acknowledged rights; they tolerate violations of their rights with apparent approval. They pretend to give their permission for subtle humiliations which they really believe no permission can make legitimate. Are such persons still servile despite their moral knowledge?

The answer, I think, should depend upon why the deferential role is played. If the motive is a morally commendable one, or a desire to avert dire consequences to oneself, or even an ambition to set an oppressor up for a later fall, then I would not count the role player as servile. The Uncle Tom, for instance, is not servile in my sense if he shuffles and bows to keep the Klan from killing his children, to save his own skin, or even to buy time while he plans the revolution. Similarly, the Deferential Wife is not servile if she tolerates an abusive husband because he is so ill that further strain would kill him, because protesting would deprive her of her only means of survival, or because she is collecting atrocity stories for her book against marriage. If there is fault in these situations, it seems inappropriate to call it *servility*. The story is quite different, however, if a person continues in his deferential role just from laziness, timidity, or a desire for some minor advantage. He shows too little concern for his moral status as a person, one is tempted to say, if he is willing to deny it for a small profit or simply because it requires some effort and courage to affirm it openly. A black who plays the Uncle Tom merely to gain an advantage over other blacks is harming them, of course; but he is also displaying disregard for his own moral position as an equal among human beings. Similarly a woman throws away her rights too lightly if she continues to play the subservient role because she is used to it or is too timid to risk a change. A Self-Deprecator who readily accepts what he knows are violations of his rights may be indulging his peculiar need for punishment at the expense of denying something more valuable. In these cases, I suggest, we have a kind of servility independent of any ignorance or confusion about one's rights. The person who has it may or may not be blameworthy, depending on many factors; and the line between servile and nonservile role playing will often be hard to draw. Nevertheless, the objectionable feature is perhaps clear enough for present purposes: it is a willingness to disavow one's moral status, publicly and systematically, in the absence of any strong reason to do so.

My proposal, then, is that there are at least two types of servility: one resulting from misunderstanding of one's rights and the other from placing a comparatively low value on them. In either case, servility manifests the absence of a certain kind of self-respect. The respect which is missing is not respect for one's merits but respect for one's rights. The servile person displays this absence of respect not directly by acting contrary to his own rights but indirectly by acting as if his rights were nonexistent or insignificant. An arrogant person ignores the rights of others, thereby arrogating for himself a higher status than he is entitled to; a servile person denies his own rights, thereby assuming a lower position than he is entitled to. Whether rooted in ignorance or simply lack of concern for moral rights, the attitudes in both cases may be incompatible with a proper regard for morality. That this is so is obvious in the case of arrogance; but to see it in the case of servility requires some further argument.

IV

----

4. The problem of the immorality of servility is examined here from a Kantian perspective. In the following paragraph Hill explicitly maps out the Kantian argument.

The objectionable feature of the servile person, as I have described him, is his tendency to disavow his own moral rights either because he misunderstands them or because he cares little for them. The question remains: why should anyone regard this as a moral defect? After all, the rights which he denies are his own. He may be unfortunate, foolish, or even distasteful; but why *morally* deficient? One sort of answer, quite different from those reviewed earlier, is suggested by some of Kant's remarks. Kant held that servility is contrary to a perfect nonjuridical duty to oneself.[4] To say that the duty is perfect is roughly to say that it is stringent, never overridden by other considerations (e.g., beneficence). To say that the duty is nonjuridical is to say that a person cannot legitimately be coerced to comply. Although Kant did not develop an explicit argument for this view, an argument can easily be constructed from materials which reflect the spirit, if not the letter, of his moral theory. The argument which I have in mind is prompted by Kant's contention that respect for persons, strictly speaking, is respect for moral law.[5] If taken as a claim about all sorts of respect, this seems quite implausible. If it means that we respect persons only for their moral character, their capacity for moral conduct, or their status as "authors" of the moral law, then it seems unduly moralistic. My strategy is to construe the remark as saying that at least one sort of respect for persons is respect for the rights which the moral law accords them. If one respects the moral law, then one must

----

[4]See Immanuel Kant, *The Doctrine of Virtue,* Part II of *The Metaphysics of Morals,* ed. by M. J. Gregor (New York: Harper & Row, 1964), pp. 99–103; Prussian Academy edition, Vol. VI, pp. 434–37.

[5]Immanuel Kant, *Groundwork of the Metaphysics of Morals,* ed. by H. J. Paton (New York: Harper & Row, 1964), p. 69; Prussian Academy edition, Vol. IV, p. 401; *The Critique of Practical Reason,* ed. by Lewis W. Beck (New York: Bobbs-Merrill, 1956), pp. 81, 84; Prussian Academy edition, Vol. V, pp. 78, 81. My purpose here is not to interpret what Kant meant but to give a sense to his remark.

respect one's own moral rights; and this amounts to having a kind of self-respect incompatible with servility.

The premises for the Kantian argument, which are all admittedly vague, can be sketched as follows:

First, let us assume, as Kant did, that all human beings have equal basic human rights. Specific rights vary with different conditions, but all must be justified from a point of view under which all are equal. Not all rights need to be earned, and some cannot be forfeited. Many rights can be waived but only under certain conditions of knowledge and freedom. These conditions are complex and difficult to state; but they include something like the condition that a person's consent releases others from obligation only if it is autonomously given, and consent resulting from underestimation of one's moral status is not autonomously given. Rights can be objects of knowledge, but also of ignorance, misunderstanding, deception, and the like.

Second, let us assume that my account of servility is correct; or, if one prefers, we can take it as a definition. That is, in brief, a servile person is one who tends to deny or disavow his own moral rights because he does not understand them or has little concern for the status they give him.

Third, we need one formal premise concerning moral duty, namely, that each person ought, as far as possible, to respect the moral law. In less Kantian language, the point is that everyone should approximate, to the extent that he can, the ideal of a person who fully adopts the moral point of view. Roughly, this means not only that each person ought to do what is morally required and refrain from what is morally wrong but also that each person should treat all the provisions of morality as valuable—worth preserving and prizing as well as obeying. One must, so to speak, take up the spirit of morality as well as meet the letter of its requirements. To keep one's promises, avoid hurting others, and the like, is not sufficient; one should also take an attitude of respect towards the principles, ideals, and goals of morality. A respectful attitude towards a system of rights and duties consists of more than a disposition to conform to its definite rules of behavior; it also involves holding the system in esteem, being unwilling to ridicule it, and being reluctant to give up one's place in it. The essentially Kantian idea here is that morality, as a system of equal fundamental rights and duties, is worthy of respect, and hence a completely moral person would respect it in word and manner as well as in deed. And what a completely moral person would do, in Kant's view, is our duty to do so far as we can.

The assumptions here are, of course, strong ones, and I make no attempt to justify them. They are, I suspect, widely held though rarely articulated. In any case, my present purpose is not to evaluate them but to see how, if granted, they constitute a case against servility. The objection to the servile person, given our premises, is that he does not satisfy the basic requirement to respect morality. A person who fully respected a system of moral rights would be disposed to learn his proper place in it, to affirm it proudly, and not to tolerate abuses of it lightly. This is just the sort of disposition that the servile person lacks. If he does not understand the system, he is in no position to respect it adequately. This lack of respect may be no fault of his own, but it is still a way in which he falls short of a moral ideal. If, on the other hand, the servile person knowingly disavows his moral rights by pretending to approve of violations of them, then, barring special explanations, he shows an indifference to whether the provisions of morality are honored and publicly acknowledged. This avoidable display of indifference, by our Kantian premises, is contrary to the duty to respect morality. The disrespect in this second case is somewhat like the disrespect a religious believer might show towards his religion if, to avoid embarrassment, he laughed congenially while nonbelievers were mocking the beliefs which he secretly held. In any case, the servile person, as such, does not express disrespect for the system of moral rights in the obvious way by violating the rights of others. His lack of respect is more subtly manifested by his acting before others as if he did not know or care about his position of equality under that system.

---

5. Hill provides an analogy to illustrate the Kantian argument. Why are the rules of the club important in the analogy? At the end of the analogy, Hill draws his conclusion from the Kantian argument.

The central idea here may be illustrated by an analogy. Imagine a club, say, an old German dueling fraternity. By the rules of the club, each member has certain rights and responsibilities. These are the same for each member regardless of what titles he may hold outside the club. Each has, for example, a right to be heard at meetings, a right not to be shouted down by the others. Some rights cannot be forfeited: for example, each may vote regardless of whether he has paid his dues and satisfied other rules. Some rights cannot be waived: for example, the right to be defended when attacked by several members of the rival fraternity. The members show respect for each other by respecting the status which the rules confer on each member. Now one new member is careful always to allow the others to speak at meetings; but when they shout him down, he does nothing. He just shrugs as if to say, 'Who am I to complain?' When he fails to stand up in defense of a fellow member, he feels ashamed and refuses to vote. He does not deserve to vote, he says. As the only commoner among illustrious barons, he feels that it is his place to serve them and defer to their decisions. When attackers from the rival fraternity come at him with swords drawn, he tells his companions to run and save themselves. When they defend him, he expresses immense gratitude—as if they had done him a gratuitous favor. Now one might argue that our new member fails to show respect for the fraternity and its rules. He does not actually violate any of the rules by refusing to vote, asking others not to defend him, and deferring to the barons, but he symbolically disavows the equal status which the rules confer on him. If he ought to have respect for the fraternity, he ought to change his attitude. Our servile person, then, is like the new member of the dueling fraternity in having insufficient respect for a system of rules and ideals. The difference is that everyone ought to respect morality whereas there is no comparable moral requirement to respect the fraternity.

The conclusion here is, of course, a limited one. Self-sacrifice is not always a sign of servility. It is not a duty always to press one's rights. Whether a given act is evidence of servility will depend not only on the attitude of the agent but also on the specific nature of his moral rights, a matter not considered here. Moreover, the extent to which a person is responsible, or blameworthy, for his defect remains an open question. Nevertheless, the conclusion should not be minimized. In order to avoid servility, a person who gives up his rights must do so with a full appreciation for what they are. A woman, for example, may devote herself to her husband if she is uncoerced, knows what she is doing, and does not pretend that she has no decent alternative. A self-contemptuous person may decide not to press various unforfeited rights but only if he does not take the attitude that he is too rotten to deserve them. A black may demand less than is due to him provided he is prepared to acknowledge that no one has a right to expect this of him. Sacrifices of this sort, I suspect, are extremely rare. Most people, if they fully acknowledge their rights, would not autonomously refuse to press them.

An even stronger conclusion would emerge if we could assume that some basic rights cannot be waived. That is, if there are some rights that others are bound to respect regardless of what we say, then, barring special explanation, we would be obliged not only to acknowledge these rights but also to avoid any appearance of consenting to give them up. To act as if we could release others from their obligation to grant these rights, apart from special circumstances, would be to fail to respect morality. Rousseau held, for example, that at least a minimal right to liberty cannot be waived. A man who consents to be enslaved, giving up liberty without *quid pro quo,* thereby displays a conditioned slavish mentality that renders his consent worthless. Similarly, a Kantian might argue that a person cannot release others from the obligation to refrain from killing him: consent is no defense against the charge of murder. To accept principles of this sort is to hold that rights to life and liberty are, as Kant believed, rather like a trustee's rights to preserve something valuable entrusted to him: he has not only a right but a duty to preserve it.

Even if there are no specific rights which cannot be waived, there might be at least one formal right of this sort. This is the right to some minimum degree of respect from others. No matter how willing a person is to submit to humiliation by others, they ought to show him some respect as a person. By analogy with self-respect, as presented here, this respect owed by others would consist of a willingness to acknowledge fully, in word as well as action, the person's basically equal moral status as defined by his other rights. To the extent that a person gives even tacit consent to humiliations incompatible with this respect, he will be acting as if he waives a right which he cannot in fact give up. To do this, barring special explanations, would mark one as servile.

V

Kant held that the avoidance of servility is a duty to oneself rather than a duty to others. Recent philosophers, however, tend to discard the idea of a duty to oneself as a conceptual confusion. Although admittedly the analogy between a duty to oneself and a duty to others is not perfect, I suggest that something important is reflected in Kant's contention.

***

6. The topic for the remainder of the article is the idea of a duty to oneself.

***

Let us consider briefly the function of saying that a duty is *to* someone. *First,* to say that a duty is *to* a given person sometimes merely indicates who is the object of that duty. That is, it tells us that the duty is concerned with how that person is to be treated, how his interests and wishes are to be taken into account, and the like. Here we might as well say that we have a duty *towards,* or *regarding* that person. Typically the person in question is the beneficiary of the fulfillment of the duty. For example, in this sense I have a duty to my children and even a duty to a distant stranger if I promised a third party that I would help that stranger. Clearly a duty to avoid servility would be a duty to oneself at least in this minimal sense, for it is a duty to avoid, so far as possible, the denial of one's own moral status. The duty is concerned with understanding and affirming one's rights, which are, at least as a rule, for one's own benefit.

Second, when we say that a duty is *to* a certain person, we often indicate thereby the person especially entitled to complain in case the duty is not fulfilled. For example, if I fail in my duty to my colleagues, then it is they who can most appropriately reproach me. Others may sometimes speak up on their behalf, but, for the most part, it is not the business of strangers to set me straight. Analogously, to say that the duty to avoid servility is a duty to oneself would indicate that, though sometimes a person may justifiably reproach himself for being servile, others are not generally in the appropriate position to complain. Outside encouragement is sometimes necessary, but, if any blame is called for, it is primarily self-recrimination and not the censure of others.

Third, mention of the person to whom a duty is owed often tells us something about the source of that duty. For example, to say that I have a duty to another person may indicate that the argument to show that I have such a duty turns upon a promise to that person, his authority over me, my having accepted special benefits from him, or, more generally, his rights. Accordingly, to say that the duty to avoid servility is a duty to oneself would at least imply that it is not entirely based upon promises to others, their authority, their beneficence, or an obligation to respect their rights. More positively, the assertion might serve to indicate that the source of the duty is one's own rights rather than the rights of others, etc. That is, one ought not to be servile because, in some broad sense, one ought to respect one's own rights as a person. There is, to be sure, an asymmetry: one has certain duties to others because one ought not to violate their rights, and one has a duty to oneself because one ought to affirm one's own rights. Nevertheless, to dismiss duties to oneself out of hand is to overlook significant similarities.

Some familiar objections to duties to oneself, moreover, seem irrelevant in the case of servility. For example, some place much stock in the idea that a person would have no duties if alone on a desert island. This can be doubted, but in any case is irrelevant here. The duty to avoid servility is a duty to take a certain stance towards others and hence would be inapplicable if one were isolated on a desert island. Again, some suggest that if there were duties to oneself then one could make promises to oneself or owe oneself a debt of gratitude. Their paradigms are familiar ones. Someone remarks, "I promised myself a vacation this year" or "I have been such a good boy I owe myself a treat." Concentration on these facetious cases tends to confuse the issue. In any case the duty to avoid servility, as presented here, does not presuppose promises to oneself or debts of gratitude to oneself. Other objections stem from the intuition that a person has no duty to promote his own happiness. A duty to oneself, it is sometimes assumed, must be a duty to promote one's own happiness. From a utilitarian point of view, in fact, this is what a duty to oneself would most likely be. The problems with such alleged duties, however, are irrelevant to the duty to avoid servility. This is a duty to understand and affirm one's rights, not to promote one's own welfare. While it is usually in the interest of a person to affirm his rights, our Kantian argument against servility was not based upon this premise. Finally, a more subtle line of objection turns on the idea that, given that rights and duties are correlative, a person who acted contrary to a duty to oneself would have to be violating his own rights, which seems absurd.[6] This objection raises issues too complex to examine here. One should note, however, that I have tried to give a sense to saying that servility is contrary to a duty to oneself without presupposing that the servile person violates his own rights. If acts contrary to duties to others are always violations of their rights, then duties to oneself are not parallel with duties to others to that extent. But this does not mean that it is empty or pointless to say that a duty is to oneself.

My argument against servility may prompt some to say that the duty is "to morality" rather than "to oneself." All this means, however, is that the duty is derived from a basic requirement to respect the provisions of morality; and in this sense every duty is a duty "to morality." My duties to my children are also derivative from a general requirement to respect moral principles, but they are still duties *to* them.

Kant suggests that duties to oneself are a precondition of duties to others. On our account of servility, there is at least one sense in which this is so. Insofar as the servile person is ignorant of his own rights, he is not in an adequate position to appreciate the rights of others. Misunderstanding the moral basis for his equal status with others, he is necessarily liable to underestimate the rights of those with whom he classifies himself. On the other hand, if he plays the servile role knowingly, then, barring special explanation, he displays a lack of concern to see the principles of morality acknowledged and respected and thus the absence of one motive which can move a moral person to respect the rights of others. In either case, the servile person's lack of self-respect necessarily puts him in a less than ideal position to respect others. Failure to fulfill one's duty to oneself, then, renders a person liable to violate duties to others. This, however, is a consequence of our argument against servility, not a presupposition of it.

READING QUESTIONS

1. What seems to be missing from people who are servile?
2. How could a utilitarian theory actually support servility?
3. How does each of the three servile models demonstrate a lack of regard for his or her moral rights?
4. How does a person show a proper Kantian respect for the moral law?
5. How does a failure to fulfill a duty to oneself suggest that a person will violate duties to others?

---

[6]This, I take it, is part of M. G. Singer's objection to duties to oneself in *Generalization in Ethics* (New York: Alfred A. Knopf, 1961), pp. 311–18. I have attempted to examine Singer's arguments in detail elsewhere.

Susan Wolf

S hould people strive for moral perfection? Should we try to be the very best people we can be? In "Moral Saints," Susan Wolf, professor of philosophy at Johns
Hopkins University, criticizes the notion that the ideally moral person—the moral
saint—provides an appropriate moral model. The moral saint, according to Wolf, is
the person "whose every action is as morally good as possible." Although the continual sacrifice of one's own interests to the interests of others appears commendable, the moral saint almost surely will fail to develop the nonmoral interests, skills,
and relationships we consider necessary for a healthy human life. Wolf contends
that a close analysis of the life of the moral saint calls into question the common assumption that it is, in her words, "always better to be morally better."

Published in 1983, this article has special relevance to virtue ethics, the ethical
theory that has its historical foundation in the ancient Greek ethics of Plato and, especially, Aristotle. Virtue ethics offers an alternative to the action-based ethical theories of utilitarianism and Kantian deontology. While action-based theories focus on
the kinds of *actions* that the ethical person should take, virtue or character-based
theories such as virtue ethics focus on the *character* of the moral person. The question to be answered in virtue ethics is, What kind of person should I be? rather than,
What kind of acts should I perform? For an article that was instrumental in directing philosophical attention to the value of a virtue-based ethical theory in this century, see "Modern Moral Theory" by G. E. M. Anscombe, elsewhere in this volume.
For an introduction to the historical basis for this approach to ethics, see the readings from Plato and Aristotle.

Moral Saints

Many people may take it for granted that being the most moral person
possible is an ideal goal in any moral theory, even if human weakness and
frailty make it impossible, or at least highly unlikely, that anyone will realize this goal. The person who selflessly dedicates himself or herself to
helping others and making the world a better place certainly seems laudable. But have you ever thought about what it would really be like to
know, or even be, one of those people whom Susan Wolf calls a "moral
saint"?

In this influential article, Wolf suggests that this ideal would not fit in
well with the way we commonly think of morality. Someone who is this selfless would somehow be lacking in other qualities that we think are important, even vital, for living a good life. Nor does the notion of the moral saint

From Susan Wolf, "Moral Saints," *The Journal of Philosophy, 79,* 8 (August 1982), 419–39. Reprinted
by permission of the publisher.

fit in with the two dominant moral theories, utilitarianism and Kantian theory. Wolf draws some important lessons about moral theories from this most
interesting examination of the pinnacles of moral perfection.   ✒

1. In this initial paragraph, Wolf defines what she means by "moral saints."
This definition will figure importantly in the remainder of the essay.

I don't know whether there are any moral saints. But if there are, I am glad that neither I nor those about whom I care most are among them. By *moral saint* I mean a
person whose every action is as morally good as possible, a person, that is, who is
as morally worthy as can be. Though I shall in a moment acknowledge the variety
of types of person that might be thought to satisfy this description, it seems to me
that none of these types serve as unequivocally compelling personal ideals. In other
words, I believe that moral perfection, in the sense of moral saintliness, does not
constitute a model of personal well-being toward which it would be particularly rational or good or desirable for a human being to strive.

Outside the context of moral discussion, this will strike many as an obvious point.
But, within that context, the point, if it be granted, will be granted with some discomfort. For within that context it is generally assumed that one ought to be as morally
good as possible and that what limits there are to morality's hold on us are set by features of human nature of which we ought not to be proud. If, as I believe, the ideals
that are derivable from common sense and philosophically popular moral theories do
not support these assumptions, then something has to change. Either we must change
our moral theories in ways that will make them yield more palatable ideals, or, as I shall
argue, we must change our conception of what is involved in affirming a moral theory.

2. Wolf describes what she intends to do in this paper.

In this paper, I wish to examine the notion of a moral saint, first, to understand
what a moral saint would be like and why such a being would be unattractive, and,
second, to raise some questions about the significance of this paradoxical figure for
moral philosophy. I shall look first at the model(s) of moral sainthood that might be
extrapolated from the morality or moralities of common sense. Then I shall consider
what relations these have to conclusions that can be drawn from utilitarian and
Kantian moral theories. Finally, I shall speculate on the implications of these considerations for moral philosophy.

Moral Saints and Common Sense

Consider first what, pretheoretically, would count for us—contemporary members
of Western culture—as a moral saint. A necessary condition of moral sainthood
would be that one's life be dominated by a commitment to improving the welfare of

I have benefited from the comments of many people who have heard or read an earlier draft of this
paper. I wish particularly to thank Douglas MacLean, Robert Nozick, Martha Nussbaum, and the
Society for Ethics and Legal Philosophy.

others or of society as a whole. As to what role this commitment must play in the individual's motivational system, two contrasting accounts suggest themselves to me which might equally be thought to qualify a person for moral sainthood.

First, a moral saint might be someone whose concern for others plays the role that is played in most of our lives by more selfish, or, at any rate, less morally worthy concerns. For the moral saint, the promotion of the welfare of others might play the role that is played for most of us by the enjoyment of material comforts, the opportunity to engage in the intellectual and physical activities of our choice, and the love, respect, and companionship of people whom we love, respect, and enjoy. The happiness of the moral saint, then, would truly lie in the happiness of others, and so he would devote himself to others gladly, and with a whole and open heart.

On the other hand, a moral saint might be someone for whom the basic ingredients of happiness are not unlike those of most of the rest of us. What makes him a moral saint is rather that he pays little or no attention to his own happiness in light of the overriding importance he gives to the wider concerns of morality. In other words, this person sacrifices his own interests to the interests of others, and feels the sacrifice as such.

Roughly, these two models may be distinguished according to whether one thinks of the moral saint as being a saint out of love or one thinks of the moral saint as being a saint out of duty (or some other intellectual appreciation and recognition of moral principles). We may refer to the first model as the model of the Loving Saint; to the second, as the model of the Rational Saint.

The two models differ considerably with respect to the qualities of the motives of the individuals who conform to them. But this difference would have limited effect on the saints' respective public personalities. The shared content of what these individuals are motivated to be—namely, as morally good as possible—would play the dominant role in the determination of their characters. Of course, just as a variety of large-scale projects, from tending the sick to political campaigning, may be equally and maximally morally worthy, so a variety of characters are compatible with the ideal of moral sainthood. One moral saint may be more or less jovial, more or less garrulous, more or less athletic than another. But, above all, a moral saint must have and cultivate those qualities which are apt to allow him to treat others as justly and kindly as possible. He will have the standard moral virtues to a nonstandard degree. He will be patient, considerate, even-tempered, hospitable, charitable in thought as well as in deed. He will be very reluctant to make negative judgments of other people. He will be careful not to favor some people over others on the basis of properties they could not help but have.

Perhaps what I have already said is enough to make some people begin to regard the absence of moral saints in their lives as a blessing. For there comes a point in the listing of virtues that a moral saint is likely to have where one might naturally begin to wonder whether the moral saint isn't, after all, too good—if not too good for his own good, at least too good for his own well-being. For the moral virtues, given that they are, by hypothesis, *all* present in the same individual, and to an extreme degree, are apt to crowd out the nonmoral virtues, as well as many of the interests and personal characteristics that we generally think contribute to a healthy, well-rounded, richly developed character.

In other words, if the moral saint is devoting all his time to feeding the hungry or healing the sick or raising money for Oxfam, then necessarily he is not reading

Victorian novels, playing the oboe, or improving his backhand. Although no one of the interests or tastes in the category containing these latter activities could be claimed to be a necessary element in a life well lived, a life in which *none* of these possible aspects of character are developed may seem to be a life strangely barren.

The reasons why a moral saint cannot, in general, encourage the discovery and development of significant nonmoral interests and skills are not logical but practical reasons. There are, in addition, a class of nonmoral characteristics that a moral saint cannot encourage in himself for reasons that are not just practical. There is a more substantial tension between having any of these qualities unashamedly and being a moral saint. These qualities might be described as going against the moral grain. For example, a cynical or sarcastic wit, or a sense of humor that appreciates this kind of wit in others, requires that one take an attitude of resignation and pessimism toward the flaws and vices to be found in the world. A moral saint, on the other hand, has reason to take an attitude in opposition to this—he should try to look for the best in people, give them the benefit of the doubt as long as possible, try to improve regrettable situations as long as there is any hope of success. This suggests that, although a moral saint might well enjoy a good episode of *Father Knows Best,* he may not in good conscience be able to laugh at a Marx Brothers movie or enjoy a play by George Bernard Shaw.

An interest in something like gourmet cooking will be, for different reasons, difficult for a moral saint to rest easy with. For it seems to me that no plausible argument can justify the use of human resources involved in producing a *paté de canard en croute* against possible alternative beneficent ends to which these resources might be put. If there is a justification for the institution of haute cuisine, it is one which rests on the decision *not* to justify every activity against morally beneficial alternatives, and this is a decision a moral saint will never make. Presumably, an interest in high fashion or interior design will fare much the same, as will, very possibly, a cultivation of the finer arts as well.

A moral saint will have to be very, very nice. It is important that he not be offensive. The worry is that, as a result, he will have to be dull-witted or humorless or bland.

---

3. When the moral saint is compared to our usual ideals, we find a great discrepancy. Even if you do not know who all these people are, can you still understand her point?

This worry is confirmed when we consider what sorts of characters, taken and refined both from life and from fiction, typically form our ideals. One would hope they would be figures who are morally good—and by this I mean more than just not morally bad—but one would hope, too, that they are not *just* morally good, but talented or accomplished or attractive in nonmoral ways as well. We may make ideals out of athletes, scholars, artists—more frivolously, out of cowboys, private eyes, and rock stars. We may strive for Katharine Hepburn's grace, Paul Newman's "cool"; we are attracted to the high-spirited passionate nature of Natasha Rostov; we admire the keen perceptiveness of Lambert Strether. Though there is certainly nothing immoral about the ideal characters or traits I have in mind, they cannot be superimposed upon the ideal of a moral saint. For although it is a part of many of these ideals that the characters set high, and not merely acceptable, moral standards for themselves, it is also essential to their power and attractiveness that the moral strengths go, so to speak, alongside of specific, independently admirable, nonmoral ground projects and dominant personal traits.

When one does finally turn one's eyes toward lives that are dominated by explicitly moral commitments, moreover, one finds oneself relieved at the discovery of idiosyncrasies or eccentricities not quite in line with the picture of moral perfection. One prefers the blunt, tactless, and opinionated Betsy Trotwood to the unfailingly kind and patient Agnes Copperfield; one prefers the mischievousness and the sense of irony in Chesterton's Father Brown to the innocence and undiscriminating love of St. Francis.

It seems that, as we look in our ideals for people who achieve nonmoral varieties of personal excellence in conjunction with or colored by some version of high moral tone, we look in our paragons of moral excellence for people whose moral achievements occur in conjunction with or colored by some interests or traits that have low moral tone. In other words, there seems to be a limit to how much morality we can stand.

---

4. Wolf uses an analogy to counter a presumed criticism. Can you state the analogy about the Olympic swimmer?

One might suspect that the essence of the problem is simply that there is a limit to how much of *any* single value, or any single type of value, we can stand. Our objection then would not be specific to a life in which one's dominant concern is morality, but would apply to any life that can be so completely characterized by an extraordinarily dominant concern. The objection in that case would reduce to the recognition that such a life is incompatible with well-roundedness. If that were the objection, one could fairly reply that well-roundedness is no more supreme a virtue than the totality of moral virtues embodied by the ideal it is being used to criticize. But I think this misidentifies the objection. For the way in which a concern for morality may dominate a life, or, more to the point, the way in which it may dominate an ideal of life, is not easily imagined by analogy to the dominance an aspiration to become an Olympic swimmer or a concert pianist might have.

A person who is passionately committed to one of these latter concerns might decide that her attachment to it is strong enough to be worth the sacrifice of her ability to maintain and pursue a significant portion of what else life might offer which a proper devotion to her dominant passion would require. But a desire to be as morally good as possible is not likely to take the form of one desire among others which, because of its peculiar psychological strength, requires one to forgo the pursuit of other weaker and separately less demanding desires. Rather, the desire to be as morally good as possible is apt to have the character not just of a stronger, but of a higher desire, which does not merely successfully compete with one's other desires but which rather subsumes or demotes them. The sacrifice of other interests for the interest in morality, then, will have the character, not of a choice, but of an imperative.

Moreover, there is something odd about the idea of morality itself, or moral goodness, serving as the object of a dominant passion in the way that a more concrete and specific vision of a goal (even a concrete *moral* goal) might be imagined to serve. Morality itself does not seem to be a suitable object of passion. Thus, when one reflects, for example, on the Loving Saint easily and gladly giving up his fishing trip or his stereo or his hot fudge sundae at the drop of the moral hat, one is apt to wonder not at how much he loves morality, but at how little he loves these other things. One thinks that, if he can give these up so easily, he does not know what it *is* to truly love them. There seems, in other words, to be a kind of joy which the Loving Saint, either by nature or by practice, is incapable of experiencing. The Rational Saint, on the other hand, might retain strong nonmoral and concrete desires—he simply denies himself the opportunity to act on them. But this is no less troubling. The Loving Saint one might suspect of missing a piece of perceptual machinery, of being blind to some of what the world has to offer. The Rational Saint, who sees it but forgoes it, one suspects of having a different problem—a pathological fear of damnation, perhaps, or an extreme form of self-hatred that interferes with his ability to enjoy the enjoyable in life.

In other words, the ideal of a life of moral sainthood disturbs not simply because it is an ideal of a life in which morality unduly dominates. The normal person's direct and specific desires for objects, activities, and events that conflict with the attainment of moral perfection are not simply sacrificed but removed, suppressed, or subsumed. The way in which morality, unlike other possible goals, is apt to dominate is particularly disturbing, for it seems to require either the lack or the denial of the existence of an identifiable, personal self.

This distinctively troubling feature is not, I think, absolutely unique to the ideal of the moral saint, as I have been using that phrase. It is shared by the conception of the pure aesthete, by a certain kind of religious ideal, and, somewhat paradoxically, by the model of the thorough-going, self-conscious egoist. It is not a coincidence that the ways of comprehending the world of which these ideals are the extreme embodiments are sometimes described as "moralities" themselves. At any rate, they compete with what we ordinarily mean by "morality." Nor is it a coincidence that these ideals are naturally described as fanatical. But it is easy to see that these other types of perfection cannot serve as satisfactory personal ideals; for the realization of these ideals would be straightforwardly immoral. It may come as a surprise to some that there may in addition be such a thing as a *moral* fanatic.

---

5. Another criticism is considered. After imagining some examples, she makes her main point.

Some will object that I am being unfair to "commonsense morality"—that it does not really require a moral saint to be either a disgusting goody-goody or an obsessive ascetic. Admittedly, there is no logical inconsistency between having any of the personal characteristics I have mentioned and being a moral saint. It is not morally wrong to notice the faults and shortcomings of others or to recognize and appreciate nonmoral talents and skills. Nor is it immoral to be an avid Celtics fan or to have a passion for caviar or to be an excellent cellist. With enough imagination, we can always contrive a suitable history and set of circumstances that will embrace such characteristics in one or another specific fictional story of a perfect moral saint.

If one turned onto the path of moral sainthood relatively late in life, one may have already developed interests that can be turned to moral purposes. It may be that a good golf game is just what is needed to secure that big donation to Oxfam.

Perhaps the cultivation of one's exceptional artistic talent will turn out to be the way one can make one's greatest contribution to society. Furthermore, one might stumble upon joys and skills in the very service of morality. If, because the children are short a ninth player for the team, one's generous offer to serve reveals a natural fielding arm or if one's part in the campaign against nuclear power requires accepting a lobbyist's invitation to lunch at Le Lion d'Or, there is no moral gain in denying the satisfaction one gets from these activities. The moral saint, then, may, by happy accident, find himself with nonmoral virtues on which he can capitalize morally or which make psychological demands to which he has no choice but to attend. The point is that, for a moral saint, the existence of these interests and skills can be given at best the status of happy accidents—they cannot be encouraged for their own sakes as distinct, independent aspects of the realization of human good.

It must be remembered that from the fact that there is a tension between having any of these qualities and being a moral saint it does not follow that having any of these qualities is immoral. For it is not part of commonsense morality that one ought to be a moral saint. Still, if someone just happened to want to be a moral saint, he or she would not have or encourage these qualities, and, on the basis of our commonsense values, this counts as a reason *not* to want to be a moral saint.

One might still wonder what kind of reason this is, and what kind of conclusion this properly allows us to draw. For the fact that the models of moral saints are unattractive does not necessarily mean that they are unsuitable ideals. Perhaps they are unattractive because they make us feel uncomfortable—they highlight our own weaknesses, vices, and flaws. If so, the fault lies not in the characters of the saints, but in those of our unsaintly selves.

To be sure, some of the reasons behind the disaffection we feel for the model of moral sainthood have to do with a reluctance to criticize ourselves and a reluctance to committing ourselves to trying to give up activities and interests that we heartily enjoy. These considerations might provide an *excuse* for the fact that we are not moral saints, but they do not provide a basis for criticizing sainthood as a possible ideal. Since these considerations rely on an appeal to the egoistic, hedonistic side of our natures, to use them as a basis for criticizing the ideal of the moral saint would be at best to beg the question and at worst to glorify features of ourselves that ought to be condemned.

The fact that the moral saint would be without qualities which we have and which, indeed, we like to have, does not in itself provide reason to condemn the ideal of the moral saint. The fact that some of these qualities are good qualities, however, and that they are qualities we *ought* to like, does provide reason to discourage this ideal and to offer other ideals in its place. In other words, some of the qualities the moral saint necessarily lacks are virtues, albeit nonmoral virtues, in the unsaintly characters who have them. The feats of Groucho Marx, Reggie Jackson, and the head chef at Lutèce are impressive accomplishments that it is not only permissible but positively appropriate to recognize as such. In general, the admiration of and striving toward achieving any of a great variety of forms of personal excellence are character traits it is valuable and desirable for people to have. In advocating the development of these varieties of excellence, we advocate nonmoral reasons for acting, and in thinking that it is good for a person to strive for an ideal that gives a substantial role to the interests and values that correspond to these virtues, we implicitly acknowledge the goodness of ideals incompatible with that of the moral saint. Finally, if we think that it is *as* good, or even better for a person to strive for one of these ideals than it is for him or her to strive for and realize the ideal of the moral saint, we express a conviction that it is good not to be a moral saint.

Moral Saints and Moral Theories

I have tried so far to paint a picture—or, rather, two pictures—of what a moral saint might be like, drawing on what I take to be the attitudes and beliefs about morality prevalent in contemporary, commonsense thought. To my suggestion that common-sense morality generates conceptions of moral saints that are unattractive or otherwise unacceptable, it is open to someone to reply, "so much the worse for commonsense morality." After all, it is often claimed that the goal of moral philosophy is to correct and improve upon commonsense morality, and I have as yet given no attention to the question of what conceptions of moral sainthood, if any, are generated from the leading moral theories of our time.

---

6. Wolf has been considering moral saints from the viewpoint of commonsense morality. She now considers how moral saints would fit into the two dominant moral theories. We look first at utilitarianism.

A quick, breezy reading of utilitarian and Kantian writings will suggest the images, respectively, of the Loving Saint and the Rational Saint. A utilitarian, with his emphasis on happiness, will certainly prefer the Loving Saint to the Rational one, since the Loving Saint will himself be a happier person than the Rational Saint. A Kantian, with his emphasis on reason, on the other hand, will find at least as much to praise in the latter as in the former. Still, both models, drawn as they are from common sense, appeal to an impure mixture of utilitarian and Kantian intuitions. A more careful examination of these moral theories raises questions about whether either model of moral sainthood would really be advocated by a believer in the explicit doctrines associated with either of these views.

Certainly, the utilitarian in no way denies the value of self-realization. He in no way disparages the development of interests, talents, and other personally attractive traits that I have claimed the moral saint would be without. Indeed, since just these features enhance the happiness both of the individuals who possess them and of those with whom they associate, the ability to promote these features both in oneself and in others will have considerable positive weight in utilitarian calculations.

This implies that the utilitarian would not support moral sainthood as a universal ideal. A world in which everyone, or even a large number of people, achieved moral sainthood—even a world in which they *strove* to achieve it—would probably contain less happiness than a world in which people realized a diversity of ideals involving a variety of personal and perfectionist values. More pragmatic considerations also suggest that, if the utilitarian wants to influence more people to achieve more good, then he would do better to encourage them to pursue happiness-producing goals that are more attractive and more within a normal person's reach.

These considerations still leave open, however, the question of what kind of an ideal the committed utilitarian should privately aspire to himself. Utilitarianism requires him to want to achieve the greatest general happiness, and this would seem to commit him to the ideal of the moral saint.

One might try to use the claims I made earlier as a basis for an argument that a utilitarian should choose to give up utilitarianism. If, as I have said, a moral saint would be a less happy person both to be and to be around than many other possible ideals, perhaps one could create more total happiness by not trying too hard to promote the total happiness. But this argument is simply unconvincing in light of the empirical circumstances of our world. The gain in happiness that would accrue to oneself and one's neighbors by a more well-rounded, richer life than that of the moral saint would be pathetically small in comparison to the amount by which one could increase the general happiness if one devoted oneself explicitly to the care of the sick, the downtrodden, the starving, and the homeless. Of course, there may be psychological limits to the extent to which a person can devote himself to such things without going crazy. But the utilitarian's individual limitations would not thereby become a positive feature of his personal ideals.

The unattractiveness of the moral saint, then, ought not rationally convince the utilitarian to abandon his utilitarianism. It may, however, convince him to take efforts not to wear his saintly moral aspirations on his sleeve. If it is not too difficult, the utilitarian will try not to make those around him uncomfortable. He will not want to appear "holier than thou"; he will not want to inhibit others' ability to enjoy themselves. In practice, this might make the perfect utilitarian a less nauseating companion than the moral saint I earlier portrayed. But insofar as this kind of reasoning produces a more bearable public personality, it is at the cost of giving him a personality that must be evaluated as hypocritical and condescending when his private thoughts and attitudes are taken into account.

Still, the criticisms I have raised against the saint of commonsense morality should make some difference to the utilitarian's conception of an ideal which neither requires him to abandon his utilitarian principles nor forces him to fake an interest he does not have or a judgment he does not make. For it may be that a limited and carefully monitored allotment of time and energy to be devoted to the pursuit of some nonmoral interests or to the development of some nonmoral talents would make a person a better contributor to the general welfare than he would be if he allowed himself no indulgences of this sort. The enjoyment of such activities in no way compromises a commitment to utilitarian principles as long as the involvement with these activities is conditioned by a willingness to give them up whenever it is recognized that they cease to be in the general interest.

This will go some way in mitigating the picture of the loving saint that an understanding of utilitarianism will on first impression suggest. But I think it will not go very far. For the limitations on time and energy will have to be rather severe, and the need to monitor will restrict not only the extent but also the quality of one's attachment to these interests and traits. They are only weak and somewhat peculiar sorts of passions to which one can consciously remain so conditionally committed. Moreover, the way in which the utilitarian can enjoy these "extracurricular" aspects of his life is simply not the way in which these aspects are to be enjoyed insofar as they figure into our less saintly ideals.

The problem is not exactly that the utilitarian values these aspects of his life only as a means to an end, for the enjoyment he and others get from these aspects are not a means to, but a part of, the general happiness. Nonetheless, he values these things only because of and insofar as they *are* a part of the general happiness. He values them, as it were, under the description "a contribution to the general happiness." This is to be contrasted with the various ways in which these aspects of life may be valued by nonutilitarians. A person might love literature because of the insights into human nature literature affords. Another might love the cultivation of roses because roses are things of great beauty and delicacy. It may be true that these features of the respective activities also explain why these activities are happiness-producing. But, to the nonutilitarian, this may not be to the point. For if one values these activities in these more direct ways, one may not be willing to exchange them for others that produce an equal, or even a greater amount of happiness. From that point of view, it is not because they produce happiness that these activities are valuable; it is because these activities are valuable in more direct and specific ways that they produce happiness.

To adopt a phrase of Bernard Williams, the utilitarian's manner of valuing the not explicitly moral aspects of his life "provides (him) with one thought too many."[1] The requirement that the utilitarian have this thought—periodically, at least—is indicative of not only a weakness but a shallowness in his appreciation of the aspects in question. Thus, the ideals toward which a utilitarian could acceptably strive would remain too close to the model of the commonsense moral saint to escape the criticisms of that model which I earlier suggested. Whether a Kantian would be similarly committed to so restrictive and unattractive a range of possible ideals is a somewhat more difficult question.

7. Having considered the moral saint within a framework of utilitarianism, Wolf now examines how the ideal of a moral saint would fit into a Kantian theory.

The Kantian believes that being morally worthy consists in always acting from maxims that one could will to be universal law, and doing this not out of any pathological desire but out of reverence for the moral law as such. Or, to take a different formulation of the categorical imperative, the Kantian believes that moral action consists in treating other persons always as ends and never as means only. Presumably, and according to Kant himself, the Kantian thereby commits himself to some degree of benevolence as well as to the rules of fair play. But we surely would not will that *every* person become a moral saint, and treating others as ends hardly requires bending over backwards to protect and promote their interests. On one interpretation of Kantian doctrine, then, moral perfection would be achieved simply by unerring obedience to a limited set of side-constraints. On this interpretation, Kantian theory simply does not yield an ideal conception of a person of any fullness comparable to that of the moral saints I have so far been portraying.

On the other hand, Kant does say explicitly that we have a duty of benevolence, a duty not only to allow others to pursue their ends, but to take up their ends as our own. In addition, we have positive duties to ourselves, duties to increase our natu-

---

[1] "Persons, Character and Morality" in Amelie Rorty, ed., *The Identities of Persons* (Berkeley: Univ. of California Press, 1976), p. 214.

ral as well as our moral perfection. These duties are unlimited in the degree to which they *may* dominate a life. If action in accordance with and motivated by the thought of these duties is considered virtuous, it is natural to assume that the more one performs such actions, the more virtuous one is. Moreover, of virtue in general Kant says, "it is an ideal which is unattainable while yet our duty is constantly to approximate to it."[2] On this interpretation, then, the Kantian moral saint, like the other moral saints I have been considering, is dominated by the motivation to be moral.

Which of these interpretations of Kant one prefers will depend on the interpretation and the importance one gives to the role of the imperfect duties in Kant's overall system. Rather than choose between them here, I shall consider each briefly in turn.

----

8. Two interpretations of Kantian theory are developed, one in this paragraph and one in the next.

On the second interpretation of Kant, the Kantian moral saint is, not surprisingly, subject to many of the same objections I have been raising against other versions of moral sainthood. Though the Kantian saint may differ from the utilitarian saint as to *which* actions he is bound to perform and which he is bound to refrain from performing, I suspect that the range of activities acceptable to the Kantian saint will remain objectionably restrictive. Moreover, the manner in which the Kantian saint must think about and justify the activities he pursues and the character traits he develops will strike us, as it did with the utilitarian saint, as containing "one thought too many." As the utilitarian could value his activities and character traits only insofar as they fell under the description of "contributions to the general happiness," the Kantian would have to value his activities and character traits insofar as they were manifestations of respect for the moral law. If the development of our powers to achieve physical, intellectual, or artistic excellence, or the activities directed toward making others happy are to have any moral worth, they must arise from a reverence for the dignity that members of our species have as a result of being endowed with pure practical reason. This is a good and noble motivation, to be sure. But it is hardly what one expects to be dominantly behind a person's aspirations to dance as well as Fred Astaire, to paint as well as Picasso, or to solve some outstanding problem in abstract algebra, and it is hardly what one hopes to find lying dominantly behind a father's action on behalf of his son or a lover's on behalf of her beloved.

Since the basic problem with any of the models of moral sainthood we have been considering is that they are dominated by a single, all-important value under which all other possible values must be subsumed, it may seem that the alternative interpretation of Kant, as providing a stringent but finite set of obligations and constraints, might provide a more acceptable morality. According to this interpretation of Kant, one is as morally good as can be so long as one devotes some limited portion of one's energies toward altruism and the maintenance of one's physical and spiritual health, and otherwise pursues one's independently motivated interests and values in such a way as to

----

[2] Immanuel Kant, *The Doctrine of Virtue*, Mary J. Gregor, trans. (New York: Harper & Row, 1964), p. 71.

avoid overstepping certain bounds. Certainly, if it be a requirement of an acceptable moral theory that perfect obedience to its laws and maximal devotion to its interests and concerns be something we can wholeheartedly strive for in ourselves and wish for in those around us, it will count in favor of this brand of Kantianism that its commands can be fulfilled without swallowing up the perfect moral agent's entire personality.

Even this more limited understanding of morality, if its connection to Kant's views is to be taken at all seriously, is not likely to give an unqualified seal of approval to the nonmorally directed ideals I have been advocating. For Kant is explicit about what he calls "duties of apathy and self-mastery" (69/70)—duties to ensure that our passions are never so strong as to interfere with calm, practical deliberation, or so deep as to wrest control from the more disinterested, rational part of ourselves. The tight and self-conscious rein we are thus obliged to keep on our commitments to specific individuals and causes will doubtless restrict our value in these things, assigning them a necessarily attenuated place.

A more interesting objection to this brand of Kantianism, however, comes when we consider the implications of placing the kind of upper bound on moral worthiness which seemed to count in favor of this conception of morality. For to put such a limit on one's capacity to be moral is effectively to deny, not just the moral necessity, but the moral goodness of a devotion to benevolence and the maintenance of justice that passes beyond a certain, required point. It is to deny the possibility of going morally above and beyond the call of a restricted set of duties. Despite my claim that all-consuming moral saintliness is not a particularly healthy and desirable ideal, it seems perverse to insist that, were moral saints to exist, they would not, in their way, be remarkably noble and admirable figures. Despite my conviction that it is as rational and as good for a person to take Katharine Hepburn or Jane Austen as her role model instead of Mother Theresa, it would be absurd to deny that Mother Theresa is a morally better person.

I can think of two ways of viewing morality as having an upper bound. First, we can think that altruism and impartiality are indeed positive moral interests, but that they are moral only if the degree to which these interests are actively pursued remains within certain fixed limits. Second, we can think that these positive interests are only incidentally related to morality and that the essence of morality lies elsewhere, in, say, an implicit social contract or in the recognition of our own dignified rationality. According to the first conception of morality, there is a cut-off line to the amount of altruism or to the extent of devotion to justice and fairness that is worthy of moral praise. But to draw this line earlier than the line that brings the altruist in question into a worse-off position than all those to whom he devotes himself seems unacceptably artificial and gratuitous. According to the second conception, these positive interests are not essentially related to morality at all. But then we are unable to regard a more affectionate and generous expression of good will toward others as a natural and reasonable extension of morality, and we encourage a cold and unduly self-centered approach to the development and evaluation of our motivations and concerns.

---

9. Wolf draws a conclusion here and discusses what appears to constitute a dilemma. In the following paragraph, Wolf begins to explain the kind of theory she would support.

A moral theory that does not contain the seeds of an all-consuming ideal of moral sainthood thus seems to place false and unnatural limits on our opportunity to do moral good and our potential to deserve moral praise. Yet the main thrust of the arguments of this paper has been leading to the conclusion that, when such ideals are present, they are not ideals to which it is particularly reasonable or healthy or desirable for human beings to aspire. These claims, taken together, have the appearance of a dilemma from which there is no obvious escape. In a moment, I shall argue that, despite appearances, these claims should not be understood as constituting a dilemma. But, before I do, let me briefly describe another path which those who are convinced by my above remarks may feel inclined to take.

If the above remarks are understood to be implicitly critical of the views on the content of morality which seem most popular today, an alternative that naturally suggests itself is that we revise our views about the content of morality. More specifically, my remarks may be taken to support a more Aristotelian, or even a more Nietzschean, approach to moral philosophy. Such a change in approach involves substantially broadening or replacing our contemporary intuitions about which character traits constitute moral virtues and vices and which interests constitute moral interests. If, for example, we include personal bearing, or creativity, or sense of style, as features that contribute to one's *moral* personality, then we can create moral ideals which are incompatible with and probably more attractive than the Kantian and utilitarian ideals I have discussed. Given such an alteration of our conception of morality, the figures with which I have been concerned above might, far from being considered to be moral saints, be seen as morally inferior to other, more appealing or more interesting models of individuals.

This approach seems unlikely to succeed, if for no other reason, because it is doubtful that any single, or even any reasonably small number of substantial personal ideals could capture the full range of possible ways of realizing human potential or achieving human good which deserve encouragement and praise. Even if we could provide a sufficiently broad characterization of the range of positive ways for human beings to live, however, I think there are strong reasons not to want to incorporate such a characterization more centrally into the framework of morality itself. For, in claiming that a character trait or activity is morally good, one claims that there is a certain kind of reason for developing that trait or engaging in that activity. Yet, lying behind our criticism of more conventional conceptions of moral sainthood, there seems to be a recognition that among the immensely valuable traits and activities that a human life might positively embrace are some of which we hope that, if a person does embrace them, he does so *not* for moral reasons. In other words, no matter how flexible we make the guide to conduct which we choose to label "morality," no matter how rich we make the life in which perfect obedience to this guide would result, we will have reason to hope that a person does not wholly rule and direct his life by the abstract and impersonal consideration that such a life would be morally good.

Once it is recognized that morality itself should not serve as a comprehensive guide to conduct, moreover, we can see reasons to retain the admittedly vague contemporary intuitions about what the classification of moral and nonmoral virtues, interests, and the like should be. That is, there seem to be important differences between the aspects of a person's life which are currently considered appropriate objects of moral evaluation and the aspects that might be included under the altered conception of morality we are now considering, which the latter approach would tend wrongly to blur or to neglect. Moral evaluation now is focused primarily on features of a person's life over which that person has control; it is largely restricted to aspects of his life which are likely to have considerable effect on other people. These restrictions seem as they should be. Even if responsible people could reach agreement as to what constituted good taste or a healthy degree of well-roundedness, for example, it seems wrong to insist that everyone try to achieve these things or to blame someone who fails or refuses to conform.

If we are not to respond to the unattractiveness of the moral ideals that contemporary theories yield either by offering alternative theories with more palatable ideals or by understanding these theories in such a way as to prevent them from yielding ideals at all, how, then, are we to respond? Simply, I think, by admitting that moral ideals do not, and need not, make the best personal ideals. Earlier, I mentioned one of the consequences of regarding as a test of an adequate moral theory that perfect obedience to its laws and maximal devotion to its interests be something we can wholeheartedly strive for in ourselves and wish for in those around us. Drawing out the consequences somewhat further should, I think, make us more doubtful of the proposed test than of the theories which, on this test, would fail. Given the empirical circumstances of our world, it seems to be an ethical fact that we have unlimited potential to be morally good, and endless opportunity to promote moral interests. But this is not incompatible with the not-so-ethical fact that we have sound, compelling, and not particularly selfish reasons to choose not to devote ourselves univocally to realizing this potential or to taking up this opportunity.

Thus, in one sense at least, I am not really criticizing either Kantianism or utilitarianism. Insofar as the point of view I am offering bears directly on recent work in moral philosophy, in fact, it bears on critics of these theories who, in a spirit not unlike the spirit of most of this paper, point out that the perfect utilitarian would be flawed in this way or the perfect Kantian flawed in that.[3] The assumption lying behind these claims, implicitly or explicitly, has been that the recognition of these flaws shows us something wrong with utilitarianism as opposed to Kantianism, or something wrong with Kantianism as opposed to utilitarianism, or something wrong with both of these theories as opposed to some nameless third alternative. The claims of this paper suggest, however, that this assumption is unwarranted. The flaws of a perfect master of a moral theory need not reflect flaws in the intramoral content of the theory itself.

Moral Saints and Moral Philosophy

In pointing out the regrettable features and the necessary absence of some desirable features in a moral saint, I have not meant to condemn the moral saint or the person who aspires to become one. Rather, I have meant to insist that the ideal of moral sainthood should not be held as a standard against which any other ideal must be

---

[3]See, e.g., Williams, op. cit. and J. J. C. Smart and Bernard Williams, *Utilitarianism: For and Against* (New York: Cambridge, 1973). Also, Michael Stocker, "The Schizophrenia of Modern Ethical Theories," *The Journal of Philosophy.* LXIII, 14 (Aug. 12, 1976): 453–466.

judged or justified, and that the posture we take in response to the recognition that our lives are not as morally good as they might be need not be defensive.[4] It is misleading to insist that one is *permitted* to live a life in which the goals, relationships, activities, and interests that one pursues are not maximally morally good. For our lives are not so comprehensively subject to the requirement that we apply for permission, and our nonmoral reasons for the goals we set ourselves are not excuses, but may rather be positive, good reasons which do not exist *despite* any reasons that might threaten to outweigh them. In other words, a person may be *perfectly wonderful* without being *perfectly moral*.

Recognizing this requires a perspective which contemporary moral philosophy has generally ignored. This perspective yields judgments of a type that is neither moral nor egoistic. Like moral judgments, judgments about what it would be good for a person to be are made from a point of view outside the limits set by the values, interests, and desires that the person might actually have. And, like moral judgments, these judgments claim for themselves a kind of objectivity or a grounding in a perspective which any rational and perceptive being can take up. Unlike moral judgments, however, the good with which these judgments are concerned is not the good of anyone or any group other than the individual himself.

Nonetheless, it would be equally misleading to say that these judgments are made for the sake of the individual himself. For these judgments are not concerned with what kind of life it is in a person's interest to lead, but with what kind of interests it would be good for a person to have, and it need not be in a person's interest that he acquire or maintain objectively good interests. Indeed, the model of the Loving Saint, whose interests are identified with the interests of morality, is a model of a person for whom the dictates of rational self-interest and the dictates of morality coincide. Yet, I have urged that we have reason not to aspire to this ideal and that some of us would have reason to be sorry if our children aspired to and achieved it.

The moral point of view, we might say, is the point of view one takes up insofar as one takes the recognition of the fact that one is just one person among others equally real and deserving of the good things in life as a fact with practical consequences, a fact the recognition of which demands expression in one's actions and in the form of one's practical deliberations. Competing moral theories offer alternative answers to the question of what the most correct or the best way to express this fact is. In doing so, they offer alternative ways to evaluate and to compare the variety of actions, states of affairs, and so on that appear good and bad to agents from other, nonmoral points of view. But it seems that alternative interpretations of the moral point of view do not exhaust the ways in which our actions, characters, and their consequences can be comprehensively and objectively evaluated. Let us call the point of view from which we consider what kinds of lives are good lives, and what kinds of persons it would be good for ourselves and others to be, the *point of view of individual perfection*.

---

[4]George Orwell makes a similar point in "Reflections on Gandhi," in *A Collection of Essays by George Orwell* (New York: Harcourt Brace Jovanovich, 1945), p. 176: "Sainthood is . . . a thing that human beings must avoid. . . . It is too readily assumed that . . . the ordinary man only rejects it because it is too difficult; in other words, that the average human being is a failed saint. It is doubtful whether this is true. Many people genuinely do not wish to be saints, and it is probable that some who achieve or aspire to sainthood have never felt much temptation to be human beings."

Since either point of view provides a way of comprehensively evaluating a person's life, each point of view takes account of, and, in a sense, subsumes the other. From the moral point of view, the perfection of an individual life will have some, but limited, value—for each individual remains, after all, just one person among others. From the perfectionist point of view, the moral worth of an individual's relation to his world will likewise have some, but limited, value—for, as I have argued, the (perfectionist) goodness of an individual's life does not vary proportionally with the degree to which it exemplifies moral goodness.

It may not be the case that the perfectionist point of view is like the moral point of view in being a point of view we are ever *obliged* to take up and express in our actions. Nonetheless, it provides us with reasons that are independent of moral reasons for wanting ourselves and others to develop our characters and live our lives in certain ways. When we take up this point of view and ask how much it would be good for an individual to act from the moral point of view, we do not find an obvious answer.[5]

The considerations of this paper suggest, at any rate, that the answer is not "as much as possible." This has implications both for the continued development of moral theories and for the development of metamoral views and for our conception of moral philosophy more generally. From the moral point of view, we have reasons to want people to live lives that seem good from outside that point of view. If, as I have argued, this means that we have reason to want people to live lives that are not morally perfect, then any plausible moral theory must make use of some conception of supererogation.[6]

If moral philosophers are to address themselves at the most basic level to the question of how people should live, however, they must do more than adjust the content of their moral theories in ways that leave room for the affirmation of nonmoral values. They must examine explicitly the range and nature of these nonmoral values, and, in light of this examination, they must ask how the acceptance of a moral theory is to be understood and acted upon. For the claims of this paper do not so much conflict with the content of any particular currently popular moral theory as they call into question a metamoral assumption that implicitly surrounds discussions of moral

---

[5]A similar view, which has strongly influenced mine, is expressed by Thomas Nagel in "The Fragmentation of Value," in *Mortal Questions* (New York: Cambridge, 1979), pp. 128–141. Nagel focuses on the difficulties such apparently incommensurable points of view create for specific, isolable practical decisions that must be made both by individuals and by societies. In focusing on the way in which these points of view figure into the development of individual personal ideals, the questions with which I am concerned are more likely to lurk in the background of any individual's life.

[6]The variety of forms that a conception of supererogation might take, however, has not generally been noticed. Moral theories that make use of this notion typically do so by identifying some specific set of principles as universal moral requirements and supplement this list with a further set of directives which it is morally praiseworthy but not required for an agent to follow. [See, e.g., Charles Fried, *Right and Wrong* (Cambridge, Mass.: Harvard, 1979).] But it is possible that the ability to live a morally blameless life cannot be so easily or definitely secured as this type of theory would suggest. The fact that there are some situations in which an agent is morally required to do something and other situations in which it would be good but not required for an agent to do something does not imply that there are specific principles such that, in any situation, an agent is required to act in accordance with these principles and other specific principles such that, in any situation, it would be good but not required for an agent to act in accordance with those principles.

theory more generally. Specifically, they call into question the assumption that it is always better to be morally better.

The role morality plays in the development of our characters and the shape of our practical deliberations need be neither that of a universal medium into which all other values must be translated nor that of an ever-present filter through which all other values must pass. This is not to say that moral value should not be an important, even the most important, kind of value we attend to in evaluating and improving ourselves and our world. It is to say that our values cannot be fully comprehended on the model of a hierarchial system with morality at the top.

The philosophical temperament will naturally incline, at this point, toward asking, "What, then, *is* at the top—or, if there is no top, how *are* we to decide when and how much to be moral?" In other words, there is a temptation to seek a metamoral—though not, in the standard sense, metaethical—theory that will give us principles, or at least, informal directives on the basis of which we can develop and evaluate more comprehensive personal ideals. Perhaps a theory that distinguishes among the various roles a person is expected to play within a life—as professional, as citizen, as friend, and so on—might give us some rules that would offer us, if nothing else, a better framework in which to think about and discuss these questions. I am pessimistic, however, about the chances of such a theory to yield substantial and satisfying results. For I do not see how a metamoral theory could be constructed which would not be subject to considerations parallel to those which seem inherently to limit the appropriateness of regarding moral theories as ultimate comprehensive guides for action.

This suggests that, at some point, both in our philosophizing and in our lives, we must be willing to raise normative questions from a perspective that is unattached to a commitment to any particular well-ordered system of values. It must be admitted that, in doing so, we run the risk of finding normative answers that diverge from the answers given by whatever moral theory one accepts. This, I take it, is the grain of truth in G. E. Moore's "open question" argument. In the background of this paper, then, there lurks a commitment to what seems to me to be a healthy form of intuitionism. It is a form of intuitionism which is not intended to take the place of more rigorous, systematically developed, moral theories—rather, it is intended to put these more rigorous and systematic moral theories in their place.

READING QUESTIONS

1. What are the two models of moral saint?
2. Why is it unlikely that a moral saint would be interested in gourmet cooking?
3. If the Loving Saint were to give up his hot fudge sundae, what is the inference we would most likely make?
4. Which of the two kinds of moral saint will the utilitarian prefer? Why?
5. What type of moral theory does Wolf support?

Michael Ruse and Edward O. Wilson

Evolutionary ethics describes a kind of moral philosophy that has been rapidly gaining interest and adherents in the last half of the twentieth century. A kind of naturalistic ethics, evolutionary ethics takes as its starting point the biological nature of human development. Given that human beings have evolved over time, everything human, including morality, should be recognized as a product of that development. The attempt to connect morality to human development has its roots primarily in the work of Charles Darwin, who wrote *Origin of Species* in 1859. But any theory of ethics that attempted to place the foundation of morality in nature was seriously undercut when G. E. Moore published *Principia Ethica* in 1903. In this landmark book, Moore charged that moral philosophers who attempted to place morality on a natural footing committed what he called the **naturalistic fallacy**. Moore emphasized a criticism of naturalistic theories of morality that had originated with David Hume a century and a half earlier: One commits a fallacy (reasons incorrectly) when moving from the **descriptive** statement "People do X" to the **prescriptive** (or normative) statement that "People *ought* to do X." Descriptive statements merely *describe* an action or situation, whereas prescriptive statements place a value on an action or situation. In moral philosophy this problem is described as either the problem of deriving an "ought" from an "is" or the problem of deriving a prescriptive statement from merely descriptive statements.

Moore's criticism silenced naturalistic theories of ethics (of which evolutionary ethics is a type) for a time. But eventually, philosophers and scientists again turned their attention to the chain that connects ethics and human biology. In a previous section we read in the work of John Dewey from 1929 a theory that challenged those who would deny the viability of naturalistic theories. However, it was not until the advent of sociobiology in the 1970s that a new enthusiasm for evolutionary ethics (and other naturalistic ethics) was generated. Today, as more and more attention is given to science and technology, philosophers increasingly use the tools and conclusions of science to investigate that most human of activities, morality.

Michael Ruse, professor of philosophy at Guelph University in Canada, and Edward O. Wilson, the eminent Harvard biologist, have each written extensively on evolutionary ethics. In this paper, which they co-authored, they argue that moral philosophy should be turned into an applied science. We should take seriously the lessons learned by science, especially biology, concerning the development of the human species. If this is done, moral philosophers can develop rules of conduct that are scientifically justified, and the gap between *is* and *ought* will be bridged.

Moral Philosophy as Applied Science
〰️ 〰️

Many people believe that in order for morality to have any force, God must exist. In fact, some people have argued that you should believe in God simply because the entire moral structure of human life will collapse

From Michael Ruse and Edward O. Wilson, "Moral Philosophy as Applied Science," *Philosophy*, Vol. 61 (1996), 173–192. Reprinted by permission of Cambridge University Press.

otherwise. Philosophers, as we know, use reason and argumentation rather than the authority of God to seek the truths about morality. Yet throughout the history of Western philosophy, most of the powerful thinkers in ethics were convinced of the reality of God. They arrived at their conclusions about moral philosophy using reason, but these conclusions (for the most part) were consistent with what they had learned from their religions. Immanuel Kant is a good example of this kind of philosopher.

However, other philosophers have long questioned the necessity of a foundation for morality provided by God. Especially in the twentieth century, increasing numbers of moral philosophers have tended to consider ethics without any reference to God at all. In this reading, the authors tackle head-on the supposed link between God and human values. No such values, they argue, exist. Human values are a product of human beings, themselves a product of an extremely long process of evolutionary change. What kind of morality exists when you take the "scientific" view of human existence? The authors find a robust version of human morality that will vary surprisingly little from the morality we now embrace.   ✍

(1) For much of this century, moral philosophy has been constrained by the supposed absolute gap between *is* and *ought,* and the consequent belief that the facts of life cannot of themselves yield an ethical blueprint for future action. For this reason, ethics has sustained an eerie existence largely apart from science. Its most respected interpreters still believe that reasoning about right and wrong can be successful without a knowledge of the brain, the human organ where all the decisions about right and wrong are made. Ethical premises are typically treated in the manner of mathematical propositions: directives supposedly independent of human evolution, with a claim to ideal, eternal truth.

While many substantial gains have been made in our understanding of the nature of moral thought and action, insufficient use has been made of knowledge of the brain and its evolution. Beliefs in extrasomatic moral truths and in an absolute is/ought barrier are wrong. Moral premises relate only to our physical nature and are the result of an idiosyncratic genetic history—a history which is nevertheless powerful and general enough within the human species to form working codes. The time has come to turn moral philosophy into an applied science because, as the geneticist Hermann J. Muller urged in 1959, 100 years without Darwin are enough.[1]

(2) The naturalistic approach to ethics, dating back through Darwin to earlier pre-evolutionary thinkers, has gained strength with each new advance in biology and the brain sciences. Its contemporary version can be expressed as follows:

---

[1] H. J. Muller is quoted by G. G. Simpson in *This View of Life* (New York: Harcourt, Brace & World, 1964), 36.

Everything human, including the mind and culture, has a material base and origulated during the evolution of the human genetic constitution and its interaction with the environment. To say this much is not to deny the great creative power of culture, or to minimize the fact that most causes of human thought and behavior are still poorly understood. The important point is that modern biology can account for many of the unique properties of the species. Research on the subject is accelerating, quickly enough to lend plausibility to the belief that the human condition can eventually be understood to its foundations, including the sources of moral reasoning.

This accumulating empirical knowledge has profound consequences for moral philosophy. It renders increasingly less tenable the hypothesis that ethical truths are extrasomatic, in other words divinely placed within the brain or else outside the brain awaiting revelation. Of equal importance, there is no evidence to support the view—and a great deal to contravene it—that premises can be identified as global optima favoring the survival of any civilized species, in whatever form or on whatever planet it might appear. Hence external goals are unlikely to be articulated in this more pragmatic sense.

Yet biology shows that internal moral premises do exist and can be defined more precisely. They are immanent in the unique programs of the brain that originated during evolution. Human mental development has proved to be far richer and more structured and idiosyncratic than previously suspected. The constraints on this development are the sources of our strongest feelings of right and wrong, and they are powerful enough to serve as a foundation for ethical codes. But the articulation of enduring codes will depend upon a more detailed knowledge of the mind and human evolution than we now possess. We suggest that it will prove possible to proceed from a knowledge of the material basis of moral feeling to generally accepted rules of conduct. To do so will be to escape—not a minute too soon—from the debilitating absolute distinction between *is* and *ought*.

---

1. The first two sections present the need that the authors perceive for a biologically based ethical theory. In this paragraph, they describe the process by which organisms evolve, or natural selection. Notice that the talk is about genes and chromosomes.

---

(3) All populations of organisms evolve through a law-bound causal process, as first described by Charles Darwin in his *Origin of Species*. The modern explanation of this process, known as natural selection, can be briefly summarized as follows. The members of each population vary hereditarily in virtually all traits of anatomy, physiology, and behavior. Individuals possessing certain combinations of traits survive and reproduce better than those with other combinations. As a consequence, the units that specify physical traits—genes and chromosomes—increase in relative frequency within such populations, from one generation to the next.

This change in different traits, which occurs at the level of the entire population, is the essential process of evolution. Although the agents of natural selection act directly on the outward traits and only rarely on the underlying genes and chromosomes, the shifts they cause in the latter have the most important lasting effects. New variation across each population arises through changes in the chemistry of the genes and their relative positions on the chromosomes. Nevertheless, these changes (broadly referred to as mutations) provide only the raw material of evolution. Natural selection, composed of the sum of differential survival and reproduction, for the most part determines the rate and direction of evolution.[2]

Although natural selection implies competition in an abstract sense between different forms of genes occupying the same chromosome positions or between different gene arrangements, pure competition, sometimes caricatured as "nature red in tooth and claw," is but one of several means by which natural selection can operate on the outer traits. In fact, a few species are known whose members do not compete among themselves at all. Depending on circumstances, survival and reproduction can be promoted equally well through the avoidance of predators, more efficient breeding, and improved cooperation with others.[3]

In recent years there have been several much-publicized controversies over the pace of evolution and the universal occurrence of adaptation.[4] These uncertainties should not obscure the key facts about organic evolution: that it occurs as a universal process among all kinds of organisms thus far carefully examined, that the dominant driving force is natural selection, and that the observed major patterns of change are consistent with the known principles of molecular biology and genetics. Such is the view held by the vast majority of the biologists who actually work on heredity and evolution.[5] To say that not all the facts have been explained, to point out that forces and patterns may yet be found that are inconsistent with the central theory—healthy doubts present in any scientific discipline—is by no means to call into question the prevailing explanation of evolution. Only a demonstration of fundamental inconsistency can accomplish that much, and nothing short of a rival explanation can bring the existing theory into full disarray.

There are no such crises. Even Motoo Kimura, the principal architect of the 'neutralist' theory of genetic diversity—which proposes that most evolution at the molecular level happens through random factors—allows that "classical evolution theory has

---

[2] See the following widely used textbooks: J. Roughgarden, *Theory of Population Genetics and Evolutionary Ecology: An Introduction* (New York: Macmillan, 1979); D. L. Hartl, *Principles of Population Genetics* (Sunderland, Mass.: Sinauer Associates, 1980); R. M. May (ed.), *Theoretical Ecology: Principles and Applications,* 2nd ed. (Sunderland, Mass.: Sinauer Associates, 1981); J. R. Krebs and N. B. Davies (eds.), *Behavioural Ecology: An Evolutionary Approach,* 2nd ed. (Sunderland, Mass.: Sinauer Associates, 1984).

[3] Reviews of the various modes of selection, including forms that direct individuals away from competitive behavior, can be found in E. O. Wilson, *Sociobiology: The New Synthesis* (Cambridge, Mass.: Belknap Press of Harvard University Press, 1975); G. F. Oster and E. O. Wilson, *Caste and Ecology in the Social Insects* (Princeton University Press, 1978); S. A. Boorman and P. R. Levitt, *The Genetics of Altruism* (New York: Academic Press, 1980); D. S. Wilson, *The Natural Selection of Populations and Communities* (Menlo Park, Calif.: Benjamin/Cummings, 1980).

[4] For example, the debate over 'punctuated equilibrium' versus 'gradualism' among paleontologists and geneticists. For most biologists, the issue is not the mechanism of evolution but the conditions under which evolution sometimes proceeds rapidly and sometimes slows to a crawl. There is no difficulty in explaining the variation in rates. On the contrary, there is a surplus of plausible explanations, virtually all consistent with Neo-Darwinian theory, but insufficient data to choose among them. See, for example, S. J. Gould and N. Eldredge, "Punctuated Equilibria: The Tempo and Mode of Evolution Reconsidered," *Paleobiology* 3 (1977), 115–151; and J. R. G. Turner, "'The hypothesis that explains mimetic resemblance explains evolution': the gradualist–saltationist schism," in M. Grene (ed.), *Dimensions of Darwinism* (Cambridge University Press, 1983), 129–169.

[5] See footnote 2.

demonstrated beyond any doubt that the basic mechanism for adaptive evolution is natural selection acting on variations produced by changes in chromosomes and genes. Such considerations as population size and structure, availability of ecological opportunities, change of environment, life-cycle 'strategies', interaction with other species, and in some situations kin or possibly group selection play a large role in our understanding of the process."[6]

(4) Human evolution appears to conform entirely to the modern synthesis of evolutionary theory as just stated. We know now that human ancestors broke from a common line with the great apes as recently as six or seven million years ago, and that at the biochemical level we are today closer relatives of the chimpanzees than the chimpanzees are of gorillas.[7] Furthermore, all that we know about human fossil history, as well as variation in genes and chromosomes among individuals and the key events in the embryonic assembly of the nervous system, is consistent with the prevailing view that natural selection has served as the principal agent in the origin of humanity.

2. In the third sentence, the authors signal that the upcoming topic will be of great importance: they mention the "several key developments" that will be explained in the following paragraphs.

It is true that until recently information on the brain and human evolution was sparse. But knowledge is accelerating, at least as swiftly as the remainder of natural science, about a doubling every ten to fifteen years. Several key developments, made principally during the past twenty years, will prove important to our overall argument for a naturalistic ethic developed as an applied science.

The number of human genes identified by biochemical assay or pedigree analysis is at the time of writing 3,577, with approximately 600 placed to one or the other of the twenty-three pairs of chromosomes.[8] Because the rate at which this number has been accelerating (up from 1,200 in 1977), most of the entire complement of 100,000 or so structural genes may be characterized to some degree within three or four decades.

Hundreds of the known genes affect behavior. The great majority do so simply by their effect on general processes of tissue development and metabolism, but a few have been implicated in more focused behavioral traits. For example, a single allele (a variant of one gene), prescribes the rare Lesch–Nyhan syndrome, in which people curse uncontrollably, strike out at others with no provocation, and tear at their own lips and fingers. Another allele at a different chromosome position reduces the ability to perform on certain standard spatial tests but not on the majority of such tests.[9] Still another allele, located tentatively on chromosome 15, induces a specific learning disability.[10]

---

[6] M. Kimura, *The Neutral Theory of Molecular Evolution* (Cambridge University Press, 1983).

[7] C. G. Sibley and J. E. Ahlquist, "The Phylogeny of the Hominoid Primates, as Indicated by DNA-DNA Hybridization," *Journal of Molecular Evolution* 20 (1984), 2–15.

[8] We are grateful to Victor A. McKusick for providing the counts of identified and inferred human genes up to 1984.

[9] G. C. Ashton, J. J. Polovina and S. G. Vandenberg, "Segregation Analysis of Family Data for 15 Tests of Cognitive Ability," *Behaviour Genetics* 9 (1979), 329–347.

[10] S. D. Smith, W. J. Kimberling, B. F. Pennington and H. A. Lubs, "Specific Reading Disability: Identification of an Inherited Form through Linkage Analysis," *Science* 219 (1982), 1345–1347.

These various alterations are of course strong and deviant enough to be considered pathological. But they are also precisely the kind usually discovered in the early stages of behavioral genetic analysis for any species. *Drosophila* genetics, for example, first passed through a wave of anatomical and physiological studies directed principally at chromosome structure and mechanics. As in present-day human genetics, the first behavioral mutants discovered were broadly acting and conspicuous, in other words those easiest to detect and characterize. When behavioral and biochemical studies grew more sophisticated, the cellular basis of gene action was elucidated in the case of a few behaviors, and the new field of *Drosophila* neurogenetics was born. The hereditary bases of subtle behaviors such as orientation to light and learning were discovered somewhat later.[11]

We can expect human behavioral genetics to travel along approximately the same course. Although the links between genes and behavior in human beings are more numerous and the processes involving cognition and decision making far more complex, the whole is nevertheless conducted by cellular machinery precisely assembled under the direction of the human genome (that is, genes considered collectively as a unit). The techniques of gene identification, applied point by point along each of the twenty-three pairs of chromosomes, are beginning to make genetic dissection of human behavior a reality.

Yet to speak of genetic dissection, a strongly reductionist procedure, is not to suggest that the whole of any trait is under the control of a single gene, nor does it deny substantial flexibility in the final product. Individual alleles (gene-variants) can of course affect a trait in striking ways. To take a humble example, the possession of a single allele rather than another on a certain point on one of the chromosome pairs causes the development of an attached earlobe as opposed to a pendulous earlobe. However, it is equally true that a great many alleles at different chromosome positions must work together to assemble the entire earlobe. In parallel fashion, one allele can shift the likelihood that one form of behavior will develop as opposed to another, but many alleles are required to prescribe the ensemble of nerve cells, neurotransmitters, and muscle fibers that orchestrate the behavior in the first place. Hence classical genetic analysis cannot by itself explain all of the underpinnings of human behavior, especially those that involve complex forms of cognition and decision making. For this reason behavioral development viewed as the interaction of genes and environment should also occupy center stage in the discussion of human behavior. The most important advances at this level are being made in the still relatively young field of cognitive psychology.[12]

---

3. The authors tell us they are now ready for the main topic: morality. The focus is upon evidence that moral behavior produces an evolutionary advantage.

---

(5) With this background, let us move at once to the central focus of our discussion: morality. Human beings, all human beings, have a sense of right and wrong, good and bad. Often, although not always, this 'moral awareness' is bound up with

---

[11] See J. C. Hall and R. J. Greenspan, "Genetic Analysis of *Drosophila* Neurobiology," *Annual Review of Genetics* 13 (1979), 127–195.

[12] See, for example, the recent analysis by J. R. Anderson, *The Architecture of Cognition* (Cambridge, Mass.: Harvard University Press, 1983).

beliefs about deities, spirits, and other supersensible beings. What is distinctive about moral claims is that they are prescriptive; they lay upon us certain obligations to help and to cooperate with others in various ways. Furthermore, morality is taken to transcend mere personal wishes or desires. "Killing is wrong" conveys more than merely "I don't like killing." For this reason, moral statements are thought to have an objective referent, whether the Will of a Supreme Being or eternal verities perceptible through intuition.

Darwinian biology is often taken as the antithesis of true morality. Something that begins with conflict and ends with personal reproduction seems to have little to do with right and wrong. But to reason along such lines is to ignore a great deal of the content of modern evolutionary biology. A number of causal mechanisms—already well confirmed in the animal world—can yield the kind of cooperation associated with moral behavior. One is so-called 'kin selection'. Genes prescribing cooperation spread through the populations when self-sacrificing acts are directed at relatives, so that they (not the cooperators) are benefited, and the genes they share with the cooperators by common descent are increased in later generations. Another such cooperation-causing mechanism is 'reciprocal altruism'. As its name implies, this involves transactions (which can occur between non-relatives) in which aid given is offset by the expectation of aid received. Such mutual assistance can be extended to a whole group, whose individual members contribute to a general pool and (as needed) draw from the pool.[13]

Sociobiologists (evolutionists concerned with social behavior) speak of acts mediated by such mechanisms as 'altruistic'. It must be recognized that this is now a technical biological term, and does not necessarily imply conscious free giving and receiving. Nevertheless, the empirical evidence suggests that cooperation between human beings was brought about by the same evolutionary mechanisms as those just cited. To include conscious, reflective beings is to go beyond the biological sense of altruism into the realm of genuine nonmetaphorical altruism. We do not claim that people are either unthinking genetic robots or that they cooperate only when the expected genetic returns can be calculated in advance. Rather, human beings function better if they are deceived by their genes into thinking that there is a disinterested objective morality binding upon them, which all should obey. We help others because it is 'right' to help them and because we know that they are inwardly compelled to reciprocate in equal measure. What Darwinian evolutionary theory shows is that this sense of 'right' and the corresponding sense of 'wrong', feelings we take to be above individual desire and in some fashion outside biology, are in fact brought about by ultimately biological processes.

----

4. How can biology be consistent with human free will? The authors give a detailed account of the relation between the two.

Such are the empirical claims. How exactly is biology supposed to exert its will on conscious, free beings? At one extreme, it is possible to conceive of a moral code produced entirely by the accidents of history. Cognition and moral sensitivity might

----

[13] See footnote 3.

evolve somewhere in some imaginary species in a wholly unbiased manner, creating the organic equivalent of an all-purpose computer. In such a blank-slate species, moral rules were contrived some time in the past, and the exact historical origin might now be lost in the mists of time. If proto-humans evolved in this manner, individuals that thought up and followed rules ensuring an ideal level of cooperation then survived and reproduced, and all others fell by the wayside.

However, before we consider the evidence, it is important to realize that any such even-handed device must also be completely gene-based and tightly controlled, because an exact genetic prescription is needed to produce perfect openness to any moral rule, whether successful or not. The human thinking organ must be indifferently open to a belief such as "killing is wrong" or "killing is right," as well as to any consequences arising from conformity or deviation. Both a very specialized prescription and an elaborate cellular machinery are needed to achieve this remarkable result. In fact, the blank-slate brain might require a cranial space many times that actually possessed by human beings. Even then a slight deviation in the many feedback loops and hierarchical controls would shift cognition and preference back into a biased state. In short, there appears to be no escape from the biological foundation of mind.

It can be stated with equal confidence that nothing like all-purpose cognition occurred during human evolution. The evidence from both genetic and cognitive studies demonstrates decisively that the human brain is not a *tabula rasa*. Conversely, neither is the brain (and the consequent ability to think) genetically determined in the strict sense. No genotype is known that dictates a single behavior, precluding reflection and the capacity to choose from among alternative behaviors belonging to the same category. The human brain is something in-between: a swift and directed learner that picks up certain bits of information quickly and easily, steers around others, and leans toward a surprisingly few choices out of the vast array that can be imagined.

This quality can be made more explicit by saying that human thinking is under the influence of 'epigenetic rules', genetically based processes of development that predispose the individual to adopt one or a few forms of behaviors as opposed to others. The rules are rooted in the physiological processes leading from the genes to thought and action.[14] The empirical heart of our discussion is that we think morally because we are subject to appropriate epigenetic rules. These predispose us to think that certain courses of action are right and certain courses of action are wrong. The rules certainly do not lock people blindly into certain behaviors. But because they give the illusion of objectivity to morality, they lift us above immediate wants to actions which (unknown to us) ultimately serve our genetic best interests.

The full sequence in the origin of morality is therefore evidently the following: ensembles of genes have evolved through mutation and selection within an intensely social existence over tens of thousands of years; they prescribe epigenetic rules of mental development peculiar to the human species; under the influence of the rules certain choices are made from among those conceivable and available to the culture; and finally the choices are narrowed and hardened through contractual agreements and sanctification.

---

[14] The evidence for biased epigenetic rules of mental development is summarized in C. J. Lumsden and E. O. Wilson, *Genes, Mind, and Culture* (Cambridge, Mass.: Harvard University Press, 1981) and *Promethean Fire: Reflections on the Origin of Mind* (Cambridge, Mass.: Harvard University Press, 1983).

In a phrase, societies feel their way across the fields of culture with a rough biological map. Enduring codes are not created whole from absolute premises but inductively, in the manner of common law, with the aid of repeated experience, by emotion and consensus, through an expansion of knowledge and experience guided by the epigenetic rules of mental development, during which people sift the options and come to agree upon and to legitimate certain norms and directions.[15]

5. The supposed objectivity of ethics is denied. What kind of evidence do they give?

(7) We believe that implicit in the scientific interpretation of moral behavior is a conclusion of central importance to philosophy, namely that there can be no genuinely objective external ethical premises. Everything that we know about the evolutionary process indicates that no such extrasomatic guides exist. Let us define ethics in the ordinary sense, as the area of thought and action governed by a sense of obligation—a feeling that there are certain standards one ought to live up to. In order not to prejudge the issue, let us also make no further assumptions about content. It follows from what we understand in the most general way about organic evolution that ethical premises are likely to differ from one intelligent species to another. The reason is that choices are made on the basis of emotion and reason directed to these ends, and the ethical premises composed of emotion and reason arise from the epigenetic rules of mental development. These rules are in turn the idiosyncratic products of the genetic history of the species and as such were shaped by particular regimes of natural selection. For many generations—more than enough for evolutionary change to occur—they favored the survival of individuals who practiced them. Feelings of happiness, which stem from positive reinforcers of the brain and other elements that compose the epigenetic rules, are the enabling devices that led to such right action.

It is easy to conceive of an alien intelligent species evolving rules its members consider highly moral but which are repugnant to human beings, such as cannibalism, incest, the love of darkness and decay, parricide, and the mutual eating of feces. Many animal species perform some or all of these things, with gusto and in order to survive. If human beings had evolved from a stock other than savanna-dwelling, bipedal, carnivorous man-apes we might do the same, feeling inwardly certain that such behaviors are natural and correct. In short, ethical premises are the peculiar products of genetic history, and they can be understood solely as mechanisms that are adaptive for the species that possess them. It follows that the ethical code of one species cannot be translated into that of another. No abstract moral principles exist outside the particular nature of individual species.

It is thus entirely correct to say that ethical laws can be changed, at the deepest level, by genetic evolution. This is obviously quite inconsistent with the notion of

[15] A new discipline of decision-making is being developed in cognitive psychology based upon the natural means—one can correctly say the epigenetic rules—by which people choose among alternatives and reach agreements. See, for example, A. Tversky and D. Kahneman, "The Framing of Decisions and the Psychology of Choice," _Science_ 211 (1981), 453–458; and R. Axelrod, _The Evolution of Cooperation_ (New York: Basic Books, 1984).

morality as a set of objective, eternal verities. Morality is rooted in contingent human nature, through and through.

Nor is it possible to uphold the true objectivity of morality by believing in the existence of an ultimate code, such that what is considered right corresponds to what is truly right—that the thoughts produced by the epigenetic rules parallel external premises.[16] The evolutionary explanation makes the objective morality redundant, for even if external ethical premises did not exist, we would go on thinking about right and wrong in the way that we do. And surely, redundancy is the last predicate that an objective morality can possess. Furthermore, what reason is there to presume that our present state of evolution puts us in correspondence with ultimate truths? If there are genuine external ethical premises, perhaps cannibalism is obligatory.

(8) Thoughtful people often turn away from naturalistic ethics because of a belief that it takes the good will out of cooperation and reduces righteousness to a mechanical process. Biological 'altruism' supposedly can never yield genuine altruism. This concern is based on a half-truth. True morality, in other words behavior that most or all people can agree is moral, does consist in the readiness to do the 'right' thing even at some personal cost. As pointed out, human beings do not calculate the ultimate effect of every given act on the survival of their own genes or those of close relatives. They are more than just gene replicators. They define each problem, weigh the options, and act in a manner conforming to a well-defined set of beliefs —with integrity, we like to say, and honor, and decency. People are willing to suppress their own desires for a while in order to behave correctly.

---

6. Here is a response to critics of naturalistic ethics. It is important to notice, also, the defense they give against the charge of moral relativism.

That much is true, but to treat such qualifications as objections to naturalistic ethics is to miss the entire force of the empirical argument. There is every reason to believe that most human behavior does protect the individual, as well as the family and the tribe and, ultimately, the genes common to all of these units. The advantage extends to acts generally considered to be moral and selfless. A person functions more efficiently in the social setting if he obeys the generally accepted moral code of his society than if he follows moment-by-moment egocentric calculations. This proposition has been well documented in the case of pre-literate societies, of the kind in which human beings lived during evolutionary time. While far from perfect, the correlation is close enough to support the biological view that the epigenetic rules evolved by natural selection.

It should not be forgotten that altruistic behavior is most often directed at close relatives, who possess many of the same genes as the altruist and perpetuate them through collateral descent. Beyond the circle of kinship, altruistic acts are typically reciprocal in nature, performed with the expectation of future reward either in this world or afterward. Note, however, that the expectation does not necessarily employ a crude demand for returns, which would be antithetical to true morality.

---

[16] This is the argument proposed by R. Nozick in *Philosophical Explanations* (Cambridge, Mass.: Belknap Press of Harvard University Press, 1981) in order to escape the implications of sociobiology.

Rather, I expect you (or God) to help me because it is right for you (or God) to help me, just as it was right for me to help you (or obey God). The reciprocation occurs in the name of morality. When people stop reciprocating, we tend to regard them as outside the moral framework. They are 'sociopathic' or 'no better than animals'.

The very concept of morality—as opposed to mere moral decisions taken from time to time—imparts efficiency to the adaptively correct action. Moral feeling is the shortcut taken by the mind to make the best choices quickly. So we select a certain action and not another because we feel that it is 'right', in other words, it satisfies the norms of our society or religion and thence, ultimately, the epigenetic rules and their prescribing genes. To recognize this linkage does not diminish the validity and robustness of the end result. Because moral consistency feeds mental coherence, it retains power even when understood to have a purely material basis.

For the same reason there is little to fear from moral relativism. A common argument raised against the materialist view of human nature is that if ethical premises are not objective and external to mankind, the individual is free to pick his own code of conduct regardless of the effect on others. Hence philosophy for the philosophers and religion for the rest, as in the Averrhoist doctrine. But our growing knowledge of evolution suggests that this is not at all the case. The epigenetic rules of mental development are relative only to the species. They are not relative to the individual. It is easy to imagine another form of intelligent life with non-human rules of mental development and therefore a radically different ethic. Human cultures, in contrast, tend to converge in their morality in the manner expected when a largely similar array of epigenetic rules meet a largely similar array of behavioral choices. This would not be the case if human beings differed greatly from one another in the genetic basis of their mental development.

Indeed, the materialist view of the origin of morality is probably less threatening to moral practice than a religious or otherwise nonmaterialistic view, for when moral beliefs are studied empirically, they are less likely to deceive. Bigotry declines because individuals cannot in any sense regard themselves as belonging to a chosen group or as the sole bearers of revealed truth. The quest for scientific understanding replaces the hajj and the holy grail. Will it acquire a similar passion? That depends upon the value people place upon themselves, as opposed to their imagined rulers in the realms of the supernatural and the eternal.

READING QUESTIONS

1. Although natural selection implies competition, other means exist by which natural selection can operate. Name two.

2. How do the authors counter the criticism that evolutionary theory does not have all the facts and that facts inconsistent with the theory may arise?

3. What is distinctive about moral claims?

4. How can the authors explain altruistic behavior in terms of biological processes?

5. What analogy do the authors draw between human moral codes and common law?

6. What is the biological explanation of moral feeling (feelings that certain acts are right and others wrong)?

Virginia Held

Feminism, the social movement that seeks to uncover and eliminate the biases that lead to the subordination of women in society, caught the public's attention in the late twentieth century. Its impact has been felt in most aspects of contemporary society, and philosophy, including moral philosophy, has benefited from a significant amount of attention and criticism by feminists. Although the traditional ethical theories—**utilitarianism, Kantian duty theory, virtue ethics,** and **social contract theory**—remain prominent, the recent development of feminist ethics has attracted significant attention and interest. All of the traditional theories have strong historical roots; Mill, Kant, Aristotle, and Hobbes would probably all recognize the modern versions of their theories. But feminist ethics is a thoroughly modern phenomenon. Historically, many women writers, and some men, have spoken out about women's concerns for human rights often accorded only to men. (For example, in this volume see Mary Wollstonecraft's *A Vindication of the Rights of Women.*) But not until recently has the movement gathered enough momentum to make the concerns of women a topic of conversation throughout the philosophical community. Yet even though it lacks a distinct historical tradition, feminist ethics assuredly deserves a place in a historical anthology of moral philosophy; it is tightly linked to historical theories in large part by being a reaction against them. The need for a feminist theory has arisen from perceived weaknesses in the historical theories, specifically a failure to appreciate and value the distinctive experience of women. In "Feminism and Moral Theory," representative of recent work in feminist ethics, Virginia Held of the City University of New York explains the need for a feminist theory in moral philosophy.

Held questions whether any single moral theory can adequately account for the different contexts of human activity. For example, a moral theory developed for the courtroom may not be adequate in the context of political bargaining since it fails to take account of the special concerns of the political arena. Likewise, the reigning traditional moral theories do not adequately account for the context of women's moral lives because they fail to recognize the special concerns that make up the experiences of women. These theories were (and still are perhaps) based on the experiences of men. Women typically held roles different from those of men and, until recently, their experience was mostly confined to the context of the family. Women's experience, therefore, provides a different perspective on what questions a moral theory must answer. Only when women's unique experience is taken into account can we determine whether a feminist ethical theory serves the contexts of women's lives better than the traditional models. A feminist moral theory is necessary, argues Held, to determine how to evaluate women's moral experience.

Feminism and Moral Theory

෴

Women and men are similar in many ways. As everyone knows, of course, they also differ. But the differences, whatever they may be, have seldom been taken into account by moral philosophers. This may be because

From Virginia Held, "Feminism and Moral Theory," in *Women and Moral Theory,* ed. Kittay, Rowman and Littlefield Publishers, Inc. Reprinted with permission from the publisher.

philosophers have most often been male; thus, male experience predominates in moral philosophy. Another reason may be that philosophers did not consider women to be different in ways that would make a difference to a moral theory. Sure, women are anatomically different from men, but how would that fact change what is right and what is wrong?

The increased attention given to women's issues in the last half of the twentieth century has forced philosophers to take a new look at moral theories. As philosophers have examined moral theories for their responsiveness to women's issues, a number of questions have taken on particular importance. For example, are moral theories applicable to all people, or are they made by and for men only? How have moral philosophers accounted for the kinds of lives that most women tend to lead? In this article, Virginia Held stresses the importance that women's experience has for moral philosophy. She argues that women have tended to lead different kinds of lives than men have, and these differences will matter to a moral theory. ✍

The tasks of moral inquiry and moral practice are such that different moral approaches may be appropriate for different domains of human activity. I have argued in a recent book that we need a division of moral labor.[1] In *Rights and Goods,* I suggest that we ought to try to develop moral inquiries that will be as satisfactory as possible for the actual contexts in which we live and in which our experience is located. Such a division of moral labor can be expected to yield different moral theories for different contexts of human activity, at least for the foreseeable future. In my view, the moral approaches most suitable for the courtroom are not those most suitable for political bargaining; the moral approaches suitable for economic activity are not those suitable for relations within the family, and so on. The task of achieving a unified moral field theory covering all domains is one we may do well to postpone, while we do our best to devise and to "test" various moral theories in actual contexts and in light of our actual moral experience.

What are the implications of such a view for women? Traditionally, the experience of women has been located to a large extent in the context of the family. In recent centuries, the family has been thought of as a "private" domain distinct not only from that of the "public" domain of the polis, but also from the domain of production and of the marketplace. Women (and men) certainly need to develop moral inquiries appropriate to the context of mothering and of family relations, rather than accepting the application to this context of theories developed for the marketplace or the polis. We can certainly show that the moral guidelines appropriate to mothering are different from those that now seem suitable for various other domains of activity as presently constituted. But we need to do more as well: we need to consider whether distinctively feminist moral theories, suitable for the contexts in which the experience of women has or will continue to be located, are better moral theories than those already available, and better for other domains as well.

The Experience of Women

We need a theory about how to count the experience of women. It is not obvious that it should count equally in the construction or validation of moral theory. To merely survey the moral views of women will not necessarily lead to better moral theories. In the Greek thought that developed into the Western philosophical tradition,[2] reason was associated with the public domain from which women were largely excluded. If the development of adequate moral theory is best based on experience in the public domain, the experience of women so far is less relevant. But that the public domain is the appropriate locus for the development of moral theory is among the tacit assumptions of existing moral theory being effectively challenged by feminist scholars. We cannot escape the need for theory in confronting these issues.

We need to take a stand on what moral experience is. As I see it, moral experience is "the experience of consciously choosing, of voluntarily accepting or rejecting, of willingly approving or disapproving, of living with these choices, and above all of acting and of living with these actions and their outcomes. . . . Action is as much a part of experience as is perception."[3] Then we need to take a stand on whether the moral experience of women is as valid a source or test of moral theory as is the experience of men, or on whether it is more valid.

---

1. Held begins to examine the differences between men's and women's moral experience.

Certainly, engaging in the process of moral inquiry is as open to women as it is to men, although the domains in which the process has occurred have been open to men and women in different ways. Women have had fewer occasions to experience for themselves the moral problems of governing, leading, exercising power over others (except children), and engaging in physically violent conflict. Men, on the other hand, have had fewer occasions to experience the moral problems of family life and the relations between adults and children. Although vast amounts of moral experience are open to all human beings who make the effort to become conscientious moral inquirers, the contexts in which experience is obtained may make a difference. It is essential that we avoid taking a given moral theory, such as a Kantian one, and deciding that those who fail to develop toward it are deficient, for this procedure imposes a theory on experience, rather than letting experience determine the fate of theories, moral and otherwise.

We can assert that as long as women and men experience different problems, moral theory ought to reflect the experience of women as fully as it reflects the experience of men. The insights and judgments and decisions of women as they engage in the process of moral inquiry should be presumed to be as valid as those of men. In the development of moral theory, men ought to have no privileged position to have their experience count for more. If anything, their privileged position in society should make their experience more suspect rather than more worthy of being counted, for they have good reasons to rationalize their privileged positions by moral arguments that will obscure or purport to justify these privileges.[4]

If the differences between men and women in confronting moral problems are due to biological factors that will continue to provide women and men with different experiences, the experience of women should still count for at least as much as the experience of men. There is no justification for discounting the experience of women as deficient or underdeveloped on biological grounds. Biological "moral inferiority" makes no sense.

The empirical question of whether and to what extent women think differently from men about moral problems is being investigated.[5] If, in fact, women approach moral problems in characteristic ways, these approaches should be reflected in moral theories as fully as are those of men. If the differing approaches to morality that seem to be displayed by women and by men are the result of historical conditions and not biological ones, we could assume that in nonsexist societies, the differences would disappear, and the experience of either gender might adequately substitute for the experience of the other.[6] Then feminist moral theory might be the same as moral theory of any kind. But since we can hardly imagine what a nonsexist society would be like, and surely should not wait for one before evaluating the experience of women, we can say that we need feminist moral theory to deal with the differences of which we are now aware and to contribute to the development of the nonsexist society that might make the need for a distinctively feminist moral theory obsolete. Specifically, we need feminist moral theory to deal with the regions of experience that have been central to women's experience and neglected by traditional moral theory. If the resulting moral theory would be suitable for all humans in all contexts, and thus could be thought of as a human moral theory or a universal moral theory, it would be a feminist moral theory as well if it adequately reflected the experience and standpoint of women.

That the available empirical evidence for differences between men and women with respect to morality is tentative and often based on reportage and interpretation, rather than on something more "scientific,"[7] is no problem at all for the claim that we need feminist moral theory. If such differences turn out to be further substantiated, we will need theory to evaluate their implications, and we should be prepared now for this possibility (or, as many think, probability). If the differences turn out to be insignificant, we still need feminist moral theory to make the moral claim that the experience of women is of equal worth to the experience of men, and even more important, that women themselves are of equal worth as human beings. If it is true that the only differences between women and men are anatomical, it still does not follow that women are the moral equals of men. Moral equality has to be based on moral claims. Since the devaluation of women is a constant in human society as so far developed, and has been accepted by those holding a wide variety of traditional moral theories, it is apparent that feminist moral theory is needed to provide the basis for women's claims to equality.

We should never forget the horrors that have resulted from acceptance of the idea that women think differently from men, or that men are rational beings, women emotional ones. We should be constantly on guard for misuses of such ideas, as in social roles that determine that women belong in the home or in educational programs that discourage women from becoming, for example, mathematicians. Yet, excessive fear of such misuses should not stifle exploration of the ways in which such claims may, in some measure, be true. As philosophers, we can be careful not to conclude that whatever tendencies exist ought to be reinforced. And if we succeed in making social scientists more alert to the naturalistic fallacy than they would otherwise be, that would be a side benefit to the development of feminist moral theory.

Mothering and Markets

When we bring women's experience fully into the domain of moral consciousness, we can see how questionable it is to imagine contractual relationships as central or fundamental to society and morality. They seem, instead, the relationships of only very particular regions of human activity.[8]

---

2. After giving reasons that women's moral experience needs to be taken into account in a moral theory, Held begins to articulate what that experience is.

The most central and fundamental social relationship seems to be that between mother or mothering person and child. It is this relationship that creates and recreates society. It is the activity of mothering which transforms biological entities into human social beings. Mothers and mothering persons produce children and empower them with language and symbolic representations. Mothers and mothering persons thus produce and create human culture.

Despite its implausibility, the assumption is often made that human mothering is like the mothering of other animals rather than being distinctively human. In accordance with the traditional distinction between the family and the polis, and the assumption that what occurs in the public sphere of the polis is distinctively human, it is assumed that what human mothers do within the family belongs to the "natural" rather than to the "distinctively human" domain. Or, if it is recognized that the activities of human mothers do not resemble the activities of the mothers of other mammals, it is assumed that, at least, the difference is far narrower than the difference between what animals do and what humans who take part in government and industry and art do. But, in fact, mothering is among the most human of human activities.

Consider the reality. A human birth is thoroughly different from the birth of other animals, because a human mother can choose not to give birth. However extreme the alternative, even when abortion is not a possibility, a woman can choose suicide early enough in her pregnancy to consciously prevent the birth. A human mother comprehends that she brings about the birth of another human being. A human mother is then responsible, at least in an existentialist sense, for the creation of a new human life. The event is essentially different from what is possible for other animals.

---

3. Held considers the way that human mothering is unique. Why is language so important?

Human mothering is utterly different from the mothering of animals without language. The human mother or nurturing person constructs with and for the child a human social reality. The child's understanding of language and of symbols, and of all that they create and make real, occurs in interactions between child and caretakers. Nothing seems more distinctively human than this. In comparison, government can be thought to resemble the governing of ant colonies, industrial production to be similar to the building of beaver dams, a market exchange to be like the relation between a large fish that protects and a small fish that grooms, and the conquest by force of arms that characterizes so much of human history to be like the aggression of packs of animals. But the imparting of language and the creation within and for each individual of a human social reality, and often a new human social reality, seems utterly human.

An argument is often made that art and industry and government create new human reality, while mothering merely "reproduces" human beings, their cultures, and social structures. But consider a more accurate view: in bringing up children, those who mother create new human *persons*. They change persons, the culture, and the social structures that depend on them, by creating the kinds of persons who can continue to transform themselves and their surroundings. Creating new and better persons is surely as "creative" as creating new and better objects or institutions. It is not only bodies that do not spring into being unaided and fully formed; neither do imaginations, personalities, and minds.

Perhaps morality should make room first for the human experience reflected in the social bond between mothering person and child, and for the human projects of nurturing and of growth apparent for both persons in the relationship. In comparison, the transactions of the marketplace seem peripheral; the authority of weapons and the laws they uphold, beside the point.

The relation between buyer and seller has often been taken as the model of all human interactions.[9] Most of the social contract tradition has seen this relation of contractual exchange as fundamental to law and political authority as well as to economic activity. And some contemporary moral philosophers see the contractual relation as the relation on which even morality itself should be based. The marketplace, as a model for relationships, has become so firmly entrenched in our normative theories that it is rarely questioned as a proper foundation for recommendations extending beyond the marketplace. Consequently, much moral thinking is built on the concept of rational economic man. Relationships between human beings are seen as arising, and as justified, when they serve the interests of individual rational contractors.

In the society imagined in the model based on assumptions about rational economic man, connections between people become no more than instrumental. Nancy Hartsock effectively characterizes the worldview of these assumptions, and shows how misguided it is to suppose that the relationship between buyer and seller can serve as a model for all human relations: "the paradigmatic connections between people [on this view of the social world] are instrumental or extrinsic and conflictual, and in a world populated by these isolated individuals, relations of competition and domination come to be substitutes for a more substantial and encompassing community."[10]

Whether the relationship between nurturing person (who need not be a biological mother) and child should be taken as itself paradigmatic, in place of the contractual paradigm, or whether it should be seen only as an obviously important relationship that does not fit into the contractual framework and should not be overlooked, remains to be seen. It is certainly instructive to consider it, at least tentatively, as paradigmatic. If this were done, the competition and desire for domination thought of as acceptable for rational economic man might appear as a very particular and limited human connection, suitable perhaps, if at all, only for a restricted marketplace. Such a relation of conflict and competition can be seen to be unacceptable for establishing the social trust on which public institutions must rest,[11] or for upholding the bonds on which caring, regard, friendship, or love must be based.[12]

The social map would be fundamentally altered by adoption of the point of view here suggested. Possibly, the relationship between "mother" and child would be recognized as a much more promising source of trust and concern than any other, for reasons to be explored later. In addition, social relations would be seen as dynamic rather than as fixed-point exchanges. And assumptions that human beings are equally capable of entering or not entering into the contractual relations taken to characterize social relations generally would be seen for the distortions they are. Although human mothers could do other than give birth, their choices to do so or not are usually highly constrained. And children, even human children, cannot choose at all whether to be born.

It may be that no human relationship should be thought of as paradigmatic for all the others. Relations between mothering persons and children can become oppressive for both, and relations between equals who can decide whether to enter into agreements may seem attractive in contrast. But no mapping of the social and moral landscape can possibly be satisfactory if it does not adequately take into account and provide appropriate guidance for relationships between mothering persons and children.

Between the Self and the Universal

Perhaps the most important legacy of the new insights will be the recognition that more attention must be paid to the domain *between* the self—the ego, the self-interested individual—on the one hand, and the universal—everyone, others in general—on the other hand. Ethics traditionally has dealt with these poles, trying to reconcile their conflicting claims. It has called for impartiality against the partiality of the egoistic self, or it has defended the claims of egoism against such demands for a universal perspective.

In seeing the problems of ethics as problems of reconciling the interests of the self with what would be right or best for everyone, moral theory has neglected the intermediate region of family relations and relations of friendship, and has neglected the sympathy and concern people actually feel for particular others. As Larry Blum has shown, "contemporary moral philosophy in the Anglo-American tradition has paid little attention to [the] morally significant phenomena" of sympathy, compassion, human concern, and friendship.[13]

Standard moral philosophy has construed personal relationships as aspects of the self-interested feelings of individuals, as when a person might favor those he loves over those distant because it satisfies his own desires to do so. Or it has let those close others stand in for the universal "other," as when an analysis might be offered of how the conflict between self and others is to be resolved in something like "enlightened self-interest" or "acting out of respect for the moral law," and seeing this as what should guide us in our relations with those close, particular others with whom we interact.

Owen Flanagan and Jonathan Adler provide useful criticism of what they see as Kohlberg's "adequacy thesis"—the assumption that the more formal the moral reasoning, the better.[14] But they themselves continue to construe the tension in ethics as that between the particular self and the universal. What feminist moral theory will emphasize, in contrast, will be the domain of particular others in relations with one another.

The region of "particular others" is a distinct domain, where it can be seen that what becomes artificial and problematic are the very "self" and "all others" of standard moral theory. In the domain of particular others, the self is already closely entwined in relations with others, and the relation may be much more real, salient, and important than the interests of any individual self in isolation. But the "others" in the picture are not "all others," or everyone," or what a universal point of view could provide. They are particular flesh and blood others for whom we have actual feelings in our insides and in our skin, not the others of rational constructs and universal principles.

Relationships can be characterized as trusting or mistrustful, mutually considerate or selfish, and so forth. Where trust and consideration are appropriate, we can find ways to foster them. But doing so will depend on aspects of what can be understood only if we look at relations between persons. To focus on either self-interested individuals or the totality of all persons is to miss the qualities of actual relations between actual human beings.

Moral theories must pay attention to the neglected realm of particular others in actual contexts. In doing so, problems of egoism vs. the universal moral point of view appear very different, and may recede to the region of background insolubility or relative unimportance. The important problems may then be seen to be how we ought to guide or maintain or reshape the relationships, both close and more distant, that we have or might have with actual human beings.

Particular others can, I think, be actual starving children in Africa with whom one feels empathy or even the anticipated children of future generations, not just those we are close to in any traditional context of family, neighbors, or friends. But particular others are still not "all rational beings" or "the greatest number."

In recognizing the component of feeling and relatedness between self and particular others, motivation is addressed as an inherent part of moral inquiry. Caring between parent and child is a good example.[15] We should not glamorize parental care. Many mothers and fathers dominate their children in harmful or inappropriate ways, or fail to care adequately for them. But when the relationship between "mother" and child is as it should be, the caretaker does not care for the child (nor the child for the caretaker) because of universal moral rules. The love and concern one feels for the child already motivate much of what one does. This is not to say that morality is irrelevant. One must still decide what one ought to do. But the process of addressing the moral questions in mothering and of trying to arrive at answers one can find acceptable involves motivated acting, not just thinking. And neither egoism nor a morality of universal rules will be of much help.

Mothering is, of course, not the only context in which the salient moral problems concern relations between particular others rather than conflicts between egoistic self and universal moral laws; all actual human contexts may be more like this than like those depicted by Hobbes or Kant. But mothering may be one of the best contexts in which to make explicit why familiar moral theories are so deficient in offering guidance for action. And the variety of contexts within mothering, with the different excellences appropriate for dealing with infants, young children, or adolescents, provide rich sources of insight for moral inquiry.

The feelings characteristic of mothering—that there are too many demands on us, that we cannot do everything that we ought to do—are highly instructive. They give rise to problems different from those of universal rule vs. self-interest. They require us to weigh the claims of one self-other relationship against the claims of other self-other relationships, to try to bring about some harmony between them, to see the issues in an actual temporal context, and to act rather than merely reflect.

For instance, we have limited resources for caring. We cannot care for everyone or do everything a caring approach suggests. We need moral guidelines for ordering our priorities. The hunger of our own children comes before the hunger of children we do not know. But the hunger of children in Africa ought to come before some of the expensive amusements we may wish to provide for our own children. These are moral problems calling to some extent for principled answers. But we have to figure out what we ought to do when actually buying groceries, cooking meals, refusing the requests of our children for the latest toy they have seen advertised, and sending money to UNICEF. The context is one of real action, not of ideal thought.

Principles and Particulars

When we take the context of mothering as central, rather than peripheral, for moral theory, we run the risk of excessively discounting other contexts. It is a commendable risk, given the enormously more prevalent one of excessively discounting mothering. But I think that the attack on principles has sometimes been carried too far by critics of traditional moral theory.

4. Other critics of the traditional types of moral theories are the focus here.

Noddings, for instance, writes that "To say, 'It is wrong to cause pain needlessly,' contributes nothing by way of knowledge and can hardly be thought likely to change the attitude or behavior of one who might ask, 'Why is it wrong?' . . . Ethical caring . . . depends not upon rule or principle" but upon the development of a self "in congruence with one's best remembrance of caring and being cared-for."[16]

We should not forget that an absence of principles can be an invitation to capriciousness. Caring may be a weak defense against arbitrary decisions, and the person cared for may find the relation more satisfactory if both persons, but especially the person caring, are guided, to some extent, by principles concerning obligations and rights. To argue that no two cases are ever alike is to invite moral chaos. Furthermore, for one person to be in a position of caretaker means that that person has the power to withhold care, to leave the other without it. The person cared for is usually in a position of vulnerability. The moral significance of this needs to be addressed along with other aspects of the caring relationship. Principles may remind a giver of care to avoid being capricious or domineering. While most of the moral problems involved in mothering contexts may deal with issues above and beyond the moral minimums that can be covered by principles concerning rights and obligations, that does not mean that these minimums can be dispensed with.

Noddings's discussion is unsatisfactory also in dealing with certain types of questions, for instance those of economic justice. Such issues cry out for relevant principles. Although caring may be needed to motivate us to act on such principles, the principles are not dispensable. Noddings questions the concern people may have for starving persons in distant countries, because she sees universal love and universal justice as masculine illusions. She refrains from judging that the rich deserve less or the poor more, because caring for individuals cannot yield such judgments. But this may amount to taking a given economic stratification as given, rather than as the appropriate object of critical scrutiny that it should be. It may lead to accepting that the rich will care for the rich and the poor for the poor, with the gap between them, however unjustifiably wide, remaining what it is. Some important moral issues seem beyond the reach of an ethic of caring, once caring leads us, perhaps through empathy, to be concerned with them.

On ethical views that renounce principles as excessively abstract, we might have few arguments to uphold the equality of women. After all, as parents can care for children recognized as weaker, less knowledgeable, less capable, and with appropriately restricted rights, so men could care for women deemed inferior in every way. On a view that ethics could satisfactorily be founded on caring alone, men could care for women considered undeserving of equal rights in all the significant areas in which women have been struggling to have their equality recognized. So an ethic of care, essential as a component of morality, seems deficient if taken as an exclusive preoccupation.

That aspect of the attack on principles which seems entirely correct is the view that not all ethical problems can be solved by appeal to one or a very few simple principles. It is often argued that all more particular moral rules or principles can be derived from such underlying ones as the Categorical Imperative or the Principle of Utility, and that these can be applied to all moral problems. The call for an ethic of care may be a call, which I share, for a more pluralistic view of ethics, recognizing that we need a division of moral labor employing different moral approaches for different domains, at least for the time being.[17] Satisfactory intermediate principles for areas such as those of international affairs, or family relations, cannot be derived from simple universal principles, but must be arrived at in conjunction with experience within the domains in question.

Attention to particular others will always require that we respect the particularity of the context, and arrive at solutions to moral problems that will not give moral principles more weight than their due. But their due may remain considerable. And we will need principles concerning relationships, not only concerning the actions of individuals, as we will need evaluations of kinds of relationships, not only of the character traits of individuals.

Birth and Valuing

To a large extent, the activity of mothering is potentially open to men as well as to women. Fathers can conceivably come to be as emotionally close, or as close through caretaking, to children as are mothers. The experience of relatedness, of responsibility for the growth and empowerment of new life, and of responsiveness to particular others, ought to be incorporated into moral theory, and will have to be so incorporated for moral theory to be adequate. At present, in this domain, it is primarily the experience of women (and of children) that has not been sufficiently reflected in moral theory and that ought to be so reflected. But this is not to say that it must remain experience available only to women. If men came to share fully and equitably in the care of all persons who need care—especially children, the sick, the old—the moral values that now arise for women in the context of caring might arise as fully for men.

---

5. Many women's experiences could be experienced by men. After listing several experiences unique to women, she concentrates on one very important one not available to men.

There are some experiences, however, that are open only to women: menstruating, having an abortion, giving birth, suckling. We need to consider their possible significance or lack of significance for moral experience and theory. I will consider here only one kind of experience not open to men but of obviously great importance to women: the experience of giving birth or of deciding not to. Does the very experience of giving birth, or of deciding not to exercise the capacity to do so, make a significant difference for moral experience and moral theory? I think the answer must be: perhaps.

Of course birthing is a social as well as a personal or biological event. It takes place in a social context structured by attitudes and arrangements that deeply affect how women experience it: whether it will be accepted as "natural," whether it will be welcomed and celebrated, or whether it will be fraught with fear or shame. But I wish to focus briefly on the conscious awareness women can have of what they are doing in giving birth, and on the specifically personal and biological aspects of human birthing.

It is women who give birth to other persons. Women are responsible for the existence of new persons in ways far more fundamental than are men. It is not bizarre to recognize that women can, through abortion or suicide, choose not to give birth. A woman can be aware of the possibility that she can act to prevent a new person from existing, and can be aware that if this new person exists, it is because of what she has done and made possible.

In the past we have called attention to the extent to which women do not control their capacity to give birth. They are under extreme economic and social pressure to engage in intercourse, to marry, and to have children. Legal permission to undergo abortion is a recent, restricted, and threatened capacity. When the choice not to give birth requires grave risk to life, health, or well-being, or requires suicide, we should be careful not to misrepresent the situation when we speak of a woman's "choice" to become a mother, or of how she "could have done other" than have a child, or that since she chose to become a mother, she is responsible for her child." It does not follow that because women are responsible for creating human beings, they should be held responsible by society for caring for them, either alone, primarily, or even at all. These two kinds of responsibility should not be confused, and I am speaking here only of the first. As conscious human beings, women can do other than give birth, and if they do give birth, they are responsible for the creation of other human beings. Though it may be very difficult for women to avoid giving birth, the very familiarity of the literary image of the woman who drowns herself or throws herself from a cliff rather than bear an illegitimate child should remind us that such eventualities are not altogether remote from consciousness.

Women have every reason to be justifiably angry with men who refuse to take responsibility for their share of the events of pregnancy and birth, or for the care children require. Because, for so long, we have wanted to increase the extent to which men would recognize their responsibilities for causing pregnancy, and would share in the long years of care needed to bring a child to independence, we have tended to emphasize the ways in which the responsibilities for creating a new human being are equal between women and men.[18] But in fact, men produce sperm and women produce babies, and the difference is enormous. Excellent arguments can be made that boys and men suffer "womb envy"; indeed, men lack a wondrous capacity that women possess.[19]

Of all the human capacities, it is probably the capacity to create new human beings that is most worth celebrating. We can expect that a woman will care about and feel concern for a child she has created as the child grows and develops, and that she feels responsible for having given the child life. But her concern is more than something to be expected. It is, perhaps, justifiable in certain ways unique to women.

---

6. The responsibility of bearing children is the focus here. Do you see how her analysis of the situation goes far deeper than ordinary views of women's responsibility?

Children are born into actual situations. A mother cannot escape ultimate responsibility for having given birth to this particular child in these particular circumstances. She can be aware that she could have avoided intercourse, or used more effective contraception, or waited to get pregnant until her circumstances were different; that she could have aborted this child and had another later; or that she could have killed herself and prevented this child from facing the suffering or hardship of this particular life. The momentousness of all these decisions about giving or not giving life can hardly fail to affect what she experiences in relation to the child.

Perhaps it might be thought that many of these issues arise in connection with infanticide, and that if one refrains from killing an infant, one is responsible for giving the infant life. Infanticide is as open to men as to women. But to kill or refrain from killing a child, once the child is capable of life with caretakers different from the person who is responsible for having given birth to the child, is a quite different matter from creating or not creating this possibility, and I am concerned in this discussion with the moral significance of giving birth.

It might also be thought that those, including the father, who refrain from killing the mother, or from forcing her to have an abortion, are also responsible for not preventing the birth of the child.[20] But unless the distinction between suicide and murder, and between having an abortion and forcing a woman to have an abortion against her will, are collapsed completely, the issues would be very different. To refrain from murdering someone else is not the same as deciding not to kill oneself. And to decide not to force someone else to have an abortion is different from deciding not to have an abortion when one could. The person capable of giving birth who decides not to prevent the birth is the person responsible, in the sense of "responsible" I am discussing, for creating another human being. To create a new human being is not the same as to refrain from ending the life of a human being who already exists.

Perhaps there is a tendency to want to approve of or to justify what one has decided with respect to giving life. In deciding to give birth, perhaps a woman has a natural tendency to approve of the birth, to believe that the child ought to have been born. Perhaps this inclines her to believe whatever may follow from this: that the child is entitled to care, and that feelings of love for the child are appropriate and justified. The conscious decision to create a new human being may provide women with an inclination to value the child and to have hope for the child's future. Since, in her view, the child ought to have been born, a woman may feel that the world ought to be hospitable to the child. And if the child ought to have been born, the child ought to grow into an admirable human adult. The child's life has, and should continue to have, value that is recognized.

Consider next the phenomenon of sacrifice. In giving birth, women suffer severe pain for the sake of new life. Having suffered for the child in giving the child life, women may have a natural tendency to value what they have endured pain for. There is a tendency, often noted in connection with war, for people to feel that because sacrifices have been made, the sacrifice should have been "worth it," and if necessary, other things ought to be done so that the sacrifice "shall not have been in vain." There may be a similar tendency for those who have suffered to give birth to assure themselves that the pain was for the good reason of creating a new life that is valuable and that will be valued.

Certainly, this is not to say that there is anything good or noble about suffering, or that merely because people want to believe that what they suffered for was worthwhile, it was. A vast amount of human suffering has been in vain, and could and should have been avoided. The point is that once suffering has already occurred and the "price," if we resort to such calculations, has already been paid, it will be worse if the result is a further cost, and better if the result is a clear benefit that can make the price, when it is necessary for the result, validly "worth it."

The suffering of the mother who has given birth will more easily have been worthwhile if the child's life has value. The chance that the suffering will be outweighed by future happiness is much greater if the child is valued by the society and the family into which the child is born. If the mother's suffering yields nothing but further suffering and a being deemed to be of no value, her suffering may truly have been in vain. Anyone can have reasons to value children. But the person who has already undergone the suffering needed to create one has a special reason to recognize that the child is valuable and to want the child to be valued so that the suffering she has already borne will have been, truly, worthwhile.

These arguments can be repeated for the burdens of work and anxiety normally expended in bringing up a child. Those who have already borne these burdens have special reasons for wanting to see the grown human being for whom they have cared as valuable and valued. Traditionally, women have not only borne the burdens of childbirth, but, with little help, the much greater burdens of child rearing. Of course, the burdens of child rearing could be shared fully by men, as they have been partially shared by women other than natural mothers. Although the concerns involved in bringing up a child may greatly outweigh the suffering of childbirth itself, this does not mean that giving birth is incidental.

The decision not to have children is often influenced by a comparable tendency to value the potential child.[21] Knowing how much care the child would deserve and how highly, as a mother, she would value the child, a woman who gives up the prospect of motherhood can recognize how much she is losing. For such reasons, a woman may feel overwhelming ambivalence concerning the choice.

---

7. How men and women value children may differ. Notice that her argument focuses on biological differences.

Consider, finally, how biology can affect our ways of valuing children. Although men and women may share a desire or an instinctive tendency to wish to reproduce, and although these feelings may be equally strong for both men and women, such feelings might affect their attitudes toward a given child very differently. In terms of biological capacity, a mother has a relatively greater stake in a child to which she has given birth. This child is about one-twentieth or one twenty-fifth of all the children she could possibly have, whereas a man could potentially have hundreds or thousands of other children. In giving birth, a woman has already contributed a large amount of energy and effort toward the production of this particular child, while a man has, biologically, contributed only a few minutes. To the extent that such biological facts may influence attitudes, the attitudes of the mother and father toward the "worth" or "value" of a particular child may be different. The father might consider the child more easily replaceable in the sense that the father's biological contribution can so easily and so painlessly be repeated on another occasion or with another woman; for the mother to repeat her biological contribution would be highly exhausting and painful. The mother, having already contributed so much more to the creation of this particular child than the father, might value the result of her effort in proportion. And her pride at what she has accomplished in giving birth can be appropriately that much greater. She has indeed "accomplished" far more than has the father.

So even if instincts or desires to reproduce oneself or one's genes, or to create another human being, are equally powerful among men and women, a given child is, from the father's biological standpoint, much more incidental and interchangeable: any child out of the potential thousands he might sire would do. For the mother, on the other hand, if this particular child does not survive and grow, her chances for biological reproduction are reduced to a much greater degree. To suggest that men may think of their children as replaceable is offensive to many men, and women. Whether such biological facts as those I have mentioned have any significant effect on parental attitudes is not known. But arguments from biological facts to social attitudes, and even to moral norms, have a very long history and are still highly popular; we should be willing to examine the sorts of unfamiliar arguments I have suggested that can be drawn from biological facts. If anatomy is destiny, men may be "naturally" more indifferent toward particular children than has been thought.

Since men, then, do not give birth, and do not experience the responsibility, the pain, and momentousness of childbirth, they lack the particular motives to value the child that may spring from this capacity and this fact. Of course, many other reasons for valuing a child are felt by both parents, by caretakers of either gender, and by those who are not parents, but the motives discussed, and others arising from giving birth, may be morally significant. The long years of child care may provide stronger motives for valuing a child than do the relatively short months of pregnancy and hours of childbirth. The decisions and sacrifices involved in bringing up a child can be more affecting than those normally experienced in giving birth to a child. So the possibility for men to acquire such motives through child care may outweigh any long-term differences in motivation between women and men. But it might yet remain that the person responsible for giving birth would continue to have a greater sense of responsibility for how the child develops, and stronger feelings of care and concern for the child.

That adoptive parents can feel as great concern for and attachment to their children as can biological parents may indicate that the biological components in valuing children are relatively modest in importance. However, to the extent that biological components are significant, they would seem to affect men and women in different ways.

Morality and Human Tendencies

So far, I have been describing possible feelings rather than attaching any moral value to them. That children are valued does not mean that they are valuable, and if mothers have a natural tendency to value their children, it does not follow that they ought to. But if feelings are taken to be relevant to moral theory, the feelings of valuing the child, like the feelings of empathy for other persons in pain, may be of moral significance.

To the extent that a moral theory takes natural male tendencies into account, it would at least be reasonable to take natural female tendencies into account. Traditional moral theories often suppose it is legitimate for individuals to maximize self-interest, or satisfy their preferences, within certain constraints based on the equal rights of others. If it can be shown that the tendency to want to pursue individual self-interest is a stronger tendency among men than among women, this would certainly be relevant to an evaluation of such theory. And if it could be shown that a tendency to value children and a desire to foster the developing capabilities of the particular others for whom we care is a stronger tendency among women than among men, this too would be relevant in evaluating moral theories.

8. A crucial point about the valuing of children is being made here. The focus is on the reasons that might be given for valuing them.

The assertion that women have a tendency to value children is still different from the assertion that they ought to. Noddings speaks often of the "natural" caring of mothers for children.[22] I do not intend to deal here with the disputed empirical question of whether human mothers do or do not have a strong natural tendency to love their children. And I am certainly not claiming that natural mothers have greater skills or excellences in raising children than have others, including, perhaps, men. I am trying, rather, to explore possible "reasons" for mothers to value children, reasons that might be different for mothers and potential mothers than they would be for anyone else asking the question: why should we value human beings? And it does seem that certain possible reasons for valuing living human beings are present for mothers in ways that are different from what they would be for others. The reason, if it is one, that the child should be valued because I have suffered to give the child life is different from the reason, if it is one, that the child should be valued because someone unlike me suffered to give the child life. And both of these reasons are different from the reason, if it is one, that the child should be valued because the continued existence of the child satisfies a preference of a parent, or because the child is a bearer of universal rights, or has the capacity to experience pleasure.

Many moral theories, and fields dependent on them such as economics, employ the assumption that to increase the utility of individuals is a good thing to do. But if asked *why* it is a good thing to increase utility, or satisfy desire, or produce pleasure, or *why* doing so counts as a good reason for something, it is very difficult to answer. The claim is taken as a kind of starting assumption for which no *further* reason can be given. It seems to rest on a view that people seek pleasure, or that we can recognize pleasure as having intrinsic value. But if women recognize quite different assumptions as more likely to be valid, that would certainly be of importance to ethics. We might then take it as one of our starting assumptions that creating good relations of care and concern and trust between ourselves and our children, and creating social arrangements in which children will be valued and well cared for, are more important than maximizing individual utilities. And the moral theories that might be compatible with such assumptions might be very different from those with which we are familiar.

A number of feminists have independently declared their rejection of the Abraham myth.[23] We do not approve the sacrifice of children out of religious duty. Perhaps, for those capable of giving birth, reasons to value the actual life of the born will, in general, seem to be better than reasons justifying the sacrifice of such life.[24] This may reflect an accordance of priority to caring for particular others over abstract principle. From the perspectives of Rousseau, of Kant, of Hegel, and of Kohlberg, this is a deficiency of women. But from a perspective of what is needed for late twentieth century survival, it may suggest a superior morality. Only feminist moral theory can offer a satisfactory evaluation of such suggestions, because only feminist moral theory can adequately understand the alternatives to traditional moral theory that the experience of women requires.

NOTES

1. See Virginia Held, *Rights and Goods: Justifying Social Action* (New York: Free Press, Macmillan, 1984).
2. See Genevieve Lloyd, *The Man of Reason: "Male" and "Female" in Western Philosophy* (Minneapolis: University of Minnesota Press, 1984).
3. Virginia Held, *Rights and Goods,* p. 272. See also V. Held, "The Political 'Testing' of Moral Theories," *Midwest Studies in Philosophy* 7 (1982): 343–63.
4. For discussion, see especially Nancy Hartsock, *Money, Sex, and Power* (New York: Longman, 1983), chaps. 10, 11.
5. Lawrence Kohlberg's studies of what he claimed to be developmental stages in moral reasoning suggested that girls progress less well and less far than boys through these stages. See his *The Philosophy of Moral Development* (San Francisco: Harper & Row, 1981); and L. Kohlberg and R. Kramer, "Continuities and Discontinuities in Child and Adult Moral Development," *Human Development* 12 (1969): 93–120. James R. Rest, on the other hand, claims in his study of adolescents in 1972 and 1974 that "none of the male-female differences on the Defining Issues Test . . . and on the Comprehension or Attitudes tests were significant." See his "Longitudinal Study of the Defining Issues Test of Moral Judgment: A Strategy for Analyzing Developmental Change," *Developmental Psychology* (Nov. 1975): 738–48; quotation at 741. Carol Gilligan's *In a Different Voice* (Cambridge: Harvard University Press, 1982) suggests that girls and women tend to organize their thinking about moral problems somewhat differently from boys and men; her subsequent work supports the view that whether people tend to construe moral problems in terms of rules of justice or in terms of caring relationships is at present somewhat associated with gender (Carol Gilligan, address at Conference on Women and Moral Thought, SUNY Stony Brook, March 21, 1985). Other studies have shown that females are significantly more inclined than males to cite compassion and sympathy as reasons for their moral positions; see Constance Boucher Holstein, "Irreversible, Stepwise Sequence in the Development of Moral Judgment: A Longitudinal Study of Males and Females." *Child Development* 47, no. 1 (March 1976): 51–61.
6. For suggestions on how Gilligan's stages, like Kohlberg's, might be thought to be historically and culturally, rather than more universally, based, see Linda Nicholson, "Women, Morality, and History," *Social Research* 50, no. 3 (Autumn 1983): 514–36.
7. See, e.g., Debra Nails, "Social-Scientific Sexism: Gilligan's Mismeasure of Man," *Social Research* 50, no. 3 (Autumn 1983): 643–64.

8. I have discussed this in a paper that has gone through several major revisions and changes of title, from its presentation at a conference at Loyola University on April 18, 1983, to its discussion at Dartmouth College, April 2, 1984. I will refer to it as "Non-Contractual Society: A Feminist Interpretation." See also Carole Pateman, "The Fraternal Social Contract: Some Observations on Patriarchy," paper presented at American Political Science Association meeting, Aug. 30–Sept. 2, 1984, and "The Shame of the Marriage Contract," in *Women's Views of the Political World of Men,* edited by Judith Hicks Stiehm (Dobbs Ferry, N.Y: Transnational Publishers, 1984).

9. For discussion, see especially Nancy Hartsock, *Money, Sex, and Power.*

10. Ibid., p. 39.

11. See Held, *Rights and Goods,* chap. 5.

12. Ibid., chap. 11.

13. Lawrence A. Blum, *Friendship, Altruism and Morality* (London: Routledge and Kegan Paul, 1980), p. 1.

14. Owen J. Flanagan, Jr., and Jonathan E. Adler, "Impartiality and Particularity," *Social Research* 50, no. 3 (Autumn 1983): 576–96.

15. See, e.g., Nell Noddings, *Caring: A Feminine Approach to Ethics and Moral Education* (Berkeley: University of California Press, 1984) pp. 91–94.

16. Ibid., 91–94.

17. Participants in the conference on Women and Moral Theory offered the helpful term "domain relativism" for the version of this view that I defended.

18. See, e.g., Virginia Held, "The Obligations of Mothers and Fathers," repr. in *Mothering: Essays from Feminist Theory,* edited by Joyce Trebilcot (Totowa, N.J.: Rowman and Allanheld, 1984).

19. See Eva Kittay, "Womb Envy: An Explanatory Concept," in *Mothering,* edited by Joyce Trebilcot. To overcome the pernicious aspects of the "womb envy" she skillfully identifies and describes, Kittay argues that boys should be taught that their "procreative contribution is of equal significance" (p. 123). While boys should certainly be told the truth, the truth may remain that, as she states elsewhere, "there is the . . . awesome quality of creation itself—the transmutation performed by the parturient woman" (p. 99).

20. This point was made by Marcia Baron in correspondence with me.

21. In exploring the values involved in birth and mothering, we need to develop views that include women who do not give birth. As Margaret Simons writes, "we must define a feminist maternal ethic that supports a woman's rights not to have children." See Margaret A. Simons, "Motherhood, Feminism and Identity," *Hypatia, Women's Studies International Forum* 7, 5 (1984): 353.

22. E.g., Noddings, *Caring,* pp. 31, 43, 49.

23. See Gilligan, *In a Different Voice,* p. 104; Held, "Non-Contractual Society: A Feminist Interpretation"; and Noddings, *Caring,* p. 43.

24. That some women enthusiastically send their sons off to war may be indicative of a greater than usual acceptance of male myths rather than evidence against this claim, since the enthusiasm seems most frequent in societies where women have the least influence in the formation of prevailing religious and other beliefs.

READING QUESTIONS

1. Why should men's moral experience be more suspect rather than worthy of being counted?

2. What relationship does Held argue is the most central and fundamental social relationship?

3. What relation has traditionally been seen as the model of human interactions?

4. List two experiences that are unique to women and two experiences that are potentially available to men as well.

5. Women bear the burden of childbirth. What other burden does Held cite that women traditionally bear that is even greater?

6. Held considers possible reasons that women may believe that children are valuable. What is one that she gives? What point is she making about this kind of reason?